SECOND EDITION

THE PSYCHOLOGY OF PREJUDICE

TODD D. NELSON

California State University–Stanislaus

PEARSON

Boston ∎ New York ∎ San Francisco
Mexico City ∎ Montreal ∎ Toronto ∎ London ∎ Madrid ∎ Munich ∎ Paris
Hong Kong ∎ Singapore ∎ Tokyo ∎ Cape Town ∎ Sydney

Series Editor: Susan Hartman
Editorial Assistant: Therese Felser
Marketing Manager: Laura Lee Manley
Production Editor: Beth Houston
Editorial Production Service: Omegatype Typography, Inc.
Composition Buyer: JoAnne Sweeney
Electronic Composition: Omegatype Typography, Inc.
Cover Administrator: Joel Gendron

For related titles and support materials, visit our online catalog at www.ablongman.com.

Between the time website information is gathered and then published, it is not unusual for some sites to have closed. Also, the transcription of URLs can result in typographical errors. The publisher would appreciate notification where these occur so that they may be corrected in subsequent editions.

Library of Congress Cataloging-in-Publication Data

Nelson, Todd D.
    The psychology of prejudice / Todd D. Nelson.—2nd ed.
      p. cm.
    Includes bibliographical references and index.
    ISBN 0-205-40225-9
      1. Prejudices. I. Title.

BF575.P9N45 2006
303.3'85—dc22

                    2005050980

Printed in the United States of America
10 9 8 7 6 5 4   10 09 08

Photo Credits: Page 2, Joseph Schuyler/Stock Boston; p. 8, Bettmann/Corbis; p. 34, David Turnley/Corbis; p. 43, AP/Wide World Photos; p. 53, From Intergroup conflict and cooperation: The Robber's Cave Experiment by M. Sherif, O. J. Harvey, B. Jack White, W. R. Hood and C. W. Sherif (1961). Norman, OK: Institute of Group Relations; p. 58, Photofest; p. 80, Felicia Martinez/PhotoEdit; p. 88, Bettmann/Corbis; p. 113, Elliott Erwitt/Magnum Photos; p. 140, Weissman/Globe Photos; p. 170, Tony Freeman/PhotoEdit; p. 172, Bill Aron/PhotoEdit; p. 196, AP/Wide World Photos; p. 200 (top), David Young-Wolff/PhotoEdit; p. 200 (bottom), Richard Hutchings/Corbis; p. 207, © 1998 The Procter & Gamble Company; p. 210, Bonnie Kamin/PhotoEdit; p. 235, Mark Richards/PhotoEdit; p. 243, Mary Kate Denny/PhotoEdit; p. 249, Jeffrey Myers/Stock Boston; p. 254; Jean Claude Lejeune/Stock Boston; p. 267 (left), Foto Marburg/Art Resource, NY; p. 267 (right), AP/Wide World Photos.

Dedicated to my children, Brandon, Logan, Jaden, and Alexis
I love you

CONTENTS

■ ■ ■ ■ ■

CHAPTER SIX

Experiencing Prejudice   134

CHAPTER SEVEN

Ageism   165

CHAPTER EIGHT

Sexism   199

PREFACE

PURPOSE OF THIS TEXT

It can be said that there is a law—"Nelson's Law" has a nice ring to it, and it sounds better than "the law of supply and demand"—concerning the relationship between the number of courses currently offered on a subject at colleges worldwide and the number of textbooks available to professors and students. This relationship is usually nicely proportional. However, it does not work very well for professors and students of courses that are not as common as, for example, Introduction to Psychology. For these less common courses, there usually are very few, if any, textbooks from which to choose. This has always been the case for courses on stereotyping, prejudice, and discrimination. Until about 20 years ago, such courses were rarely offered, even though researchers have been investigating stereotypes for nearly a century. But as the world becomes increasingly interconnected (through increased travel and especially because of the Internet), there has been a growing awareness of the benefits of creating and integrating courses on stereotyping and prejudice into the curriculum. Today, colleges are adding such courses, but there is a problem: very few textbooks on prejudice exist. Some texts are not entirely useful for psychology students because they are written from the theoretical and empirical standpoint of sociological research on prejudice. The psychologically oriented prejudice textbooks that are available are either too dense and cover too much, or the research and theory they cover are dated. Professors have either adopted these books or made do by assigning journal articles and chapters from scholarly books to read. The problem with that approach is that it tends to induce sleepiness, confusion, and boredom in students.

When I developed a seminar on stereotyping, these issues confronted me as I examined for use in my course the few available books on prejudice that have been used as textbooks. All too often, I found that the topics, experiments, and theories that I think are important in understanding prejudice were insufficiently covered, if at all, in these books. To address this problem, I decided to write this textbook. In writing the text, my goal was to present an in-depth, research-based, and applied focus on the study of prejudice and stereotyping. The text is written for the advanced undergraduate or first-year graduate student who has had some exposure to course work in social psychological research and methodology. The study of prejudice and stereotyping is exciting, challenging, and interesting. There is much we know, and much we do not yet know about what causes, maintains, and reduces prejudice. This book is intended to stimulate critical thinking about the issues surrounding our attempts to understand prejudice. I hope that as you read it, your questions will be answered, and more important, you will think of additional issues that you want addressed by future theory and research. Who knows, you may have so many questions that you will be moved to become a prejudice researcher yourself!

ORGANIZATION OF THE TEXT

The textbook is organized into 10 chapters, each addressing a different aspect of the study of prejudice and stereotyping. Chapter 1 introduces the field and provides historical background to the birth of research on stereotypes. It presents issues surrounding definitions of basic concepts, and it explains the empirical and theoretical trends in the field of social psychology that led to the current social-cognition approach that dominates much of social psychology, and certainly much of the field of prejudice research. Chapter 2 gets the reader in-depth into the basic social-cognitive principles that underlie the formation and maintenance of prejudice and stereotyping. Chapter 3 reflects recent empirical and theoretical trends by focusing on the influence of affect and cognition on the tendency to be influenced by prejudice and to use stereotypes in social judgments. Chapter 4 addresses the question of whether certain personality types tend to be prone to feel prejudice and to think of others in terms of stereotypes. Chapter 5 examines how the face of prejudice has changed over the decades, from an overtly and openly expressed hostility in the past to a predominantly subtle, almost imperceptible negative attitude. Chapter 5 also examines the problems that researchers face when trying to measure prejudiced attitudes. Chapter 6 reflects a very recent focus in the field: the attempt by researchers to investigate the effects of prejudice, stereotyping, and discrimination on the targets of prejudice. Chapter 7 is devoted to an underexamined but very important type of prejudice: prejudice against older persons. By about the year 2030, the population of those in the United States older than 65 years will double, and by the year 2011, the baby boomers will start to retire, a transition that some researchers term the "graying of America." This chapter attempts to understand why many people—especially Americans—have strong stereotypes and prejudice against older persons. Chapter 8 focuses on another major type of prejudice that is still unfortunately very much alive and well today: sexism. We examine how prejudice against women originates in historical, religious, and cultural causes and also how it affects career opportunities—or lack thereof—for women. Chapter 9 explores the ways that researchers have attempted to reduce prejudice and stereotyping, and why those efforts have often fallen short. We focus on the factors that seem to make people resist giving up their cherished stereotypes in favor of individuating others. We will also discuss prejudice-reduction efforts that have worked, and how researchers are currently addressing prejudice reduction. Finally, Chapter 10 reviews the state of research on three stigmatized groups that have received much less empirical attention: those who are overweight, those who are homosexual, and those who are physically challenged. We will present what we do know about those specific prejudices, and we'll describe what issues currently face prejudice researchers in these areas. The chapter then explores the current trends in the study of prejudice and stereotyping and addresses several (of an uncountable many) unanswered questions about prejudice that still confront researchers.

FEATURES

This book possesses many unique features that make it useful from both the student's and professor's perspectives. First, it has been developed as an in-depth examination of the entire field of prejudice, thus making it well-suited for advanced undergraduate and first-year graduate courses on prejudice. Although I cover the field fairly comprehensively, there will be some issues that are either too complex or too tangential to be covered in a book like this. This book is written so as not to be overly dense or to go off on tangents that distract the reader from the issues under discussion in each chapter.

Second, I've written the book in a conversational style, presenting questions to the reader directly and taking the opportunity (where possible) to relax the atmosphere with humor. This reflects my approach to lecturing as well as my philosophy of teaching. I want to create a fun, challenging, and thought-provoking atmosphere in my lectures, and I hope that same goal has been accomplished in this book.

Third, the discussions in the book are based heavily on the empirical literature on prejudice and stereotyping and reflect the past and current theoretical and empirical approaches to understanding prejudice. Related to this point, I present my analysis and evaluation of the experimental findings where possible, rather than merely presenting the findings with no interpretation or context. As a student, I always appreciated hearing what authors thought of the research they were evaluating, and I hope my perspective on the literature is helpful to you as well.

Fourth, each chapter focuses in detail on describing and critically evaluating one or two experiments. This is intended to help the reader understand some of the important methodological, theoretical, and scientific issues researchers need to grapple with when studying prejudice. Of course, if more studies were analyzed in this fashion, students might find it a bit overwhelming, and the book would likely be two to three times as long, so the current approach is, in my experience, palatable for the student while still accomplishing the instructional goals of the professor.

Finally, each chapter ends with a glossary of terms and a list of discussion questions that are designed to provoke stimulating discussions about controversial and not easily answered questions concerning prejudice in society today.

NEW FEATURES IN THE SECOND EDITION

In the three or so years that have passed between the publication of the first edition and the second edition, research on prejudice and stereotyping has continued at a fast pace. Going back through and updating, changing, modifying, and adding material to the text has been fun, because at the end of that writing process, I always get a nice sense of where the field is. The edition you now hold in your hands is an up-to-date version of the first edition, with references current as of 2005. It includes many improvements and additions, including the following:

- Over 230 new references
- A new section on sexist humor
- A new section on the neurobiology of prejudice
- More extensive, updated lists of web links relevant to prejudice research
- Summary sections at the end of each chapter

- Expanded sections that cover research on homosexuals, the overweight, and the physically challenged
- An expanded section on implicit stereotyping and prejudice

An Instructor's Manual will be available to all qualified adopters. Please contact your local Allyn and Bacon representative. If you do not know who the representative in your area is, please visit our website at www.ablongman.com.

I hope you enjoy the second edition. I am deeply gratified to have learned from my colleagues in the field that they found the first edition an excellent resource for their courses on prejudice. I am even more excited to hear that their students also enjoyed the first edition. I hope faculty and students alike find the second edition as interesting and informative as the first.

ACKNOWLEDGMENTS

Many people were instrumental in the production of this book, and I would like to take a moment to thank them. First, I am grateful for the tireless effort that my former editor at Allyn & Bacon, Carolyn Merrill, devoted to this project. When I proposed this book to her, she immediately recognized the need for such a book and was unhesitating in her outstanding guidance and encouragement of my writing of it. Throughout the long process of putting the first edition together, Carolyn was a reliable and unwavering source of support and vision, helping me as I navigated what was for me the uncharted waters of writing a book. I am also indebted to Lara Zeises, Carolyn's editorial assistant, for her excellent work in pointing out the many important details that require attention during the production of a book. Finally, to the creative production staff and everyone at Allyn & Bacon, I want to express my sincere gratitude for your efforts. Susan Hartman, executive editor at Allyn & Bacon, was especially instrumental in helping the second edition come together so wonderfully. I am very grateful to her.

A number of excellent reviewers helped me immensely as I revised my initial manuscript for final production. Many professionals in the field reviewed a few chapters. The following hardy souls reviewed the *entire manuscript (wow!)* and offered indispensable wisdom, insight, and critiques, which I attempted to incorporate into the book you now are reading: Nilanjana Dasgupta, New School University; Karen Howe, College of New Jersey; James Johnson, University of North Carolina at Wilmington; Keith Maddox, Tufts University; Gretchen Sechrist, State University of Buffalo–North Campus; and William Woody, University of Northern Colorado. I want to thank each of them for their thoughtful reviews and for helping me make this book even better.

When I initially decided to write this, my first book, I really did not know what to anticipate. I knew it would take a while, but it has ended up taking more than seven years and has involved nearly all of my free time outside of teaching and conducting research. Although I loved writing this book, the process has left little time for me to devote to my family. So I want to express my deepest gratitude and appreciation to my entire family for their infinite patience during the time it took to work on this book, and for being understanding about me working on my days off and trekking in to my office on weekends.

■ ■ ■ ■ ■

CHAPTER ONE

INTRODUCTION TO THE STUDY OF STEREOTYPING AND PREJUDICE

Throughout time, humans have had a tendency to form groups (Brewer & Miller, 1996). Membership in a group can be restricted on the basis of special skills, family relations, gender, power, and a host of other factors. By forming such groups, humans have found that it is possible to construct their environment such that their daily lives are easier; for example, through division of labor among various groups in the society. Through specialization of skills and the order within the society imposed by the power certain groups are given over the larger society (e.g., government), people found that they could live longer, happier, and more fulfilling lives than if people were each to fend for themselves or only for their own group. Thus, it is reasonable to suggest that "groups are the basic building blocks of society" (Forsyth, 1999, p. 2).

Groups are not unique to humans. Some researchers theorize that the tendency to form groups is such a basic part of the nature of animals, including humans, and has conveyed survival benefits so successfully that it has (e.g., fighting off predators, raising offspring successfully) withstood time and evolution. (Buss, 1995). In addition to the tremendous benefits to individuals in groups, however, there are some disadvantages and complications that group life brings, such as mate competition and mate retention. Something else tends to happen too when people form groups. They tend to form closer ties to members of their own group, and they tend to be suspicious and rejecting of members of other groups (Fiske, 2002). That is, group members tend to favor their own groups (called **ingroups**) over other groups to which they do not belong (termed **outgroups**). Even when group membership is based on the most arbitrary criteria (e.g., randomly assigning people to group A or to group B, an example of a **minimal group**), people tend to show preferences for members of their own group over those of other groups (Brewer, 1979).

Although such preferences may have adaptive utility from evolutionary and practical perspectives, they form the basis for negative feelings about other groups (**prejudice**) and for believing that certain characteristics are associated with other groups (forming **stereotypes**), often because the outgroup members are perceived to be antithetical to the ingroup's welfare or values (Neuberg, Smith, & Asher, 2000). Moreover, such ingroup preferences may underlie more severe negative behavior toward other groups, such as intergroup hostility and violence. This discussion certainly paints a pessimistic picture of the nature of prejudice and stereotyping. If, as evolutionary psychology suggests, ingroup preferences and hostility toward outgroups are adaptive, and therefore innate, there is little

1

Each one of us is a part of several groups. Being part of a group defines who we are as individuals, and we derive our self-esteem in part from our membership in groups. However, groups also lead us to look more favorably on our other group members than on those who are not in our groups.

we can do to avoid prejudice and stereotyping. Are prejudice and stereotyping unavoidable? Are they part of our human nature? We will explore these and many other questions throughout this book. A logical analysis of intergroup hostility suggests that there is no rational basis for disliking others simply because they belong to another group. Other groups, like our ingroups, comprise people who have the same right as we do to life and to the pursuit of their dreams. Unfortunately, humans are often far from logical in their thinking (Fiske & Taylor, 1991; Nisbett & Ross, 1980; Plous, 1993), and ingroup favoritism and negative attitudes toward members of other groups remain a pervasive aspect of human society today.

Why is the study of prejudice and stereotyping important? Aside from a need to understand the negative influence such thinking has on the thoughts, feelings, and behavior of people in their daily lives, and how they relate to the targets of their prejudice, it is important to understand that such negative attitudes form the basis for subsequent negative intergroup behavior. Virtually all of history's wars, battles, and other acts of group violence have been driven by some form of prejudice, stereotyping, and/or discrimination (Eidelson & Eidelson, 2003). For example, in the Spanish Inquisition, the American Civil War, the American slave trade, the Holocaust, and the genocide in Rwanda and Yugoslavia, the intergroup prejudice and hostility led to unparalleled bloodshed. Interestingly, some of the most intense intergroup hostility has been based on a difference in religious beliefs. For example, Catholics and Protestants in Northern Ireland have engaged in battles among themselves for decades, leading to great loss of life among each group.

There are those who believe that prejudice and stereotyping are no longer a problem in the United States. For example, some suggest that racism has declined dramatically as a result of desegregation, the Voting Rights Act of 1965, and affirmative action policies in hiring (McConahay, 1986). While it is the case that *overt* expressions of racial prejudice and intergroup hatred have declined dramatically, racial prejudice and stereotypes have by no means disappeared. Virtually any group (racial, age, gender, religious, etc.) one can imagine has been the object of prejudices and stereotypes by other groups or individuals. Our country—indeed, the world—has a long way to go to fully address its prejudices. Sadly, one only need look at newspaper headlines for examples of intergroup violence that are driven purely by prejudice:

- In 2002 gay actor Trev Broudy suffered a brutal attack outside his West Hollywood apartment. The baseball bat beating to his head left him in a coma for more than a week. A succession of strokes and brain surgeries wiped out his memory of the attack. He was also rendered blind, unable to speak, and unable to think clearly.
- In Laramie, Wyoming, in 1998 two young men savagely beat Matthew Sheppard, an openly gay college student, because he was gay. They tied his battered body to a fence in freezing temperatures and left him for dead. Although he was found by a passerby about 30 hours later, he slipped into a coma and died a few days later.
- In 1998 in Jasper, Texas, three white men offered a ride to James Byrd Jr., a Black man, who was walking on the side of the road. The men drove Byrd to a remote location, where they severely beat him, tied his feet to a logging chain, and tied the chain to the back end of their pick-up truck. They then dragged the still-conscious Byrd behind their truck down a remote country road, where Byrd's body quickly disintegrated and he was decapitated as his body hit a storm drain in a ditch near the road.

In the following chapters of this book, we will examine the past and present research and theory on the motivations (the why), the situations and contexts (the when), the individual difference variables and traits (the who), and the affective and cognitive processes (the how) that lead to stereotyping and prejudice. The intent of the present book is to provide an advanced-level undergraduate or first-year graduate student with an in-depth and broad-ranging analysis of stereotyping and prejudice. The text is intended to help the student understand the issues, theories, and important empirical experiments that bear upon each problem in stereotyping and prejudice, and to understand the most up-to-date research, theories, and conclusions of the leading researchers in the field. Stereotyping and prejudice are indeed complex in their origin, and one of the main goals of this book is to provide a coherent picture of the conditions under which stereotyping and prejudice are more, or less, likely to occur.

Another primary focus of the book is to examine whether and how stereotyping and prejudice can be reduced or eliminated. Are such ways of thinking innate and therefore unavoidable? Or are they examples of faulty thinking or "lazy" thinking? Could we eliminate prejudice and stereotyping if we all just *decide* to heed L.A. riots beating victim

Rodney King in his famous plea, "Can we all just get along, please?" As we will see in the coming chapters, such an ideal is very difficult to attain, and it doesn't appear to be the case that people can simply decide to not use stereotypes (Bargh, 1999).

We begin our discussion with a look back, to understand the origins of the concepts *stereotype* and *prejudice* and the various definitions of these words. We will then examine some famous, classic studies of intergroup prejudice and stereotyping. Finally, we will conclude with a discussion of how the rise of social cognition changed the way researchers understand prejudice and stereotyping.

DEFINING STEREOTYPING

Lippmann's "Stereotype"

What is a stereotype? Interestingly, the word *stereotype* originally derives from a term to describe a printing process in which fixed casts of material are reproduced (Ashmore & Del Boca, 1981). This term was adopted by social scientists when journalist Walter Lippmann (1922) used the word *stereotype* to describe the tendency of people to think of someone or something in similar terms—that is, as having similar attributes—based on a common feature shared by each. He said that we all have "pictures in our heads" (p. 3) of the world outside and that these representations are more like templates into which we try to simplify the sometimes confusing information we receive from the world.

Lippmann was prescient in two respects. First, he was remarkably accurate in his speculation about the origin of stereotyping, when he wrote "We pick out what our culture has already defined for us, and we tend to perceive that which we have picked out in the form stereotyped for us by our culture" (1922, p. 55). In other words, stereotypes tell us what social information is important to perceive and to disregard in our environment. This process tends to confirm preexisting stereotypes by paying attention to stereotype-consistent information and disregarding information that is inconsistent with our stereotypes. Subsequent research has shown that, indeed, the content of stereotypes is largely determined by the culture in which one lives (Jones, 1997; Stephan & Rosenfield, 1982; Triandis, 1994). We will discuss this further in the next chapter.

Stereotyping: From Bad to Neutral

As with most concepts in psychology, there are a number of ways that researchers have defined *stereotype* over the decades. Though Lippmann did not express any particular evaluation of the nature of stereotyping, researchers soon began to regard stereotyping as a very negative, lazy way of perceiving social groups. In other words, stereotyping was seen as an outward indicator of irrational, nonanalytic cognition (Stroebe & Insko, 1989). Some researchers (e.g., Adorno, Frenkel-Brunswik, Levinson, & Sanford, 1950) characterized stereotypes as examples of rigid thinking. Many regarded stereotyping as an external sign of the stereotyper's moral defectiveness (Jones, 1997).

However, researchers began to move away from the inclusion of assessments of the morality or correctness of the stereotype or the stereotyper (Ashmore & Del Boca, 1981;

Stephan & Rosenfield, 1982). In his pioneering work, *The Nature of Prejudice,* Allport (1954) was ahead of his time in moving away from including evaluative assessments of the "goodness" of stereotyping or those who stereotype. He defined a stereotype by writing that "a stereotype is an exaggerated belief associated with a category" (p. 191). Other researchers presaged the social-cognition revolution movement in social psychology (e.g., Brown, 1965; Fishman, 1956; Vinacke, 1957) in that they argued that stereotyping ought to be examined as a normal psychological process.

The Social-Cognitive Definition

In the early 1970s, with the birth of social cognition, researchers came to regard stereotyping as a rather automatic process of categorization that many cognitive and social psychologists believe is inherent in the very nature of the way humans think about the world (Fiske & Taylor, 1991; Hamilton & Sherman, 1994). Let us consider a few of the more popular definitions of stereotyping by researchers in the area. Brigham (1971) defined stereotyping as "a generalization made about a . . . group concerning a trait attribution, which is considered to be unjustified by an observer" (p. 31). A problem with this is the last half of the definition: "which is considered to be unjustified by an observer." A stereotype is *any* generalization about a group whether an observer (either a member of the stereotyped group or another observer) believes it is justified or not. By definition, a generalization about a group is bound to be unjustified for some portion of the group members. The question of the justification of a stereotype is virtually synonymous with the question of the accuracy of a stereotype (Lee, Jussim, & McCauley, 1995). This is a controversial issue, and one we will explore later.

Other researchers have adopted Hamilton and Trolier's (1986) definition of a stereotype as "a cognitive structure that contains the perceiver's knowledge, beliefs, and expectations about a human group" (p. 133). Yet, this definition tends to be too broad to accurately capture the true meaning of a stereotype. Although Hamilton and Trolier have included within their definition the notion that a stereotype is the association between a group and one's beliefs about the group, the definition also includes one's *knowledge and expectations* about the group. A problem with the inclusion of these components is that it makes the definition too broad and inconsistent with traditional definitions of a stereotype (Fiske, 1998). Hamilton and Trolier's definition sounds more like the definition of a **schema** than of a stereotype. Judge for yourself by examining Fiske and Taylor's (1991) definition of *schema:* "A schema may be defined as a cognitive structure that represents knowledge about a concept or type of stimulus, including its attributes and the relations among those attributes" (p. 98).

Schemas are therefore broader cognitive structures that contain our knowledge of a stimulus, our expectations for the motives or behavior of the stimulus (if a living being), and our feelings toward the stimulus (Stangor & Schaller, 1996; Taylor & Crocker, 1981). Stereotypes are much more specific and are subsumed within a schema. For example, one's schema of librarians may contain knowledge about that occupation (they work with books), expectations for motives of librarians (they are there to help you locate books and other information within the library), how to feel about librarians (you feel positive because they are helping you), and one's beliefs (stereotypes) about librarians (all librarians are introverted and have poor fashion sense).

Another popular definition of stereotypes, by Ashmore and Del Boca (1981), defines stereotypes as "a set of beliefs about the personal attributes of a group of people" (p. 16). This definition is more consistent with the essence of many past definitions of stereotype because it restricts the meaning of *stereotype* to a generalization about a group of people. Most social-cognition researchers today define stereotype in this fashion (e.g., Gardner, 1994; J. M. Jones, 1997; Kunda, 1999; Schneider, 2004; Wilder, 1993; Worschel & Rothgerber, 1997; Wright & Taylor, 2003). Therefore, this book will use Ashmore and Del Boca's definition of stereotype.

Cultural and Individual Stereotypes

A useful but infrequently used distinction must be made when discussing the definition of *stereotype*. Specifically, it is important to differentiate between **cultural** and **individual stereotypes** (Allport, 1954; Ashmore & Del Boca, 1979, 1981). A cultural stereotype describes "shared or community-wide patterns of beliefs" (Ashmore & Del Boca, 1981, p. 19), whereas an individual stereotype describes the beliefs held by an individual about the characteristics of a group. This difference is important both theoretically and methodologically. Ashmore and Del Boca (1981) suggest that adjective rating scales, such as those used by Katz and Braly (1933, discussed later in this chapter) tend to assess cultural stereotypes. Any other measure of stereotype content in which the respondent's answers are restricted to the stereotype content choices offered by the measure tends to provide an inaccurate measure of the person's stereotype of the group. This is important, because one's cultural stereotype about a group may not be the same as one's individual stereotype about the group. In these cases, assessing a person's knowledge about the stereotypes of the group in their culture yields no information on whether the individual personally believes the stereotype or whether there are other ideas about the group that may tend to drive one's attitude toward the group (Devine, 1989). The question is, which of these two—cultural or individual stereotypes—tends to predict future behavior and attitudes toward a given group? While early thinking, exemplified by Lippmann (1922), suggested that "we tend to perceive that which we have picked out in the form stereotyped for us by our culture" (p. 55), contemporary researchers tend to be interested primarily in assessing individual stereotypes, because many experiments have demonstrated that these are most directly related to that person's specific thoughts, feelings, and behavior toward the group (Dovidio, Brigham, Johnson, & Gaertner, 1996; Esses, Haddock, & Zanna, 1993; Fazio & Olson, 2003; Kunda, 1999; Stangor, Sullivan, & Ford, 1991).

Is a Stereotype an Attitude?

There is some debate concerning the nature of stereotypes. Some researchers believe that a stereotype is similar to an **attitude.** An attitude is a general evaluation of some object (Eagly & Chaiken, 1993). Any attitude is usually viewed as falling somewhere on a good-bad, or favorable-unfavorable dimension. For example, you may have a favorable attitude toward soccer but an unfavorable attitude toward table tennis. Researchers have traditionally viewed attitudes as comprising three components: a behavioral component, an affective component, and a cognitive component (Breckler, 1984; Eagly & Chaiken, 1998). Thus, some theorists define stereotypes as intergroup attitudes, partitioned into these three components. However, the majority of researchers in this area agree that stereotypes represent only the cognitive portion of any intergroup attitude (Dovidio et al., 1996; Fiske, 1998; Hamilton & Sherman, 1994). The other two components of an intergroup attitude, affect and behavior, correspond to prejudice and discrimination, respectively. **Discrimination** is defined as any negative behavior directed toward an individual based on their membership in a group. We will define and discuss prejudice in more detail below. In sum, although a stereotype is not an attitude, an intergroup attitude is composed of one's thoughts or beliefs about, feelings toward, and behavior toward a particular group.

Positive versus Negative Stereotypes

You may have noticed that the definition of *stereotype* just given does not indicate anything about the affective valence (positive or negative) of the stereotype. When most people think of stereotypes, they think of a "bad" characteristic associated with a group of people (e.g., having undesirable traits, such as laziness). However, researchers do not regard stereotypes as being bad or good (Allport, 1954). Rather, they are merely generalizations about a group. You no doubt are aware of many more negative stereotypes about various groups than positive stereotypes associated with those groups. Positive stereotypes are simply beliefs that attribute desirable or positive characteristics to a group. For example, such a stereotype exists in the United States about Asians and their intelligence. Specifically, this positive stereotype might be phrased, "All Asians excel at mathematics and science." The stereotype suggests that the whole group has a very desirable characteristic. So, why would people resent being the object of positive stereotyping? Throughout this book, we will explore this question and discuss the major factors that lead to the formation of positive and negative stereotypes.

DEFINING PREJUDICE

To have prejudice about something can mean many things, depending on one's frame of reference for the term. As Gardner (1994) suggests, the word *prejudice* can be taken literally to indicate a prejudgment about something. At a further level of specificity, prejudice can suggest an evaluation, either positive or negative, toward a stimulus. For example, you might be prejudiced in favor of your favorite football team when it is playing another team (i.e., you have a preformed positive evaluation of your team, relative to the other team). Finally, Gardner specified another definition of prejudice, in which the individual has a *negative* evaluation of another stimulus (Gardner, 1994). As you read these different perspectives on prejudice, you may notice that the last two use the term "evaluation." Essentially, an evaluation is an attitude, as we discussed earlier. This brings us to a controversial point in the prejudice literature.

In a famous photograph, Elizabeth Eckford ignores the hateful taunts of whites who oppose her attending the previously all-white Central High School in Little Rock, Arkansas (circa 1957). Because such open expressions of racism are far less frequent today, some believe that prejudice and discrimination are problems of the past. But much research shows that prejudice is still very much a problem in the United States and elsewhere, and that expressions of racism have changed from being overt to being very subtle.

Prejudice as Negative Affect

Early theorists tended to define prejudice in terms of its affective basis. In his influential book *The Nature of Prejudice* Allport (1954) defined prejudice as "an antipathy [intense dislike] based upon a faulty and inflexible generalization. It may be felt or expressed. It may be directed toward a group as a whole, or toward an individual because he is a member of that group" (p. 9). From this classic perspective, prejudice is seen as a strong negative feeling about someone based on a generalization one has about that person's group. This view corresponds most clearly with the traditional view of an intergroup attitude as composed of cognition, affect, and behavior, as discussed earlier. In such a model, prejudice is the affective component of the intergroup attitude. Most researchers (but not all, see Fiske, 1998; Schneider, 2004), however, soon abandoned the prejudice-as-emotion definition, in favor of more complex definitions of prejudice (Dovidio, et al., 1996; Hamilton, Stroessner, & Driscoll, 1994; Stephan & Stephan, 1993). Why the move toward defining prejudice as an attitude? We will consider this, and then we will arrive at a working definition of *prejudice* for our purposes in this book.

Prejudice as an Attitude

During the 1960s, and especially with the rise of social cognition in the early 1970s, researchers started regarding prejudice as an evaluation of a stimulus (usually, a social group). As such, prejudice is essentially an attitude. Like an attitude, therefore, prejudice is seen by most researchers to have cognitive, affective, and behavioral components (Dovidio & Gaertner, 1986; Dovidio et al., 1996; Harding, Proshansky, Kutner, & Chein, 1969; Jones, 1997). One problem with the earlier definitions of prejudice concerns the focus on the negative affect toward the outgroup. This unnecessarily limits the definition of prejudice, because prejudice can also refer to positive prejudice in favor of one's ingroup (ingroup favoritism) (Eagly & Chaiken, 1993; Jones, 1997). Most research, however, tends to focus on the more familiar negative type of prejudice.

Prejudice can be based on affective (e.g., anger), cognitive (e.g., beliefs linking hostility to the outgroup), or behavioral (e.g., avoidant or hostile) sources and can result in cognitive, behavioral, or affective expressions of prejudice. It seems, though, that affect is a common, influential basis upon which most prejudice is based. Stangor, Sullivan, and Ford (1991) found that the best predictor of negative outgroup prejudice is not negative feelings about the outgroup but, rather, a lack of positive emotions. Based on these findings, some have suggested that stronger, more obvious forms of prejudice are more likely to be based on strong negative emotions, whereas more subtle types of prejudice may be based on an absence of positive feelings about the outgroup (Brewer, 1998; Pettigrew & Meertens, 1995). In an interesting study, Jackson, Hodge, Gerard, Ingram, Ervin, and Sheppard (1996) assessed the cognitions, affect, and behaviors of 869 White college students toward various minority groups. They found that affect and behavior were the strongest predictors of group attitudes. The authors suggest that the quality of an intergroup interaction therefore is most dependant on "how good people feel, not how well they think of group members" (p. 314).

A recent, interesting approach by Eagly and Diekman (2005) suggests that prejudice should be regarded as an "attitude-in-context." According to this model, prejudice is not inflexible; rather, it depends on the match (or lack thereof) between the social role into which the stereotyped individual is trying to fit and the beliefs of the perceiver about the attributes that are required for success in that role. If the role is highly valued, the prototypical member (e.g., Caucasian) in that role will tend to be viewed only slightly more positively than a role-incongruent (e.g., African American) individual in that position. Eagly and Diekman argue that prejudice is most likely to be displayed toward a disadvantaged group when that group tries to move into roles for which they are believed by the majority group to be unqualified (Eagly & Karau, 2002). This is a promising conceptualization of prejudice, and one that deserves further empirical and theoretical attention.

There have been some critics of the prejudice-as-attitude approach, however. Criticism centers around a couple of core problems. First, some theorists assert that an attitude (or evaluation) is not the same as affect (Fiske, 1998; Zanna & Rempel, 1988). If prejudice is an affect-based reaction to a stimulus group (as Allport, 1954, suggests it is), then it cannot be the case that an evaluation of the group is the same thing as prejudice. Second, Devine (1995) asserts that the notion that prejudice has an affective, cognitive, and behavioral component is problematic because research shows that the three components are not always consistent. For example, Devine (1989) found that low-prejudice individuals know about stereotypes of their outgroups, and LaPiere (1934) found that people's expressed attitudes did not match their behavior toward the outgroup.

Prejudice as a "Social Emotion"

In an insightful paper, Smith (1993) draws on appraisal theories of emotion and self-categorization theory to suggest a new conceptualization of prejudice. Self-categorization theory (Turner, 1987) states that people view themselves as a member of a social category or group (e.g., a racial, national, ethnic, religious group, etc.). According to this theory, intergroup interactions will make salient (or bring to conscious awareness) particular group categorizations, depending on the nature of the group interaction. For example, when I interact with someone of a different religious belief, my religious self-categorization may be most salient. Or, if I interact with a French citizen, my self-categorization as a U.S. citizen may be most salient. These distinctions serve to enhance the perception of the outgroup as homogeneous (we will discuss this further in Chapter 2). Turner also suggests that these self-categorizations tend to be strongly linked to one's self-identity, and as such, when they are salient, any self-relevant information in the interaction has affective and motivational consequences (Smith, 1993).

According to Smith and Ellsworth (1987), an **appraisal** is a set of cognitions that are attached to a specific emotion. Emotion, in appraisal theory, is triggered by an assessment of the adaptive significance and self-relevance of the people and events in one's environment. For example, the emotion of fear might be elicited when one perceives that a situation or individual is out of one's control or unpleasant and blocks one from attaining one's goals (e.g., to stay alive, stay healthy, etc.). Smith (1993) suggests that appraisals invariably involve the self, because they have relevance to one's goals in some fashion. There are two key differences in Smith's conceptualization of prejudice that make it a unique and very useful model of prejudice. First, he says that it is too vague to say that prejudice is a positive or negative feeling about another group. Our emotional reactions to other groups are quite specific, such as anger, fear, disgust, excitement, happiness, or serenity (Bodenhausen, 1993). Second, the traditional conception of prejudice suggests that if we are prejudiced against another group (e.g., lawyers), then we should react with the same negative affect to all members of the group every time we encounter them. But, this does not fit with reality. Many prejudiced people can dislike the group as a whole, and most of its members, but have genuinely positive attitudes and affect toward a specific member of that group (e.g., a friend, a neighbor, a celebrity).

Some have suggested that this reaction can be explained in terms of **subtyping,** whereby the prejudiced individual maintains a negative affect toward the group but creates a separate category (e.g., friend, coworker, etc.) for specific members, thereby allowing the perceiver's stereotypes to persist in the face of what would otherwise be a stereotype-disconfirming case (Weber & Crocker, 1983). However, Smith contends that this obscures the fact that how we react to other people does not depend on the type of group member they are, but who a person is, in what context, and how we appraise that individual in terms of our goals. So, how we react to any given outgroup member depends on (1) what self-category is salient for us at that moment (e.g., Nelson & Wischusen, 1999), (2) in what context the interaction occurs (competitive, cooperative, etc.), and (3) how that person helps or hinders our movement toward salient personal or group goals at that time. This is a much richer conceptualization of prejudice than has been proposed in the past, and it goes a long way toward capturing the complexity of affect, cognition, behavior, and motivation in intergroup interactions. We will return to this further when we discuss social-identity theory (Tajfel & Turner, 1979).

If all these approaches to defining prejudice seem a bit confusing, you are not alone. Among today's prejudice researchers, there is little consensus and much debate over how precisely prejudice should be defined. Definitions differ on several issues, as discussed. An important consideration is how to measure prejudice. Some suggest that concepts such as affect, emotion, or feelings presuppose a physiological reaction (Oatley, 1993; Zajonc, 1998). As such, our ability to measure feelings or affect toward outgroups is not as precise as our measurements of people's evaluations, attitudes, or beliefs about other groups (Walter Stephan, personal communication, June 7, 1999). It is not practical to have a definition of prejudice that contains a concept that is not easily measured. Thus, in addition to the aforementioned theoretical reasons for conceptualizing prejudice as an attitude, the movement to view prejudice in this way was also strongly initiated by the practical constraints of how to measure prejudice. Currently, prejudice is most commonly measured by standardized self-report measures that assess the endorsement of statements about the characteristics of a group, feelings about the group, and behavior toward the group and its members (Dovidio et al., 1996).

Given the myriad definitions of *prejudice,* how should it be defined? Before we address this question, it is important to note that there really is no single "correct" definition. The way one defines *prejudice* often depends on the specific research questions one is looking at, as well as the way the investigator intends to measure prejudice. However, researchers can generally agree on a few points (Devine, 1995; Jones, 1997).

Prejudice:

1. Occurs between groups
2. Involves an evaluation (positive or negative) of a group
3. Is a biased perception of a group
4. Is based on the real or imagined characteristics of the group

Therefore, for the purposes of this book, we will define *prejudice* as *a biased evaluation of a group, based on real or imagined characteristics of the group members.* Note that this definition allows for both positive and negative prejudice, such as the favorable attitudes one has for one's ingroups, compared to the negative attitudes one has toward outgroups, respectively. Although the definition of *prejudice* as encompassing an evaluation (attitude) does not resolve the debate over whether prejudice ought to be considered an attitude, an emotion, or a social emotion, we will use this definition to be consistent with the majority of the contemporary researchers in this area.

THE LINK BETWEEN STEREOTYPING
AND PREJUDICE

It seems intuitive that stereotypes should be strongly related to prejudice and to discrimination. Thinking about a group will elicit from memory the schema about the group, including the stereotypes, affect, and behavioral tendencies toward members of that group (Collins & Loftus, 1975). As you will recall, this is based on the notion that an intergroup attitude comprises one's beliefs about, evaluations of, and behavior toward a group. The representations of these concepts tend to be grouped and linked together in memory under the organizing structure of a schema.

The idea that stereotypes and prejudice should be strongly related was also supported by the balance theory (Heider, 1958) as well as Fishbein and Ajzen's (1975) theory of reasoned action (Stroebe & Insko, 1989). According to the balance theory, one's attitudes, behavior, and evaluation (and affect) toward another person should be cognitively consistent, or else one experiences a state of "imbalance," which is an aversive state of "cognitive arousal." Festinger (1957) called this "cognitive dissonance." One way to think of this is that when we say one thing and do another we feel foolish or hypocritical. Balance theory says that it does not make sense for one to have positive attitudes toward, for example, lawyers but to tell negative jokes about them. According to the theory of reasoned action, our beliefs about a group will be determined by our attitudes toward a group. So, in this model, it could never be the case that the beliefs (stereotypes) about the group would not be consistent with one's attitudes (or prejudice) toward the group.

There were some researchers, however, who said that beliefs, attitudes, and behavior were weakly or inconsistently related. In the late 1960s, Wicker (1969) published a seemingly devastating criticism of the attitude–behavior relationship. He reviewed 42 studies and concluded that there was virtually no evidence that people have stable attitudes that guide their behavior. Though this criticism aroused a lot of attention among social scientists, causing others to question the validity and utility of the whole field of attitude research (Elms, 1975), researchers showed that the explanation for Wicker's results was simple. Wicker examined the relation between attitudes and single acts. However, much research has shown that actions are multiply determined by a number of other factors besides attitudes (Fishbein & Ajzen, 1975). Thus, Fishbein and Ajzen argued, the relationship between an attitude and subsequent attitude-relevant behavior is much stronger if one "aggregates" multiple behaviors into a single behavior measure. In this way, the behavioral measure is much more likely to show consistency around a true behavioral tendency (Eagly & Chaiken, 1993).

However, more criticism existed concerning the specific relation between ethnic attitudes and behavior toward members of ethnic groups. In Brigham's comprehensive review of the literature (1971), he concluded that the relationship between stereotypes of a group and behavior toward that group was quite weak. According to Dovidio et al. (1996), Brigham reached that conclusion based on an imprecise consideration of the methodological variations between all the studies he reviewed for his paper. Dovidio and his colleagues performed a sophisticated statistical analysis called meta-analysis on a dozen studies and found that not only were stereotyping and prejudice related, they were strongly related.

EARLY PERSPECTIVES
IN STEREOTYPING RESEARCH

Like other subfields within psychology, social psychology has gone through a number of evolutions in the foci of its theories, methodology, and phenomena under investigation. In this section, we will discuss some of the major approaches to understanding stereotyping and prejudice, and we will conclude with a discussion of the current dominant approach, the social-cognition perspective.

Measurement

In the early 1900s, when social psychology was in its infancy as a scientific discipline, researchers were primarily concerned with understanding and cataloging the content of stereotypes. The Katz and Braly (1933) study was a prime example of this empirical focus. In what has been widely acknowledged as the first empirical study of stereotyping, Katz and Braly (1933) investigated the content of the stereotypes that Whites had regarding 10 different ethnic groups (Ashmore & Del Boca, 1981; Hamilton, et al., 1994; Stroebe & Insko, 1989). Students at Princeton University were given a list of adjectives and asked to specify which adjectives were associated with various ethnic groups. The content of the stereotype, therefore, consisted of those adjectives that were most frequently indicated for a particular group.

Research was focusing on refining ways to assess, through various attitude measurement techniques (e.g., Likert-type, Thurstone, Guttman attitude scales, etc.), the way people evaluated their world. Attitude research was an important cornerstone of social psychology, and it remains so today. The reason for this is straightforward. If, as social psychologists believe, the best way to predict someone's actions in a given context is to know how they think about that context and the stimuli within it (i.e., their attitudes), then knowing the individual's attitude ought to allow the researcher to predict with a fair degree of accuracy the individual's behavior in that context. For example, if I know that John has a positive attitude toward Bruce but a negative attitude toward Bill, I would likely be accurate in predicting that John's verbal and nonverbal behavior toward Bruce would be characterized as friendly, whereas his behavior toward Bill would likely be cold, aloof, or even rude. While such a prediction seems fairly obvious, the assumption upon which it rests—that attitudes predict and are related to subsequent attitude-relevant behavior—has been a contentious one, as we have already discussed. After much controversy, researchers today do agree that attitudes can allow one to predict subsequent attitude-relevant behavior with a fair degree of accuracy (Eagly & Chaiken, 1993). The next question for the researcher then becomes, what is the best way to measure stereotyping and prejudice? We will discuss this in detail in Chapter 5.

Individual Differences in Stereotyping

From the 1930s through the 1950s, a popular approach to understanding stereotyping was to examine the factors that lead individuals to stereotype others. That is, what sort of enduring personality characteristics or motivations would cause one person, but not another, to stereotype other people? The influential research of Hovland, Janis, and Kelly (1953) on factors that enhance persuasion was indicative of this approach. Among the results from their extensive program of research, Hovland et al. found that persuasion messages were more likely to be successful when directed toward a certain type of audience. Specifically, people who were less educated, distracted, and lower in self-esteem tended to be persuaded more easily than to other people. Research on attitude formation and change during this time was dominated by assumptions from theories of learning and reinforcement (Eagly & Chaiken, 1993). The theories of Hull (1943), Skinner (1953), Miller & Dollard (1941), and other learning theorists suggested that a primary reason that certain attitudes are formed and maintained is that the expression of such attitudes was followed by reinforcing events (e.g., social approval).

Recall that during this period in American history, the racial climate was one of deep division, and society was segregated. African Americans had very few rights that Caucasians enjoyed. Indeed, other groups, such as women and members of the Communist Party, were stereotyped and given unequal status in society. The motivational-reinforcement theories suggest that the prevalence of prejudice and stereotyping at that time was attributable to the need for social approval and self-esteem. If people felt poorly about themselves and their lot in life, all they needed to do was to publicly derogate a particular stereotyped group, and they could find ready allies in complete strangers who felt the same motives and negative attitudes. Thus, stereotyping can be explained by Thorndike's (1911) Law of Effect, which says that any behavior that is followed by a positive event will be more likely to be performed again in the future. From this perspective, then, Hovland et al.'s (1953) findings about the susceptibility to persuasion among individuals who are less educated and who have lower self-esteem seems to fit nicely with the motivations such individuals have to attempt to enhance their self-esteem.

Other researchers suggested that prejudice and stereotyping arose out of feelings of aggression (Dollard, Doob, Miller, Mowrer, & Sears, 1939). In their "frustration–aggression" theory, Dollard et al. suggest that frustration leads to aggression, and a special type of aggression is feelings of prejudice toward others. There is some interesting indirect evidence that bears on this theory. Hovland and Sears (1940) reported a negative correlation between the price of cotton and the number of lynchings of African Americans in the southern states of the United States between 1882 and 1930. That is, as the price dropped (meaning worse economic times), the greater the number of lynchings. Hepworth and West (1988) later reanalyzed these data and confirmed Hovland and Sears' conclusions, with one specification: that the rates of lynching were highest when hard economic times followed a period of positive growth in the economy. In a recent paper, however, Green, Glaser, and Rich (1998) found problems with Hepworth and West's analyses, and they made a compelling case that, in fact, there is no relation between economic downturn and rates of lynching. They suggest that this is because frustration as a result of hard economic times tends to dissipate fast. Also, in the absence of a strong political figure directing that frustration toward a scapegoat outgroup, the frustration is not focused into outgroup hostility (e.g., hate crimes) before it dissipates.

Another problem with this "scapegoat theory of prejudice" (Jones, 1997), is that it suggests that frustration leads to aggression (and prejudice) toward any salient stimulus or group, not necessarily African Americans. However, the evidence in support of the theory focuses primarily on hostility toward African Americans, and little evidence has been reported that would show such displaced frustration against other groups. Another problem is that subsequent research has shown that not all frustration leads to aggression (or prejudice), and not all prejudice is caused by frustration. Berkowitz (1989) reformulated the frustration–aggression theory to better account for such situations by stipulating that *any* negative affect (not just a frustrating event) is likely to elicit aggressive feelings. This is especially the case when the negative affect results from an unanticipated thwarted goal.

In addition to the motivational approaches, other research has investigated the question of whether some people have so-called prejudiced personalities. Exemplifying this perspective was the research by Adorno, Frenkel-Brunswick, Levinson, & Sanford, 1950 on what they referred to as the "authoritarian personality." Adorno et al. believed some people's personality characteristics caused them to be prejudiced. According to this view, a child's early experiences with their parents determine whether they will develop a prejudiced personality. Driven by unconscious impulses created out of these early child–parent interactions, the child (and later as an adult) tends to seek out and adopt prejudiced attitudes. If this sounds psychodynamic, you are not alone. Most researchers characterize this view of prejudice as having strong psychodynamic roots (Fiske, 1998; Hamilton et al., 1994). What characterizes the authoritarian individual is a rigid adherence to middle-class values, submissiveness to authority, close-mindedness, black-and-white thinking, preoccupation with power relationships (e.g., leader–follower, strong–weak), cynicism, and condemnation of those who are perceived to be violating traditional values. Interestingly, although the distribution of authoritarian personalities varies within a given country, factors that threaten one's values will increase the tendency of the individual to display authoritarian characteristics (Sales, 1973). In essence, then, people with an authoritarian personality are strongly attached to the status quo (Simonton, 1990). Anything that threatens this will be met with hostility and prejudice. We will discuss the supportive evidence and criticisms of the authoritarian-personality approach to the origin of prejudice in much more detail in Chapter 4. The authoritarian-personality explanation generated much research, but with the rise of group-level approaches to stereotyping and prejudice, the focus on individual-level factors receded into the background.

Group-Level Explanations

From the close of the 1950s to the early 1970s researchers began to focus on cultural and broader group-level explanations for stereotyping and prejudice (Duckitt, 1992). Duckitt (1992) describes the shift from an individual-differences focus to a group-level focus as originating in two factors. First, individual-level explanations were unable to adequately explain why there was much more prejudice and racism in the southern states of the United States. The fact that prejudice existed on such a large scale could not be accounted for by either authoritarian personality or frustration. Second, the rise of the civil-rights movement in the late 1950s highlighted the institutionalized nature of racism in the United States and showed that less-prejudiced people were condoning racism right alongside the more blatant racists. This meant that there must be something else, something on a larger scale that better accounts for why Caucasians were prejudiced against African Americans.

A popular approach was to explain prejudice and stereotyping as a result of a perceived group threat. In other words, if one perceived that a member of an outgroup (and, by association, that person's whole outgroup) impeded one's goals, such an event may evoke in the perceiver the idea that that outgroup poses a threat to one's ingroup generally, not just to one's personal goals (Fiske & Ruscher, 1993). Such a perception could arise from the view that the outgroup's goals are incompatible with the goals of one's ingroup, or that those goals interfere with one's ingroup goals. Anything that blocks one (or one's group) from reaching a desired goal should elicit a reaction of frustration, anxiety, anger, and so forth directed toward the blocking agent.

Another group-level approach was the explanation of prejudice as the result of competition for scarce resources. This was the prediction from the **realistic-conflict theory** (Campbell, 1965; Sherif, Harvey, White, Hood, & Sherif, 1961). According to this theory, prejudice and stereotyping of outgroups arises when groups compete against one another for scarce resources (e.g., jobs, food, land, etc.). Much research supports the notion that such competition enhances prejudice against and stereotypes about one's competing outgroups (Brown, 1995). We will discuss Realistic Conflict Theory in detail in Chapter 2. As the 1960s ended, theoretical developments in cognitive and social psychology converged to give rise to the current approach to understanding stereotyping and prejudice: the social-cognition perspective.

THE SOCIAL-COGNITION REVOLUTION

By the late 1950s, psychology as a field had begun to shift from an emphasis on learning theory and behaviorism to embrace a more cognitive approach to understanding the causes of behavior. Many prominent researchers have even agreed on the date of birth for this "cognitive science": September 11, 1956 (Gardner, 1985). On that date, researchers met at the Massachusetts Institute of Technology for a symposium on information theory. Seminal talks were delivered by Herbert Simon, George Miller, and Noam Chomsky. These researchers and others (e.g., Von Neumann, 1958) noted that the computer provided a useful analog of how the mind processes information (i.e., it takes in information, does something with the information, and produces an output). This information-processing model of cognition soon dominated many areas of psychology. These advances had a tremendous impact on social psychology.

Cognitive-Consistency Theories

From the late 1950s through the 1960s, researchers focused on cognitive-consistency theories of behavior. The most notable of these was Festinger's (1957) cognitive-dissonance theory. Dissonance theory suggested that people are motivated to maintain consistent cognitions (or consistency between cognitions and behaviors) and that the lack of cognitive consistency led to an aversive physiological state (dissonance). Festinger (1957) proposed that people are strongly motivated to reduce this drive state by changing either their behavior or their cognitions. Festinger used the example of a smoker to illustrate dissonance. Suppose a smoker knows that smoking is bad for their health but smokes anyway. These behaviors are cognitively inconsistent and should produce dissonance, motivating them to change either their behavior or the way they think about it. Many behavioral tendencies, especially addictive habits such as smoking, are very difficult to abandon. Thus, the easiest route by which the smoker can reduce their dissonance is changing their attitude toward smoking (from thinking about its harmful effects to convincing themself that it has not been *proved* to be harmful). It should be noted that the cognitive inconsistency did not need to be an exact, true inconsistency to arouse dissonance. Even perceived inconsistencies aroused the same negative drive state. This is a major point to which we will return in a moment. Some saw cognitive-consistency theory as a way to reduce prejudice and stereotyping. It seems quite elegant in its simplicity: all one needs to do is to show the prejudiced person that there is an inconsistency between how they think of themself (i.e., as a good, fair person) and their negative attitudes and behavior toward outgroup members, and dissonance will be aroused. The dissonance will cause the person to change their attitudes and behavior toward the outgroup. Unfortunately, cognitive-consistency theories fell out of favor with social cognition researchers (and stereotype researchers in particular) because it could not account for many instances of blatant inconsistency in attitudes and behavior (Fiske & Taylor, 1991). It became clear that people often behaved in ways that were inconsistent with their attitudes and that they did not appear to be bothered by that fact.

Attribution Theory

In the late 1960s and throughout the 1970s social psychologists embraced attribution theory as a model of much processing of social information (Jones, Kanouse, Kelley, Nisbett, Valins, & Weiner, 1972; Jones, 1985). The central question in attribution is, to what do we attribute the causes of another person's (and our own) behavior? The causes are attributed to either internal characteristics of the person (e.g., personality traits) or to the situational pressures or other environmental factors external to the individual (e.g., the constraints of a job). According to this perspective, we are all "naive scientists" (Heider, 1958) testing our own theories of the causes of other people's behavior. From the standpoint of attribution theory, stereotyping and prejudice emerge as a result of cognitive processes that lead people to disproportionately suspect negative (threatening) motivations or causes for the behavior of outgroup members. At the heart of attribution theory, like cognitive-dissonance theory, was a core notion that was to become the cornerstone of the social-cognition approach to social psychology and to theories of stereotyping and prejudice in particular: the best predictor of an individual's behavior or attitudes in relation to a stimulus is the individual's construal of the stimulus, not the influence of the objective qualities of the stimulus on the perceiver (Fiske & Taylor, 1991; Jones, 1985). Behaviorism suggests that if one can understand the lawful relationships between an organism and its environment, then one will be able to predict the organism's behavior from an assessment of the characteristics of the environmental stimuli present at any given moment. This perspective suggests that we all react to the same stimuli in the same way. However, humans do not react the same way to a given stimulus. If 10 people stand in Chicago's Art Institute, looking at Seurat's famous painting *A Sunday at La Grande Jatte,* their perceptions of that stimulus (and their reactions to it) would likely be different for each person. It is the same for any stimulus in the environment: the way we think about it determines our reactions to it.

Let me give you an example I use in my classes (silly as it is, students love to see me act this out) to illustrate this point. Suppose you and I are on an elevator, with no one else on the elevator with us. You are minding your own business as the elevator doors close and it begins to move, when suddenly I walk over to you and step on your foot. How would you react? Most people would become quite angry at such an unprovoked attack. But why? Because in quickly ascertaining the most likely cause of my behavior, they see no obvious external force (environmental factor) that made me do what I just did. Thus, the only attribution left is a personality explanation (and a hostile personality I must have to do such a thing!). Now, suppose we are on a crowded elevator, and you are standing behind me, and I back up to let others get in the elevator. In the process, I step on your foot. Would you react with the same anger? Likely not, because you have noticed that the most likely explanation for my behavior is the fact that others forced me to step back, and I accidentally stepped on your foot in doing so. The interesting point here is a powerful one: objectively it is the same act (stepping on your foot), but your behavior, affect, and attitude toward me are quite different depending on your construal, or interpretation, of the reasons for my behavior. We will explore this in further detail throughout the book.

The "naive scientist" approach suggested that people will use a rational thought process to arrive at an accurate assessment of the causes of another's behavior. A problem with this view soon emerged as more attribution research was conducted. There were many instances in which people had plenty of access to information and plenty of time to arrive at a thoughtful attributional judgment, and yet their judgments reflected something else. Research revealed that people are often irrational, inefficient thinkers and that they allow biases and shortcuts to influence their thinking (Nisbett & Ross, 1980). For this and other reasons, research in attribution theory declined by the end of the 1970s, supplanted by an ever more sophisticated view of the biases, tendencies, and limitations of cognition that can contribute to reliable phenomena that enhance the tendency to form and maintain stereotypes and prejudice about others. Before we conclude this brief history of the cognitive revolution in social psychology, it is important to make something clear about the nature of this revolution. It is not the case that social psychology was devoid of any emphasis on cognition prior to these theoretical shifts in the late 1950s and 1960s. To the contrary, Zajonc (1980) has rightly noted that social psychology has always been strongly interested in cognition. At the infancy of the field, the dominant area of research was the study of attitudes (Allport, 1935). The study of social influence, altruism, and attraction all have heavy emphases on how people think about their environment. So, rather than going from no cognitive emphases to a strong cognitive emphasis, it is more accurate to say that the field went from a moderate to heavy emphasis on cognition, with alternating periods of waxing and waning interest in cognitive explanations of social behavior (Jones, 1985).

THE SOCIAL-COGNITION VIEW OF STEREOTYPING
AND PREJUDICE

In 1969 Tajfel published a landmark paper entitled "Cognitive Aspects of Prejudice." In it he suggested that the origin of stereotyping and prejudice cannot be adequately understood unless one considers their cognitive aspects. He preceded the social-cognition movement in social psychology by a few years and was one of the first to assert that stereotyping originates from a process of social categorization. Tajfel showed that social categorization had a major impact on how a perceiver views others, and this was a fundamental principle for the social-cognitive approach (Ashmore & Del Boca, 1981; Hamilton & Sherman, 1994). This also marked a significant shift in the way stereotyping was viewed. If it was the case that stereotyping was a product of the inherent limitations of our cognitive systems (as suggested by Tajfel), then the view of stereotyping as an external sign of the individual's moral failings was not entirely correct. Rather, Tajfel asserted that stereotyping was a result of a very adaptive, efficient categorization process of cognition (Rothbart & Lewis, 1994).

Categorization

That the brain had limitations on the amount of information processing it could handle was not news to psychologists. Indeed, about 15 years earlier, Miller (1956) showed this with his famous paper on the limited capacity of short-term memory. What was novel was the connection between categorization and stereotyping, and that categorization was an inevitable aspect of human cognition. At any given second, there are hundreds, even thousands, of different stimuli that can be perceived in our immediate environment. If we constantly had to think carefully about every one of those stimuli (or even a small subset thereof), in order to understand its nature and function, we would never get anything done. Instead, we learn about different stimuli and tend to group them in terms of common features, attributes, or functions. This categorization process then becomes so well practiced as to become automatic, and it frees up our consciousness to attend to things that are novel in our environment, or to our current task (Fiske & Neuberg, 1990). Thus, categorization helps us reduce the complexity of the stimuli in our social environment.

Many researchers agree that the primary way we categorize other people is in terms of who is like us, and who is not like us (Jones, 1982; Tajfel, 1969). That is, we group people into "us" and "them" (Perdue, Dovidio, Gurtman, & Tyler, 1990). Although we can categorize people on the basis of virtually any real or perceived feature, most categorization takes place with the fastest and most immediately available ways of categorizing others: in terms of race, gender, and age. These have been termed **"basic," or "primitive," categories** (Brewer, 1988; Fiske & Neuberg, 1990) to denote the notion that they seem to occur rather automatically, without conscious effort to initiate such categorization (Smith, 1990).

There is an important difference between the categorization of physical objects and the categorization of people, however. With physical objects, such as a pencil, there is usually only one way to categorize the object (e.g., a pencil is a writing instrument). There are, however, many ways to categorize a person (e.g., by race, gender, occupation, hair color, style of clothes, religion, etc.), and the way we categorize the target individual depends on the involvement, motivations, and interests of the perceiver (Kunda, 1999; Spears, Oakes, Ellemers, & Haslam, 1997). Bodenhausen and Macrae (1998) suggested that when we are confronted with multiple ways of categorizing another person, we will usually focus on one primary categorization and inhibit information that makes us think of other categories for that person. The stereotypes we have for another person, and the biasing effects of that initial categorization are often determined by chance factors. For example, research by

Macrae, Bodenhausen, and Milne (1995) investigated how people would categorize a Chinese woman who appeared in a short videotape. When participants saw her in a context that made salient her race (i.e., she was eating with chopsticks), they recognized Chinese stereotypic words faster than female stereotypic words on a subsequent reaction-time assessment. When these researchers showed another group of participants the same woman, this time in a video clip in which she was applying makeup, participants were faster at recognizing female stereotype words than they were at recognizing Chinese stereotype words.

Other research indicates that how we categorize someone (e.g., based on a role, gender, occupation, or race) is determined by the fit between these categories and the knowledge that is accessible in memory at that moment. Thus, if the characteristics "educated," "logical" and "competitive" are accessible when one is forming an impression of a particular target, we may tend to use the category "lawyer" to guide our further impressions of the target, as opposed to the individual's gender, race, or other possible categories of membership (Stapel & Koomen, 1998). Additionally, the relationship of the two individuals in the social context is an important factor that will determine how the target person is perceived. As Spears, Doosje, and Ellemers (1997) note, the involvement of the perceiver in the social context invalidates the idea that there is a theoretical fixed point of reference for the perceiver to view other individuals. In other words, it is incorrect to say that the perceiver does not influence, but is influenced by, the target person, and from that alone they categorizes the target. This is an important point, and one to which we will return shortly, in our discussion of the motivated tactician.

Categorizing people makes it easy to develop stereotypes about them. If I categorize a group of people on the basis of a similar characteristic they share (e.g., that they are all women), one thing that begins to happen is that I will start to infer (or guess) that because they share one characteristic, they share a number of other characteristics as well. That seems like a reasonable assumption, because things and people in categories do indeed often share not just one but many attributes (e.g., tables, dogs, men, police officers, etc., may share similar features with other members of their category). However, the problem comes in when these inferences are based on faulty or no evidence at all. For example, suppose I infer that because I know so much about my sister, I know what most women are like. I know what their interests, abilities, tendencies, emotions, personalities, and social skills are like. How do I know all this? Because I know one of those category members (my sister) very well. Thus, I am making the following syllogism: *I know what my sister is like. My sister is a woman. I know what women are like.* I am inferring characteristics about the whole group based on information about one of the specific group members. Is such an inference accurate? Of course not. Is it efficient? You bet it is. But wait. Why would someone sacrifice accuracy for efficiency? Is it not better to be correct in one's assessments of others? Let's explore this in more detail.

The Cognitive Miser

As research on the influences of the cognitive system on social perception developed throughout the 1970s, a recurring theme emerged in the data: people overwhelmingly embrace efficiency rather than accuracy in their perceptions of the social world. This view of the perceiver is often referred to as the "cognitive miser" model (Taylor, 1981). The essence of this view is that people are much more concerned with developing ways of thinking about the world that are fast and efficient (Fiske & Taylor, 1991). Slow yet more accurate cognitive processes are not valued as highly by individuals. The main goal seems to be to arrive at the fastest judgments or evaluations possible. There are a couple of reasons for this. First, if one is able to form an impression quickly, the anxiety associated with not knowing how to behave toward, or what to expect from the target individual is eliminated. Second, there are few, and often no, negative outcomes for arriving at inaccurate assessments of others. For example, walking down the street, you rather automatically categorize virtually everyone you notice (i.e., people who receive even the most minimal attention in your perceptual field). Those dozens of categorizations have no discernible effect on the those people because you do not interact with them; indeed, you may never see most of them again in your life. So the benefits of thinking that you know a lot about those categorized persons and what you might expect from them far outweigh the remote possibility that such an inaccurate categorization would lead to a negative consequence (e.g., getting into a hostile confrontation with the target individual who found out about your inaccurate assessment of them). However, as we will see throughout the remainder of this book, merely thinking of someone in terms of stereotypes can have strong effects on one's behavior and attitudes in that context and in future intergroup situations.

The cognitive-miser model of social perception heavily emphasizes the role of cognition and does not include other factors, such as affect or motivation. This aspect of the model symbolizes a problem that many critics had with the social-cognition movement in social psychology. Many said that social-cognition theories being developed were almost entirely cognition and very little social (Spears, Oakes, et al., 1997). The role of the self, affect, motivation, and other factors receded into the theoretical background in favor of explanations that attempted to understand how the cognitive system worked, and the limitations of that system. However, this criticism is not really a fair one to level at social cognition, because it suggests that researchers were not looking at the whole system—the social and the cognitive together—in understanding how we categorize and stereotype others. Yet, this is the nature of scientific progress (Kuhn, 1970). Specifically, in order to understand the influence of a particular factor on a system, scientists must first understand the nature of the factor itself, uninfluenced by other factors. Once that is established, it is introduced to other factors in varying combinations in different situations to understand how it interacts with other elements in the environment. This was precisely what was happening with the cognitive revolution in social psychology. As researchers began to understand the limitations and extent of cognitive influences in social categorization, the scientific pendulum swung back once again to the roles of affect and motivation in categorization.

The Motivated Tactician

This view of the social perceiver incorporates the cognitive perspective but also includes the motivational and affective factors into an understanding of how intergroup social interactions and social categorization influence the attitudes, affect, and behavior of the perceiver (Fiske & Taylor, 1991; Pendry & Macrae, 1994). According to this perspective, the perceiver is an integral part of the social context, with motivations that vary depending on the dynamic nature of the context. These motivations can bias how the person perceives any other individual, depending on how it best suits the perceiver's salient needs, values, or goals at that given time. This view reflects the richness of the research on affective and motivational states that had developed while social cognition dominated social psychology and intergroup research in particular. Once the parameters and limits of the cognitive factors in social perception were becoming clear, researchers returned to their earlier emphases on motivation (e.g., Adorno et al., 1950; Festinger, 1957) and affect (e.g., Dollard et al., 1939).

From the cognitive-motivational approach, categorization elicits the need to view one's ingroups positively relative to one's outgroups (see Chapter 4 for a more detailed discussion of this point; Duckitt, 1992). Thus, the social perceiver may sometimes think about the target individual in a considered manner in order to enhance accuracy, and sometimes they may elect to consider the other person in a heuristic fashion, to maximize speed or to enhance one's self-esteem (Fiske & Taylor, 1991; Tajfel & Turner, 1979). Researchers have been increasingly interested in understanding the role of motivation (e.g., Kruglanski, 1996) and affect (Mackie & Hamilton, 1993) in intergroup perception. Today, there is a consensus that motivation plays an important role in social cognition, and in outgroup perception specifically (Geen, 1995; Gollwitzer & Moskowitz, 1996). In their review of the literature on motivation and stereotyping, Kunda and Sinclair (1999) concluded that people are more likely to apply a stereotype to a target when it supports their desired impression of the person. Thus, **motivation** is defined in this research as the impetus to do some behavior (or avoid doing some behavior) and to keep doing it, in order to meet one's goals. Interestingly, the authors also argue that people can be motivated to inhibit the activation of a stereotype when they believe it will hinder their personal goals or social interactions. Indeed, there is much evidence to suggest that stereotype inhibition can occur with sufficiently motivated persons (Bodenhausen & Macrae, 1998). We will discuss stereotype inhibition in greater detail in Chapter 2.

WHY THE EMPHASIS ON AFRICAN AMERICAN– WHITE INTERGROUP RELATIONS?

Throughout this text, most of the studies, experiments, and theories we will discuss feature the specific stereotyping and prejudice history between two specific groups, African Americans and Caucasians. Some readers will no doubt wonder why this is the case and may even conclude that it reflects a biased view of prejudice and stereotyping research. Let me assure you that this emphasis reflects no such bias. There are several reasons why I (and other researchers) tend to draw heavily on the theory and data concerning African American and White intergroup relations.

First, the vast majority of the empirical and theoretical literature on prejudice and stereotyping has examined prejudice between African Americans and Caucasians (Dovidio et al., 1996; Jones, 1997). Thus, there is a wealth of scientific information available that gives the researcher a more complete picture of the various factors that contribute to the development and maintenance of prejudice and stereotyping. Second, many agree with Jones (1997) that relations between African Americans and Caucasians tend to reveal stronger, more intense psychological and emotional reactions than the relations among other groups.

As a result, racial attitudes tend to be stronger, less susceptible to change, and consensual (Dovidio et al., 1996). Finally, the political, social, and cultural history of the United States is such that the relationship between African Americans and Caucasians has played a major role in shaping the course of wars (e.g., the Civil War), legislation (e.g., *Brown vs. Board of Education,* the Civil Rights Act of 1964, affirmative action, antidiscrimination laws, etc.), and public policy. It is important to understand how the relations between these groups has affected, and still affects, the United States (Dovidio et al., 1996).

It is important to note that the emphasis of prejudice researchers on African American–White relations does not assume that the processes, factors, and findings that follow from this research will generalize to prejudice and stereotyping between all types of groups (racial, age, religious, etc.). Accordingly, this text focuses on the ways that prejudice and stereotyping are similar and different for various stereotyped groups. One of the aims of this text, however, is to start with the broad database culled from the research on Caucasians and African Americans and attempt to ascertain to what degree the basic cognitive, affective, and behavioral factors that lead to prejudice between these two groups will likely generalize to the ways people think about other stereotyped groups. In so doing, we may begin to have a better understanding of how prejudice and stereotyping arise, how they are maintained, and hopefully, how we can reduce or eliminate prejudice and stereotypes.

SUMMARY

The study of stereotyping and prejudice has come a long way, from its beginnings in the 1930s to the very sophisticated theoretical models of present-day researchers. Since the so-called cognitive revolution in social psychology, the number of journal articles on theoretical and empirical studies of stereotyping and prejudice has grown tremendously. A search of the literature indicates that from 1977 to 2004 approximately 1,913 articles on prejudice have been published. This interest in prejudice keeps growing among researchers for both theoretical and applied reasons. Because it is the nature of humans to belong to various groups, the way we think about and behave toward members of our own and other groups has important implications for our lives and the lives of others in our community (and, more generally, the world). Because stereotyping and prejudice often have a strong, negative impact on social life, researchers are continually attempting to address these problems through research and theory.

Over the last 60 years, research in stereotyping and prejudice has illuminated the content of stereotypes, improved the ways we measure stereotyping and prejudice, and investigated the individual and group-level factors that contribute to the formation and maintenance of prejudice. We have also learned much about how to conceptualize the roles of personality, emotion, cognition, and, more recently, motivation in understanding the nature of stereotyping and prejudice. In the remainder of this book, you will read about the important issues, theories, and problems that have been addressed by research, and you will also learn about enduring problems that continue to challenge investigators today. This book will present the major, as well as some interesting minor, theories that have been proposed over the decades, and we will attempt to put them into historical and empirical context in order to discern the utility of these theories to present-day research and real-world problems. An aim of this book is to present an extensive treatment of the field of stereotyping and prejudice research, highlighting both the classic theories and studies and the most up-to-date research. Another goal I have for this book, as well as for my teaching generally, is to convey to students the excitement that can accompany understanding prejudice, how that understanding can be applied to existing social problems that arise from prejudice, and how fascinating social psychology is. When I was a college freshman in 1985 (wow, a long time ago!), I was blown away by how fascinating my course on introductory psychology was. I really looked forward to class, studied long hours for each exam, and did well in the class because I was intrigued and interested in how researchers addressed the complexity of social life. Today, I am continually excited by a myriad of research domains within my profession, and I hope you, too, will discover that excitement as you read this book.

GLOSSARY

appraisal   A set of cognitions that are attached to a specific emotion.

attitude   A general evaluation of some object. This evaluation usually falls along a good–bad or favorable–unfavorable dimension.

basic (primitive) categories   Categories into which people are grouped rather automatically upon perception. These categories are race, gender, and age.

cultural stereotype   Consensually or widely shared beliefs about a group.

discrimination   Negative behavior toward someone based on their membership in a group.

individual stereotype   The beliefs held by an individual about the characteristics of a group.

ingroup   Any group with which one affiliates themself. Any group to which one belongs.

minimal group   Groups formed on arbitrary or random criteria (e.g., random assignment).

motivation   The impetus to do some behavior (or avoid doing some behavior), and to keep doing it, in order to meet one's goals.

outgroup   Any group with which one does not affiliate themself. Any group to which one does not belong.

prejudice   A biased evaluation of a group, based on real or imagined characteristics of the group members.

realistic-conflict theory   States that prejudice and stereotyping arise from the competition between groups for scarce, valued resources.

schema   A hierarchically organized, cognitive structure that represents knowledge about a concept or type of stimulus, and its attributes and the relations between those attributes.

stereotype   A set of beliefs about the personal attributes of a group of people.

subtyping   The process whereby a new category is created to accomodate stereotype-inconsistent members of a group about which one holds negative stereotypes.

DISCUSSION QUESTIONS

1. Why do humans form groups? What are the ways that human versus animal groups differ in function or origin?

2. Is it possible for humans to form groups and not categorize other groups of humans? If so, how can societies eliminate the tendency to categorize and generalize other groups?

3. How are cultural stereotypes maintained and transmitted to members of the culture?

4. Do you believe that prejudice is primarily an affect or cognition-based concept (or both)? Why?

5. How are stereotyping and prejudice linked? Is it possible to be prejudiced toward another group and not have stereotypes about that group (or vice versa)?

6. What is it about the early childhood environment of the authoritarian-personality adult, that

would lead that individual to develop prejudice toward others?

7. Why do you suppose that a strong motive like the motivation for consistency (e.g., as the basis for cognitive-dissonance theory) is routinely violated by those who are prejudiced toward other groups? Are prejudiced people behaving inconsistently? If not, how are they avoiding dissonance?

SUGGESTED KEY READINGS

Allport, G. W. (1954). *The nature of prejudice.* Reading, MA: Addison-Wesley.

Dovidio, J. F., & Gaertner, S. L. (1986). Prejudice, discrimination, and racism: Historical trends and contemporary approaches. In J. Dovidio & S. Gaertner (Eds.), *Prejudice, discrimination, and racism* (pp. 1–34). New York: Academic Press.

Jones, E. E. (1985). Major developments in social psychology during the past five decades. In G. Lindzey & E. Aronson (Eds.), *Handbook of social psychology* (Vol. 1, 3rd ed., pp. 47–107). New York: Random House.

Jones, J. M. (1997). *Prejudice and racism.* New York: McGraw-Hill.

Plous, S. (Ed.). (2003). *Understanding prejudice and discrimination.* New York: McGraw-Hill.

INTERNET RESOURCES: RESEARCHERS, REFERENCES, AND ORGANIZATIONS DEVOTED TO THE STUDY OF PREJUDICE

www.understandingprejudice.org Perhaps the best, most comprehensive prejudice website on the Internet. Contains hundreds of links, demonstrations, and a multimedia archive.

www.apa.org/pubinfo/hate The American Psychological Association's report on hate crimes.

www.antiracism.net Anti-Racism Net

www.naacp.org National Association for the Advancement of Colored People

www.adl.org Anti-Defamation League

CHAPTER TWO

ORIGIN AND MAINTENANCE OF STEREOTYPES AND PREJUDICE

In the introduction, we discussed the various ways researchers have defined the concepts *stereotype* and *prejudice*. In so doing, we also necessarily discussed the nature of stereotyping and prejudice, because if one wants to define something, it makes sense to try to first have a firm handle on what that something is. In this chapter, we will explore in greater detail the nature of stereotyping and prejudice, and we will focus in particular on how each begins and on what factors facilitate their maintenance in our culture, in our memories, and in our daily social interactions. Questions about the origin and maintenance of stereotyping and prejudice have generated perhaps the most empirical and theoretical work among researchers, and there is a clear reason for this disproportionate focus on the origin issue: if we can understand how stereotypes and prejudice originate and are maintained, we will be in a much better position to discover effective ways to reduce or even to try to eliminate the often harmful effects of stereotypes and prejudice. This is a very applied focus, in the tradition of some of the best research in social psychology. Indeed, the individual whom most social psychologists regard as the father of modern social psychology, Kurt Lewin, suggested that social science, and psychology in particular, ought to have a very strong applied focus with the aim of addressing social problems and informing social policy and legislation with the goal of improving the welfare of humanity (Lewin, 1951). Let us now turn to an in-depth examination of the fruits of this research over the last 70 years, to begin to understand the origin of stereotyping and prejudice.

THE FORMATION OF STEREOTYPES

Categorization

As you will recall from our coverage of the history of research on stereotyping in Chapter 1, the way researchers, and indeed society, regarded stereotypes has changed dramatically over the decades. Specifically, stereotyping was once regarded as a sign of the moral deficiency of the stereotyper, or even as an indicator of repressed unconscious hostility. However, developments in cognitive psychology in the 1960s led to some changes in our understanding of how the mind perceives and processes information. With the advent of the computer, and its useful analog of information processing (input, operate, output) to the human brain, researchers began to realize something astonishing about perception, cognition, and memory, and this had revolutionary implications for the study of stereotypes and prejudice. In short, cognitive psychologists found that the human brain seems to almost automatically classify or categorize similar objects in the environment (Gardner, 1985). This tendency is pervasive and has been shown in children as young as 6 months old (Ramsey, Langlois, & Hoss, 2004). This led prejudice researchers to change their conceptualization of the nature of stereotyping. Stereotypes were no longer regarded as the product of lazy thinking by the uneducated or those with moral deficiencies. Instead, most researchers have taken Allport's (1954) lead and now regard stereotypes as a natural consequence of cognition (Fiske, 1998). Let us turn now to a more in-depth consideration of the reasons we categorize people, and the influence of categorization on person perception.

Why We Categorize

When we encounter a person, we tend to automatically assess that person on the basis of our perception of that person's features. The question you may have at this point is, why do we categorize at all? The reason is that humans have a limited-capacity cognitive system that cannot simultaneously process all the available information in our social environment. Because we have a need to understand and even anticipate the behavior of others, humans have developed ways around our limited cognitive system. One of the best ways is categorization. We categorize people (and objects, ideas, etc.) on the basis of shared features, or even shared time and space. Based on Aristotle's principle of association, we assume that things that are similar on the basis of one feature or because they occur together will likely have other notable similarities on a number of dimensions (Lundin, 1979). For example, consider the category of blond-haired people. In the United States, there are a number of assumptions made about blond-haired people, and these assumptions suggest that one's hair color will lead to some similarity in behavior, personality, or attitudes among the category members. You have probably heard the phrase "Blonds have more fun." This assumes that people with this similar feature (1) are fun people, (2) tend to attract fun people, or (3) are more likely to be involved in fun activities, or any combination of the three. But, why would we categorize people on the basis of their hair color? It does not seem to be a useful way of categorizing people. We might just as well categorize people on the basis of the length of their right thumbnail. The basis for categorizing people can be very logical—for example, according to their support of a particular political candidate, we would assume these category members share many similar attitudes on a number of social and political issues—or they can be quite illogical—as in the case of categorizing people according to the color of their hair or skin color. As we will see throughout this text, human cognition is often anything but rational and logical (Kahneman, Slovic, & Tversky, 1982). In the social perception process, there are many factors that bias the way we perceive and evaluate other people. We turn now to a discussion of how categorization influences our perception of social information.

Types of Categorization

When we perceive an individual, we tend to classify that person along a few broad categories: race, gender, and age (Brewer, 1988; Fiske & Neuberg, 1990). These are the major ways we first categorize someone because these are the most immediate and obvious features of an individual, and because these categories yield much information about useful distinctions in social behavior between those in different groups. These categories, often refereed to as basic categories, or primitive categories, have been accorded special status by researchers because these categorizations have strong influences on how the perceiver interprets most (if not all) of the other information about the perceived individual (Fiske, Lin, & Neuberg, 1998; Hamilton & Sherman, 1994). This process occurs so quickly that with repeated use the categorization of an individual can become virtually automatic and nonconscious (Fiske & Neuberg, 1990; Gilbert, 1989). Basic categories are used so often in perceiving people that they are central points around which stereotypes develop. Some research has suggested that merely being exposed to a face of a White or Black person (Banaji & Greenwald, 1994; Fazio, Jackson, Dunton, & Williams, 1995) or words associated with a gender group (e.g., *nurse, mechanic, Black, White;* Banaji & Hardin, 1996; Dovidio, Evans, & Tyler, 1986), for example, can instantaneously (i.e., within milliseconds) evoke the associated cognitions, beliefs, and feelings one has for that group.

Others, however, have suggested that stereotypes are not automatically activated for all stimuli (Bargh, 1989). Specifically, some research has indicated that upon perceiving category words (e.g., *Hispanic, woman, accountant*) we automatically think of associated stereotypes for that category, yet when seeing a member of one of these groups, we do not automatically think of all of the stereotypes for the groups (racial, gender, age, etc.) to which the person belongs (Macrae, Bodenhausen, Milne, Thorn, & Castelli, 1997). This makes sense if we consider that category labels do not require the perceiver to categorize the object, because the label precategorizes the object for the perceiver. So, thinking of the category name (e.g., *woman*) automatically evokes the associated stereotypes. However, perceiving a face requires the individual to make a categorization, and the categorization can fall on any of a number of different salient dimensions (occupation, gender, age, race, etc.). Macrae and his colleagues suggest that the way the person categorizes a picture of an individual depends on the perceiver's motives, cognitions, and affect. Only when the perceiver wants to quickly evaluate the target in the picture do stereotypes become activated as a useful means of arriving at an attitude toward the target.

Ingroups and Outgroups

As we learned earlier in the book, people tend to form groups for a variety of reasons and motivations, to satisfy a variety of purposes, and these groups are formed on the basis of a virtually limitless array of membership criteria. Sometimes, we get together for an occasion, or we have a task to do, or we share a common interest. For decades, researchers have been interested in understanding the dynamics of groups and how the attitudes, motivation, and cognitions of individuals change as a function of their membership in a group. One of the most basic ways we partition people in our social environment is into **ingroups** (groups to which we belong) and **outgroups** (groups to which we do not belong; Allport, 1954). One's ingroups can be quite numerous. For example, ingroups for me would be males, males in Modesto, California, professors, psychology professors, male professors, 38-year-olds, people of Norwegian descent, people who grew up in Minneapolis, Minnesota, and so on. How you partition people in these groups depends on your current, salient motives, fears, goals, and expectations (Allport, 1954). If I am at work, the most salient ingroup for me may be my fellow professors. When I am at a Starting Line concert, the most salient ingroup may be my fellow Starting Line fans. This has implications for how I would cognitively process information about a given individual in a particular environment. At the concert, I am most cognizant of being a member of the group "Starting Line fans," and the concert environment provides certain expectations for me as I perceive the behavior of my ingroup concertgoers. For example, at the concert, jumping up and down is seen as normative behavior. Because of this, an individual doing this behavior likely would not grab my attention, and thus I would not remember them engaging in that behavior. However, at the workplace, my salient ingroup is my fellow professors, and my expectations for their normative behavior are different. Seeing a colleague jump up and down (like a concert attendee) at the workplace would be very unusual, it would capture my attention, and I would remember that incident (and that strange professor!). Indeed, research by Taylor (1981) and her colleagues (Taylor, Fiske, Etcoff, & Ruderman, 1978) demonstrated the effect of one's salient groups on perception and memory for social information. These researchers found that when participants were exposed to a discussion group of African Americans and Caucasians, participants were generally accurate at recalling the race of the person who made a particular comment but were less accurate at specifying the particular individual who made the statement. Thus, it appears that people tended to perceive and remember the information in terms of race categories, and not in terms of the individual identity.

Dividing people into groups to which we either belong or do not belong has a number of implications for how we think about a given individual. Individuals who are part of an outgroup are perceived to share similar characteristics, motives, and other features. However, when it comes to our own ingroups, we like to think that our groups comprise unique individuals who happen to share one or two common features (e.g., one's occupation). Thus, we think that the outgroup members are "all alike," whereas our ingroup members are as different as snowflakes. Interestingly, those outgroup members who most closely resemble what one believes is the typical or representative member of an outgroup will be more likely to be perceived stereotypically than those who have fewer of the stereotyped characteristics of the typical outgroup member (Maddox, 2004). This bias can also affect criminal sentencing. Blair, Judd, and Chapleau (2004) found that Whites and Blacks who had the same criminal histories received the same sentences. However, within each race, those with more "African" features (i.e., those typical of Blacks) received significantly harsher sentences. The tendency to think in these terms has been referred to as **outgroup homogeneity** and **ingroup bias** (or **favoritism),** respectively (Hamilton, 1976; Ostrom & Sedikides, 1992). Perceiving outgroups as all alike, and our ingroups as diverse helps us satisfy two major goals: we greatly simplify our social environment by categorizing others in that way, and we enhance our self-concept by thinking that we do not belong to a homogeneous, cookie-cutter type of group in which all members are similar in many dimensions. Rather, we attribute great individuality and a host of other positive attributes to our ingroup members (Hamilton & Trolier, 1986).

When we perceive outgroup members to be similar, how exactly are they similar? The reasoning among researchers used to be that thinking favorably about one's group meant, in part, that one was motivated to distinguish one's group favorably relative to other groups, and this provided the basis for not merely outgroup homogeneity but outgroup derogation (Devine, 1995). In other words, in favoring our ingroups, we also tend to put down, or attribute negative characteristics to, outgroups. However, research has shown that the assumption that we derogate outgroups is not necessarily supported (Brewer, 1979, 1999; Perdue, Dovidio, Gurtman, & Tyler, 1990; Quattrone & Jones, 1980). That is, contrary to a prevailing assumption in the prejudice literature, research indicates that favoring our ingroups does not necessarily mean that we also must dislike outgroups. In one study, researchers examined the facilitative/inhibitory aspects for trait descriptors of one's ingroups versus outgroups (Perdue, et al., 1990, Experiment 3). Participants' reaction times to positive person descriptors were faster when preceded by a priming word that denotes one's ingroup (i.e., words such as *us, we, our*). Their reaction times were slower to negative person descriptors when preceded by those ingroup primes. This is a clear indication of favoritism for one's ingroups, in that the ingroup word primes one to recognize positive information about one's groups and inhibits or impairs one's recognition of negative information pertaining to one's ingroups. When participants were presented with outgroup priming words (i.e., *they, them*), their reaction times to negative person descriptors was *not* facilitated. So, thinking about outgroups does not necessarily lead one to be prone to readily process and accept negative information about that outgroup (Brewer, 1979). On the other hand, it should be noted that it is the case that the more an outgroup is seen as homogeneous, the greater the likelihood for perceivers to use group or stereotype labels to process information about the outgroup (and its members). This thinking can in fact lead to outgroup derogation and outgroup discrimination (Miller & Brewer, 1986).

Exposure to members of a stereotyped outgroup can lead to either a more homogeneous (and more stereotyped) or heterogenous (and more positive) view of the outgroup, depending on the context. Specifically, when the outgroup member does something bad, or has negative characteristics, one's stereotypes of the outgroup will be reinforced, and the interaction reduces the likelihood that the perceiver will wish to interact further with the group, and the perceiver's evaluation of the group becomes more negative (Rosenfield, Greenberg, Folger, & Borys, 1982). In one study, Henderson-King (1994) examined how White males would react to a White or African American couple having an argument or a neutral conversation. Henderson-King specifically wanted to find out how this reaction would affect their interaction with a subsequent White or African American confederate who asked him for directions. Results indicated that, after watching the Black couple argue, participants interacted with the Black confederate for a shorter period of time (showing avoidance behaviors). Similarly, Henderson-King and Nisbett (1996) found that when White participants were exposed to an African American being rude to the experimenter, they were more likely to stereotype African Americans and avoid further contact with an African American. Interestingly, even hearing about an African American committing a crime can lead Caucasians to reinforce their stereotypes of African Americans and to perceive African Americans as less variable as a group than Caucasians (Henderson-King, 1999). Positive encounters with members of the stereotyped group tend to lead perceivers to show more sympathetic beliefs about the group (Bodenhausen, Schwarz, Bless, & Wanake, 1995) and be open to further interactions with that outgroup (Rosenfield, et al., 1982).

Research has revealed an even more fundamental element of ingroup versus outgroup categorization: the dimension on which people are viewed as ingroup or outgroup members does not need to be a meaningful one (e.g., racial, political) in order for ingroup and outgroup biases to occur (Tajfel, Flament, Billig, & Bundy, 1971). In a classic series of experiments, Tajfel and his colleagues (1971) asked people to estimate how many dots were on a page. He then assigned people to groups ostensibly based on their ability to correctly estimate the number of dots (or to come as close as possible to the correct number). Unbeknownst to the participants, their scores on the task were not recorded, and they were arbitrarily assigned to their group. They were then asked to allocate resources given to them to either a fellow group member or a member of the other group. Results showed that participants tended to allocate more resources to their ingroup members. These results have been taken to imply that groups that have no meaningful basis for their membership, known as **minimal groups,** would exhibit the same ingroup favoritism found in more meaningful ingroups (i.e., groups based on, for example, race or gender; Brewer, 1979). Minimal groups are called that because they have none of the usual features of group structure: a coherent group structure, face-to-face interaction, a set of norms for the group members, interactions with other groups, and so forth (Brown, 1995). Researchers have found that even when people are arbitrarily assigned to a group (e.g., when the experimenter flips a coin to determine group membership) they display ingroup favoritism or outgroup homogeneity (Billig & Tajfel, 1973; Rabbie & Horwitz, 1969). These data are interesting in that they suggest that the basis for ingroup favoritism may be neither a perceived dispositional similarity nor mere arbitrary categorization but the common fate of one's group members that seems to be the catalyst for ingroup favoritism and outgroup homogeneity (Rothbart & Lewis, 1994). Specifically, being grouped together with others tends to make salient in the group members the generalized norm of preference for group members over others, and this seems to be a plausible, if economical, explanation for the pervasive ingroup favoritism found among virtually any group (Horwitz & Rabbie, 1989). Ingroup favoritism and outgroup negativity tend to be initiated and perpetuated by our motivation to see our groups as special, and better than other groups. Two experiments reported by Sherman, Klein, Laskey, and Wyer (1998) suggest that we rather implicitly (i.e., without our conscious awareness) remember positive information about our ingroups and negative information about outgroups. We tend to explain away or otherwise conveniently forget negative information about our ingroups and positive information about outgroups. Again, this tendency is so pervasive, and well learned, that it becomes automatic early in life and perpetually influences the way we remember ingroup- and outgroup-relevant information.

Recent research by Boldry and Kashy (1999) indicates that outgroup homogeneity tends to be strong but that ingroup favoritism is not as universal as we thought. Their data suggest that group status moderates the tendency to engage in ingroup favoritism, such that low-status groups tend to show outgroup favoritism and high-status groups showed ingroup favoritism only on one of several dimensions. These data are more interesting because they were collected not from artificially created groups (e.g., minimal groups) in the laboratory but from naturally existing groups (junior versus freshman college classes). These results also suggest that more research is needed to examine the influence of context variables (such as group status) on perceptions of ingroups and outgroups. Future research would do well to examine the relation between the self-relevance of the status of the group and one's ingroup and outgroup perceptions. For example, one might expect that as the status of the group is more self-relevant and important to one's own self-concept, the influence of that group on one's perceptions of ingroups and outgroups would be much stronger.

Social Learning

In psychology, it has long been a truism that children learn many of their values, attitudes, and other information about the world from their parents (Eagly & Chaiken, 1993). Through direct or observational learning of the rewards and norms that one's society (and one's parents, or other significant others) have for believing and behaving according to certain attitudes, children begin to acquire beliefs and values about the world. In the search for clues as to the origin of stereotypes and prejudice, much research has focused on the role that parents (and significant others) play in the development of stereotypes in their children (Clark, 1963; Katz, 1983; Pettigrew, 1958; Rosenfield & Stephan, 1981). By age 5, children show distinct recognition of, and preferences for, some groups over others (including race and gender preferences; Goodman, 1952). Allport (1954) suggested that there is a definite link between the prejudiced attitudes of parents and the development of such attitudes in their children. Allport supported the idea that children of parents who were authoritarian (i.e., parents who expected the child to obey, to never disagree, and to keep quiet and who were more strict disciplinarians) were more likely to develop prejudiced attitudes. Allport also argued that it is important to distinguish between the teaching and the development of stereotyped attitudes and prejudice. Some parents explicitly and directly teach their children about their attitudes and values, and they specifically communicate their stereotypes and prejudices to the child. Other children develop prejudiced attitudes as a result of observation of the stereotyped attitudes and behaviors of their parents in an unhealthy, negative home atmosphere. In these instances, Allport suggests, "Prejudice was not *taught* by the parent, but was *caught* by the child from an infected atmosphere" (1954, p. 300). In a moment, we will return to the influence of authoritarian parents and the taught-versus-caught distinction.

Childhood Intergroup Contact.   Some interesting research by Wood and Sonleitner (1996) suggests that childhood interracial contact is a good predictor of adult endorsement of outgroup stereotypes and prejudiced attitudes. The authors had White adults indicate whether, when they were growing up, they lived in a neighborhood in which Blacks also lived, they belonged to any clubs or churches in which Blacks were also members, and they ever attended a school that also had Blacks attending. These questions formed the index of childhood interracial contact. The participants also indicated their endorsement of anti-Black stereotypes and prejudice. Results indicated that people who had more interracial contact showed the least amount of stereotyping and were significantly less prejudiced that those who were rather isolated from Blacks when they were children.

While these results are interesting and encouraging, some important limitations of this study should be noted. First, the measures collect no data on age of first interracial contact. It would be interesting and revealing to find out whether interracial contact at a very early age (e.g., before age 6) is the most potent inoculation to forming prejudiced attitudes and stereotyped beliefs, or if interracial contact at any age through adolescence is sufficient to inhibit the development of prejudiced attitudes. Second, the questions that make up the index of contact do not really assess the specific nature of the contact between the respondent and Blacks. Is casual contact (e.g., with someone who works at a store where one shops) enough to help children form positive intergroup attitudes toward Blacks, or is it important to have friends, teachers, or other close contacts, who are Black in order to prevent the development of negative attitudes and prejudiced feelings toward Blacks? Finally, the questions that make up the index of contact only really assess the potential for contact, not necessarily actual contact. One could answer in the affirmative to all three questions and yet never have had any contact, or have had only very superficial contact, with Black individuals as a child. Thus, while these data are interesting, we need to be cautious in interpreting these results and to remember that more research is needed on this issue before we can get a clear picture of how childhood interracial contact might influence racial attitudes.

Value Transmission in Families.   When examining the origin of stereotyping and prejudice, early researchers examined whether and how strongly we develop preferences for groups influences the way we think about others and at what age these preferences manifest themselves. That is, are some people born prejudiced toward different groups, or is prejudice learned? Much evidence suggests that racial attitudes are not inborn, and neither is it the case that race does not influence a child's perception of the world until years later. Rather, research suggests that racial attitudes gradually develop in the first years of life (Clark, 1963). Indeed, research repeatedly has shown that most 3- and 4-year-olds show an awareness of racial cues and even show a preference for one race over others (Katz, 1983). As children get older, their attitudes about racial groups become more coherent, complex, and intense. Indeed, there is little difference between the racial attitudes of 6th graders and those of high-school students (Clark, 1963). So, children clearly *learn* prejudiced attitudes and stereotypes about others. But where do they learn these attitudes?

It is important to understand the enormous influence that parents and other family members can have on children in terms of what children learn about other groups and how they feel toward them. Parents are a first and powerful source of information about the world, and children are strongly influenced by this information. Recall that Allport (1954) suggested that children develop stereotypes and prejudice either through direct teaching by their parents (or other family members) or these attitudes are "caught" in a family environment that promotes such negative outgroup attitudes. Indeed, research supports this assertion. Overt instruction in prejudiced attitudes, as in the case of highly prejudiced individuals (e.g., White supremacists) certainly has a strong impact on the very young child's intergroup attitudes, leading the child to espouse with the same fervor and conviction the negative beliefs and feelings toward the outgroups as those voiced by the parents. Prejudice can also be learned indirectly. Jokes, overt and subtle intergroup behavior, and derogatory labels (or slang words) used by parents in reference to other groups can have a strong influence on the attitudes the child develops about those groups (Katz, 1983; Rohan & Zanna, 1996). It is interesting to note that in the early years of life the child does not really comprehend the meaning or impact of these stereotypes and thus cannot really internalize these attitudes (Aboud, 1988). Thus, at the early ages of life (approximately before age 10 or so), children are essentially parroting the outgroup sentiments of their parents (Rohan & Zanna).

One of the major sources of stereotypes and prejudice is our parents: our first teachers. Children learn the values and beliefs of their parents and tend to internalize those same beliefs. In this way, stereotypes and prejudice often are transmitted within families from generation to generation.

What, then, do we know about the influence of the parents on their children's attitudes toward other groups? To what extent do the stereotypes and prejudices of the parent match those of their children? In a review of the literature and based on their own research, Rohan and Zanna (1996) found that there is support for the notion that parents and their adult children are very similar in intergroup attitudes. The biggest factor that seemed to influence the degree of parent and child intergroup attitude similarity was whether the parents exhibited Right-Wing Authoritarianism (RWA: see Chapter 4; Altemeyer, 1996). The attitudes of adult children of low-RWA parents were very similar to those of their parents. The relationship between the intergroup attitudes of high-RWA parents and those of their children was a bit more complex, depending on whether the child saw the parent as responsive (encouraging discussion of problems, explaining the reasons behind requests). Those who viewed their high-RWA parents as responsive were much more attitudinally similar to their parents, compared to those who viewed their parents as unresponsive. While more research is needed to expand on and clarify these findings, it appears that children will adopt attitudes and values similar to those of their parents, except when they perceive their parents as both demanding (a major feature of high RWAs) and unresponsive. That is, the lack of attention and consideration of the unresponsive high-RWA parent for the child seems to make the child much less willing to adopt similar attitudes and values (perhaps because there is little incentive for doing so).

Influence of Stereotypes on Cognition in Children.   Stereotypes have a strong influence on a child's perception of their ingroups and outgroups. Corenblum, Annis, and Young (1996) and Aboud (2003) found that majority-group children held more positive attitudes toward their own group and more negative attitudes toward outgroups. Interestingly, minority-group members also held more positive views of the majority group than of even their own ingroup. When asked to explain successful performances of majority group members, both majority-group children and minority-group children made positive, internal, and optimistic attributions. Both groups, however, attributed successful performances of minority-group members to luck. Majority- and minority-group members tend to remember more positive and few negative behaviors about the majority group and more negative and fewer positive behaviors about the minority group (Corenblum, 2003). McKown and Weinstein (2003) found that between ages 6 and 10, majority-group children move from being virtually oblivious to others' stereotypes about their ingroup to being able to infer others' stereotypes. These researchers also found that children from stigmatized groups are aware of stereotypes about their group from a very young age and that they tend to show effects of the stereotype threat (see Chapter 6) on stereotype-relevant tasks; that is, their anxiety about confirming poor stereotypic performance on the task impedes their performance. Stereotypes also influence overall cognitive performance in children in much the same way that they do in adults. Ambady, Shih, Kim, and Pittinsky (2001) found that activation of negative stereotypes impeded, but positive stereotypes facilitated, performance on a math test in young children (kindergarten to grade 2) and older children (grades 6–8).

Stereotypes and Prejudice in the Media.   From a very young age, children are exposed to stereotypes and prejudice. We just explored how a first major influence, parents, plays a role in the development of stereotyped beliefs and negative outgroup affect. As children internalize the values of their parents, they are also paying attention to the overt and covert messages about intergroup relations they receive from movies, television, magazines, video games, and all other types of media. A prevalent heuristic among both children and adults seems to be, "If it is in the media, it must be true" (Huff, 1954). In other words, we use the media as a tool to help us decide the pervasiveness and acceptability of our beliefs and attitudes. If one routinely sees stereotypes portrayed in the media, then one may come to believe that these attitudes represent the normal, or mainstream, view of society. Stereotypes are portrayed in all types of media. As one example, try to think of the last time you saw a commercial on television in which a male is shown cleaning the house, cooking, or caring for the children. Most of you will have a fair amount of difficulty thinking of examples of these situations in commercials. That is just one example of how commercials on television portray, and seem to endorse, sexist gender roles for men and women (see Chapter 8 for a more extensive discussion of sexism in the media).

Another example of the intergroup beliefs that people can form from the media is the portrayal of crime in the United States. Specifically, a common belief among many Americans is that African Americans (more than other racial groups) are more likely to engage in criminal activity. One reason this belief exists is that African Americans seem to be disproportionately represented in the news as the perpetrators of crime, and Caucasians are more likely to be portrayed as the victim of such crimes. But, if the media merely report the news, and it happens to be the case that African Americans are more often identified as the perpetrator of the crime, then should it not be reasonable to assume that African Americans are indeed more likely to engage in criminal activity?

To answer that question, we need to be clear on the assumptions on which the question rests. It assumes that the media are objective reporters of news and are not selectively leaving out some news stories or are otherwise biased in their portrayal of the news (specifically, crime reports). In other words, if the media were mere unbiased conduits of the actual statistical frequency of the crimes committed by all racial groups, and one saw a disproportionate number of one group as the perpetrators of the crime, then it would be entirely reasonable to suggest that that group (for whatever reasons) was more likely compared to other racial groups, to engage in criminal activity.

However, several studies suggest that the media is often less than objective in reporting the incidence of crimes committed by African Americans relative to other racial groups (see van Dijk, 1991, for a review). In an analysis of the portrayal of persons of color that Caucasians in three local television newscasts, Romer, Jamieson, and deCoteau (1998) found that, over 14 weeks of newscasts, persons of color were much more likely to be presented as perpetrators of crimes, and Caucasians were more likely to be shown as the victim of those crimes. Romer et al. also found that the frequency of crimes by persons of color that were reported on the newscasts were about 20% higher than what would be predicted based on actual statistics compiled by the FBI. Certainly this indicates that there is some bias and that the actual frequency with which African Americans commit crimes is far lower than is portrayed in the media. Indeed, Chideya (1995) cites data from the U.S. Bureau of Justice Statistics that indicates over half of violent crimes are committed by Caucasians, and 64% of victims of violent crimes identified their attacker as Caucasian. Such biased portrayals of African Americans in the media can indeed lead to the formation of an artificial, or illusory (see section on illusory correlations later in this chapter), correlation between African Americans and criminal behavior, and this of course tends to lead to the formation and maintenance of negative stereotypes about African Americans. A recent study by Dixon and Maddux (in press) found that heavy news viewers, compared to those who only occasionally watched the news, were more uncomfortable being exposed to a dark-skinned perpetrator of a crime, and they were more likely to remember the perpetrator if he was a dark-skinned Black male. The heavy news viewers also had more favorable views of the victim when the perpetrator was Black. Unfortunately, it is easy to see how the very real bias in the media can perpetuate stereotypes of racial groups.

Implicit Theories

We all have our own ideas of what personality characteristics seem to "go together" in people, and we also have our own ideas about the nature of personality. Researchers refer to these beliefs as **implicit theories** because these beliefs and heuristics guide one's processing of social information and help us to evaluate (and sometimes stereotype) others (Jones, 1982). Once we have categorized someone as having a certain characteristic, we are more likely to assume that that person has a whole host of related characteristics, the specifics of which are determined by the content of one's implicit theory of personality

(Jones, 1982; Schneider, 1973). Moreover, people form their own beliefs about the nature of personality. Specifically, research indicates that some people, termed *entity theorists,* believe that one's personality traits are fixed and cannot be changed, while others, termed *incremental theorists,* believe that one's personality traits are flexible and can be modified (Levy, Plaks, & Dweck, 1999). Entity theorists tend to believe that because traits are fixed, they are stable indicators of behavior. They also believe that behavior is consistent. As a result, they should also be more likely to infer a host of related target-personality characteristics based on an isolated behavior by the target. On the other hand, incremental theorists should be less likely to make such an inference, because they are more cognizant of the belief that behavior (and personality) is less predictable just based on one sample of behavior. In five experiments, Levy, Stroessner, and Dweck (1998) found that, compared to incremental theorists, entity theorists did indeed tend to use stereotypes more often in their judgments of outgroups, form more extreme judgments about the outgroup, and attribute stereotyped characteristics to inborn qualities within the outgroup individual. Thus, one's implicit theories about the content and nature of personality can have a profound effect on one's subsequent beliefs (i.e., stereotypes) about other groups.

The Efficiency of Stereotypes

Ever since Lippmann (1922) coined the term *stereotype,* researchers have noted the utility of stereotypes for simplifying the way we think about our complex social environment (Allport, 1954; Fiske & Neuberg, 1990; Jones, 1997; Taylor, 1981). Stereotypes enable the perceiver to very quickly arrive at an evaluation of a target individual on the basis of very little information (i.e., race, gender, age). This is useful because we can then devote more energy to other demanding cognitive tasks. But why would we be willing to make inaccurate assessments of others in order to move on to other types of thinking? One could argue that to succeed in life it is important, perhaps most important, that one make more accurate assessments of others in one's social world. That is indeed a compelling, logical argument, but it is largely impractical, and here is the reason. Humans have a strong need to have a predictable, somewhat-ordered world (Maslow, 1970). To think carefully about every person one encounters, reads about, or thinks about in an effort to form an accurate evaluation of the person would require an enormous expenditure of cognitive energy (to say nothing of time!). Although a careful social perceiver would be much more likely to be accurate in their assessments of others, they would get little else accomplished that day. Instead, we tend to reserve our considered cognitive efforts for those instances in which we are motivated to be accurate in our assessment of a select other person (i.e., a prospective employee, a prospective mate, a teammate, etc.). For the rest of the population, we play the odds that the stereotypes we use will yield at least some accurate information about the target individual, or—and here's an important point—at least give us the feeling that we know a lot about the target person. Instead of assuming that our instant impressions of others (largely based on some stereotypes) were fact, we would do well to consider recasting our stereotyped impressions as "hunches to be verified" Newcomb (1959, p. 214). With this in mind, Newcomb suggests, people would be more likely to have the advantages of both efficiency and accuracy in their evaluations of others.

So, stereotypes are an integral part of cognitive life. But, do they really save us cognitive energy? In a series of clever experiments, Macrae, Milne, and Bodenhausen (1994) examined the assumption that stereotypes function as cognitive-resource preserving tools. They examined the ability of participants to do two cognitive tasks at one time: form an impression of a target individual while also monitoring a prose passage. For some participants, the impression-formation task also included stereotype labels of the target, whereas for others no stereotype label was provided. If stereotypes facilitate fast judgments of others and conserve cognitive energy for other resources, one should find that those who were given the stereotype labels would be able to devote more cognitive effort to the prose-monitoring task (a paragraph describing Indonesia) and the impression-monitoring task, as compared to those who did not get the label. Indeed, the results indicated that those who were provided with the stereotype label were able to recall twice as many personality descriptors for the target and to recall more of the paragraph information than those given no stereotype label. Macrae et al. suggest that the stereotype labels enabled participants to devote less attention to forming an impression of the target and more attention to remembering stereotype-associated personality descriptors and the paragraph information in the prose-monitoring task. These results suggest that stereotypes do in fact function as energy-saving tools in social perception.

In general, much research shows that when we are confronted with a lot of information about a target, and we are required to make a social judgment about that individual, we are more likely to use stereotypes in our assessment of the target (Bodenhausen & Lichtenstein, 1987; Fiske & Neuberg, 1990). On the other hand, when our cognitive task is simple, we are much less likely to rely on stereotypes in our assessment of the other person, because our cognitive capacity to think carefully about the other person's attributes is not taxed by the need to process a lot of information about the person to arrive at an evaluation (Bodenhausen & Lichtenstein). Research by Sherman and Bessenoff (1999) also indicates that people use stereotypes to guide their memory retrieval about an individual. These researchers put half of their participants under a cognitive load, and the other half was not under a cognitive load while doing a task. Those in the cognitive-load condition were asked to hold an eight-digit number in their mind while simultaneously deciding which trait-related behaviors (from three lists of behaviors) described the target they were told about at the beginning of the study (either a priest or skinhead). Sherman and Bessenoff found that when an individual's cognitive capacity was constrained by the simultaneous cognitive tasks, they were not able to accurately recall the episodic memories (target behaviors), and they relied on stereotypes about the target to help them decide which target behaviors were associated with the target. Thus, when our recall for individuating behavioral information about a person is compromised by a limited cognitive capacity, we may tend to rely on stereotypes in our social judgments about that person. Stereotypes therefore help simplify the cognitive task before us, and they enable us to quickly come to an evaluation about another person.

HOW AND WHY STEREOTYPES ARE MAINTAINED

Because stereotypes enable the perceiver to make a judgment about another individual extremely quickly, they nicely satisfy a major goal of cognitive life: to arrive at the fastest judgments possible, using the least amount of cognitive effort. The issue of whether the judgments are at all accurate is secondary to the utility of the stereotype in helping the person quickly evaluate another individual and move on to devote more thought and time to other cognitive tasks. That is, for most people, it is more important to arrive at any evaluation, whether or not it is an accurate assessment. Thus, stereotypes are difficult to give up, even though most people agree that they are undesirable, promote often-inaccurate evaluations of others, and can lead to strained relationships between groups of people.

People are therefore confronted with the cognitive dissonance aroused by the thought that one has stereotypes of others that guide one's social judgments and the thought that one is a good, fair, and rational thinker. According to dissonance theory, one of these cognitions must change in order for dissonance to be alleviated. Which one changes? It is almost always the cognition that is most amenable to change (i.e., the most weakly held conviction), and in this case it is—you guessed it—one's cognitions about stereotyping. Rather than think that we use stereotypes to evaluate others, we simply do not allow ourselves to come to such a conclusion, and we instead convince ourselves that we are indeed a fair, logical thinker, by making our social judgments after a considered assessment of the information about the target individual. In other words, we often either do not realize, or do not consciously acknowledge, that we do indeed stereotype others. This self-delusion helps us maintain our cherished stereotypes while reducing the possibility for cognitive dissonance related to our self-concept. How, then, do we continue to use stereotypes without being consciously aware of their influence? How are stereotypes maintained in the face of stereotype-disconfirming evidence? In the next section we will discuss the various ways that people maintain their stereotypes of others, and we will review the research on the factors that facilitate stereotype maintenance in daily social judgments.

Selective Attention to Stereotype-Relevant Information

We are constantly exposed to a wide variety of information that pertains to our stereotypes of others. Some of the information is consistent with our stereotypes, other information is stereotype inconsistent. Stereotype-inconsistent information is usually perceived as dissonance-arousing, because it is threatening to one's self-concept (though people usually do not consciously perceive such information as threatening). In other words, if I learn that the way I think about others and the way I interpret and categorize others is unsound, I may feel foolish. Rather than do that, I will change the way I think about the validity of the stereotype-inconsistent information. One way to do this is to use the heuristic that I will only pay attention to information that confirms what I already believe (my stereotypes), and to pay no attention to stereotype-inconsistent information. Indeed, research indicates that this is, in fact, what most people do, and this explains how they maintain their stereotypes in the face of stereotype-inconsistent information (Bodenhausen & Lichtenstein, 1987; Dijkserhuis & Knippenberg, 1996; Fiske & Neuberg, 1990; Rothbart, Evans, & Fulero, 1979; Wigboldus, Dijksterhuis, & Van Knippenberg, 2003).

One of the nice features of stereotypes is that they help us anticipate likely motives, attitudes, and behaviors of others, and they therefore provide us with a comfortable sense of what to expect in our daily social interactions. These expectations certainly guide our behavior, and they also guide our perceptions of social information. In a metaanalysis of 54 experiments, Stangor and McMillan (1992) reviewed the literature on the influence of such expectations on memory for expectancy-consistent and expectancy-inconsistent information. Their results indicated that memory tends to be better for expectancy-incongruent than for expectancy-congruent information. This is in line with much of the cognitive literature on memory that shows that our attention is grabbed by unusual or surprising information, and therefore, we are more likely to remember that information. However, Stangor and McMillan found that when it comes to strong expectancies, which describes most stereotypes, we are more prone to remember expectancy- or stereotype-consistent information (see also Bodenhausen, 1988).

Interestingly, when it comes to stereotypes about our own group, we remember things differently. Koomen and Dijker (1997) presented participants with stereotype-consistent and -inconsistent information about their own groups (Dutch versus Turkish) and about an outgroup. Their memory for this information was then tested for accuracy. With regard to stereotype-relevant information about an outgroup, the results indicated that participants remembered more stereotype-confirming information than disconfirming information. However, when it came to stereotype-relevant information about their own group, participants were more likely to remember stereotype-inconsistent information. This supports earlier research (e.g., Park & Rothbart, 1982), and suggests that we like to think of our own groups as consisting of unique individuals and other groups as consisting of people who share common characteristics and who are more similar than different. Koomen and Dijker's findings show that one way we can do this is by focusing on stereotype-inconsistent information (stereotype disconfirming) about our group, and stereotype-consistent information about other groups. Recent research by Sherman, Stroessner, Conrey, and Azam (in press) found that high-prejudice but not low-prejudice persons pay more attention to stereotype-inconsistent behaviors in order to attribute them to external factors and stereotype-consistent behaviors to internal (personality) factors.

Human memory and cognition are nothing if not flexible and adaptive to the challenges presented by an ever-changing world. If we are to survive, we need to develop flexible cognitive mechanisms for processing and remembering important information related to how we interact with the world and others in it. Consider, then, the adaptiveness of a cognitive system that rather blindly processes only one kind of information, and ignores all other information, when there is really no good reason to do so. Such is the case with stereotypes. Recall that some research has shown that stereotypes facilitate the processing of stereotype-consistent, but not stereotype-inconsistent, information (Rothbart, et al., 1979). For example, Macrae, Stangor, and Milne (1994) found that people who had stereotypes activated in their memory were subsequently able to more efficiently process stereotype-relevant (specifically, stereotype-consistent) information.

However, recent research suggests that this may not represent the full picture of how we process stereotype-relevant information. Sherman, Lee, Bessenoff, and Frost (1998) argued that our cognitive system must be more adaptive and flexible in processing social information than is characterized by past research that suggested that we only perceive and remember stereotype-consistent information. In a series of experiments, Sherman and his colleagues found that stereotypes are efficient because they facilitate the processing of both stereotype-consistent and -inconsistent information when cognitive capacity to process information is low. Sherman et al. (in press) found that when we are under a cognitive load (due to any number of factors, such as information overload, parallel tasks, etc.), stereotypes enable us to process stereotype-consistent information more quickly and to devote more cognitive resources to stereotype-inconsistent (and thus, surprising and attention-getting) information. As a result, less attention is given to stereotype-consistent information, and this information is thus weakly encoded in memory. Because most of our attention is given to stereotype-inconsistent information, this information is encoded in greater detail and our memory for the specifics of this information is better. In a follow-up series of experiments, Sherman and Frost (2000) replicated these findings and suggested that although perceivers will have stronger stereotype-consistent impressions of a target, their memory for the specific stereotype-relevant information may be poor. This can lead perceivers to be easily misled (and often inaccurate) in their recollections of the target's behavior or characteristics.

Indeed, there is a compelling argument to be made for the idea that the act of categorizing something (or someone) can reduce one's openness to revision of that initial categorization, even in the face of evidence that the initial assessment was incorrect. Von Hippel, Sekaquaptewa, and Vargas (1995) argue that stereotypes bias the way we perceive (and interpret) the world, specifically affecting the way information is encoded. Von Hippel and his colleagues suggest that stereotypes lead perceivers to encode social information in ways that will facilitate the maintenance of the stereotype. This is a different perspective on how stereotypes influence our social judgments, because it suggests that stereotypes have their strongest influence at the actual perception of the social information, and not later when one is trying to recall that social information (e.g., information about an individual one has perceived). As evidence for this hypothesis, Von Hippel et al. cite research by Wyatt and Campbell (1951) in which participants saw a series of blurred pictures and were asked to generate guesses as to what the pictures might be. Later, participants were shown the pictures in gradually increasing focus and were asked to modify, if they felt it necessary, their initial guesses. Results indicated that the initial guess about the picture interfered with an individual's ability to accurately perceive (and identify) the subsequently presented clear picture. Von Hippel and his colleagues recount the results of their own program of research on this issue, as well as a number of other studies, which all support the idea that once we categorize an ambiguous (or even unambiguous) stimulus, our later perception of categorization-inconsistent information is impaired, thus facilitating the perpetuation of the initial stereotype in the perceiver's memory.

Subcategorization

Most researchers agree that stereotypes have a basic hierarchical structure, in which the category information tends to become more complex and differentiated as time goes on (Fiske & Neuberg, 1990; Sherman, 1996; Stangor & Lange, 1994; Stephan, 1989; Taylor, 1981; Weber & Crocker, 1983). The information about the group tends initially to be stored in terms of superordinate abstract stereotypes that apply to all group members. When stereotype-discrepant information confronts us (as in the case of encountering an individual who has stereotype-inconsistent characteristics), we form **subcategories** (also known as subtypes), which are separate categories for the deviant individual (Weber & Crocker, 1983). We do this because the stereotype-inconsistent member of the stereotyped group is seen as unrepresentative of the whole group, so stereotypes that apply to the group do not appear to apply to the particular group member. Another reason subcategories are created is to enable us to maintain our stereotypes for the group in the face of stereotype-disconfirming evidence. Because we have such a strong motivation to keep our stereotypes (for cognitive simplicity and efficiency), we are motivated to keep our stereotypes intact and safe from the threat presented when we encounter an outgroup member who does not fit the group stereotype. Subcategorization allows stereotypers to have their cake and eat it too. It also enables one to think of oneself as not prejudiced toward that particular group. Because stereotypes are predominantly negative, it is likely that deviant (stereotype-disconfirming) group members will represent positive qualities and characteristics not typically associated with the outgroup. As a result, we are more likely to have positive affect for, and evaluate positively, those individuals for whom we have created subcategories. For example, a White person may create subcategories for Michael Jordan, Oprah Winfrey, an African American friend and coworker, and so forth. In this way, they can convince themself that they are not prejudiced because, according to him, some of his best friends or people he admires are African American.

When an individual is seen as representative of a group and shows stereotype-inconsistent characteristics, people will be more likely to modify their stereotypes about that group, to perceive more variability among group members (Rothbart & Lewis, 1988). In this way, the group is seen as being more heterogeneous and comprising individuals, and less as a homogeneous ("they-are-all-alike") collective. To the extent that this happens, the stereotypes of the group are less useful for the perceiver because they are less applicable to the target group. However, when the perceived individual is not seen as representative of the group, then it is easier for perceivers to regard that person as a deviant, and any of the individual's stereotype-inconsistent characteristics will be less likely to influence or dispel the stereotypes the perceiver has about the group as a whole. Research indicates that when we can explain away as a fluke a member of a stereotyped group who does not fit the stereotype, we will do so (Kunda & Oleson, 1995). When we can explain the person's stereotype-inconsistent characteristics as being attributable to some aspect of the situation, or to vague stereotype-relevant information, or otherwise have a ready variable that would allow us to explain the origin of the group-deviant characteristic, we will use it as a way to subcategorize the group member (Garcia-Marques & Mackie, 1999; Kunda & Oleson; Rothbart & Lewis, 1988).

Illusory Correlations

In our attempt to make sense of the social world, we often try to notice when events co-occur, or covary (Kelley, 1967). That is, we are trying to figure out what things are correlated. In so doing, we can develop a sense of what to expect, and even predict when events should occur. If we know that variable A is present, and we know that variable A is highly correlated with variable G, then we can make a prediction that variable G should also be present in that situation. For example, police and insurance companies tend to be aware of a correlation between a driver's gender and age and the tendency to break the speed limits (or get into an accident). They assume that being a young male (age 16–28) is highly correlated with the tendency to drive fast and get into auto accidents. This is a legitimate assumption because statistics support the notion that these factors are positively correlated (U.S. Department of Transportation, 1999). However, we often perceive a relationship between variables that are only weakly correlated or not correlated at all. Researchers call these perceived relationships **illusory correlations** (Hamilton & Gifford, 1976; Hamilton & Rose, 1980). Illusory correlations can lead to both the formation and maintenance of stereotypes. When one perceives a distinctive group (e.g., an outgroup or a minority group) behaving undesirably (e.g., committing a crime), we are more likely to notice that event, because it is an unusual occurrence. The co-occurrence of the distinctive group and the undesirable behavior can lead to the perception of a link between the group and the supposedly natural tendency to do the undesirable behavior. The more cognition and attention devoted to this co-occurrence, the more this illusory correlation is accessible in memory, and thus the more likely it is to influence subsequent judgments of the target group (Hamilton & Sherman, 1994). This is the beginning of a stereotype for that ougroup.

Illusory correlations also form as a result of the influence of one's existing stereotypes of others. Recall that stereotypes tend to bias our perception of stereotype-relevant information such that we pay attention only to information that confirms our stereotypes, and we pay less attention to information that is inconsistent with the stereotype. Therefore, when making an assessment about a member of a stereotyped outgroup, one will draw on

How do prejudiced perceivers regard members of a stereotyped group, such as singer Michael Jackson, who do not fit the stereotypes of that group? They usually will subcategorize the individual. In this way, the target person is put into a special group in the perceiver's mind. This prevents the perceiver from having to change their perception of the stereotyped group (in light of the stereotype-inconsistent exemplar Mr. Jackson). The perceiver then can claim that they are not prejudiced, because they think highly of the (stereotype-inconsistent) group member.

one's knowledge, beliefs, expectations, and stereotypes of that group. As an example, suppose you believe that older people are grumpy. You will tend to notice and remember only those examples of grumpy older persons that you met, (or were exposed to via other means: media, friends, relatives, etc.), and not those examples of either happy older persons or grumpy younger persons. In this way, stereotypes lead you to perceive a strong (illusory) correlation between grumpiness and being old.

Interestingly, some recent research also suggests that a motivation to perceive order and predictability in the world can enhance the likelihood of forming illusory correlations. Lieberman (1999) asked participants in a study to describe what would happen to them when they die and how they feel thinking about their death, and others were asked to describe what would happen to them if they watched television. The first group had their mortality made salient, and the second group did not. According to the terror-management theory (Solomon, Greenberg, & Pyszczynski, 1991a), when we think about our mortality, it arouses a need for stability, predictability, and order in the world. Then Lieberman presented participants in each condition with either ambiguous or unambiguous information about a target group. The need for order is more easily satisfied when we have clear information. Lieberman predicted that those in the mortality-salient condition, when presented with ambiguous information, should be more likely to form illusory correlations between the negative behaviors listed and the minority group than those who did not have their mortality made salient. This is exactly what he found, suggesting that the motivation for order and predictability (in this case, initiated by mortality salience) led participants to attempt to fashion order from the ambiguous target-group information by forming illusory correlations. Regardless of the fact that it is an inaccurate way of thinking of a group, these participants were much more interested in obtaining a predictable sense of what the minority group was like. As we mentioned in the first chapter, all people tend to be cognitive misers, tending to be more interested in cognitive efficiency and the speed of judgments than in the accuracy of their evaluations. It appears however, that under certain conditions (e.g., mortality salience), this tendency can be supercharged, and this increases the chances for heuristic, stereotypical thinking about other groups.

Motivation

Stereotypes and prejudice have many different sources. In addition to the many cognitive biases, heuristics, and other capacity limitations of our cognitive system, we also form and maintain prejudice on the basis of motivation to do so. That is, we may have a specific interest in perceiving another group as inferior to our own group, and our effort and energy directed at meeting that goal is what most researchers would refer to as motivation. Motivation is a nebulous concept and has a myriad of definitions. It is hard to pin down, but for our purposes we will define motivation as those processes that energize and direct behavior toward a goal (Reeve, 1997). When we are motivated to do something, we have a goal (or more than one goal) in mind, and we find that goal of sufficient import to initiate actions to attain that goal. For example, if you are reading a book and your roommate comes home and asks you if you want to go out to a nightclub, you may not feel sufficiently motivated to do all the behaviors necessary for going out (i.e., getting cleaned up, putting on nice clothes, getting money from the ATM, etc.). However, if an important goal of yours (to meet a potential boyfriend or girlfriend) can be pursued (i.e., your roommate says that the person you are interested in is going to be at the nightclub), then you may suddenly find yourself with more than enough energy to get ready to go out with your roommate.

Similarly, some people tend to be more motivated than others to form accurate impressions of others and to not rely on stereotypes in their social perceptions. Stangor and Ford (1992) have suggested that people can be identified as either perceiving others in an "accuracy-oriented" or "expectancy-confirming" manner. Some people are very concerned with arriving at the most accurate perception of individuals they perceive, based on the target person's qualities, characteristics, interests, and so forth. Such individuals are very motivated to avoid any bias in their evaluations of others. Research indicates that these accuracy-oriented individuals tend to be much less likely to rely on stereotypes in their evaluations of others, as compared with those who are not motivated to be accurate in their social perceptions (Hilton & Darley, 1991; Pendry & Macrae, 1996). Others are motivated to perceive people according to expectations they may have of that individual (i.e., expectations for the target person's behavior based on stereotypes about the target's group) (Neuberg, 1994). These individuals attend to expectancy-confirming behavior in the target, and they disregard (forget) instances of expectancy-disconfirming behavior in targets. Chaiken, Giner-Sorolla, and Chen (1996) suggest that this latter group is acting from a "defensive" orientation, because these individuals are seeking to defend their prejudices and preexisting beliefs. The defensive motivation stems from the need to maintain one's belief in the current societal system of group hierarchy (and inequality) and the predictable structure of the social status quo.

Of course, people are sometimes accuracy oriented and sometimes expectancy oriented, and it is rarely the case that a person is only one or the other. However, it turns out that, in general, accuracy-oriented people are in very short supply. Indeed, Taylor (1981) made the point that most people are *not* motivated to think carefully about others, individuating each person they perceive, because to do so would require more cognitive energy than they are willing to devote to routine cognitive tasks such as social perception. Additionally, perceivers reason that there is no harm done in using heuristic strategies (such as relying on stereotypes) in evaluating others, and that, for example, if you categorize a person you pass in the mall on the basis of their ethnic group and associated stereotypes, it is not a problem because no one will know of this evaluation. Thus, many people are not motivated to avoid using stereotypes in social perceptions because there is usually no good motivation to think carefully about others and expend that much cognitive energy in our social evaluations.

Research by Kunda and her colleagues (Klein & Kunda, 1992; Kunda, 1990) suggests that people do not merely believe whatever they want (or expect) to believe about outgroups. To convince themselves that they are objective in their evaluations of others, people attempt to construct justifications for their evaluations and beliefs. They do this by searching their memory for belief-supporting target information, and they pass over target-relevant information that does not support their beliefs. Thus, their objectivity is illusory, because their search was motivated by a biased goal. For example, when Klein and Kunda (1992) told participants that they were about to interact with a schizophrenic individual, the participants expressed more positive stereotypes about schizophrenics, than did the nonmotivated participants, who were told they would merely view an interaction with a schizophrenic. In this way, participants who have a self-interest to view another person positively (because they would like the upcoming interaction to go well, and not be uncomfortable) will generate more positive information about the target. Kunda and Sinclair (1999) further suggest that the activation, application, and inhibition of stereotypes tends to be guided by motivated reasoning. In other words, if one has a goal of disparaging a particular group, then one may activate negative stereotypes (that they may or may not normally activate when thinking about others), apply them to people to whom they might not have otherwise applied those stereotypes, and inhibit information in their memory that is incompatible with the goal of forming a negative impression of the group members (i.e., positive information about that individual, or positive stereotypes).

Unfortunately, being motivated to avoid stereotyping others may not be sufficient to actually individuate others in one's social judgments. Pendry and Macrae (1994) examined the influence of processing goals and attentional capacity on an individual's use of stereotypes in judgments of others. They reasoned that when one's outcomes were dependent on another individual (e.g., they would win a cash prize if they worked well with another participant—an elderly woman—to generate the best solutions to some word problems), one would be less likely to rely on stereotypes in an assessment of the other person. If one is to do well on a task with a partner, it is important to have an accurate sense of one's partner's capabilities. Relying on cognitive shortcuts, such as stereotypes, would be an impediment to that goal in this situation, which is why participants should be motivated to think carefully about their elderly partner, with the goal of forming an accurate impression of her.

Other participants were told that they may win a cash prize based on their performance alone, and thus their outcomes were independent of the performance of their elderly partner. In these conditions, Pendry and Macrae predicted, participants would not be motivated to think carefully when forming an evaluation of their partner, and they would thus be more influenced by stereotypes in their perceptions of their elderly partner. Results indicated support for these predictions. However, something interesting happened when the attentional capacity of participants was manipulated. When Pendry and Macrae had half of the participants read the self-description of their partner (a precompleted demographic sheet, ostensibly filled out by their elderly partner, but in fact there was no elderly partner; participants were only led to believe she was in the adjoining lab room and they would meet soon) while simultaneously doing a digit-rehearsal task, their attentional capacity reached its limit. They were then asked to complete an evaluation of their partner's personality. The other half of the participants did not have their attentional capacity depleted. They read their partner's information at their leisure and then completed an evaluation of their partner's personality. Results indicated that when outcome-dependent participants' attention was depleted, they were equally likely as those who were in the outcome-independent condition to rely on stereotypes in their evaluation of their partner. The results of the Pendry and Macrae experiment, as well those of other, similar studies (e.g., Moreno & Bodenhausen, 1999), suggest that if we are to avoid stereotyping others, we need both the will and the cognitive means to do so.

ORIGINS OF PREJUDICE

Our discussion of motivation as it relates to creating and maintaining stereotypes provides a nice bridge to the next section of this chapter, which centers on the origin of prejudice. Recall from Chapter 1 that stereotyping and prejudice are almost always integrally related

(Dovidio et al., 1996). Feelings of prejudice always encompass stereotyped beliefs about outgroups, and endorsement of stereotypes usually carries an accompanying negative affect and evaluation of the outgroup in question. Note that stereotyping and prejudice are almost always related. This is because there are some instances where one may not have prejudice toward the outgroup in question, and may have knowledge of (but not personally endorse) stereotypes (Devine, 1989). Because stereotyping and prejudice are linked in our social perceptions, it is important, therefore, to understand the origin of prejudice, how it interacts with stereotyping in ways that maintain the stereotype, and how stereotypes can promote the maintenance of prejudice toward outgroups. Most researchers conceptualize prejudice as originating out of a motivational impetus (Brown, 1995; Fiske, 1998; Jones, 1997). That is, the reason one endorses stereotypic beliefs and holds negative feelings toward another group is to attain one's own psychological goals. More specifically, we tend to dislike others in order to feel better about ourselves. Let us turn now to an examination of the various theories that discuss the genesis and structure of prejudice.

Social-Identity Theory

In the last 30 years, perhaps no other theory of prejudice has had as strong an impact on the field of prejudice research than the **social-identity theory** (SIT) by Tajfel and Turner (1979, 1986). According to the SIT, we all have a need for positive self-regard, and this need fuels motivational and cognitive biases in social perception aimed at helping us feel good about ourselves. The theory says that there are essentially two ways we can obtain positive self-regard: by one's own achievements and by the groups to which one belongs. If I create, accomplish, or achieve some goal, I should feel good about myself and my abilities. My self-esteem should naturally be high as I bask in the glow of my accomplishment. However, in those instances where one has not particularly achieved or accomplished something to one's satisfaction, positive self-regard may be obtained by thinking about one's social identity, that part of one's self-concept that is based on one's membership in social groups. In other words, if I feel like my self-esteem is a bit low (if I have no personal achievements to boost my self-esteem), I may try to restore my self-regard by considering that I belong to one or more groups that are highly regarded in society. By doing so, I can bolster my deflated self-esteem and thus meet the strong need—which we all have, according to the theory—for high self-esteem.

SIT states that because people naturally partition their social environment into "us" and "them" groupings, people are motivated to perceive their own groups as superior to other groups on important, valued dimensions. This creates a bias in favor of their own group, and against outgroups. The theory suggests that one way to increase one's positive feeling about one's ingroup is to derogate (evaluate negatively) outgroups. What happens when one's ingroup has traditionally been of lower status, or had been of high status but that status is being questioned or is fading? The SIT says that in these instances we will tend to highlight the unique, or distinctive, nature of our group (Spears, Doosje, & Ellemers, 1997) in order to shield it from a potential decline in status. Another way we maintain the perceived high status of our group is by derogating deviant or stereotype-confirming ingroup members, or others that reflect poorly on the ingroup, in an effort to maintain the status of one's ingroup.

So the SIT says that we are highly motivated to show ingroup bias (favoritism) for our ingroups, and we are also motivated to negatively evaluate outgroups (and members thereof). According to the SIT, this intergroup bias is the core reason that prejudice toward outgroups will emerge. However, the SIT has not fared as well under empirical scrutiny. Research has shown, for example, that although we do tend to favor our ingroups, and this bolsters our self-esteem (e.g., Chin, 1995; Hirt, Zillman, Erickson, & Kennedy, 1992), there is little evidence that we also engage in outgroup derogation (but see Fein & Spencer, 1997, for evidence that prejudice emerges solely from outgroup derogation) as a way of enhancing self-esteem (Branscombe & Wann, 1994; Brewer, 1979; Jetten, Spears, & Manstead, 1996). Thus, we can be prejudiced toward outgroups even if we do not derogate those outgroups, because we are favoring our own ingroups (Jones, 1997). Recall from our definition of prejudice (in Chapter 1) that prejudice does not only mean negative affect directed toward an outgroup, it can also refer to a preference for or favoring of one's ingroups.

The main tenet of the SIT, that people engage in group comparisons to enhance their self-esteem, has also been the subject of increasing criticism in the last decade (Abrams & Hogg, 1988; Hogg & Abrams, 1990). Critics of the self-esteem-enhancing motive proposed by the SIT point to the finding that people who have low self-esteem sometimes identify *more* with their embattled ingroup, instead of seeking a higher-status group (Brewer & Brown, 1998; Long & Spears, 1997). Other research indicates that it is those with high self-esteem who show a greater identification with low-status groups than those who have low self-esteem. Thus, although self-esteem may not be a prime motive in the dynamics of social identity and ingroup–outgroup relations, it remains an important part of the motivations that drive social identity processes. The theoretical and empirical issues with self-esteem, and the lack of empirical support for the derogation of outgroups as a strategy for self-esteem enhancement led many researchers to turn to other theories of motivation that may better explain the origins of prejudice.

Optimal Distinctiveness Theory

Recall that the social-identity theory suggests that people sometimes feel a need to identify strongly with a particular group, in order to enhance their self-esteem. Brewer (1991) suggests that our social motives are governed by an alternating tension between our need to be our own unique person and our need to belong to groups. In her optimal distinctiveness theory (ODT), Brewer (1991) suggests that it is aversive to us to be too extreme in our needs for uniqueness and belongingness. In these cases, an individual's sense of worth and security is in jeopardy, and this motivates the individual to find groups that can help provide a balance between these opposing needs. The ODT therefore predicts that we will feel isolated and alone if we feel strong uniqueness at the expense of belongingness. But too much enmeshment of one's social identity into a group can also have negative consequences. Indeed, there is recent evidence that if one's social identity is strongly salient, (i.e., one's personal identity recedes into the background in favor of belongingness) there is an increased tendency to evaluate outgroups in terms of shared ingroup stereotypes about the outgroups (Haslam, Oakes, Reynolds, & Turner, 1999).

Therefore, one reason that exclusive groups are so valued is that they tend to provide just the right balance between uniqueness and belongingness (Brewer & Brown, 1998).

This theory, then, accounts well for the findings discussed earlier that sometimes people more strongly identify with low-status groups. Specifically, the ODT says that when the need for uniqueness is strong, people will value membership in minority groups (because these groups can fulfill the need for uniqueness) more than membership in a majority group. They will value such allegiance irrespective of any gulf in status between the minority and majority. So, according to the ODT, if we want to be able to predict when and with what group an individual will identify, we need to know more than the status of the individual's ingroups relative to their outgroups. To be more accurate in our prediction of intergroup behavior, we need to understand the balance between the belongingness and uniqueness motives in the individual. This theory has much intuitive appeal, and it elegantly addresses many of the holes that plagued the SIT. Although only a few studies have tested the ODT, they have generally indicated support for the predictions of the ODT (Brewer, Manzi, & Shaw, 1993; Hornsey & Hogg, 1999; Leonardelli & Brewer, 2001). More research is needed if we are to have a better understanding of the exent to which the ODT allows us to predict general intergroup behavior, and group identification and prejudice in particular.

Scapegoat Theory

Some theorists have suggested that the likelihood of intergroup conflict is often tied to economic conditions, and that when the times get tough economically, people are more likely to take their frustration out on outgroups. In one of the earliest studies of this idea, Hovland and Sears (1940) analyzed the relationship between the number of lynchings (most of which occurred in the southern United States) and the economy of the South. They operationalized "economy" by measuring the farm value of cotton, and the per-acre value of cotton, because cotton was a major product of the South, and it would therefore be a good index of economic impact for the population studied. Hovland and Sears charted the economy from 1882 to 1930 and found, in line with their predictions, that lynchings were more frequent during hard economic times (i.e., when cotton prices were low) and less frequent during times of prosperity.

Why would people be motivated to dislike another group when that outgroup had nothing to do with the source of their frustration and anger? In Hovland and Sears's (1940) study, why would Caucasians commit such violence against African Americans when the price of cotton fell? One explanation that has empirical support is known as the **scapegoat theory** (Allport, 1954; Berkowitz & Green, 1962). This theory postulates that when an individual becomes thwarted from a particular goal, they may feel anger, irritation, or disappointment. In general, we tend to feel negative when something prohibits us from attaining what we want. The anger or hostility we feel toward that frustrating agent may be, in many ways, similar to the negative emotion associated with our views of a disliked outgroup. What happens then, according to the theory, is that because both the frustrating agent and the outgroup arouse similar emotions, they tend to become associated in the individual's memory. As Berkowitz and Green suggest, "There is an acquired equivalence between the frustrator and the minority group which mediates the generalization of the aggressive responses from the former to the latter" (p. 295). Some have suggested that the scapegoat theory may be one contributing factor to wars, and conflict between groups, from the beginning of human history (Allport, 1954). For example, throughout the past several thousand years, an often-scapegoated group has been Jewish persons (Allport, 1954). Many scholars suggest that Hitler was able to rally his country around his ideas because, in part, he introduced a common scapegoat—the Jews—for Germany's economic plight following its defeat in World War I (e.g., see Goldhagen, 1996). While the scapegoat theory has intuitive appeal, it has received mixed empirical support. A problem with the theory has been the fact that many studies have shown that when people are frustrated, they are no less and no more prejudiced toward disliked outgroups than they are toward other, liked outgroups (Brown, 1995). Another problem with the theory is that it cannot explain the choice of targets (scapegoats). For example, the theory is not able to predict which disliked outgroup the Germans in the 1930s would choose as their scapegoat (Stroebe & Insko, 1989). As a result, researchers have turned to another approach to understanding intergroup prejudice, relative deprivation.

Relative Deprivation

People routinely compare themselves to others, in order to assess how their attitudes, cognitions, feelings, or behaviors compare to others in their environment (Festinger, 1954). We also tend to compare our situation to that of others. That is, we are interested in knowing if the things we have (status, power, wealth, possessions, employment, etc.) are equal to, lesser than, or greater than other individuals (and outgroups) in our society. For example, suppose everyone in your neighborhood has a satellite dish for their televisions, while you have cable (or, gasp, a regular antenna that gets four stations). Your neighbors enjoy hundreds of channels from which to select their programs, whereas your setup provides you with just a small fraction of that amount. In comparing yourself to your neighbors, you may experience what Davis (1959) called "relative deprivation." That is, your situation is lesser than that of others (you are deprived of an important quality, Z, relative to a particular group). In his formal statement of **relative deprivation theory**, Davis suggests that when people (1) decide that they want Z, (2) compare themselves with similar others who have Z, and they (3) feel entitled to Z, they will feel deprived.

In the intergroup context, then, the theory suggests that feelings of prejudice and hostility toward outgroups arise out of a feeling of relative deprivation with regard to that outgroup in terms of an important goal (e.g., good educational opportunities, jobs, housing). As with the scapegoat theory, the empirical literature on relative deprivation has yielded only intermittent support. Bernstein and Crosby (1980) note that this may be due, in large part, to the fact that relative deprivation is defined differently by different researchers. Although four versions of the theory (including Davis's version) have been popular, they adhere to the basic elements of Davis's model. Despite the mixed empirical support, the theory has continued to generate substantial interest among researchers (with 81 articles and chapters from 1968 to 2000), and research on relative deprivation appears to be attracting more empirical and theoretical attention (Walker & Smith, 2002). This research has also suggested a further refinement in Davis's original formulation. Runciman (1968) suggested that it is important to distinguish between egoistic relative deprivation and fraternal relative deprivation. The former is the type of situation in which an individual compares their life to that of other individuals (as in my example of the satellite dish). Fraternal relative deprivation, however, involves a comparison of how one's ingroup fares relative to an outgroup with regard to a desired goal. Subsequent theory (Crosby, 1976) and research (e.g., Guimond & Dube-Simard, 1983; Vanneman & Pettigrew, 1972) have supported this distinction, and the data indicate that although fraternal relative deprivation is strongly related to negative outgroup perceptions, egoistic relative deprivation does not appear to be related to negative outgroup evaluations. Thus, people make a distinction between personal deprivation as compared with individual others, and the deprivation status of one's group relative to another group's advantage, and feelings of prejudice only emerge when one's group is perceived to be at a disadvantage in comparison with another group.

Realistic Conflict Theory

As research on the notion of relative deprivation suggests, it only appears to be the case that we will develop feelings of hostility and prejudice toward another group if we believe that our ingroup as a whole is at a disadvantage, relative to an outgroup, with regard to an important goal. But why do you suppose we do not feel outgroup hostility and prejudice toward other groups when we feel that our own situation is worse than that of other individuals? One possibility is that it may arouse greater feelings of helplessness and threat to believe that one's ingroup is at a disadvantage relative to another group. As individuals, there is not much we can do to control or affect the standing of our group compared with an outgroup, and that sense of powerlessness may be a strong contributor to the prejudice that arises between groups when those groups vie for similar goals. In other words, if we cannot change the disadvantaged status of our group relative to an outgroup, one way we can vent this frustration and also try to equalize the two groups is by bringing down the other group by directing feelings of prejudice toward the outgroup.

But, we have much more control over our own situation, and a feeling of relative deprivation compared to other individuals (in one's ingroup or outside of one's ingroup) would tend to arouse in oneself either a sense of increased motivation to reduce that discrepancy, or a sense of dejection (if one believes one cannot reduce that discrepancy). In this situation, it would not make any sense to foster prejudice toward an outgroup for the feelings of deprivation one feels at the egoistic (and individual) level, because railing against outgroups would not really better one's individual situation.

Closely related to relative deprivation are our feelings toward outgroups against whom our group is competing for a scarce resource. Notice, here the shared goal is complicated by scarcity, and that may mean that one group achieves the goal and the other one does not. In this instance, the goal is thus a finite, zero-sum scenario (i.e., there is only one winner, and there must be a loser; two cannot share or each get the prize). Campbell (1965) suggested that these cases represent realistic conflicts, because they are based on competition for real resources. In his **realistic conflict theory (RCT),** Campbell suggested that when two groups are in competition for scarce resources, feelings of hostility and prejudice toward the other group will emerge. Zárate, Garcia, Garza, and Hitlan (2004) demonstrated that realistic-conflict-induced prejudice tends to emerge when people perceive an outgroup as having similar work-related personality traits and abilities. Interestingly, however, when perceivers were asked to evaluate an outgroup's similarity to themselves on non-work-related traits, they were less prejudiced against those who were rated as more similar.

In a classic demonstration of Campbell's prediction, Sherif and his colleagues (Sherif et al., 1961) conducted an experiment with a group of 22 11-year-old boys who were going to a summer camp at Robber's Cave national park. Sherif had designed the whole camp experience as a study of the RCT and had obtained permission from the boys' parents and school administrators to include the boys in this experiment. The boys were selected on the basis of similar (above-average) IQ scores (median score of 112), good school performance, and no physical, psychological, or emotional problems. Of course, the boys were unaware that their camp experience was designed to examine the tenets of RCT. Sherif trained the camp counselors, and, essentially, they were to remain fairly nondirective (within reason), allowing the boys to choose what activities they would like to do, and so forth. Sherif's plan was to have 11 boys ride to camp on one bus and set up camp at the other end of the park, unaware of the other group of 11 boys at the opposite end of the park.

During phase one, which lasted about a week, the boys in each group were oblivious to the existence of the other. Sherif wanted them each to form an ingroup identity, choose a name for their group (one called themselves the Eagles, and the other boys called themselves the Rattlers), and do activities to foster friendships and group unity and loyalty (such as pitching tents, serving meals, climbing on dams, making signs, etc.). After this initial phase, the two groups were introduced to each other. During phase two, Sherif brought the two groups together to compete in a series of sporting events, and the winning team would receive a team trophy, $5, and medals and pocket knives for each member of the winning team. Thus, the boys were competing for a scarce resource. As the RCT would predict, the boys during this stage started to show a great deal of outgroup prejudice. They referred to the other team members as "sneaky," and "stinkers," whereas they described their own group members as "brave" and "friendly." They raided each others' cabins and stole items from the other groups, and their dislike for the outgroup members was evident in their prejudiced feelings about and stereotypes of outgroup members. When asked who their friends were, the boys invariably listed only ingroup members as their friends. At the end of phase 2, the winning team (the Rattlers) was announced, and that team was given their prizes.

During the final phase of the camp experience (phase 3), Sherif wanted to reduce the prejudice that had been produced through competition. He first decided to test the **contact hypothesis,** which suggests that prejudice can be eliminated (or reduced) if two groups are brought into contact with each other (Allport, 1954). The idea here is that because prejudice is often born out of ignorance and fear, having people get together with outgroup members (with whom they normally have little contact) would result in them forming intergroup friendships, and their prejudices would subside (we will discuss the contact hypothesis in greater detail in Chapter 9). To test this prediction, the boys were asked to sit among the outgroup members at the camp cafeteria, alternating every seat with an ingroup member, an outgroup member, an ingroup member, and so on. Unfortunately, this did not result in decreased prejudice, but rather a food fight between groups. Prejudice was still high between groups. Sherif then decided to test another prediction made by the RCT. Campbell (1965) speculated that when the goals of two groups are compatible, the attitudes of one group toward the other group should be more tolerant, if not outright friendly.

Sherif introduced two situations in which the goals of the two groups were compatible. In each instance, the goal could not be accomplished without the assistance of the other group, so all the boys needed to work together to solve what Sherif referred to as a **superordinate goal.** In theory, the superordinate goal should work to reduce ingroup–outgroup distinctions and cause the individuals to reconceptualize their group affiliation in terms of a unified, inclusive group, thereby abandoning—or at least relegating to a lesser role—their former, separate group affiliations. In one situation, the camp's water supply malfunctioned (a paper sack had clogged the faucet of the camp water supply). The boys worked together to brainstorm ideas on how to clear the faucet of the obstruction, and they were successful. In the other situation, Sherif arranged for the bus that was to take them home from the camp to break down. Specifically, the boys were told it would not start. The boys again worked together to think of a way to get it to start (manually, by getting the bus to move and having the driver try the ignition). They decided to hook a rope to the truck, and all the boys pulled the bus, which enabled the driver to start the truck. After these

In Sherif et al.'s Robber's Cave experiments, the two groups meet for the first time. Each group is eyeing the other suspiciously, and prejudice between the groups is forming quickly, because (as the realistic conflict theory predicts) they must compete for scarce resources. If you think about human history, much prejudice can be explained as originating, in part, through a similar process.

events, Sherif and the counselors noticed a dramatic decline (if not absence) in hostility between the groups. Indeed, each group started regarding outgroup members in positive terms, and some even formed outgroup friendships. As an epilogue to this classic experiment, on the way home the boys chose to ride on one bus (not two separate buses), and the Rattlers decided to spend their $5 for ice cream for all of the boys.

Subsequent lab and field research on the realistic conflict theory has yielded data supportive of the theory (Brown, 1995; Jones, 1997), although critics have noted a couple of problems with the theory (Brewer & Brown, 1998). One is that subsequent research has indicated that ingroup identification is harder to eliminate than the Sherif et al. (1961) data would lead one to believe. Thus, even though two groups may be motivated to work together on a superordinate goal, they still tend to identify themselves along their separate group identities, and not as a larger, single group. As such, it becomes more difficult to not think in terms of "us and them," and the associated prejudices and stereotypes about the outgroup therefore become that much more difficult to eliminate. However, in a recent analysis, Hornsey and Hogg (2000) contend that maintaining one's separate group identity is not only all right, but essential to intergroup harmony. These researchers suggest that as long as groups can maintain their important group identity *and* successfully locate these identities within the "context of a binding superordinate identity" (p. 143), the likelihood of intergroup tension will be greatly reduced. A second problem is that, even before the Rattlers and Eagles were to formally compete for the prizes, they expressed a desire—almost immediately upon learning of the other groups' existence—to compete and win against "them." Recall that such a finding does not fit with the RCT, because according to that theory, feelings of hostility toward an outgroup will only emerge when one's group is competing for a scarce resource with that outgroup. Some researchers (e.g., Fiske & Rusher, 1993; Perdue, et al., 1990) have suggested that it may be the case that merely seeing someone else as an "outgroup" member can arouse negative affect in a perceiver. Such a possibility would nicely explain the anomalous findings in the Sherif et al. study and speak to the growing literature on the automaticity of stereotyping and prejudice (see our discussion of implicit stereotyping, in Chapter 3).

SUMMARY

In this chapter, we examined research and theory on the factors that contribute to the formation of prejudice and stereotypes, and the reasons that stereotypes and prejudice persist, even in the face of stereotype-inconsistent information. Research in social cognition has led to great advances in our understanding of the nature of stereotyping, showing, for example, that stereotyping is the result of the mind's normal tendency to categorize stimuli in the environment, and not the product of a deviant mind or maladjusted personality. Of course, such a conclusion does not in any way suggest that we ought to condone the endorsement of stereotyped beliefs. Rather, it clarifies that stereotyping is an outgrowth of the innate tendency of the human brain to categorize the world, in order to greatly simplify the amount of information it must deal with at any given moment. With this perspective, researchers have been able to identify the cognitive tendencies and processes (e.g., illusory correlations or subcategorization) whereby we maintain this simplified view of the world and the cognitive efficiency (and frequent inaccuracy) that stereotypes afford us in our daily lives. These tendencies tend to be somewhat automatic, and as such are difficult to control. But knowing of stereotypes does not imply that one endorses them, and this is an important distinction in our understanding of the difference between high- and low-prejudice persons (which we will discuss in detail in the next chapter). We then explored the reasons why some people dislike other groups, and our discussion focused on the motivational factors that lead to the development and maintenance of such prejudices. Motivational theories for prejudice have tended to implicate the self, self-esteem, and group identity as factors that lead one to actively dislike other groups, in order to feel better about oneself or one's ingroups. Current researchers are focusing on motivational explanations of prejudice, because they have the most explanatory power and theoretical promise as a tool for understanding the nature of prejudice, and we will explore this further in Chapter 10, in our discussion of future trends and unanswered questions in prejudice research.

GLOSSARY

contact hypothesis   The prediction that intergroup prejudice will diminish or be eliminated when the two groups are brought into contact with one another.

illusory correlation   The overestimation of the association between two variables that are either related weakly or not at all.

implicit theories   Our individual beliefs about the nature of personality and the behaviors, attitudes, and values associated with certain types of individuals.

ingroup   Any group to which one believes he or she belongs.

ingroup bias (favoritism)   The tendency to favor, and have positive affect for, members of one's own group, and to attribute more positive characteristics to one's ingroups than to outgroups.

optimal-distinctiveness theory   Suggests that our social motives are governed by an alternating tension between our need to be our own unique person and our need to belong to groups. We are therefore motivated to find and affiliate with groups that can help provide a balance between these opposing needs.

outgroup   Any group to which a person does not belong.

outgroup homogeneity   The belief that members of outgroups are more similar to each other than are members of one's ingroups ("they all look alike").

minimal groups   A group formed on the basis of some (sometimes trivial) criteria, and which are otherwise devoid of the normal aspects of group life, such as face-to-face interaction, group norms, interactions with other groups, and a group structure.

realistic conflict theory   A theory of intergroup conflict which states that when groups are competing for scarce resources, prejudice and hostility between the groups will result.

relative deprivation theory   States that when groups perceive that they are at a disadvantage, relative to an outgroup, in their attainment of important group goals, the group that feels disadvantaged or deprived will feel prejudice and resentment toward the other group.

scapegoat theory   Postulates that when an individual becomes thwarted from a particular goal, they may feel anger, irritation, or disappointment. That anger is similar to the negative affect we feel toward disliked outgroups, and, eventually, the outgroup is blamed for the ingroup's failure to attain their goal, and the ingroup feels prejudice toward the outgroup.

social-identity theory   States that the need for positive self-esteem motivates individuals to perceive people in the environment in terms of ingroups and outgroups. Suggests that people can attain positive self-esteem either by their own accomplishments or by affiliating with high-status groups.

subcategories   Special, separate cognitive categories for deviant (i.e., stereotype-disconfirming) members of a stereotyped outgroup, so that a stereotype can remain intact.

superordinate goal   A task which, if it is to be completed successfully, requires the cooperative efforts of two (or more) groups.

DISCUSSION QUESTIONS

1. After reviewing the research on the automatic nature of stereotyping, what do you think about Macrae et al.'s (1997) suggestion that seeing a category word will evoke the associated stereotypes, but seeing a member from that category may not necessarily evoke stereotypes (because the perceiver may categorize the individual on another salient dimension)?

2. How do your salient ingroups change as you go from one social situation to another, and as you go from one social interaction to the next? How do you think this influences (or does not influence) your tendency to perceive others according to their category membership (and to evoke various stereotypes about other persons)?

3. In your own experiences, what sources of stereotypes (e.g., parents, television, magazines, friends, etc.) have been most prevalent and influential?

4. Can you identify some major stereotypes that are communicated in today's media (movies, magazines, television)? What are some specific examples of prejudiced or stereotypical messages or portrayals of a group?

5. How much do feelings and thoughts of relative deprivation contribute to prejudice in the United States today?

6. How would realistic conflict theory explain anti-immigrant attitudes?

SUGGESTED KEY READINGS

Devine, P. G. (1989). Stereotypes and prejudice: Their automatic and controlled components. *Journal of Personality and Social Psychology, 56,* 5–18.

Fiske, S. T., & Neuberg, S. L. (1990). A continuum of impression formation, from category-based to individuating processes: Influences of information and motivation on attention and interpretation. In M. P. Zanna (Ed.), *Advances in experimental social psychology* (Vol. 23, pp. 1–74). New York: Academic Press.

Jones, J. M. (1997). *Prejudice and racism* (2nd ed.). New York: McGraw-Hill.

Kunda, Z., & Sinclair, L. (1999). Motivated reasoning with stereotypes: Activation, application, and inhibition. *Psychological Inquiry, 10,* 12–22.

Tajfel, H., & Turner, J. C. (1986). The social identity theory of intergroup behavior. In S. Worchel & W. G. Austin (Eds.), *Psychology of intergroup relations* (pp. 7–24). Chicago: Nelson-Hall.

INTERNET RESOURCES: RESEARCHERS, REFERENCES, AND ORGANIZATIONS DEVOTED TO THE STUDY OF PREJUDICE

http://psychclassics.yorku.ca/Sherif   The complete report (from the original 1961 book) of Sherif's famous Robber's Cave experiment.

www.psych.ucla.edu/faculty/taylor   Home page of Dr. Shelley Taylor, a prominent social psychologist and pioneer in social cognition research and theory.

www.psych.ucsb.edu/people/faculty/Hamilton/index.php   Home page of Dr. David Hamilton, a pioneer in social-cognition theory and research.

http://webscript.princeton.edu/~psych/psychology/research/fiske/index.php   Home page of Dr. Susan Fiske, an eminent social psychologist and expert on stereotyping. Her recent work has focused on the influence of power on gender stereotyping.

CHAPTER THREE

FEELING VERSUS THINKING IN THE ACTIVATION AND APPLICATION OF STEREOTYPES

Suppose you have a stereotype about people who live in the upper Midwest (the Dakotas, Minnesota, Wisconsin). Based on your extensive knowledge of midwesterners (you watched the movie *Fargo* once), you believe you have a pretty good idea of what people in that strange land are like. Among many of your firmly held convictions about midwesterners are the beliefs that they all have a strange accent and their speech is peppered by funny words and phrases such as "youbetcha," "yah," "shuure," and "oh geeez." Having spent the first 22 years of my life in Minnesota (Minneapolis, to be exact), and having been to the Dakotas and Wisconsin, I can assure you that midwesterners are nothing like your stereotype (okay, maybe some are). You have developed a stereotype, and it leads you to a number of assumptions, beliefs, expectations, and perhaps negative feelings about midwesterners.

When I meet you and tell you where I was raised, will you react to me on the basis of your stereotypes or your negative feelings (prejudices) about people from the Midwest? In other words, when we have stereotypes about other groups, are our behaviors, thoughts, and feelings guided primarily by our beliefs or by our affect associated with the group? This is a difficult question to address, and one that has intrigued prejudice researchers for decades. When you are in a certain mood, are you more or less likely to rely on stereotypes when you are evaluating outgroup members? Can we just decide to not stereotype? What are the cognitive and affective factors that lead us to be more likely to stereotype others? In this chapter, we explore these and many other questions in detail and attempt to understand the complex interaction of mood and cognition as they enhance or inhibit our ability to carefully evaluate other individuals in our environment. We also discuss, in detail, the fascinating current research on implicit cognition and explore why it is the case that exposure to subliminally presented information can indeed enhance our tendency to stereotype others. Unfortunately, we will not be able to explain why, after a 5-minute phone conversation with my sister, who lives in Fargo, North Dakota, I find myself saying "youbetcha" for the rest of the day.

MOOD

Since the early 1970s, research on stereotyping has been dominated by a social-cognitive perspective, which focuses on how people think about others and about themselves (Hamilton, 1981a; Stephan, 1985). Discussions of stereotyping during the 1970s and early 1980s centered on understanding the processes involved in the way perceivers processed social information and how breakdowns or biases in this information processing increased the reliance of the individual on stereotypes for making social judgments (Brewer & Kramer, 1985; Hamilton & Trolier, 1986; Taylor & Crocker, 1981). A major benefit of the cognitive approach to stereotyping has been the demonstration of the important influence of expectations about social groups on social judgments and attitudes and behavior toward out-

Our views of other groups are often guided by stereotypes, which can form on the shakiest bits of "information." Countless viewers of the movie Fargo *formed stereotypes about midwesterners. Our views of other groups very frequently are based on fictitious events, hearsay, or single-case encounters with outgroup members—not very scientific. Unfortunately, most people care less about being accurate in their social perceptions than they do about coming to a quick evaluation of another person.*

groups. Examples of this type of theorizing include research demonstrating that intergroup discrimination can originate from categorization (e.g., Tajfel, 1970); that the context-based salience of outgroup members can affect how those persons are perceived (e.g., Taylor et al., 1978); and that biases in the way distinctive information about outgroup members is perceived can lead to an increased tendency to stereotype outgroup members (e.g., Hamilton & Gifford, 1976).

During this period of cognitive dominance in the social–psychological investigation of stereotyping, the investigation of the influence of affect on stereotyping (an area of research pursued with much less vigor) continued. Yet, amid the emphasis on cognition, a few researchers called for the examination of the role of affect in stereotyping (e.g., Fiske, 1982; Hamilton, 1981a). Toward the end of the 1980s, researchers began to take a closer look at the influence of affect on cognitive processes (e.g., Forgas, 1990; Isen, 1987; Schwarz, 1990). This change was precipitated by the development of several theoretical perspectives concerning the nature and structure of emotion (e.g., Frijda, 1988; Ortony, Clore, & Collins, 1988). In an influential article, Zanna and Rempel (1988) argued that attitudes toward different attitude objects might be more or less determined by affective, rather than cognitive, sources. Researchers soon began investigating more directly the effects of positive versus negative moods on the tendency to stereotype others in social judgments (Mackie & Hamilton, 1993).

In addition to the growing empirical basis for returning to the investigation of emotion's effects on stereotyping, there were theoretical and intuitive reasons for such a renaissance of emotion experiments in intergroup perception. Traditionally, emotions were thought to contribute importantly to the development and endurance of stereotypes (Allport, 1954; Lippmann, 1922). The history of intergroup relations is replete with evidence that intense emotions guide the thoughts and actions of people in intergroup contexts (Katz, 1981). Affect plays a major role in the way that information about social groups and group members is processed. Affect influences the accessibility of constructs in memory and thus may determine which of many social representations are primed, and which characteristics in a given representation become activated (Forgas, 1992; Stangor, 1990). Affect may also influence the extent to which the individual exerts information processing effort (Schwarz, 1990; Stangor & Lange, 1994). Affect also becomes associated with social-group labels through learning processes (Bower & Cohen, 1982; Clark, Milberg, & Erber, 1988). When affect and physiological arousal are associated with group members, they will influence how information about the outgroup member is interpreted, how the perceiver responds to the outgroup member, and whether the perceiver tends to interact with members of the target group in the future. Below, we consider the findings reported thus far in this rapidly growing area of investigation.

Types of Intergroup Affect

In one step toward specifying further the nature of affect in the intergroup context, Bodenhausen (1993) has introduced the useful distinction between **incidental affect** and **integral affect.** The former is defined as affect that is elicited by situations unrelated to the intergroup context, and the latter is affect that is elicited within the intergroup context and involves the stereotyped outgroup. Integral affect can also arise merely from thinking about the outgroup. Bodenhausen notes that much research on stereotyping has utilized incidental affect, but surprisingly few studies have examined the influence of integral affect on judgments of members of stereotyped outgroups. It is useful to make a further distinction regarding integral affect. It is reasonable to suggest that individuals should have a rather stable feeling toward the outgroup as a whole, which may be termed **chronic outgroup affect.** In addition, people can also have an affective reaction within an interaction with a specific outgroup member, and this can be termed **episodic outgroup affect.** Below, we consider the research evidence on chronic and episodic racial affect, as well as incidental affect.

Chronic Outgroup Affect.   Attitudes have traditionally been viewed as stable, enduring evaluations of an **attitude object** (Fishbein & Ajzen, 1975; Petty & Cacioppo, 1981). An attitude object is defined as anything about which one forms an attitude (e.g., idea, person, object). This idea certainly holds true for the notion of outgroup attitudes. In his classic treatise, *The Nature of Prejudice,* Allport (1954) defined a stereotype as "a fixed idea that accompanies a category" (p. 191). Because one's outgroup attitude was believed to be a stable evaluation of the outgroup and its members, it was assumed that any evaluation of the outgroup member in the future, regardless of the context, would be a direct result of the simple recall of the perceiver's stored evaluation of the outgroup member. Because any attitude (or "evaluation" of the attitude object) has incorporated within it both a cognitive and affective component (Breckler & Wiggins, 1989; Eagly & Chaiken, 1993), it is reasonable to suggest that the affect associated with the attitude is also an enduring feature of the evaluation of the attitude object. In other words, each time the attitude object is perceived or remembered, the evaluation will trigger beliefs and other information associated with the object, as well as enduring feelings associated with the attitude object (Dovidio & Gaertner, 1993; Fiske & Pavelchak, 1986). This process also holds when considering enduring intergroup attitudes. The affect that one feels toward the outgroup, as a result of one's enduring attitude toward the outgroup can be termed *chronic outgroup affect.* This affect is distinct from affective reactions to an interaction with a *specific member* of the outgroup. In order to better understand the affect that accompanies this enduring outgroup attitude, it is useful to examine further the nature of the enduring outgroup attitude.

The attitudes of White Americans toward African Americans have been increasingly liberal and egalitarian since the mid-1960s, suggesting to some that prejudice in this country has decreased and that Caucasians are more egalitarian toward African Americans today than they were three decades ago (Schuman, Steeh, & Bobo, 1985). Much research suggests however, that although the overt form of hostility and prejudice toward African Americans may be much less prevalent, prejudice continues to exist in a more subtle form (Crosby, Bromley, & Saxe, 1980; Devine & Elliot, 1995; Gaertner, 1976; Gaertner & Dovidio, 1977, 1981; McConahay & Hough, 1976; Sears & Allen, 1984). Gaertner and Dovidio (1986) use the phrase **aversive racism** to describe the prejudice toward African Americans that characterizes many White Americans' attitudes. Aversive racists, according to Gaertner and Dovidio (1977), truly believe they are egalitarian and regard themselves as nonprejudiced. However, they also possess negative feelings about African Americans. If they can do so in a subtle, easily rationalizable fashion, these individuals may express negative attitudes toward African Americans yet feel no affective consequences (i.e., guilt, shame, sadness) from doing so, thereby preserving the self from threatening conflict-related negative affect (Monteith, 1996a).

Gaertner and Dovidio (1986) suggested that this anti-Black affect has a number of possible sources. Differences in physical appearance between Caucasians and African Americans can fuel this negative affect (e.g., Margaret Mead's statement that people "must be taught to hate, but the appreciation and fear of difference is everywhere," as cited in Gaertner & Dovidio, 1986, p. 63). The multiple effects of mere categorization of people into ingroups and outgroups has biasing effects for the perceiver on the perception and evaluation of people, irrespective of objective evaluations of the individual being perceived (Billig & Tajfel, 1973). People in the ingroup are (1) assumed to be more similar in beliefs, (2) evaluated more favorably, (3) the recipients of more positive behavior by the perceiver than are members of outgroups, and (4) found to be more attractive by the perceiver (Brewer, 1979). Some suggest that social and cultural factors also contribute to the anti-Black affect felt by aversive racists. These anti-Black feelings are fostered by traditional cultural stereotypes of Blacks in the United States as lazy, ignorant, poor, and more likely to commit crimes (Karlins, Coffman, & Walters, 1969). Finally, some research suggests that Caucasians tend to see Black culture in the United States as promoting values that are at odds with the Protestant work ethic (Jackson et al., 1996).

Central to low-prejudice individuals' self-concept is their belief that they possess egalitarian values. Their negative feelings about African Americans are often kept out of awareness so that such feelings do not threaten their view of themselves as egalitarian and nonprejudiced. When a situation threatens to make these negative feelings salient, low-prejudice individuals try to dissociate themselves from these feelings and often act more positively in ways that will convince them and others that they are not prejudiced (Gaertner & Dovidio, 1986; Monteith, 1993).

Because much affect in intergroup contexts involving stereotyped groups tends to be negative, empirical attention has been devoted to the influence of such affective states on judgments of the members of the stereotyped outgroup. In general, when people feel negative affect, they are especially likely to describe racial outgroups using unfavorable characteristics (Esses & Zanna, 1995). The particular negative affective state that has been investigated the most is anxiety, because it is commonly experienced by individuals in an intergroup interaction (Dollard et al., 1939; Gaertner & Dovidio, 1986; Stephan & Stephan, 1985; Wilder, 1993). Stephan and Stephan (1985) developed a theoretical model of intergroup anxiety. In this model, anxiety has a disruptive effect on the behaviors, thoughts, and feelings of the outgroup member and the perceiver. This anxiety can also lead to increased stereotyping by the perceiver, an avoidance of future intergroup interaction, and attempts by the perceiver to control others (Fiske, Morling, & Stevens, 1996). According to Stephan and Stephan, the amount and conditions of intergroup contact are crucial determinants in whether the individual will experience anxiety prior to, or during, interactions with the outgroup. When there has been minimal contact, and/or the contact has been characterized by conflict, the individual will tend to feel more anxiety prior to or during the intergroup interaction. Research by Wilder (1993; Wilder & Shapiro, 1989) and others (e.g., Rankin & Campbell, 1955) supports the notion that anxiety may be a common emotion felt among interactants in intergroup contexts. Moreover, anxiety may promote stereotyping of outgroup members by an affective consistency process (cuing more negative cognitions) or through increased reliance on expectancies (and schemas) regarding outgroup members as a result of a reduction in cognitive capacity (Bodenhausen, 1993). Stereotyping may also occur through a combination of each of these two processes.

Research by Dijker (1987) suggests that an important determinant of the type of chronic racial affect that the perceiver feels in the intergroup context is the degree to which the outgroup member is culturally dissimilar from the perceiver. Dutch participants in Dijker's research were surveyed about the way they believe they would feel and behave in response to various scenarios involving various forms of contact with different ethnic groups. Dijker identified four types of emotion that appeared to be strongly related to ethnic attitudes: positive mood, anxiety, irritation, and concern. More personal forms of contact were associated with decreased anxiety and more positive mood with an ethnic group that is culturally similar (Surinamers) to the Dutch perceivers. On the other hand, close contact tended to be more negative with a group that is more culturally dissimilar from the Dutch perceivers (Turks).

Some research also suggests that intergroup affect is a better determinant of attitudes and behavior toward ethnic groups than are cognitions about the ethnic group (Esses, Haddock, & Zanna, 1993; Stangor, Sullivan, & Ford, 1991), but others suggest that our cognitions about members of the outgroup influence how we feel about the outgroup. For example, Dijker and Frijda (1988, as cited in Esses et al., 1993) reported evidence that supports the notion that the characteristics (positive traits, ethnic appearance) that we attribute to members of an ethnic group may influence how we feel about that group and our attitudes toward that ethnic group. In other words, many of the reported causes of emotions in the intergroup context were related to characteristics of members of the ethnic outgroup.

In sum, there appears to be a solid empirical basis for the notion that the intergroup context brings with it an emotional component for the interactants, and that factors such as proximity and degree of personal contact in the intergroup context, physical and personality characteristics of the outgroup members, and the cultural similarity of the outgroup to the perceiver's ethnic group tends to influence the strength and valence of the emotion felt by each individual in the intergroup interaction. This emotion, then, has various disruptive/biasing effects on the individual's perception of information, and it tends to increase reliance on the use of stereotypes in processing information about the outgroup member in the intergroup context.

Episodic Outgroup Affect.   One's intergroup-related affect can also be a result of a specific interaction with a specific individual member of the outgroup. This affect can also result from the imagined interaction with an individual from the outgroup. This intergroup-related affect, or episodic outgroup affect, can be similar or different in valence from one's chronic outgroup affect toward the outgroup. The reason researchers have been interested in what is here termed episodic outgroup affect is that it can often have a strong impact on an individual's chronic, enduring outgroup affect, and, it is believed, the individual's enduring attitudes toward the outgroup. In this way, researchers have theorized, it may be possible to change negative chronic outgroup affect (and, hence, negative outgroup attitudes) toward the outgroup by the opposing impact of positive episodic outgroup affect.

Incidental Affect.   Feelings that have no origination associated with the outgroup can be characterized as incidental affect. A pervasive theme in the extant literature has been that affect in one context can influence social judgments in another context (e.g., Isen, 1987; Wyer & Srull, 1989). Thus, it is reasonable to suggest that incidental affect (arising in a context having nothing to do with intergroup attitudes) can subsequently influence an individual's proclivity to use stereotypes in social judgment. There is some research evidence that supports this assertion. Stroessner and Mackie (1993) induced incidental happiness or sadness in participants by having them watch amusing or depressing 5-minute clips of television programs. Participants were then asked to estimate outgroup variability. Results indicated that both incidental sadness and happiness significantly reduced the perception of outgroup variability. In research reported by Esses and her colleagues (1993), incidental happy or sad affect was induced (via the Velten procedure and recall-of-events procedure; Izard, 1972), and this affect had an impact on participants' subsequent judgments of characteristics associated with six different ethnic groups. Specifically, incidental sad affect increased the tendency of participants to use negative stereotypes in descriptions of Pakistanis and Native Americans. Interestingly, participants who felt incidental happiness were more likely to provide especially favorable stereotypes of their own ethnic ingroup. Research also indicates that incidental anxiety seems to facilitate the use of stereotypes in making social judgments (Baron, Inman, Kao, & Logan, 1992; Baron, Logan & Lilly, 1994; Stephan, 1985), as well as increase the perception of outgroup homogeneity (Wilder & Shapiro, 1989). In sum, it appears that affect induced in a context unrelated to the outgroup can have an impact on attitudes toward and judgments about the outgroup.

Influence of Positive Affect

Recent research has focused on the effects of positive affect (usually happiness) and negative affect on social judgments. First, let us consider how positive affect seems to influence intergroup perception. Positive affect appears to influence how people categorize others. In a wide range of cognitive processing tasks, positive affect has been shown to reduce the extent of systematic processing (Hamilton, Stroessner, & Mackie, 1993; Isen, Means, Patrick, & Nowicki, 1982). People who are happy tend to process information less analytically; they rely on heuristic cues, initial judgments, decisional shortcuts, and other simplifying strategies (Bless, Hamilton, & Mackie, 1992; Mackie & Worth, 1991); and they are more likely to use stereotypes in their judgments of others (Park & Banaji, 2000). An exception to this general finding is that when happy people are confronted with an outgroup individual who radically diverges from the outgroup, the happy person has no problem giving up their reliance on stereotypes in making judgments about that target (Krauth-Gruber & Ric, 2000).

This research supports the contemporary notion in social cognition research that people are more likely to stereotype when they are under increased cognitive constraints due to influences such as distraction, or demands brought on by other complex, simultaneous cognitive processing (Bodenhausen & Lichtenstein, 1987; Fiske & Neuberg, 1990). However, some research suggests that this view may need to be revised somewhat. Results from a series of experiments investigating the effects of happiness on stereotyping led Bodenhausen, Kramer, and Süsser (1994) to conclude that there is "little support for the idea that happiness promotes stereotypic thinking by constraining the perceiver's capacity for more systematic thought" (p. 628). These researchers suggest that happy people are just not very motivated to expend the cognitive effort required to avoid using stereotypes in intergroup judgment. However, according to Bodenhausen et al. (1994), if such an effort were to have an effect on the individual's well-being, then the individual would likely not stereotype (a conclusion supported by Forgas, 1989). The question then remains: do people stereotype when they are in a good mood because they do not want to think carefully about the other individual (i.e., a motivational issue) or because the positive affect cognitively clogs their finite cognitive resources to individuate the target individual (a cognitive capacity issue)? We will explore this issue in the next section.

Effects of Negative Affect

Unfortunately, the pervasive affect that is felt among interactants in an interracial context is often decidedly negative (Allport, 1954; Bodenhausen, 1993). This is true even for those who think of themselves as egalitarian (Gaertner & Dovidio, 1986). Thus, it is important for researchers to understand the specific effects that different negative emotions can have on the way individuals think about and behave toward members of ethnic outgroups. In research on the effects of anger and sadness on stereotyping, Bodenhausen, Sheppard, and Kramer (1994) found that angry participants tended to make more stereotypic judgments, whereas participants who were sad did not differ from neutral-affect participants in their use of stereotypes. In fact, research on the effects of sadness on subsequent social judgments has often found that mildly sad individuals engage in more systematic, careful cognitive processing of information and are less likely to rely on stereotypes than are angry and happy individuals (Bodenhausen, 1993). Incidental anger and anxiety tend to lead to increased use of stereotypes in social judgments, whereas sadness (for a discussion of mildly depressed persons, see Bodenhausen, Sheppard et al., 1994) does not lead to an increased tendency to stereotype others (Park & Banaji, 2000).

Research has also examined the effects of various negative affective states on people's tendency to stereotype others. Unlike the research on the effects of positive affect on stereotyping, the data from research investigating negative affect yields a picture that is less clear. On the one hand, research in the persuasion literature indicates that sad people tend to seek and consider more information and process persuasive messages more completely (Bless, Bohner, Schwarz, & Strack, 1990; Sinclair, 1988). In contrast, some have found that sad subjects exhibit no decrements in memory performance, and this is especially true when the task is resource intensive (Ellis & Ashbrook, 1988). Similarly, subjects in a negative mood have been found to do less attributional processing (Sullivan & Conway, 1989) and generate fewer complex hypotheses (Silberman, Weingartner, & Post, 1983). The most common negative moods that have been investigated are sadness and anger, because these are most likely to occur naturally in the intergroup context. Bodenhausen (1993) suggests that although it is likely that other negative emotions (such as guilt, embarrassment, anxiety, and fear) may have a similar influence on the tendency of individuals to stereotype, it is important that researchers investigate the influence on stereotyping of these different negative moods (the same suggestion is made for the various positive moods, such as joy, serenity, and elation). As a case in point, one recent study by Skitka, Bauman, and Mullen (2004) found that tolerance for different political views appears to be differentially influenced by anger versus fear. When people feel fear or anger, they are less tolerant of others' political views. However, the routes to the decreased tolerance are different for each emotion. The effect of fear appears to be mediated by personal threat and ingroup enhancement. The influence of anger is mediated by moral outrage and outgroup derogation. Much more work is needed to uncover the specific mediating variables that influence the effects of various emotions on prejudice.

Interestingly, it may be the case that merely subliminally evoking information related to affect, but not actually activating that affective state, may be enough to activate behavioral tendencies of approach or avoidance associated with the emotion. In two experiments, Ric (2004) found that activation of information related to sadness leads to an increased reliance on stereotypes. Nonconscious activation of information related to happiness decreases reliance on stereotypes in social judgments. These data are intriguing, and their contrast with other affect-stereotyping studies merits further research in order to delineate the conditions under which various affective states, and information related to those states, will either enhance or inhibit the use of stereotypes in social perception.

Motivational versus Cognitive-Capacity Deficits

Do people stereotype when they are experiencing happiness, sadness, or anger because they are not motivated to expend the cognitive energy that it takes to individuate members of a stereotyped outgroup, or is it the case that people simply cannot think carefully about others because of a decreased cognitive capacity? The answer is, it depends. There is good basis for positing each of these possibilities. Regarding positive moods, Schwarz and his colleagues have suggested that positive mood conveys the message that because all is well with their environment, they do not need to focus on new information (Clore, Schwarz, & Conway, 1994; Schwarz & Bless, 1991; Schwarz & Clore, 1988). Thus, these people may be motivated to maintain their good mood and avoid activity that negates it (Worth & Mackie, 1987). Other researchers suggest that positive moods may activate the abundant positively valenced material in memory, and this material then consumes the cognitive capacity of the individual (Bower, 1981; Isen, 1987; Mackie & Worth, 1989).

A similar debate is occurring in the literature over whether there is a cognitive-capacity limitation imposed by negative moods or whether negative moods reduce motivation to process social information in a systematic fashion. Mackie and her colleagues (Mackie & Worth, 1989, 1991) have reported several experiments that support the idea that negative moods create a diminished cognitive capacity in the individual. An equally impressive array of experiments support the idea that negative moods affect the individual's motivation to process information systematically (Bless et al., 1990; Innes & Ahrens, 1991). If it seems that this brief review of the controversy surrounding the debate between proponents of the diminished-capacity notion and those who support the reduced-motivation hypothesis does not present a resolution of the debate, it is because there currently *is* no resolution (Hamilton et al., 1993). Indeed, many researchers agree that it is likely the case that investigating the separate effects these two factors have on the influence of mood on stereotyping may be fruitless because they are inexorably linked together (Bodenhausen, Sheppard et al., 1994; Eagly & Chaiken, 1993; Mackie, Asuncion, & Rosselli, 1992; Pendry & Macrae, 1994).

In an interesting paper, Martin, Ward, Achee, and Wyer (1993) presented data suggesting that moods do not have stable implications (as is implied in the previously mentioned research). Rather, they have different meanings depending on the person's interpretation of the mood. The authors suggest that with different interpretations, the same mood can have different effects. Positive moods will tell people to continue their tasks (or cognitive processes) if the mood reflects the individual's enjoyment (having a good time), but the positive mood will tell people to stop what they are doing if the mood reflects the level of goal attainment (goal attained, so stop and relax). On the other hand, negative moods will tell people to stop when the mood reflects the level of enjoyment (not having fun), but to continue when it reflects the person's level of goal attainment (goal not attained, keep working). It may be the case that the investigation of the dynamic interplay of the motivational, cognitive capacity, and hedonic contingency processes will yield further insight into the influence of affect on the tendency to stereotype (Pendry & Macrae, 1994).

COGNITION

Implicit Cognition

That some psychologists propose that cognition occurs outside of awareness, and that these processes can influence behavior and overt cognitive processes comes as no surprise to researchers within psychology. For centuries, philosophers have speculated on the existence of such cognitive processes (e.g., Descartes, 1637), and the birth of American psychology also saw several advocates for the proposition that humans have what James (1890) termed "sub-conscious," and Freud (1900/1953) termed "unconscious" cognitive processes. But what may be surprising is the recent revitalized interest in the notion of cognitive processes occurring outside conscious awareness. In the last decade, researchers within the cognitive-neuroscience domain of psychology (as well as other cognitive and social psychologists) have found compelling evidence for the idea that cognitive processes do function outside of consciousness and that these processes can influence overt thoughts and behaviors (Schacter, 1992). Does this mean that uncontrolled, unconscious cognition can affect our behavior and attitudes? More specifically, will low-prejudiced people stereotype others and show prejudice as a result of unconscious cognitions? In the next section, we will examine the evidence that suggests the existence of unconscious cognition.[1] We will then explore the implications of these findings for research on stereotyping and prejudice.

Subliminal Messages.   Have you ever seen the now-famous vodka advertisement that features a close-up picture of a drink of vodka on ice (see Figure 3.1)?

For decades, people have sworn that there is a tiny picture of a nude woman's chest hidden subtly in the recesses of the ice and liquor. The rumor suggests that the advertisers and makers colluded to plant the picture in the advertisement so that it will work at a **subliminal** level (to perceive something without being consciously aware of the perception) to influence people, especially men, to purchase that brand of vodka. In other words, even though viewers of the advertisement may not consciously realize the presence of the subliminal stimulus, their attitudes and behavior can still be influenced by the perception of the stimulus below the level of awareness. For decades, the concept of subliminal messages has been part of American culture. People have readily believed that their behavior (e.g.,

---

1. It is important to note that my use of the word *unconscious* is strictly a generic use of the word, and it implies no psychoanalytic theoretical usage. Because of its simplicity, I have elected to use *unconscious cognition* to describe the cognitive processes below the level of awareness (very strictly, the phrase implies cognition that is not conscious; that is, *un*conscious).

PEOPLE HAVE BEEN TRYING TO FIND THE BREASTS IN THESE ICE CUBES SINCE 1957.

The advertising industry is sometimes charged with sneaking seductive little pictures into ads.

Supposedly, these pictures can get you to buy a product without your even seeing them.

Consider the photograph above. According to some people, there's a pair of female breasts

hidden in the patterns of light refracted by the ice cubes.

Well, if you really searched you probably *could* see the breasts. For that matter, you could also see Millard Fillmore, a stuffed pork chop and a 1946 Dodge.

The point is that so-called "subliminal advertising" simply

doesn't exist. Overactive imaginations, however, most certainly do.

So if anyone claims to see breasts in that drink up there, they aren't in the ice cubes.

They're in the eye of the beholder.

ADVERTISING
ANOTHER WORD FOR FREEDOM OF CHOICE.
American Association of Advertising Agencies

FIGURE 3.1 Subliminal mind control? Since the 1950s, Americans have believed in the power of subliminal messages to influence their attitudes. Some have charged that certain advertisers have constructed print ads that contain a subliminal symbol or message that subtly influences a reader's attitude to be more favorable toward the product. Taking advantage of this common belief, the American Association of Advertising Agencies created this clever public-service message, which attempts to debunk the myth of subliminal advertising. (Copyright © AAAA. Reprinted with permission of the American Association of Advertising Agencies.)

weight loss, quitting smoking, even self-esteem enhancement) can be altered via presentation of a message below the level of awareness that is perceived by the unconscious and therefore strongly impacts behavior. But, can subliminal messages really work? Are we subject to the subtle mind influences of the proverbial Orwellian Big Brother? Researchers have addressed the degree to which subliminal perception can actually occur.

You probably have seen television ads for subliminal self-help tapes (which feature messages that are supposedly presented below the level of conscious recognition) that claim to have a tremendous effect on your attitudes and behavior. In a compelling study, Greenwald, Spangenberg, Pratkanis, and Eskenazi (1991) examined the effectiveness of subliminal self-esteem and memory-enhancement audiotapes. Unbeknownst to participants in the study, the labels of the tapes were switched, so that people who thought they were getting the memory tape were in fact getting the self-esteem tape, and vice versa. Participants completed brief measures of self-esteem and memory tasks. After two weeks, participants came back to the lab and were tested on their self-esteem levels and memory abilities once again. Participants who believed they had the self-esteem tapes truly believed that their self-esteem increased as a result of the tapes. Those who thought they had memory-enhancement tapes believed their memories were improved. In fact, their second testings showed no difference in self-esteem or memory abilities compared to their scores before the tapes. Greenwald (1991) and his colleagues concluded that complex subliminal messages (i.e., sentences) cannot be detected below the level of awareness. However, very simple symbols, sounds, or words may be perceived below the level of awareness. Thus, while we may not be subject to complex persuasion messages or subliminal "mind control" by others, the fact that we can perceive simple symbols, faces, or words below the level of conscious awareness has some very interesting and surprising implications for research on stereotyping and prejudice. As you will soon see, a new area of research shows that it is very hard to avoid stereotyping.

Implicit Memory

Why can researchers use the term "unconscious" today without blushing with embarrassment? In large part, this is because of the research by cognitive neuroscientists on amnesic patients. For decades, it was believed that amnesics had an inability to transfer verbal information from short-term memory to a long-term memory store. But a study by Warrington and Weiskrantz (1970, Experiment 2) dramatically showed that the performance of amnesics on implicit tests of memory (e.g., tests of word-fragment identification, and word-stem completion—considered implicit because they tap priming from a previous study of the words by asking subjects to simply produce the first words that come to mind) is often virtually identical to that of controls. Yet, on explicit tests of memory (such as free recall or recognition—explicit because subjects are attempting to recall specific words to which they were recently exposed) amnesics consistently showed significantly inferior performance relative to controls. These findings have been replicated a number of times with other patient populations and different tasks (Roediger, 1990). These results have wide-ranging implications for researchers: implicit measures of retention reflect unconscious learning, because the amnesic patient is almost always unaware that they know the material when tested with explicit measures, but the subject performs similarly to normals on tests that implicitly tap memory. Thus, the amnesic will show normal retention *if* the test of memory is an implicit one (Schacter, 1987).

Until the mid-1980s, these phenomena were discussed in terms of a unified explicit-memory system. But a paper by Graf and Schacter (1985) can be regarded as a watershed in the current study of unconscious cognition. In this paper, the authors, citing findings from several studies with amnesics, made an important distinction between what they termed **implicit memory** (unintentional, nonconscious form of retention) and **explicit memory** (conscious recollection of previous experiences). This distinction, although similar to the conscious–unconscious, controlled–automatic, and other distinctions of the past, was different in that it was based on several systematic empirical demonstrations and it used new methodology that allowed such access into the implicit memory.

It appears, then, that research with amnesics that tests explicit and implicit memory shows that when implicit (but not explicit) measures are used to tap previously studied words, the memory performance of the amnesic patients is equal to that of controls. Again, the crucial point to be made here is that the type of measure one uses (implicit or explicit) will determine whether one will gain access to an implicit memory. What does this mean for people with normal (nonamnesic) memory? Do they also have an implicit memory system? Following Graf and Schacter's paper (1985), much research was initiated with other populations (e.g., normals) to determine the existence of implicit memory in others. This research revealed that normal subjects do show a dissociation between explicit and implicit memory on implicit and explicit tasks (Jacoby & Dallas, 1981; Jacoby & Witherspoon, 1982; Smith & Branscombe, 1988; Srinivas & Roediger, 1990). These results are impressive considering that in normals, explicit memory retention may exert opposite effects on the two types of memory test, rather than affecting performance on one and not affecting performance on the other (as is the case with amnesics).

Implicit Stereotyping

For nearly 20 years, social-cognition research has emphasized the dichotomy between cognitive processes that are intentional versus those that are not intended by the actor. This dichotomy has alternatively been labeled the difference between cognitive processes that are automatic versus controlled (Devine, 1989), unconscious versus conscious (Kihlstrom, 1990), intended versus unintended (Uleman & Bargh, 1989) aware versus unaware (Lewicki, Hill, & Czyzewska, 1992), and mindful versus mindless (Langer, 1989). As Abelson (1994) has rightly noted, these various dichotomies may belie the theoretical inclinations of the researcher more than they reflect distinct subsystems within cognitive activity. That is, perhaps these diverse research domains may be subsumed under a more inclusive distinction between implicit and explicit processes (Greenwald & Banaji, 1995). Such a characterization avoids any accompanying theoretical interpretations and ties the study of unconscious cognition to the work on implicit versus explicit memory processes.

Recent research has shown that whether one will stereotype another may be influenced by previous exposure to information, information the subject is unaware of at the time of subsequent testing. This process is referred to as **implicit stereotyping.** As Greenwald and Banaji (1995) explain, "Implicit stereotypes are the introspectively unidentified (or inaccurately identified) traces of past experience that mediate attributions of qualities to members of a social category" (p. 15). In their influential theory of "implicit social cognition," Greenwald and Banaji made two important points about implicit cognition (and this applies to implicit stereotyping as well). First, the effect of implicit cognition is demonstrated only when a past experience (such as an attitude formation, or exposure to a cognitive priming procedure or another type of biasing information such as the chronic accessibility of self-esteem) affects some future behavior or thought without the awareness of the subject that this experience has influenced their thoughts or behaviors. Second, the measure of implicit cognition should not be an explicit measure of the type already discussed (e.g., any type of self-report measure, or recognition or recall measure; see Dovidio and Fazio, 1992, for a more detailed discussion of implicit measures). This second point requires a bit of elaboration. In virtually all studies on stereotyping, self-esteem, and attitude measurement, researchers have often implied a consciousness in their operational definitions of these constructs. As just discussed, much research has shown that implicit cognition differs from self-reportable (conscious) cognition (Roediger, 1990). To the extent that this is true, then, those measures that presume introspection (such as self-report measures) are not appropriate for the study of the effects of implicit cognition on thought and behavior. Researchers must instead rely on measures that provide evidence of the operation of implicit cognition, such as word-fragment identification or special priming tasks.

To enable access to evidence of implicit stereotyping, researchers often employ a priming methodology. In the prototypical priming task, a prime stimulus (often a word) is presented briefly to the participant. Then, participants are asked to respond as quickly as possible to questions about related and unrelated target words (for example, the participant may simply be asked to judge whether the target character strings are real words or simply strings of letters) in reaction-time measures (such as response latency measures on a computer: how fast one can hit the appropriate keys in response to the stimulus presented on the screen). According to the spreading-activation model of memory (Collins & Loftus, 1975), when one thinks of a concept, related concepts are automatically activated in memory, and the time it takes to access those related concepts is markedly reduced as a result of the spreading activation. On the reaction-time task, the faster the participant's response to the target word, the greater the facilitative effect of the prime on the target word, and, we infer, the stronger the association between the prime and the target word. Because the spreading-activation effect is an automatic process, reaction-time measures can give researchers a window to the participant's cognitive network, unimpeded by psychological defenses, or concerns about social desirability (Gaertner & McLaughlin, 1983).

Using a priming methodology does not mean one has evidence concerning implicit cognition. There has been some debate about the reliability of some implicit stereotyping methods. Some find only modest reliability between those measures and other implicit and explicit measures of stereotyping (Kawakami & Dovidio, 2001), whereas others (Cunningham, Preacher, & Banaji, 2001) find that the reliability is fine. Recall that implicit processes are indicated only when we are reasonably certain that the participant was influenced by exposure to prior stimuli but shows no awareness of such influence (Greenwald & Banaji, 1995). Therefore, if one uses a priming task, it is important to verify that the participant was exposed to the stimulus but is not aware of the influence of the stimulus on their later judgments or behavior. Next, we will explore some studies that have used priming methods to assess implicit stereotyping.

In one of the first experiments using a priming task to examine stereotypes, Dovidio, Evans, and Tyler (1986) presented White participants with a prime of the word *black* or *white* for 2 seconds, then asked participants to respond as fast as they could to the question about the target traits (i.e., a yes or no answer about whether the trait could ever be true of the prime category) that followed the prime and remained on the screen until the participant responded. Dovidio and his colleagues found that participants had faster reaction times to positive stereotyped-trait words (e.g. *ambitious, practical*) that followed the prime *white*. When the prime was *black,* participants responded faster to negatively stereotyped words (e.g., *lazy, imitative*). These results are interesting in that they establish a facilitative effect for the activation of an outgroup (Black) and the recognition of negative, stereotyped words associated with that group. However, these data do not demonstrate an implicit stereotyping effect, because the presentation of the prime is too long. Recall that to establish an implicit stereotyping effect, the individual must not be aware of the influence of the prime on their responses to the subsequent words. In the Dovidio et al. (1986) procedure, participants were not only aware of the prime category, they were asked to consciously make decisions about the relationship between the target characteristics and the prime category.

The Implicit Association Test

A different, and very popular, method of assessing implicit attitudes is called the Implicit Association Test (IAT; Greenwald, McGhee, & Schwartz, 1998). This measure has captured the interest and imagination of researchers worldwide, and it has generated a tremendous amount of empirical attention. The IAT can be found on the web (https://implicit. harvard.edu/implicit/demo/index.jsp), and it can also be adapted for use offline in lab experiments (e.g., see Olson & Fazio, 2004a). The IAT works like this. Participants are presented with a target concept or category (such as Black, White, old, young, male, female, etc.) paired with an associated attribute discrimination (e.g., pleasant, unpleasant, good, or bad). Suppose the first pairing is Black/Good and White/Bad. Thus, they are led to understand that anytime they see a photo of an African American, or a positive trait word (e.g., intelligent, honest), they are to hit the appropriate key on the computer keyboard (as designated in the instructions) as soon as possible. Thus, it is a reaction-time measure, intended to discern the degree of association one has between target categories and various traits. In other words, if the individual has a lot of positive characteristics strongly associated in their memory with the word *Black,* they will be especially quick to react (show the shortest response latency) to the Black/good pairing test, and he or she should be much slower to react to the Black/bad pairing test items.

The test proceeds for 15 to 20 minutes, alternating to present new pairings of the various categories and attribute-discrimination terms. At the end of the test, the response latencies are calculated to give an overall preference that the individual holds for one category or the other. The results can show a slight, moderate, or strong preference for one category, or the results can be inconclusive (for a number of reasons). Again, a preference for one category over the other only suggests that, for that person, the pairing of *good* or *bad* to a particular category (old or young, for example) is a close one, resulting in the lowest response latencies across all trait pairings. What does this mean? If, for example, the results indicated that the individual shows a moderate preference for women, does it mean the person is prejudiced against men? No. It merely suggests that, for that person, there is a stronger association between certain traits and the category.

The IAT and priming measures are similar, but they are different in some important respects. Most notably, the IAT measures associations to a category, while priming measures assess the average responses to individual category exemplars (i.e., individual photos), the IAT gives an estimate of the strength of the association between the category as a whole, and positivity/negativity (Fazio & Olson, 2003). Research by Olson and Fazio (2003) has found that a priming procedure, such as that used by Fazio et al. (1995) has little correspondence in its results to the results of an IAT taken by the same participant. However, when people are told to explicitly categorize exemplar faces in the priming procedure according to their racial category, the results of the priming measure and IAT were correlated. Olson and Fazio (2003) argue that normally people do not always categorize by race (e.g., they may categorize by gender or attractiveness). The priming procedure used by Fazio et al. (1995) may be a superior measure of judgments and behavior toward individual Blacks, and the IAT may be a better measure of associations between the category *Black,* and trait descriptors. A recent paper by Conrey, Sherman, Gawronski, Hugenberg, and Groom (2004) suggests that one reason IAT and other implicit cognition measures may not correspond is that the tasks involved in each could be differentially affected by one or more of four processes: automatic activation of an association, ability to determine a correct response, success at overcoming the activated associations, and response biases in the absence of other response guides.

It is important to note that automatically activated evaluations of an outgroup can be significantly influenced by moderating variables. One such factor is one's motivation to control prejudiced responses (high restraint). Olson and Fazio (2004b) found that for high-restraint persons with automatically activated negative attitudes toward Blacks, a major fear is that reporting negative attitudes would lead to disfavor or dispute. So, by reporting overly positive attitudes (which is what they did), their fear is addressed. More interesting is the fact that high-restraint people with positive attitudes toward Blacks *also* attenuate the attitudes they report. Their fear appears to be that they will be perceived as bending over backward too much, showing too positive an attitude. So, they actually reported attitudes that were less positive than their automatically activated positive attitudes toward Blacks. Other research shows a significant moderating effect of perceived outgroup variability. Lambert, Payne, Ramsey, and Shaffer (2005) found that the predictive validity of implicit attitudes is four times greater if the outgroup is perceived as homogeneous. Even more astounding is that when group variability is not taken into account, implicit attitudes were not able to predict impressions of the target.

Although the IAT has been shown to have good convergent and discriminant validity, and very good reliability (Gawronski, 2002; Greenwald & Nosek, 2001), and has been shown in some studies to be related to explicit attitude measures and to predict attitude-relevant behavior (McConnell & Leibold, 2001), there are a number of caveats, special conditions (e.g., affective valence of stimulus items, Govan & Williams, 2004; cross-situational instability, Steffens & Buchner, 2003), moderating variables, and potential confounds (e.g., slower cognitive processing leads to higher IAT prejudice scores and lower IAT self-esteem scores, McFarland & Crouch, 2002; or IAT effects may be due to a mere acceptance effect, Mitchell, 2004, or word familiarity and frequency, Ottaway, Hayden, & Oakes, 2001) to the IAT (some of which we have discussed). The IAT is by no means a panacea for measuring implicit attitudes. It is important that researchers who wish to use the IAT are fully aware of what, exactly, it is measuring and that they address the limiting factors, moderating variables, and confounds that could influence their results with the IAT.

In an influential paper, Devine (1989) investigated stereotype activation in White participants who had high or low self-reported prejudice toward African Americans (as measured on McConahay's [1986] Modern Racism Scale [MRS]). Results indicated that high- and low-prejudiced individuals automatically activated stereotypes about African Americans. But this does not mean that everyone is prejudiced. Rather, it indicates that people in a given society have knowledge of the cultural stereotypes for various groups (Lepore & Brown, 1997), and this knowledge is automatically activated when the person thinks about the group. Devine's results make the important distinction between knowledge of cultural stereotypes and personal beliefs about outgroups (personally believing the stereotypes). When presented with target characteristics that are associated in memory with a stereotype of a particular group, people will then automatically think of that stereotype. What was especially interesting about this research was that while the automatic activation was equally strong and inescapable in both groups, only the low-prejudice individuals were motivated to engage in controlled, effortful cognitive processes designed to inhibit the effects of the automatic stereotype activation. Therefore, according to Devine's **dissociation model,** there is no correlation between explicit measures of prejudice (i.e., the MRS) and the degree of implicit stereotyping in low-prejudice individuals. Of course, high-prejudice persons should (and Devine's results confirmed this) show a high correlation between their self-reported prejudice scores and measures of their implicit stereotyping.

Later research has emerged that challenges the assumption that low-prejudice and high-prejudice persons automatically activate stereotypes when exposed to category labels (e.g., Blacks). Lepore and Brown (1997) found that although both high- and low-prejudice White persons were aware of negative stereotypes of Blacks, there is a difference in how high- and low-prejudice Caucasians respond to being exposed to either a stereotype or a category label. Lepore and Brown found that when a stereotype of Blacks was primed (e.g., *musical*) participants were more negative in their ratings of a target person (see Figure 3.2).

However, when the category label was primed (e.g., *Blacks*), only high-prejudice persons gave negative ratings of the target, whereas low-prejudice persons tended to have more positive impressions (see Figure 3.3).

Lepore and Brown (1997) suggest that the reason Devine (1989) found no difference between low- and high-prejudice Caucasians in automatic-stereotype activation was because Devine's experiments incorporated a mixture of both stereotype and category primes. Thus, according to Lepore and Brown, high-prejudice people have strong stereotypic associations with the category label that are activated when primed with the label or a stereotypic associated concept. On the other hand, low-prejudice people, they suggest, do not have such associations at the automatic level, and, therefore, when they are primed with the category label, they do not have automatic access or activation of stereotypic concepts.

Lepore and Brown (1997) suggested that Devine's model of a conscious inhibition of automatic stereotyping needs to be revised in light of these data and the weight of other

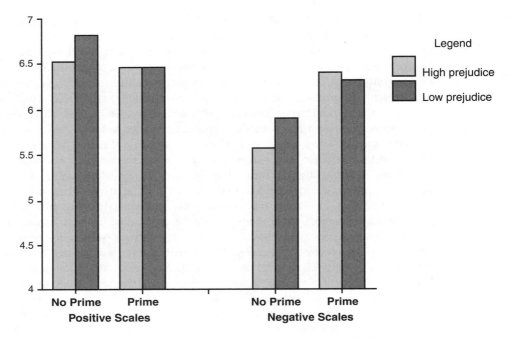

FIGURE 3.2   Influence of priming a stereotype on ratings of a target person. In their research, Lepore and Brown (1997) found that high- and low-prejudice participants tended to respond to an ethnically nondescript target individual in essentially the same ways when they were primed with a stereotype about blacks (e.g., *musical*). (Copyright © 1997 by the American Psychological Association. Reprinted with permission.)

studies suggesting that stereotypes are a functional mechanism to conserve cognitive resources (e.g., Macrae, Milne, & Bodenhausen, 1994; Snyder & Meine, 1994a). However, in a compelling investigation, Fazio and Dunton (1997) showed that such conscious inhibition is precisely how low-prejudiced persons operate. Their data showed that for some people (e.g., high-prejudice and some low-prejudice persons) categorizing an individual by race is a highly automatic process. This makes subsequent similarity judgments for high-prejudice persons very fast and efficient (one of the main benefits of stereotyping, as discussed in Chapter 2). However, for low-prejudice persons who are highly motivated to control prejudiced responses, such categorization needed to be overridden by a time-consuming, conscious search for other attributes by which to classify the target individual. In a related set of experiments, Blair and Banaji (1996) found that implicit stereotyping effects can be overridden when perceivers have an intention to think about counterstereotypic information, and when they have sufficient cognitive resources available (for example, when they are not distracted, tired, or in a hurry). Recent data obtained by Wyer (2004) mirrors the conclusions of Fazio and Dunton, and Blair and Banaji, and in fact shows that low-prejudice persons not only seek out stereotype-disconfirming evidence, they are able to do so when their cognitive resources are constrained. Therefore, these data, along with Devine's (1989) results, show that for some low-prejudice persons, the conscious inhibition of auto-

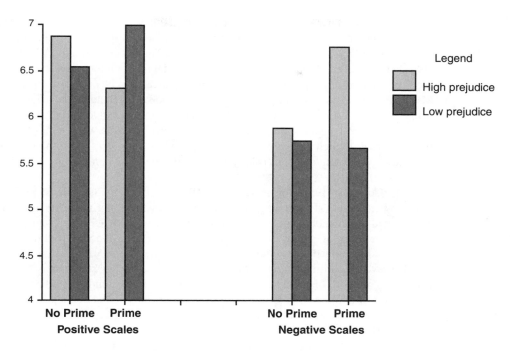

FIGURE 3.3   Influence of priming a category on ratings of a target person. Conversely, Lepore and Brown (1997) found that priming participants with a category (i.e., *Blacks*) had a differential effect on high- versus low-prejudice participants. High-prejudice participants rated the target more negatively compared to low-prejudice participants (see far-right side of Figure 3.3). (Copyright © 1997 by the American Psychological Association. Reprinted with permission.)

matic racial categorization (and possible prejudiced responses) is indeed a reality, and it may be the means by which they maintain their view of themselves as nonprejudiced. Inhibition of prejudiced responses may not be entirely efficient, but it works, at least in certain situations (More on this later when we discuss stereotype suppression).

Devine's (1989) model has been challenged in another respect. Wittenbrink, Judd, and Park (1997) presented participants with a very brief prime (15 milliseconds) that was not consciously perceptible. The prime was either the word *black* or *white* or a neutral nonword (e.g. *xdofger*) or a filler noun (e.g., *lemon, table*). Participants were asked to judge whether subsequent adjectives were words or nonwords. The adjectives were positive or negative stereotypical adjectives that were characteristic of either Caucasians or African Americans. Results revealed evidence of implicit stereotyping and implicit prejudice. Implicit stereotyping was demonstrated in that there was a greater facilitation when the stereotypical words matched the prime that preceded it. That is, people recognized the stereotypical words about Caucasians faster when they followed the prime *white* than when the words followed the other primes. Implicit prejudice was shown in that positive stereotyped words were facilitated more following the *white* prime than the *black* prime. However, negatively stereotyped words were facilitated more following the *black* prime than the *white* prime. These data suggest support for the idea that group labels facilitate access to stereotype-consistent traits and inhibit access to stereotype inconsistent traits (Blair & Banaji, 1996; Dijksterhuis & Knippenberg, 1996). The data reported by Wittenbrink et al. (1997) challenge Devine's (1989) dissociation model in that they found that implicit prejudice scores were highly correlated with explicit measures of prejudice (in this case, the MRS). Recent experiments by Cunningham, Nezlek, and Banaji (2004) support Wittenbrink et al.'s assertion that explicit and implicit attitudes are indeed correlated. According to Devine (1989), there should be little or no correlation between explicit measures of prejudice and implicit measures in low-prejudiced persons. To shed some further light on these divergent opinions, let us briefly examine the evidence concerning the centerpiece of this issue, the MRS.

McConahay (1986) formulated the MRS, a self-report measure of prejudiced attitudes toward Blacks. He found good reliability and validity for the scale and found that it represented a nonreactive measure of racial attitudes. The MRS was designed to measure subtle expressions of negative feelings about Blacks, contrasted with traditional overt hostility in "old-fashioned" measures of racism. The scale was very popular, and still is to this day. However, mounting evidence over the years has led many researchers to abandon the MRS as a measure of prejudice. Some suggest that it confounds prejudice with political conservativism (Sniderman & Tetlock, 1986). Others have found that it is a highly variable, highly reactive measure and is highly correlated with traditional (old-fashioned) measures of racism (Dovidio, Kawakami, Johnson, Johnson, & Howard, 1997). In a compelling programmatic series of experiments, Fazio et al. (1995) found that the MRS was uncorrelated with unobtrusive (priming) measures of prejudice, and it was a highly reactive measure in that White participants responded in a less prejudiced manner when interacting with a Black experimenter. Fazio et al., (1995) concluded that researchers ought to utilize priming procedures (such as those described above) to accurately assess prejudiced attitudes. The MRS can best be thought of as a measure of one's willingness to express prejudiced attitudes, rather than a true measure of a person's intergroup attitudes. The serious problems with the MRS may account for the variability between Devine's (1989) and Wittenbrink et al.'s (1997) conclusions. (We will discuss the MRS in more detail in Chapter 5.)

Implicit stereotyping has also been demonstrated concerning gender stereotypes (Banaji & Greenwald, 1995). In an experiment by Banaji, Hardin, and Rothman (1993), subjects were assigned to either a dependence or aggression condition. Some subjects were then primed (in what was described as a separate experiment) with trait behaviors. The subjects were asked to unscramble 45 four-word sentences that were either neutral in meaning or contained 30 trait-relevant behaviors (such as "*N* abuses an animal" for the aggressive trait). Then, in the second experiment the subject read about a male or female performing slightly trait-relevant behaviors. Then the subject rated the person on the target trait and other traits. Results indicated evidence of implicit gender stereotyping. Those who were primed with a dependence prime judged the female as more dependent than the male. Likewise, those primed with the aggressive trait rated the male as more aggressive than the female. Similar implicit gender stereotyping effects have been reported by Banaji and Hardin (1996).

Implicit stereotype activation not only makes stereotype-consistent concepts more accessible (and more likely to influence social perception and judgments), it also influences overt behavior. In a series of experiments, Bargh, Chen, and Burrows (1996) found that when participants were implicitly primed with an elderly stereotype, they walked more slowly down the hallway after the experiment concluded than those who were not primed with the elderly stereotype. Another experiment revealed that when non-Black participants were implicitly primed with an African American face prior to the start of a computer task, they tended to react with more hostility to an irritating post-task request from the experimenter, compared with those who were not primed. Similarly, Chen and Bargh (1997) found that subliminal activation of African American stereotypes in White perceivers resulted in stereotype-consistent behavior (i.e., hostility) by the perceivers toward an African American interaction partner. This behavior was detected by the partner and was responded to in kind, which the perceivers used as supportive evidence for their stereotypes of African Americans. These results confirm the importance of considering stereotyping in a dynamic interaction context, rather than simply (as has traditionally been the case in prejudice research) assessing the attitudes of the majority about the minority (Devine, Evett, & Vasquez-Suson, 1996). In other words, social interactions are not unidirectional processes whereby one individual influences, but is not influenced by, the other. Each person contributes information in a moment-by-moment, bidirectional, dynamic interaction. The subtle cues in the overt and nonverbal behavior of one individual are detected by another and reacted to, and this reaction can be taken as evidence by the first individual that may confirm or disconfirm stereotypes, prejudices, or other thoughts about their partner. While this makes much intuitive sense, it is a very recent approach to understanding prejudice, and we will discuss it in greater detail in Chapter 10.

The priming paradigm used so often in implicit stereotyping experiments assumes that people respond to implicit category name primes (e.g. *African American*) the same way they would to seeing a member of a stereotyped outgroup. Some researchers, however, suggest that there are fundamental differences in the activation of stereotype-related concepts in each instance. Macrae, Bodenhausen, Milne, Thorn, and Castelli (1997) presented participants with a prime photograph for 255 milliseconds and then had them judge whether a letter string was a word or nonword (a lexical decision task). The prime was either a picture of a woman's face or a household item (e.g., a chair). The words to be judged were either stereotypically associated with women (e.g. *caring, tender*) or counterstereotypic (e.g., *assertive, decisive*), or they were pronounceable nonwords. Macrae and his colleagues theorized that it is only when one thinks semantically about the prime stimulus that the related concepts to the stimulus are activated. He and his colleagues wanted to investigate the long-held notion that thinking about group names (or seeing a member of that group) automatically activates related concepts. To test this, participants were assigned to one of three processing conditions. In the feature-detection condition, participants were asked to attempt to detect the presence or absence of a white dot on the prime photo. In the semantic-judgment condition, participants were to indicate whether the stimulus was an animate or inanimate object. Those in the exposure condition were asked simply to report the detection of a prime stimulus. Results indicated that facilitation for stereotypic words only occurred in the semantic-judgment condition. Simply being exposed to the prime (as in the feature-detection and exposure conditions) did not facilitate recognition of stereotype-consistent words. Other research supports this finding (e.g., Gilbert and Hixon, 1991).

We are thus in a dilemma. How can one reconcile the very different conclusions reached by Macrae et al. with the dozens of other priming studies? Macrae et al. suggest one explanation. Almost all of the other priming studies have presented the category label as a prime. The evidence from these studies suggests that this is sufficient to activate stereotypes and their related concepts. But when we perceive people (either photos, or in person), Macrae and his colleagues suggest, stereotype activation is not automatic, because we must detect the stimulus *and* make a categorization. This effortful cognitive activity precludes activation of the stereotype unless one pays more attention to the stimulus at a deeper level of processing (i.e., a semantic level). Only in that instance, will the perception of a person activate the stereotype. However, such an explanation cannot adequately explain why Chen and Bargh (1997) found significantly higher hostile behaviors (as rated by coders) among those exposed to a subliminal prime (26 milliseconds) photo of an African American face compared to those exposed to a subliminal prime photo of a White face. Clearly, being implicitly primed with a photo activated associated negative feelings about African Americans in the non-Black participants, and these negative feelings influenced their behavior (made them feel more negative and behave in a more hostile fashion). Thus, the explanation that Macrae et al. offer for why their findings differ from other prime studies does not appear to be well founded in light of the evidence that suggests that one does not need to semantically consider the stimulus individual in order to activate associated stereotypes and prejudices about that person (Bargh, 1999).

In sum, research from cognitive neuroscience labs, using systematic procedures, strictly controlled conditions, and new technologies and methods, has demonstrated the existence of two separate memory systems: an implicit and an explicit memory system. The former system has been shown to have significant effects on the conscious thought and behavior of individuals, without the subject's awareness of the influence of the memory. Researchers in social psychology are examining the effects of various automatic versus controlled cognitive processes, but they have just begun to examine the implications of the implicit/explicit cognition for fundamental social–psychological phenomena. Using measures that tap the implicit cognition processes, implicit-memory research has opened up a new area of research that has implications for virtually all researchers within psychology.

The next step is to investigate the parameters of the implicit-memory effects, and how implicit memory interacts with affective, motivational, personality variables. A crucial issue that has yet to be addressed fully concerns whether people are still responsible for the effects of their implicit stereotyping. If implicit stereotyping occurs (and we have reviewed the solid evidence that suggest that it does), and, by definition, it occurs without the awareness, control, or intention of the individual, then are they still responsible for stereotype-consistent behavior or feelings that arise in response to implicit stereotyping? This is an interesting question. Banaji and Greenwald (1995) take the controversial position that the implicit stereotyping data support the idea that society should rethink the issue of personal responsibility when it comes to stereotyping in everyday situations. They argue that it is unwise to blame or punish individuals who have shown implicit stereotyping, because it is out of the person's control. Instead of focusing on (they suggest, futile) efforts to control implicit stereotyping at an individual level, Banaji and Greenwald propose a purely behavioristic solution to implicit stereotyping. They suggest that society ought to instead "modify environments such that the operation of implicit stereotypes is inhibited" (p. 197). Many other researchers (e.g., Fiske, 1989) are critical of a position that removes all personal responsibility for implicit stereotyping. Fiske (1989) argues that if society adopted the position that people "just can't help" stereotyping, it would remove any pressure, incentive, and sanctions that would promote stereotype reduction. To avoid such a perspective, Fiske suggests that researchers refocus their energies on understanding stereotype reduction as a combination of knowledge and motivation (see also Allport, 1954). People who have self-insight about their prejudices, and know they are undesirable, should be motivated to avoid using them (or allowing them to influence their thinking). While there is some merit to this idea, much research attests to the failure of even highly motivated individuals to avoid stereotypic thinking (Banaji & Hardin, 1996; Bargh, 1999; Devine, 1989; Dovidio et al., 1997; Fazio & Dunton, 1997; Pendry & Macrae, 1994). So, are people responsible for their implicit stereotyping? Currently, this is an unresolved issue, and more research is needed to further refine our understanding of the parameters of implicit stereotyping.

Stereotype Suppression

In this chapter, we have been reviewing the research on the ways various cognitive and affective processes enhance the likelihood of using stereotypes in social judgment. Why, then, are we talking about suppressing stereotypes in this chapter? A good question, because in Chapter 9 we will cover the theory and research on ways to control, or even eliminate, stereotyping and prejudice. But there is a good reason for talking about stereotype suppression when speaking of stereotype activation. As researchers have learned, it appears that when we try not to think of something (thinking about someone in terms of stereotypes about their group, for example), in many cases the unwanted thought springs back to mind even more frequently and with greater strength than when we are not trying to suppress a thought. In other words, the very act of trying to inhibit thoughts of stereotypes makes them even more likely to intrude upon your thoughts!

Sometimes, the thoughts that intrude on our consciousness are disturbing or just plain unwanted. How can we avoid such unpleasant experiences? When we do not want to think of something, a simple solution is just to try to "not think of it." Can this work with stereotyping? If you think of or see a member of a minority group, can you just tell yourself not to think of stereotypes that are associated with that group? Some of you may think you can do this; other readers may believe it a difficult task. Research in social cognition has been addressing these questions for the past 8 years or so, and we have learned much about our ability to control unwanted thoughts (including stereotypes). Below, we will briefly review the rapidly growing research on this intriguing question and attempt to discover the limits, if any, to such cognitive control over stereotyping.

Thought Suppression. Don't think of a pink elephant. This (very difficult) task illustrates the heart of the problem we encounter when we try to control unwanted thoughts. We need to think of the thought we are supposed to not think of so we can know what we are supposed to not think about. (Huh? What did he say?). To clarify this further, let's take a step back for a second to briefly review the theory behind thought suppression. In a pioneering series of experiments (Wegner, 1989, 1994; Wegner & Erber, 1992; Wegner & Pennebaker, 1993), Wegner and his colleagues have shown that, ironically, when we try to not think of a concept, it actually becomes even *more* available to our conscious awareness.

Thought-suppression research shows how hard it is to try to not think of something (such as a polka-dotted elephant). For this reason, trying to not think of stereotypes in your evaluation of other people is extremely difficult and often results in an ironic tendency to think even more about those stereotypes! If I told you that it is very important for you to not think of this image of a polka-dotted elephant for the remainder of the day, not only would you be unsuccessful, you might be likely to think of the image even more frequently than if I had given you no thought-suppression instructions.

The reason is that normal mental control works by the joint function of two processes. One is an intentional operating process that scans our consciousness for mental contents that will bring about a desired mental state (i.e., no unwanted thoughts of [x]). The other is an ironic monitoring process that searches for mental contents that indicate the failure to reach that desired state. So, to use our elephant example, the intentional process searches for information pertinent to pink elephants, and the ironic processes search for indications that we have not avoided thinking about pink elephants. The intentional process is our consciousness in trying to suppress the unwanted thought. This process takes a lot of cognitive effort. The ironic process operates in the background to check for instances when we need to exercise mental control. This process requires less effort and runs consistently and rather independently of conscious control. The consistent nature of the ironic monitor is the source of the hyperaccessible nature of the unwanted thought. That is, because it searches for signs of the unwanted thought, it increases the accessibility of the unwanted thought to conscious awareness. Normally, however, this hyperaccessibility does not impinge on our consciousness because the intentional operating process prevails. When mental capacity is compromised in some fashion, however, (e.g., when we are busy, or when several tasks demand our attention), that leaves less cognitive capacity to devote to the intentional operating process, and then the ironic process prevails, making the unwanted thought hyperaccessible to our consciousness. Across a number of experiments, Wegner (1994) showed that his theory of mental control nicely models what happens to unwanted thoughts under cognitive loads. However, hyperaccessibility of unwanted thoughts has been demonstrated in the absence of cognitive loads, as we will examine in the next section (Macrae, Bodenhausen, Milne, & Jetten, 1994). It appears that we cannot always think what we want. Of course, such a finding has tremendous implications for intergroup stereotypic perception, prejudiced attitudes, and discriminatory behavior, because it suggests that even the most well-intentioned perceiver who is cognitively busy can still think stereotypically about another person (Pendry & Macrae, 1994). Next, we examine the research on stereotype suppression, to determine the conditions under which stereotypes may become hyperaccessible, and the implications of such a consequence on social perception.

Suppressing Stereotypes.   There are a number of things that we would rather not think about, including stereotypes of others. For most people, thinking about others in terms of stereotypes is a negative experience because it brings about feelings of discomfort, guilt, and shame (Allport, 1954). This is especially true in those individuals who pride themselves on their egalitarian attitudes (Devine, Monteith, Zuwerink, & Elliot, 1991). In an effort to avoid these negative feelings, people may try to recognize when they are beginning to stereotype and quickly "push it out of mind." That is, they put forth a concerted conscious effort to not think about someone in terms of a stereotype (to engage in **stereotype suppression**). This seems to be a reasonable solution to the problem of stereotyping: if one is truly motivated to avoid stereotyping, one can do just that with enough conscious effort. However, Wegner's (1994) thought-suppression research mentioned earlier should give the reader reason to be skeptical about such a simple (and intuitively appealing) solution to stereotyping.

Research by Bodenhausen and Macrae (1998) suggests that suppressing stereotypes is a difficult task indeed. They argue that the attempt to banish stereotypic thoughts from one's mind may be successful for a short while, but soon the unwanted stereotypic thoughts will tend to return with more intensity and frequency to influence the individual's thoughts, feelings, and behavior. This ironic result occurs because of the mechanics of the process of thought suppression. Specifically, Bodenhausen and Macrae suggest that this rebound effect is due to the repeated activation of the unwanted stereotype by the monitoring process, and, therefore, the residual activation of the concept dissipates more slowly in the stereotype suppressor's mind as compared with those who did not engage in stereotype suppression.

To test this hypothesis, Macrae, Bodenhausen, et al. (1994) showed a picture of a male skinhead to male and female participants. Participants were asked to spend 5 minutes writing about a typical day in the life of that target individual (the skinhead). Half of the participants were told about the negative influence of stereotypes and how these thoughts may bias one's perceptions of another person. These participants were asked to try very hard to avoid thinking (i.e., to suppress any stereotypic thoughts that may arise) about the target in stereotypical terms. The other half of the participants were given no instructions to avoid stereotyping the target. All participants were then shown another photo of a different skinhead. Participants were again asked to spend 5 minutes writing about the typical day of this individual. This time, no instructions to avoid stereotyping were given to the subjects. The stories were rated for their degree of stereotypicality. Results for the stories about the first target indicated that, as hypothesized, stereotype suppressors were successful in greatly reducing the degree of stereotypic content in their thinking, as revealed in their stories, compared with nonsuppressors, who showed more stereotype content in their stories. However, the content of the stories for the second target revealed quite a different pattern. While the nonsuppressors showed virtually the same degree of stereotype content in their stories, those who previously suppressed their stereotypic thoughts now showed significantly more stereotypic thinking than nonsuppressors. These data support the idea that suppressing stereotypic thinking may work in the short term, but later those thoughts come back (rebound) with even more strength and can influence attitudes and behavior. Recent work by Gordijn, Hindriks, and Koomen (2004) extends these findings by showing that the suppression rebound results not only in hyperaccessibility of the specific suppressed stereotype but in a greater tendency to use stereotypes in general in subsequent social judgments. Moreover, Gordijn et al.'s data suggest that the hyperaccessibility of suppressed stereotypes only seems to occur in those who have a low motivation to suppress stereotypes. A recent paper by Newman, Caldwell, Chamberlin, and Griffin (2004) suggests a different route by which prejudice emerges in suppressing cognition. When participants were told that their ingroup had negative characteristics, and they were told to suppress thoughts about one of these attributes, they subsequently projected that attribute to an outgroup. In other words, thinking favorably about one's group entails suppressing the shortcomings of one's group, and this suppression tends to be expressed in one's evaluations of outgroup members. These data are provocative and highlight the need for more research to explicate the influence of motivation on stereotype suppression (Fiske, 2004).

Several experiments have demonstrated the reliability of these findings, indicating that when people are reminded to think in egalitarian ways (i.e., to avoid thinking of stereotypes), they are able to do so (for a short while at least). But what happens when people are not explicitly asked to avoid stereotyping others? Do they suppress their stereotypic thoughts on their own? Some research indicates that some people do indeed do this (Macrae, Bodenhausen, & Milne, 1998). Macrae and his colleagues found that when people were made to feel self-focused (directing their attention and thoughts toward themselves), they were much less likely (compared with non-self-focused individuals) to describe others in stereotypic terms. Macrae et al. (1998) relied on a substantial amount of data on self-focus effects that suggest that when people think of themselves as the object of attention (by others or themselves), they are more likely to think of their own values, attitudes, morals, and standards for the behavior they are engaging in at that instant, and to attempt to bring their behavior in line with these standards (Deiner & Wallbom, 1976; Duval & Wicklund, 1972). It is important to note, however, that increased self-focus will only reliably lead to spontaneous stereotype suppression efforts among those who have egalitarian values and standards for interpersonal perception (Macrae et al., 1998).

What happens when self-focus is enhanced in high-prejudice people? The results are mixed. Some data suggest that the self-focus enhances adherence to the social norms (i.e., do not stereotype, do not break laws) rather than personal beliefs (Deiner & Srull, 1979). In other words, high-prejudice people would tend to adhere to the social norms (e.g., do not be prejudiced) rather than to their own prejudiced personal beliefs. Support for this comes from recent research by Monteith, Spicer, and Tooman (1998). They found that when social norms against stereotyping others were salient, high-prejudice persons did not experience stereotype rebound effects. Other researchers (e.g., Froming, Walker, & Lopyan, 1982) propose that the type of self-focus is crucial in determining the degree to which people will adhere to their personal beliefs or social norms when they are self-focused. Froming et al. suggest that private self-focusing devices (e.g., a mirror, or hearing one's own voice) promote adherence to personal standards, whereas public enhancement of self-focus (i.e., being in front of an audience, or the subject of evaluation by other people) leads the individual to follow social norms. Thus, it appears that more research is needed before we are able to make conclusions about the effects of self-focus on high-prejudice individuals.

So far, we have reviewed several studies that suggest that avoiding stereotyping is very difficult and that even when we are able to do so, it lasts only a short time and the stereotypic thoughts come back even more stronger and more frequently. Is it really that dire? Are we just doomed to stereotype each other? Research suggests that this is a bit of an exaggeration, and that some people *are* able to avoid the rebound effects of stereotype suppression (Rudman, Ashmore, & Gary, 2001). Monteith et al. (1998) found that low-prejudice persons did not show stereotype rebound. They concluded that when people are motivated to not use stereotypes and they have well-practiced, alternate ways of thinking about other individuals, they will be able to avoid stereotypic thinking and will not suffer stereotype rebound effects (see also Sherman, Stroessner, Loftus & Deguzman, 1997, for a similar argument). There is substantial empirical evidence to support this contention (Devine, 1989; Monteith, 1993). A recent paper by Dunn and Spellman (2003) suggests that, for people who do not believe in stereotypes, thinking about a stigmatized individual's characteristics tended to inhibit access to stereotypical information, and they were much less likely to stereotype that individual. Interestingly, the inhibition process works the other way as well: thinking about stereotypical traits decreases the likelihood of thinking about the outgroup member as an individual. Indeed, Macrae, Bodenhausen et al. (1994) agree with the idea that, like many things, practicing nonprejudiced responses can help one create a dominantly nonprejudiced way of thinking: "If stereotype activation can become routinized, automated, and triggered by external stimulus cues, then there is no compelling reason why stereotype inhibition should not take a similar course" (p. 815).

SUMMARY AND ISSUES FOR FUTURE RESEARCH

There is much we do not yet know about the interface between affect and cognition as they influence stereotyping and prejudice, and there are important research domains that require further study.

First, investigators should consider the physiological arousal of the individual. As Bodenhausen (1993) argued, "A useful place to begin considering the impact of emotions on the use of stereotypes in social judgment may be with their physiological aspects" (p. 17). Research has indicated that when physiological arousal is either too high or too low, people increasingly rely on stereotypes in social judgment (Bodenhausen, 1990). Others have also found that high arousal is associated with increased stereotyping (e.g., Kim & Baron, 1988). Bodenhausen (1993) has suggested that those mood states associated with happiness (such as, joy, elation, contentment, and serenity) may likely be variations on the same happiness theme. Research using sophisticated physiological measures (Cacioppo & Tassinary, 1990; Cacioppo, Martzke, & Tassinary, 1986) can and should be conducted to discover whether these various moods are associated with different levels of physiological arousal, and, therefore, different tendencies to be associated with stereotypic thinking. A similar procedure should be taken with various negative moods, such as fear and anxiety.

A second issue for researchers to consider when they are investigating the influence of affect on stereotyping is the following important distinction: that between integral and incidental affect (Bodenhausen, 1993). Many researchers agree that affect that arises in one context can affect social judgments in another context (e.g., Forgas & Bower, 1988; Schwarz & Clore, 1988). Although much is known about the influence of moods on information processing, comparatively little is known about the impact of everyday mood states in intergroup contexts, such as guilt (for exceptions, see Devine et al., 1991; Nelson, 1996) fear, and pride (Stangor & Lange, 1994). These different mood states should be investigated within the intergroup context to assess the effects of integral affect on stereotyping. The degree of the impact of affect on the individual's tendency to stereotype another person is the greatest in the actual intergroup contact situation. As an example, consider the following suggestion for future research in this area.

Third, the fascinating research program of Wegner and his colleagues (Wegner, Erber, & Zanakos, 1993) on the ironic processes in the mental control of mood and mood-related thought is worthy of the attention of researchers investigating the processes whereby integral affect leads to stereotyping. Specifically, Wegner (1993) found that when people attempted to control mood-related thoughts under a cognitive load, they tended to show increased accessibility of those thoughts in the opposite direction of intended control. What does this mean for affective processes in stereotyping? To the extent that individuals are aware of their usually negative emotional moods (whether this is negative depends on the degree of hostility and prejudice the person feels toward members of stereotyped outgroups) when in contact with members of stereotyped outgroups (and is trying to suppress these feelings), and to the degree that the individual is under an increased utilization of their cognitive capacity (for whatever reason; task involvement, distraction, etc.), they may be susceptible to the ironic result that the undesired mood and mood-related thoughts are even *more* accessible. Bodenhausen and Macrae (1996) have conducted some research that generally confirms these ideas. However, the complex interactions between the influences of mood, cognitive capacity, and memory certainly necessitate further research in order to begin to flesh out some of the separate and interrelated effects each of these has on the relation between moods and stereotyping.

I would like to suggest two more directions for research on the affect/cognition interface in stereotyping. Researchers should continue work on implicit-stereotyping phenomena (Banaji & Greenwald, 1994; Banaji et al., 1993; Galinsky, Martorana, & Ku, 2003). Especially important in this regard are efforts to find new ways to measure implicit attitudes. For example, a recent paper by Vanman, Saltz, Nathan, and Warren (2004) found that facial electromyography (EMG) from smiling and frowning muscles in the face was directly related to racial discrimination. Additionally, more studies are needed to look at dispositional characteristics associated with mood and their influence on stereotyping. For example, Basso, Schefft, and Hoffman (1994) investigated the moderating effect of affect intensity (AI) on the influence of positive and negative affect on cognitive tasks. Given the same emotion-eliciting stimulus, people who are low in AI will experience a much weaker affective arousal than those who are high in AI. High-AI people tend to be susceptible to more frequent mood shifts. The researchers found that the cognitive performance of those low in AI was enhanced by positive mood and disrupted by negative mood. The performance of those high in AI was disrupted by positive mood and facilitated by negative mood. While the empirical examination of the affect-cognition interface as it bears on stereotyping and prejudice is a relatively recent occurrence, we have learned much about how our moods and the way we think can influence how we feel about members of outgroups. Much more research is needed to help complete our understanding of the affect/cognition influence, but this domain of research inquiry is certainly proving to be an exciting field in which to work.

GLOSSARY

attitude object Any idea, object, or person about which one forms an attitude.

aversive racism A type of racism in which the individual believes they are nonprejudiced, but they still harbor negative feelings about the outgroup.

chronic outgroup affect One's stable feeling toward the outgroup.

dissociation model Devine's model of prejudice, which states that there is no relationship between explicit (i.e., self-report) measures of prejudice (like the Modern Racism Scale) and the degree of implicit stereotyping in low-prejudice persons. Low-prejudice persons are able to inhibit their stereotypical thoughts soon after such thoughts are activated, resulting in no correlation between explicit measures of prejudice and measures of the automatic activation of stereotypes in low-prejudice persons.

episodic outgroup affect One's affective reaction to a specific member of the outgroup.

explicit memory Conscious recollection of memories. All the episodic and general information that is in long-term memory and that is available for conscious recollection.

implicit memory An unintentional, nonconscious form of memory. Stimuli can be perceived without awareness, and this information can later influence thoughts, feelings, and behaviors.

implicit stereotyping The introspectively unidentified (i.e., nonconscious) traces of past experience that influence perceptions of outgroup members. Exposure to prior stereotype-relevant information below the level of awareness can later influence one's attitudes, feelings, and behavior toward the relevant outgroup.

incidental affect Affect that arises in situations unrelated to the intergroup context.

integral affect Affect that originates within the intergroup situation and involves the stereotyped outgroup. This type of affect can also arise from merely thinking about the outgroup.

stereotype suppression The conscious effort to avoid thinking about stereotypes. Results in stereotype rebound in some low-prejudice persons.

subliminal Perception of a stimulus without conscious awareness of perceiving the stimulus.

DISCUSSION QUESTIONS

1. Do you think that when you are interacting with a member of an outgroup your reaction to that person tends to be based on integral affect, or incidental affect? Why?

2. What percentage of Caucasians in the United States do you believe would be classified as aversive racists? Why?

3. Why do you suppose happiness enhances the tendency to think about others in terms of stereotypes? Do you favor the motivational or cognitive-capacity explanations?

4. What are the implications of the research on implicit stereotyping for efforts to understand the origin of prejudice and stereotyping?

5. Do you think that most people would have an easy or a difficult time suppressing a stereotype? What other factors would help one to suppress a stereotype (a certain type of personality, motivation, etc.)?

SUGGESTED KEY READINGS

Devine, P. G. (1989). Stereotypes and prejudice: Their automatic and controlled components. *Journal of Personality and Social Psychology, 56,* 5–18.

Fiske, S. T., & Neuberg, S. L. (1990). A continuum of impression formation, from category-based to individuating processes: Influences of information and motivation on attention and interpretation. In M. P. Zanna (Ed.), *Advances in experimental social psychology* (Vol. 23, pp. 1–74). New York: Academic Press.

Mackie, D. M., & Hamilton, D. L. (1993). *Affect, cognition, and stereotyping: Interactive processes in group perception.* New York: Academic Press.

Pendry, L. F., & Macrae, C. N. (1994). Stereotypes and mental life: The case of the motivated but thwarted tactician. *Journal of Experimental Social Psychology, 30*(4), 303–325.

INTERNET RESOURCES: RESEARCHERS, REFERENCES, AND ORGANIZATIONS DEVOTED TO THE STUDY OF PREJUDICE

http://implicit.harvard.edu/implicit   The Implicit Association Test, an online measure of racism, ageism, and sexism.

www.psych.northwestern.edu/psych/people/faculty/bodenhausen   Home page of Dr. Galen Bodenhausen, a leading social-cognition researcher on

the influence of affect on stereotyping, as well as a pioneer of stereotype-suppression research,

CHAPTER FOUR

THE PREJUDICED PERSONALITY: ARE SOME PEOPLE MORE LIKELY TO FEEL PREJUDICE?

In the early 1970s television sitcom *All in the Family,* Carroll O'Connor played the character Archie Bunker, a working-class man who was a cab driver and lived a modest life. One of the reasons the show was so popular with American viewers was that Archie was a stubborn, ignorant, prejudiced, and selfish character who was also portrayed as sometimes very vulnerable, sensitive, sentimental, and caring toward others. Archie was, in his own words, an equal-opportunity bigot. He was prejudiced toward anyone who was different from himself (his narrow ingroup was white, middle-class men who were Protestants). He was indeed a complex man, and American viewers embraced the show because it addressed important social issues (e.g., prejudice, women's rights, abortion) and showed how ridiculous prejudice is.

You may know some people like Archie, people who are prejudiced toward several groups. They seem to dislike most everyone who is different from themselves and their own groups. In these instances, it is intuitive to think that there is something about the personality of these persons that makes them dislike other groups so much. We arrive at such a conclusion because we think, what are the odds that someone will find faults with so many different groups, or what are the odds that all these groups will truly have these shortcomings? The more likely explanation is that there is something about the perceiver that colors the way they view the groups, such that fault is found with all the groups. Explanations for the prejudice exhibited by Archie Bunker, and often found in society in general, attribute prejudiced attitudes to a flaw in the perceiver's personality.

In this chapter, we will explore the ways that psychologists have sought to describe and understand what might be referred to as the prejudiced personality. A primary question that we will address is, is there such a thing as a prejudiced personality? That is, is there a definite constellation of characteristics or traits that can be identified which, when they co-occur in an individual, can predict prejudiced behavior, attitudes, feelings, and thoughts with good reliability? We will also examine the many other individual-difference variables that tend to influence the tendency to use stereotypes or hold prejudiced attitudes. We will conclude with a discussion of the current state of inquiry into the prejudiced personality and the direction of future research on individual differences in prejudice.

Indirectly, one of the major influences on theory and research in psychology was the terrible reign of the Nazis in Germany from 1933 to 1945. Many brilliant and creative intellectuals (most notably, Gestalt psychologists from Germany, who had a tremendous influence on American psychologists' research and theory) in the field of psychology fled

Some people, such as Archie Bunker, the All in the Family *sitcom character, seem to harbor not one or two but many stereotypes and prejudices. This observation led researchers to investigate the idea that certain personality types may lead one person to be more prejudiced than another.*

from Germany to the United States and elsewhere as the grip of Nazi rule became tighter in Europe in the late 1930s. In addition, much research and theory was initiated to attempt to explain the unexplainable: the horror of the genocide of Jewish, homosexual, gypsy, and physically challenged individuals at the hands of the Nazis. When the allies discovered and freed the prisoners in the German death camps, the world was stunned at the barbarism and cruelty of the Nazis in committing millions of innocent people to death.

Up until that time, psychologists had explained prejudice as a psychodynamic process of unconscious defense mechanisms (Duckitt, 1992). This approach fit well with the perceived ubiquity of prejudice, because psychological defense mechanisms were also believed to be a common aspect of every person's mind. Prejudice was therefore seen as a defensive projection of one's frustrations, fears, and hostility outward against innocent outgroups. With the full realization of the horror of the Nazi regime, psychologists began to examine how it was that a whole society could allow such an atrocity to take place. Theorists reasoned that no normal person could be capable of such horrific behavior, so there must have been some sort of mass hysteria, or other characterological flaw, within the Nazis and, more generally, the Germans themselves (see Goldhagen's [1996] controversial book on this point) that would account for such behavior on this scale. Thus, research into the prejudiced personality began in earnest.

PSYCHODYNAMIC PERSPECTIVES

Authoritarianism

One of the first attempts to examine the prejudiced personality was put forth by Adorno and his colleagues (1950), with their description of what they called the "authoritarian personality." According to Adorno et al., some people have personality structures that are flawed in such a way that they are conditioned to be especially likely to adopt prejudiced attitudes. Adorno and his colleagues interviewed and tested hundreds of individuals and found that for a subset of these persons—the **authoritarians**—certain patterns of prejudice, childhood upbringing, and relationships with parents tended to be quite common. Specifically, authoritarians tended to grow up in homes in which the parents or guardians were strict disciplinarians, often using harsh discipline to keep the children from misbehaving and to punish them when they disobeyed the parent or guardian. Authoritarians were more likely to be submissive to authority, to adhere strictly to middle-class traditions and values, and to think very rigidly (in either–or, all-or-nothing thinking terms—no gray areas (Fiske, 1998).

Adorno et al. also found that authoritarians, more than other individuals, tended to hold prejudices against not just one group but many groups (essentially, anyone who is different from the authoritarian). Adorno et al. believed that authoritarians hated deviant impulses (e.g., fear, aggression, sex) and were also more likely to externalize these unacceptable impulses to others via projection (Harding et al., 1969). In other words, this psychodynamic approach to understanding the nature of the prejudiced personality suggests that these unacceptable impulses are displaced to stereotyped groups. Thus, the authoritarian person does not believe they have these negative qualities, but these undesirable characteristics are attributed to various minority groups. In sum, the authoritarian's fear of and dependency on the parents, coupled with their hatred and suspicion of them tends to be the impetus to displace or channel these unacceptable parent-related impulses and their own negative impulses into hostility toward minority groups.

Authoritarian personality characteristics can also be found in some minority-group members (Harding et al., 1969). For example, Jewish persons who are high on a measure of antidemocratic values and attitudes (called the F [for facism] scale) not only are prejudiced toward other groups, they are more likely to be anti-Semitic. Although much evidence points to a strong correlation between the way the parents raise the child and the child's subsequent tendency to evidence prejudice, it is unclear what process accounts for the correlation. Specifically, is the correlation a result of the child developing the authoritarian personality characteristics and hence a greater intolerance of minority groups, or is it simply a result of the child internalizing the parents' values and ethnic attitudes (Harding et al.)?

Character-Conditioned Prejudice

Allport (1954) elaborated on Adorno et al.'s theory of authoritarian personality and suggested that such a personality is a strong contributor in developing prejudiced attitudes. Like Adorno et al., Allport discussed the prejudiced personality in psychodynamic terms. Allport believed that the prejudiced personality emerged out of a "crippled" ego (p. 396). Specifically, this individual feels threatened, insecure, and fearful of virtually everything. In trying to overcome these insecurities, the person develops a prejudiced view of others as a way of projecting their fears and self-doubts onto others. In addition to projection, Allport suggested that people with a prejudiced personality tend to repress their fears and insecurities so that they can avoid facing their anxieties and shortcomings. This repression leads to the development of many of the same characteristics possessed by the authoritarian individual: ambivalence toward parents, moralism, a need for definiteness, and dichotomization (categorical, black-or-white thinking).

Problems with the Psychodynamic Approach

After enjoying much prominence and garnering a tremendous amount of research attention, interest in the psychodynamic explanation for a prejudiced personality waned. There were four main reasons for the decline of empirical interest in the theory (Fiske, 1998; Monteith, Zuwerink, & Devine, 1994). First, researchers became more and more critical of psychoanalytic approaches to personality. For example, Smith and Rosen (1958) found an inverse correlation between authoritarian personality scores (higher scores on the F scale) and a measure of what they termed "world-mindedness." World-mindedness is a concept that indicates one's attitudes toward and acceptance of people from other countries (low scores indicate greater intolerance). Smith and Rosen suggest that their scale and the F scale measure essentially the same personality characteristics, and yield similar results (i.e., the high scorer on the F scale tends to score very low on the world-mindedness scale, and vice versa).

In another line of inquiry, Martin and Westie (1959) suggested that prejudice may be a result of an intolerant personality. These individuals tended to be suspicious of politicians, intolerant of ambiguity (i.e., they were prone to categorical, rigid thinking), more superstitious, and inclined to believe in mystical and bizarre definitions of reality. Additionally, those with an intolerant personality scored lower on measures of compassion, sympathy, and trust and higher on measures of conservatism than those who have a tolerant personality. These findings mirror many of those reported by Adorno and his colleagues concerning the authoritarian personality type. However, the important point about both the world-mindedness and the tolerant-personality approaches is that each nicely measures the same constellation of personality characteristics and uncovers the same findings as those of Adorno et al., but they do so without assuming the psychodynamic processes that were the supposed causal force in creating the authoritarian personality.

Second, methodological and other conceptual problems with the notion of the authoritarian personality caused many researchers to conclude that the approach was unsatisfactory under scientific standards. The primary measures of authoritarianism, the F scale (facism), the A-S scale (for anti-Semitism), and the E scale (ethnocentrism), were worded in such a way that it was unclear whether high scores indicated agreement with the authoritarian beliefs (an example item from the F scale is "obedience and respect for authority are the most important virtues children should learn") or an acquiescence bias (agreeing with most or all items on a measure; Devine, 1995). Third, the theory only explained the presence of prejudice in a small subset of the population and did not explain why many people who did not have an authoritarian personality did show prejudice toward at least one other group. Similarly, it could not account for the fact that prejudice was stronger in some regions (e.g., anti-Black prejudice has typically been stronger in the southern United States than in other parts of the country) than others (Pettigrew, 1959). Fourth, the authoritarian-personality perspective suggests that there is little hope of changing an authoritarian individual to be more accepting of others (Eberhardt & Fiske, 1996). This is because authoritarians are not introspective, they do not believe there is anything about their personality that needs to be changed or improved, and they will resist attempts by others to convince them of the error of their authoritarian views of the world. By the late 1960s research on authoritarianism was so contradictory and confusing that researchers abandoned work on the concept.

RIGHT-WING AUTHORITARIANISM

Science has a funny way of sparking new lines of research on old concepts. Such was the case with a renewed look at authoritarianism by Altemeyer (1981). In 1965, Altemeyer was asked in his PhD-candidacy exam to explain the problems with the F scale and response sets with regard to measuring authoritarianism. His answer to the question was not sufficient, and he had to write a paper on the subject to demonstrate his knowledge of authoritarianism. Thus began what Altemeyer (1994) calls "a case study in overcompensation" (p. 132). That is, he sought not just to show that he knew the essentials of authoritarianism but that he really wanted to master the research literature on authoritarianism. In his research on the authoritarian personality, Altemeyer (1981, 1994, 1996) found that the Adorno et al. (1950) definition of a prefacist personality (i.e., the authoritarian) was quite vague. Adorno and his colleagues believed it was based on a constellation of nine related traits that were in fact very ill defined. An example is the "superstition and sterotypy" trait, which was supposed to refer to "the belief in mystical determinants of the individual's fate; the disposition to think in rigid categories" (Adorno et al., p. 228). Superstition and stereotypy are not the same thing and, therefore, such a definition that has the two representing one trait results in an ill-defined and conceptually messy construct. It is perhaps no wonder that Altemeyer found little correlation and covariance between these nine traits.

He did, however, find that three of these traits seemed to show a strong relationship with each other. These traits, which Altemeyer conceptualizes as "attitudinal clusters," are authoritarian submission, authoritarian aggression, and conventionalism. Authoritarian submission indicates a strong degree of submission to perceived legitimate authorities in one's society. Authoritarian aggression suggests a general aggression and hostility directed toward outgroups, that is viewed as acceptable by recognized authorities. Finally, conventionalism is defined as a strong adherence to social norms and traditions that are perceived as sanctioned by recognized authorities (Altemeyer, 1994). Altemeyer termed this constellation of attitudes **right-wing authoritarianism** (RWA), to denote its difference from Adorno et al.'s Freudian-based authoritarianism while also acknowledging its basis in at least part of Adorno et al.'s theory.

In his extensive research on RWA over the last 25 years, Altemeyer has found that people who are identified as high RWAs, as measured by Altemeyer's RWA scale (see Altemeyer, 1981) tend to be conservative politically, wish to restrict personal freedoms (for example, they tend to endorse the notion that the Bill of Rights ought to be abolished!), are more punitive toward criminals, and tend to hold more orthodox religious views (see Box 4.1).

They are also very prejudiced toward their outgroups. Scores on the RWA scale correlate highly with measures of ethnocentrism and hostility toward homosexuals. Interestingly, high RWAs tend to show more prejudiced attitudes when their answers on the questionnaires are anonymous. Much research has shown that people who are high RWAs

BOX 4.1

1997 RIGHT-WING AUTHORITARIANISM SCALE

Instructions: This survey is part of an investigation of general public opinion concerning a variety of social issues. You will probably find that you *agree* with some of the statements, and *disagree* with others, to varying extents. Please indicate your reaction to each statement by blackening a bubble on the bubble sheet, according to the following scale:

Blacken the bubble labeled

-4   if you *very strongly disagree* with the statement
-3   if you *strongly disagree* with the statement
-2   if you *moderately disagree* with the statement
-1   if you *slightly disagree* with the statement
+1   if you *slightly agree* with the statement
+2   if you *moderately agree* with the statement
+3   if you *strongly agree* with the statement
+4   if you *very strongly agree* with the statement

If you feel exactly and precisely *neutral* about an item, blacken the "0" bubble. You may find that you sometimes have different reactions to different parts of a statement. For example, you might very strongly disagree (-4) with one idea in a statement, but slightly agree (+1) with another idea in the same item. When this happens, please combine your reactions, and write down how you feel "on balance" (i.e., a -3 in this case).

1. The established authorities generally turn out to be right about things, whereas the radicals and protesters are usually just "loud mouths" showing off their ignorance.

2. Women should have to promise to obey their husbands when they get married.

3. Our country desperately needs a mighty leader who will do what has to be done to destroy the radical new ways and sinfulness that are ruining us.

4. Gays and lesbians are just as healthy and moral as anybody else.*

5. It is always better to trust the judgment of the proper authorities in government and religion than to listen to the noisy rabble-rousers in our society who are trying to create doubt in people's minds.

6. Atheists and others who have rebelled against the established religions are no doubt every bit as good and virtuous as those who attend church regularly.*

7. The only way our country can get through the crisis ahead is to get back to our traditional values, put some tough leaders in power, and silence the troublemakers spreading bad ideas.

8. There is absolutely nothing wrong with nudist camps.*

9. Our country *needs* free thinkers who will have the courage to defy traditional ways, even if this upsets many people.*

10. Our country will be destroyed someday if we do not smash the perversions eating away at our moral fiber and traditional beliefs.

11. Everyone should have their own lifestyle, religious beliefs, and sexual preferences, even if it makes them different from everyone else.*

12. The "old-fashioned ways" and "old-fashioned values" still show the best way to live.

13. You have to admire those who challenged the law and the majority's view by protesting for women's abortion rights, for animal rights, or to abolish school prayer.*

14. What our country really needs is a strong, determined leader who will crush evil and take us back to our true path.

15. Some of the best people in our country are those who are challenging our government, criticizing religion, and ignoring the "normal way things are supposed to be done."*

16. God's laws about abortion, pornography, and marriage must be strictly followed before it is too late, and those who break them must be strongly punished.

17. It would be best for everyone if the proper authorities censored magazines so that people could not get their hands on trashy and disgusting material.

18. There is nothing wrong with premarital sexual intercourse.*

19. Our country will be great if we honor the ways of our forefathers, do what the authorities tell us to do, and get rid of the "rotten apples" who are ruining everything.

20. There is no "ONE right way" to live life; everybody has to create their *own* way.*

21. Homosexuals and feminists should be praised for being brave enough to defy "traditional family values."*

22. This country would work a lot better if certain groups of troublemakers would just shut up and accept their group's traditional place in society.

23. There are many radical, immoral people in our country today, who are trying to ruin it for their own godless purposes, whom the authorities should put out of action.

24. People should pay less attention to the Bible and the other old forms of religious guidance, and instead develop their own personal standards of what is moral and immoral.*

25. What our country needs *most* is discipline, with everyone following our leaders in unity.

26. It's better to have trashy magazines and radical pamphlets in our communities than to let the government have the power to censor them.*

27. The facts on crime, sexual immorality, and the recent public disorders all show we have to crack down harder on deviant groups and troublemakers if we are going to save our moral standards and preserve law and order.

28. A lot of our rules regarding modesty and sexual behavior are just customs that are not necessarily any better or holier than those that other people follow.*

29. The situation in our country is getting so serious, the strongest methods would be justified if they eliminated the troublemakers and got us back to our true path.

30. A "woman's place" should be wherever she wants to be. The days when women were submissive to their husbands and social conventions belong strictly in the past.*

31. It is wonderful that young people today have greater freedom to protest against things they don't like, and to make their own "rules" to govern their behavior.*

32. Once our government leaders give us the "go ahead," it will be the duty of every patriotic citizen to help stomp out the rot that is poisoning our country from within.

Note: Only items 3–32 are scored. Items 1 and 2 are "table-setters" to help familiarize the respondent with the subject matter and with the −4 to +4 response format. Items with an asterisk after them are reverse scored.

From "The Other 'Authoritarian Personality,'" by B. Altemeyer. In *Advances in experimental social psychology,* Vol. 30, copyright © 1998 by Academic Press, reprinted with permission of the publisher. All rights of reproduction in any form are reserved.

tend to be prejudiced toward virtually everyone. In summarizing this research, Altemeyer (1994) quipped that RWAs are "equal-opportunity bigots" (p. 136).

RWA individuals are both fearful and self-righteous. Altemeyer (1988) has found that these two factors account for the strong link between RWA scores and prejudice. Where do these tendencies originate? Altemeyer (1994) speculates that most children form rather authoritarian attitudes, but for most kids, these attitudes and beliefs are modified with experience, and they tend to be low on RWA by their late teens or early twenties. High RWAs, however, may not get these experiences, and because they tend to have circles of like-minded high-RWA friends, they do not appreciate the extent of their prejudice and RWA attitudes. Unfortunately, this lack of self-insight is a major reason why it is not very easy to change the rigid attitudes and prejudices of high-RWA individuals. However, RWAs might respond to information that indicates they are violating their cherished ideals (i.e., that shows them how their prejudiced attitudes contradict their strong belief in values such as equality or freedom). Faced with this information, they might be willing to change their beliefs, in order to feel more attitudinally consistent and to reduce cognitive dissonance that would surely arise with such a realization. The RWA construct is a very promising one, and more research is needed to further examine the utility of the RWA personality as a predictor and moderator of attitudes toward others. Recent research by Cunningham, Nezlek, and Banaji (2004) has found support for the fundamental idea that prejudice finds a home in people with rigid ideologies, as was predicted by Adorno and also by Altemeyer. Cunningham and his colleagues found that people who are high in explicit prejudice are also high in implicit prejudice, and that people who demonstrate a rigid, right-wing ideology tend to be prejudiced toward many disadvantaged groups that have little in common. This supports Adorno's theorizing that authoritarian individuals tend to be equal-opportunity bigots, so to speak, and are prejudiced toward essentially any outgroup.

RELIGION

It is rather counterintuitive to think that religious beliefs and attitudes could be associated with intolerance and prejudice. One would think that if anyone were nonprejudiced, it would be someone who is religious. We think this because the vast majority of religions place great emphasis on compassion for one another, peace, tolerance, and love for others (Batson & Burris, 1994). Research suggests, though, that there is a positive correlation between being more religious and having less tolerance and more stereotyped cognitions about others (Adorno, et al., 1950; Allport & Kramer, 1946; Batson & Ventis, 1982; Gough, 1951; Rowatt, Tsang, Kelly, LaMartina, McCullers, & McKinley, 2004). Some have suggested that the reason for this correlation is that, with greater adherence to strict tenets of religious scripture (for example, literal readings of the Bible, Torah, Koran, etc.) comes an increase in the tendency to think in rigid, either–or terms that partitions the world into a basic good–bad dichotomy (Adorno et al.). As we have been learning throughout this book, much social-cognition research suggests that anything that works to inhibit the considered processing of information about other individuals increases the likelihood that one will rely on heuristics (e.g., stereotypes) when evaluating others (Kunda, 1999). This early research suggested that there was a strong link between prejudice and intolerance and the type of thinking fostered with greater religiosity.

Committed versus Consensual Religiosity

On the other hand, there are a number of studies that found little correlation between religion and prejudice (Evans, 1952; Martin & Nichols, 1962; Parry, 1949). What might account for these divergent conclusions? In an attempt to address this question, Allen and Spilka (1967) suggest that these different findings result from using different methods to assess religiosity. Specifically, they argue that much of this early research tended to rely on measures of religiosity that are too simplistic, such as church attendance, membership, or denominational preference. These indexes tell us nothing about the crucial factor that underlies the particular connection between an individual's social attitudes and one's religious beliefs. In other words, Allen and Spilka suggest that it is very important to assess how each individual participant focuses and organizes their religious beliefs. By doing this, we can get a much more accurate understanding of the relationship between religion and prejudice.

In their research, Allen and Spilka (1967) assessed religiosity on not one but eight different measures, and they obtained participant attitudes on various social issues via six different measures of social opinion. They also conducted an interview with each participant and coded the responses according to five cognitive components: content, clarity, complexity, flexibility, and importance. Based on these codings, participants were classified as either having "committed" or "consensual" religious beliefs. Essentially, a **committed religious** orientation is one that allows an individual to hold a wide range of belief categories through which one can evaluate the world, and one's ideas about the world and others tend to be more complex and open-minded. Committed individuals show a greater tolerance for diversity, and they are more likely to thoughtfully consider different ideas, beliefs, and opinions. **Consensual religious** individuals tend to interpret religion more literally and concretely, tend to make more generalizations about religious topics (i.e., are more likely to make broad characterizations, and think in categorical terms), and they are relatively unreceptive to different ideas and opinions. As you might imagine, the results indicated that the distinction between committed and consensual religious individuals is a useful one because it provides a more specific articulation of the relationship between prejudice and religious beliefs. In particular, the data showed that consensual religiosity was closely associated with prejudiced attitudes, and committed religious beliefs were strongly associated with greater tolerance and nonprejudiced attitudes.

Extrinsic versus Intrinsic Religious Orientation

In another attempt to examine the relationship between religion and prejudice, Allport and Ross (1967) examined two different types of religious individuals. They suggested that it is useful to differentiate between an **extrinsic** and an **intrinsic religious orientation.** Extrinsic people use religion for their own purposes, attend church infrequently, and tend to be more prejudiced toward others. Intrinsic people are those who have internalized the values of their religion, live life according to these beliefs, attend church regularly, and tend to be more egalitarian. Although Allport and Ross found supportive evidence for the extrinsic–intrinsic dichotomy, other researchers have been critical of the distinction (Hunt & King, 1971), and some data suggest that the Religious Orientation Scale (ROS; devised by Allport and Ross to measure intrinsic or extrinsic religious orientation) is not useful in assessing the religious beliefs of participants in nontraditional religions (e.g., Unitarians) (Strickland & Weddell, 1972). Contrary to what would be predicted of intrinsic and extrinsic individuals, Strickland and Weddell found that Unitarian individuals scored more extrinsically than those who had a traditional religious denomination (Baptists), but they were less prejudiced.

The intrinsic–extrinsic distinction came under scrutiny again in a study by Batson, Naifeh, and Pate (1978). Batson and his colleagues noted that the measures of religious orientation (the ROS) and prejudice were self-report measures. As much research has shown, the accuracy of self-report measures is often questionable because of the social-desirability concerns of the respondent (Eagly & Chaiken, 1993). That is, people tend to respond to attitude questionnaires in ways that avoid social disapproval and gain social approval (i.e., responding how they think they ought to respond, not how they really think about an attitude issue). This is especially likely to occur on measures of sensitive topics, such as religious beliefs and prejudiced attitudes. Batson et al. (1978) suggested that the association between the intrinsic religious orientation and prejudice was influenced by social desirability. They gave a measure of racial prejudice, a measure of social desirability, and six measures of religious orientation to 51 White participants. Participants were led to believe that they would be discussing their religious and racial attitudes later with either a White or African American interviewer. Participants were asked to indicate their ratings of how much they would like each interviewer (White or African American, as indicated by photos of the interviewer attached to the interviewer's personal information sheet) to interview them. To the degree that people rated the White interviewer higher, these ratings were used as an index of racial prejudice. Results indicated that, as predicted, an intrinsic religious orientation was strongly associated with high scores on measures of social desirability, and negatively associated with racial prejudice. Interestingly, when the effects of social desirability were statistically controlled in the analyses, the negative correlation between intrinsic orientation and racial prejudice nearly disappeared. This suggests that being intrinsically oriented does not necessarily mean that one is nonprejudiced, but it does mean that one is much more concerned with presenting oneself as more religious and egalitarian than one actually is.

In another examination of the relationship between religious orientation and prejudice, Morris, Hood, and Watson (1989) suggested that it is important to further specify religious orientation in terms of intrinsic (I), extrinsic (E), indiscriminately antireligious (IA) and indiscriminantly proreligious (IP). Their results suggest that IA and I persons were lower in racial prejudice compared to E and IP individuals. This pattern was unchanged when accounting for concerns about social desirability. Morris et al. suggest that the high scores on the social-desirability measure for Is differ in meaning from IPs. For Is, they suggest that the high social desirability scores indicate that the person is reporting something that is actually true (that is, that the person genuinely, for example, rarely lies) and is not concerned with appearing socially desirable, but is in fact desirable socially. IPs, on the other hand, may indeed be concerned with responding according to how they think they should respond to gain social approval. This is an interesting interpretation, and we will revisit the social-desirability issue in our discussion of religion as a quest.

While Batson and his colleagues (1978) showed that not all intrinsically oriented religious individuals are low in prejudice, research by Herek (1987) indicates that Is are tolerant of only *certain* types of individuals. Herek gave measures of religious orientation, racism, and attitudes toward homosexuals to White heterosexual undergraduate students. The data indicated that an intrinsic orientation was not positively correlated with racism, but an extrinsic orientation was positively correlated with racism. Thus far, the data support Allport and Ross's (1967) findings. Unfortunately, Herek did not measure social-desirability concerns, so it is likely that the results may be subject to that bias. The novel contribution of this study was the findings with regard to attitudes toward a much less acceptable group for religious individuals, homosexuals. Herek found that Is were more prejudiced than Es toward homosexuals. Herek suggests that having an intrinsic religious orientation does not foster greater tolerance toward others, only unequivocal acceptance of specific others who are accepted by Judeo-Christian teachings.

Religion as Quest

In the Batson et al. (1978) study, Batson and his colleagues examined the relationship between another religious orientation and prejudice. They called this other orientation a "quest" orientation (measured with Batson's [1976] Interactional scale). This orientation sees religion as a "process of questioning, doubting, and reexamination in response to the contradictions and tragedies of life" (Batson et al., 1978, p. 33). Results indicated that the quest orientation did not correlate positively with social desirability, and higher scores on the quest orientation were negatively correlated with prejudice. Batson et al. (1978) suggested that a quest orientation may correlate more positively with prosocial behavior, such as compassion for others. Some researchers have been skeptical of the utility and validity of the quest orientation (Griffin, Gorsuch, & Davis, 1987; Morris et al., 1989). For example, Griffin et al. examined religious orientation in Seventh-Day Adventists in the Carribean (measuring prejudice against Rastafarians). Because both participants and targets of prejudice were Black, the study examined cultural influences on prejudice. While strength of commitment to the church, church attendance, and an intrinsic orientation were significantly correlated with prejudice, extrinsic and quest orientations were not related to prejudice (they were neither positively nor negatively correlated). Griffin et al. suggest that it is too simplistic to measure a broad religious orientation and correlate it with prejudice, and that a more accurate assessment of the relation of prejudice and religious beliefs must take into account the influence of the cultural and religious context. That is, Griffin et al. suggest that in this culture and context, the Seventh-Day Adventist church promoted an intolerant attitude among its members toward the Rastafarians, who they regarded as a cult at odds with the church teachings. Therefore, being highly religious also meant that one was very intolerant toward the group that was regarded negatively by one's church. These results are quite consistent with and supportive of Herek's (1987) findings that religion fosters both tolerance of groups accepted by the church and intolerance of groups not acceptable to the church.

On the other hand, support for the quest orientation and its relationship to nonprejudiced attitudes has been growing among a number of prejudice researchers (e.g., Altemeyer & Hunsberger, 1992; Hunsberger, 1995; McFarland, 1989). Altemeyer and Hunsberger (1992) found that whereas religious fundamentalism (the belief that there is only one, unchanging truth about humanity and God, that these truths must be followed strictly, and that only those who follow these truths have a special relationship with God) and prejudice were highly correlated, people who had a quest orientation showed little or no prejudice toward a wide variety of groups. These results are especially interesting because Alte-meyer and Hunsberger used a different (yet valid and reliable) measure of quest orienta-tion than what was used in Batson et al.'s (1978) and most other researchers' studies. This bolsters the argument for the validity of the quest orientation and our confidence in the quest–prejudice association, because two different measures of quest have shown the same negative correlation with prejudiced attitudes. Not surprisingly, these data also showed that high RWAs tended to be more prejudiced and were more likely to score high on measures of religious fundamentalism.

Let us return to the issue of religious orientation, social desirability, and prejudice. Batson et al. (1978) found data to suggest that the low prejudice scores of intrinsic-oriented individuals were merely an artifact of social-desirability concerns, and when social-desirability scores are accounted for in the analyses, the negative correlation between prejudice and intrinsic orientation disappears. Before we reject the oft-reported support for Allport and Ross' (1967) negative correlation between intrinsic orientation and prejudice, more studies are needed. To that end, Batson, Flink, Schoenrade, Fultz, and Pych (1986) designed a conceptual replication of the Batson et al. (1978) study, with specific focus on examining prejudice via overt and covert measures. Batson et al. (1986) used an attribu-tional ambiguity procedure to examine the prejudice of individuals who had an intrinsic, extrinsic, and quest orientation.

The basic procedure (first used by Snyder, Kleck, Strenta, & Mentzer, 1979) examines prejudiced responses to situations in which it is very obvious that prejudice is the basis for one's behavior (the overt, unambiguous context) and in which there is a ready alternative ex-planation for one's behavior (the covert, ambiguous context). White participants completed measures of religious orientation in a pretesting session. They were contacted 3–4 weeks later to participate in the ostensibly separate experiment (participants were not told that their religious orientation scores were related to their selection for the study). Participants were told that the main experiment was concerned with reactions to movies. They were led to a large theater, where they were seated at a chair near the entrance. The middle of the theater had a partition, forming two smaller theaters containing screens and chairs, and participants were told that they could select the theater in which they would like to watch the movie. In each of the theaters, participants could see another subject (who was a con-federate) filling out a questionnaire prior to the start of the film. In one of the theaters, the confederate was African American, and in the other theater the confederate was White.

Half of the participants were told that one of the movie projectors had broken and they could only show the same movie in each theater (this was the overt, unambiguous condition). The other half of the participants were told that there would be different movies in each theater, and they were given a brief description of each movie to help them choose which movie they would like to see (the covert, ambiguous condition). The experimenter left the subject and confederate, 5 minutes later the film ended, and participants completed questions about the movie and then were debriefed. If Batson and his colleagues were cor-rect, we would expect that intrinsic individuals would show no prejudice in the overt condi-tion, because they are very concerned with appearing nonprejudiced. Thus, they would be more likely to choose to sit with the African American confederate than opt to sit in the other theater with the White, because to sit with the White would indicate only one reason for such a choice: prejudice (they did not want to sit with the African American student). In the covert condition, however, Batson et al. (1986) predicted that intrinsics would tend to choose not to sit with the African American confederate but to sit in the other theater with the White. Here, their intolerant attitudes can be expressed without concern for being seen as prejudiced, because the choice to sit in the other theater can be explained as an interest in the other movie, and not as an expression of prejudice. Batson et al. (1986) also predicted that the choice to sit with a White would be negatively correlated with a quest orientation, regardless of the overt or covert nature of the situation.

Results indicated that, as predicted, intrinsic individuals tended to choose to sit with the African American confederate in the overt condition. However, they chose to sit with the White confederate in the ambiguous, covert situation. Also as predicted, those who scored high on the quest orientation tended to sit with the African American confederate in both the overt and covert conditions. Indeed, they were significantly more likely to sit with the African American confederate in the covert condition. Batson and his colleagues suggest that, taken together with the results of the Batson et al. (1978) study, these results show that an intrinsic religious orientation is less related to tolerance and low prejudice, and more related to the desire to appear nonprejudiced. In sum, the available evidence from a number of studies indicates that people who have an intrinsic religious orientation score lower on self-report measures of prejudice, but they do not tend to score lower on these measures compared to nonreligious persons (Batson & Burris, 1994). Although the evidence suggests that religion does not stimulate prejudice (though it may foster intolerance toward certain, unacceptable outgroups [Herek, 1987]), it does not curtail prejudice either. This conclusion does not apply, however, to those who have a quest religious orientation. Much evidence suggests that these individuals do indeed tend to be of low prejudice and show a greater tolerance of outgroups, regardless of the self-presentation aspects of the situation.

A recent paper by Rowatt and Franklin (2004) makes the case that as agreement with orthodox Christian beliefs increases, scores on measures of implicit racial prejudice actually decrease. The key here is that Rowatt and Franklin specify that the Christian beliefs need to emphasize tolerance and acceptance of others. Another important finding is that this association (more Christian beliefs leading to less prejudice) only happens when one controls for the moderate effects of RWA on prejudice. These results suggest that lowering RWA attitudes could reduce implicit prejudice.

Much more research is needed in this area to further clarify the complex interrelationship between religious orientation, fundamentalism, RWA, and prejudice toward various groups, and this research should utilize more behavioral measures of prejudice (to avoid the social-desirability problem inherent in earlier research). Experiments of this sort can clarify the nature of the quest orientation, for example, and begin to clarify the development of the nonprejudiced and prejudiced religious individual. Of further empirical interest would be examining whether various religious orientations and personality traits allow one to be more receptive to changing one's religious intolerance to more tolerant views of others.

NEED FOR COGNITION

Some people tend to dispositionally enjoy cognitive activity. Others find effortful cognition aversive. The rest of the world falls somewhere between these extremes. This is the basic notion behind Cacioppo and Petty's (1982) concept of the **need for cognition.** Cacioppo and Petty suggest that the need for cognition (NC) describes an individual difference variable that refers to the motivational state of an individual to think about the world. Those high in the need for cognition (HNC) tend to think about, seek, and ponder information relevant to the relationships among people, events, and objects in their environment. Individuals with a low need for cognition (LNC), on the other hand, are neither motivated to nor excited by thinking about their environment. They prefer to avoid extensive cognition, and instead they rely on more heuristic types of thinking that allow them to make quick judgments with the least cognitive effort.

Much of the extant work on NC has been applied to the question of susceptibility to various persuasion contexts. Overall, dozens of studies indicate that HNC persons are least susceptible to distraction or other heuristic cues that would lead to biased (or nonrational) conclusions about the persuasion message. LNC persons, on the other hand, are indeed susceptible to these peripheral cues in persuasion messages, and they tend to be equally persuaded by weak and strong rationales for changing one's attitude in the direction intended by the persuader (Petty & Wegener, 1998).

To the degree that NC causes an individual to seek more information about the world and avoid fast and (often inaccurate) heuristic judgments, that person should be less likely to rely on stereotypes when thinking about others. Interestingly, very few studies have addressed this question. A recent paper by Crawford and Skowronski (1998) reported the results of four experiments on the relationship between NC and memory for stereotype-consistent and inconsistent information. Contrary to what one would expect, their data do not support the simple prediction that HNC persons would be less likely to use stereotypes in social judgments. HNC individuals remembered more stereotype-consistent information about a target than did LNC persons, but they were unaffected by target-relevant stereotypes when forming impressions of a given target. In contrast, LNC persons tend to rely on stereotypes when forming impressions of a target, but when they later recall information about that target, their recollections tend to be unaffected by stereotypes. Yet, data reported by Florack, Scarabis, and Bless (2001) found support for the idea that people are more likely to base their social judgments on automatic associations between traits and categories (implicit stereotypes) if they are LNC. So, at present, more research is needed to attempt to further explicate these divergent results, to give us a better understanding of the influence of the need for cognition on the tendency to use stereotypes in social judgments.

These data are also consistent with the now rather substantial literature on the influence of situational and person variables on behavior (e.g., Ross & Nisbett, 1991) that suggests that behavior is a function of both situation pressures and individual personality characteristics (Lewin, 1951a). More specifically, this research indicates that it is important to note that there are some situations that impose a stronger influence on the cognition and behavior of the individual (strong situations) and some situations exert very little influence on the individual's thoughts and behavior (weak situations; Mischel, 1977). When the situational forces are strong—for example, when it is important to think carefully about another person, in order to form an accurate evaluation of them—then both HNC and LNC individuals tend to demonstrate more extensive and careful cognition. Similarly, when the influence of the situation is very minimal in an evaluation context, then HNC and LNC persons show equally minimal levels of cognitive elaboration in their evaluations. The difference between HNC and LNC individuals in levels of careful cognition is greatest when the situation exerts a moderate level of influence (Cacioppo, Petty, Feinstein, & Jarvis, 1996).

NEED FOR STRUCTURE

People also differ in the degree to which they desire clear, certain, or unambiguous knowledge (i.e., structure; Jamieson & Zanna, 1989). In this conceptualization, knowledge can refer to norms, emotions, attitudes, and any other information that is accessible to an individual. Kruglanski (1980, 1990) suggests that people with a high **need for structure** prefer to halt the acquisition of further information about the world with regard to a particular aspect of knowledge. That is, these individuals seek a definite, clear answer, and the process of further information gathering would pose a threat to the stability and clarity of one's current state of thinking, because such information might contain knowledge-inconsistent, or challenging information.

Much research has supported the validity of the need-for-structure construct as an individual-difference variable that influences social judgments (Kruglanski, 1996; Neuberg & Newsom, 1993). Need for structure is conceptualized as both a stable characteristic of one's personality and as a situationally induced motivational state. Thus, some people have a consistent tendency to prefer a definite, clear state of knowledge about the world, whereas others do not show such a preference, and in fact are comfortable with (and may welcome) inconsistent, ever-changing information about the world (Kaplan, Wanshula, & Zanna, 1993; Kunda, 1999; Webster, 1993).

A number of studies have shown that the need for structure can influence social judgments (Moskowitz, 1993; Neuberg & Newsom, 1993). In one such experiment, Neuberg and Newsom (Study 4) asked participants who were either high in the need for structure (HNS) or low in the need for structure (LNS; as assessed by the personal need for structure scale) to read a brief paragraph about either a male or female student who was having difficulty both in a math course and with a boyfriend or girlfriend. Participants then were asked to give their evaluations of the target on different dimensions assessing traditional female sex stereotyped characteristics (e.g., emotionality, irrationality, gullibility). Results indicated that HNS participants were more likely than LNS participants to stereotype a target, and they were more likely to ascribe female characteristics to a woman target than to a male target. LNS participants showed no difference in their ratings of the male and female targets. These data suggest that HNS persons may be more likely to use a stereotype to help them arrive at a social evaluation in ambiguous situations. Schaller, Boyd, and Yohannes (1995) found that HNS persons were more likely than LNS individuals to form stereotypes about other groups. However, an HNS orientation does not mean that a person is doomed to always think heuristically about others. Schaller et al.'s data also indicated that the effects of the need for structure on stereotyping are diminished when the individual perceiver is motivated to form an accurate impression of the target person. Similarly, when the situation is unambiguous, individuals who have an HNS and an LNS tend to form similar impressions of others (Neuberg & Newsom, 1993).

Need for structure can be enhanced by conditions that restrict one's ability to consider information relevant to a judgment. Such factors include emotions, distraction, too much information, and time pressure to arrive at a judgment (Kaplan, et al., 1993). In the lab, need for structure has been experimentally induced by telling participants that they have very little time in which to do the task. The judgments and performance of these participants are compared with those of participants who were not time restricted in their tasks. Researchers using this manipulation have found that increased time pressure leads participants to rely on stereotypes in making their evaluations of a target (Jamieson & Zanna, 1989; Kaplan et al.; Kruglanski & Freund, 1983). The research on the need for structure suggests that the degree to which one will use stereotypes as a judgmental heuristic in their social judgments depends, in part, on the extent to which that individual has a need for certainty (Kaplan et al.).

NEED FOR COGNITIVE CLOSURE

As an individual-difference variable, the **need for cognitive closure** has also been regarded as an influential factor in the process by which we make social judgments. The need for cognitive closure has been defined as the "need for an answer on a given topic, any answer, as compared to confusion and ambiguity" (Kruglanski, 1990, p. 337). According to Kruglanski (1990), the need for cognitive closure is proportionate to the perceived costs for not attaining closure and the perceived rewards for getting cognitive closure. For example, one reward could be the ability to act on one's decision/answer about the topic, while a cost for failing to get cognitive closure might entail missing a deadline for a decision (Kruglanski, 1990). Kruglanski (1990) notes that the need for cognitive closure appears to be a similar construct to authoritarianism and dogmatism, in that they, too, deal with intolerance of ambiguity. Those constructs, however, are tied to politically conservative attitudes, whereas the need for cognitive closure is viewed as a content-free motive.

The need for cognitive closure directly influences two tendencies in the individual: a tendency toward urgency, in which the person has a desire to seize on closure rapidly, and a tendency toward permanence, in which the individual wishes to preserve (or freeze) a certain state of knowledge and block out subsequent information that might negate or invalidate the belief (Kruglanski & Webster, 1996). This motivational state has significant effects on the way the individual processes information, and it leads the person to think more heuristically, make more errors in social judgments, and rely on any salient cues to make a fast judgment. One of the pernicious aspects of this need is the permanence tendency. The need for cognitive closure delivers a double hit to the social perceiver by (1) leading them to an often erroneous judgment and then (2) motivating the individual to avoid seeking further information relevant to the accuracy of that assessment.

The need for cognitive closure can be conceptualized as a need that varies with the specific demands of the situation. This is one reason why, for example, researchers have been successful in experimentally inducing a heightened need for cognitive closure in subjects by introducing a time constraint for the subject to perform the required experimental tasks. Need for cognitive closure is thus enhanced when a judgment on the issues is required. It can be reduced by a fear of making an invalid evaluation, as in the case of forming an accurate impression of another individual (especially one who has power over your outcomes).

Research has also demonstrated that the need for cognitive closure represents a dimension of individual differences that functions as a stable personality characteristic that affects our thoughts and behavior across situations (Dijksterhuis, Knippenberg, Kruglanski, & Schaper, 1996; Webster & Kruglanski, 1994). Like the need for structure, the data support the contention that the effects of a situational enhancement of the need for cognitive closure are virtually identical to the effects obtained with those with a characteristically high need for cognitive closure (Kruglanski & Webster, 1996; Webster, 1993). While the need for closure has a significant effect on the information processing of the individual in a range of cognitive tasks (see Kruglanski & Webster for a more detailed discussion), we are interested in how this need influences stereotyping tendencies. Generally, those who are high in the need for cognitive closure tend to rely on stereotypes to a greater extent in their social judgments compared to those low in the need for cognitive closure (De Dreu, Koole, & Oldersma, 1999; Dijksterhuis et al., 1996; Shah, Kruglanski, & Thompson, 1998; Webster & Kruglanski, 1994; Webster, Kruglanski, & Pattison, 1997). For example, research by Dijksterhuis et al. found that participants who were high in the need for cognitive closure tended to recall more stereotype-consistent information about a target group, while those low in the need for cognitive closure recalled more stereotype-inconsistent information. Their results also showed that individuals high in the need for cognitive closure evaluated the target group more stereotypically and were more likely to see the target group as homogeneous (i.e., an outgroup homogeneity bias) than those low in the need for cognitive closure. In a related vein, experiments by Webster and her colleagues (1997) and Shah et al. (1998) support Dijksterhuis et al. (1996) in that they suggest that the enhanced tendency of individuals who are high in the need for cognitive closure to rely on stereotypes in social judgments may be due to an increased tendency to favor one's ingroup and to derogate outgroups.

Looking at the need for cognition, the need for structure, and the need for cognitive closure, one might be tempted to argue that they are all essentially measuring a general tendency to avoid ambiguity, and that the distinctions between them are really conceptually insignificant. However, let us carefully examine that conclusion. In order to claim that one has identified a construct that is unique from another psychological construct, one needs data that speak to the distinctiveness of the construct (i.e., data on the discriminant validity of a concept) from already-existing constructs. Webster and Kruglanski (1994) set out to provide evidence for the distinctiveness of the need for cognitive closure and need for structure from each other and compared to the need for cognition. They first compared the two primary scales designed to assess the need for structure and the need for cognitive closure. They noted that each scale shares two common aspects: items that tap a preference for order and a preference for predictability. So, scores on each scale should be slightly correlated, but not highly correlated, because each scale also assesses different characteristics that make up each construct. Results indicated that the two scales did indeed show a small correlation ($r = .24$). The data also showed that the need for cognition scale was slightly negatively correlated with the need for cognitive closure ($r = -.28$). As one's need to think about a concept increases, the need to close off information processing about that concept decreases. Thus, it is evident that the need for cognition and need for cognitive closure scales do not reflect the same construct. Webster and Kruglanski (1994) conclude that although the scales for the need for cognitive closure and need for structure are partially related (in that they share overlap in their measurement of preference for order, and preference for predictability), they are assessing different constructs.

SOCIAL-DOMINANCE ORIENTATION

Some people exhibit a preference for inequality among social groups. Specifically, these individuals want their group to dominate and be superior to other groups. Such individuals are regarded as possessing a high **social-dominance orientation** (SDO; Pratto, Sidanius,

Stallworth, & Malle, 1994). An SDO is an attitude toward intergroup relationships which says that groups are different and organized into a hierarchical structure within society, and thus some groups are subordinated and of lesser status than others. High-SDO persons seek to maintain this structure by promoting group inequity and policies that help maintain the dominance one group over another. Low-SDO persons seek to reduce group inequity and eliminate the hierarchical structure of society's groups. Research by Pratto et al. (1994), suggests that SDO has good discriminant and predictive validity and is a reliable index of an individual's attitudes and affect toward outgroups, and toward minority outgroups in particular. Their data showed that SDO was strongly correlated with anti-Black racism and sexism. Pratto and her colleagues (1994) found evidence to support the idea that a high SDO is strongly correlated with conservative political views, and opposition to programs and policies that aim to promote equality (such as affirmative action, laws advocating equal rights for homosexuals, women in combat, etc.). However, it is important to remember that an SDO does not only refer to those who are high in social-dominance orientation. Like any other individual-difference variable, there are those who are less extreme in this dimension. Low-SDO individuals tend to hold attitudes that attenuate social hierarchies. In other words, they favor programs and policies that promote equality and hold more liberal political views.

It should be noted that social-dominance theory (Sidanius, 1993), upon which the concept of SDO is based, does not make any specifications about the foundation of prejudiced attitudes (i.e., genetics, fairness, political conservativism, etc.), it just states that the ideology behind the outgroup prejudice describes groups as unequal. Such a foundation provides a "legitimizing myth," and these beliefs tend to be highly correlated with SDO (Pratto, et al., 1994; Quist & Resendez, 2002). To have an impact, legitimizing myths must be widely accepted in a society. They stabilize oppression by providing a self-evident truth about the rationale for the differential status of certain groups within society. In this way, legitimizing myths help society minimize group conflict by promoting the superiority of one group over another (Crandall, 2000; Pratto, et al., 1994). Next, we will examine in some detail the relevant empirical findings on SDO and attempt to come to some conclusions about the utility of considering SDO as an individual difference variable that predicts prejudice and stereotyping.

Who tends to be high on measures of social-dominance orientation? According to Sidanius (1993), the answer can be found in a fundamental dichotomy of society: organizations that favor the strong over the weak (that promote the dominance of a group over another, or hierarchy-enhancers), and those that promote the interests of the weak over the strong (hierarchy-attenuators). People in institutions/organizations that are hierarchy enhancing should be more likely to hold high-SDO attitudes and beliefs. Those in hierarchy-attenuating institutions should hold attitudes that are consistent with a low SDO. In the United States, one such system that nicely embodies both ends of the SDO is the criminal-justice system. In order to examine the predictions of social dominance theory in this context, Sidanius, Liu, Shaw, and Pratto (1994) gave a questionnaire assessing social status, social and political attitudes, SDO, and other demographic information to police officers, public defenders, jurors, and university students.

Based on the social-dominance theory, Sidanius, Liu et al. (1994) predicted that police would tend to have the most conservative, hierarchical attitudes (consistent with a high SDO), and public defenders would have the lowest scores on a measure of SDO, owing to the nature of their position in the criminal justice system (defending the "weak" [individual] against the "strong" [the state]). They also predicted that average citizens (the jurors) would have the next-highest SDO scores, and university students would have low (but slightly higher than public defenders) SDO scores. They made these predictions based on to the fact that university students tend to hold more liberal, equality-favoring social and political attitudes than the general public. Results indicated support for these predictions.

It should be noted that the differences between these individuals on SDO may not be attributed solely to the influence of the institution or occupational role of the individual. That is, while some occupations clearly do foster attitudes that promote or attenuate social hierarchies, it is important to remember that there is a subject self-selection issue in these data. Specifically, it may be the case that those people who have a high SDO are drawn to positions that favor those attitudes, and those who have a low SDO wish to work in positions that foster their social attitudes. Indeed, results reported by Sidanius, Pratto, Martin, and Stallworth (1991) found that students who were preparing for careers in hierarchy-enhancing positions tended to have significantly higher SDO scores than those preparing for hierarchy-attenuating careers.

Research on SDO also shows reliable differences between men and women in the degree to which they have a social-dominance orientation. Throughout history, most societies have accorded special status to males and granted them most (in some cases, all) of the political, social, economic, and legal power in society. Thus, it seems reasonable to predict that, to the degree that these cultural and societal traditions are present in a given society, men should prefer to maintain their special status, and should support policies, legislation, and attitudes that promote the dominance of men over women. Data reported by Pratto, Stallworth, and Sidanius (1997) suggest that men do hold more conservative political views, compared with women, who tend to be more liberal politically and supportive of programs concerned with equal rights. Although the United States has made long strides toward equality between men and women and is far more egalitarian than other countries toward women, women in the United States still face discrimination, prejudice, and stereotyping left over from the patriarchical sexism in American society (Swann, Langlois, & Gilbert, 1999).

Based on the history of the unequal status of men and women in the United States, Sidanius, Pratto, and Bobo (1994) predicted that men should have a higher SDO than women. Sidanius, Pratto et al. (1994) conducted a survey of a large ($N = 1,897$) sample of men and women in Los Angeles, asking respondents for their demographic information, political attitudes, and attitudes on a number of social issues. They found that, indeed, men had significantly higher SDO scores than did women. Interestingly, this difference did not vary when accounting for cultural, situational, and demographic factors. The sexism prevalent in U.S. society, coupled with traditional gender beliefs about men and women, also affects the occupations women attain in the United States. Pratto, Stallworth, Sidanius, and Siers (1997) asked college students to rate what types of jobs they would prefer to have after they graduate (Study 1). They found that men tended to prefer hierarchy-enhancing positions and women favored hierarchy-attenuating occupations, and this was correlated with the higher scores of men compared to women on measures of SDO. Results indicated that these preferences still hold even among men and women who have the same SDO levels (Study 2). Pratto, Stallworth, Sidanius et al. (1997) also had students rate the appropriateness of six applicants, based on their résumés for different occupations. Half the subjects read about three jobs that were hierarchy-enhancing and two that were hierarchy-attenuating, and the other half read about three hierarchy-attenuating and two hierarchy-enhancing positions (Study 3). The résumés differed in that three applicants had prior experience in hierarchy-enhancing positions, and the other three had prior hierarchy-attenuating job experience. The data showed that people filled the hierarchy-attenuating positions with hierarchy-attenuating applicants, and the hierarchy-enhancing positions were filled with hierarchy-enhancing applicants.

However, a gender bias also was clearly evident in the hiring decisions of the student participants. They tended to hire more women (about 50% more) for the hierarchy-attenuating positions and more men (also about 50% more) for the hierarchy-enhancing occupations. A replication of Study 3 was conducted with a sample of actual business persons who made hiring and personnel decisions (Study 4). The results were similar to those of Study 3; businesspersons hired more people with hierarchy-attenuating job experience for hierarchy-attenuating positions, and more people with hierarchy-enhancing job experience for hierarchy-enhancing positions. They also showed the same gender bias in their hiring decisions, in that they hired more women for hierarchy-attenuating positions, and more men for the hierarchy-enhancing positions. What is also interesting is that both men and women respondents showed these hiring biases. This latter finding may be in line with the prediction of social-dominance theory that people are socialized to believe in the legitimacy of the status differences between groups, and this helps maintain the social hierarchy by quelling desires of the subordinate groups to question or attempt to change the social order (see Pratto, et al., 1994; and Sidanius, 1993, for more details).

Recall that those high in SDO tend to oppose programs that are designed to eliminate or reduce inequality between groups. Research by Pratto et al. (1994) showed support for this aspect of social-dominance theory. High-SDO persons did indeed oppose a wide range of political and social programs that would attenuate the social hierarchy. Pratto et al. (1994) also found that high SDO scores were also strongly correlated with measures of sexism and anti-Black prejudice. This brings up an interesting question of how to interpret these findings. Does opposition to programs that promote social and economic equality and that reduce the hierarchy between groups in society indicate racism or sexism? Moreover, what is the relation between SDO and racism? One explanation suggests that opposition to these programs is based not on racism or sexism but on a "principled conservatism" (Sidanius, Pratto, & Bobo, 1996). This perspective suggests that opposition to such programs is based not on racism but on a "concern for equity, color-blindness, and genuine conservative values" (Sidanius, et al., 1996, p. 476).

Furthermore, some principled-conservatism theorists have suggested that racism and conservatism are independent, and only very weakly correlated among the highly educated, who truly understand the concepts of conservative values and attitudes. In an effort to examine the relationship between education, SDO, and racism, Sidanius and his colleagues (1996) asked approximately 4,600 Euro-Americans to complete a survey in which they were asked about their political and social attitudes, and their social-dominance orientation was assessed. Results indicated partial support for the principled-conservatism position that opposition to affirmative action cannot be completely understood by racism or SDO. However, the data suggest several problems for the principled-conservativism position. Contrary to what conservatism theorists would predict, correlations among SDO, political conservatism, and racism were strongest among the most well educated, and weakest among the least well educated. Political conservatism and racism are related, according to Sidanius, Pratto, and Bobo (1996), because conservatives tend to be more invested in the hierarchical structure of society and in maintaining the inequality of the present status quo in society. These results are therefore supportive of the explanation that SDO, not political conservativism, is a better predictor of racial attitudes among the highly educated. Sidanius et al. (1996) conclude that racism can be conceptualized as a special case of a social-dominance orientation.

A study by Pratto and Shih (2000) found that people high in SDO do not differ from those low in SDO on measures of implicit group prejudice. When primed with the word *our,* high and low SDOs were equally likely to respond faster to recognizing positive adjectives, and slower to recognize negative adjectives. When primed with *them,* both groups were faster to recognize negative adjectives, and slower to recognize positive adjectives. This mirrors findings by other researchers (e.g., Perdue et al., 1990). However, two interesting things happened when the researchers conducted another, similar experiment, this time preceded by a threat to the participant's group status (these student participants read an essay about the declining prestige of their university). First, high SDOs were significantly more likely to show implicit outgroup discrimination and prejudice than low SDOs. Second, recall that most research on social-identity theory has not indicated that people derogate outgroups to enhance their self esteem. Pratto and Shih, however, found that under group threat, high SDOs responded with strong forms of ingroup favoritism and outgroup derogation. Similar results were reported in a study by Quist and Resendez (2002). This fascinating result speaks to the current zeitgeist in contemporary models of prejudice concerning the importance of contextual, or situational, variables in determining whether an individual will show prejudice (Duckitt, Wagner, du Plessis, & Birum, 2002; Eagly & Diekman (2005); Fiske, Cuddy, Glick, & Xu, 2002).

It should be emphasized again that RWA and SDO do not describe personality traits, but rather, they are better conceptualized as ideological beliefs (Duckitt et al., 2002) that influence personality traits and intergroup attitudes. A recent analysis by Guimond, Dambrun, Michinov, and Duarte (2003) found that a dominant social position influences prejudice, and that SDO is a mediator of that relationship. In other words, people who find themselves in a dominant social position are more likely to adopt higher SDO beliefs (to justify and solidify their status), and these beliefs are what influence prejudice toward outgroups (and those who would threaten or compete for that desired social position). These results are perhaps the strongest yet in support of the idea that whether one adopts RWA- or SDO-like attitudes or shows prejudice is largely due to social-contextual (social-position) variables. Because people move in and out of these daily (and at a more macro level, in their lives, moving up or down socioeconomically, for example), the salience and type of one's particular social identity (e.g., age, national, personal, gender) or social context at a given moment is likely to be the key determinant of whether SDO or RWA attitudes will be evoked and whether the person will display prejudice (Reynolds, Turner, Haslam, & Ryan, 2001).

Finally, if you're thinking that many of these personality traits, individual difference variables, needs, and ideological beliefs seem to have a common thread somehow, a recent meta-analysis supports your hunch. Jost, Glaser, Kruglanski, and Sulloway (2003) analyzed 88 studies, from 12 countries, with over 22,000 subjects, and found that death anxiety (Greenberg, Pyszczynski, & Solomon, 1986), intolerance of ambiguity, openness to experience, uncertainty, needs for closure and structure, and threat of loss of position or self-esteem all contribute to the degree of one's overall political conservativism. Jost et al. suggest that these results show that political conservatives stress resistance to change and justification of inequality and are motivated by needs that are aimed at reducing threat and uncertainty. These data are compelling and are exciting for prejudice researchers in that they provide fertile ground for further theoretical refinements about the connections between individual difference variables and prejudice.

SUMMARY

At the outset of this chapter, we sought to address the question of whether or not people can have a prejudiced personality. If we define such a personality as consisting of a certain group of traits that lead the individual to be more likely to dislike outgroups, the available research evidence suggests that there is no support for the concept of a prejudiced personality. As research on the prejudiced personality concept waned in the late 1960s, the field turned its attention to different ways of examining prejudice, and today researchers tend to view prejudice in very cognitive terms, as an inevitable product of social categorization (Duckitt, 1992). In contemporary research on prejudice, attempts to identify a prejudiced personality are virtually nonexistent (Monteith, Zuwerink, & Devine, 1994). However, some psychologists have recently proposed a new addition to the DSM-IV-TR (the Diagnostic and Statistical Manual of Mental Disorders; American Psychiatric Association, 2000) called Intolerant Personality Disorder (Guindon, Green, & Hanna, 2003). Guindon and her colleagues suggest that intolerance is the basis of racism, sexism, homophobia, and virtually any other sort of prejudice. This is an intriguing suggestion, and the authors make a compelling case for the creation of a new DSM personality disorder. More research on this idea, as well as more debate is needed on what such an addition would mean (e.g., would stereotyping be considered a pathology?) in clinical practice and daily life.

Why have most prejudice researchers not given much attention to the idea that there may be a prejudiced personality? One reason this is the case is that personality approaches underestimate the powerful impact of situational forces on behavior and attitudes (Brown, 1995; Ross & Nisbett, 1991). Another problem with the personality approach is that it cannot account for why different groups become targets of prejudice, or why different cultures show differing levels of prejudice toward outgroups (Stroebe & Insko, 1989). Finally, such approaches cannot account for what Brown (1995) calls the "historical specificity of prejudice" (p. 34). That is, why is it the case that prejudice toward certain outgroups has rather suddenly erupted in society, only to recede again (i.e., Nazi anti-Semitism, American anti-Japanese attitudes in World War II)? If some people had prejudiced personalities, we would expect a constant level of prejudice from them throughout their lives, as well as toward all outgroups (as in the authoritarian and right-wing-authoritarian individuals).

While these criticisms have rightly been leveled at the prejudiced-personality approach, it is still very worthwhile to examine individual differences in the tendency to stereotype others and develop prejudiced attitudes. As we have seen, there is much evidence to support the idea that people differ on several important trait-like dimensions, which leads them to be more or less likely to think of others in a heuristic way, and to be more prejudiced toward others (Heaven & St. Quintin, 2003). As an example, one recent paper by Graziano, Bruce, Sheese, and Tobin (2004) found strong correlations between the trait dimension of agreeableness and prejudice. People high in agreeableness are motivated to maintain positive relationships with others. Graziano and colleagues reported data from several studies that showed that people low in agreeableness were more prejudiced than those high in agreeableness. These results are supported by data from Carter, Hall, Carney, and Rosip (2004) that shows a strong correlation between low agreeableness and a greater acceptance of stereotyping. Graziano et al. speculate that this may be explained by low-agreeable persons having a bias toward negativity and not being willing to suppress it. Much more research is needed to better understand the influence of trait dimensions on expressions of prejudice.

Research on the need for cognition, need for structure, and need for cognitive closure has demonstrated solid evidence for the validity and reliability of these constructs and has shown that when people who are low in the need for cognition, or high in the need for structure or cognitive closure, they are more susceptible to making stereotyped social judgments. Similarly, people who are motivated to keep their ingroup superior and dominant over other groups are more likely to endorse stereotypes and be prejudiced toward those outgroups. Altemeyer's work on right-wing authoritarianism suggests that those who are submissive, aggressive, conventional, fearful, and self-righteous tend to be more likely to be prejudiced toward anyone who is different from them.

Finally, research on religious attitudes shows that even the most religious individuals (intrinsic religious orientation) can be prejudiced toward others, especially groups that are unacceptable to the church (e.g., homosexuals), and that only those who have a quest religious orientation (and those who are nonreligious) are truly nonprejudiced. It is important that further research in this area be continued, in order to help us get a better understanding of the stable trait-like characteristics that make people more or less likely to be prejudiced toward and to stereotype others.

GLOSSARY

authoritarianism   Rigid personality characterized by categorical thinking, submissiveness to authority, and adherence to middle-class values. These individuals tend to dislike anyone who is different from themselves and thus tend to have stereotypes and prejudice toward many groups.

committed religiosity   Religious viewpoint that allows an individual to hold a wide range of categories about which one can evaluate the world, and one's ideas about the world and others tends to be more complex and open-minded.

consensual religiosity   Religious viewpoint in which the individual tends to interpret religion more literally and concretely, make more generalizations about religion, and be unreceptive to different ideas and opinions.

extrinsic religious orientation   Describes an individual who uses religion for their own purposes, attends church infrequently, and tends to be more prejudiced toward others.

intrinsic religious orientation   Describes a person who has internalized their religious values and lives according to these beliefs, attends church regularly, and tends to be more egalitarian.

need for cognition   An individual-difference variable that describes the dispositional motivation of an individual to think about the world; the higher this motivation is, the more the individual enjoys thinking about, seeking, and pondering problems and information about the world.

need for cognitive closure   An individual-difference variable in which persons who have this motivation tend to need an answer—any answer—on a given topic, so that they may arrive at a conclusion (and not have confusion or ambiguity about the topic), even if the conclusion is incorrect.

need for structure   An individual-difference variable in which those who have a high degree of this motivation tend to desire clear, certain, or unambiguous knowledge (structure) about a topic.

right-wing authoritarianism   Personality style in which the individual tends to be politically conservative, more punitive toward criminals, more likely to endorse orthodox religious views, and very prejudiced toward outgroups.

social-dominance orientation   An attitude toward intergroup relations in which the individual believes that groups are different, that they are organized hierarchically in society, and that some groups naturally are higher in status than others. These individuals strongly prefer and seek to maintain the inequality among groups.

DISCUSSION QUESTIONS

1. In your opinion, what is it about some people that makes them seem to hold prejudices against virtually all outgroups? Is there something about their personality (e.g., the authoritarian personality) that predisposes them to think about others in terms of stereotypes?

2. Do you know any people who could be classified as a right-wing authoritarian? Can you name any famous people who might fit this profile? Do you think that the number of RWAs tends to fluctuate with trends in the political and/or economic landscape? Why?

3. Why do you think that having an intrinsic religious orientation leads one to be tolerant toward some groups and prejudiced against other groups (e.g., homosexuals)?

4. Do you think that it would be possible to reduce prejudice through parents, teachers, and society encouraging children to develop an appreciation for the ambiguity, and uncertainties of life, thus developing a high need for cognition, low need for structure, and low need for cognitive closure?

5. What are some legitimizing myths you can think of that provide the rationale for the different status (power, legal, economic, wealth, social, etc.) of groups in the United States and in the world?

SUGGESTED KEY READINGS

Altemeyer, B. (1988). *Enemies of freedom: Understanding right-wing authoritarianism.* San Francisco: Jossey-Bass.

Batson, C. D., & Burris, C. T. (1994). Personal religion: Depressant or stimulant of prejudice and discrimination? In M. P. Zanna & J. M. Olson (Eds.), *The psychology of prejudice* (Vol. 7, pp. 149–169). Hillsdale, NJ: Erlbaum.

Kruglanski, A. W., & Webster, D. M. (1996). Motivated closing of the mind: "Seizing" and "freezing." *Psychological Review, 103*(2), 263–283.

Sidanius, J. (1993). The psychology of group conflict and the dynamics of oppression: A social dominance perspective. In W. McGuire & S. Iyengar (Eds.), *Current approaches to political psychology* (pp. 183–219). Durham, NC: Duke University Press.

INTERNET RESOURCES: RESEARCHERS, REFERENCES, AND ORGANIZATIONS DEVOTED TO THE STUDY OF PREJUDICE

www.psych.ku.edu/faculty/dbatson/default. htm Home page of Dr. C. D. Batson, a prominent social psychologist and researcher of the quest orientation to religion.

www.psych.ucla.edu/Faculty/Sidanius Home page of Dr. Jim Sidanius, social-dominance orientation researcher.

www.understandingprejudice.org/readroom/ articles/affirm.htm Scientific article on the ten myths about affirmative action.

CHAPTER FIVE

OLD-FASHIONED VERSUS MODERN PREJUDICE

WHERE HAVE ALL THE BIGOTS GONE?

In the past, Caucasians were comfortable with openly expressing prejudiced racial attitudes, because the culture in American society was such that overt hostility toward other races, discrimination, and segregation of other races from the Caucasian-dominated culture were the norm. Thus, it was not until the late 1920s that serious attention was paid to the problem of prejudice and stereotyping. Though it took American society over 30 more years to acknowledge its deep racial prejudice, researchers in the 1920s and 1930s were beginning to tackle questions such as: What is a stereotype and how does it form (Lippmann, 1922)? What is the content of racial stereotypes (Katz & Braly, 1933)? How strongly do prejudiced attitudes correspond to behavior in interracial interactions (LaPiere, 1934)? Implicit in these questions (and the answers the researchers were obtaining in their data) were the beginnings of a shift in the way prejudiced people were viewed. As J. M. Jones (1997) describes it, "There was a tendency to consider individuals who answered a question in a certain way not only as prejudiced, but as morally inferior human beings" (p. 42). As a result in this shift in perspective, prejudice and stereotyping were no longer viewed as a normal part of being human, but rather were beginning to be seen as problems to be understood and reduced or eliminated whenever possible. That is, prejudice was no longer a natural thing; it signified that the individual *chose* that negative view of certain others, either through a moral defect, mental laziness (as first discussed by Lippmann and later developed by social cognition researchers), or both.

Therefore, stereotypes were coming to be understood as attitudes (negative evaluations, rather than pictures in our head) that some people endorse but others do not (Jones, 1997). Here was a turning point in understanding prejudice and stereotyping. If the basis of prejudice, stereotyping, and discrimination was a negative attitude (and not something inherent about being human), then if we can understand the nature of those attitudes we can understand the nature of stereotyping and prejudice and then be in a much better position from which to address ways to reduce or eliminate stereotyping and prejudice. Why were some people prejudiced and others not prejudiced? Is it even possible to not have prejudice? These questions (and many more) occupied the thoughts of researchers in the early part of the 20th century and will likely continue to be the focus of research for years to come, as the answers remain elusive despite tremendous advances in our knowledge over the decades.

In the sections that follow we examine how stereotyping and prejudice have changed form over the decades. We will also examine whether stereotyping and prejudice seem to be more or less prevalent today than they were in the past. The second half of the chapter will focus in some detail on the methods that social scientists have used to further the understanding of stereotyping and prejudice. We will examine the major avenues of measuring stereotypes and highlight the strengths and weaknesses of each approach. The chapter concludes with a discussion of the current state of the art in stereotype and prejudice measurement and fruitful directions for future research on measures of prejudice and stereotyping.

From Katz and Braly to Civil Rights, and Beyond

With Katz and Braly's (1933) landmark study, researchers obtained their first view of the content of racial stereotypes that Caucasians held about African Americans. Recall from our discussion of this classic study (in Chapter 1) that White college students were asked to indicate whether various traits (84 in all) described Caucasians or African Americans. Those early data suggested that Caucasians held very negative views of African Americans and very positive views of Caucasians. For instance, African Americans were viewed

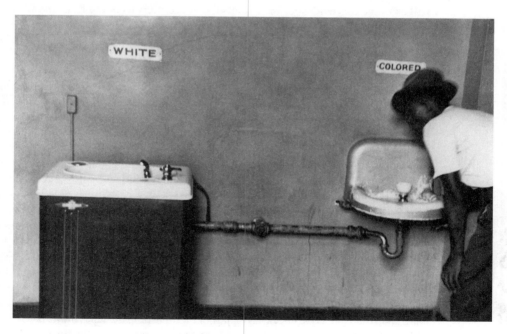

"Old-fashioned" racism is the type of openly hostile prejudice that characterized much of the seg-regated southern United States prior to the landmark Supreme Court rulings of the 1950s and the civil-rights movements of the 1950s and 1960s. Such prejudice led to state-sanctioned segregation of Blacks and Whites in all public places, based on the belief that Blacks were inferior and Whites deserved the privileged status in society, as evidenced here in a 1950 photo of segregated drinking fountains in North Carolina.

by the White respondents as "superstitious," "lazy," and "ignorant," whereas they viewed Caucasians as "industrious," "intelligent," and "ambitious." Few respondents were willing to attribute positive qualities to African Americans or negative qualities to Caucasians. However, over the years, data have been gathered using the adjective-checklist procedure to attempt to gauge whether and how Caucasians' stereotypes of African Americans are changing. These data indicate that these attitudes have become less negative and increasingly positive (Dovidio & Gaertner, 1991).

Certainly the changes in the social, legal, and political climate of the United States seem to correspond to the changes in Caucasians' self-reported stereotypes of African Americans. The changes in society, mentioned earlier, have been quite dramatic in the area of race relations. Segregation and discrimination were outlawed. Laws (Civil Rights Act of 1964) and social programs (e.g., affirmative action) were created to advance the economic status and job prospects for groups that had traditionally experienced discrimination. Movies (e.g., *Amistad*), television (e.g., *Roots*), and music were beginning to deal with stereotyping and prejudice, and other race relations issues. African Americans were being accepted into White American society on many levels. While most researchers will agree that White America has indeed reduced its negative views of and prejudice toward African Americans, there is compelling evidence to suggest that the extent of this attitude and prejudice change is not as dramatic as was once believed (Fiske, 1998; Mellor, 2003). Next, we will examine this evidence. We will also review criticisms of the Katz and Braly study and studies like it that rely on the adjective-checklist methodology for assessing stereotypes.

Are Low-Prejudice People *Really* Low-Prejudice?

method used affects stereotype detection

Some have questioned the adjective-checklist procedure of Katz and Braly as a misleading measure of the stereotyping landscape. For example, Niemann, Jennings, Rozelle, Baxter, and Sullivan (1994) point to several problems with the Katz and Braly procedure, including (1) the subjects were predominantly White, upper-class males, which limits the generalizability of the data, and (2) the method requires the subject to rely on a rather controlled cognitive process in which the individual is actively thinking about whether a particular trait "fits" into their schema for the group in question (Devine, 1989; Fiske & Neuberg, 1990). This is a limitation because much research suggests that stereotypes are activated automatically upon encountering the stimulus (group label, or other indicator of the group), and can hold a wealth of affective and other cognitive information that drives the stereotype that cannot be represented on the adjective checklist (Fiske & Neuberg, 1990; Stangor & Lange, 1994; for an exception, see Lepore & Brown, 1997). Thus, as Niemann et al. (1994) suggest, "Results using the checklist method may provide stereotypes that are more a function of the words presented on a list than of the schematic content of the respondents' stereotypes" (p. 380). Consider the following experiment. Ehrlich and Rinehart (1965) administered the Katz and Braly adjective checklist to half of their participants, and they asked the other half to simply list all of the words, traits, and characteristics they needed to adequately describe the group in question. The results showed that the words that participants used in the open-ended method were different from the words the participants checked in the Katz and Braly procedure. Subsequent research by Allen and colleagues (Allen, 1971; Potkay & Allen, 1988) has expanded this open-ended procedure to include values assigned to the words generated, and these values are analyzed to indicate the degree of favorability and unfavorability of the characterizations of the target. This technique, known as the adjective-generation technique, is a good way to ascertain the content of stereotypes at a given point in time (Allen, 1996). The differences in words generated from time A to time B can indicate how stereotypes of the target group may be changing.

Other researchers suggest that the Katz and Braly procedure does not, as commonly believed, measure knowledge about stereotypes, but rather personal beliefs about the truth of the stereotype. This position is exemplified by Devine and Elliot (1995), in their analysis of the decline in racial stereotypes. Devine and Elliot suggest that it is important to distinguish between personal beliefs about stereotypes, and knowledge about the stereotypes, and their analysis of the participant responses to the adjective-checklist data accumulated over the years (e.g., Gilbert, 1951; Karlins et al., 1969) suggests that some participants construed the task as an assessment of their stereotype knowledge and others thought it was a measure of their personal beliefs about African Americans and Caucasians. Devine and Elliot compared these earlier data to more contemporary adjective-checklist data on racial attitudes (Dovidio & Gaertner, 1986). Their analysis supports the notion that the adjective checklist, as it has been administered over the decades, is actually measuring personal beliefs (or willingness to publicly state those beliefs) about the truth of racial stereotypes. Thus, as we have seen earlier in this chapter, it is not surprising, given the change in U.S. society on racial issues over the last 50 years, that the personal beliefs of Caucasians, or Caucasians' willingness to publicly state such beliefs, about stereotypes of African Americans indicate a strongly diminished support of those stereotypes.

So, this analysis would suggest that some progress *has* been made in reducing the negative personal beliefs that Caucasians have about African Americans. But what about the negative stereotypes of African Americans that used to be common in the United States? Have they diminished? According to Devine and Elliot (1995), the answer is, unfortunately, no. Their data suggest that when Caucasians are asked about their knowledge (not personal beliefs) about the stereotypes of African Americans, their responses indicate a high degree of negativity in the traits selected as stereotypical of African Americans. These contemporary ratings are virtually identical to the negative adjective rating data collected since 1933. This suggests that although personal beliefs in negative stereotypes of African Americans appear to have decreased, knowledge of the cultural stereotype of African Americans has remained the same. In other words, Caucasians rather unanimously know about the negative things (and few positive things) that are stereotypically associated with African Americans via their early learning from parents or through other exposure to such information in society. Yet what has seemed to change is their willingness to personally believe, and also overtly express, such negative racial attitudes.

In sum, the available evidence suggests that stereotypes themselves have not changed much over the last century, but the form in which they are expressed has changed. Before the social, legal, and political climate of the United States changed dramatically with the civil-rights movement of the late 1950s and 1960s, stereotypes and prejudice were fairly easy to assess. Researchers could use simple self-report measures (e.g., Katz and Braly's [1933] adjective-checklist procedure) to understand the content and extent of negative affect directed at other groups. However, the Civil Rights movement (and legislation) changed the social landscape with regard to stereotyping and prejudice. Stereotyping and prejudice went underground, so to speak. The negative affect and stereotypes remained, but in a subdued, subtle form.

This new form of prejudice was not adequately conceptualized by models of stereo-typing and prejudice that were applied prior to the 1960s. Researchers needed different theories that could better address these contemporary expressions of prejudice. The theo-ries had to account for the ambivalence that seemed to characterize the attitudes of Cauca-sians toward African Americans in the post-Civil Rights environment. On the one hand, most Caucasians seemed to have an underlying association between African Americans and undesirable characteristics and values, and on the other hand, most Caucasians overtly embraced egalitarianism, the values of equality for all, and nondiscrimination. Another way to think about this fundamental ambivalence that characterizes current expressions of racism and prejudice is the "trouble with equality." The hard-won fight for the civil rights of African Americans in society was an easy rallying point for most justice-minded Americans, because the overt discrimination, prejudice, and segregation of one group of people in a democratic society violated all standards of morality, ethics, and justice. Thus, that fight was for the *freedom* of African Americans. However, the post-civil rights era can be thought of as the search for the *equality* of African Americans. Next we discuss three major theories of contemporary forms of prejudice and racism that attempt to explain the origins of the ambivalence that Caucasians experience in their attitudes toward African Americans. We will examine the basic tenets of each, as well as the empirical support for each theory. Following this, we move into a discussion of ways to measure stereotyping and prejudice. As the endorsement of negative stereotypes and expressions of prejudice have changed over the decades, researchers have had to modify the methods and instru-ments they use to assess prejudice.

MODERN RACISM

According to McConahay (1983, 1986), the theory of **Modern Racism** asserts that some Whites are ambivalent toward African Americans, conflicted between their anti-Black feelings and their beliefs that racism and discrimination are wrong. For modern racists, the issue is not whether African Americans should be equal, but how that equality should be implemented in policy, law, and employment. As with the symbolic-racism perspective (see the next section), the theory of modern racism suggests that modern racists have a problem with giving what they deem special treatment (e.g. hiring preferences, as in af-firmative action) to African Americans, because they believe it violates the work ethic that says that advancement in life should be based on achievements and hard work rather than on "unfair" shortcuts. Modern racists believe that (1) discrimination is a thing of the past; (2) African Americans are too pushy, trying to get into places where they are not welcome; (3) the demands of African Americans are unfair; and (4) African Americans' gains (bol-stered by social programs that provide economic, housing, and other opportunities) are undeserved and unfair (McConahay, 1986).

Modern racists do not consider themselves to be racists, for two reasons. First, they regard racism as associated with pre-civil-rights, "old-fashioned" racism, in which open hatred and feelings of superiority are shown by the racist (McConahay, 1986). Second, their subtle negative feelings toward African Americans are disguised, in order to prevent the dissonance associated with acknowledging the hypocrisy of prejudice and egalitar-ian values, as negative attitudes toward *anyone* who violates what they believe are traditional American values (McConahay & Hough, 1976). The theory of modern racism has good empirical support (e.g. McConahay, Hardee, & Batts, 1981), and the self-report scale (called the "Modern Racism Scale") that McConahay (1986) has devised to measure this subtle prejudice has been shown to have fair reliability and validity (McConahay, 1986). For over a decade, the Modern Racism Scale (MRS) was one of the most widely used measures of contemporary prejudice toward African Americans. However, recall from our discussion in Chapter 3 that there are a number of criticisms of the MRS that led researchers to search for better ways to measure racial attitudes (Biernat & Crandall, 1999). The strongest criticism is that modern racism is not conceptually distinct from old-fashioned racism (Fazio, et al., 1995). We will discuss these criticisms in more depth, and the new measures a little later in the chapter. Next, we turn to the theory of symbolic racism.

SYMBOLIC RACISM

Kinder and Sears (1981; Sears, 1988) have proposed a different approach to understanding the origins of the prejudice of contemporary White Americans toward African Americans. They suggest that old-fashioned overt racism has been replaced with what they term **symbolic racism.** This is defined as a "blend of anti-Black affect and traditional American moral values embodied in the Protestant Ethic" (Kinder & Sears, 1981, p. 416). According to this view, Whites who would be classified as symbolic racists tend to resist changing the racial status quo (i.e., White dominance) in all areas of life—economically, socially, and politically. The use of the term *symbolic* is used to describe this resistance that originates not out of self-interest but out of the general belief that Blacks violate traditional American values (such as self-reliance, individualism, hard work, obedience).

The symbolic racist can also deny holding racist attitudes (and may, in fact, believe that they are not prejudiced), because, in their view, a racist is one who exhibits "old-fashioned" racist beliefs of the inherent superiority of one race over another, as well as negative affect toward a group based on such beliefs. The negative affect and negative attitudes that symbolic racists may hold toward another group are converted into derision for groups that do not seem to value traditional American values. According to this position, then, symbolic racists would have no problem with other groups if those other groups were self-reliant, hard working, and individualistic. However, because their view of how closely the other group is adhering to those values is tainted by their prejudice, it is unlikely that that group would ever be perceived as adhering to those ideals. In this way, symbolic racists are able to keep their negative affect and stereotypes of the outgroup, and even express these sentiments overtly, while still claiming that the source of such negative evaluations is an objective difference between Whites and the outgroup in their support of traditional American values.

Critics of the symbolic racism concept argue that (1) it is an ill-defined concept (Bobo, 1988; Eagly & Chaiken, 1993) and (2) other explanations, such as realistic group conflict (Bobo, 1983) and social-dominance theory (Sidanius, Devereux, & Pratto, 1992), can just as easily explain Whites' opposition to social programs that reduce the inequity between Blacks and Whites. Perhaps the most damaging attack on symbolic racism comes from numerous studies that suggest that symbolic racism does not appear to be a distinct concept from more traditional (old-fashioned) forms of racism (Lea, Bokhorst, & Colenso,

1995; Raden, 1994; Schuman, Steeh, Bobo, & Krysan, 1997; Sniderman & Tetlock, 1986; Weigel & Howes, 1985). However, the debate is not settled on the concept of symbolic racism. Indeed, Eagly and Chaiken (1993) and Wood (1994) have noted that one of the redeeming qualities of the theory is that it rightly highlights the importance of the link between values and racial attitudes. Research by Katz and Hass (1988) indicates that value conflict in Whites leads to ambivalent attitudes toward Blacks, and it would be interesting to explore what implications this ambivalence may have for the strength with which prejudicial feelings and beliefs are held (Thompson, Zanna, & Griffin, 1995).

A recent paper by Sears and Henry (2003) presented results from several studies designed to further refine the theoretical and conceptual underpinnings of symbolic racism. Their research showed that symbolic racism is grounded in what they call "Black individualism," which is a concern that Blacks do not live up to conservative values (such as those embodied in the Protestant work ethic), and specifically the value of individualism. These data represent the first empirical test of the basis for symbolic racism and make the compelling argument that symbolic racism is indeed distinct from the similar aversive and modern-racism constructs.

AVERSIVE RACISM

According to Gaertner and Dovidio (1986), the racist history of American culture combined with the cognitive tendency to categorize information (Fiske & Taylor, 1991) results in subtle yet commonplace racist beliefs and feelings in White Americans. **Aversive racism** is a term Gaertner and Dovidio use to describe White Americans who possess these racist beliefs and feelings alongside strong egalitarian values. Thus, aversive racism reflects an ambivalence in Caucasians between their learned negative attitudes (from early childhood to adulthood) toward African Americans, and their commitment to egalitarian values and beliefs. Because egalitarian ideals and beliefs are central to the aversive racist's self, they may deny conscious awareness of their negative attitudes and prejudice toward African Americans. Indeed, they will take great pains to not do or say anything that appears to be prejudiced, because they truly believe that they are not prejudiced. However, their underlying biases may be expressed as pro-White behaviors, such as ingroup favoritism, rather than old-fashioned prejudicial expressions of outgroup derogation. When they are in a situation in which it is unclear whether there are social prohibitions against expressing negative racial beliefs, the aversive racist's negative feelings about African Americans may be expressed in subtle, easily justifiable (Crandall & Eshleman, 2003) ways. However, when the social norms are clearly antiprejudice, then the aversive racist will not behave in a racist fashion and may even appear very strongly egalitarian (Aberson & Ettlin, 2004; Katz, 1981; McConahay, Hardee, & Batts, 1981). In contrast to "old-fashioned" racism, in which the racist openly displays hatred for, and beliefs of superiority to, African Americans, aversive racists experience more subtle feelings of "discomfort, uneasiness, disgust, and sometimes fear" in the presence of African Americans (Gaertner and Dovidio, 1986, pp. 62–63).

In a recent paper, Dovidio and Gaertner (2000) analyzed data from 1988 to 1989 on hiring decisions of White participants regarding Black and White job applicants, and they compared those data with similar data gathered 10 years later, in 1998–1999. The theory of aversive racism suggests that self-reported expressions of prejudice should decline over time but that subtle, underlying prejudice should remain constant. Consistent with this theory, results of the analysis found that self-reported prejudice levels of the 1998–1999 participants were lower than their counterparts a decade earlier. When presented with a clearly superior Black applicant, participants did not show any underlying prejudice against the applicant or preference for the White applicant, and they tended to hire the well-qualified minority. When the qualifications of the Black applicant were rather ambiguous, however, their subtle, underlying hostility toward Black applicants emerged, and the White participants tended to prefer to hire the White candidate. A recent meta-analysis of helping studies showed the presence of aversive racism. Caucasians showed no discrimination in helping Caucasians versus Blacks, but when they could rationalize their decision to not help with reasons not related to race (e.g., if helping would entail more time, risk, or effort), Caucasians gave less help to Blacks than to Whites (Saucier, Miller, Doucet, in press).

SUMMARY OF CONTEMPORARY THEORIES OF PREJUDICE

Symbolic and modern racism differ from aversive racism in that they are found primarily in political conservatives, whereas aversive racism is associated with liberals (Dovidio & Gaertner, 1996), but these theories are all very similar. For example, Ward (1985) found support for the common argument made by modern, aversive, and symbolic racism theories that negative racial attitudes are acquired early in childhood (primarily through parental attitudes), and that this forms the basis for a stable bedrock of anti-Black affect beneath later egalitarian beliefs learned through school, peers, and society. The theories of modern, symbolic, and aversive racism also suggest that because Caucasians' negative affect toward Blacks manifests itself subtly in terms of opposition to social programs and voting behavior that are aimed at bringing more Blacks into society, they actually may have little awareness of their negative feelings toward Blacks (Dovidio et al., 1996).

Another important feature is the common thread of racial ambivalence that runs throughout these contemporary theories of prejudice. By virtue of growing up in America, Caucasians learn, via American society, culture, parents, and peers, what stereotypes are associated with various groups, and feelings of negative affect get attached to these groups in the Caucasian's memory. However, society also teaches equality, freedom, nondiscrimination, and values that embody the Protestant work ethic—hard work, independence, and self-sufficiency—which Caucasians also tended to embrace. The clashes with regard to perceptions of how various racial outgroups violate these cherished values lead Whites to feel ambivalent, or conflicted, toward Blacks. The stronger their ambivalence, the more inconsistent their behavior will be toward Blacks. The determining factor in whether negative attitudes toward Blacks may be displayed tends to hinge on the context. Relatively minor aspects of the situation can influence the Caucasian's racial attitude and behavior to be either positive or negative toward Blacks (Crocker, Major, & Steele, 1998; Fiske, 1998).

The similar motivational and behavioral manifestations of prejudice in modern, aversive, and symbolic racists suggests support for the underlying theme of racial ambivalence that characterizes many Caucasian's racial attitudes in contemporary American society. As we have seen, however, there is much disagreement over whether some of these theories (e.g., those of modern and symbolic racism) are really identifying distinct forms of racism or whether they are simply old wine in new bottles, (a relabeling of old-fashioned racism). Clearly, the expression of racial prejudice and stereotyping has changed over the decades, but has the form of prejudice changed? That is, are the contemporary theories of prejudice describing a conceptually distinct type of prejudice? We will take up this question at the end of the chapter. First, let us consider the ways that researchers attempt to assess prejudice and stereotyping.

MEASURES OF STEREOTYPING AND PREJUDICE

One of the biggest challenges for researchers studying prejudice and stereotyping involves the question of how best to accurately measure prejudiced attitudes. This is a formidable obstacle for researchers. Consider the questions that must be addressed in order to devise a sound measure of prejudice. What is the nature of the motivation that underlies the expression of prejudice and stereotypes about others (Allport, 1954)? Is the prejudice more likely to be expressed under certain affective or cognitive conditions (Mackie & Hamilton, 1993)? Are some personality types more likely to be prejudiced (e.g., Adorno et al., 1950)? Once the nature of the prejudice, and its relation to personality and situational influences (e.g., cognitive load) have been identified, the researcher can then attempt to create a self-report measure to measure the participant's level of that particular type of prejudice. Below, we will examine the various ways researchers have attempted to measure prejudice and stereotyping. We will address the criticisms and supportive evidence for each approach. Last, we will examine the current state of the science of measuring prejudice and discuss the future trends in measuring prejudice.

The Self-Report Questionnaire

There is an old saying among social scientists, "If you want to know how someone feels about something, ask them." This practical approach to ascertaining the attitude of an individual has guided psychologists, sociologists, opinion pollsters, and other researchers for over 60 years. Sometimes, as in opinion polls or interviews, the respondent is asked about their attitudes on a variety of topics, then the questioner records the reply on the questionnaire or in the computer database. However, this is not the most popular method of obtaining attitude data, because of its labor-intensive nature. Interview methods such as this require an interviewer, and attitudes of individuals can only be ascertained one person at a time (i.e., one interviewer and one respondent). A much more efficient way to find out how people feel about something is to have them complete a questionnaire themselves, (or a self-report). In this method, a researcher can administer hundreds of questionnaires simultaneously to hundreds of participants. The self-report quickly became, and remains, the most popular method of attitude assessment in psychology today. The big advantage of self-report questionnaires is their efficiency: one can obtain a large volume of attitude data from lots of people very quickly. For example, the researcher could mail out hundreds (or thousands) of questionnaires to potential respondents or deliver an equal number of questionnaires to various classes on a college campus, obtaining the data from student volunteers. Sometimes, the researcher does not even need to be present: the potential subject could stop by the Psychology Department to pick up a questionnaire packet (complete with informed consent, the questionnaire(s), and a debriefing sheet), and return it to the department later.

However, self-report measures have some serious drawbacks. First, the responses to the questions are usually restricted to the response alternatives provided on the questionnaire (unless it is a free-response, open-answer format in which the individual can write anything they want in response to the question). Thus, the researcher gets a general, if somewhat imprecise, measure of the respondent's attitudes. Second, and perhaps more important, people do not always provide their true attitudes on self-report measures. This may be due to a couple of reasons. The sensitive nature of an issue may prevent people from being conscious or aware of their true, underlying attitudes toward it. A good example of this is racial attitudes. In the past, stereotyping others and holding prejudiced attitudes were the norm, and there were no legal or societal prohibitions against overtly displaying such negative attitudes. Over time, this has changed dramatically, and it is no longer tolerated in mainstream society. However, old habits die hard, and research on modern racism, aversive racism, and symbolic racism suggests that many people's negative feelings toward other groups may not have been eliminated, they are just hidden more carefully.

Even some people who believe they are low in prejudice still harbor underlying negative racial attitudes. Consider the following quote by Pettigrew (1987, as cited by Devine et al., 1991). "Many Southerners have confessed to me, for instance, that even though in their minds they no longer feel prejudice toward Blacks, they still feel squeamish when they shake hands with a Black. These feelings are left over from what they learned in their families as children" (p. 817). Thus, the anxiety and cognitive dissonance that are aroused with awareness of the underlying attitude may motivate such individuals to shut off those feelings from awareness, to deny their existence, in order to maintain a desired image of their self as a person with no prejudice. Other individuals may be aware of their negative feelings toward other groups, but they do not express these attitudes, because of the negative social (and sometimes legal) consequences for such behavior. Thus, interpersonally and on questionnaires they express little or no prejudice while they may indeed harbor negative attitudes toward certain groups. This tendency to present oneself in a positive light is termed **social desirability,** and it presents a big obstacle for the attitude researcher. In these situations, the person who is providing their attitudes is concerned with presenting responses that are socially acceptable and hiding any attitudes that are socially unacceptable. Because the researcher only wants to get the honest, accurate responses from the individual, they must take extra measures to enhance the likelihood that the respondent will provide their true attitudes, even if they are unpopular.

There are several ways that the researcher can decrease the influence of social desirability in the subject's responses. For a majority of experiments investigating attitudes, the researcher can tell the subjects that their responses will be completely anonymous. If it cannot be anonymous, the next best thing is to make the responses confidential (i.e., only the principal investigator or other responsible professionals will have access to the data, and for research purposes only). This helps alleviate any anxiety that subjects may have about their responses being attributable to them. Another instruction that researchers will give to subjects when asking for their attitudes on various issues is that it is important for subjects to provide their honest responses, not how they think they should respond (i.e., not the socially desirable response). Honesty in responding to the questionnaire or the researcher's questions is emphasized as paramount, in the hope of appealing to the participant's desire to be a good subject by correctly following directions and helping the researcher.

Finally, virtually all respondents to attitude measures are tempted to try to figure out the purpose of the attitude questionnaire (what it is measuring; for example, whether the person is prejudiced against homosexuals). Aspects of a questionnaire and testing situation that encourage subjects to make their own hypotheses about what answers are expected or what is being measured are called **demand characteristics,** and these represent an unwanted bias in the research. If the subject is responding to his or her own ideas of what the questionnaire is measuring, or what the researcher wants the subject to say, then they are not providing their truthful opinions on the items. In these instances, the researcher may use "filler items" in the questionnaire, in order to make the purpose of the questionnaire less obvious to the respondent (to "throw them off the scent"). Filler items are those items that have no relation to the hypotheses under investigation, and are included in the questionnaire as a way to distract the respondent from the hypotheses of the researcher. For example, one may only be interested in responses to 7 items dealing with attitudes toward homosexuality, and there may be 43 other items that examine other issues (such as attitudes toward recycling). This often has the intended effect of making it difficult for the respondent to formulate hypotheses of what is under investigation in the questionnaire, and without the bias of that potential demand characteristic, participants should be more likely to provide their honest responses to the items. The problem with these techniques is that they are not a guarantee that there will be no social desirability or other biases in the participant's responses. In fact, research suggests that these techniques designed to enhance the validity of self-report measures are only partially effective (Schuman & Kalton, 1985). Thus, researchers have developed other methods of collecting attitude information.

The Bogus Pipeline

The **bogus-pipeline technique**, devised by Jones and Sigall (1971), was in part inspired by a paper by Karlins et al. (1969). Karlins et al. reported that Caucasians in the United States reported more favorable attitudes toward African Americans over the course of many decades and that they showed little prejudice or stereotyping of African Americans, according to their responses on the questionnaires in the study. Jones and Sigall believed that such a sudden shift in how Whites viewed Blacks was unlikely, especially given the turbulent interracial climate of the 1960s. Jones and Sigall suspected that attitudes had not changed dramatically, but people's willingness to express overt negative racial attitudes was likely diminishing. Thus, they reasoned, some of the respondents in the Karlins et al. study were more likely providing the socially appropriate attitudes about other races and keeping their prejudices to themselves. Sigall and Page (1971) designed a study to examine this, using an apparatus that subjects are led to believe can assess one's true attitudes. In other words, subjects are told that the experimenter will have a direct reading, or a pipeline, to their attitudes on the issues under examination. The apparatus looks much like a polygraph machine, with dials, lights, buzzers, and electromyographic (EMG) electrodes that are attached to the person's arms.

The procedure for the bogus-pipeline study (as it was carried out by Sigall and Page [1971]) is as follows. One half of the participants are assigned to a rating condition in which they indicate their attitudes on the issue in question (e.g., racial attitudes) aloud when the experimenter asks the question. The other half are assigned to an EMG condition, in which they are asked to provide their ratings by turning a wheel, attached to a computer, that moves a dial to the left or right, corresponding to more negative or more positive attitudes (or disagreement versus agreement) to the question being asked of the participant. Participants in the rating condition were asked to turn the wheel device to move the pointer to the number (from a range of –3 to +3) that corresponds to their attitude on the item. For half of the rating-condition participants, the experimenter read a list of 22 traits (e.g., "superstitious," "ambitious"), and asked the participant to indicate on the wheel device how representative each trait was of "Americans." The other half of the participants were asked to indicate how representative each trait was of "Blacks." Typically, these ratings indicated that participants (in the Sigall and Page study, all participants were White, and were all males) rated both Americans and Blacks positively.

In the EMG condition, participants were told of the EMG machine, and that the intent of the study was to further validate the measures it provides. Participants in this condition were first given a five-item inventory asking their attitudes on relatively neutral topics such as music, sports, or movies. The experimenter then took the questionnaire and led the participant into the room that had the EMG machine at the wall opposite the door. The experimenter casually placed the completed questionnaire on a table by the door as they entered, and he left the door slightly ajar. The subject was seated at the machine with their back to the wall. As the experimenter explained the EMG machine and procedure to the subject, another researcher silently retrieved the questionnaire, copied the answers, and returned the questionnaire to the table.

After the experimenter had explained the procedure, electrodes were attached to the participant's forearm. The experimenter explained that the machine was able to assess the participant's "implicit muscle movements," and that these would tell the experimenter the strength with which the participant was about to turn the wheel (i.e., the strength and direction of the participant's attitude on the item in question). In order to convince the participant of the accuracy of the machine, the experimenter asked the participant to hold the wheel and concentrate on the answers they gave to the five-item inventory they completed earlier. The experimenter read the question and turned a switch on the machine. The machine buzzed for a few seconds and then was silent as the needle, controlled by the researcher's associate in the other room, who had copied the participant's answers, moved to a number. On the fourth item, the experimenter asked the subject to try to "trick" the machine by moving the wheel in the opposite direction of his attitude, and to think about the opposite attitude as well. The machine was not "fooled," and it gave the attitude number that the subject had indicated earlier on the questionnaire. After the fifth item, the experimenter retrieved the subject's questionnaire from the table, compared it with the machine's readings, and showed the subject that the machine was extremely accurate. The participant is then read the 22 traits and asked to provide his honest attitudes about each of them. As with the rating condition, half of the participants in the EMG condition are asked about the typicality of the traits for "Americans," and the other half are asked how well these traits describe "Blacks."

When the results from the rating and EMG conditions were compared, some very striking differences emerged. Generally speaking, EMG participants were more confident than their rating condition peers that "Americans" had more positive traits, and less negative traits. For example, ratings participants thought that the trait "honest" was not very typical (−.27) of Americans, but EMG participants thought it was more typical (+.60). Ratings subjects thought that Americans were not lazy (−.40), and EMG participants were even more adamant that this was the case (−.80).

The results for perceptions of Blacks were different, however. Generally, while ratings participants evaluated Blacks rather favorably, EMG participants rated Blacks as having more undesirable and few desirable traits. For example, ratings participants thought that the trait "unreliable" was not indicative of Blacks (−.67), while EMG participants believed that it was characteristic of Blacks (+.27). On the trait of "honesty," ratings participants believed that it was characteristic of Blacks (+.60), whereas EMG participants believed that it was not very typical of Blacks (−.33).

These results supported Jones and Sigall's suspicions that the dramatic decline in prejudiced attitudes that was reported by Karlins et al. (1969) did not reflect a revolution in the attitudes of Whites toward Blacks. Many Whites were not as low-prejudice as their egalitarian responses on self-report measures of prejudice would suggest. Thus, while negative attitudes of Whites toward Blacks had not declined dramatically, what had changed was the willingness of Whites to overtly express these negative racial attitudes. As Sigall and Page (1971) describe the results, the EMG participants provided more negative attitudes toward Blacks (compared with those in the ratings condition) because they believed that the machine could accurately assess their attitudes, and if they attempted to portray themselves as those in the ratings condition (i.e., as nonprejudiced), the machine would show to the researcher that the subject had lied. Thus, rather than risk being seen as a liar, the subject indicates (via his negative responses about Blacks) that he is prejudiced!

Does the bogus-pipeline technique work, and is it a viable means to accurately assess prejudice? Although Schlenker, Bonoma, Hutchinson, and Burns (1976) were unable to completely replicate Sigall and Page's (1971) findings, and others found no differences between self-reported attitudes and attitudes provided via the bogus pipeline (Broverman, Bloom, Gunn, & Torok, 1974; Cherry, Byrne, & Mitchell, 1976), the bulk of the research suggests that it does indeed reduce attitude distortion, (as influenced by social desirability and other self-presentational goals; Page & Moss, 1975; Riess, Kalle, & Tedeschi, 1981; Quigley-Fernandez & Tedeschi, 1978). A recent comprehensive meta-analysis of 31 bogus-pipeline studies also showed that the technique does work to reduce socially desirable responding and leads to more truthful responses from the participants (Roese & Jamieson, 1993). Interestingly, other research in which the subject is led to believe that their self-reported attitudes will be validated later for accuracy shows similar reductions in attitude distortion (e.g., Evans, Hansen, & Mittelmark, 1977; Hill, Henderson, Bray, & Evans, 1981).

While the data indicate that the bogus-pipeline (and variations thereof) is a particularly accurate (i.e., little attitude distortion) measure of attitudes, it is almost never used in modern prejudice research. The reason is simple: conducting research with bogus-pipeline-type measures is very labor intensive. The experiment involves elaborate deception and extensive training of the experimenters, and the experimenter needs to devise an accurate replica of an EMG machine (the bogus pipeline) and convince today's more psychologically savvy subjects that the machine is valid and that the experimenter is being up-front with the subject.

Measuring Stereotyping

Though it was once a useful gauge of stereotypes, the Katz and Braly adjective checklist is rarely used in contemporary research, owing to the aforementioned problems associated with the measure. Other researchers have used a "diagnostic ratio" measure of stereotyping (McCauley & Stitt, 1978). This procedure asks the participant to provide estimates of the percentage of the target group who possess a given characteristic (e.g., honesty), and also what percentage of people in general possess the given characteristic. To the degree that participants' responses for the target group differ from those they indicated for the general population, positive or negative attributes (depending on the perceived differences on the trait[s] in question) are thus attributed to the target group. Perhaps because of to its perceived complexity, the diagnostic ratio measure of stereotyping has not been a very popular method for assessing stereotyping (Allen, 1996). In the last decade, researchers have come back to the free-response technique, exemplified by the Adjective Generation Technique (AGT) procedure (Potkay & Allen, 1988), as a robust and accurate measure of the stereotypes individuals hold about outgroups at a given time (e.g., Devine, 1989; Esses, Haddock, & Zanna, 1994). Free-response measures also have a distinct advantage over earlier measures of stereotyping in that they can more accurately predict subsequent prejudice-related behavior toward the outgroup (Stangor, Sullivan, & Ford, 1991). The down side to free-response measures of stereotyping is that (1) they are not always better predictors of prejudice and discrimination, and (2) the task of coding the free-response data generated by the participants is often time consuming and requires lengthy reliability analyses that some researchers might consider too labor intensive (Stangor & Lange, 1994). Nevertheless, if the goal is to understand the content of stereotypes toward a certain target at a particular time, free-response measures are an excellent method to achieve that end.

A primary approach to research in stereotyping and prejudice is to ascertain the conditions that facilitate and inhibit the use of stereotypes in making judgments about others. In other words, when are we more or less likely to use a stereotype when thinking about, or forming an impression of, another person? One useful approach to assessing the proclivity to use stereotypes in social judgments is to examine the degree to which participants in a study use the category membership of the target as a heuristic in helping them arrive at conclusions about that target. Though a variety of measures exist, a popular version has been Bodenhausen's (1990) Student Court Questionnaire (SCQ). Participants are asked to read a short description about a disciplinary hearing that will be held against a student on campus, involving either academic dishonesty or possession of drugs. The paragraph presents a brief outline of the offense and the evidence that implicates the defendant. However, the information is ambiguous as to the guilt or innocence of the defendant (i.e., there is equal evidence of innocence and guilt). Participants are then asked, on eight Likert-type items, about the likelihood that the defendant is guilty, severity of punishment if he is guilty, and so forth. There are two versions of the SCQ. One names the defendant in the paragraph with an ethnically nondescript name, such as Dan Jensen. The other version is identical to the first except for the name of the defendant, which is a name that may be construed as sounding African American, such as Darnell Jackson. Within all experimental conditions, half of the participants get the nondescript version, and the other half get the African American version. To the degree that responses on the two versions of the questionnaire differ significantly in terms of judgments of greater guilt, more severe punishment deserved, and so forth for the African American defendant, the researcher can then conclude that the independent variable for that condition either increased, or had no effect on, the tendency to use a stereotype in social judgments. The SCQ is popular because it is nonreactive, easy to administer and score, very brief, and has little or no demand characteristics associated with it. Using this measure (and variants thereof), researchers have found that when people are happy (Bodenhausen, Kramer, & Süsser, 1994) they are more likely to use a stereotype in their judgments about a target. Research also indicates that people are more likely to stereotype others when they are angry, but not when they feel sad (Bodenhausen, Sheppard, & Kramer, 1994). Research also indicates that when people are cognitively busy they are more likely to use stereotypes when thinking about a target (Bodenhausen & Lichtenstein, 1987; Fiske & Neuberg, 1990).

Measuring Prejudice

In addition to discovering the conditions under which stereotyping is likely to occur, researchers have been equally interested in understanding the relation between negative intergroup affect (prejudice) and subsequent attitudes and behavior toward outgroups. To this end, there has been a considerable amount of effort directed toward devising self-report measures of prejudice. Recall that a good self-report measure must be fairly nonreactive, reliable, relatively short, valid, and easy to score and interpret if it will be useful to the research community. Questionnaires on sensitive issues such as prejudice have an additional burden of overcoming inevitable response biases caused by social desirability, reactivity, and unawareness of one's underlying attitudes (as in the case of aversive racists, and, to a lesser extent, modern and symbolic racists). As a result of these difficult measurement obstacles, some theorists have suggested that contemporary forms of prejudice cannot be measured via self-report questionnaires (Gaertner & Dovidio, 1986).

Nevertheless, many researchers have devised self-report measures of prejudice, with varying degrees of success. While there are far too many to discuss in this chapter (for a comprehensive review of published prejudice measures, see Biernat & Crandall, 1999), we will focus on the most popular measure of prejudice, the modern-racism scale (MRS; McConahay, Hardee, & Batts, 1981; McConahay, 1986). McConahay (1986) designed the MRS to measure the subtle form of anti-Black prejudice that characterizes prejudice today, as described by the theory of modern racism. The scale comprises of seven statements to which the respondent indicates their agreement or disagreement on a 5-point Likert scale. Agreement with the items indicates the presence of modern racist beliefs, such as the belief that discrimination is no longer a problem in the United States, that Blacks get unfair special treatment in government policy, and that they should not "push themselves where they are not wanted." The inability to empathize with the plight of Blacks is also an indicator of modern racism (as in the reverse-scored item "It is easy to understand the anger of Black people in America"). In order to avoid reactivity, social desirability, and demand characteristics, most researchers also randomly intersperse many more filler items that tap similar social attitudes between the seven MRS items, in order to conceal the true purpose of the measure. The reader will note that the basis for the items is quite similar to the beliefs that underlie the symbolic- and aversive-racism theories. For that reason, many researchers have used the MRS as a measure of general, subtle prejudice that characterizes some Caucasians' attitudes toward African Americans in contemporary American society.

Of course, one of the first questions researchers ask about any measure is, is it valid and reliable? McConahay (1986) reported that the test–retest reliability was between .72 to .93, and that it showed fair convergent validity (Biernat & Crandall, 1999). The problem with the MRS is that it does not show very good discriminant validity. Specifically, it does not fail to correlate with measures of a different construct, old-fashioned racism (McConahay [1986] reported correlations between old-fashioned and modern racism between .33 and .66). Other researchers have found similar high correlations (.65, Weigel & Howes, 1985; .86, Swim, Aikin, Hall, & Hunter, 1995) between measures of old-fashioned racism and scores on the MRS (Weigel & Howes, 1985). Another problem with the MRS is that, contrary to McConahay's (1986) assertions, it does appear to be reactive. Jackson and Fazio (1995) found that when high-prejudice individuals (as indicated by earlier MRS scores) completed the MRS again with an African American experimenter, they shifted their responses on the MRS to appear less prejudiced. Those who were given the MRS by a White experimenter showed no significant attitude shift. The researchers suggest that the shift in the African American experimenter condition indicates the reactivity of the scale, and that subjects respond in socially desirable ways in certain situations.

Priming and Reaction Times: The True Measure?

For the reasons stated, the MRS has become less popular as a means to measure prejudice. Researchers have recently investigated the merits of reaction-time methods for measuring prejudice. Reaction-time measures are desirable in assessing racial attitudes because they bypass the controlled cognitions that may mask underlying negative racial affect (Dovidio & Gaertner, 1996). Research by Gaertner (Dovidio & Gaertner, 1993; Gaertner & McLaughlin, 1983) found that White participants were more likely to associate positive characteristics with the racial category word *White* than with the word *Black*. There were no differences in association however, between negative characteristics and the group labels. In other words, this research supports the research discussed earlier in this chapter which concluded that though many Caucasians are still prejudiced against African Americans, the prejudice seems to take the more mild form of favoritism toward the ingroup, rather than outgroup derogation.

Let us consider a recent compelling series of studies reported by Fazio et al. (1995), in which they wanted to examine the relationship between participant MRS scores and reaction times to (positive and negative) words that follow photos of faces of different races. Based on earlier research by Fazio and his colleagues (Fazio, Sanbonmatsu, Powell, & Kardes, 1986), Fazio et al. (1995) reasoned that people tend to associate negative or positive words and traits with different racial groups, and these words are automatically activated in memory upon seeing a member of that group. According to the spreading-activation theory of memory, this activation should facilitate the recognition of the related words (Collins & Loftus, 1975). Upon presentation of an African American face, the degree to which Caucasians show faster recognition times for certain words and not others would indicate the types of words that are most strongly associated with African Americans (the same applies with photos of individuals of other ethnicities and races).

Because activation of category-related concepts in memory is an automatic process, it cannot be corrupted by social desirability, reactivity, or other biases that taint self-report measures (Dovidio & Fazio, 1992; Fazio, 1990). Thus, if White participants show faster recognition for negative words (and not for positive words) following the African American photo prime, and faster recognition times for positive words following photos of individuals of their own race, we would conclude that the individual is prejudiced against African Americans, and favors their own race (ingroup bias). Fazio et al. (1995) asked participants whose MRS scores were in the top and bottom 10% of the pretesting sample (i.e., the most high- and low-prejudice individuals) to participate in a study of word meanings and recognition of faces. They randomly presented 48 photos of Caucasian, African American, Asian, and Hispanic students' faces (which were obtained from volunteers prior to the study) to the participant for 315 milliseconds. The faces served as the prime for the subsequent presentation of trait words. Participants then saw a randomly presented trait word and were asked to press a key labeled either "good" or "bad," depending on their categorization of that trait. As shown in Figure 5.1, the results indicated that when White participants viewed an African American prime, they showed greater facilitation for the recognition of negative traits words, but when they saw a White prime, they showed greater facilitation for positive trait words. This pattern did not differ between those who scored high or low on the MRS. African American participants showed the opposite result. The authors found the same results when using participants with a range of MRS scores (rather than just the top and bottom 10%; Experiment 2).

Using this reaction-time measure of prejudice, Fazio et al. (1995) have demonstrated a strong case for the idea that the MRS is a highly reactive and blatant measure of prejudice. When high and low MRS scorers took the reaction-time measure of prejudice, the results indicated that both low-prejudice and high-prejudice Caucasians showed stronger negative attitudes linked to the African American category, and stronger positive attitudes linked to the White category (this finding was supported by similar findings reported by Wittenbrink, Judd, & Park, 1997). Finally, the data obtained in Fazio et al.'s (1995) second experiment revealed that participants' scores on the MRS were not correlated with the reaction-time measure of prejudice. This indicates that the two measures are not assessing the same construct. Even stranger than the lack of correspondence is the fact that the MRS and the reaction-time measure were weakly ($r = .28$, < p .06) negatively correlated. That is, those with the lowest (least prejudiced) scores on the MRS showed the highest amount of negativity (fastest facilitation for most negative traits following the African American prime) on the reaction-time measure.

Rather than being a nonreactive measure of prejudice toward African Americans, the MRS should be thought of as a measure of one's willingness to express negative racial attitudes (Biernat & Crandall, 1999; Jackson & Fazio, 1995). What can we conclude from the fact that both high- and low-prejudice persons (as indicated by MRS scores) showed facilitation for negative trait words following the African American prime? Does that mean that all Caucasians are prejudiced toward African Americans? No. Recall that the MRS measures one's willingness to express negative feelings toward African Americans, while the reaction-time measure used in Fazio et al.'s research seems to measure something else. Despite Fazio et al.'s assertions that reaction-time measures are indeed

based in memory

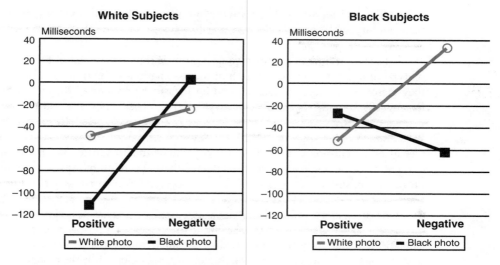

FIGURE 5.1   Ingroup favoritism and priming. In a series of compelling experiments, Fazio and his colleagues showed that when we think of our own group (primed by a photograph of a person from our ingroup), we are quicker to recognize positive trait words, and slower to recognize negative trait words. However, when participants were primed with a photograph from a member of their outgroup, they were faster at recognizing negative trait words and slower to recognize positive trait words. The effect holds for both Black and White participants. This research suggests that activation of one's ingroup category facilitates cognitive access to positive information, and activation of outgroup categories facilitates cognitive access to negative information. Note: the higher the mean recognition time as plotted on the y axis (the less negative, in terms of milliseconds), the greater the facilitation of the prime for recognition of the trait words. (Copyright © 1995 by the American Psychological Association. Reprinted with permission.)

a true indicator of prejudice, the reaction-time methodology appears to be assessing the strength of the association between the category and associated traits. Faster facilitation to various words gives the researcher an indication of the strength of the associations, and the most-facilitated words following the category prime give an indication of the content of the stereotype that the individual has for that prime category.

The fact that these two measures are tapping different constructs would account for the lack of correlation between them in Fazio et al.'s Study 2, but it would not account for the weak negative correlation, which is an odd finding and one that Fazio et al. do not attempt to interpret. This explanation would also account for the finding that both high- and low-prejudice Caucasians showed more facilitation to negative words following the African American prime than with the White prime. Specifically, the results indicate that Caucasians are more likely to associate negative traits with African Americans. But, as Devine (1989) has demonstrated, there is an important difference between knowledge of the stereotype and personally believing or endorsing the stereotype. She found that high- and low-prejudice Caucasians had the stereotype automatically activated upon presentation of the category, but that low-prejudice individuals quickly suppressed the expression of such stereotypes and high-prejudice individuals showed no attempt to suppress expression of their stereotypes. Thus, knowing the stereotype does not mean that one personally believes or endorses the prejudice.

If reaction-time measures give us a glimpse into the content of the individual's stereotype of a group, and the strength of the association of the traits and the category, are they therefore an inappropriate method for measuring prejudice? Maybe not. Lepore and Brown (1997) found that while high and low prejudiced individuals did not differ in the content of the traits associated with African Americans, they did differ in the strength of the associations between the category "African Americans" and positive and negative traits (see also Wittenbrink et al., 1997). They speculate that this difference between high- and low-prejudice individuals results from the facilitating and inhibiting effects of the category on related positive and negative words. Lepore and Brown suggest that high-prejudice Caucasians tend to have stronger associations between the category label and negative characteristics, and that although their associations between the category "African American" and positive traits are activated, these are inhibited. For low-prejudice persons, the same positive and negative traits are also activated upon thinking of the category, but the associations for positive traits are facilitated in recognition while the associations for negative traits are inhibited. Thus, Lepore and Brown propose that high- and low-prejudiced persons have the same positive and negative traits associated with a category, but that the strength of these specific associations differs between the two groups due to different patterns of facilitation and inhibition.

If this sounds similar to the model proposed by Devine (1989), it is, with one important difference. Both models, and the results of the Fazio et al. (1995) studies, suggest that high- and low-prejudice persons know the stereotypical information associated with a given racial outgroup (in these experiments, the outgroup was African Americans, but the model can apply to other outgroups). Devine says that low-prejudice persons consciously inhibit the activated stereotype. Lepore and Brown say that the inhibition of the stereotype also occurs, but that it is automatic (nonconscious). Recent research by Stewart, Weeks, and Lupfer (2003) indicates that high- and low-prejudice Whites spontaneously stereotype African Americans. Using a variant of an implicit priming technique, the researchers assessed the degree to which people remembered seeing trait words associated with pictures of White or Black persons. Results indicated that high- and low-prejudice White participants were much less likely to remember a pairing of a Black photo with positive traits. Stewart et al. suggest that these data support the idea that both high- and low-prejudice persons spontaneously activate *and* apply stereotypes, and that this indicates that no inhibition of stereotypes is occurring for low-prejudice persons. It is important to remember that the Stewart et al. study employed a different, implicit measure of prejudice activation and application, and it may be this different method that accounts for why their findings diverge from those of Devine and Lepore and Brown. Which approach best accounts for the differences between high- and low-prejudice persons? At this point, the evidence is mixed, and there is a need for much more future research on the subject before we can arrive at a definitive conclusion.

As measures of the content and strength of stereotypical information associated with outgroups, reaction-time measures are perhaps the best method researchers have today. However, much more research is needed on reaction-time as a measure of prejudice, in order to demonstrate the conditions under which high- and low-prejudice persons can be

[handwritten: associations ≠ feelings]

distinguished in terms of their negative feelings toward the outgroup, and not only in terms of the strength of the associated traits with the outgroup category. Currently, researchers must infer the presence of prejudice (negative feelings toward the group) from knowing that a given person has stronger associations between negative traits and the category. However, in order to be more confident about an individual's prejudice, paper-and-pencil measures, and even reaction-time measures, should be correlated with the individual's verbal and nonverbal behaviors in intergroup contexts.

One move in this direction is a measure called the racial-argument scale, by Saucier and Miller (2003). The scale asks people to indicate how well arguments support conclusions that are either supportive or negative toward Blacks. The scale is an indirect measure of prejudice against Blacks because respondents do not feel defensive about giving their impression about the strength of pro- or anti-Black arguments. The scale has been shown to have good reliability and validity, it can predict positive or negative behavior against Blacks, and it looks like a promising measure of prejudice for future research. As Devine et al. (1996) cogently argue, researchers currently know very little about the dynamics of interracial interaction. By understanding the verbal and nonverbal behavior of the majority and minority member in such a context, we can begin to understand the reciprocal nature of negative expectancy confirmation, misattribution, and misunderstandings that perpetuate prejudices. Such a context also provides for a more externally valid measure of outgroup prejudice.

SUMMARY: IS THERE SUCH A THING AS MODERN PREJUDICE?

Earlier in this chapter, we left unanswered the question of whether current expressions of prejudice differ in form from the prejudice expressed in the past. That is, are theories of so-called modern prejudice describing a qualitatively different type of prejudice from old-fashioned, or overt, prejudice, or are they describing new ways to measure the more subtle contemporary versions of old-fashioned prejudice? This is a difficult question, and one that researchers are still attempting to answer. One step in this direction comes from a paper by Klienpenning and Hagendoorn (1993). They suggest that when one looks at the components of attitudes toward ethnic groups (such as stance on segregation, rights for outgroups, threat from outgroup members, and adjustment of outgroups), people can be reliably distinguished along a continuum of attitudes toward ethnic groups. That is, the nonracist represents the absence of negative attitudes toward other ethnic groups, followed (in increasing order of negativity toward ethnic outgroups) by aversive racists, symbolic racists, and biological (old-fashioned) racists. Given the consistent findings of strong correlations between the various measures of the categories of modern prejudice and old-fashioned prejudice, Kleinpenning and Hagendoorn's model accounts for the correlations by suggesting that these measures *should* be correlated to some degree because they all assess various degrees of prejudice toward ethnic outgroups. Kleinpenning and Hagendoorn suggest that today's prejudice is not independent of, but rather is a first step toward, old-fashioned prejudice. Whether old-fashioned, overt, and openly hostile, or covert, subtle, and virtually undetectable, research shows that each type of prejudice still results in negative behavior, affect, and cognitions about the stereotyped target, and that of course

[handwritten: modern prejudice = start of old prejudice]

can have negative influences on the individuals who are targets of such prejudice. In the next chapter, we turn to an in-depth examination of how prejudice, both overt and subtle, affects those who are its targets.

GLOSSARY

aversive racism   Anti–African American prejudice, in individuals who believe they are very egalitarian, but who also have negative feelings and attitudes toward African Americans. This prejudice is more likely to be expressed as ingroup favoritism, rather than outgroup derogation.

bogus-pipeline technique   Attitude-assessment technique that reduces the social-desirability response bias but is very labor intensive. The participant is connected to a device similar to a lie detector, and the participant is led to believe that the device will give the experimenter an accurate reading of the participant's true attitudes.

demand characteristics   Aspects of an experimental situation that lead participants to form their own

hypotheses about what the experiment is about (and what behavior the experimenter would like them to show).

modern racism   A subtle form of prejudice that is only expressed when the individual believes it is safe, acceptable, or easily rationalizable.

social desirability   Presenting oneself and one's attitudes as very positive, in order to give the most socially acceptable attitude/behavior, even if it deviates from one's true attitudes.

symbolic racism   Anti–African American prejudice originating out of the belief that African Americans violate traditional American values.

DISCUSSION QUESTIONS

1. Do you believe that stereotyping and prejudice (any type: racial, ethnic, gender, age, etc.) has declined or increased over the past century? What do you think accounts for the increase or decrease?

2. What are the legitimizing myths that modern racists hold about African Americans? In what ways do they rationalize their prejudice toward African Americans?

3. What, in your opinion, is the best way to measure prejudice and endorsement of stereotypes?

4. What are the strengths and weaknesses of Fazio's reaction-time measure of prejudice?

5. In your opinion, will prejudice and stereotyping always be a part of our society, never decreasing, but merely changing focus or form? Why?

SUGGESTED KEY READINGS

Allport, G. W. (1954). *The nature of prejudice*. Reading, MA: Addison-Wesley.

Devine, P. G., & Elliot, A. J. (1995). Are racial stereotypes really fading? The Princeton trilogy revisited. *Personality and Social Psychology Bulletin, 21*(11), 1139–1150.

Gaertner, S. L., & Dovidio, J. F. (1986). The aversive form of racism. In J. F. Dovidio & S. L. Gaertner (Eds.), *Prejudice, discrimination, and racism* (pp. 61–89). New York: Academic Press.

McConahay, J. B. (1986). Modern racism, ambivalence, and the modern racism scale. In J. F. Dovidio & S. L. Gaertner (Eds.), *Prejudice, discrimination, and racism* (pp. 91–125). New York: Academic Press.

Sears, D. O. (1988). Symbolic racism. In P. A. Katz & D. A. Taylor (Eds.), *Eliminating racism: Profiles in controversy* (pp. 53–84). New York: Plenum.

INTERNET RESOURCES: RESEARCHERS, REFERENCES, AND ORGANIZATIONS DEVOTED TO THE STUDY OF PREJUDICE

http://departments.colgate.edu/psychology/web/ dovidio.htm Home page of Dr. John Dovidio, a leading researcher of prejudice, discrimination, and stereotyping.

www.udel.edu/psych/fingerle/sgaertner.htm Home page of Dr. Sam Gaertner, another leading prejudice researcher.

www.udel.edu/psych/fingerle/jones.htm Internet site for Dr. James Jones, a prominent prejudice researcher, and author of the excellent book *Prejudice and racism* (1997).

www.psy.ohio-state.edu/faculty/fazio Home page of Dr. Russell Fazio, prominent social cognition researcher.

www.understandingprejudice.org/links/racthen.htm Many links to the history of the civil-rights movement, slavery, and Japanese internment during World War II.

www.understandingprejudice.org/links/racnow.htm Links to diversity, multiculturalism, affirmative action, and other race- and ethnicity-specific Internet resources.

CHAPTER SIX

EXPERIENCING PREJUDICE

In the search for understanding the processes that lead to the formation, maintenance, and reduction of stereotypes and prejudice, researchers have taken a certain view of the process that is implicit in one underlying common fact about all the writings, experiments, and theorizing that characterized the research: prejudice originated and was maintained within the majority perceiver of the minority target. It is a fairly intuitive notion to think that if a perceiver holds prejudice toward a target, and if we want to understand the processes that lead to the formation, maintenance, and reduction of that prejudice, we need to understand more about that perceiver. Indeed, this is how much of the research literature has approached prejudice and stereotyping.

We know much about how various personality characteristics are more likely to foster prejudice (Adorno et al., 1950), and how various affective states (Bodenhausen, 1993), expectancies (Devine et al., 1996), cognitive capacity (Mackie & Worth, 1991) and motivational deficits (Isen & Simmonds, 1978) can lead to increased reliance on stereotypes in social judgments. As Devine et al. (1996) note, though, this literature gives us only an incomplete picture of the context in which stereotyping occurs. Stereotyping and prejudice are not processes that involve a perceiver regarding an inactive target of stereotyping. Rather, stereotyping and prejudice occur in a dynamic social context involving the perceiver and target reacting to each other. It is a two-way street, involving feedback from the target that often confirms the expectations of the perceiver, with the perceiver's behavior often then confirming the expectations of the target. This will be discussed as we proceed, but suffice it to say that it is important, if we want to understand stereotyping and prejudice more thoroughly, that we consider the perspective of the target in this social interaction. In this chapter, we will explore what it means to be the target of prejudice and stereotyping. What effect does it have on one's motivations, expectancies, self-esteem, and approach to interactions with members of the stereotyping majority? We will also explore how the target's expectations influence the perceiver in the social context, and how individual expectations bias the way they view the social interaction, such that they emerge from the situation with their stereotypes of the other newly confirmed and their prejudices strengthened.

SOCIAL STIGMA

Suppose I asked you, "Have you always been normal?" Your reply may likely be, "What do you mean by 'normal'?" By "normal" I mean mainstream in your attitudes, dress, appearance, and personality. Normal in that these aspects of yourself are not extreme in any respect, such that you fit in with the majority of society at any given point in your life. When I put it that way, it is likely that you might have a difficult time answering my initial question in the affirmative. At some point in our lives, it is likely that we have all been unusual in some respect. Perhaps you had a leg brace as a child or wore glasses or wore a funny-looking hat during winter (because it was the only one you had) or you had a bad case of acne. Perhaps you were quite short, your pituitary glad was active early and you were significantly taller than your peers, or you were brighter or less bright compared with your peers. The examples are endless.

The point, for our purposes in this chapter, is to think back to those times, to remember as vividly as you can how people regarded your uniqueness. How were you treated, and how did it make you feel? How did others' treatment influence your self-esteem and your attitudes toward those others? It is likely that the treatment from others was not especially positive, and this probably made you feel negative toward those others and about yourself. No one likes to be the subject of negative evaluations made by others. That is precisely why so many people try to fit in with the majority: so they will not be singled out for ridicule or treated negatively by others. Such treatment is fairly overt among children, who, not having learned socially sophisticated methods of expressing disapproval, will have no compunction about telling everyone and the individual in question about the target's deficiencies (sometimes entailing laughter, cruel jokes, and/or physical hostility). Among adults, those negative evaluations may take the form of subtle negative comments, rude behavior, or other subtle expressions of prejudice. For many people, these unusual aspects about them are temporary (e.g., wearing braces on your teeth or having acne), and they are no longer subject to ridicule as time goes on. But for others, being the object of negative evaluations from society is something they deal with each day of their lives.

Noted sociologist Erving Goffman (1963) referred to the unusual characteristics that engender negative evaluations as being indicators of **stigma.** The stigmatized person is one who is "reduced in our minds from a whole and usual person to a tainted, discounted one" (Goffman, 1963, p. 3). Stigmas are characteristics that mark the individual as "deviant, flawed, limited, spoiled or generally undesirable" (Jones, Farina, Hastorf, Markus, Miller, Scott et al., 1984, p. 8). The reader will note that stigma encompasses all the more familiar situations where prejudice is shown (i.e., racial, religious, gender, age, sexual orientation), but it also covers any physical, behavioral, psychological marker that elicits negative evaluation from society. Goffman (1963) denoted three types of stigmas: "abominations of the body" (e.g., physical deformities, being overweight, etc.; Crandall, 1994), "blemishes of individual character" (e.g., drunkenness), and "tribal stigmas of race, nation, and religion" (e.g., prejudice against another race; p. 4).

Researchers know much about how nonstigmatized persons view stigmatized individuals (e.g., Heatherton, Kleck, Hebl, & Hull, 2000; J. M. Jones, 1997), but comparatively little research has been conducted on the experiences of the stigmatized person and how stigmatized and nonstigmatized individuals regard each other in social interactions. In this chapter we will explore in some detail the extant research that has addressed the problem of understanding how the stigmatized are influenced by prejudice, stereotyping, and discrimination. We will also address ways to understand how prejudice is maintained and, indeed, reinforced as a result of intergroup interactions. Finally, the chapter concludes with a look at unanswered questions and empirical challenges prejudice researchers should address in the future.

GROUP IDENTIFICATION

Previous research indicates that individuals faced with external threats (such as prejudice) show stronger ingroup identification (Janis, 1968). Research has confirmed this general effect with Jewish persons (Dion & Earn, 1975; Radke, Trager, & Davis, 1949; Rollins, 1973), African Americans (Cross & Strauss, 1998), and women (Swim & Hyers, 1999, as cited in LaFrance & Woodzicka, 1998). However, subsequent research has indicated that whether the individual has already strongly personally identified with their stigmatized group will have a major impact on the degree to which that individual disassociates from the group. Doosje and Ellemers (1997) found that people differ in the degree to which they identify with their stigmatized group. High-identifiers are much more likely to associate themselves with their group, even when—especially when—it has a negative image. High identifiers derive much of their self-esteem from their identification as a group member. They are much more likely to seek collective strategies against group threat. They tend to make it clear that they are fully committed, loyal group members, who are, to coin a phrase, in it for the long run. Low identifiers, on the other hand, are much more likely to dissociate themselves from the group, especially when the group has a negative image. They feel no special affinity toward, or derive no self-esteem from, their group. Doosje and Ellemers conclude that low identifiers "seem quite prepared to let the group fall apart" when the group is threatened or has a negative image (p. 271). Low identifiers are thus much more individualistic and opportunistic in that they will only identify themselves with the group when it would positively affect their social identity.

STEREOTYPE THREAT

For most groups, there exist at least a few widely known stereotypes. From early on, children learn these stereotypes (Jones, 1997) and are aware that their own group and other groups are sometimes negatively viewed by others (Rosenberg, 1979). In addition to the negative implications that stereotypes of one's group have for one's self-concept and self-image, such stereotypes represent another problem with which one must contend. Specifically, individuals in stereotyped groups often find themselves ever-vigilant about not behaving in ways that confirm stereotypes about one's group. Doing so would appear to lend evidence to support the legitimacy of the stereotype in the eyes of others, and even in the individual's own view. Occasionally, individuals in stereotyped groups will engage in performance-limiting behavior (e.g., practicing less before an athletic event, or not studying prior to an exam), in order to provide them with a ready excuse for their expected poor performance on the stereotype-relevant dimension (Stone, 2002).

Steele and Aronson (1995; Steele, Spencer, & Aronson, 2002) refer to this situation as **stereotype threat.** On the face of it, it would seem that if you were aware of the stereotype and you decided to behave in ways that disconfirm the stereotype, you would behave in that counterstereotypical fashion, and that would be it. No problem, no hassle. But that is not the end of the matter. Research indicates that for many stereotypes the negative implications of confirming the stereotype are important enough that they can impair one's ability to behave in a counterstereotypic way (Baumeister, 1984; Steele & Aronson; Steele, 1997; Aronson, Quinn, & Spencer, 1998). In other words, the anxiety that one feels in thinking about possibly confirming the stereotype can be so debilitating that it actually impairs one's performance on the stereotype-relevant dimension, thereby having the paradoxical effect of confirming the stereotype. Recent research suggests that stereotype threat has its effect through the mediating influence of a drop in working-memory capacity (Schmader & Johns, 2003).

The effects of stereotype threat are especially likely to occur in people who strongly identify with the group about which the stereotype exists (Nosek, Banaji, & Greenwald, 2002; Schmader, 2001; Pronin, Steele, & Ross, 2004) and in individuals who are self-conscious of their stigmatized status (Brown & Pinel, 2003; Pinel, 2002). Recent research shows that people under stereotype threat actually fare worse physiologically than their non-threatened counterparts (Blascovich, Spencer, Quinn, & Steele, 2001). Specifically, Black participants in a threatened condition showed significantly higher blood pressure than their nonthreatened counterparts. The researchers suggest that this may help explain the higher incidence of coronary heart disease and high blood pressure among Black persons.

In the research on this relatively new area of inquiry, most of the attention has focused on stereotypes that revolve around intellectual ability and performance. For African Americans, a common stereotype suggests that African Americans perform poorly compared with others on measures of intellectual ability (Steele, 1992). As Cose (1993) describes,

> In some places things are much as they were when I was a schoolboy and heard one teacher say that Blacks had "lazy tongues," and another announce that he didn't care whether anyone learned anything since he was getting paid anyway, and yet another explain, when challenged over handing out brain-deadening assignments, that kids like us were incapable of handling difficult material. Scholastic attainment may not generally be discouraged in so brutal a manner, but legions of Black kids still have it instilled in them that they are not particularly intelligent; and at least partly as a result of such indoctrination, many give up on academic achievement at a very young age. (p. 162)

In fact, statistics on results of standardized aptitude and intelligence tests over the decades suggest that African Americans consistently average about 15 points less on such measures compared to Caucasians (Loehlin, Lindzeg, & Spuhler, 1975). Most researchers agree that some of the reasons for this gap are the socioeconomic disadvantages that African Americans experience that affect their academic environment, cultural biases embedded into standardized intelligence tests, and discrimination and prejudice that they face from others (Schiele, 1991). However, this does not explain the finding that even when African Americans and Caucasians have the same preparation, African Americans still achieve less (i.e., poorer subsequent GPA, time to graduation, etc.; Steele & Aronson, 1995). Steele and Aronson (1995; see Figure 6.1) suggest that the debilitating effects of stereotype threat may account for the gap in subsequent achievement between similar-scoring African Americans and Caucasians. They found that when African American participants believed that a difficult verbal test was a measure of their intellectual ability (compared to those who were not told this), they underperformed compared to Caucasians in the ability-diagnostic condition (intellectual ability) but performed as well as Caucasians in the nondiagnostic condition.

They also found that just making the stereotype salient impaired the performance of African Americans on the task, even in nondiagnostic conditions (see Figure 6.2). A

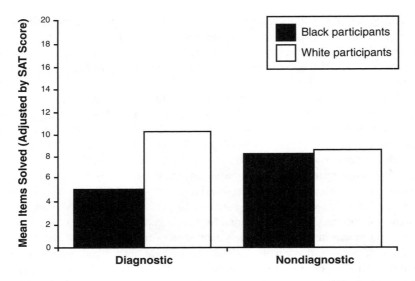

FIGURE 6.1   Stereotype threat and performance on a difficult verbal test. When Steele and Aronson (1995) presented Black and White students with a test of verbal ability, the way the test was introduced had an impact on the Black students' performance. Steele and Aronson told half of the participants that the test was diagnostic of intellectual ability (stereotype-threat condition) and the other half were told that it was a problem-solving task unrelated to intellectual ability. This graph shows that after statistically controlling for participants' SAT verbal scores, Blacks and Whites performed equally in the nondiagnostic condition. However, when Blacks believed there was a danger that their performance on the test potentially could confirm a stereotype about Blacks (the diagnostic condition), the anxiety associated with that belief impaired their performance relative to Whites in the same condition. (Copyright © 1995 by the American Psychological Association. Reprinted with permission.)

recent, intriguing meta-analysis of the literature by Walton and Cohen (2003) suggests that this disparity may also be due to what they term "stereotype lift." That is, nonstigmatized persons seem to experience a performance enhancement when they engage in a downward comparison between themselves and a member of a stereotyped outgroup. So, even when Black and White people are similarly prepared educationally and have the same abilities, the influence of stereotype lift may be a contributing factor that might explain continued performance discrepancies between the Black and White individuals.

Being a member of a stereotyped group can also affect the degree of one's self-confidence about performance on the stereotype-relevant dimension. Research by Aronson and Inzlicht (2004) found that those who were higher in "stereotype vulnerability" (the "tendency to expect, perceive, and be influenced by stereotypes about one's social category") tended to be the least in touch with the quality of their performances on a stereotype-relevant task. They were not able to accurately predict what they knew relative to the demands of the test. As a result of this inaccuracy, their academic (stereotype domain related) self-confidence was subject to stronger fluctuations (see related work on rejection sensitivity by Mendoza-Denton, Downey, Purdie, Davis, & Pietrzak, 2002).

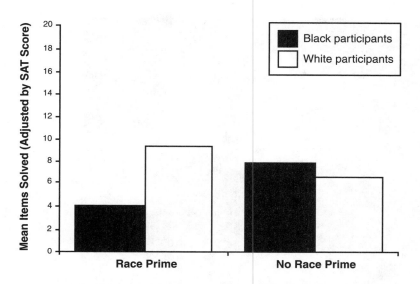

FIGURE 6.2   The slightest prime unleashes stereotype threat. Steele and Aronson (1995) also found that it does not take much priming at all to activate feelings of stereotype threat. In one variation of the study described in Figure 6.1, Steele and Aronson did not tell participants anything about the diagnostic nature of the verbal test. However, they primed half of the participants to think about their race merely by having the participants indicate their race in a demographic questionnaire. That simple difference was enough to cause Black participants to feel stereotype threat when doing the verbal test, and, as can be seen in this graph, their performance suffered compared to that of Whites who also had their race primed. (Copyright © 1995 by the American Psychological Association. Reprinted with permission.)

Research with women reveals similar results, implicating the stereotype-threat effects. For women, a commonly held stereotype has been that they are less capable in science and mathematics (Aronson, et al., 1998; Smith & White, 2002). Quinn and Spencer (1996, as cited by Aronson et al., 1998) manipulated the diagnosticity of a math exam (i.e., by either telling participants that the math exam was diagnostic or not diagnostic of their math ability) for male and female participants who had matched math backgrounds and skills (as measured by their SAT scores and calculus grades). Results indicated that when women believed that the exam was diagnostic, they performed poorly compared with their male counterparts. When women believed it was not diagnostic, they performed as well as the other male participants. Simply completing a math test in a group in which she is the sole woman (with two other men) seems to make salient the stereotype of women's poor math performance, and women in these situations do indeed perform poorly compared with women completing a math test in a group of two other women (Inzlicht & Ben-Zeev, 2000; Sekaquaptewa & Thompson, 2003).

In addition to examining race and gender, researchers have looked at the stereotype threat attached to being older (Hess, Auman, Colcombe, & Rahhal, 2003) and to being poor. When individuals of low socioeconomic status believe that they might confirm a common stereotype of them (specifically, that they perform poorly on measures

A stereotype about women is that they are not as adept as men are at mathematical and scientific reasoning. In the 1980s, in what was to bring a tremendous amount of negative publicity, toy maker Mattel released a talking Barbie doll that had a repertoire of a few sentences, one of which was "Math is hard!" Following a storm of controversy after the doll hit the store shelves, Mattel quickly removed that particular Barbie doll.

of intellectual ability relative to those who are not poor), their performance suffers on perceived diagnostic measures, relative to those who are not poor. When the exam is seen as being nondiagnostic, they do just as well as their more affluent peers (Croizet & Claire, 1998). Finally, some investigators have found a stereotype threat effect in Whites who take the Implicit Association Test (thus, a finding of a preference for White) arising from their anxiety about obtaining a score that might indicate they are racist (Frantz, Cuddy, Burnett, Ray, & Hart, 2004).

The stereotype threat is not subject to change, however. Aronson, Fried, and Good (2001) told African American participants that the characteristic under study, and about which there was a stereotype about their group's performance—in this case, intelligence—was a malleable, not a fixed, characteristic. This led participants to be more resistant to the influence of stereotype threat, and they showed better performance on the intelligence tests and their grade point averages were higher. However, the ability to be unaffected by a stereotype against one's group becomes much more difficult to the degree that one's identity is closely tied to membership in that group (Schmader, 2001). Other research has shown that stereotype-threat effects can be reduced significantly when people from the stereotyped group are individuated (i.e., making one's own abilities salient, and distancing oneself from the group); in these cases they outperform their nonindividuated counterparts (Ambady, Paik, Steele, Owen-Smith, & Mitchell, 2004). One study found that simply reminding women about great achievements that other women had made tended to significantly reduce the stereotype threat on their mathematics test scores (McIntyre, Paulson, & Lord, 2003).

In an interesting twist on stereotype-threat research, Cheryan and Bodenhausen (2000) examined the influence of salient positive stereotypes on one's task performance. That is, if the stereotype about your group is that you do especially well on a task, could that stereotype potentially enhance or impair one's performance? Cheryan and Bodenhausen focused on the stereotype that Asians have a special aptitude for mathematical problems. Asian American women were exposed to an identity-salience manipulation, in which they were to complete a survey about either their ethnic group (e.g., "Overall, my race is considered good by others"), their gender, or their individual identity. They then completed a test of math skills. The results revealed that when participants' ethnic identity was made salient, their math performance was significantly worse than when their personal identity or gender identity was made salient. Research by Ambady and her colleagues (Ambady, Shih, Kim, & Pittinsky, 2001; Shih, Pittinsky, & Ambady, 1999) found just the opposite, though: when Asian American women had their ethic identity made salient, they performed better on a math test than when either no identity or their gender was made salient. Thus, more research is needed to identify the specific additive and individual effects that stereotypes about one's various ingroups can have on one's cognitions and behaviors. On the subject of anti–Asian American prejudice, recent work by Lin, Kwan, & Cheung (2005) suggests that this prejudice has two major components: envy of the (perceived) excessive intellectual competence, and disdain for their (perceived) low sociability. Curiously, Lin et al. found that it is the low sociability (and not the perceived high intellectual competence) that primarily drives anti–Asian American prejudice. These data support the central tenet of Fiske's (1998; Fiske, Xu, Cuddy, & Glick, 1999) stereotype-content model (SCM), which says that many stereotypes and prejudices can be located along two dimensions: competence and warmth. There are a number of studies published in support of SCM, and it appears to be a fruitful model for understanding the roots of many different types of prejudice.

The evidence accumulated to date indicates support for the notion that stereotypes about one's group can impair one's performance on salient ego- and identity-relevant tasks (Stone, Lynch, Sjomeling, & Darley, 1999). Paradoxically, although stereotype-threatened individuals are motivated to do well on the tasks, they tend to be inefficient in their work, largely because their attention is split between their alternating assessment of the correct answers to the task and their worry that their performance may confirm a stereotype of their group (Steele & Aronson, 1995).

It is important to remember that the results from experiments by Steele and Aronson (1995) and others that demonstrate stereotype threat effects do not show that reducing stereotype threat eliminates differences in performance between stereotyped groups and nonstereotyped groups. Recall that in these studies the groups were matched for equivalent stereotype-task (e.g., a math test) ability prior to the experiment. Introducing the stereotype threat impaired the performance of members of the stigmatized group. When the threat was not present, their performance matched that of their nonstigmatized counterparts. However, this only shows the debilitating effects of stereotype threat and in no way should be misinterpreted as suggesting that eliminating stereotype threat therefore eliminates group differences on stereotype-relevant task performance (Sackett, Hardison, & Cullen, 2004).

So, why do stereotype threatened individuals who score similarly to nonstereotype threatened persons (e.g., European Americans) on intelligence and aptitude tests achieve less than their European American counterparts? Steele (1992, 1997) suggests that the answer may lie in a process called **disidentification**. In disidentification, individuals disengage their identity from the achievement domain in question, such that their self-esteem and sense of self-competence is preserved and shielded from the negative effects of associating identity with performance on a stereotype-relevant dimension (Aronson et al., 1998). In practical terms, then, a woman may disidentify with achievement in science and mathematics, and African Americans may disidentify from academics (Major, Spencer, Schmader, Wolfe, & Crocker, 1998; Osborne, 1995). Again, the disidentification process allows the stigmatized to retain their self-esteem.

This is an interesting point that bears some elaboration. Intuitively, it would seem clear that people who are stigmatized should have lower overall self-esteem compared to nonstigmatized persons. Yet, much research suggests that this is not the case. In fact, research suggests that African Americans, for example, show self-esteem that is as high or higher than European Americans (Crocker & Major, 1989; Porter & Washington, 1979). Interestingly, although the stigmatized are more likely than the nonstigmatized to show disidentification, they are less likely to see the stereotype-threat dimension (e.g., academics) as unimportant (Crocker & Major, 1989; Major & Schmader, 1998). Thus, although disidentified stigmatized individuals agree that the stereotype-threat dimension is important, it is not important for them and for their self-identity.

What might trigger disidentification? Major and Schmader (1998) suggest that, by either devaluing the importance of the stereotype-threat domain or discounting the validity and self-diagnosticity of outcomes on the stereotype-threat dimension, the stigmatized can psychologically disengage from the stereotype-threat dimension and protect their self-esteem. Indeed, some disenchanted African Americans may devalue academic achievement by derogating other African Americans who pursue achievement in academics by saying they are "acting White" (Fordham, 1988; Fordham & Ogbu, 1986). In other words, the belief is that achievement in academics is something that Whites can accomplish, and African Americans who aspire to academic achievement are selling out and disidentifying themselves from their African American identity.

Indeed, some academics have suggested that African Americans who achieved academic success did so by adopting behaviors and attitudes that distanced themselves from their culture of origin, and that this results in increased depression, anxiety, and identity confusion (Fordham, 1988; Fordham & Obgu, 1986). In a careful examination of these predictions, Arroyo and Zigler (1995) found that academically achieving African Americans were more likely to experience feelings of depression and anxiety compared with their peers who were not academically successful. However, it appears that achievement in academics does not necessarily lead to confusion regarding racial identity. Arroyo and Zigler (1995) found that both high- and low-achieving African Americans were more likely to negatively evaluate, and psychologically distance themselves from, their racial group when they believed that their group was negatively evaluated by others. Thus, para-doxically, achieving academic success can have important psychological consequences for African Americans.

There is some evidence to suggest that these processes may arise in the individual's early teen years. Osborne (1995) found that the correlation between African Americans' self-esteem and academic outcomes remained strong until about the eighth grade. Then, Osborne writes, "something happened to weaken their identification. . . . It is probable that the African American students . . . may begin to see the academic environment as discriminatory and lacking in rewards, and begin disidentifying" (p. 453). Steele (1997) suggests that the "something" that happened is stereotype threat. In one experiment (cited in Steele, 1997), he varied the strength of the threat that female subjects were under by telling some subjects that differences between men and women in mathematics ability was due either to genetic differences (in other words, an innate limitation of being female) or to social/learned causes (i.e., discrimination, social roles). Participants' identification with mathematics and math-related careers was measured either before or after taking a

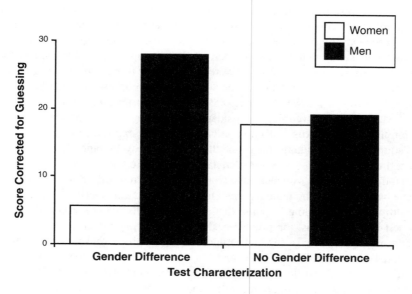

FIGURE 6.3 **The experience of stereotype threat for women.** Steele and his colleagues (1995) also examined stereotype threat among women. As with the experiment procedure described for Figure 6.1, Steele et al. invited males and females who were good at math, and who considered math ability to be an important part of their identity, to take a difficult math test. For half of the participants, the test was described as generally showing gender differences in performance on the test. As can be seen in this graph, when women believed the test did not show gender differences in performance, they performed just as well as men. However, when women were led to believe that males and females perform differently (activating the stereotype about women not being as adept as men at math), their performance on the test was much worse than men in the same condition. (Copyright © 1995 by the American Psychological Association. Reprinted with permission.)

difficult math test. Results indicated that women under stronger stereotype threat (i.e., the genetic limitation females have in mathematics) tended to disidentify more with math careers than women under weak stereotype threat (see Figure 6.3).

Stereotype threat has implications for how one perceives one's ingroup, and, importantly, one's relation to the ingroup. Lee and Ottati (1995) investigated how one's social identity may be affected by stereotype threats that are either consistent or inconsistent with self-perceived stereotypes about one's ingroup. According to Tajfel and Turner's social-identity theory (SIT; 1986), we derive our identity and self-esteem through two avenues. One is through our own accomplishments, and the other is through our group membership. SIT suggests that when one belongs to a devalued or threatened group, continued identification with the group threatens one's self-esteem. Threatened individuals may therefore disidentify with their ingroup in order to protect their self-esteem.

Lee and Ottati (1995) examined how Chinese participants would respond to negative stereotypic threats that are inconsistent or consistent with one's ingroup perceptions. They found that negative stereotypes that are inconsistent with the ingroup stereotype lead ingroup members to increase their perceptions of ingroup homogeneity, or solidarity/unity. That is, participants' identification with their ingroup increased. However, when participants were exposed to a negative stereotype-consistent threat (that is partially consistent with stereotypes about those who are Chinese), the participant had a more difficult time denying the validity of the stereotype expression. Participants protected their social identity by emphasizing that not all members of their group are characterized by the negative stereotype. In doing so, participants were emphasizing more ingroup heterogeneity, which may reflect a weakening identification with their ingroup as a whole (Arndt, Greenberg, Schimel, Pyszczynski, & Solomon, 2002; Spears, Doosje et al., 1997).

Although this psychological disidentification may be a temporary response to a particular situation (Markus & Kunda, 1986), continued exposure to stereotype threat may lead stigmatized individuals to chronically disengage psychologically from the stereotype-threat dimension (Major & Schmader, 1998). What are the consequences for the stigmatized individual who has disidentified from the stereotype-threat domain? Disidentification can be both adaptive and maladaptive. On the one hand, disidentification can be viewed as a healthy, effective coping response that allows the individual to protect their self-concept and self-identity against the prejudice, discrimination, and disadvantage the stigmatized person may encounter in the stereotype-threat domain (Crocker et al., 1998; Major & Schmader). However, Steele (1997) and Major and Schmader note that the paradox of disidentification is that while it saves the self-esteem, it imperils the individual's chances for success and achievement in domains that society may regard as important.

There are ways to reduce stereotype threat. Steele (1997) suggests that it is not enough to merely prevent disidentification of stigmatized students. It is important to simultaneously enhance the individual's identification with the stereotype-threatened domain. Techniques such as Aronson's jigsaw classroom (see Chapter 9) can be an effective way to help students enjoy school and can lead to higher self-esteem and higher exam scores (Aronson & Bridgeman, 1979; Wolfe & Spencer, 1996). Steele (1997) suggested some additional useful strategies: optimistic student–teacher relationships, challenge instead of remediation, stressing that intelligence is expandable, affirming domain belonging, valuing multiple perspectives, having visible successful role models, and building self-efficacy.

Recent evidence suggests that such an approach may work (Steele, Spencer, Hummel, Carter, Harber, Schoem, & Nisbett, 1998, as cited in Aronson et al., 1998). Steele et al. (1998) implemented a program for the reduction of stereotype threat and enhanced domain identification for African American college freshman at the University of Michigan. The researchers used three ways to reduce stereotype threat: (1) students were honorifically recruited for the program with an emphasis on their being bright enough to have been admitted to the University of Michigan (this taps into domain belonging), (2) students participated in weekly seminars to get to know each other and share common problems, and (3) participants attended subject-matter workshops that exposed them to advanced material outside the material discussed in class. Results after 4 years of the program indicated that participants had grade point averages about 4/10 higher than nonprogram peers, and they were more likely to finish college. Interviews with participants indicated that the program did, in fact, reduce stereotype threat and increase domain identification, leading to better grades (Aronson et al., 1998).

SELF-ESTEEM

It seems intuitive that those who are stigmatized quickly become aware of the negative way that many in society view them. This should have a negative effect on the self-esteem of the stigmatized. However, the data are mixed on this issue. Some research concludes that stigmatized persons suffer no damage to their self-esteem, and, in some cases, their self-esteem is higher than that of nonstigmatized counterparts (Porter & Washington, 1979; Rosenberg, 1979; Simmons, Brown, Bush, & Blyth, 1978). In fact, studies have failed to show decreased self-esteem for such stigmatized groups as African Americans, the physically challenged, developmentally disabled, or mentally disabled (for a review, see Crocker & Major, 1989). Other studies have indicated that some stigmatized individuals (e.g., overweight persons; Crocker et al., 1993) do suffer lower self-esteem. What seems to account for why some stigmatized individuals are able to protect their self-esteem and others seem to feel miserable about themselves has much to do with the perceived controllability (and hence, the justifiability) of the stigma (Crocker, Cornwell, & Major, 1998). Those individuals who believe that their stigmatizing condition is controllable (and thus indicates some personal flaw on their part) may be more likely to feel that negative evaluations of them are justified, and will be more likely to feel lower self-esteem. However, believing that one's stigma is uncontrollable will lead the stigmatized individual to resist the "blame" for the stigma, to attribute negative evaluations to prejudice, and to maintain self-esteem (Crocker & Major, 1994).

A comprehensive meta-analysis of 261 comparisons of self-esteem differences between Caucasians and African Americans revealed that, in general, African Americans tend to have higher self-esteem than Caucasians (Gray-Little & Hafdahl, 2000). A separate meta-analysis by Twenge and Crocker (2002) came to the same conclusion. Although this finding had also been reached in earlier studies, Gray-Little and Hafdahl note that past researchers would disregard the findings as flawed, because of the assumption that members of a stereotyped group would have to have lower self-esteem as a result of the larger society's generally negative views of African Americans, but not of Caucasians. Gray-Little and Hafdahl further suggest that the reason for the higher self-esteem of African Americans lies in the fact that they do not, as had been assumed, base their self-worth on the way others view them. If they did, it might be the case that they would feel more negative about themselves. However, Gray-Little and Hafdahl found that the reference group for African Americans is other African Americans, and not society. They are a distinctive minority group, and by embracing that distinctiveness and their positive ethnic/racial identity, they maintain self-esteem as high as, and often higher than that of their White counterparts.

Another explanation for the inconsistent findings concerning the influence of prejudice on the self-esteem of the target of prejudice centers on a problem with the way researchers have conceptualized and measured self-esteem. In a recent analysis, Crocker and Quinn (2000) argued that researchers assumed that self-esteem was a stable aspect of personality, and that when the target of prejudice would experience prejudice, stereotypes, or discrimination, they would internalize the shame or psychological pain, and this then would damage the individual's self-esteem. However, the literature on self-esteem does not support these assumptions. Crocker and Quinn make the compelling case that it is more accurate to conceptualize self-esteem as a kind of working model that is multiply determined and constructed by the situational, motivational, and interpersonal factors in a given situation, and by one's salient beliefs and values at that time. Such a conceptualization would account well for the inconsistency in the self-esteem studies, and it is important to continue research on this intriguing perspective to examine whether it holds up to empirical and theoretical scrutiny, and to ascertain its parameters with regard to the data.

Denial of Discrimination

Other research has revealed another way by which stigmatized individuals maintain their self-esteem. Researchers have found that, often, stigmatized persons are able to deny that they have been personally discriminated against, or that they have suffered prejudice, discrimination, or other mistreatment related to their stigma (Crosby, 1984). This denial of personal discrimination has been found in African Americans (Abeles, 1976) and women (Crosby, 1984; Hodson & Esses, 2002), in addition to other minority groups. What is especially interesting about these data is that the stigmatized person acknowledges that their group suffers discrimination and prejudice in society but claims that they have not personally had such negative experiences. Such a disconnect (or cognitive distortion) allows the stigmatized person to avoid the uncomfortable reality that the world may not be a just or fair world (Lerner, 1980), and that their life may be negatively (and seemingly unavoidably) affected by their stigma (Crosby, 1984). Some research suggests that making an attribution to discrimination also helps protect one's self-esteem (Major, Kaiser, & McCoy, 2003). However, other studies on the effects of such attributions show greater stress responses and decreased self-esteem (e.g., King, 2003). Thus, the data on this issue are mixed, and more research is needed (Major, Quinton, & McCoy, 2002). Given the negative implications of believing the latter two statements about the world, it is easy to understand why stigmatized persons would deny personal discrimination. Such a perspective appears to hold no negative psychological, emotional, or adjustment consequences, and it may be an adaptive way to deal with the unfair treatment one often receives as a result of being a member of a stigmatized group.

What determines whether a member of a stigmatized group perceives the behavior of a nonstigmatized person as discrimination or prejudice? Research by Major and her colleagues (2002a) makes a compelling case that the degree to which the stigmatized individual believes in an ideology that legitimizes existing status differences between groups will influence his/her perceptions of personal communication. The more an individual does *not* endorse such an ideology and instead believes in individual mobility of group members, the less likely it is that negative behavior/evaluations from the nonstigmatized individual will be interpreted as instances of discrimination or prejudice. Another factor that can influence whether a stigmatized group member attributes behavior of a nonstigmatized individual to prejudice and/or discrimination is the social costs involved with doing so. Kaiser and Miller (2001, 2003) found that stigmatized individuals who make such attributions to discrimination are perceived as complainers and were generally less favorably evaluated by others.

Self-Fulfilling Prophecy

Attributing negative feedback from a nonstigmatized individual to prejudice often, but not always, works as a technique for the stigmatized to protect their self-esteem. Sometimes, the ubiquity of the stereotype about one's stigmatized group can indeed influence one's self-concept. For example, Stephan and Rosenfield (1982) analyzed several studies and literature reviews of the attitudes of Blacks and Whites toward their own groups and toward the other group and found that Whites' views of their own group was largely positive (with the exception of the characteristic "materialistic"), and their view of Blacks was very negative (with the exception of "musical," "peace-loving," and "proud"). Blacks tended to view Whites in very negative terms as well (with the exception of attributing the positive characteristics "intelligent" and "industrious" to Whites). Finally, while Blacks viewed their own group in positive terms, they also believed some negative stereotypes about their group (they attributed the characteristics "lazy" and "superstitious" to Blacks).

What might explain the process whereby a stigmatized group comes to accept and believe some negative stereotypes about itself? One possible mechanism whereby this may occurs is through a **self-fulfilling prophecy.** The self-fulfilling prophecy refers to the phenomenon by which a perceiver's expectations about a target eventually lead that target to behave in ways that confirm those expectations (Rosenthal & Jacobson, 1968). Thus, some researchers have hypothesized that one reason for the finding that some stigmatized groups view themselves as having a small number of stereotypic, negative characteristics is that the group members have internalized the negative views of the group that the majority members (and, to a large extent, society) directly and indirectly communicate to them (Word, Zanna, & Cooper, 1974). Allport (1954) believed that this may occur in minority groups because if the minority group acknowledged that their group had as much worth as other groups in society, it would bring about tremendous psychological discomfort in that it causes the stigmatized individual to question the structure of social reality (Crosby, 1984).

The process works as follows. The majority member's stereotype influences how they interact with the member of the minority group. These behaviors elicit behaviors that fit the majority member's initial expectancies (Hamilton & Trolier, 1986). This may be difficult to ignore, if you are a member of the stigmatized group. If you are finding that your fellow stigmatized colleagues are demonstrating the stereotyped characteristics (in response to the expectancies of the nonstigmatized group, see Snyder & Swann, 1978), and you recall yourself acting the same way, it is not surprising, then, that you accept as valid that your group (including you) tends to demonstrate that characteristic. In other words, faced with the evidence from within and outside the stigmatized group that points to that conclusion, the stigmatized individual may be likely to internalize that stereotype for their group.

However, it is important to note that self-fulfilling prophecies do not occur when the target is aware of the perceiver's expectations (Hilton & Darley, 1985). While the self-fulfilling prophecy is a robust phenomenon (Rosenthal & Rubin, 1978), recent research indicates that its effect in maintaining stereotypes and eliciting stereotypic behavior in stigmatized individuals is limited. Jussim and Fleming (1996) reviewed the literature on self-fulfilling prophecy effects in intergroup interactions and found that most of the naturalistic studies show that the effect of the stereotyped expectations on the stigmatized tends to be quite small (correlation of .2, and a .2 regression coefficient). Thus, although the idea that self-fulfilling prophecies may elicit more stereotype-consistent behaviors in the stigmatized (and may even lead them to believe their group possesses some negative stereotyped characteristics), and although it is an interesting explanation for the data reported by Stephan and Rosenfield (1982), there is little data supporting it as a factor in the stereotype-relevant behavior of the stigmatized.

In sum, Major and her colleagues (Crocker & Major, 1989; Major & Schmader, 1998) suggest four ways the stigmatized can maintain their self-esteem:

1. Attributing the negative evaluations and reactions of others to prejudice
2. Devaluing outcomes on which their group compares poorly with other groups (recall the discussion on stereotype threat)
3. Comparing one's stigmatized ingroup with other stigmatized groups, rather than to nonstigmatized groups
4. Psychologically disengaging their self-esteem from feedback in domains in which their group is at a disadvantage.

Self-esteem in stigmatized individuals seems to be fairly resilient against the negative influence of others' prejudice and stereotyping.

INTERGROUP INTERACTIONS

Research has yielded little information on how the expectations and affective states of majority and minority groups in actual intergroup interactions influence their perceptions of the behavior of their interaction partner. Past research has attempted to understand the perceptions of an imagined intergroup interaction partner (e.g., Devine et al., 1996; Islam & Hewstone, 1993; Stephan & Stephan, 1985). In one such experiment, Langer, Fiske, Taylor, and Chanowitz (1976) found that people experience discomfort and a desire to avoid interactions with physically different (e.g., pregnant women and physically challenged) persons because they are conflicted over whether to stare at the individual. They found that the tendency to stare at an outgroup member comes primarily from curiosity about a group with whom the subjects infrequently come into contact. Interestingly, people did not derogate the physically different persons, so staring (and avoidance behavior) was not attributable to feelings of disgust or dislike. Staring and avoidance were reduced when people had more time to get accustomed to the physically different person, via simple habituation.

However, prior research has tended only to address majority and minority groups separately. Research on the majority groups (e.g., Caucasians, the young, heterosexuals) has explored how stereotypes and prejudices arise in these individuals (in order to reduce or even eliminate such negative intergroup attitudes). Investigations with minority groups (e.g., African Americans, homosexuals, the elderly) have examined how minority-group members feel about their stigma and how the stigma influences their self-perceptions and behavior toward others (Devine et al., 1996). However, in order to assess how affect, perceptions, and expectations influence the way one perceives the outgroup member in an intergroup context, it is important to understand the dynamics of the intergroup interaction.

Dynamic Nature of Interactions

Devine et al. (1996) make the compelling argument that researchers today must turn their attention toward understanding the dynamic *live* interactions between majority- and minority-group members, and how their thoughts, feelings, and behavior both change the interaction and are changed by their perception of the interaction on a moment-by-moment basis. As I have mentioned throughout this text, much research suggests that the typical intergroup interaction is characterized by some (or a significant degree of) anxiety (see Fiske, 1998; Stephan & Stephan, 1985). The potential causes for the anxiety are different for each member in the intergroup interaction. For high-prejudice majority members, anxiety may reflect their discomfort (sometimes driven by strong negative feelings, such as disgust or anger) with the minority group, and their preference to avoid the minority group altogether (Devine, Monteith, Zuwerink, & Elliot, 1991; Monteith, 1993). The behaviors of the minority-group individual in response to the high-prejudice majority member are likely to be seen by the latter as supportive evidence for their stereotypes. For low-prejudice individuals, however, it is important to distinguish between those who have had many intergroup experiences (i.e., they are intergroup skilled) from those who have had few intergroup interactions (i.e., intergroup unskilled). Both groups are highly motivated to indicate to the minority group individual that they are not prejudiced. Intergroup-skilled majority members have a good idea of how best to present their low-prejudice self to the other individual, and they feel little or no anxiety in the interaction. This is conveyed to the minority member through a relaxed behavior and demeanor. The model contends that in this situation the minority member is thus less likely to misinterpret the behavior of the low-prejudice majority member as an indicator of underlying prejudice. Rather, the minority-group member is likely to respond in similar fashion.

In the case of the low-prejudice, intergroup-unskilled majority member, Devine and her colleagues (1996) suggest that the intergroup context holds the potential for much misunderstanding, because of the different motivations, expectations, and perceptions the majority and minority individuals bring to the interaction. The intergroup-unskilled individual is in a very difficult spot. Because they have had little intergroup contact, they do not know what behaviors are appropriate, what might (unintentionally) communicate prejudice where it does not exist, and what to expect from the minority member. This uncertainty leads to anxiety. This anxiety is evidenced in more avoidant nonverbal behaviors, such as decreased eye contact, nervous laughter, and increased interpersonal distance (Word et al., 1974). These behaviors often result in conveying precisely the opposite impression to the minority-group member: that the majority member is nervous because they are uncomfortable around minorities as a result of feelings of prejudice toward the minority. According to Devine and her colleagues, and depending on the minority individual's own prejudice level toward the majority member (Ashburn-Nardo, Knowles, & Monteith, 2003; Dasgupta, 2004; Rudman, Feinberg, & Fairchild, 2002), at this point in the interaction the minority member may respond with withdrawal, dismissal (being indifferent to the majority-group member), or hostility. Next, if the majority individual does not perceive that the minority member's reaction is in response to perceived prejudice, they may perceive the minority's behavior as an indicator of prejudice toward the majority. Thus, intergroup interactions can often be fraught with misunderstandings, misperceptions, and reaffirmed prejudices. As is the case in social interactions in general, the perceived motives and expectations can often affect one's behavior toward the other person, and this often results in confirmed expectations and behavior confirmation (Snyder & Swann, 1978).

An experiment by Weitz (1972) shows that it is easy to see why minority-group members might be suspicious of the true attitudes and motives of the majority-group interaction partner. She asked 80 male Caucasians to participate in an interaction with another individual. Racial attitudes were measured earlier (all participants selected for the study were low in self-reported prejudice toward African Americans) and then the experimenter asked the partner to read some information about the partner with whom the male would interact. Among this information was whether the interaction partner was either African American or Caucasian. Measures of anxiety in the participant's voice (participants recorded a brief taped message) and behavior (participants were asked to choose how long and how closely they would like to work on the task with the partner, whether they would like to wait with the partner, and how far apart they should sit during the task) were taken to assess whether there was any discrepancy between attitudes and behavior. Results indicated that very favorable racial attitudes were strongly correlated with avoidant, unfriendly behavior. Thus, while they claimed to be low in prejudice, their nonverbal behavior indicated otherwise. This certainly represents a confusing situation for the minority at the receiving end of this behavior. Weitz suggests that because vocal and behavioral cues are more illustrative (more trustworthy), the minority would more than likely pay attention to these cues and respond in like fashion (i.e., negatively toward the Caucasian). Unfortunately, this would likely contribute to the Caucasian's unease and confirm their negative feelings about the minority group, and prejudice and misunderstanding would thus be perpetuated by both interactants.

What if one's stigmatized status was not obvious (e.g., being on welfare), would that individual's interaction with the nonstigmatized differ in important ways from interactions between visibly stigmatized persons and the nonstigmatized? It is an interesting question. One might imagine that the immediate and obvious nature of some stigmas (e.g., race, gender, physical characteristics) would tend to make stigmatized persons in these groups more defensive, more alert to signs that they are being treated unfairly by others. This could most assuredly influence how that person approaches interactions with a nonstigmatized person. In an experiment to examine this question, Frable, Blackstone, and Scherbaum (1990) did find that whether one's stigma is visible or invisible makes a big difference in that person's interaction with a nonstigmatized person. Forty-four pairs of women were unobtrusively videotaped while they waited for the experimenter to begin the study. Their interpersonal behavior, attitudes toward their interaction partner, and memory for the interaction and environment were measured. Some participants had invisible stigmas (they had been raped, they were bisexual, or they were victims of incest), and others' stigmas were visible (they were more than 60 pounds overweight, they were African American, or they had severe facial acne). Stigmatized persons were always paired with a nonstigmatized person. Results indicated that invisible and overtly stigmatized persons reacted differently to the interaction.(Individuals with invisible stigmas were more likely to take their partner's perspective, to remember what occurred in the interaction, and to remember details about what the partner said.)Those with visible stigmas were much less likely to remember the interaction details, though they remembered details about the partner's appearance and the room. Frable et al. (1990) suggest that invisible deviants need to pay close attention to all information that might be relevant to exposing their condition. In that respect, paying attention to what was said is very important. Those with visible stigmas have a "spoiled identity" (Goffman, 1963), and are engaged in a kind of damage control in that they are more vigilant about nonverbal behavior in an effort to ascertain the true attitude of the nonstigmatized person toward their stigmatized group.

Interestingly, an analysis of the participants' perceptions of the interaction and their attitudes toward their partner showed that nonstigmatized participants displayed a lot of effort, encouraging their partners to participate, and they tended to talk, smile and initiate conversation. Although the stigmatized person participated, the nonstigmatized participant did not remember their partner's contributions, and, in fact, reported that they disliked their stigmatized partner. Because the nonstigmatized person tended to devalue the contribution (or distort the extent of their own contribution and effort in the interaction), their negative preconceptions and stereotypes of the stigmatized group were more likely to be confirmed. These findings again illustrate the difficulty of overcoming stereotypes and the potential for misunderstanding in intergroup interactions.

To put it simply: if you enter a social interaction expecting it to go poorly, it is likely to turn out poorly. A study by Ickes (1984) supports this conclusion. Ickes examined the unstructured interactions of intergroup dyads composed of Blacks and Whites. Results revealed that although White dyad members displayed more smiling, gazing, and talking relative to their Black partner, they also perceived the interaction as more stressful and uncomfortable. Ickes concluded that these results are likely due to differences between Blacks and Whites in terms of intergroup contact experiences. By virtue of their minority status, Blacks are much more likely to have contact with Whites (and thus should feel more comfortable in interactions with Whites) than Whites are to have contact with Blacks. Thus, the lack of intergroup experience can lead to anxiety about the intergroup interaction. The more anxiety one feels, the more one is likely to perceive the reaction of an interaction partner to oneself as more negative (Pozo, Carver, Wellens, & Scheier, 1991).

Devine's model of the dynamic nature of intergroup interactions is an important contribution to the extant prejudice and stereotype literature. It clearly articulates how expectations, motivations, and prejudices can influence and be influenced by the perceptions of the other individual's behavior. The model is also unique in attempting to explain how moment-to-moment changes in social interactions influence both interactants. The model is also unique in taking into account the perspective, expectations, motivations, and behavior of the minority individual in the intergroup context in an analysis of how these factors influence and are influenced by the majority individual. Understanding this dynamic process is an important next step to understanding the complexity of intergroup interactions. Testing a dynamic model such as this in an experimental setting does, however, pose daunting challenges for the researcher.

First, in a typical social–psychological experiment, there usually are clearly defined causal variables, and the researcher is interested in examining the effects on participants when this variable is manipulated. In other words, there is a unidirectional, linear cause and effect implicit in the experiment. Although this makes life easy for the experimenter, such experiments represent an incomplete picture of how natural social interactions affect (and are affected by) the interactant's behavior. As we have seen, the behavior of the majority (or minority) member in the intergroup context does not occur in a vacuum. Rather, behavior, expectations, and perceptions change and are changed by the other's behavior. Second, this dynamic model suggests that there is no single, clear cause and effect in a continuous interaction; rather, there are many many miniature cause–effect sequences all encompassed in a dynamic feedback loop (for further discussion, see Nelson, 1993). For these reasons, we know very little about how the dynamics of the intergroup interaction influence the interactants. We will revisit this discussion on the dynamic nature of intergroup interactions in greater detail in Chapter 10. Next we explore how expectations, metastereotypes, and intergroup anxiety affect intergroup interactions.

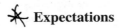 **Expectations**

Another factor that fuels the negative expectancies for the intergroup interaction is the notion that the majority and minority have different perspectives from which they approach an understanding of the world. As Gates (1995, as cited by Jones, 1997b) suggests, "People arrive at an understanding of themselves and the world through narratives—narratives purveyed by schoolteachers, newscasters, "authorities," and all the other authors of our common sense. Counternarratives are, in turn, the means by which groups contest the dominant reality and the network of assumptions that supports it. . . . Much of Black history is simply counternarrative" (p. 57). Thus, the narratives and counternarratives define reality for various individuals. Jones (1996) suggests that oftentimes the reason why the minority approaches contact with the majority with negative expectations is that the majority "are strongly biased toward their own experiences, values, beliefs, and the products of their culture" while the minority "who have so often been victimized by those very beliefs and cultural outcroppings, mistrust them and ultimately dislike them" (p. 257).

Intergroup Anxiety

Most of the past research on reactions to the outgroup has typically involved imagining (or reading) an intergroup scenario, and how you might think and feel in such a situation. Ideally, we would like data that speak to how people react in an actual intergroup interaction (in order to compare the data for how we think we would react to how we actually react). Unfortunately, there exist few studies that compare anticipated with actual behaviors in the intergroup context. However, the direction of the research in stereotyping seems to be changing to answer Devine et al.'s (1996) call to explore the uncharted waters of expectations and impressions of other individuals in live intergroup interactions.

In one such experiment, Hyers and Swim (1998) examined the reactions of minority and majority members in an actual intergroup interaction. African American or European American women participated in triads in which they were either the sole representative of their ethnic group (i.e., one African American and two European Americans) or they were a nonsolo member. The subject was being covertly videotaped while they worked on a group task. Each group consisted of one subject and two confederates. They were told that they were to decide the 10 best occupations that would be useful for starting a new society on a desert island. They were to provide their suggestions to the group with justification for their responses. After the group task was completed, the participants were ostensibly interviewed separately (however, only the participant was interviewed; the confederates, unbeknownst to the participant, were not interviewed). The participant was told that the purpose of the study was to examine how the group interacted, and she was told that she was videotaped. After the subject agreed to authorize the use of the videotape for the study, she viewed her reactions on the videotape and wrote down her thoughts and feelings about different points of the group task. Hyers and Swim expected that, because European American women likely did not have as much intergroup experience, they would feel more negative affect than African American subjects. But this hypothesis was not supported. Also, whether the subject was the sole representative of her ethnic group did not influence her reactions to the intergroup encounter. Results did indicate that European American women showed decreased task attention. The authors suggested that African Americans showed little affective, cognitive, or behavioral negative experiences in the intergroup interaction largely because of their greater intergroup experience.

→ reference my father

✷ Metastereotypes

Sigelman and Tuch (1997) introduced the term **metastereotype** to refer to one's perceptions of another group's stereotypes of one's group. For example, what do Whites believe that Blacks believe about Whites? Similarly, what stereotypes about Blacks do Blacks believe Whites endorse? If minorities share a common experience in their stigmatization at the hands of the majority, it seems logical that the majority might have a common view of how the minority group views them. To examine metastereotypes, Vorauer, Main, and O'Connell (1998) examined White Canadians' perceptions of how Aboriginal Canadians viewed them. Results indicated that White Canadians have a common negative stereotype about how they are viewed by Aboriginal Canadians, and that the belief in these metastereotypes was associated with more negative affect and expectancies regarding potential intergroup interactions. Additionally, when the White Canadians endorsed these metastereotypes, they experienced decreased self-esteem and worsened self-concept clarity.

While there is a substantial literature on the stereotypes that majority members have about minorities, we know relatively little about the perceptions of minorities of the majority members, and little to nothing about their metastereotypes. To address this issue, Sigelman and Tuch (1997) examined data gathered from the National Opinion Research Center (Davis & Smith, 1990) on Blacks' perceptions of Whites' views of Blacks. The attitudes of Blacks and Whites toward each other were also examined. Finally, the degree of stereotype endorsement for each group was examined. The authors uncovered some surprising data.

Two thirds of the Black participants in the survey indicated that they believed that Whites endorsed *every* stereotype about Blacks. This is not as alarming when one considers that the researchers also found that most Whites in the survey did, in fact, view Blacks in very stereotyped terms. It appears, therefore, that the metastereotypes of the Black participants were largely accurate. However, not all Blacks were as strong in their belief that Whites endorsed stereotypes about Blacks. The data from the survey revealed that Black women, younger Blacks, and higher-income Blacks were less likely than their older, male, and lower-income counterparts to view Whites as holding positive stereotypes (positive views) about Blacks. According to Sigelman and Tuch, it seems that those who have more contact with Whites are least likely to believe that Whites hold positive views of Blacks.

Intergroup interactions are also doomed when the interactants are prejudiced against each other's groups. Pettigrew (1979) suggested that the prejudice of the individual taints their perception of both positive and negative behavior on the part of the disliked outgroup member. When the outgroup member does something that is perceived as negative, the prejudiced perceiver is more likely to attribute the action to internal, genetically determined factors than when the same act is committed by an ingroup member. When the prejudiced perceiver views a positive action from the outgroup member, they will most likely attribute it to luck, exceptional effort, or the "exceptional case" (in other words, subtyping; Weber & Crocker, 1983).

ATTRIBUTIONAL AMBIGUITY

One of the most fundamental components of our social lives concerns the attempt to understand the behavior of other people. In trying to understand others' behavior toward us, we try to decide whether an individual's actions were caused by some internal force or stable characteristic about the individual (e.g., a enduring personality trait), or a situational force (e.g., a role the individual is playing, or that the person was forced to behave in some fashion). This is the basic problem of attribution. To which of these two major causes do we attribute others' behavior? For most people, there are always various individuals and situations that make it difficult to arrive at a clear answer to the attribution question. Yet, there is a difference between the stigmatized and nonstigmatized, in terms of their daily experiences in understanding the causes of others' behavior toward them. Most of the time, for most nonstigmatized individuals, this task is fairly straightforward: other people behave toward them based on the personality or performance of the nonstigmatized individual. Stigmatized individuals, on the other hand, face a different set of circumstances.

In attempting to understand the reasons for others' behavior toward them, the stigmatized are confronted with another possible causal explanation: others' reaction (often based on stereotypes and prejudices) to their stigma. Thus, because the stigmatized are well familiar with the stereotypes and prejudices that exist about their group (Jones, 1997), they are continually faced with deciding whether to attribute others' behavior toward them as a reaction to their stigma (and thus, to stereotypes and prejudice), or to their reaction to the aspects of the stigmatized individual that are not associated with the stigma (i.e., the stigmatized person's personality). This constant attributional calculus has been termed **attributional ambiguity** (Crocker & Major, 1989; Major & Crocker, 1993). Major and Crocker suggest that the chronic uncertainty that the stigmatized experience regarding the causes of others' behavior toward them has important consequences for the self-esteem, mood, motivation, and interpersonal behavior of the stigmatized. For example, it is one thing to believe that the store manager told you that the job they listed in the want ads has been filled, but quite another to believe that the manager told that to you because of the color of your skin (or your gender, age, or the fact that you are in a wheelchair, etc.).

For many stigmatized people, self-esteem can be protected by regarding the negative behavior of others toward them as a reflection of underlying prejudice, and not as a consequence of their personal traits (Goffman, 1963, Jones et al., 1984). Some readers who are members of nonstigmatized groups might respond, "That sounds like an awfully cynical way to go about life." Before you rush to such an assessment, consider the following. If you had a noticeable stigma, one that is associated with a number of negative stereotypes, you likely would come to learn, as you grew up, that this stigma was universally noticed by others. Given this, you are faced with the very difficult task of understanding what the motives are for the behavior of the nonstigmatized outgroups toward you. Given the pervasiveness of prejudice and stereotypes in American society, it is likely that most people are aware of, and some percentage of them believe, stereotypes about your group. The assessment you need to make is a probability assessment (Fiske & Taylor, 1991; Kahneman et al., 1982). Specifically, what is the likelihood that the nonstigmatized individual with whom I am interacting is behaving according to some stereotypes they have about my group?

In answering this question, trying to understand the (potential) stereotyper and the context in which the behavior occurred is helpful. It is useful to attempt to find out if the stereotyper had the ability and motivation (and background learning history) that would enable them to behave in nonstereotyped ways. What the stigmatized person is attempting to understand here is the *intent* of the stereotyper (Fiske, 1989). The reasons for the behavior of the nonstigmatized person may be clear with an assessment of the context in which the negative intergroup behavior occurred. If it is nondominant, then other persons surrounding the stereotyper are thinking and acting in nondiscriminatory terms, and, in this instance, a basic perceptual contrast effect reveals that the behavior of the stereotyping majority member is especially likely to be regarded as caused by their own prejudice. However, if the context is such that everyone else is emitting similar stereotyping behaviors as the individual in question, the question of intent becomes cloudier, and the context holds a fair amount of attributional ambiguity for the stigmatized individual.

One way to avoid the frustration of trying to ascertain the true motive behind the other's behavior is to just assume that no behavior that others exhibit toward you is related to your stigma. This is an "innocent until proven guilty" approach. While apparently logical and reasonable, this perspective has some self-relevant pitfalls that make it unattractive. You know that such a perspective is a fair way to view others, but American society is, more often than not, unfair in the way your stigmatized group is viewed (Fiske, 1998; Swim & Stangor, 1998). Given that conclusion, your conclusion is likely to be that most (not all) nonstigmatized outgroup members will react to you based in some part on their stereotypes and prejudices about your stigmatized group (the "guilty until proven innocent" approach).

In a fascinating experiment, Kleck and Strenta (1980) investigated the effects of having negatively valued characteristics on one's perceptions of an interaction partner. Women participants were told that they would be interacting with another participant (who was a confederate) in a brief discussion of tactics people use to make friends. Participants were randomly assigned to one of three characteristics conditions: allergy, epilepsy, or a facial scar. Participants were told that the experimenter wanted to assess whether the partner's behavior would be affected by the participant's physical condition. Participants were asked to complete a biographical questionnaire and indicate their condition on the second page (unbeknownst to the participant, the partner/confederate was not shown the second page). Those in the scar condition had a very noticeable fake scar applied to their face. Participants confirmed the presence of the scar with a mirror and were asked not to touch it or discuss it unless the partner mentioned it. Before the participant interacted with the partner, the experimenter informed her that he needed to moisturize the scar so that the adhesive would not crack. While doing so, he removed the scar—without the participant's knowledge. The experimenter then brought the participant's biographical information to the partner in the other lab room, and then the two were brought together and seated in a room. After a 6-minute discussion, they went back to their separate lab rooms, and the participant evaluated the partner's behavior, and provided her attitude toward the partner.

Results indicated that participants who were in the negative stigma conditions (scar and epilepsy) believed that their conditions had a strong impact on the behavior of the partner. Those in the allergy condition did not have this belief about their partner. Specifically, scar and epilepsy participants were more likely to perceive that their partner was tense and patronizing. Additionally, they believed that their partner liked them less and found them less attractive. These data highlight the strong influence of expectancies in clouding our perceptions of others' reactions to us. Even though there was no stigma presented to the confederate, and the confederate's behavior toward the participant was virtually the same for all participants, those who believed that their partner was regarding them as negatively stigmatized perceived their partner's behaviors as reflecting tension and derision toward the participant (similar findings were obtained in experiments by Santuzzi & Ruscher, 2002). Our expectancies about someone can cause us to regard that person's normal, innocuous behavior as symptomatic of the attributed motive, characteristic, or personality of the other individual (Fiske & Taylor, 1991; Rosenhan, 1973).

With this assessment, it would be difficult to take the "innocent until proven guilty" perspective, because you are making your self-esteem and self-identity vulnerable to the negative effects of others' behavior, which is likely based on unfair, stereotype-based evaluations of you. In short, you may perceive that you are treated fairly, when in fact, the probability is that you are not being treated fairly. In that instance, you may feel foolish, gullible, and hurt. To protect the self, the stigmatized individual may take a "guilty until proven innocent" approach to interacting with nonstigmatized individuals (Jones, et al., 1984; Major & Crocker, 1993; Swim, Cohen, & Hyers, 1998), but such an approach comes with its own consequences. Kaiser, Major, and McCoy (2004) found that individuals who are members of a stereotyped group and who are pessimists (i.e., viewing others' behavior toward them as likely due to prejudice) are more likely to feel more stressed at (potentially) prejudiced intergroup interactions, and they tend to believe they have fewer resources for coping with it. Optimists, on the other hand (i.e., taking an "innocent until proven guilty" attribution to others' behavior toward them) report more coping resources and much less stress at perceiving potential prejudice directed toward them.

Research also indicates that positive feedback from nonstigmatized individuals to the stigmatized can present an attributionally ambiguous situation. To what does the stigmatized person attribute the positive evaluation they have received? Is it due to a patronizing, artificial positive evaluation of the person that is related to their stigma, or to purely the performance or personal characteristics of the stigmatized individual? In other words, the stigmatized individual may ask him/herself, "Did this person give me this positive feedback because I am Black (or a woman, or Hispanic, Asian, etc.) and they don't want to appear prejudiced, or is it because they really like me (or what I did) for who I am as a person?" This is a difficult question to answer in most instances.

Consider the following illustration of the problem. Several studies have demonstrated that nonstigmatized individuals give more positive ratings to stigmatized (compared to nonstigmatized) individuals in impression-formation experiments (e.g., Carver, Glass, Snyder, & Katz, 1977). This led some researchers to explain the findings in terms of a sympathy effect. Further analysis indicates, however, that there could be three possible explanations for these findings. They may reflect true positive biases of the majority members, they may reflect unconscious distortions of true negative feelings, or, finally, they may represent conscious distortions of true negative feelings, due to social-desirability effects (Carver, Glass, & Katz, 1978).

In a clever experiment, Carver, Glass, and Katz (1978) investigated how White females evaluated Black and physically handicapped target individuals. Participants were asked to read a transcript of an interview with the target individual (either a male Caucasian, or a male Black, or a physically handicapped male) who was described as being of lower socioeconomic status, who had no plans for the future, and who had few friends. Basic demographics of the target individual, and their group identifier, if any (e.g., "handicapped" or "Black") were provided at the top of the interview transcript. Participants in the control condition read the transcript and then provided their ratings of the target individual. The other half of the participants were given a bogus-pipeline procedure (recall our discussion of this method from Chapter 5). Participants' arms, chest, and fingertips were hooked up to what appeared to be a very real physiological measuring device. It was explained that this would allow researchers a direct assessment of the participant's reaction to the interview transcript and that the researcher would thus know what the participant's true attitudes were toward the target. Allegedly, as a measure of reliability, however, participants were asked to complete the rating sheet (as the control-condition participants had), so that the investigator could compare the two types of attitude information.

Results indicated that participants in the control and bogus-pipeline conditions were identical in their ratings of the handicapped individual. They also agreed in their ratings of the male Caucasian. As predicted, ratings of the handicapped person were significantly higher than ratings of the Caucasian. Control-condition participants who read about a Black interviewee rated him as positively as the ratings that the handicapped individual garnered. However, participants who were in the bogus-pipeline condition rated the Black target significantly lower than those in the other conditions. Carver et al. (1978) explained these data as suggesting that perceptions of stigmatized individuals are not homogeneous. It appeared that the favorable ratings of the handicapped reflected a true underlying positive attitude toward the handicapped, whereas the favorable ratings of the Black target seemed to reflect an attempt to cover underlying negative feelings toward Blacks. The authors explain the difference in reaction to the two targets as possibly attributable to different perceptions of the degree to which each target has hurdles in life he must overcome. They speculate that perhaps participants gave handicapped persons more "credit" (consistent with Kelly's augmentation principle, 1971) for having to overcome physical, mental, and social difficulties.

They may have conversely regarded the Black individual as not facing as many difficult challenges in life as the handicapped. Another possible explanation may be that observers viewed the negative life circumstances of the Black person as being related to lack of motivation, while the situation for the handicapped individual could have been attributed to circumstances beyond his control (Carver, et al., 1978).

If we could experimentally manipulate the situation, such that sometimes the nonstigmatized person's reaction (positive or negative) to the stigmatized person is based only on an evaluation of the stigmatized person's character (and not the stigma), and less clear at other times, we might be able to more clearly understand the consequences for the self-esteem of the stigmatized. Well, just such an experiment has been published (you knew I was going to say that, didn't you?). Crocker, Voelkl, Testa, and Major (1991, Experiment 2) asked African American students to participate in an experiment ostensibly on friendship. When each participant arrived at the lab, they were told that another participant had arrived earlier and was seated in an adjacent room (there really was no other participant). The experiment room in which the African American participant was seated had a one-way mirror (obscured by closed blinds) in the wall to the adjacent room (where the other participant was supposedly seated). The African American participants were told that the experimenters were interested in same-race and cross-race friendship formation and that in this instance the participant would be paired with a White participant. Participants were asked to complete a self-description questionnaire (that did not indicate their race) and a measure of self-esteem. Participants were told that their responses would be shared with the other participant, who would use it to determine whether the two of them could become friends.

Participants were next told that either the blinds would be raised so their partner could see them (but they could not see their partner) and use this information in their judgment of whether they wanted to be further acquainted with the participant, or they were informed that the blinds would not be raised so that the other person would not be biased by the participant's appearance. The experimenter brought the African American participant's self-description to the next room, ostensibly to let the "other participant" evaluate it. The experimenter then brought back either a positive or negative evaluation and gave it to the participant. Participants read it and then completed a few questionnaires, including another measure of their self-esteem and a measure of current mood.

The results were quite interesting. When African American participants received positive feedback, their self-esteem increased when they believed they could not be seen, but for those who were in the blinds-up (seen) condition, positive feedback from the White partner brought about a decrease in self-esteem. In the not-seen condition, the positive feedback can only be attributed to information about the participant that was on their self-description. Thus, the conclusion the African American participant may make is, "The White person likes me because I have a good personality, and may have similar interests." Of course, we all like to be liked by others, and this type of feedback about our personality makes us feel good about ourselves. However, in the "seen" condition, the African American participant is faced with attributional ambiguity. It is unclear why they received positive feedback from the White partner. In this instance, African American participants attributed the positive feedback to a patronizing, false positive feedback that was probably given so the White participant would not appear prejudiced. Such an attribution (that it is likely that their stigma determined or influenced another's evaluation of them) led African American participants to feel worse about themselves.

Negative feedback from the White partner had different effects on the self-esteem of African American participants. When participants believed they were seen, their self-esteem remained unchanged. When they believed they were not seen, their self-esteem decreased. These data indicate that when a stigmatized individual believes that others have evaluated him/her negatively solely on the basis of a self-description (and not on race, as in the unseen condition), the only possible attribution for such an evaluation is that there is something unlikeable about the individual, which naturally makes the stigmatized individual feel negatively (and results in a decreased self-esteem). On the other hand, when a stigmatized person receives negative feedback from a nonstigmatized person who can see them, they are presented with an attributionally ambiguous situation. Here, participants resolved this ambiguity in a way that protected their self-esteem, and in terms of the most likely probable cause of the negative evaluation: they attributed the negative evaluation to the prejudice of the nonstigmatized participant. Unfortunately, although such an attribution may protect the self-esteem of the stigmatized individual, it may also result in feelings of helplessness and depression (Major & Crocker, 1993). A related study by Britt and Crandall (2000) examined whether Black and White participants accepted positive and negative feedback from an evaluator after they were informed not only about the race of their evaluator, but also about the motive of the evaluator; that is, whether the evaluator was pro- or anti-Black/Caucasian. Results indicated that Black and White participants discounted (were not affected by) positive feedback when they were seen by a pro-Black (or pro-Caucasian, respectively) evaluator. Similarly, participants tended to discount negative feedback from anti-Black (or anti-Caucasian) evaluator.

The attributional ambiguity of positive and negative feedback may also have consequences for the motivation of the stigmatized individual. Because it is unclear why the stigmatized individual received the feedback, they thus have little information about their true ability/characteristics on that dimension, and this uncertainty may lead the stigmatized person to be more likely to engage in self-handicapping behaviors (e.g., drinking and staying out late the night before an important morning exam) that are designed to provide a ready excuse for anticipated poor performance on that dimension (Arkin & Baumgardner, 1985; Berglas & Jones, 1978; Major & Crocker, 1993). This uncertainty may also result in decreased motivation to engage in behaviors on the relevant domain (e.g., academics; see the discussion of stereotype threat in Chapter 6).

The Paradoxical Effects of Affirmative Action

Members of stereotyped groups, such as racial and ethnic minorities, women, and the elderly, are sometimes the beneficiaries of programs and regulations that are designed to help them economically, occupationally, or educationally. For example, affirmative-action programs are designed to overcome the effects of past discrimination and current stereotypes and help these underrepresented minorities find good employment in the workplace. However, critics of affirmative action regard such programs as mere reverse discrimination, charging that they represent an unfair attempt to place preference on minority status above job qualifications in hiring decisions (Blanchard & Crosby, 1989; Kravitz, Klineberg, Avery, Nguyen, Lund, & Fu, 2000; Resendez, 2002). Research indicates that when both the beneficiaries and critics of affirmative action programs perceive the program as unjustified, they will each react negatively to the program (Taylor & Dube, 1986). Opposition to affirmative action may be especially likely from those who support an unequal, hierarchical social-status differential that favors their group over the stigmatized outgroup (i.e., those higher in social dominance; Federico & Sidanius, 2002). Although affirmative-action programs have succeeded in helping more minorities into the workplace, many observers have suggested that, overall, the success of the program has been limited (Murrell & Jones, 1996). Aside from any potential limitations in the program's ability to fulfill its purpose, another concern has been voiced by critics. Specifically, some argue that affirmative action may have psychological costs for those who benefit from the program. Steele (1990) suggests that it implies that the recipients of affirmative action are, a priori, inferior and in need of help from society (i.e., the majority).

There is some evidence to support this argument. Schneider, Major, Luhtanen, and Crocker (1996) reasoned that because minorities are more likely to be stereotyped as having lesser abilities, they will be more susceptible to potential negative psychological effects of offers of help from members of the majority. The idea here is that it is likely that due to the attributional ambiguity of the situation (is this majority member offering me help because they are a nice person, or because they think I am incompetent due to my minority status?) the minority member may be more likely to attribute helping behavior to veiled prejudice and stereotypes (Major, Feinstein, & Crocker, 1994). Such an attribution would clearly have implications for the minority member. Schneider et al. further hypothesized that if the minority believes that others see them as incompetent, it may negatively affect their self-esteem and views of their own work competence. Heilman, Block, and Lucas (1992) reported data to support this idea. They found that just mentioning that a woman was an affirmative-action hiree led perceivers to view her as less competent and less qualified than a non-affirmative-action female hiree or a male hiree. On the other hand, in research in which beneficiaries of affirmative action were told that their ability, as well as their group status, was taken into consideration in hiring them, they did not suffer the same negative effects (e.g. self-doubt) that those who were hired solely based on their status as a member of a minority group (Brown, Charnsangavej, Keough, Newman, & Rentfrow, 2000; Heilman, Rivero, & Brett, 1991).

In the Schneider et al. (1996) study, White and Black participants were assigned to either a help or no-help condition. Black students who received help from a White student reported lower self-esteem compared to Blacks in the no-help condition. Blacks who received help also reported more depressed affect than those who did not receive help; however, they did not evaluate the helping majority member negatively. In a related investigation, Nacoste (1985) found that when women perceived that they were given membership in a group primarily on the basis of their category membership, they felt that the admission procedure was less fair, and they displayed fewer positive emotions compared with those women admitted based on their qualifications. These results are consistent with other research that suggests that being the recipient of help can negatively influence one's self-esteem and feelings of competence (Blaine, Crocker, & Major, 1995; Fisher, Nadler, & Whitcher-Alagna, 1982; Schroeder, Penner, Dovidio, & Piliavin, 1995).

The prognosis is not as bleak as it may appear for minorities who are the beneficiaries of affirmative action. Pratkanis and Turner (1996) acknowledge that although much research suggests that the stigma attached to individuals who benefit from affirmative action is real and quite negative, further analysis reveals that the pernicious consequences for the recipient's self-esteem and competence evaluations can be short circuited. Pratkanis and

Turner suggest that when help is given to a minority individual (i.e., an affirmative-action hiring decision) who appears not to conform to societal values and is perceived to lack competence or appropriate qualifications, nonminorities feel defensive and hostile and the minority recipient tends to experience decreased self-esteem. However, if the same help is framed such that it is aimed at removing past discriminatory barriers, the minority and nonminority perceivers do not experience negative reactions to such help. When help is presented in this way, it is less threatening and is seen as social support and an indicator of societal concern for overcoming the negative effects of stereotypes and past discrimination (Crosby, Iyer, Clayton, & Downing, 2003).

Perceived Controllability of the Stigma

Some stigmas are seen as controllable (e.g., homelessness, substance abuse, being over-weight), whereas others (e.g. race, gender) are not perceived as controllable or reversible. This has tremendous implications for the affect, self-esteem, and motivation of the stigmatized individuals, as well as their reactions to nonstigmatized people. If one receives negative feedback and believes that it is linked to the nonstigmatized person's reaction to the individual's observable but noncontrollable stigma, the stigmatized person will tend to attribute the negative reaction to prejudice and not suffer any loss of self-esteem (Crocker et al., 1991). However, individuals with perceived controllable stigmas face a different set of circumstances. First, the nonstigmatized are likely to have less sympathy for, and feel more derision toward, the stigmatized person, because the stigma is believed to reflect a lack of effort, ability, or will (Crocker, et al., 1998; Hebl & Kleck, 2002; Weiner, Perry, & Magnusson, 1988). Second, when those who have perceived controllable stigmas receive this negative feedback from the nonstigmatized, they are more likely to feel decreased self-esteem and more negative affect. They do not, however, blame the nonstigmatized person for the negative evaluation. It is as if the stigmatized person says, "Yes, I know I have this negative, controllable condition. I feel bad about it. I don't blame you for noticing it, and telling me I should change it." Third, prejudice toward those who have a controllable stigma is seen as more justifiable than prejudice toward those who have an uncontrollable stigma (Rodin, Price, Sanchez, & McElligot, 1989).

To examine this unique reaction of those with stigmas that are perceived to be controllable, Crocker, Cornwell, and Major (1993) investigated the attributions of overweight and "normal"-weight women when they received positive and negative feedback from nonoverweight males. Women were led to believe that another male participant in an adjoining room was also participating in the study (in actuality, there was no other participant). The study was ostensibly about how dating relationships form and about what things people look for when they have a limited amount of information. Women were weighed, and their height was measured. On a self-description sheet, the women were to indicate these measurements, a number of other demographic and personality characteristics, and other self-descriptions. Men would ostensibly do the same. The experimenter took her self-description to the male and exchanged the sheets. Women read that the male was fit, unattached, and a pre-med major. Overweight women were shown either a positive or negative evaluation from the male, which either did or did not indicate a strong desire to date her.

The self-esteem of the female subjects before and after the feedback was measured, as were her mood and attributions for the male's feedback. Results indicated that when overweight women were rejected, they attributed it to their weight, and they did not blame the male for the negative feedback (one problem that Crocker et al. note is that measuring the subject's weight and height may have made this a salient reason for any feedback she may later receive, and this may be a possible confound). In addition, they felt significantly more (compared to their "normal"-weight counterparts) negative affect, depression, and hostility, and lower self-esteem, as a result of attributing the negative feedback to their weight.

Thus, the literature suggests that the perception by others and oneself of the controllability of one's stigma can have tremendous implications for how one is actually regarded by the nonstigmatized (e.g., with sympathy or anger), and how one feels in response to such feedback. Those with uncontrollable stigmas may be energized, in the face of negative feedback, to fight prejudice and overcome obstacles in society to achieve their goals. They do not blame themselves for their stigma; in fact, they rarely regard their situation as a stigma. Rather, they protect their self-esteem in response to negative feedback from the nonstigmatized via an attribution of prejudice. Conversely, the data indicate that those with controllable stigmas not only feel worse about about themselves and their abilities, they hold no malice toward the negative evaluator and blame themselves for their condition (Crocker & Major, 1994). They are also more likely to try to change their stigmatizing condition and regard themselves as a failure when they fail to do so (Crocker, et al., 1998).

SUMMARY

Being a member of a stigmatized group has important and lasting effects on one's self-concept, self-esteem, intergroup interactions, motivation and achievement, expectations, attributions, and affect. This chapter has illustrated how the nonstigmatized treat those with stigmas and has attempted to highlight many (but not all) of the ways that the stigmatized react to their group status and its influence on their self-identity. While self-reported prejudice toward the stigmatized has declined dramatically (Gaertner & Dovidio, 1986), much evidence suggests that what has declined is not necessarily prejudiced attitudes but the willingness to publicly state those now socially inappropriate negative attitudes (McConahay, 1986). The research we reviewed in this chapter shows that prejudice is alive and well in America, and this has important implications for the future of intergroup relations. If we are to better understand prejudice, and ways we can reduce prejudice, we need to understand more fully the perspective of those who experience prejudice and discrimination in large and small ways every day of their lives. We know much about how majority members think, feel, and behave toward minority members, but little empirical attention has been devoted to understanding prejudice from the minority's perspective (for a notable exception, see Swim & Stangor, 1998). Much more attention is needed in this neglected area of prejudice research. Finally, a more three-dimensional view of prejudice will likely be obtained when researchers begin to take Devine et al.'s (1996) challenge to tackle the methodologically and theoretically complex problem of prejudice in actual, dynamic intergroup interactions. When we consider how motives, behavior, expectancies, feelings, and attitudes all interact in response to the context and the perceptions of the partner on a moment-by-moment basis, we will have a much richer understanding of how prejudice and stereotypes are maintained and reinforced. Hopefully, we will also be closer to understanding how to reduce prejudice.

GLOSSARY

attributional ambiguity   Situation in which it is difficult for the perceiver to ascertain whether the target's behavior was influenced by the situation or by the individual's personality or attitudes.

disidentification   Process whereby members of stereotyped groups disengage their identity from a stereotype-relevant domain, in order to preserve their self-esteem.

metastereotypes   A person's beliefs regarding the stereotype that outgroup members hold about their group.

self-fulfilling prophecy   Process by which a perceiver's expectations about a target lead that target to behave in ways that confirm those expectations.

stereotype threat   Situation in which negative expectations about ability (due to stereotypes about the group's ability on that dimension) lead the stigmatized person to experience anxiety at the thought of performing poorly and confirming the stereotype. This anxiety often has the unfortunate effects of inhibiting performance and confirming the stereotype.

stigma   The possession of a characteristic or attribute that conveys a negative social identity.

DISCUSSION QUESTIONS

1. In your opinion, why do people tend to single out people who are different from themselves, treat them negatively, and form prejudices and stereotypes about them? Have you ever been the target of ridicule? If so, how did it make you feel?

2. Are there any ingroups of yours with which you feel especially strongly identified? Why?

3. What are some stereotypes about any of your ingroups? Do you think you make deliberate efforts to avoid confirming those stereotypes?

4. In what ways might increased intergroup contact reduce feelings of anxiety among individuals in an intergroup interaction?

5. In dealing with the attributional ambiguity related to their stereotyped group, how do you think members of that group interpret the behavior of others toward themselves: with a predominantly "guilty until proven innocent," or "innocent until proven guilty" approach? Why?

SUGGESTED KEY READINGS

Crocker, J., & Major, B. (1989). Social stigma and self-esteem: The self-protective properties of stigma. *Psychological Review, 96,* 608–630.

Goffman, E. (1963). Stigma: Notes on the management of spoiled identity. Englewood Cliffs, NJ: Prentice-Hall.

Heatherton, T. F., Kleck, R. E., Hebl, M. R., & Hull, J. G. (Eds.). (2000). The social psychology of stigma. New York: Guilford.

Steele, C. M. (1997). A threat in the air: How stereotypes shape intellectual identity and performance. *American Psychologist, 52*(6), 613–629.

Swim, J. K., & Stangor, C. S. (Eds.). (1998). *Prejudice: The target's perspective.* New York: Academic Press.

INTERNET RESOURCES: RESEARCHERS, REFERENCES, AND ORGANIZATIONS DEVOTED TO THE STUDY OF PREJUDICE

http://rcgd.isr.umich.edu/faculty/crocker.htm
Web page of Dr. Jennifer Crocker, social-cognition researcher, who examines stigma, attributional ambiguity, and other prejudice-related phenomena.

www.u.arizona.edu/~jeffs   Home page of Dr. Jeff Stone, a social psychologist examining stereotype threat as well as cognitive dissonance and other social-cognitive phenomena.

www-psych.Stanford.edu/~steele   Home page of Dr. Claude Steele, an eminent social psychologist and pioneer of stereotype-threat research and self-affirmation theory.

CHAPTER SEVEN

AGEISM

One of my pet peeves is people who drive slowly. After a few seconds of trailing behind a pokey vehicle while the rest of the traffic whizzes by, I start to think that the hapless driver ahead of me really has no conception of the written rules (and unwritten rules, like giving a wave to people who let you pull in front of them) of the road. In these instances, I may think (and I suspect many others have these same thoughts): "That person must have either just gotten their license (typically, we think of a young, and inexperienced, teenager), or they got it 50 years ago" (we think of an elderly, and slow, person).

No, this is not a call for revolution against the slow drivers of the world (an interesting idea, though!). Rather, this nicely illustrates some stereotypes people have about others based on the perceived or actual age of the target individual. Butler (1969) coined the term **ageism** to refer to stereotyping, prejudice, and discrimination based on age. Typically, we refer to ageism with respect to stereotyping and prejudice against older people. Our society tends to be decidedly pro-youth, and antiaging. Evidence bearing on this assertion is a recent finding that both young and older people seem to have easy access to stereotypes about aging, but access to stereotypes about the young appears to be much more limited (Chasteen, Schwarz, & Park, 2002). However, we certainly have stereotypes about young people, as my example shows, and this chapter will discuss what is sometimes referred to as juvenile ageism (Montessori, 1974; Westman, 1991). In this chapter, we will discuss the origins of ageism, cross-cultural differences in attitudes toward older persons (and young people), the effects of ageism on the target individual, the accuracy of age stereotypes, and finally, ways to try to reduce ageist thinking about others (Nelson, 2002).

WHY AGEISM? (AND WHAT ABOUT OTHER "-ISMS?")

According to the U.S. Bureau of the Census (2000), the number of people over age 65 is expected to double by the year 2030. The main reason? The baby boomers (those born between 1946 and 1964) are getting older. In many ways, ever since the explosive growth of the U.S. population at the end of World War II, U.S. society and its economy have been influenced by the largest segment of its population: the baby boomers. Now that these individuals are nearing retirement, society is again responding to their needs. Researchers, physicians, and policy makers are moving to address the anticipated mushrooming of the population of older adults (Abeles, 1987).

This is not to say that, because a special chapter is devoted to it in this book, prejudice and stereotyping based on age are more important than other types of prejudice (e.g., religious prejudice). That is certainly not the case. The reasons ageism is given a special chapter are threefold. First, ever since 1945, academicians, policy makers, and politicians have focused on the baby boomers because of the unique phenomenon they represent. The baby boomers are a large spike, if you will, in the gradual rise of the American population. As a result, it has been easy to focus on this segment of the population as a sort of litmus test to gauge what society as a whole ought to be concerned with at any given time. In other words, what are the baby boomers' interests, buying habits, special needs, and so forth? In general, during the 1960s, the boomers were at the center of a counter culture movement, changing politics, music, art, and society. In the 1980s, the boomers were trading in their bell-bottom jeans and beads for Armani power suits, BMW's, and corporate careers. They were in their 40s, living in the suburbs, concerned with acquiring material possessions and providing for their families. Society again changed with them, catering to these trends. Now, as this large segment of the population retires from work and enters their "golden years," society is moving (with mixed success) to address the issues and concerns of older baby boomers.

Second, and perhaps more important, ageism is given its own chapter because of the relative lack of attention it has received from researchers who specialize in the study of stereotyping; social psychologists (Montepare & Zebrowitz, 1998; Pasupathi, Carstensen, & Tsai, 1995). Specifically, social psychologists typically have been concerned with the effects of sexism and racism, to the virtual neglect of what some researchers refer to as the third -ism—ageism (Barrow & Smith, 1979). Consider the coverage of aging in introductory and advanced psychology textbooks. Whitbourne and Hulicka (1990) found that, in general, undergraduate textbooks in psychology (including developmental psychology) either do not discuss the aging process in any detail or, when it is discussed, many authors present the aging process in an inaccurate or condescending fashion. Why might this be the case? One would think that psychologists would be sensitive to the psychology of aging and to ageism in particular (unfortunately, this is not always true, as we will learn later in the chapter). Is it possible that Levenson (1981) is correct in pointing to the ageist attitudes of the researchers and text authors as the cause for the lack of coverage of aging? That might explain some of these cases. However, another, more parsimonious explanation is that age as an important factor influencing social behavior is not salient to many psychologists because the majority of them are aging baby boomers themselves (Montepare & Zebrowitz, 1998).

Third, the aging process represents a unique set of factors for researchers in prejudice and stereotyping. The way most research has addressed prejudice is from the standpoint of the perceptions, attitudes, and beliefs of the minority and majority members toward each other, and the factors that contribute to, maintain, and reduce prejudice. By definition, each individual is a permanent member of various groups (racial, socioeconomic, religious, sexual orientation, gender, etc.). We permanently belong to some groups (e.g., race), and other groups (e.g., religion) are more interchangeable. Aging is an interesting, and altogether much-overlooked, process in social psychology. We all will (if we are fortunate) grow old ourselves someday. Aging is different, therefore, from examining racism or sexism because the members of an outgroup (the young) will eventually become part of an ingroup (the elderly; Snyder & Meine, 1994). As you will read, there is clear, strong evidence that our society fosters negative stereotypes about older persons. But why are many young people prejudiced against a group which they will inevitably join? We will address this and other questions when we discuss the origins of and motivations for ageism.

Whatever the reasons for the lack of attention paid to aging and ageism, it is clear that much more attention needs to be focused on the influence of age prejudice on social perception, policy, health care, and the target of such prejudice. This chapter will discuss in some detail the research and theories on ageism. We begin with a discussion of what ageism is, the origins of ageism, and cross-cultural differences in age prejudice. The chapter will then address the impact of ageism on the victim of age prejudice and conclude with suggested ways to reduce age prejudice.

DOES AGEISM REALLY EXIST?

It might seem more than a bit obvious that the answer to this question should be an unequivocal yes. We all know of examples of prejudice toward people based on their age group membership. However, social scientists approach such questions with an empirical focus. In order to address whether ageism is a prevalent phenomenon in society, researchers have conducted dozens of experiments and surveys over the last several decades in order to measure the attitudes of society toward its older citizens. The results have been mixed, with some data suggesting that ageism is not a valid, reliable phenomenon, while other results suggest quite the opposite. Below, the possible reasons for these divergent conclusions are explored.

Ever since the 1950s, researchers have had data indicating that society as a whole has a negative view of aging and older people (e.g., Tuckman & Lorge, 1953). A number of scholars since that time have concluded that the available evidence suggests a strong presence of ageism in the United States (Barrow & Smith, 1979; Falk & Falk, 1997; Nuessel, 1982; Palmore, 1982). However, an almost equal number of researchers have found little evidence for pervasive ageist attitudes in America (Bell, 1992; Crockett & Hummert, 1987; Green, 1981; Lutsky, 1980). Which conclusion is correct? Before I address that question, consider your own attitudes toward older people. You may say, "Most people may be prejudiced toward older people, but not me. I have elderly grandparents (or parents), an elderly boss, and an older professor, and I really like all of them." This statement highlights the heart of the conundrum that has plagued attitude research among gerontological and psychological studies of ageism over the decades, and it serves to clarify why we have two separate literatures—with two different conclusions—on attitudes toward aging (Cook, 1992).

Specifically, researchers have typically used two approaches in dealing with the issue of how to measure ageism. Some have asked participants to indicate their attitudes toward "older people" in general. Most often, these researchers find solid evidence for ageist thinking about older people. However, those studies that ask participants to indicate their attitudes toward specific older individuals most often find very positive attitudes toward older persons (sometimes, more positive than attitudes toward younger individuals). Why the different results? The way the question is asked has a major impact on the type of answers people will give. This is especially the case with attitude research in general, and research on all types of prejudice in particular. It turns out that different conceptions of "older people" are evoked when one accesses a generic prototype of older people (often a vague, negative impression, formed by years of exposure to subtle and pervasive stereo-types). Conversely, if you are asked to give your impression of a specific older person, it is usually more difficult to see or recall confirmatory evidence of a negative stereotype (and this is especially the case when people are asked to give their attitudes about an older friend, coworker, or relative); thus, the overall impression is often a positive one (Crockett & Hummert, 1987).

If it seems a bit strange that people would endorse two opposing impressions of older persons, recall our discussion of subcategorization (in Chapter 2). Remember that ste-reotypes are wonderfully fast cognitive mechanisms, allowing great speed and efficiency (but not accuracy) in the processing of information and in impression formation. Because people are "cognitive misers" (Taylor & Fiske, 1991), they are often reluctant to abandon stereotypes (even though the individual is often faced with repeated instances of stereotype inaccuracy as a judgmental heuristic) because stereotypes require little effortful cognition but they still get the job of social perception done fast. When faced with the cognitive dis-sonance of having a negative attitude toward older people in general and having an older friend, loved one, or relative, people may be inclined to create a subcategory for their friend or relative. This allows people to have the best of both worlds: no dissonance about their older friend, and they get to keep their stereotype of older people as a group.

Indeed, Americans have a number of subcategories for older people (Braithwaite, Gibson, & Holman, 1986; Braithwaite, Lynd-Stevenson, & Pigram, 1993; Brewer, Dull, & Lui, 1981; Hummert, 1990; Schmidt & Boland, 1986). In a series of careful experiments, Brewer and her colleagues (Brewer et al., 1981) found that people have a generally nega-tive view of the superordinate category "older people," but they have several subcategories of older people (which Brewer et al. term "basic categories," based on Rosch's [Rosch & Lloyd, 1978] theory of natural categories). Brewer et al. found that when one encounters an elderly individual, information about the elderly person tends to be organized in terms of these subcategories, and not according to the superordinate age category. However, it ap-pears to be the case that age does influence how we perceive another person. We first sort the world according to general categories (e.g., race, age, gender), and that categorization limits (or influences) how subsequent person perception occurs and the impressions one has of the target individual. According to Brewer et al., when we do not have further spe-cific information that allows us to place the individual in a subcategory, the superordinate category is used as a kind of default for thinking about (and stereotyping) the individual.

It appears that people not only think about older people in specific ways, but in *many* specific ways. Schmidt and Boland (1986) had university students sort out 99 personality traits into groups. Participants were told to place into each group all the traits that would be found within the same older person. They were told they could use any number of groups, and to put traits that did not seem to belong in any group into a "miscellaneous" pile. Par-ticipants generated from 2 to 17 groups (M = 6.46), indicating that people have a number of subcategories for older people. These subcategories were organized in a hierarchical structure, with a cluster of negative subcategories, positive subcategories, and general traits (e.g., "retired," "poor eyesight") at the top of the hierarchy. Consistent with prior research, Schmidt and Boland found a mixture of negative subcategories and positive subcatego-ries of the elderly, with twice as many negative as positive subcategories. The negative subcategories were: "despondent," "mildly impaired," "vulnerable," "severely impaired," "shrew/curmudgeon," "recluse," "nosy neighbor," and "bag lady/vagrant." The positive subcategories were termed "John Wayne conservative," "liberal matriarch/patriarch," "sage," and "perfect grandparent."

Hummert (1990) found support for 8 of Schmidt and Boland's (1986) 12 subcategories ("perfect grandparent," "liberal matriarch/patriarch," "vulnerable," "despondent," "severely impaired," "shrew/curmudgeon," "recluse," and "John Wayne conservative"). It should be noted, though, participants in Hummert's research used different traits to arrive at several of the subcategories, indicating that although there was a good deal of cross-sample agreement in the subcategories themselves, there was less agreement about what constituted each subcategory. Hummert's participants also included two other subcategories not found in Schmidt and Boland's research: "flexible senior citizen" and "self-centered older person."

In sum, perceptions of older people are much more complex than was once thought. Overall, people have a more negative attitude toward older people than toward younger people (Kite & Johnson, 1988; Kite, Stockdale, Whitley, & Johnson, 2005). However, this conclusion must be qualified with the strong evidence for the idea that people have multiple, often contradictory, views of older people (Brewer et al., 1981; Hummert, 1990; Kite & Johnson; Kite & Wagner, 2002; Schmidt & Boland, 1986). This research indicates that one's attitude toward older people depends in large part on how the attitude is solicited. People have mostly positive views of *specific* older persons (e.g., their older relatives, friends, coworkers) but more negative, stereotyped, views of older people as a group. We have many specific ways of subcategorizing older people, but it appears that we have many more negative subcategories than positive subcategories.

AGE STEREOTYPES: CONTENT AND USE

Duffer, blue-hair, old fart, coot, geezer, old fogy, spinster. These are just a few of the many negative slang terms we have for older people (Nuessel, 1982). As Nuessel (1982) points out, the fact that U.S. society has far fewer positive terms for older people (e.g., mature, veteran, venerable) indicates the presence of a strong individual and institutional ageism (Coupland & Coupland, 1993). A number of research reviews support Nuessel's argument (Bytheway, 1995; Levin & Levin, 1980; Palmore, 1982). Butler (1980) has distinguished two types of ageism, benign and malignant. **Benign ageism** is a subtle type of prejudice that arises out of the conscious and unconscious fears and anxiety one has of growing old. **Malignant ageism** is a more pernicious stereotyping process in which older people are regarded as worthless. As with "old-fashioned" racism (see Chapter 5), one is less likely to see blatant examples of malignant ageism in society today. Because of its subtle nature, benign ageism is much more common. In the following sections of this chapter, we will explore the origins, maintenance, and reduction of both types of ageism.

In U.S. society, old age is perceived as being virtually synonymous with decline and loss of physical and mental capacities. Stereotypes about the elderly suggest that older people are tired, slow, ill, forgetful, uninformed, isolated, and unproductive (Lehr, 1983).

In both overt and covert ways, American society tells us that it is undesirable to be older. Youth is valued, and being an elder means being a member of a stereotyped group. Ageism is one of the most institutionalized and socially condoned prejudices in America today.

Research suggests that Americans regard older adults as "warm but incompetent" (Cuddy & Fiske, 2002). Such perceptions lead them to treat older people with pity, but not respect. Television, movies, and books convey to children from a very young age a predominant stereotype of older people as isolated, inactive, asocial, poor, and disagreeable (Sorgman & Sorensen, 1984). Ageism is one of the most unnoticed and socially condoned forms of prejudice (Ansello, 1978; Falk & Falk, 1997). People need look no farther than their local greeting card store to find such ageism. A pervasive theme in birthday cards is some variant of a sarcastic, negative comment about being another year older, or "over the hill." Ageism is fostered by the focus on youth and all the characteristics of youth in American society. Billions of dollars a year are spent by people seeking to mask the signs of their aging through cosmetics, wigs, hair pieces and plastic surgery. The clear message is that it is undesirable to be old.

POSITIVE ATTITUDES AND POSITIVE STEREOTYPES

Some research suggests that society's attitude toward older people is changing, becoming more positive. Bell (1992) found that media, and in particular, television portrayals of older people have changed in positive ways over the decades. Although television is in no way an accurate mirror of society at any given time, it does provide a glimpse into accepted images of groups, including older people. Many times, of course, these images are rife with stereotypes and negative connotations. Bell found that in the past, older people were portrayed as stubborn, eccentric, foolish, and comical characters. However, older lead characters in 1989's most-watched programs by the older (age 55 and over) demographic (i.e., *Murder She Wrote*, *Matlock*, *Jake and the Fatman*, *In the Heat of the Night*, and *The Golden Girls*) were portrayed as active, admired, powerful, affluent, and sexy. Bell concludes that these positive views—what he terms "positive stereotypes"—of older people are an improvement and that they help to reverse the past negative stereotypes of older people.

Do positive stereotypes reverse negative ones? Are there any negative effects of such positive stereotypes? Potentially. Palmore (1999) suggests that such positive stereotypes are indicative of what he calls "positive ageism," which is prejudice and discrimination in favor of the aged. Positive ageism assumes that older people are in need of special care, treatment, or economic assistance. However, like the debate with affirmative action, some researchers suggest that because older people are better off medically and economically than they were in the past, special programs and policies that are geared toward older people should be made available to people of all ages (Neugarten, 1982). Essentially, any special discounts, benefits, or treatments that are available only to older persons and not to younger individuals constitute age discrimination. Palmore (1999) identified eight common positive stereotypes people have of older people. Specifically, older people are believed to be kind, happy, wise, dependable, affluent, politically powerful, enjoying more freedom, and trying to retain their youth. However, there is little evidence to support the factual basis for any of these stereotypes. The reality is that older people are as likely as younger people to have these characteristics.

If people do believe that older persons have these positive characteristics, why focus on this positive stereotyping as an undesirable thing? Does it not lead to more positive attitudes? Not really. The majority of the research evidence suggests that people generally have more negative than positive views of older people and of aging (Kite & Johnson, 1988). Although there is no research that indicates that positive stereotyping leads to negative attitudes toward older people, there is much evidence to suggest that well-intentioned, positive stereotypes of older people—what Palmore (1999) terms "pseudopositive attitudes"—can lead to patronizing language and behavior toward older people and a loss of self-esteem in older persons.

EFFECTS OF PSEUDOPOSITIVE ATTITUDES

Patronizing Language

Like the old saying goes, the road to hell is paved with good intentions. Oddly enough, people with very positive attitudes toward older people often seem to communicate with

From a very young age, American children learn that youth is valued and that older people have undesirable characteristics. The increasing lack of contact between children and elders (e.g., grandparents) tends to provide fertile ground for the maintenance of stereotypes about elders. As a result, many children regard older persons with a degree of condescension and prejudice.

older people according to negative stereotypes about older persons. Two major types of negative communication have been identified by researchers: **overaccommodation** and **baby talk.** In overaccommodation, younger individuals become overly polite, speak louder and slower, exaggerate their intonation, have a higher pitch, and talk in simple sentences with elders (Giles, Fox, Harwood, & Williams, 1994). This is based on the stereotype that older people have hearing problems, decreasing intellect, and slower cognitive functioning. Overaccommodation also manifests itself in the downplaying of serious thoughts, concerns, and feelings expressed by older people (Grainger, Atkinson, & Coupland, 1990). In one study (Kemper, 1994), caregivers at a nursing home were found to speak in simple, short sentences. They repeated their sentences and spoke more slowly to older adults. Interestingly, this pattern did not vary as a function of the cognitive state or physical health of the individual. What seemed to trigger this overaccommodating speech style was simply the age of the individual. That is, all older persons were treated this way, which indicates a strong influence of a negative stereotype influencing the behavior of these caregivers.

A more negative, condescending form of overaccommodation is what is termed "baby talk" (Caporael, 1981). Baby talk is a "simplified speech register . . . [with] high pitch and exaggerated intonation" (Caporael & Culbertson, 1986). As the term implies, people often use it to talk to babies (primary baby talk) but such intonation is also used when talking to pets, inanimate objects and adults (secondary baby talk). In one of the first experiments on this phenomenon, Caporael filtered out the content of secondary baby talk directed to adults and had young adults attempt to differentiate it from primary baby talk. Participants were unable to distinguish between the two types of baby talk, which indicates that the only thing that distinguishes secondary baby talk from primary baby talk is the content. The exaggerated tone, simplified speech, and high pitch of the talk is virtually identical. Caporeal, Lukaszewski, and Culbertson (1983) found that older people who have lower functional abilities preferred secondary baby talk to other types of speech, because it conveys a soothing, nurturing quality. This is interesting because older persons who have higher cognitive and social functioning regard secondary baby talk as disrespectful, condescending, and humiliating (Giles et al., 1994). In addition to these features, secondary baby talk is ageist and insulting because it connotes a dependency relationship (i.e., the target of the secondary baby talk is dependent on the speaker; Caporael & Culbertson, 1986). The use of this type of speech appears to be associated with the stereotype that all older persons have deficits in cognitive abilities and therefore need special communication at a slower, simpler level. Cross-cultural research also indicates that both primary and secondary baby talk appear to be universal, occurring in small preliterate societies as well as modern industrialized cities (Caporael & Culbertson).

Patronizing Behavior

Because many physical changes happen to the body as we get older, appearance often provides a cue to trigger stereotypes of older people. As we get older, our movement and reflexes may become slower, our hair turns grey (or we may lose our hair), our skin becomes more wrinkled, and our sight and hearing may begin to worsen. Therefore, many people regard old age as a time of decreased function and ability, and any positive changes in intellect and health lie in one's past, rather than the future (Lieberman & Peskin, 1992). In this very pessimistic view, then, life, growth, and vitality lie behind the individual rather than in the future.

We all show some physical signs of aging as we get older. Some individuals also show some mental signs of aging. It is the individuals whose signs of physical and mental aging are more severe who are more likely to be noticed and remembered and to confirm stereotypes about old age (Montepare & Zebrowitz, 1998). **Infantilization,** one of the more pernicious stereotypes about older people, is the belief that elders are like children because of their inferior (to young and middle-aged adults) mental and physical ability (Gresham, 1973). How do we treat children? We talk slowly to them, we use simple words, we help them with many things (assuming they are not able to do the task by themselves), and we do not consider their thoughts/opinions as seriously as those of young or middle-aged adult. Older people are often treated in much the same way.

Think of your images of boy or girl scouts. Now think of a busy intersection in a large city. Then think of an older man or woman standing waiting for the light to turn green to cross the street. It is likely that your next thought was, well, boy and girl scouts always try to do good deeds, and helping an older person across the street is a great example of a good deed. So, they probably helped the elder individual across the street. Why would you think that? I never told you that the older person needed or wanted help, so why would it be good to try to help the person with a simple task such as crossing the street? To many people, it seems self-evident that most older people would welcome such an offer. However, many experiments in the altruism literature suggest that the reason the offer to help another can be misconstrued is that the offer implicitly suggests to the target that they *needs* help (Newsom, 1999; Schroeder et al., 1995). In other words, the recipient of the offer to help believes they are perceived as incompetent, unable, or otherwise impaired in their ability to perform the task.

You think to yourself, that's strange, why would someone think that? Try this. Think how you might feel if you were the person waiting to cross the street and someone came up to you and offered to help you cross the street. You might feel angry, hurt, and maybe a loss of self-esteem. This is precisely how many older adults feel when they are treated like children. In a society such as the United States that constantly reminds older persons that they are not highly valued, the elder adult must struggle to maintain their self-esteem and sense of dignity. Being offered help by others can undercut one's self-esteem and sense of competence and freedom. Of course, if one does not already have a high self-esteem, it would stand to reason that threats to self-esteem wouldn't be perceived as such. The research supports this idea. People with high self esteem are much less likely to request help than those with lower self-esteem (Nadler & Fisher, 1986). In sum, patronizing behavior and even well-intended offers of assistance can have negative consequences for the self-esteem of the older individual.

Effects of Pseudopositive Attitudes on Older People

According to Arluke and Levin (1984), infantilization creates a self-fulfilling prophecy in that older people come to accept and believe that they are no longer independent, contributing adults (they must assume a passive, dependent role; Butler, Lewis, & Sunderland, 1991). The acceptance of such a role and loss of self-esteem (that one derives from feeling like a useful, valued member of society) in an older individual occurs gradually over the course of their life as they are continually exposed to society's subtle and not-so-subtle infantilization of older people (Ansello, 1978; Rodin & Langer, 1980). When older people come to believe and act according to these age myths and stereotypes, such stereotypes and treatment are maintained and reinforced (Golub, Filipowicz, & Langer, 2002; Grant, 1996). The following is just one example of many cited by Arluke and Levin (1984) as evidence of infantilization of older people:

> In a suburban small town newspaper, a recent article reported that the patients at a local nursing home "held their very own Christmas party." The article went on to indicate that patients "planned the party, made the invitations, decorated the cookies made by the chef, and took part in the entertainment, which included a group singing Christmas carols." The article thanked a local drugstore for supplying "Santa's gifts." The intentions were admirable, but the message rang loud and clear: Old people are like big children. (p. 9)

Arluke and Levin argue that by accepting such a role and the childlike behavior that accompanies such acceptance, older people are faced with three negative consequences. First, the social status of older people is diminished through the decrease in responsibility and increased dependency. Second, when society sees childlike behavior in an older person, it may feel justified in its use of psychoactive medication, institutionalization, or declarations of legal incompetency. Finally, the political power of older people is reduced when older people come to believe their ability and impact on society is limited.

The cumulative effect of hearing from others that one is old will eventually bring about corresponding changes in behavior and an self-image in the older individual via a self-fulfilling prophecy effect (Levy, 2003). This negative self-perception about aging can have a strong connection to one's overall physical health and longevity. A study by Levy, Slade, Kunkel, and Kasl (2003) found that older people who had more positive self-perceptions about aging lived about 7.5 years longer than those with a more negative self-perception of aging. In a series of studies, Giles and his colleagues (Giles et al., 1994; Giles, Fox, & Smith, 1993) found that elder adult targets of overaccommodation appear (to independent raters) to "instantly age" in that they look, talk, move, think, and sound older than control participants (those who were not recipients of overaccommodation). Harris, Moniz, Sowards, and Krane (1994) reported that when undergraduates believed they were making a teaching video for an older partner (in another room), they were more overtly anxious and showed signs of withdrawal and negative affect. Students who watched this videotape answered fewer questions correctly, rated the teacher less positively, and felt worse about their own performance.

These data represent indirect evidence for the notion that anxiety and negative expectancies directed toward an older target lead that target to also feel anxiety and generalized negative affect (about oneself and one's young interaction partner) and to suffer performance deficits as a result. This makes sense if we consider what Cooley (1902) said about the self. A major part of who we are, who we believe our "self" is, is derived from our social interactions (Cooley called this the "looking-glass self") and the feedback about our self that others give us. If you hear from your family, friends, society, and even professionals in overt and subtle ways that you are an older person with decreased abilities, you may start to believe it yourself. After all, what is the likelihood that they are all wrong and you are right? This is the insidious effect of ageism on the self-concept of older individuals.

Patronizing talk also affects the way elders view other elders. Giles and his colleagues (1993) also found that the older victim of patronizing talk was seen by older (but not young) raters as helpless, weak, and less alert. Why would older persons be harsher judges of one of their own than younger individuals were? According to social-identity theory (Tajfel & Turner, 1979) part of one's self-esteem is derived from their group memberships. Much research has shown that it is uncomfortable to have a member of one of those core groups verify negative stereotypes about that group. When that happens, the easiest way to protect one's self-esteem is to keep that group in high regard, and the best way to do this is to derogate the unusual member and distinguish them from the group as a nonmember or a rare aberration.

While it is certainly true that ageism can have a negative effect on one's self-esteem, it is fortunately not the case that all older persons have low self-esteem. Interestingly, research suggests that the self-esteem scores of older people living independently in the community tend to be almost double the scores found in high-school students (Cottrell & Atchley, 1969). Why would this be the case? According to Atchley (1982), aging affects the self in three ways. First, one develops a stable self-concept. The longer one has lived, the more opportunities one has had to test themself over various situations. Snyder's (1987) research on self-monitoring (the tendency to present different selves to others depending on the self-presentation concerns of each situation) confirms this point. Snyder has found that as one gets older, one's self-monitoring scores drop, indicating a more stable, coherent self. Second, the reduction in the social roles one has as one gets older reduces the possibility for conflict between various aspects of the self. Third, aging is not a difficult period of working to develop oneself but is a time of simply maintaining one's self, roles, and abilities. Therefore, it appears that most older people have very positive self-images that are quite resistant to change or damage from others. So, what predicts a vulnerability to ageism, resulting in lower self-esteem among some older persons? Atchley (1982) suggests that a likely factor is the lack of adequate defenses for the self. The more times one has confirmed one's self, the stronger the negative information needed to make a dent in one's positive self-image. However, some people never develop a firm concept of their self, and they are left feeling confused and acting inconsistently. These people cannot test who they are and therefore are vulnerable to negative information about themselves. Atchley also notes two other factors that contribute to a low self-esteem among some elders: loss of physical capacity and loss of control over one's environment.

AGEISM IN THE HELPING PROFESSIONS

One might think that if there was any person who would be least likely to hold stereotypes about and be prejudiced against older persons, it would be those whose job it is to help older persons. Sadly, research has shown that counselors, educators, and other professionals are just as likely as other individuals to be prejudiced against older people (Troll & Schlossberg, 1971). For example, Reyes-Ortiz (1997) suggested that many physicians have a negative or stereotypical view of their older patients. Specifically, older patients are often viewed by doctors as "depressing, senile, untreatable, or rigid" (p. 831). Physicians may feel frustrated or angry when confronted with cognitive or physical limitations of older people and may approach treatment with a feeling of futility. Levenson (1981) argued that "medical students' attitudes have reflected a prejudice against older persons surpassed only by their racial prejudice" (p. 161). He suggests that the medical community implicitly trains its doctors to treat patients with an age bias, putting little value on geriatrics in the medical-school curriculum, and approaching the treatment of older people with a noticeable degree of apathy or even disdain. Research supports Levenson's contention. Madan, Aliabadi-Wahle, and Beech (2001) found that medical students were significantly more likely to recommend breast-conserving and reconstruction therapeutic options for younger than for older patients. According to Levenson, doctors all too often think that because old age is unstoppable, illnesses that accompany old age are not that important, because such illnesses are seen as a natural part of the aging process.

Curiously, the perpetuation of the myth of aging as a state of continual physical and cognitive decline leads to the continued treatment focus on disease management versus prevention and to decreased optimism about the prognosis of medical problems in old age (Madey & Gomez, 2003). Much evidence suggests that many of the "usual" disease processes associated with aging (e.g., osteoporosis, diabetes, blood pressure) can be changed and addressed proactively (Grant, 1996). Indeed, the expectation that older people have cognitive and physical deficits can be debilitating to the older individual in terms of self-esteem and performance. However, age stereotypes do not appear to affect the decision by older persons to use health and self-care information (Wagner & Wagner, 2003). They are just as likely as younger persons to utilize health and self-care information. Avorn and Langer (1982) found that when nursing-home residents were helped with a jigsaw puzzle versus simply encouraged, they rated the task as more difficult, believed themselves to be less able, and their performance on the puzzle was much poorer.

Treatment for older people by psychologists also shows evidence of stereotypes and ageist views. Many therapists are what Kastenbaum (1964) calls "reluctant therapists" when it comes to older clients, because of many pervasive stereotypes therapists may have about older people (e.g., older people do not talk much, or they talk too much; Garfinkel, 1975). Even when presenting with the same symptoms, older persons are less likely than younger clients to be referred for psychiatric assessments (Bouman & Arcelus, 2001; Hillerbrand & Shaw, 1990). As an indicator of the presumption of a poorer prognosis for the older client, Ford and Sbordonne (1980) found that psychiatrists were more likely to recommend drug therapy rather than psychotherapy for the treatment of depression. Gatz and Pearson (1988) suggest that this may not reflect ageism in professionals but rather a tendency to exaggerate the competency and excuse the failings of older clients (in an effort to be nondiscriminatory). However, there is a lack of compelling evidence to support this speculation. Because of methodological problems and mixed evidence for ageism in psychological services to older people (e.g., Dye [1978] found no ageism in diagnoses of depression), it is unclear whether there is a strong ageist bias among mental-health professionals. Rather, it may be the case that therapists are more influenced by misconceptions about normal aging processes, and thus, ageist thinking can be addressed in clinical training with increased emphasis on understanding the normal and abnormal aspects of the aging process (Gatz & Pearson; Kane, 2002).

The mixed data on the issue of ageism among psychological therapists has led some researchers to the conclusion that the bias observed in the delivery of psychological services indicates not ageism, but a healthism (stereotypes about individuals who are in poor physical health; Gekoski & Knox, 1990; James & Haley, 1995). In their national survey of doctoral-level psychologists, James and Haley found that psychologists continue to rate the psychological prognosis of older individuals as worse than younger clients presenting with the same symptoms. These authors also found that psychologists gave worse interpersonal ratings for persons with poor physical health than those with no health problems. In a similar design with undergraduate raters, Gekoski and Knox found that only people in poor health were rated negatively on personality measures. This is a problem, however, because there is no reason why, for example, people in poor physical health should be rated worse on personality dimensions (e.g., generous–selfish). Because older adults frequently present with health problems, this may bias psychologists in assessing the presence and extent of any mental-health problems (Grant, 1996; James & Haley). Grant suggests several ways that elements of age bias (and healthism) among medical and psychological health care providers can be changed. Professionals need to (1) continually assess their own attitudes toward older people, (2) confront ageism and healthism where it arises, (3) institute geriatrics programs in hospitals and mental-health practices, and (4) integrate into their training a thorough knowledge of healthism and ageism, as well as become well versed on what happens when humans age. Related to this last point, professionals need to understand the flexibility of aging and the heterogeneity of older people as an age category (i.e., older people do not fit into one stereotype).

ORIGINS OF AGEISM

A contributing factor to stereotyping and prejudice against older people is what Bunzel (1972) refers to as **gerontophobia.** This is defined as an irrational fear, hatred, and/or hostility toward older people. It is a fear of one's own aging and of death. Because older persons are often associated with aging and dying, people displace their fear of death into stereotypes and prejudice toward older people, in an effort to distance themselves from death (Levin & Levin, 1980). Ageism may also be increasing along with the quality of medical care. Atchley (1977) suggested that because the life expectancy in industrialized societies has increased greatly over the centuries, death no longer appears to strike randomly at any age. Rather, we are much more likely to die later in life. As a result, old age has come to be associated with death.

Age Grading of Society

Western society (the United States in particular) has developed to separate the generations in a way that is "contrary to the natural state of living" (Peacock & Talley, 1984, p. 14). In school, we learn to play only with children our own age. We learn that we need to be a certain age to vote, drive a car, drink alcohol, get married, and retire. This **age grading** (also called age stratification) of society communicates implicit and explicit expectations (i.e., age norms) about behaviors that are expected and appropriate at various ages (Lehr, 1983; Palmore, 1999). Age grading has tremendous implications for the attitudes we have toward members of society and for the opportunities and quality of life people enjoy. In some cultures, older people are held in the highest respect and hold positions of power and leadership (these are often—but not always—more primitive cultures). Such societies are referred to as **gerontocratic societies** (Palmore, 1999). In the United States, however, the middle-aged are more likely to hold more respect and power than younger and older persons.

From Sage to Burden

Older people have not always been perceived in a negative light. In most prehistoric and agrarian societies, older people were often (but not always) held in high regard, holding positions of power, respect, and high social status. Elders were the teachers. They passed on norms, culture, traditions, values, and religious beliefs to the younger members of their society. In such societies, older people were almost universally accorded some prestige (Branco & Williamson, 1982). During biblical times, people who lived to an old age (i.e., age 50 or older was considered old at that time) were said to be given a long life by God to fulfill a divine purpose (Branco & Williamson, 1982). In prerevolutionary America, attitudes toward older people were also positive. Living to old age was still a fairly rare event (only 2% of the population lived to age 60 or older), and older people were respected as sage and powerful individuals (power because of a greater likelihood of land ownership and positions of power as a result of their elder status; Secouler, 1992). However, the time period between 1770 and 1850 heralded a changing attitude toward older people. As great advances were made in medicine, people lived longer, and this created a new, large population of elders that the younger society was not prepared to deal with. Society began to associate old age with negative qualities, and older people were seen no longer as wise teachers, but as nonproductive burdens to be marginalized into the fringes of society.

As a result of the change toward a youth-oriented culture that coincided with the industrial revolution, older people no longer had a productive, valued role in society. Society institutionalized this ageism in forced retirement at age 65 (McCann & Giles, 2002). Consider this for a moment. Much research indicates that a large part of how we define ourselves is tied to what we do for our career (Deaux, 1996). We are what we do, and when our occupation is suddenly gone, learning new roles for oneself can be a very difficult process. Before retirement, an older person can feel that they are a valued member of society because they are contributing to and producing for society. For many older individuals, depression often sets in when they believe that because they are no longer employed, they are a worthless burden to society (Wigdor, 1983). Indeed, this depression can exact a severe toll. As Wigdor explains, "The grief associated with loss of work and the loss of power in our society for men who identified closely with their positions in the corporate structures, and its relation to depression, is evidenced by the relatively high suicide rate in white males over 65" (p. 53). Below, we examine two major theories that speak to the origins of this negative attitude toward older people.

Modernization

According to the theory of modernization, older people have lost prestige and respect as society has become modernized. Before modernization, there was a strong emphasis on close ties with an extended family, but after modernization the fundamental structure of society changed. The close bonds were likely to be severed, and the normal family unit was changed from an extended family to a nuclear family (parents and children, with no grandparents living in the same household). Before modernization, tradition, culture, and values were valued and passed on by elders. Older people no longer were a rarity (due to improvements in medicine), so their status diminished. Retirement became popular and part of society's way of focusing the efforts of society on youthful, strong, and fast workers. Finally, experience in a position was not as valuable as being able to adapt to new approaches and new technologies and to conceptualize new approaches for the future (Branco & Williamson, 1982). While the theory of modernization is an intuitively appealing one, research investigating its explanatory power has yielded mixed results (more on this later in the section "Cross-cultural Differences in Ageism").

Idealism

According to the theory of idealism, the increasingly negative attitudes toward older people did not come about with the industrial revolution (circa 1850), but between 1770 and 1840, when the American and French revolutions took place (Branco & Williamson, 1982). Whereas before this period older people were revered and respected, the revolutions sparked a social and political change that demanded equality and liberty. No longer were elders held in superior status and higher regard by virtue of their age. Rather, as the U.S. Constitution stated, the new philosophy for the government and the new American society was that "all men are created equal." The moral authority of older people to dictate what happened to their families was eliminated in the emphasis on personal liberty (Branco

& Williamson). No longer did the society value tradition (and, by association, its elders, who represent the past and traditions). Instead, a high value was placed on innovation, change, and new ideas (Branco & Williamson). According to an idealist perspective then, a change in values and beliefs, not social structures, was the most influential force leading to the negative change in attitudes toward older people. Like modernization, idealism also holds much utility as an explanatory mechanism for understanding the change in attitudes toward older people. But some aspects of this theory are not supported by the research literature. For example, idealism suggests that within any historical period, it is unlikely that a society will hold both positive and negative views of older people. Yet, the bulk of the research literature suggests that Americans and the Japanese, for example, hold very mixed attitudes toward elders.

MAINTENANCE OF AGEISM

Functional Perspective

A popular approach to understanding stereotyping is to examine the motivations that underlie the formation and use of stereotypes. In other words, what are the motivations that drive stereotyping? Perhaps by understanding the motives that are served, researchers can investigate techniques aimed at reducing the prevalence of stereotypes. Because young persons will eventually (in the normal course of life) become members of the outgroup "older person," it would seem to be a threat to one's self to hold negative attitudes about older people (Snyder & Meine, 1994b). The reasons for maintaining negative attitudes are questions of motives. One way researchers have tried to understand motives for ageist thinking is through the understanding of the functions of the ageist attitudes. Examining the functions of a motive entails looking at the needs, goals, reasons, and purposes, that influence a person's thoughts, feelings, and behaviors (Edwards & Wetzler, 1998; Snyder, 1993). Snyder and Meine (1994b) suggest that, in order to understand the function of a particular stereotype, it is important to ascertain the role of the target of the stereotype, the context in which the stereotype was formed and applied, and the role of the person applying the stereotype. With regard to the functional basis of stereotypes of older people, some data suggest that such stereotypes serve an ego-protective function for the individual. That is, although other dominant functional interpretations have been offered (i.e., cognitive economy, and the social–cultural orientation function of stereotypes), it appears that a more likely—but not the only—function for stereotypes of older people is that they help individuals deny the self-threatening aspects of old age (i.e., that one will lose status and self-esteem, become physically frail, and eventually die). This is accomplished by blaming the older individuals themselves for their condition, rather than the aging process itself. Thus, young perceivers can hold on to the illusion that they will not go through the same aging process.

Edwards and Wetzler (1998) found evidence to support Snyder and Meine's (1994b) functionalist perspective on ageism. Their evidence suggests that when people encounter others who represent threats to their self (i.e., for younger persons, the older outgroup represent such a threat in that their undesirable attributes represent a possible future for the young perceiver), their perceptions of and behaviors toward the threatening individual (or that individual's group as a whole) are more likely to be negative. Edwards and Wetzler discuss this in terms of Markus and Nurius' (1986) notion of "possible selves." Specifically, we all have perceptions and images of possible future selves that represent what we might become, and, importantly for the purposes of this discussion, what we are afraid of becoming. Thoughts about the salience of any of those possible selves can induce certain moods, motivate goal-directed behavior, or influence attitudes toward those possible futures. Edwards and Wetzler suggest that, by reacting negatively to older people, their young participants were able to reduce the anxiety associated with considering older people as a future ingroup, and therefore they were able to psychologically distance themselves from older people and reduce the perceived threat to their self (and self-image as a young person). These results support the functionalist perspective that thoughts of future ingroups can exert a strong influence on one's behavior, thoughts, and feelings in the present social context.

Conflict

According to this perspective, the parts of society are not seen as working for the greater whole of society. In this view, society is composed of competing groups (racial, religious, rich versus poor, etc.). The question conflict theorists ask about some societal phenomenon is, who benefits from this social phenomenon? Conflict theory proposes a different perspective on the existence of institutions such as retirement. There are definite pluses and negatives for retirement. Most negative, however, is the loss of the status as a working (contributing) individual. People who do not work are assumed to be lazy, incompetent, or unintelligent. Stereotypes of older people are seen as serving the interests of the young and the upper class (Branco & Williamson, 1982).

Self-Threat, Self-Esteem, and Terror Management

"The average elderly person experiences a series of 'little deaths of the spirit'" (Secouler, 1992, p. 197). Secouler's view suggests that almost every older person experiences some form of humiliation. The literature on aging supports this view. The aging process in the United States certainly seems to subject the aging individual to negative expectations, lowered status, discrimination and stereotyping, infantilization, and, unfortunately not surprisingly, declining self-esteem. While research has explored in some detail gender and ethnic identity, little empirical attention has been devoted to understanding how aging affects our self-concepts (Montepare & Zebrowitz, 1998).

Just as possible selves have implications for how the young view older people, so too do they influence how older people view themselves. Linville (1987) found that the more possible selves one has, the more easily that person can handle challenging or threatening self-relevant information. Some research has indicated that young and older persons are more likely to stereotype young people in terms of a variety of features, whereas elders are primarily stereotyped in terms of their age (Bassili & Reil, 1981). Taken together with the loss of the various selves (roles) one has as one gets older, this certainly can adversely influence the older individual's self-esteem. In other words, as people age, they lose various roles and self-conceptions from which self-esteem can be derived. As discussed earlier, much of our self-concept is tied into our work-related self and our feelings of "usefulness" or contribution to society (Markus & Herzog, 1991). The experiences of retirement, bereavement, and other physical changes associated with old age may impair one's sense of control over one's life and surroundings (Rodin & Langer, 1980) and negatively influence one's self-esteem. To the degree that other possible selves are available (i.e., losing the work role at retirement but maintaining active community involvement or role as parent or spouse), self-relevant threatening information should have a diminished impact. However, it appears that older persons often have few possible selves with which to deflect self-threatening information, and therefore they are more susceptible to diminished self-esteem and to depression. Recent research suggests that older persons tend to adaptively preserve their current self, and they do not really engage in fearing what might become (i.e., worrying about a feared future possible self), and they also do not strive for unattainable possible selves (Frazier, Hooker, Johnson, & Kaus, 2000). In this way, balance, continuity, and stability help the older individual maintain a better-adjusted psychological, emotional, and even physiological state (e.g., greater perceived—and in some cases, actual—control over their body's health and susceptibility to illness; see Taylor, Helgeson, Reed, & Skokan, 1991).

Another perspective that has addressed the issue of the relationship between self-esteem and aging is terror-management theory (TMT; Greenberg, Pyszczynski, & Solomon, 1986; Pyszczynski, Greenberg, Solomon, Arndt, & Shimel, 2004; Solomon, Greenberg, & Pyszczynski, 1991b). According to TMT, culture and religion are creations that impose order and meaning on the world, and this staves off the frightening thoughts of one's mortality and the chaotic, random nature of existence. Self-esteem is derived from the perception that one has a meaningful purpose in that world. As we go through childhood, we learn to associate being good with being safe and getting rewarded with parental approval. Being good (and feeling good about oneself as a result) means being protected. Self-esteem, therefore, becomes an anxiety buffer in that it helps to deny one's mortality.

With this brief background, it should become apparent that TMT has implications for stereotyping and prejudice, and specifically how outgroups are viewed (Solomon, Greenberg, & Pyszczynski, 2000). As already mentioned, an outgroup for the young is older people. Theory and empirical evidence discussed earlier suggest that one reason stereotypes of older people exist and are maintained is that older people are anxiety-provoking reminders to the young of their own impending mortality. As Solomon, Greenberg, and Pyszczynski (1997) suggest, when their mortality is made salient to them, that young people will be especially negative in their reactions to outgroups. Thus, from a TMT perspective, because older people remind the young of their impending mortality, they are regarded by the young negatively (cast as unusual or defective persons who brought their fate—age—upon themselves) in order to deny the intense anxiety that is brought about by thoughts of one's mortality. In a series of recent experiments, Martens, Greenberg, Schimel, and Landau (2004) found that when young people see photos of older persons, they showed more cognitive accessibility to death-related concepts. When students had their mortality made salient, they psychologically increased their distance from older persons and were more likely to attribute negative characteristics to older persons. TMT represents a compelling, fascinating perspective on ageism, and certainly much more research is needed on the specific relationship of the theory to the understanding of the origins, maintenance, and reduction of ageism (Greenberg, Schimel, & Mertens, 2002).

JUVENILE AGEISM

Just as the young and middle-aged can hold prejudices and stereotypes about older people, so too can middle-aged and older people stereotype the young. This reversal of the way people normally think of ageism has been referred to as **juvenile ageism** (Westman, 1991). Juvenile ageism occurs in the denial of personhood of children, by adults who assume that children cannot make decisions for themselves, do not work, must be taught to learn, are not intelligent individuals, cannot cope with daily life without assistance, and do not know what is best for themselves (Bytheway, 1995). Although society has a much more difficult time perceiving such prejudice against the young, there is a fair amount of empirical evidence to suggest that it exists and that children are affected by it. For example, Giles and Williams (1994) found that young people perceived that elderly persons often speak to them in patronizing ways, which elicited feelings of annoyance and irritation. Young persons perceived three general types of patronizing speech: nonlistening, disapproving, and overparenting, with disapproval communicating the most negative intent. Giles and his colleagues (1994) found that patronizing speech from one direction (e.g., from a young person to an older person) is often matched by the recipient in the other direction in order to communicate their irritation at being spoken to in a patronizing way. It appears that we respect people more when they stand up to our patronizing speech. Harwood, Giles, Fox, Ryan, and Williams (1993) found that people who are assertive respondents to patronizing speech are rated as more controlling, higher status, and less nurturing. So why would adults be prejudiced toward or stereotype young people? Do the elderly dread young people, in much the same way that many researchers propose that ageism against older people results from an underlying fear of aging? Perhaps ageism by older or middle-aged people against young persons may not be an indication of dread per se, but this sort of ageism may represent anger at the fact that they are no longer young (Butler, 1980). On the other hand, ageism against young people may also arise because young people remind middle-aged and older adults of the burden of the responsibility of children and their dependency on adults (Westman). Zebrowitz and Montepare (2000) suggest that the reason stereotypes about young people have received little empirical attention is that they are so widely accepted. Teenagers are seen as moody, irresponsible, and rebellious. Interestingly, even adolescents seem to endorse stereotypes about their age group. Despite the stereotypes about adolescents, and the stigma of being seen by society as too young for a number of roles and privileges, adolescents do not seem to suffer diminished self-esteem (O'Malley & Bachman, 1983).

BELIEFS AND EXPECTATIONS ABOUT OLD AGE

Beliefs and Expectations of Young People about Aging

Older people in society are perceived by younger people to possess undesirable mental, physical, and behavioral characteristics (Montepare & Zebrowitz, 2002). Specifically, older people are often seen as being rigid in thought and values, slow in movement, aimless, a burden to family and society, behind the times, silly, and disagreeable (Barrow &

Smith, 1979; Falk & Falk, 1997, Tuckman & Lorge, 1953). Meltzer (1962) asked 141 males (all under age 60) to name which years of life are the worst. The results indicated that 80.3% of the participants said that the worst time in one's life is from age 60 on. Because these respondents were not in that age group, their answers communicate their strong negative expectations for life beyond age 60. In their study of adolescents' views of aging, Kastenbaum and Durkee (1964) found that adolescents tend to focus on the present, and considered their distant future (i.e., their older adult years) as a negative time in their lives, holding little promise and little importance. These beliefs appear to be present from very early in a person's childhood. Children (from nursery school to sixth grade) generally have few positive views of old age, have little contact with older people, and fear old age because of its association with death (Jantz, Seefeldt, Caalper, and Serock, 1976; Montepare & Zebrowitz, 2002).

As a result of the little contact many children have with older people, much of children's knowledge of older people is gained through their school books. Unfortunately, these books can be, and often are, biased against elders. Ansello (1978) examined 656 books for grades K–3 and found that only 16% contained an older character. Only 4% of those books had an older person as the main character. Older people were often portrayed as retired, problem creators (rarely problem solvers), and dependent. Interestingly, children's books mirror the ambivalence of society's attitudes toward older people. Ansello's data indicated that the most frequent personality descriptors for an older person were: poor (17.3%), sad (6.77%), wise (4.51%), and dear (3.76%). Isaacs and Bearison (1986) found that children as young as 4 tended to speak less to older than to middle-aged adults, and they looked at older people less and initiated fewer conversations. Programs that bring children into more frequent contact with older people (such as Foster Grandparents) can have a strong impact on stereotypes about old age, thereby reducing the likelihood of negative attitudes toward older people as the child grows to adulthood (Glass & Trent, 1980; Murphey, Myers, & Drennan, 1982).

Expectations of Older People about Aging

Rothbaum (1983) asked young (ages 30–45) and older (ages 55–70) participants to rate the degree to which older and young people possess various positive and negative characteristics. Results from three studies indicated that older persons had a much more positive view of the characteristics associated with older people than did younger respondents (see similar findings by Wentura & Brandtstadter, 2003). Rothbaum suggests that this may reflect an attempt of older people to maintain their self-esteem or to obtain higher status. This is indeed a possibility, as we will examine later in a discussion of terror-management theory (Greenberg, Pyszczynski, & Solomon, 1986). On the other hand, data collected by Brewer and Lui (1984) present a different view of how older people view themselves. Brewer and Lui found that older individuals (aged 70 and older) held the same negative stereotypes about the category "senior citizen" as younger persons did. However, when asked to assign personality traits to people in a "like-me" category, older participants made many complex and specialized trait assignments, suggesting a greater differentiation (individuation) for persons in the older individual's own subgroup. These results fit well with what we know about the basic processes involved in the outgroup homogeneity bias. But wait, aren't the results of Rothbaum's studies and those of Brewer and Lui at odds? Rothbaum's data suggests that older people have a positive view of older people, while Brewer and Lui found that older people have a negative view of the category "senior citizens." Who is right? Before I address this question, consider the seminal work by Neugarten (1974) on the lack of homogeneity among older people.

Neugarten (1974) made an important distinction between what she calls the "young-old" and the "old-old." The young-old are those individuals between the ages of 55 and 75. A majority of the young-old are active, economically independent, healthy, and still working. Many still have living parents, which also contributes to their feeling of youthfulness. The old-old are those individuals who are 75 and older. Neugarten (1974) suggested that many of society's negative stereotypes about older people (e.g., being sick, poor, slow, miserable, disagreeable, and sexless) are actually derived from perceptions of the old-old and are especially inaccurate generalizations of the young-old. In recent research to examine these differentiations between the types of elders, Hummert, Garstka, Shaner, and Strahm (1995) found that young, middle-aged, and elderly individuals tended to choose older ages (i.e., the old-old) for negative stereotypes (e.g., "severely impaired"), especially for stereotypes associated with health problems (indicating the healthism discussed earlier), and they associated younger age ranges (the young-old) with positive stereotypes (e.g., "activist").

Neugarten's (1974) analysis helps us address the apparent divergent findings of Rothbaum (1983) versus Brewer and Lui (1984). Rothbaum asked participants to rate, on a Likert-type scale, the degree to which the age-stereotyped (positive and negative) characteristics were characteristic of 30–45-year-olds or 55–70-year-olds. There are a few problems with the design of Rothbaum's study in particular that may explain the data he obtained. First, the older participants were asked to do a forced-choice type of questionnaire, in which the trait either had to be characteristic of 30–45-year-olds or 55–70 year olds (or equally characteristic of each group). This is a problem in that previous research suggests that positive and especially negative age-stereotyped characteristics are associated with the old-old. The older participants were exactly in the young-old category, and yet they had to associate the old-old age-stereotyped older person characteristics with their ingroup. Given this design, it may not be surprising that when one is asked to rate the characteristics that one has just associated with one's ingroup, the ratings are going to be positive. This is certainly consistent with an ingroup bias. It may very well be that Rothbaum would have obtained results similar to Brewer and Lui had he allowed his participants to associate the age-stereotyped older person characteristics with an old-old outgroup (i.e., age 70 or older). In other words, the young-old persons likely would have endorsed negative stereotypes of the old-old outgroup and (as in Rothbaum's 1983 studies) associated more positive characteristics with their own young-old ingroup. You may be thinking, okay, but why did Brewer and Lui's elderly participants (age 70 or older, in the old-old category) associate negative stereotyped characteristics with their own ingroup?" Good question, but consider the setup of the study (in particular, Study 2) and the answer will become clear. The old-old participants (all women) were asked to sort characteristics into piles on the basis of whether they were "like me," "like other old people," or "like young women." As you can see, when deciding whether to associate stereotypic older person characteristics with oneself or "other old people," people are much more likely (as Brewer and Lui and others have found) to associate stereotypes with a general outgroup than with oneself.

AGE DISCRIMINATION

As a result of the stereotype of old age as a period of decline and decreased ability, and due to the increased youth-oriented nature of Western society, older people in the United States find themselves a frequent victims of age discrimination when they apply for, or try to maintain, employment. Rosen and Jerdee (1976) found that business managers had a very negative view of older (age 60) workers compared with younger (age 30) workers. They believed that older people were less adaptable, less capable, and more rigid. They were seen as slower (physically and mentally) and less capable of learning new ideas. On the other hand, they were viewed as more trustworthy, reliable, and dependable. In a meta-analysis of age-discrimination studies, Finkelstein, Burke, and Raju (1995) found that younger participants (ages 17–29) tended to rate younger workers more favorably than older workers. The researchers also found support for Rosen and Jerdee's results in that younger participants rated older workers as more stable than young workers. Older raters (ages 30–60), however, showed no such ingroup bias: they did not show a bias against any age group. There are two major problems with these findings. First, the age groups were not as conceptually clear as we would like them to be. This is especially true for what they referred to as the older workers. In the study, young and middle-aged adults are lumped into the older-person age group. A better solution would be to have the older workers limited to individuals ages 55–75 or aged 75 and older. Second, a major confound was the difference between the young and old participants. The young participants were all students, whereas the older participants were all business managers. This may be a likely explanation for why the older participants showed no preference in assigning personality traits to workers in each age group and why they did not seem to rely on age stereotypes in their judgments. Finkelstein (1997) asked 324 managers from various companies to evaluate different job applications. She found that older workers (age 59) were perceived as less interpersonally skilled and less beneficial to an organization, and they were less likely to be interviewed than younger applicants (age 28). When confronted with evidence of their ageist hiring practices, employers often deny any age bias in hiring and attribute the small numbers of older persons in their company to factors outside their control (McVittie, McKinlay & Widdicombe, 2003).

Frequently, older people are not hired, are not promoted to positions of more responsibility, or have their employment terminated due to stereotyped conceptions of the mental (and physical) abilities of older individuals. However, it is not inaccurate to say that people show varying degrees of cognitive decline as they age. Yet, many older individuals show great mental acuity and a sharp intellect. How is this possible? According to Hambrick and his colleagues (1999), the reason that the work performance of older people does not decline even when there is some cognitive decline is that many jobs are based on knowledge and experience more than cognitively based skills like reasoning. Other researchers have found research to contradict the old saying "An old dog can't learn new tricks." Czaja and Sharit (1998) found in their research that older people were perfectly able to learn new computer tasks. These experiments also revealed that although older people do tend to do their work more slowly than younger people, they tended to be very accurate in their work.

Despite the fact that many older persons experience little if any decline in memory and other cognitive abilities, the stereotypes of older people and the feedback elders receive from others about expected declines in their physical and cognitive functioning lead many older persons to buy into the stereotype of old age. This, coupled with the negative view of old age that has pervaded American society leads many elders to look to their future with a grim resignation. How do older persons deal with information that they are getting older? There are three reactions older persons tend to have. First, the older person may accept their aging with confidence, optimism, and an active, vibrant lifestyle. Second, they may attempt to deny such information by cognitively identifying with a younger age group. Third, they may simply avoid the possibility of such age-related feedback altogether. As an example of this last reaction, consider the reactions of many older persons who were contacted by phone for a study of memory (and, unknown to potential participants, of test anxiety; Whitbourne, 1976). As Whitbourne (1976) writes,

> Nine of the forty persons who had been telephoned refused to participate altogether. Five of these said that they were refusing because they did not want to be tested on anything. Three more elders agreed to volunteer on the phone, but refused when they arrived for testing and saw that it was a memory task (the experiment had been referred to as a study on "adult learning" over the phone). Another five persons went partly through the first trial, but would go no further. They complained that they did not want their memory tested, that they were fatigued, and that the task was more difficult than they had expected. Four other elders managed to complete the experiment, but exhibited severe emotional reactions (p. 207).

Clearly, it appears that many of these older individuals did not want information about their memory that had the potential to suggest that their abilities were declining. Moreover, there may be another motive behind their refusal to do the memory task. Some of these participants may have felt the threat of confirming a stereotype about older people (i.e., that older people are often confused, forgetful, and cognitively slower than younger persons). As discussed in chapter 8, Steele (1995) has found that one reason members of stereotyped groups perform poorly on behavioral and cognitive measures of ability may be due to the increased anxiety felt in the testing situation. The anxiety experienced by the minority-group member may be triggered by a fear of poor performance on the task, thereby confirming a negative stereotype about the individual's ingroup.

PROMINENCE OF AGE AS A VARIABLE IN SOCIAL PERCEPTION

Leading theories of social perception suggest that certain features about a person are more likely to be noticed than others, and, as a result, these features form the basis for categorization of the individual (Brewer, 1988; Fiske & Neuberg, 1990). In other words, when we see an individual, the most immediately noticeable features are the person's race, gender, and age group. Because these three variables are most consistently used to process information about another individual, some researchers refer to these as **primitive categories** (Hamilton & Sherman, 1994). There is some debate about whether researchers should accord primary status to these variables and not others (for example, eye color, height, etc.). However, much research attests to the fact that when certain variables are consistently used in processing social information (such as age, gender, and race), these variables are more accessible as a category for future categorization (Bargh, 1994). The more these categories are used, the more automatically they are activated to process social information. Is age as automatically activated as other salient characteristics of an individual, such as gender and race?

Research by Perdue and Gurtman (1990) suggests that age is indeed an automatically activated category for processing social information. Participants were presented with a random sequence of positive and negative traits on a computer screen and were asked to determine whether the trait was a good or bad quality to have, indicating their decision by pressing an appropriate key on the keyboard. Immediately prior to the presentation of each word, participants were presented with a priming word. The priming word (either *old* or *young*) was presented for 55 ms, and then masked (overwritten) with the target trait. The researchers wanted to discover if the subliminal presentation of the prime would make that category more accessible for processing the traits, and, if so, would it facilitate positive or negative traits? Before we find out, it is important to understand the basis for the hypotheses and the method. This experiment is based upon the popular spreading-activation network model of memory (Collins & Quillian, 1969), which states that memory is organized into a network or web of associated concepts, called nodes. Each time a node is activated (thought about consciously or unconsciously), the related concepts are activated. The stronger the link or association between the node and its related concept, the faster the related concept will be activated. The question for our purposes here is, does thinking about "older person" make positive or negative associated traits more accessible? Simply put, is the nature of our concept of older people predominantly negative, or positive?

Now for the results (see Figure 7.1). The data indicated that when the *old* prime was presented, negative traits were much more accessible (faster reaction time for the trait-judgment task) than when the *young* prime was presented. Conversely, when the *young* prime was presented, positive traits were much more accessible than when the *old* prime was presented.

These results indicate that when age categories are activated, even outside of conscious awareness, they have a strong influence on the way social information is processed. Perdue and Gurtman suggest that these data indicate an automatic ageism because the concept "old" facilitates accessibility to negative traits in an unconscious and unintentional fashion. In other words, it appears to be the case that, for most people in the United States, when we encounter (or think of) an older individual, we are most likely to think of negative characteristics associated with that age group, and this may negatively influence how we perceive the individual.

Maybe some of the participants in Perdue and Gurtman's (1990) experiments were prejudiced toward older people. How do we know that their concept of automatic ageism reflected an *unintentional* negative bias against older people? We don't, because Perdue and Gurtman did not assess their participant's consciously held attitudes toward older people. In an experiment by Hense, Penner, and Nelson (1995) on implicit stereotyping of older people, participants showed greater implicit memory for words consistent with negative stereotypes about older people, than for words inconsistent with such stereotypes. This supports Perdue and Gurtman's findings. Additionally, Hense et al. found that there were no differences between those high and low in conscious prejudice toward older people with respect to the degree of implicit memory for negative stereotypes. These results sup-

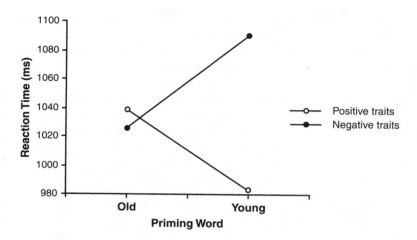

FIGURE 7.1 Automatic ageism. When Perdue and Gurtman (1990) primed participants with the word *old*, they were faster at recognizing negative trait words, relative to the recognition of the same words among those primed with the word *young*. When people were primed with the the word *young*, they were quicker to recognize positive trait words. Those primed with the word *old* were much slower to recognize positive trait words. These data support the notion that merely thinking about a category label can activate stereotype-consistent (negative) information when the category describes an outgroup, and positive, ingroup-flattering information when the category is one's ingroup. (Reprinted from *Journal of Experimental Social Psychology, 26,* C. W. Perdue and M. B. Gurtman, "Evidence for the automaticity of ageism" 199–216, Copyright © 1990, with permission from Elsevier.

port the assertion that implicit (or unconscious) cognition operates independently of conscious cognition with respect to stereotypes (Devine, 1989; Greenwald & Banaji, 1995). With respect to age categories, both high- and low-prejudice individuals are more likely to have access to (or knowledge of) negative information about older people, so both groups appear prejudiced on implicit measures of stereotyping. However, on measures of more controlled (conscious) attitudes toward older people, some individuals (low-prejudice) are able or are motivated to suppress these negative thoughts and allow only their egalitarian attitudes toward the elderly to be expressed.

A review of the literature on age in social judgments by Montepare and Zebrowitz (1998) suggests that age is indeed a prominent variable in the processing of social information. As Brewer et al. (1981) suggested earlier, age (like gender and race) seems to greatly influence social categorization, stereotyping, and impression formation. Stereotypes about older people can be triggered not only by the categorization of the person as older, but also by their physiognomic (facial features and structure) cues. Hummert (1994) found that undergraduates associated positive stereotypes (e.g., "liberal," "perfect grandparent") of older persons with physiognomic cues indicative of the young-old (e.g., little or no wrinkles or gray hair), and more negative stereotypes (e.g., inflexible, recluse) were associated with physiognomic cues indicative of the old-old (e.g., gray hair, wrinkled skin). In a study of voting behavior, Sigelman and Sigelman (1982) found that the candidate's age had a significantly greater effect on voting behavior than did the candidate's race or gender.

Young voters preferred young candidates and disliked older candidates. Bassili and Reil (1981) found that young and old perceivers were more likely to stereotype young targets in terms of a variety of features, whereas older targets were stereotyped primarily on the basis of their age. On the other hand, other researchers have argued that it is rare that age alone is the predominant factor influencing person perception and stereotype formation (e.g., Braithwaite et al., 1986). Braithwaite and her colleagues (1986) argue that because we rarely form impressions of individuals solely on the basis of age, it does not make sense to ask participants about their feelings about fictitious old and young people (that is, to manipulate only the age of the target person in a paper-and-pencil measure of attitudes toward the target person and elderly in general). Such data are not generalizable to the real world. A meta-analysis of the ageism literature by Kite and Johnson (1988) supports this reasoning. Kite and Johnson conclude that age-related information does not influence attitudes in the most common situations, in which one individual is evaluating another person. Consistent with other research, Kite and Johnson assert that age information does influence attitudes toward older people when one is comparing an older and younger person on various dimensions. In sum, the available research evidence suggests that age information exerts a strong influence on social perception, social categorization, stereotyping, and self-perceptions (Montepare & Zebrowitz, 1998).

CONTACT WITH OLDER PEOPLE

Like other forms of prejudice, it seems logical that ageism could be short circuited by increased contact with older people. As we will see in Chapter 9, however, this simple contact is a notoriously poor intervention in changing prejudiced feelings and reducing stereotypes. It may come as no surprise then, to learn that research on intergenerational contact has yielded mixed results (Lutsky, 1980). Some have found that more frequent contact with an elderly person is associated with more positive attitudes toward older people (Braithwaite et al., 1986; Gatz, Popkin, Pino, & VandenBos, 1984). An equal number of studies have found no relationship between contact frequency and attitudes toward older people (Ivester & King, 1977). However, most research supports the revisions of the contact hypothesis in that it is not the frequency with which one has contact with an older person, but the *type* of contact which seems to be more powerful in reducing prejudice and stereotyping of the elderly (e.g., Knox, Gekoski, & Johnson, 1986).

Negative Expectations about Intergenerational Contact

A major determinant of the type or quality of contact between young and old people is the ways each age group talk to each other. Of course, we will feel much better about an interaction with another individual if we believe it was an enjoyable experience for both parties, with no feelings of awkwardness or discomfort. In the intergenerational context as well as in other interracial and cross-gender interactions, our expectations often color how we perceive our interactions. Giles and Coupland (1991) found that older individuals believe that young people are skeptical about the value of talking (especially to an older person). The young responded with a much more negative perception of older people. Young people in this research saw the elderly as placing a great value on small talk, and perceived a strong element of egocentricism and assertiveness on the part of the elderly person in dialogue. Older people also sound frail and vulnerable when they speak, according to younger perceivers (Giles et al., 1994).

Negative Schemas about Older People

These expectations lead to biased schemas with which young individuals perceive information. In one experiment (Giles et al., 1994), young-adult participants read the text of an interview of a motorist who was involved in an accident. The participants were to make a number of conclusions about liability and cause of the accident based on interviews and evidence. When participants believed the motorist was 62 years old, the use of an older-person schema became apparent in participant's conclusions about the motorist's statement "I didn't know what to think" (i.e., the conclusion drawn was that the older motorist was confused). However, when other participants read the same scenario but believed that the motorist was a young adult, they attributed the same quote to his "wishing to withhold judgment given the complexity of the issues at hand" (p. 133). In a follow-up replication study, older motorists were viewed by younger perceivers as rambling, weak, and vague (Giles, Henwood, & Coupland, 1992). Carver and de la Garza (1984) conducted a similar experiment and found that when young participants believed the motorist was 84 years old, participants tended to seek more information about the auto accident in the passage pertaining to the physical, mental, and sensory state of the older motorist. When the motorist was believed to be age 22, participants focused their questions on speeding and alcohol consumption. Participants were ageist in their information seeking about the likely cause of the accident for the older motorist (i.e., the stereotype of older people as having mental and physical deficits), and also for the young motorist, in that the participants were more likely to attribute criminal behavior (drunk driving) to the younger—but not to the older—motorist. Both older and young people tend to make similar attributions for success and failure when it comes to an older or younger target. Specifically, when Banziger and Drevenstedt (1982) asked older and young participants to give the most likely reasons for success or failure of an older or younger target on a written driver's examination, age was cited as the main cause for the older target's failure. Conversely, age was perceived as the main reason for the younger target's success.

Do older people have poor communication skills, as the schemas and expectations of young people suggest? According to Boone, Bayles, and Koopmann (1982), there is no evidence to suggest that people over age 65 have more communication-skills deficits than the younger people. Research by Gold, Andres, Arbuckle, and Schwartzman (1988) supports this assertion. Gold et al. examined the stereotype that older people tend to include more "off-target verbosity" in their speech. Essentially, this is the tendency to be flighty when speaking, often incorporating unrelated and increasingly irrelevant stories or topics that stray farther from the original topic of conversation. Results indicated that there was no association between age and off-target verbosity. However, certain factors do seem to enhance the likelihood of this phenomenon. Older people who are extraverted, socially active, unconcerned with others' impressions of them, or who may be feeling stress may be more likely to engage in off-target verbosity.

Other research has revealed a different picture of the ways older people interact with younger people. Research by Coupland and colleagues (Coupland, Coupland, Giles,

Henwood, & Weimann, 1988) indicates that older people tend to engage in what Coupland et al. (1988) term "painful self-disclosure (PSD)" when talking with both older peers and younger people. Specifically, older people seem to spend about one sixth of the conversation disclosing painful, very personal information (e.g., health problems, grief over a loss, accidents they had, etc.), whereas younger persons spend significantly less (a negligible amount) time talking about such intimate details in an intergenerational context. PSDs were most often initiated by older people and were usually followed by older people discussing other unrelated PSDs. As you might imagine, hearing such painful, intimate information from another person is often an uncomfortable experience, and young interactants did, indeed, feel uncomfortable when older persons engaged in PSD. Such an interaction presents a very awkward situation for the young participant, in that there is no good way out of the topic: changing topics is seen as rude, and asking more questions about the PSDs only prolongs the experience. Giles and his colleagues (1994) found that most often, younger participants gave very minimal responses (e.g., "mmm") in order to acknowledge the older person's PSD, but to bring it to a polite halt. When interviewed after the interaction, most younger participants viewed the older person as "sad" and "underaccommodative," in that they were selfishly talking about themselves and not being socially skilled and asking questions of the younger individual (Giles et al., 1994). Unfortunately, this is a very common view of older people, as evidenced by the following response from a young research participant. Giles and his colleagues (1994) were interviewing participants about their reactions to audiotapes of young and older individuals talking. Results indicated that most of the young participants reacted negatively to evidence of painful self-disclosure on the part of the older interactant. One individual summed it up this way: "They play for sympathy, they're very much . . . like young children, they want to be the center of attention for as long as possible" (p. 140). Such a negative interaction certainly can contribute to negative stereotypes of older people and avoidance of future contact with older persons.

CROSS-CULTURAL DIFFERENCES IN AGEISM

According to Slater (1964), the past is riddled with ambivalent views of old age. The Greeks viewed aging as a calamity, as evidenced in a common saying of the period, "Whom the gods love die young." However, the Middle Eastern view is that aging is a blessing, and much wisdom, prestige, and political influence accompanies the eldest members of the community. Great age was seen as a sign of divine blessing and virtue. Before a written language was used to transmit the stories, laws, and traditions of a society, people relied on their elders to teach these things to the next generation, thereby preserving their way of life.

It is important to emphasize that much cross-cultural research indicates a diverse spectrum of attitudes toward aging. Ageism is not a universal phenomenon. Some research suggests that ageism is not even universal within the United States. For example, in traditional and modern Hawaiian families, older people are regarded with much respect and affection and are referred to as *Hula Kapuna,* which means, "precious elder" (Jensen & Oakley, 1982–1983).

Primitive societies were not great places to get old. The nomadic nature of some tribes, and the hunter–gatherer focus of others left little room for individuals who did not contribute in some way to the survival of the group. Older people in these primitive cultures were often seen as burdens on the tribe, taking but not giving. Research shows that some of these societies practiced eldercide (and abandonment) to alleviate the burden of older people from the tribe (Simmons, 1945). Similarly, in modern, industrialized cultures, older people are often not viewed as performing a valued function in society, and they suffer the consequences. Jensen and Oakley (1982–1983) suggest that ageism in America can be regarded as a subtle form of abandonment that is often more psychological than physical. Therefore, it appears that prestige of elders is greatest in cultures with a moderate level of development, where older people are seen as performing a valuable function (e.g., wise teachers, village leaders, etc.).

Slater (1964) found that older people enjoy the highest prestige in societies that are authoritarian, totalitarian, static, and collectivistic. Individual freedom is limited severely, and the society is usually governed by royalty or chiefs. Slater contends that societies that value change and innovation (such as the United States) will never accord high status to tradition, or to older people. In a recent study, Ikels, Keith, Dickerson-Putman, Draper, Fry, Glascock, and Harpending (1992) examined how people in Ireland, the United States, Hong Kong, and Botswana perceive aging. They found that age categorization of others is much less likely to occur in societies where there is little migration, in or out. In societies that experience a high rate of migration, on the other hand, age categorization is an often-used tactic in social perception.

Eastern versus Western Views

How cultures view aging has a lot to do with how they view death. Eastern cultures have traditionally viewed the self, life, and death as intertwined within the person, and in this view, death is seen as a welcome relief from the suffering of life. Death is even seen as a step up in one's spiritual journey to join one's revered ancestors (Butler, Lewis, & Sunderland, 1991). Because Western culture puts a strong emphasis on individuality and personal control, death is unwelcome. A common belief among researchers and the lay public alike has been that, generally speaking, Eastern cultures have far more respect for, and positive attitudes toward, their elders than Western cultures (Levy & Langer, 1994). These are reinforced via stereotypes in books, movies, and other popular media. However, recent research suggests that young people in Eastern cultures (specifically, Korea, Japan, China, and the Philippines) have more mixed, and sometimes more negative, views of older people than their Western counterparts (Ng, 2002; Williams, Ota, Giles, Pierson, Gallois, Ng, Lim et al., 1997). Williams et al. found a tremendous variability in the attitudes in Eastern countries toward their elders. For example, respondents in Korea felt the greatest need to be polite and deferential in intergenerational conversations, followed by those in Japan, then the Philippines. Those in China were the least likely to agree that it is important to be polite and deferential in intergenerational interactions. Williams et al. explain these counterintuitive findings in terms of increasing modernization of Eastern cultures, encroaching upon old traditions and past patterns of family hierarchy.

Research by Tien-Hyatt (1986–1987) challenges this modernization explanation. According to the modernization explanation for cross-cultural attitudes toward older people, increasing modernization leads to more negative views of older people. Tien-Hyatt's data show that Americans, who represent the highest degree of modernization, had the most positive views of aging. Respondents in China and Taiwan, societies that represent a lower degree of modernization, showed the least positive view of aging. These results also support Williams et al.'s (1997) findings that Eastern cultures show more negative views of aging than originally believed. Koyano (1989) also disabuses researchers of their belief that the Japanese have great respect and admiration for their elders. Koyano distinguishes between culturally mandated *tatemae* (how one ought to behave and feel) and *honne* (how one actually behaves and feels). The Japanese, Koyano suggests, have many traditions and even laws that mark tatemae respect for elders, but in practice, most Japanese regard their elderly with a negative honne, dismissing them as silly or infantile. To outsiders, then, Japanese culture still appears to strongly support the idea that elders hold high respect, but Koyano argues that such respect is often a feigned mask, and underneath lies indifference or negative feelings toward older people.

SUMMARY AND ISSUES FOR FUTURE RESEARCH

As in all of the chapters of this book, I have tried to present a fairly comprehensive (but not exhaustive) discussion of the research relevant to the chapter topic. When controversies or mixed results have occurred, I have tried to highlight the main issues of contention and to point to the currently favored conclusion. However, there are always unanswered questions, and there are bound to be critics of the research presented. In the following sections, I present some of the more important criticisms of the research on ageism. I also identify areas of research, and specific questions that need more empirical attention. As is the prerogative of all scientists, you can judge the merit of the research presented, and the criticisms leveled against that research, and arrive at your own conclusions.

Grant (1996) suggests several ways professionals can help fight ageism. First, professionals ought to take personal responsibility to monitor their own use of age stereotypes and eliminate these stereotypes. Next, they ought to involve older persons in policy and program decisions that affect them. Then, through research and improved professional training, those in the helping professions can learn to recognize instances of ageist thinking and behavior. Finally, we should combat ageism in society as a whole.

Measurement

A longstanding issue for researchers of the aging process is how to best measure attitudes toward aging and older people. Braithwaite and her colleagues (1986; Braithwaite et al., 1993) have suggested that the common method of comparing semantic-differential ratings of the typical younger person with the typical older person usually yields evidence for more negative attitudes toward older people than younger people. However, this method may have a strong demand characteristic in it, making these data less reliable. Specifically, asking people to give a rating to younger people and compare it with that for older people indicates to the respondent that age is the salient dimension and that the respondent is to separate them into distinct groups. Because most research indicates that the respondent will usually have positive attitudes toward younger people, and the respondent wants to differentiate the groups as much as possible, their attitude toward older people may be more negative, or even very negative (to get the most distinction between their attitudes toward younger and older persons).

You're Really as Old (or Young) as You Feel

What does it mean to be old? What does it mean to be young or middle-aged? We usually think of some socially shared consensus on what chronological-age ranges define each of these broad age groups. But, does being 55 years old mean the same thing to everyone? Highly unlikely. It is a truism (indeed, a cornerstone) of social psychology (specifically, social-cognition research) that it is not informative to measure properties of an objective stimulus and assume that most people react to the stimulus in lawful ways (although behaviorists would suggest otherwise). People are messy, and do not behave in rigid, lawful patterns in response to stimuli. It is much more informative to understand how the individual perceives or construes (thinks about) the stimulus (Markus & Zajonc, 1985). Why do two people react to the same stimulus in different ways? Because they perceive it differently. The same is true for chronological age. Different ages mean different things to different people. Thus, we need a new way to measure our attitudes toward age. Barak (1987) created a scale that measures cognitive age (an assessment of one's perceptions of the age that one feels, looks, acts, and shares interests with). The scale showed good reliability (.91) and validity. This gives a measure of the age with which one most identifies. For example, chronologically, you may be 22, but you may feel that you most identify with those in their 40s. Some general conclusions can be culled from the studies of cognitive (sometimes referred to as subjective) age. Most people in their teens and 20s report that their cognitive age is older, while those who are middle-aged and older report cognitive ages that are younger than their chronological age (Goldsmith & Heiens, 1992). It may be the case that discrepancies between one's cognitive and actual age are associated with personal fears of aging. Montepare and Lachman (1989) found that greater discrepancies in middle-aged and older adults were associated with a stronger fear of aging, whereas greater discrepancies in younger persons were associated with the least fear of aging in self-report measures. Interestingly, Montepare and Lachman's data also indicated that those persons with the smallest discrepancies between their cognitive and actual age reported the greatest satisfaction with their lives. While Barak's scale is a valuable contribution to age research, much more research is needed to develop scales that tap psychological age identity.

Stereotype Knowledge or Stereotype Belief?

Because many studies of prejudiced attitudes toward older people have utilized a semantic-differential scale in comparing older people to younger people on various attributes (e.g., satisfaction, adjustment, personality, etc.), precisely what is being measured has been called into question (Braithwaite et al., 1986; Kite & Johnson, 1988). Specifically, this method ignores the crucial distinction between knowledge of a cultural stereotype and the individual's belief or acceptance of that stereotype (Braithwaite et al., 1986; Devine, 1989). Devine (1989) has shown that people have automatically activated cognitive processes, and controlled cognitive processes with regard to stereotypes and prejudice. When encountering a member of a stereotyped minority group, both high- and low-prejudice

According to the "social clock" and common stereotypes about older people, we would not expect an elder to engage in activities that typically are the province of younger people. That is why former U.S. president George Bush's 1999 sky dive in celebration of his 75th birthday garnered so much media attention. Lending further credence to the idea that "you're as young as you feel," many active older people, such as the former president, feel quite young, even though their bodies are older.

persons automatically think of stereotypes associated with a that group. However, low-prejudice persons do not personally endorse such stereotypes, so when they become aware of these automatically activated stereotypes, they seek to inhibit these stereotypes and initiate new ways of responding to, and thinking about, the target individual. We all have fairly equal knowledge of the cultural stereotypes of various groups. What differentiates high- and low-prejudice individuals is that low-prejudice individuals do not endorse those stereotypes. However, when one is asked to compare groups designated as older people to young people, on various dimensions, what is being measured? Most likely, these questions tend to force an artificial homogenization of each group and indicate little more than the respondent's knowledge of the stereotypes of each group. The questions need to assess one's personal beliefs about members of the target group in order to approach a valid measure of prejudice.

Evaluating Prejudiced Attitudes

The multifaceted nature of people's attitudes toward older people has certainly created a challenge for researchers interested in assessing evidence of prejudice toward older people. In this chapter, we have learned that people have many views of older people. The question for researchers is twofold: (1) what constitutes one's overall view toward elders (versus a specific person)? and (2) how can researchers construct a better measure of attitudes toward older persons? Currently, the most promising approach to answering these questions is the functional-analysis perspective. That is, once we understand the motivations of the perceiver and take into account these motivations in specific contexts with the perceiver's construal of their relationship to the older target, we may make great strides in understanding the origins, maintenance, and—ideally—the reduction of ageism.

GLOSSARY

age grading   The implicit and explicit expectations of society that stipulate what behaviors, interests, privileges, and activities are appropriate at a given age of a person.

ageism   Prejudice, stereotypes, and discrimination directed at someone because of their age.

baby talk   A simplified speech register with exaggerated intonation. When directed at pets, children, or inanimate objects, it is called "primary baby talk." When directed at older persons, it is referred to as "secondary baby talk."

benign ageism   Subtle type of prejudice that arises out of one's conscious and unconscious fears and anxiety of growing old.

gerontocratic societies   Societies in which older people are held in the highest respect and hold positions of power and leadership.

gerontophobia   An irrational fear, hatred, and/or hostility toward older people.

infantilization   The belief that older persons are like children, because of their perceived inferior mental and physical ability.

juvenile ageism   Prejudice, stereotypes, and discrimination directed at an individual based on their youth.

malignant ageism   A more negative stereotyping process in which older people are regarded as worthless.

overaccommodation   A type of behavior by younger individuals toward older persons, in which the younger person is overly polite and speaks louder and in simpler sentences.

primitive categories   Describes the idea that some means of categorizing others (age, race, gender) are used so often that they become rather automatic in social perception. These categories are the bases, then, from which we develop further attitudes about the target individual.

DISCUSSION QUESTIONS

1. What are the stereotypes you have heard about elderly persons or about teenagers? To what extent do you believe that these stereotypes hold a kernel of truth? Why?

2. Do you think that (as terror-management theory would predict) if people were not afraid of death, then their attitudes toward elderly persons would be more positive and there would be few stereotypes about older persons?

3. In what ways does U.S. Society promote a bias in favor of the young? Do other countries do that as well, or are there some that respect elderly people?

4. In what ways might we, as a society, change the way that health professionals regard older persons, to reduce stereotyping and improve their attitudes toward elderly individuals?

5. Do you think that, as the idealism theory suggests, as our society continues to embrace change, innovation, and new ideas that our attitudes toward older persons will grow increasingly negative, because they represent tradition and the past?

6. Do you look forward to being an elderly person, or do you have some anxiety about it? Why?

SUGGESTED KEY READINGS

Bytheway, B. (1995). *Ageism*. Philadelphia: Open University Press.

Kite, M. E., & Johnson, B. T. (1988). Attitudes toward older and younger adults: A meta-analysis. *Psychology and Aging, 3*(3), 233–244.

Montepare, J. M., & Zebrowitz, L. A. (1998). Person perception comes of age: The salience and significance of age in social judgments. In M. Zanna (Ed.), *Advances in experimental social psychology* (Vol. 30, pp. 93–161). New York: Academic Press.

Nelson, T. D. (Ed.). (2002). *Ageism: Stereotyping and prejudice against older persons*. Cambridge, MA: MIT Press.

INTERNET RESOURCES: RESEARCHERS, REFERENCES , AND ORGANIZATIONS DEVOTED TO THE STUDY OF PREJUDICE

www.geron.org Gerontological Society of America.

http://apadiv20.phhp.ufl.edu/apadiv20.htm Division 20 of APA–Psychology and Aging.

http://falcon.jmu.edu/~ramseyil/ageism.htm Ageism resources.

www.americangeriatrics.org American Geriatrics Society.

www.asaging.org American Society on Aging.

www.ncoa.org National Council on Aging.

www.aarp.org American Association of Retired Persons.

www-unix.oit.umass.edu/~swhitbo Home page of Dr. Susan Whitbourne, a prominent researcher of aging, links on this page to dozens of interesting, informative sites on aging.

■ ■ ■ ■ ■

CHAPTER EIGHT

SEXISM

As the scene fades in, we see a couple of young children impatiently waiting for their breakfast at the kitchen table. Their father is in an apron, putting the finishing touches on a massive eight-course meal for the children's breakfast. Satisfied, the father awaits the children's expected delight at their good fortune, and at their father's accomplishment. One of the children then says to her father, "Dad, mom usually just makes us a bowl of cereal for breakfast." The commercial ends with a display of the cereal product and—the seller hopes—the viewer chuckling at the humorous scenario they just saw. While the main goal of advertising is to sell the product, there are other messages in this commercial that are subtly communicated to the viewer besides the overt message to buy that particular cereal. We find out that usually the mother prepares the children's breakfast, and dad was not aware of the kids' morning routine (presumably because he has left for work before the children have breakfast). The viewer also is led to infer that the mother is in charge of household duties (like preparing breakfast), and taking care of the children (making sure they eat breakfast, get dressed and ready for school, etc.). All this from a simple cereal commercial? Yes, and these subtle messages about male and female roles, expected and common gender behaviors in society, and, more broadly, the natural structure of the family unit are subtly but clearly communicated to the viewer in this commercial and throughout other types of media (movies, magazines, books, and television shows).

As we learned in Chapter 1, people tend to immediately group other individuals according to the basic, or primitive, categories of gender, race, and age. Throughout this text, we have been discussing racism, and in Chapter 7 we discussed prejudice against the elderly. In this chapter we will explore in some detail the factors that lead to the formation, maintenance, and reduction of prejudice against women. Negative attitudes and behavior toward someone on the basis of their gender is termed **sexism**. Though such prejudice can refer to prejudice against men, most researchers use the term *sexism* to refer to prejudice against women.

As with any prejudice and stereotype, a first question that arises when studying sexism is, *why* would society or individuals within that society be motivated to create and maintain such gross generalizations about, and negative attitudes toward, women? In this chapter we will review the major theories and current empirical work that attempt to address this question. We will also explore the content, structure, and accuracy of gender stereotypes. Finally, we will discuss ways that sexism and sexist thinking can be reduced. By the end of the chapter you will see that, like racism and ageism, sexism permeates American society. In subtle and overt forms, sexism influences our attitudes toward

Gender roles are learned first at home. Children learn the stereotypes from their parents that some behaviors and interests are "for girls" and others are "for boys." Even in today's society, gender-role stereotypes persist because such beliefs are transmitted within families from generation to generation. Look at these two families. What are the children learning about gender roles from their parents' behavior?

women, women's views of themselves, women's career choices, and countless other aspects of women's lives (Ruble & Ruble, 1982).

Stereotypes of women also can sabotage their performance on stereotype-related tasks. For example, a prevalent stereotype about women is that they are less able to understand science and mathematics and that in these subjects they perform poorly relative to men. In a test of this stereotype of women, Spencer, Steele, and Quinn (1999) found that, indeed, when the negative stereotype about the math and science abilities of women was made salient to women participants, their performance suffered relative to a group of equally qualified men. It is important to note that these male and female participants were equally matched on their mathematics ability (based on their math subsection scores on major college-entrance exams). Thus, even though males and females had demonstrated equal talent for mathematics, when women were made aware of the stereotype about women performing poorly in math, the women participants performed significantly worse compared with their male counterparts.

Thus, for members of groups about whom negative stereotypes exist, stereotype threat and the pernicious effects of stereotyping, prejudice, and discrimination can impair performance, limit opportunities, and affect one's self-concept. In this chapter we will explore the various ways that gender prejudice can manifest itself. Sexism is often minimized, downplayed, or shrugged off by society as being harmless or even humorous, and instances of sexist stereotypes and sexist behavior often go unrecognized as such. It may indeed be the case that people are not consciously aware of the presence of sexism in society or when they are being sexist toward another. Recent research suggests that gender stereotypes are so well learned that they automatically influence our perceptions and judgments, often without our conscious awareness of such bias (Banaji & Greenwald, 1995). But as we will learn in Chapter 9, much research supports the idea that the links between a group and negative thoughts and feelings can be broken and substituted with more egalitarian responses (Devine & Monteith, 1993; Monteith, 1993, 1996a). It is therefore beneficial to understand the nature of gender stereotypes, in order to learn more about how to avoid such stereotyping.

GENDER STEREOTYPES

What are women like? What are men like? From a very young age, we begin to learn from society the answers to these questions. We learn that women are not aggressive, not independent, tend to be more emotional, more easily persuaded, dislike math and science, and tend to be passive (Broverman, Vogel, Broverman, Clarkson, & Rosenkrantz, 1972). We also learn that while women are seen as polite, gentle, nurturing, compassionate, neat, indecisive, concerned with their appearance, and quiet, and men tend to be viewed as aggressive, independent, nonemotional, decisive, confident, rough, blunt, sloppy, and loud (Broverman et al., 1972). There are countless other gender stereotypes—these are just a few. Interestingly, there seems to be a remarkable cross-cultural consensus in the content of gender stereotypes. Williams and Best (1982) examined data covering 30 nations and found that men tend to be viewed as stronger, more assertive, dominant, active, and aggressive. Women are usually viewed as primarily concerned with fostering relationships with others, nurturing, and deference. Within the United States, college students have similar shared ideas about the physical appearance, clothes, and settings of specific stereotyped subgroups for males (e.g., "nerd," "ladies' man") and females (e.g., "housewife," "feminist"; Green & Ashmore, 1998).

In the research by Broverman and colleagues (1972), you may have noticed something interesting about the content of the characteristics that people used to describe men versus women. Namely, men and women were seen as complete opposites on virtually all of the traits and characteristics listed (hence the term *the opposite sex*). Men were seen as independent, and women were viewed as dependent. Men were rated as sloppy, aggressive, and decisive, while women were perceived as neat, nonaggressive, and indecisive. Why might that be the case? What incentive or reason does society have to view men and women as opposites on virtually any psychological dimension one can identify? There are many possible factors that may contribute to such a motivation, and we will examine them as the chapter proceeds. You may be thinking to yourself, Self, these data were collected over 25 years ago, and many of these stereotypes about the sexes no longer exist. Unfortunately, such an assumption appears to be incorrect. Bergen and Williams (1991) compared the prevalent gender stereotypes about men and women in 1972 and in 1988 and found no differences in the content of the stereotypes. Thus, it appears that despite the great political, economic, and social gains women have made toward more equal status over the last quarter-century, people's views of women still tend to be shaped by traditional gender stereotypes that persist today.

When we perceive that someone is either male or female, are those perceptions biased by general stereotypes about males or females, or are our perceptions of the individual guided by specific features of the person, leading to specific gender stereotypes (e.g., "male jock" or "career woman")? In three experiments by Deaux and Lewis (1984), participants were given information about the gender of a target individual, as well as role behavior or trait information, and they were asked to indicate the likelihood that the target person had gender-related characteristics. Results demonstrated that gender stereotypes are best conceptualized as a set of components, such as traits, role behaviors, occupations, and physical appearance. Making features of a component salient can lead the perceiver to think of other components of the gender stereotype. Interestingly, Deaux and Lewis found that specific gender-stereotype component information can outweigh the influence of gender in evaluations of the target. Therefore, it appears that if people just know that a target individual is a man or woman, they will draw on gender-stereotype information in their inferences about the target. However, once the perceiver knows more specific information about the target (i.e., the components discussed above, such as physical appearance, traits, etc.), the influence of the gender category will diminish in the perceiver's evaluation of the target, and the target will be viewed according to the specific component information. Swim (1993) found similar results in her studies, and she suggests that these data indicate that while participants do use gender information in their evaluations of a target, the influence of this information is weak. The reason for the weak influence of gender, according to Swim, is that participants prefer to use specific case information in their assessments of a target, rather than simple gender-category information (see also, Swim, Borgida, Maruyama, & Myers, 1989).

MEASUREMENT OF GENDER STEREOTYPES

Stereotypes about men and women suggest that people have different ideas about the behavior and personality characteristics of men and women. Indeed, the notion of the "opposite sex" suggests more than a distinction between a man and a woman; it also implies that men and women are opposite (Deaux & Kite, 1993; Deaux & Lewis, 1984). The key word here is *opposite*, not *different*. Consider this point further. Men and women are merely different sexes. They are not *opposite* in the way that we usually refer to the term. *Webster's* dictionary (Neufeldt, 1989) defines *opposite* as "1. set against; in a contrary direction, 2. entirely different; exactly contrary." Thus, the word *opposite* suggests that men and women are as different as hot and cold, or positive and negative poles of a magnet. The notion that men and women are so diametrically opposite represents a **bipolar assumption** among both researchers and the lay public alike. This assumption states that a person has characteristics that are associated with either males or females, but not both (Ruble & Ruble, 1982). This assumption tended to guide the way researchers devised measures of gender stereotypes; thus, their results were strongly tainted by the limitations of the instrument and the demand characteristics associated with such measures. For example, Broverman and colleagues (1972) presented participants with a list of dichotomous trait items. Each item listed two endpoints of a trait indicating the opposite ends of a given trait. For example, participants saw "emotional" and "nonemotional," "aggressive" and "nonaggressive," "dominant" and "submissive," etc. Participants could only indicate where on the trait the typical woman and the typical man fell. Participants could only indicate that women/men were, for example, either dominant or submissive, but not somewhere in-between. Thus, it is easy to see how this type of inherent bias in the design of the questionnaire could lead participants to indicate opposite characterizations of men and women. Interestingly, though, when participants are asked, in an open-ended questionnaire, to list the characteristics of males and females, their responses mirror very closely those results obtained by Broverman et al. (1972; Basow, 1992).

The bipolar assumption has been strongly criticized, primarily because little evidence supports the notion that men and women have either masculine or feminine traits, but not both, or that the presence of a number of supposedly masculine traits in an individual necessarily means that the individual cannot have a number of supposedly feminine traits (Bem, 1974; Spence & Helmreich, 1978). Indeed, Bem's (1974, 1993) research on gender roles reveals that many people do, in fact, often possess traits that are typically associated with males and females. As a result of the inadequacy of the bipolar model, researchers have moved to a more **dualistic view** (Spence & Helmreich), which suggests that people can have some of both **agentic** and **communal traits.** Agentic traits are those that have traditionally been associated with males, traits that indicate task orientation, assertiveness, and a striving for achievement. Communal traits, or expressive traits, are those that have traditionally been associated with women, such as the desire to foster relationships, to be sensitive, and to get along with others.

Although much research suggests that people generally have less favorable attitudes toward women than toward men (as exemplified in the Broverman et al. research discussed above; see also Burn [1996] and Deaux & Kite [1993] for a more comprehensive discussion of gender stereotypes), research by Eagly and Mladinic (1989) suggests that people actually have quite favorable attitudes toward women. Eagly and Mladinic examined the research literature on people's attitudes toward women and noticed that researchers had been using Spence and Helmreich's (1978) Attitudes Toward Women Scale (ATWS) to measure attitudes toward women, when that was not the purpose of the scale, according to Spence and Helmreich. The name of the scale is a bit misleading, because the scale actually measures attitudes toward equal rights and roles and privileges for women.

In order to gain a better assessment of attitudes toward women, and the relation of those attitudes to attitudes about equality for women, Eagly and Mladinic (1989) administered the ATWS to 203 male and female college students, also asking them to list the traits and attributes of men and women (i.e., to list their stereotypes of the typical man and typical woman) in an open-ended questionnaire. Participants were also asked to indicate their attitudes toward the equality of women and men in terms of rights and roles in society. If the ATWS really was a measure of attitudes toward women, then the evaluative content of participants' stereotypes should correlate highly with their scores on the ATWS. However, participants' questionnaire responses (their stereotypes) were completely uncorrelated with ATWS scores. As predicted, participants' scores on the ATWS were strongly correlated with their self-reported attitudes toward equal rights and roles for women. Thus, these data suggest that the ATWS measures not attitudes toward women but attitudes toward equal rights and privileges for women in society (compared with those of men). Interestingly, participants' conceptions of the typical woman in their open-ended responses show that people have quite favorable views of women.

In sum, it appears that past research using the ATWS had suggested that people have negative views of women, when in fact what was likely happening with the data was that they had negative views of the idea of male–female equality in society. It is certainly interesting that people can have positive views of women (indeed, Eagly and Mladinic's [1989] participants indicated more positive attitudes about women than men), but at the same time indicate negative attitudes toward equal rights, roles, and privileges for women. Why might that be the case? One explanation may be found in the differences between male and female participants' scores on the ATWS. Eagly and Mladinic found that men had significantly more negative attitudes toward equal rights for women than did women participants. These data support the possibility that although men and women have positive attitudes toward women in general, men may react negatively to threats to their power dominance over women in society. We will explore this notion in more detail later in this chapter, in a discussion of the power differential between men and women and how it might account for the persistence of gender stereotyping and discrimination against women.

ORIGIN OF GENDER STEREOTYPES

To understand the nature of sexism, it is helpful to examine the causes of sexist thinking and beliefs. Why are there stereotypes about, and prejudice toward, women? To answer this question, one must consider that prejudice and stereotypes against women have not one, but many different contributing sources. Each of these sources serves to strengthen what seems to be the truth of the stereotype, the legitimacy of the prejudice, and to communicate the shared beliefs of a society about the relationship of women to men. Let's consider several major factors that have led to the creation and maintenance of prejudice and stereotypes about women.

Religion

Perhaps one of the earliest and strongest influences on the perception of men versus women has been religion. Bem and Bem (1970) found that many major religions in the world (e.g., Islamic, Jewish, and Christian) have taught that women are different from, inferior to, and subservient to men. For example, the Bible reads in part, "Let the woman learn in silence with all subjection. But I suffer not a woman to teach, nor to usurp authority over the man, but to be in silence. For Adam was first formed, then Eve. And Adam was not deceived, but the woman being deceived was in the transgression" (I Timothy 2, 11–14). According to Christian teaching, because woman was derived from man, and man from God, woman was lesser than man (see Genesis, Chapter 3 in the Bible). As recently as 1998, a major religious denomination— the Southern Baptists—adopted the following into their statement of faith, "A husband is to love his wife as Christ loved the church. He has the God-given responsibility to provide for, to protect, and to lead his family. A wife is to submit herself graciously to the servant leadership of her husband even as the church willingly submits to the headship of Christ" (adopted by the Southern Baptist Convention, June 8, 1998). As a result of the church sanctioning prejudice against women, women came to be viewed as less than men in spirit and intellect (Albee & Perry, 1998; Ruble & Ruble, 1982). Research also indicates that people who are more devoutly religious are more likely to hold stereotypical gender role attitudes (Morgan, 1987), and those attitudes tend to reflect a benevolent sexism (Glick, Lameiras, & Castro, 2002).

It should be noted that most religions today have made tremendous advances in their perspective on the status of women in relation to men. Specifically, many do not adhere so rigidly to the exact wording of the Bible in terms of the equality of men and women. Indeed, there are more and more churches and religions today that give equal status to men and women. In many churches, however, women still do not enjoy all the opportunities and privileges afforded to men. Thus, despite the progress religions have made with regard to reducing or eliminating sexist ideology, there is a long way to go toward full equality between men and women in the church. In sum, religion has had a tremendous influence on the attitudes of society toward women. Unfortunately, that influence has often resulted in a view of women as inferior and subservient to men (Rakow & Wackwitz, 1998).

Social Learning

From a very young age, children are taught what it means to be a male or female in society. According to the social-learning theory (Bandura & Walters, 1963; Mischel, 1966), children learn (through reinforcement and modeling) the expectations, goals, interests, abilities and other aspects associated with their gender. Children's conceptualization of what their gender means to them is shaped by their environment, and, most importantly, by their parents. Through rewarding what are deemed gender-appropriate behaviors and punishing or discouraging supposedly gender-inappropriate behaviors (differential reinforcement), parents teach the child about their gender. Children also learn about their gender by watching their parents and important others in their environment engage in behavior (modeling). A boy gains information about being a man from observing his father's behavior, and a girl learns about being a women by watching her mother's behavior. The child then can acquire complex new behaviors via this observational learning (modeling). In his classic experiments on modeling of aggression in children, Bandura (Bandura, Ross, & Ross, 1961) showed that boys and girls were equally likely to learn to be aggressive with a toy if they previously saw a model (an adult) behave aggressively toward the toy.

There is substantial evidence to indicate that the influence of the parent in shaping the child's gender identity is substantial and lasting (Eccles, Jacobs, Harold, Yoon, Arbreton, & Freedman-Doan, 1993). In American society, gender is a fundamental dimension upon which people are understood, and gender concepts and stereotypes permeate many aspects of one's life. Additionally, Americans tend to adhere to the belief that men and women are naturally different in temperament, personality, and ability. This belief leads parents to feel the responsibility to teach their children what it means to be a boy or to be a girl. These expectations are communicated, in direct and indirect ways, through the parents' interactions with the child. Even before they begin elementary school, children have learned quite a lot about boys' versus girls' toys, clothes, hobbies, personalities, and so forth (Edelbrock & Sugawara, 1978; Serbin, Powlishta, & Gulko, 1993). As they get older, children's gender stereotypes become more rigid and resistant to change (Cann & Haight, 1983).

Interestingly, a comprehensive review of the literature on differential reinforcement and socialization by parents for boys versus girls suggests that parents do not really differentiate between boys and girls in the things they teach their children (Lytton & Romney, 1991). Why have studies failed to find evidence for a different socialization by parents for boys versus girls? According to Jacklin and Baker (1993), a likely reason is that parents are egalitarian in their socialization of children and that the stereotypic gender roles and characteristics are acquired via other socialization agents, such as the child's friends and teachers, and through the media. In her recent controversial book *The Nurture Assumption* Harris (1998) takes this point even further, stating that the influence of parents in the socialization of their children is minimal at best, and that the child's aforementioned nonparental socializing agents (especially friends) strongly shape the child's personality and gender identity. It should be noted that Harris's position is very controversial and hotly contested, and it goes against a mountain of child-development research that suggests just the opposite: parents are not only influential, they are *very* influential, in shaping the child's personality. Nevertheless, Harris is correct in noting that more empirical attention should be paid to understanding the underestimated influence of nonparental socializing agents on children.

Cultural Institutions

In addition to the role of parents in the socialization of gender information, society plays a big part in communicating to the child similar gender roles and gender stereotypes. Through television, movies, magazines, and other media, society reinforces the notion that boys and girls are indeed different, and that each gender has gender-appropriate goals, interests, abilities, and roles in society. The child learns that violating these expected roles will invite negative attention and ostracism, and generally make it more difficult to get along with others and more difficult to succeed in life. These messages about men and women are communicated very early to the child, even from the most benign sources. An analysis of animated cartoons from 1975 to 1995 indicated that males and females were still portrayed in very gender-stereotypical ways in the 1990s, just as they were in the 1970s (Thompson & Zerbinos, 1995). Male characters tend to be given more prominence, talk more, and are given nearly all of the important behaviors in the cartoon. However, the researchers noted that there has been a significant change in the degree of stereotypic portrayal of each gender since the early 1980s. Today, there are more female lead characters, and female cartoon characters are more frequently portrayed as intelligent, assertive, strong, independent, and competent.

Americans watch a lot of television. By some estimates, by age 70 an average person will have watched *ten years* of television (Center for Media Education, 1997). That amount of exposure to a particular source of information has a strong influence on a wide variety

The Peanuttiest.
Jif has more fresh roasted peanut taste
than any other leading creamy brand.

Choosy moms choose

Another strong purveyor of gender stereotypes is the media. Magazines, television, books, and movies all tend to perpetuate the idea that men and women are very different creatures who are genetically predisposed to like certain things and behave in certain ways. According to U.S. advertisements, fathers apparently do not shop for groceries for their children.

of our attitudes. Attitudes about gender are certainly influenced by continual exposure to gender-relevant information contained in television shows and commercials. Back when television emerged onto the American scene (in the late 1940s), the expectations and roles for each gender were highly divided. Men were the achievers, working at a career to support their family, and women were expected to stay at home, raise the children, and maintain the house, (doing all the housework and cooking). Shows like *Leave it to Beaver, Ozzie & Harriet,* and *Father Knows Best* reflected these expectations and communicated them to the viewer. Over the subsequent 50 years, society has undergone tremendous changes in the expectations, opportunities, and roles afforded to women. Unfortunately, however, television does not always reflect such advances.

Think about any commercial that advertises a cleaning product for the interior of the house. Recall that such a task has traditionally—and stereotypically—been the province of women. Advertisers know that the most persuasive messages are communicated by individuals similar to the target audience (Hovland et al., 1953). So, if the advertisers believe that men and women today still adhere to traditional gender roles, then their commercials should feature a woman discussing the benefits of that particular cleaning product. Indeed, this is the case today. For example, according to commercials, women are the only ones in the family who care about the foods their kids eat ("Choosy mothers choose Jif peanut butter" and "Kix cereal: kid tested, mother approved") and the health of their family ("ask Doctor Mom"). On one occasion, while perusing the meat section of my local supermarket, I noticed a box of hot dogs for children called Fun Franks by the Ball Park Franks company. The gimmick with the product was that each hot dog came in its own little bun, individually wrapped, ready for the microwave. What was amazing was the overt sexism on the front of the box. In a big white bubble, the box announced, "Hey Mom! Check out the cooking instructions on the side panel!" Apparently fathers still don't cook in 2005. Whenever I ask my students to name the last commercial they saw in which a man was touting the wonders of a laundry detergent or other household cleaner, they are stumped.

But much research indicates that they should not be surprised. Men and women still adhere to traditional divisions of labor in the household. Women are primarily responsible for the care of the children and maintaining a clean house, while men are expected to fulfill their duty as father and husband by getting a good job to provide for the family (Crosby, 1991; Thoits, 1987). Even among couples who both work full-time, women report doing 65.1% of the household labor, while men perform only 42.7% of the housework (a significant difference that is associated with a greater likelihood of depression among working women; Bird, 1999). Why would this still be the case today? According to Crosby and Jaskar (1993), men and women today look to their parents as a guide for understanding the nature of the respective roles of husband and wife in the household. Because their parents are more likely to have traditional gender roles in their marriage (which they in turn learned from their even more traditional parents, and so on back through one's lineage), their conceptions of their roles in their marriage (i.e., What are wives and husbands supposed to do? How are tasks divided?) are also likely to reflect gender-role stereotypes.

While seemingly benign, advertisements such as these convey several implicit messages to the viewer about the interests, expected roles, and abilities of men and women in society. Often, these messages are portrayed in rigid, stereotypical ways, and this constant exposure to gender stereotypes in the media influences the attitudes that the viewer has about what it is to be a male and a female in America today (Courtney & Whipple, 1983; Goffman, 1979; Gunter, 1986). Another way that gender stereotypes in advertisements influence gender attitudes is through **normative** and **informational influence** (Deutsch & Gerard, 1955). When we wish to hold a particular attitude in order to be liked by others, we are adhering to normative influence. When we wish to be correct in our attitudes, we may be more susceptible to informational influence. In this circumstance, we may adopt an attitude held by others because we believe the shared attitude of many others is more likely correct than if we developed an attitude about the issue on our own. When we see the advertisement, we often implicitly infer two things: this attitude/message is correct (otherwise why would it be published/broadcast on worldwide media?), and it is shared by many others, at least all those involved in creating the ad, and those consumers who view the ad. However, such inferences merely reflect a common heuristic about the media—"If it is in print/broadcast, it must be true" (Huff, 1954)—and illustrate the powerful, pervasive, and pernicious (there's a tongue twister!) influence of repeated exposure to gender stereotypes on the attitudes of the public about men and women.

Sexist portrayals of women in advertising take the form of pairing women and attractiveness. In a content analysis of over 4,000 television commercials, Downs and Harrison (1985) found that female performers on commercials are more likely to be associated with attractiveness stereotypes than are male performers. They also found that the pairing of a female performer and a male voice-over (what the authors suggest is the "voice of authority" in the advertising industry) seems to make the most persuasive advertisement. This finding may not surprise you, since you no doubt have noticed that advertisers today place beautiful women in advertisements that have nothing to do with the merits of the product. Why? Because women are associated with attractiveness, and attractive things evoke positive emotions, and the seller wants people to associate positive emotions with the product.

In his in-depth analysis of print advertisements, Goffman (1979) found that print ads convey sexism in many subtle ways. Men were almost always pictures in an agentic or instrumental act (i.e., doing something), whereas women were often pictured as peripheral to the action, looking on at what the man was doing. Women, far more than men, are featured in poses that draw attention to their bodies, even when the object being sold is not something worn, a camera, for example. Other things Goffman noted: men tend to be placed higher in the ad, relative to women, conveying greater stature or importance; men have their arms around women, and hold the woman's hand, not the other way around, indicating dominance in the relationship; and women are almost exclusively pictured with and nurturing children in print ads. It is rarely the case that a man was pictured in such a fashion. The impact of sexist advertisements is strong. Research by Rudman and Borgida (1995) showed that men, even those who are not prejudiced against women, who are exposed to sexist advertisements tend to think of women in more sexualized roles, and sexist stereotypes of women are made more salient for them. It should be noted that, like the changes in the gender stereotyping and sexism present in children's cartoons, print advertisements have changed with the times and are becoming less sexist. It would be interesting to see what another in-depth analysis of print advertisements would reveal about the sexism and gender stereotypes portrayed in contemporary advertising.

This objectification of women has been found in another line of fascinating research on what is termed **face-ism.** Face-ism is the greater facial prominence of depictions of men

Face-ism in action. Advertisers are more likely to use a full-body image of a woman (and rarely a man) in an advertisement, even when there is no obvious reason to do so. Research suggests that this is based on the patriarchal history of the United States, in which women were objectified, and their value was tied more closely to their physical beauty and less to their intellectual talents. Take a look at the above photograph. What does a full-body shot of a nude woman have to do with a personal digital assistant device?

in the media versus women, and greater emphasis on the whole body of women. Archer, Iritani, Kimes, and Barrios (1983) conducted a series of studies that found that men's faces were given much more prominence in three contexts: American magazines, in publications from 11 different countries, and even in artwork over the last 600 years. Archer and colleagues also found that when facial prominence was varied experimentally, and when the faces of individuals in photos were more prominent, those individuals were rated by participants as more intelligent, more ambitious, and higher in physical appearance (a term the authors later admitted was vague in that they meant physical attractiveness, but people could have read it to denote neatness, for example). Archer et al. suggest that the faceism in depictions of women versus men conveys a message about the importance of various parts of the body for each gender. Because the head is the center of mental life (one's character, intellect, personality, and identity are associated with the mind), and the data showed that people rated subjects in facially prominent photos as more intelligent and ambitious, men and women are viewed and portrayed in very different ways. Men are seen as the bright achievers, and women tend to be valued primarily for the physical attractiveness of their body. Recall that Archer et al. found that this symbolic message has been communicated in many different countries and over the last 600 years.

Not surprisingly, research indicates that gender-stereotyped portrayals of women in advertisements have negative effects on women. Schwarz, Wagner, Bannert, and Mathes (1987) found that when women were exposed to advertisements that portrayed women in traditional roles as homemakers, they reported less-positive attitudes toward political participation. These data suggest that activation of a common cultural stereotype (e.g., women as homemakers) may, for women, result in a suppression of achievement-related attitudes, or perhaps a depressed, pessimistic outlook on her own abilities and career possibilities due to the implied societal limits set forth in the traditional stereotype of women as homemakers. This interpretation is supported by an experiment conducted by Geis, Brown, Jennings, and Porter (1984). Men and women were asked to watch either sex-stereotyped commercials, commercials with the sex-roles reversed (e.g., a male talking about a product for cleaning his kitchen floors), or were asked to list their favorite television programs (this was the control condition). They were then asked to write an essay in which they describe their lives 10 years from that date. The essays were analyzed and coded for achievement-related versus homemaking themes. Results showed that women who viewed the stereotyped commercials reported less achievement imagery and more emphasis on homemaking compared with men and those in the control and role-reversed conditions (see Figure 8.1).

Interestingly, the data also indicated that when women viewed the role-reversed commercials, women's essays contained much more achievement-related themes than those of women in the sex-role stereotyped condition (see Figure 8.2).

Taken together, these studies highlight the strong influence that the media has on the attitudes of women toward themselves and their future. The media does not just reflect popular cultural stereotypes about gender, it perpetuates them and creates new gender stereotypes that negatively affect women's self-concepts and the way society views women.

Both the environment and the types of women to whom women perceivers are exposed can have a significant effect on their own tendency to engage in automatic gender stereotyping. Research by Dasgupta and Asgari (in press) found that when women are exposed to famous women who have made major contributions to various areas (e.g., law, politics, science), they are much less likely to automatically activate gender stereotypes in their subsequent judgments. Moreover, women who are exposed to more women leaders (e.g., female professors) in their daily environments are much less likely to automatically activate gender stereotypes. This suggests that a well-entrenched, automatic cognitive process (gender stereotyping activation and endorsement) can be disrupted and perhaps eliminated by exposing the individual to women who occupy leadership (counterstereotypic) positions.

Evolution versus Social Roles

Many people believe that men and women are different in terms of their personalities, interests, and abilities, and these differences are caused by their different biological makeup. In other words, men and women are hardwired differently, and this is why, for example, men are aggressive, and women are nonaggressive. According to this line of reasoning,

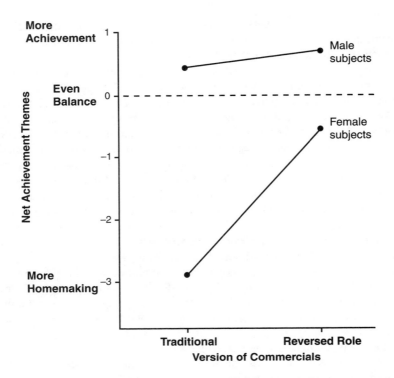

FIGURE 8.1   The influence of stereotypical and nonstereotypical commercials on women's and men's aspirations to achieve. Geis and her colleagues (1984) showed men and women either a series of gender stereotypic ("traditional") commercials or gender-role-reversed commercials, and examined its effects on participants' essays describing their views of themselves in the future. The achievement-related themes in male's essays were unchanged as a result of the type of commercial; they had more achievement-related themes in their self-views. Women who saw the sex-stereotyped commercials tended to see their futures in terms of those stereotypes: their essays revealed significantly more homemaking themes and less achievement imagery than those of men. However, when women viewed the gender-role-reversed commercials, their essays showed significantly more achievement-related themes and very little gender-stereotypical imagery. Interestingly, this type of commercial resulted in women having achievement aspirations that were nearly equal to those of men in that condition. (From Geis, Brown, Jennings, and Porter, "TV commercials as achievement scripts for women." *Sex Roles, 10* (7/8), 513–525. Copyright © 1984, by Plenum Publishing. Reprinted with permission of publisher.)

then, the *x* or *y* sex chromosome from the father (added to the mother's *x* sex chromosome) determines a woman's or man's personality, abilities, and interests in regular ways that are not stereotypical, but are just a natural outcome of the person's gender.

Evolutionary psychologists (Buss, 1995, 1996; Simpson & Kenrick, 1997) suggest that such differences are the result of the Darwinian principle of natural selection. Specifically, natural selection is the process whereby those with genetic fitness are those who are most able to adapt successfully to the environment. Successfully adapted organisms are

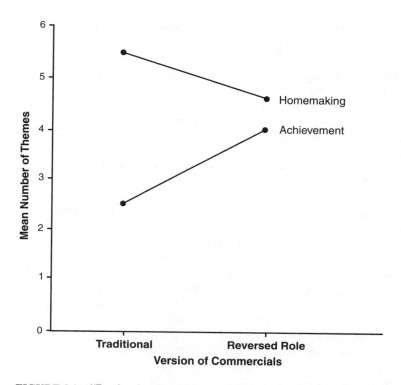

FIGURE 8.2 **"Buying into" society's gender stereotypes can influence one's aspirations for the future.** This figure shows another look at the basic effect presented in Figure 8.1. We can see that the actual number of homemaking versus achievement-related themes in women's essays shows a powerful influence of gender stereotypes. When women viewed commercials that promoted gender stereotypes, they tended to generate many more homemaking and few achievement-related themes in their views of themselves in the future. Interestingly, viewing a gender-role-reversed commercial influenced women to think of their futures in less stereotypical ways (more achievement, and less homemaking themes in their essays). (From Geis, Brown, Jennings, and Porter, "TV commercials as achievement scripts for women." *Sex Roles, 10* (7/8), 513–525. Copyright © 1984, by Plenum Publishing. Reprinted with permission of publisher.)

most likely to pass on their genes (i.e., to have offspring), and in this way, only the strongest, most adapted organisms in the species survive (Darwin, 1859). Evolutionary explanations for behavior assert that behavior and characteristics that are present today must necessarily have been adaptive, or else they would not have been passed down in the genetic code, to be observed in the organism today. More contemporary forms of evolutionary psychology have broadened the notion of genetic fitness, to inclusive fitness, which states that an organism is motivated to pass on its genes, either directly by producing offspring, or indirectly by helping a genetic relative survive and pass on its genes (Buss, 1996).

How does this apply to gender stereotypes? What evolutionary psychology suggests is that the differences between males and females, in terms of personality, characteristics, and so forth that are often labeled as stereotypes, are real, and they exist because evolutionary processes of inclusive fitness favored certain behaviors for men and different behaviors for women. While evolutionary psychology is the target of a number of criticisms (the erroneous belief that it is untestable, and therefore unfalsifiable), it is gaining popularity within mainstream psychology. A difference that many current gender researchers have with evolutionary theory is at the causal level of gender differences. Evolutionary theory suggests that gender differences today evolved out of the evolutionary drive to pass on one's genes, while researchers from other perspectives state that human biology evolved around different social structures and social roles (Caporael & Brewer, 1995; Eagly & Wood, 1999). In other words, social roles and societal structure have evolved throughout time, and with these changes males and females have placed different emphases on qualities they seek in a mate. These social changes have thus influenced what genes and what characteristics are passed down in men and women.

A bigger problem exists, however, when attempting to use evolutionary principles to explain current gender differences. It is a big leap to suggest that the specific social conditions that are present today—for example, gender differences in behavior—were also present and adaptive in the early days of humankind (Eagly & Wood, 1999). Eagly (1987) has proposed an alternative to the evolutionary and biological explanations for gender differences in behavior. According to her **social-roles theory,** gender differences that are present today come from the different social roles that men and women perform in society. Put simply, Eagly argues that it is not the case that the ability, interests, and characteristics of men and women are different because of genetics, but rather, we are different because society has taught us to do and be interested in different things, and to develop some aspects of personality more than others. Social-roles theory states that

1. Through a combination of biological and social factors, a division of labor between the sexes has emerged over time.
2. Since people behave in ways that fit the roles they play, men are more likely to wield physical, social, and economic power.
3. These behavioral differences provide a continuing basis for social perception, leading us to perceive men as dominant "by nature" and women as domestic "by nature," when in fact the differences reflect the roles they play.

We only perceive gender differences in behavior and personality because of the socialization of different behaviors and personality characteristics for boys and girls. Theoretically, then, if we socialized a girl as if she were a boy (i.e., taught her to be interested in traditional male activities and to develop what are deemed male traits, such as aggressiveness and competitiveness), she would develop interests and personality characteristics that are more similar to those that we stereotypically associate with boys. Though social-roles theory has been criticized by evolutionary theorists as an unsatisfactory explanation for gender differences in behavior (e.g., Archer, 1996), the theory has received much empirical support (Eagly, 1987; Eagly & Steffen, 1986; Eagly & Wood, 1991, 1999; Moskowitz, Suh, & Desaulniers, 1994). In making the point that men and women are more similar than they are different, social-roles theory is consistent with much of the research literature, which has arrived at the same conclusion (Basow, 1992; Deaux & LaFrance, 1998). Thus, at present, social-roles theory provides the most parsimonious account for the observed differences between men and women in their social behavior.

Power

Throughout the ages, societies have been based on a strong patriarchical structure. This foundation represents a social structure that grants men power over women (Janssen-Jurreit, 1982). In societies cross-culturally, history has recorded a remarkable consistency in the subordination of women to men (Albee & Perry, 1998; Burn, 1996). Explanations for this disparity in equality range from the stronger male physique (i.e., power deriving literally from superior physical force), the province of men to be more agentic (or instrumental) compared with women (who needed to be more geographically stationary to raise and protect the children), and the legitimization of male dominance over women by religion (Basow, 1992; Bowman, 1984) and government (Albee & Perry; Benokraitis & Feagin, 1986). All of these influences have worked to keep societies male dominated in virtually every aspect of life. The question for the present discussion is, how does this power differential lead to gender stereotyping of women?

According to Fiske (1993; Fiske & Stevens, 1993), the initial difference between men and women in terms of power can be explained by the same reason that drives sexism and prejudice against women today: control. Fiske suggests that stereotypes are a form of control. They limit the target of the stereotype, and they legitimize discrimination and prejudice against the stereotyped group. Fiske argues that power fosters the development of stereotypes about the powerless (and not vice versa). People in power do not need to think carefully about others, and they may not be personally motivated to pay attention to others, and therefore they are more likely to use rough stereotypes when thinking about others (Keltner, Gruenfeld, & Anderson, 2003). Whenever there is a power asymmetry, therefore, stereotyping of the powerless by the powerful is likely to occur, primarily because stereotyping serves the useful function of maintaining the power imbalance. The power differential between men and women is embedded and legitimized within organizational, societal, and interpersonal structures, and this serves to perpetuate the gender stereotyping the control of women (Deaux & LaFrance, 1998; Haines & Jost, 2000). Within such a power imbalance, the powerful (men) will adopt ideologies (including gender stereotypes) and beliefs that legitimize their dominance over the less powerful (women), and these ideologies help stabilize the oppression of the powerless and minimize group conflict through their institutionalization within society (Pratto, Sidanius, Stallworth, & Malle, 1994; Sidanius, 1993).

Stereotypes are both **descriptive** and **prescriptive.** According to Fiske (1993), the descriptive aspect of stereotypes tells how most people in a group behave, think, and feel. It describes the group's motives, expectations, and other aspects of behavior (e.g., Asians are good at math and science). Stereotypes thus are controlling in that they provide a point from which the stereotyped individual must start, or from which they must break free. The prescriptive aspect of stereotypes is even more controlling. This suggests how stereotyped groups *should* think, feel, and act. This limits the range of behaviors open to the stereotyped individual, and it demands conformity to some or most aspects of the stereotype in order to maintain smooth interactions with the more powerful. Indeed, Fiske and Stevens (1993) suggest that gender stereotypes are a special type of stereotype in terms of their ability to exert control: they are more prescriptive than other stereotypes. The reason for this is that we have much more experience with gender groups than we do with other groups, and this provides a larger database from which to derive the prescriptive "shoulds" that make up gender stereotypes. Recent data from Gill (2004) shows support for the idea that prescriptive stereotypes are influential. Gill found that prescriptive (and not descriptive) gender stereotypes predicted sexism, and this type of stereotyping is resistant to behavioral information that undercuts descriptive stereotypes.

ACCURACY OF GENDER STEREOTYPES

Are stereotypes about men and women accurate? Although most people would view such a possibility as preposterous, it is important to think carefully about what people mean by "accurate." Consider the fact that, most people, when given a stereotype about a group, can think of specific members of that group who have a number of characteristics that conform to that group stereotype. This, of course, does not make the stereotype accurate. Stereotypes, by definition, are broad generalizations of members of a group. A stereotype suggests that all members have similarity among themselves, and this unique constellation of characteristics sets them apart from other groups. Strictly speaking, therefore, stereotypes can never be accurate in terms of describing individuals within the group.

However, what about the famous prejudice researcher Gordon Allport's (1954) contention that stereotypes contain a "kernel of truth"? This is the idea that stereotypes are based in some small way on fact. So, for some percentage of the group, the stereotype is an accurate reflection of reality, and accurately describes the characteristics of those members. The "kernel of truth" notion is one type of accuracy—addressing the question of the actual accuracy of the stereotype in describing the characteristics of the entire group. A second part of the accuracy question is, how accurate is the group stereotype in describing an individual group member (Deaux & Kite, 1993)? To illustrate these aspects of the accuracy of stereotypes, let us consider the following example of a gender stereotype.

A common stereotype about women is that they are more emotional than men. Women seem to be more willing than men to express, talk about, and let themselves experience emotion. First, is this difference real, or is it a stereotype, and if the difference exists, what might account for the differences between men and women in terms of their emotionality? LaFrance and Banaji (1992) reviewed the scientific literature on this issue and found that women do indeed tend to express their emotions more than men, but in terms of the subjective experience of emotion (an index of emotion which typically relies on self-report measures), women are more emotional if they are asked directly, the context is interpersonal, and the emotional domain is observable. This difference may be attributable to the finding that men and women rely on different information cues to define their internal state. Men use internal physiological cues, whereas women use external situational sources of information (Roberts & Pennebaker, 1995). Interestingly, however, physiological measures of emotion indicate that there are no differences between men and women in terms of physiologically felt emotion (LaFrance & Banaji, 1992).

Thus, the LaFrance and Banaji (1992) research has illuminated the question of the accuracy of the stereotype for the whole group (i.e., it is somewhat accurate with regard to subjective emotion only). However, the issue of the accuracy of a group stereotype in describing a group member is a more complex issue. Most researchers regard stereotypes as probability estimates when applied to individuals, rather than accurate characterizations (Deaux & Kite, 1993; McCauley, Stitt, & Segal, 1980). That is, for a given stereotype, there is a certain probability that the stereotype is accurate for the particular group member under consideration. Perceivers decide, based on their own information, past experiences, biases, and other heuristics, what those probabilities are for them in that social context, at that moment. As we have seen throughout this book, some people are more likely to rely on stereotypes as accurate and may be more likely to inflate their estimates of the probability of stereotype accuracy (e.g., right-wing authoritarians). On the other hand, there is some evidence that people are more sensitive to *actual* group differences than once thought, and that their judgments about an individual may reflect both bias and accurate perceptions of distinctions between groups (Ottati & Lee, 1995). Despite this, much research suggests that people often apply group stereotypes that, although they may or may not be somewhat accurate in characterizing differences between groups, represent a "good enough" judgment about an individual that meets the cognitive demand for fast judgment and the least effortful thinking that characterizes cognition (Fiske & Neuberg, 1990; Taylor, 1981).

With regard to the accuracy of gender differences, surprisingly few sound studies have been conducted on the issue. Martin (1987) asked men and women to estimate the percentage of men and women who have various characteristics. Thus, she obtained a measure of a group's own consensus on self-perceived traits, and a measure of how that group perceives the other gender. Results indicated that males and females had very stereotypical images of each other, and they tended to exaggerate small real differences to match gender stereotypes. These results support what most stereotype researchers have concluded about stereotype accuracy: within-group variability is usually larger than is perceived, and intergroup differences tend to be exaggerated in perception in ways that conform to expected stereotypes (Kunda, 1999). In a meta-analysis of the accuracy of gender stereotypes, Swim (1994) concluded that males and females were quite accurate in their perceptions of the characteristics of the other's group. Thus, according to Swim, gender stereotypes may not be overestimates. However, Allen (1995) replicated Martin's findings, further supporting the idea that gender stereotypes are not accurate, but are substantial exaggerations of small group differences. Though research on stereotype accuracy has been lacking, it is becoming a hot area of research (see Lee et al., 1995, for a detailed discussion), and more research is needed to further clarify the nature and accuracy of gender stereotypes.

SEXIST LANGUAGE

Just as we learn about the nature of our social world and our gender roles and expectations through culture and social learning, the structure and content of our language also communicates the patriarchical nature of society, and this affects the way we think about men and women (Carroll, 1956). Think about common terms for occupations: policeman, fireman, repairman, mailman, chairman, and so on. While the use of such terms for occupations has declined with the increased sensitivity to the sexist connotations of appending *man* to an occupation, many people still use the terms to refer to both men and women in those jobs. Such a usage has been termed the "generic masculine." For decades, English textbooks and manuals on proper grammar and writing structure (e.g., Strunk & White, 1979) have taught that the use of the word *he* is understood to be a generic reference to men and women in the English language that the practice is rooted in the beginnings of the

English language (Coates, 1986). So, saying the word *mankind* refers to men and women, just as the phrase "May the best man win" refers to both sexes.

But does it really? How does the presence of masculine terms in the English language affect gender stereotypes, and how do women perceive their place in such a patriarchical system? In order to examine how the generic *he* affects interpretations of the subjects of various sentences, Gastil (1990) asked participants to read various sentences aloud and then describe whether the image of the subject was a male, a female, either male or female, or neither (no human image). Results confirmed earlier research (e.g., MacKay, 1980; Todd-Mancillas, 1981) which showed that the generic *he* tends to evoke a male image in a significant majority of the responses. Similarly, much research indicates that when children read sentences with the generic *he*, they generally do not understand that it is meant to denote male and female (Hyde, 1984; Wise & Rafferty, 1982). Use of generic masculine terms in job advertisements also affects how women perceive the appropriateness of the position for them. Research indicates that when jobs are described with masculine pronouns (e.g., "this position requires that the individual be required to show his mastery of . . . He will be responsible for overseeing . . . "), women are rated as less competent than men to do the job (Shepelak, Ogden, & Tobin-Bennett, 1984), and female applicants lose interest in the position, assuming that they are not suited for the position (Briere & Lanktree, 1983).

Basow (1992) notes many other sexist aspects of the English language that are still prevalent today. Women tend to be described in the media by their appearance, whereas men are rarely so described. For example, how many times have you heard a talk-show host introduce a female (actor, singer, etc.) as "please welcome the beautiful . . . " No mention of her skills in what she does (presumably why she is there), but a focus on her physical appearance. Rarely do we see male actors/singers introduced as "the handsome. . . . " Similarly, saying "a female doctor" or, "a woman pilot" implies that the position is normally a male occupation (because we never hear "male doctor": *doctor* implies male), and when a woman occupies such a position, it is unusual and thus must be signified as such by denoting "female." This principle applies the other way too, for primarily female-dominated positions occupied by males, such as "male nurse" or "male model."

Finally, Basow notes that the English language is sexist in the tradition of women being referred to by their relationships. Traditionally, when a woman gets married, she loses her identity and becomes Mrs. John Doe. She is Jane Doe, *wife of* John Doe. She also loses her original ("maiden") last name, and takes the husband's last name. What does that communicate to women? That their name is not important, and what is important is the male name, which is passed down to the children. After the wedding ceremony, the couple were introduced as "man and wife." These days, many of these sexist traditions are changing. Women are keeping their last names when married, and newly married couples are introduced in the ceremony in nonsexist ways, such as "John and Jane, husband and wife." However, many sexist traditions remain rooted in religion (as noted earlier) and language. In sum, although research indicates that men and women agree that sexist language is a problem and can be detrimental to women, men are less likely than women to recognize sexist language as sexist (Stewart, Verstraate, & Fanslow, 1990). This suggests that much effort ought to be put forth in schools, the media, and business to help educate people about sexism, how to recognize instances of sexism, and how to avoid using sexist language.

SEXIST HUMOR

One of the axioms of stand-up comedy is, make sure your jokes appeal to the most common denominator. That is, you will get the biggest laughs if everyone can relate to the content of the joke or story. What better way to appeal to the humor of human existence than to discuss a subject of mystery, problems, and—yes—comedy: the differences between men and women. Ever since the early days of vaudeville around the beginning of the 20th century, people have been making fun of the differences between men and women. For example, a man's idea of romance is sharing a pizza and a 12-pack of beer with his significant other while watching the sports channel, while a woman's idea of romance is a candlelight dinner at an elegant restaurant, followed by a walk on the moonlit beach. Why have such sexist ideas permeated comedy, and why do people—even those who do not fully agree with the differences between men and women—continue to find sexist humor amusing? Next, we examine the motivation for, perceptions of, and effects on women of sexist humor.

Sexist Jokes Perpetuate Gender Stereotypes

One of the first things one notices in humor that describes differences between men and women is that they are restatements of gender stereotypes. Gender stereotypes suggest that men are selfish, sloppy, beer drinkers, sports lovers, aggressive, obsessed with sex, insensitive and uncaring, and unrefined and uncultured. Women are stereotyped as vain, neurotic about everything (especially their appearance), unintelligent, petty, uninterested in things that men find interesting (e.g., sports, beer, being aggressive), and emotional. Recall that stereotypes are true for a fraction of the population, but they are in no way generalizable to the entire population or even, in most cases, a majority of the population. Most people, however, tend to disregard this fact and instead give a fair amount of credence to the truth of the message in gender-stereotypic humor. There are a couple of reasons for this.

First, relationships between men and women are often confusing. How many times have you heard someone bemoan the mysterious nature of men (or women)? To clarify our understanding of the other gender, we often rely on our schemas about that gender (Fiske & Taylor, 1991). The gender schema contains all the information we know about the gender in question, expectations for behavior (how to behave toward the person, and what behavior to expect from the other person), stereotypes, motives, and how to feel toward the other gender. Gender schemas contain a tremendous amount of information that is made accessible upon perceiving the other individual (and activating the gender schema in one's consciousness), but the downside is that much of the information can be inappropriately applied or is just plain wrong, as in the case of stereotypes. Nevertheless, as we discussed in Chapter 1, people tend to be cognitive misers (S. E. Taylor, 1981). We are usually more concerned with making a fast evaluation rather than an accurate one. Therefore, there is little incentive to disregard information that may derive from incorrect sources within the schema (i.e., stereotypes), and people may consider such information as accurate (E. E. Jones, 1990). Recall that stereotypes are valuable tools toward the goal of simplifying judgments about the environment. The more confusing and complex the environment or stimulus is, the more likely we ought to rely on cognitive heuristics to help us understand

and evaluate the stimulus. So, when it comes to understanding the other gender, people often rely on their schemas about the gender, and within those schemas are a lot of gender stereotypes.

Second, as we learned earlier in this chapter, people are exposed to gender-stereotype information from a very young age. From parents, media, friends, and other sources, we learn many generalizations about men and women and about what it is to be a man or woman. This lifetime of exposure to the same stereotypes has a profound influence on the way we think about gender. The more we encounter a piece of information, the more likely it is to be encoded in our memory as part of the schema, and this holds true for gender stereotypes (Nisbett & Ross, 1980). So, stereotypes about men and women tend to be well entrenched in our gender schemas, which is why these stereotypes become salient upon one's perceiving a male or female. Much research has demonstrated that the rate at which we can access stimulus-relevant information upon encountering a stimulus will tend to influence the way we think about that stimulus (Nisbett & Ross). Specifically, the **availability heuristic** states that our judgments about the probability of the event will be affected by the availability (or how fast an instance of the event comes to mind) of that event information (Tversky & Kahneman, 1973).

Thus, upon the initial perception of a male or female, we should have gender stereotypes made highly salient, along with other gender schema information. However, research suggests that some people are more likely than others to think about gender when perceiving the world. Bem (1981) suggested that there are those who tend to think about the world in terms of gender information, whom she calls gender schematic. Those who do not think about the world in gender terms are called gender aschematic. Stangor (1988) found that gender schematic individuals are much more likely to process information in terms of gender, made more evaluations in terms of gender stereotypes, and made more errors in memory judgments about behaviors performed by their gender. Frable (1989) found that gender schematic individuals tend to accept culturally prescribed roles for each gender and tend to endorse sexist language more than nongender schematic persons. Thus, it appears that those who think about the world in male/female terms tend to have more accessible gender schemas, more fully elaborated gender schemas, and more accessible gender stereotypes than those for whom the world is not so partitioned.

Perceptions of Sexist Humor

In examining the influence of sexist humor on the perpetuation of gender stereotyping, it is important to understand how people perceive sexist humor. Do they perceive it as sexist? If so, do they still find it humorous? Most of the research on these questions investigates the problem by presenting people with sexist and nonsexist jokes, cartoons, and humorous material and rating whether they perceive that material to be funny. Moore, Griffiths, and Payne (1987) asked men and women who had either traditional (stereotyped) or nontraditional views of male and female gender roles to view sexist and nonsexist cartoons from various publications. As one might expect, those with less-traditional views of women rated sexist cartoons as less funny than nonsexist cartoons. Interestingly, both men and women rated the sexist cartoons as significantly funnier than the nonsexist cartoons. Love and Deckers (1989) conducted a similar study, with men and women rating sexist and nonsexist cartoons, but they found that women found sexist cartoons less funny than nonsexist cartoons. Women found sexist cartoons to be less funny than did men. The authors of both of these studies interpret the data as supporting Zillman's (1983) dispositional theory of humor, which states that the more one feels sympathy for the victim of a disparaging joke, the less likely one will find that joke funny. This is certainly the case with both the nontraditional-gender-type individuals in Moore et al.'s study (1987) and the women in Love and Deckers's study (1989): each group felt sympathy for the women targets in the sexist cartoons and thus rated the cartoons as less funny.

In a different approach to the how males and females perceive sexist humor, Bill and Naus (1992) asked participants to rate the humor and acceptibility of actual sexist and nonsexist incidents. Participants' attitudes toward women were assessed by their completing the Sexist Attitudes Toward Women Scale (Benson & Vincent, 1980). An example of a sexist incident from the study is as follows: "On a work term, a female student was told by her male supervisor to 'just sit at your desk and look pretty.' This is the reply he gave her after she inquired what her duties and responsibilities would involve" (p. 663). Results indicated that sexist attitudes toward women were a predictor of greater appreciation of sexist incidents as humorous. Bill and Naus also found little difference between male and female participants in their ratings of how humorous the sexist incidents were. In both the Moore et al. (1987) and Bill and Naus studies, men and women show equal appreciation for sexist humor.

It seems rather strange that a target of derogating humor, or humor that perpetuates stereotypes, would find the humor as amusing as those who produce and distribute the humor. While researchers have yet to address the specific reasons why this might be the case, one plausible explanation may be that women may perceive sexist humor as not actually sexist, but as harmless fun about the differences between and stereotypes about the sexes. Another possibility, discussed in the next section, is that women may perceive sexist humor as sexist, but they want to get along with others, and so they do not stand up against sexism (for fear of being perceived as pushy or, worse, for doing so), but rather go along with others in perceiving the sexist humor as benign fun. Much more research is needed in this area to ascertain the reasons for the similarity between men and women in their perceptions of some types of sexist humor.

Is Sexist Humor Harmless Fun?

Some may argue that what is called sexist humor is merely innocent fun that calls attention to the differences between men and women. They may contend that perceptions of jokes about women (and men) as sexist are a minority view held primarily by humorless feminists, and that most people find them funny. However, much research suggests that sexist humor, however seemingly benign, often has negative implications for society, and specifically for women, who are the most frequent target of sexist humor; LaFrance & Woodzicka, 1998). Sexist humor may indicate a deeper hostility toward women. Freud (1905/1960) theorized that sexist humor may indicate an underlying hostility toward women and that humor is a vehicle for masking socially unacceptable hostility. In a test of this basic assumption, Ryan and Kanjorski (1998) asked 399 college students to rate 10 sexist jokes according to how funny they thought the jokes were. Participants also completed measures of rape-myth acceptance and acceptance of interpersonal violence (Burt, 1980) and attraction to sexual aggression (Malamuth, 1989). Results indicated sexist jokes seem to be enjoyed the most by men who are higher in the acceptance of violence toward women, who are more accepting of rape myths, and who tend to be aggressive with their partners. These individuals are more likely to agree that violence against women is acceptable. It is perhaps not surprising that men who have views of women as adversaries, as sexual objects, and as targets to be manipulated and dominated are more likely to enjoy humor that demeans women (LaFrance & Woodzicka). Ryan and Kanjorski interpret these findings as support for Freud's idea that sexist humor may mask underlying hostility and aggressive impulses toward women.

Interestingly, there has been very little empirical attention devoted to the effects of sexist humor on women. How do women react when they encounter an example of sexist humor? Does it hurt their self-esteem or make them angry, or are most women unaffected by sexist humor? As noted earlier, the available research on sexist humor indicates that women sometimes find sexist humor as funny as men do, and sometimes they find it less amusing than do men. In an interesting study, LaFrance and Woodzicka (1998) expanded on this literature by examining how women respond to sexist and nonsexist jokes both directly, via self-report, and indirectly, via nonverbal measures of affect. Women participants completed measures of negative attitudes toward women, identification with women, self-esteem, and negative affect. They then were asked to do a separate study involving listening to 7 audiotaped sexist or nonsexist jokes, and then rating them in terms of perceived funniness, amusement, comfort, and interest. Results indicated that women hearing sexist jokes reported feeling more angry, surprised, and hostile than women who heard nonsexist jokes.

But the picture becomes a bit more ambiguous when examining the nonverbal responses of the women to the jokes. Researchers coded facial reactions for very specific muscle movements, in order to distinguish the presence and duration of various types of facial reactions that do and do not correspond with affect states. Specifically, the researchers used Eckman and Friesen's coding system to identify smiles that have been shown to be strongly linked to positive affect (Duchenne smiles) and those that have not been shown to be associated with positive affect (non-Duchenne smiles; Eckman & Friesen, 1982). The data indicated that women who heard sexist jokes showed an equal amount of Duchenne smiles to those who heard the nonsexist jokes. This result is counterintuitive given the fact that women hearing the sexist jokes reported feeling more angry and hostile after hearing the jokes, compared with those who heard the nonsexist jokes. The only other significant behavioral difference between those hearing the sexist and the nonsexist jokes was that women who heard sexist jokes displayed more eye-rolling (a measure of contempt) than those who heard the nonsexist jokes. These data illustrate the complex nature of women's reactions to sexist humor. Their self-reports and nonverbal measures of contempt indicate a hostile, angry reaction to sexist jokes, but nonverbal measures of nonverbal behavior corresponding to positive affect indicate that women genuinely found both the sexist and nonsexist jokes to be equally amusing.

Automatic and Controlled Reactions to Sexist Humor

These results are interesting, and more research is certainly needed before we can sort out what exactly is going on with these data. On the face of it, it appears that women say they are finding the sexist jokes objectionable, but their nonverbal reactions indicate that they found the sexist jokes amusing. However, perhaps these results can be explained by Devine's (1989) work on controlled and automatic components of prejudice. Recall from our discussion in Chapter 3 that Devine showed that people all have automatic reactions to stereotyped targets (e.g., thoughts of stereotypes about the most salient group to which the target is categorized), affective reactions (e.g., fear, anger, anxiety), and behavioral reactions (e.g., distancing behavior, avoidance of eye contact), but only those who are low in self-reported prejudice are able and motivated to control these reactions and subsequently react to the target in an egalitarian fashion. Indeed, research by Banaji and her colleagues (Banaji & Greenwald, 1995; Banaji et al., 1993) shows that gender stereotypes are activated automatically upon perception of the target individual, and these stereotypes influence subsequent judgments about men and women, often without the conscious awareness of the individual.

Applying this research to LaFrance and Woodzicka's (1998) data, we can propose the following. Men and women growing up in America are exposed to countless instances of gender stereotyping, sexist remarks, and sexist humor. As we have already discussed, sexism is interwoven in many aspects of American society, and it is even culturally sanctioned (Deaux & Kite, 1993; Unger & Saundra, 1993). For example, television shows, and comedy shows in particular, are often rife with gender stereotypes. An excellent example is the show *Home Improvement*, in which the husband/father proudly exhibits virtually every known stereotype about American males and his wife is a stereotyped caricature of a mother/wife. Most comedy shows employ taped audience laughter (the so-called laugh track), inserting it in the post-production of the show (prior to broadcast) so that the producers can specifically control where the we hear an audience laughing, and how much laughter is heard (how intense and how long). While television is by no means a reflection of the real world, it is a barometer of sorts that tells viewers what society is thinking about and concerned about and what issues our leaders are dealing with. It tells us how to feel about issues, and it also tells us what shows, situations, and jokes are funny. Thus, watching comedy shows that perpetuate gender stereotypes and sexism, amid laughter from the audience, the television viewer is slowly conditioned to view gender stereotypes and sexism as not only harmless, but also funny. Thus, the well-learned, conditioned reaction to gender stereotypes and sexism may indeed be positive affect, laughter. In other words, we are primed to perceive gender stereotypes and sexism as funny.

Yet, laughing at jokes that disparage one's core ingroup should arouse dissonance. Reduction of the dissonance can be accomplished by voicing disapproval of the gender stereotype or sexist material. Indeed, LaFrance and Woodzicka's (1998) research and the results of the Ryan and Kanjorski study support the notion that only those women who endorse rape myths, have hostile attitudes toward women, and view violence against women as more acceptable report enjoyment of sexist humor. The data indicate that the majority of women report negative opinions of sexist humor. In sum, it may be the case that most women's automatic reaction to gender stereotypes and sexism in a humorous context is one of genuine amusement, followed by a more deliberate attempt to show disapproval (perhaps to relieve dissonance) of the sexist humor. It should be noted again that this is a speculative explanation of the LaFrance and Woodzicka data, but a very plausible account and a potentially fruitful avenue of investigation for future research on the reactions of women to sexist humor.

TYPES OF SEXISM

Just as the form of racial prejudice has changed from "old-fashioned" (overt) to "modern" (subtle) racism over the last four decades, so too have attitudes toward equality for women changed with the social climate. It seems strange to think that prior to 1920, women in the United States were not allowed to vote. Women were also not allowed to work in some jobs (such gender discrimination still exists, in subtle and not-so-subtle forms, in today's workplace). They were actively discouraged from having careers and encouraged to stay at home, raise children, and take care of household duties. Attitudes of men toward equality for women were openly negative, and women experienced discrimination and demeaning sexism in various forms. Society's attitudes toward gender equality have been slowly changing since World War II, when women made up the majority of the wartime workforce, stepping in to do the jobs vacated by men who were serving in the war. But the road toward equal rights has been a slow one, and it is not complete. Sexism is unfortunately alive and well in the United States, and although it does not often take an overt, openly hostile form, it is much more frequently expressed in subtle ways (Benokraitis, 1997). Next, we will examine the various forms that sexism has taken in the last 30 years.

Old-Fashioned versus Modern Sexism

The late 1960s were a time of tremendous changes in the fabric of American society. War, civil rights for African Americans, assassinations of four prominent leaders (John Kennedy, Malcolm X, Martin Luther King, Robert Kennedy), and subsequent riots in cities all over the country were deeply divisive, contentious events that tested the status quo. Amid these changes, women were beginning to be more vocal about their right to equality in society (Spence, 1993). There was a tremendous resistance to the so-called women's liberation movement in the early 1970s: only 57% of those surveyed in a Gallup poll in 1976 supported the Equal Rights Amendment (ERA), which stated that equal rights under the law cannot be denied by the federal, state, or local government (Oskamp, 1991). Ever so slowly, however, attitudes toward equality for women have changed. Gallup polls taken in 1988 indicated that 73% of respondents supported the ERA (Oskamp). Despite that encouraging statistic, sexism is by no means a thing of the past. Persistent gender stereotypes and stubborn beliefs about the natural social order for men and women in society remain today, though today it is often unacceptable to express these stereotypes overtly. Accordingly, sexism has not really decreased, but the willingness to express sexist beliefs openly has declined sharply. Sexism has taken a new, subtle form, modern sexism (Benokraitis & Feagin, 1986).

Swim et al., (1995) suggest that there are two types of sexism, **old-fashioned sexism** and **modern sexism.** Old-fashioned sexism is characterized by "endorsement of traditional gender roles, differential treatment of women and men, and stereotypes about lesser female competence" (Swim et al., 1995, p. 199). Modern sexism is indicated by the denial of discrimination against women, a hostility toward equality for women, and nonsupport of programs and legislation designed to help women. In two experiments, Swim and her colleagues showed that old-fashioned and modern sexism are distinct but related concepts. Swim et al. developed measures of old-fashioned sexism and modern sexism. Their modern sexism was based on many of the items in McConahay's (1986) modern-racism scale

(MRS). Results indicated that people who are modern sexists tend to be less sympathetic to the plight of women and more likely to also endorse old-fashioned sexist beliefs (for example, an item on the old-fashioned-sexism scale assesses the belief that women are not as logical as men; Table 8.1).

As in the case of symbolic racism (Sears, 1988), scores on the modern sexism scale correlate highly with a strong endorsement of the Protestant work ethic (to a much greater degree than the correlation between between old-fashioned sexism and the Protestant work ethic). Like Sears' (1988) measure of symbolic racism, Swim et al.'s modern-sexism sexism scale assesses attitudes toward policies designed to promote equality (e.g., affirmative action). Modern sexism, however, appears to be difficult to pinpoint, because neither men nor women find expressions of modern sexism offensive, and so this type of prejudice often goes unchallenged (Barreto & Ellemers, in press).

Neosexism

At the same time that Swim et al.'s (1995) research was published, Tougas and her colleagues (Tougas, Brown, Beaton, & Joly, 1995) reported the results of their research on what they termed **neosexism.** According to Tougas et al., neosexism is the "manifestation of a conflict between egalitarian values and residual negative feelings toward women" (p. 843). As a foundation for their research, Tougas and her colleagues made virtually identical arguments to those put forth by Swim et al. about the changing face of sexism over the decades, from a more overt, hostile prejudice toward women to a more subtle, often imperceptible type of sexism. Tougas et al. also based their measure of sexism on wording found in several of the MRS items, as well as items from other measures of symbolic racism. An examination of the items that make up the neosexism scale and the modern-sexism scale suggests that it is reasonable to conclude that the two scales measure the same construct. Moreover, though each scale has different items, the similarities and theoretical foundations of the constructs that are the foundation of each scale indicate support for the existence of a distinct type of subtle sexism that is substantially different from past expressions of sexism (which were more hostile and based on beliefs about the inferiority of women).

Tougas and her colleagues suggest that neosexism arises when one group (usually, males) believe that the interests of men are better served by a hierarchical view of the status of men and women, with men dominating society. According to Tougas et al., when neosexists perceive a threat to their preferred power advantage over women, they are more likely to resist policies aimed at promoting the equality of women, to deny the plight of women (to assert that discrimination against women is no longer a problem), and to view the world with a stronger pro-male bias. To test this idea, Tougas and her colleagues (Beaton, Tougas, & Joly, 1996) asked 123 male managers employed in a federal agency to participate in a study of their perceptions of women in management. The results indicated that as the men perceived that more and more women were entering positions of power (i.e., management), their self-reported feelings of threat increased. This was strongly associated with neosexist beliefs. The more neosexist beliefs the managers reported, the more likely it was that they evaluated the competence of a male and female with a promale bias, and the less likely the men were to support policies, such as equal pay for women, designed to promote equality for women (Beaton et al., 1996).

TABLE 8.1 The Modern Sexism Scale

	SCALE	ITEM
Old-Fashioned Sexism		1. Women are generally not as smart as men.*,a
		2. I would be equally comfortable having a woman as a boss as a man.
		3. It is more important to encourage boys than to encourage girls to participate in athletics.*
		4. Women are just as capable of thinking logically as men.
		5. When both parents are employed and their child gets sick at school, the school should call the mother rather than the father.*
Modern Sexism	Denial of continuing discrimination	1. Discrimination against women is no longer a problem in the United States.*,a
		2. Women often miss out on good jobs due to sexual discrimination.
		3. It is rare to see women treated in a sexist manner on television.*
		4. On average, people in our society treat husbands and wives equally.*
		5. Society has reached the point where women and men have equal opportunities for achievement.*
	Antagonism toward women's demands	6. It is easy to understand the anger of women's groups in America.*
		7. It is easy to understand why women's groups are still concerned about societal limitations of women's opportunities.
	Resentment about special favors for women	8. Over the past few years, the government and news media have been showing more concern about the treatment of women than is warranted by women's actual experiences.*,a

aItem was adapted from McConahay's (1986) Modern Racism Scale.

Note: Items with an asterisk required reverse scoring.

Source: Copyright © 1995, American Psychological Association. Reprinted with permission.

Benevolent versus Hostile Sexism

As we discussed earlier in this chapter, the patriarchical nature of societies throughout history has had a strong influence on the power structure within the society. Men have controlled the political, economic, and legal institutions, and, according to some recent compelling research, this has led them to form certain beliefs about the nature of men and women, and their relationship to each other. In their theory of **ambivalent sexism,** Glick and Fiske (1996) suggest that ambivalent sexists hold positive (yet stereotyped, traditional) views of some women. This is termed **benevolent sexism.** These men also have negative attitudes toward other women, and this is called **hostile sexism.** Hostile sexism is a negative attitude toward women that encompasses beliefs about the inferiority of women to men, including beliefs about lesser intelligence and competence of women relative to men. Glick and Fiske (1996) define benevolent sexism as traditional beliefs about women that evoke positive feelings in the perceiver. This type of sexism is still stereotyping, however, and it limits the target (women) because it is based on the assumption of male dominance. Hostile sexism and benevolent sexism tend to be correlated because they are based on similar beliefs about women. Both types of sexism assume women are a weaker sex and that they should occupy the domestic roles in society. Benevolent sexists want to protect women, they respect and admire women's roles as mothers and wives, and they idealize women as objects of romantic love. Hostile sexists view women as being unfit to hold positions of power, are more tolerant of wife abuse (Glick, Sakalli-Ugurlu, Ferreira, & de Souza, 2002), and are more likely to commit acquaintance rape and blame the victim for their act (Abrams, Viki, Masser, & Bohner, 2003).

Thus, Glick and Fiske (1996) suggest that hostile and benevolent sexism both serve to justify relegating women to traditional, stereotyped roles in society. What determines how ambivalent sexists will respond to a given woman? Generally speaking, if the woman violates traditional gender stereotypes (e.g., she is a career-woman or considers herself a feminist), ambivalent sexists will react with hostile sexism. One study found that benevolent sexists reacted most harshly toward a rape victim if she was married—specifically, if she was being unfaithful and then got raped—than if no information was given about her marital status (Viki & Abrams, 2002). The violation of the traditional role (wife) and values (marriage) resulted in benevolent sexists acting like hostile sexists in how negatively they regarded the victim. If a woman typifies a traditional domestic (mother, homemaker) or romantic (sex object) stereotype of a woman, they may feel benevolent sexism. In six studies, Glick and Fiske (1996) demonstrated the validity of the hostile and benevolent sexism constructs, and they developed an instrument, the Ambivalent Sexism Inventory (ASI) which had good psychometric properties as a measure of each type of sexism.

It is important to note that ambivalent sexists do not have negative attitudes toward all women. Indeed, as Eagly and Mladinic (1989) showed, most men have a very positive attitude toward women. But, what differentiates the ambivalent sexist from the nonsexist is that ambivalent sexists have strong negative reactions to some women, and positive, stereotyped reactions to other women, whereas nonsexists do not so categorize women and do not endorse such gender stereotypes. Glick and Fiske (1996) theorized that there may be two types of ambivalence that men experience upon encountering a woman. They may feel an unconflicted type of ambivalence, in which a target woman is classified into either a favored group or an unfavored group. They may also feel a conflicted ambivalence, in which a target woman evokes negative and positive feelings in the perceiver. Glick, Diebold, Bailey-Werner, and Zhu (1997) conducted two studies to examine how males classify women into subgroups and how those subgroups are evaluated by men. Glick and his colleagues predicted that ambivalent sexists would be more likely to generate a list of more polar-opposite subgroups (e.g., "whore" versus "caring"), whereas nonsexist men would generate lists of subgroups that were closer in evaluation and content (e.g., "quiet" and "nice"). Results indicated that, indeed, ambivalent-sexist men tended to classify women into polar-opposite categories (i.e., "saint" or "slut"). The data also further support Glick and Fiske's (1996) results, which indicated that hostile sexism is evoked by women who violate traditional gender roles and benevolent sexism is elicited by women who fulfilled traditional gender roles.

According to Glick et al. (1997), ambivalent sexists tend to choose to categorize women into either favored or nonfavored groups, in order to reduce any potential conflict in positive and negative attitudes they may have toward a given woman. Certainly, though, there are women who do not fit neatly into such simple categories. For example, how do ambivalent sexists deal with a homemaker who has feminist views? Glick and his colleagues (1997) suggest that when it is difficult to put a woman into one of the simple (favored versus nonfavored) categories, ambivalent sexists may try to split their evaluation of her in terms of various dimensions (for example, competence versus interpersonal), which would allow the conflicted ambivalence (and the cognitive dissonance) they feel to be reduced. Thus, they could dislike a career woman for her violation of traditional gender roles but respect her competence and achievement (an agentic dimension that men value and would therefore find it difficult to disparage or devalue).

What determines whether a woman would be seen as competent and/or likeable? The woman's relative status would influence evaluations of competence, whereas cooperative or competitive interdependence of the male perceiver and the female target would determine whether the male finds the woman likeable (Glick and Fiske, 1999). Additionally, the perception of the woman may be influenced by the personality of the male perceiver. In their research on attitudes toward women, Haddock and Zanna (1994) replicated Eagly & Mladinic's findings that men have a positive attitude toward the general category "women" but that some men have more varying attitudes toward subcategories of women. Specifically, the data suggested that men who were high in right-wing authoritarianism (RWA) tendencies were more inclined to have a very negative opinion of feminists and a more positive view of housewives. RWA individuals "maintain a strong acceptance of traditional social values and norms, possess a willingness to submit to established and legitimate authorities, and display a general willingness to aggress against others, particularly those who threaten conventional values and norms" (Haddock & Zanna, 1994, p. 28). The negative opinion that RWA males have of feminists appears to derive from the RWA males' perceived discrepancy between their values and their perceptions of the beliefs of feminists. Unfortunately, the researchers did not ask participants to elaborate on their perceptions of feminists and on how feminist values might be similar to or different from their own. Much more research is needed to clarify these findings, and we may then obtain a more developed picture of how personality type, specifically RWA, affects males' perceptions of various subgroups of women.

How do women react to hostile and benevolent sexists? To address this question, Kilianski and Rudman (1998) asked 100 female participants to read profiles of a benevolent sexist, a hostile sexist, and a nonsexist male and then provide their attitudes toward each of these men. The data indicated that women rated the nonsexist very favorably, the benevolent sexist slightly favorably, and the hostile sexist very negatively. Interestingly, Kilianski and Rudman also found that their participants did not believe that hostile and benevolent sexism could coexist within the same person. The investigators conclude that the underestimation of the coexistence of both types of sexism in men tends to lead to continued resistance to its elimination. In other words, if, as their data suggest, most women have a favorable attitude toward benevolent sexists, they are implicitly condoning the male's beliefs about traditional gender roles and unknowingly validating his other hostile sexist beliefs about male dominance and superiority over females. While these data are indeed intriguing, much more research is needed to examine the details of women's attitudes toward these varieties of sexism.

EFFECTS OF SEXISM ON WOMEN

Much research indicates that the tendency to stereotype oneself (Hogg & Turner, 1987; Lorenzi-Cioldi, 1991) and others (Chiu, Hong, Lam, Fu, Tong, & Lee, 1998) is more likely when one's gender category is made salient (Deaux & LaFrance, 1998; Fiske, 1998). This is consistent with the notion that the categories male and female are not separate stereotypes. Rather, activation of one category can make salient information about the stereotype components in the other category (Deaux & Lewis, 1984). When one is in a minority in terms of gender in a given setting, some researchers have predicted that individuals will have an increased tendency to define themselves in terms of their gender (McGuire & McGuire, 1981). Research by Cota and Dion (1986) supports this prediction. However, gender identity is very complex, and it is not enough to state that one's gender is simply male or female—it is also closely tied in with other gendered aspects of social life, such as occupation and interests, to name a few (Burn, 1996). To the extent that gender is central to one's self-concept, it would stand to reason that the influence of sexism should be stronger for such individuals. However, the findings on this issue have been mixed (Deaux & LaFrance). Thus, we must turn to other areas of inquiry to examine the influence of sexism on women. Gender stereotypes, prejudice, and discrimination have a pervasive influence on women in virtually all aspects of their lives. It is beyond the purvue of this chapter to examine *all* of the research on the effects of sexism, so we will cover just a sampling of some interesting areas of research on this issue.

When women encounter instances of sexism, how do they react? This is a fundamental question that has not received enough empirical attention, until very recently. The question is important because it asks (1) whether women notice instances of sexism, (2) whether they react privately (i.e., show no overt reaction) or publicly, (3) if they react publicly, what form that reaction takes, and (4) how instances of sexism make women feel about themselves. To investigate this question, Swim and Hyers (1999) designed two interesting experiments, one to assess women's public and private reactions to a sexist remark made by a male (Experiment 1), and another to examine the reasons for the type of reactions women indicated they would have to the remark (Experiment 2).

In the first experiment, women were pretested for their attitudes toward equal roles and privileges for women and men, for their sensitivity to sexism, for the degree to which they identify with other women, and for the degree of personal activism in reducing sexism. Women were then asked to participate in a discussion group with three other participants (who were all confederates). Sometimes there were no other women in the group (solo condition), and sometimes there would be two other females and one male in the discussion group (nonsolo condition). Participants were asked to select, from a list of 15 individuals, 12 people who would be best suited for survival on a desert island, and to list their choices aloud and explain the reasons for their selections. Confederates' responses were scripted, and in the sexist-remarks condition, a male confederate gave three sexist rationales for his selection of various females on his list (e.g., "I think we need more women on the island to keep the men satisfied"). After this task, participants viewed a videotape of their discussion group and were asked to indicate their thoughts and feelings at various points while watching the tape, as well as their perceptions of the prejudice level of the male confederate.

The videotapes were then coded by the researchers for degree of confrontation (verbal expressions of displeasure with the comment) by the participant in reaction to the sexist comments. Confrontation was further coded for whether it was direct (telling the confederate that his comment was sexist, or telling him to refrain from being sexist) or indirect (all other verbal expressions of displeasure at the comment). Results indicated that 45% of the participants confronted the male confederate in the sexist condition, but only 15% of those participants directly confronted him. Interestingly, of the remaining 55% of the women (the nonconfronters), 91% later reported that they had negative thoughts and feelings about the male confederate after he made the sexist comments. The data also indicated that those who considered themselves activists were unaffected by the sexist comment, while those who were not activists and those who endorsed traditional gender roles reported a decrease in their self-perceived performance, appearance, and self-esteem. Interestingly, confronting the confederate did not make participants feel better about themselves.

What affected the decision of women to respond or not respond to the sexist remark? The researchers hypothesized that confronting depended on the perceived costs for such behavior by the participant. There may be a social cost (such as rejection, or outright hostility) to confronting the sexist individual, and women may also be seen as impolite (violating the gender role for women that states that they ought to be polite to others). As in Experiment 1, participants in Experiment 2 were asked to read a scenario describing the group composition of a discussion group (solo or nonsolo) that did the same task and had the same sexist or nonsexist comments by the male confederate as in Experiment 1. Participants in this experiment rated the sexist and offensive nature of the comment, and indicated whether they would confront him and how they think they would confront him (behaviors, thoughts, feelings). The results indicated that 81% of the women in this experiment said they would give at least one confrontational response. Factors that would inhibit their confronting the confederate included social pressures to be polite and not respond, diffusion of responsibility for confronting (in the nonsolo condition), and worries about social retaliation. Indeed, the vast majority of the women in Experiment 2 who indicated that they would confront the male confederate chose the most polite form of confrontation (e.g., give a task-related response, such as "that is not a good reason to choose someone. Make another selection").

As another example that illustrates how socially condoned sexism is, relative to expressions of racism, one recent study found that when participants were told to imagine being confronted about being either gender or racially biased, the participants in the latter conditions reacted with more guilt and were apologetic (Czopp & Monteith, 2003). Those who were accused of gender bias were much less apologetic, and instead they reacted with amusement.

In sum, these data suggest that most women notice and think negatively about those who make sexist remarks, but less than half actually respond with some form of confrontation toward the sexist individual. Those who closely identify with women and are more committed to actively ending sexism are least personally affected (i.e., no drop in state self-esteem) and are more likely to confront sexist individuals. Swim and Hyers (1999) suggest that these data illustrate the conflict women have between their desire to confront sexism, and the social pressures (conformity, diffusion of responsibility, avoiding social rejection, gender role behavior) that inhibits confrontation. An interesting question for future research in this area is, how do the public reactions of women to sexist remarks affect those individuals who are the sources of the sexist comments?

GENDER DISCRIMINATION

Gender stereotypes have a strong impact on how men and women behave toward each other. In this section, we will discuss negative behavior directed toward an individual based on their gender. This type of behavior, gender discrimination, can be found in individuals as well as organizations. We will first discuss gender discrimination by individuals and then focus on the nature of institutionalized gender discrimination in America today. Due to the long tradition of patriarchical structure within societies in America and, indeed, all over the world, men have had a distinct political, economic, and legal advantage over women, and they have enjoyed many privileges that were, and in some cases still are, denied to women (such as the right to vote). This imbalance in power relations between men and women tends to be a perfect breeding ground for prejudice of the more powerful against the less powerful. Though prejudice and discrimination toward women today is no longer as overtly expressed as it was in the past, there is substantial evidence to suggest that men still possess negative attitudes toward different types of women (Haddock & Zanna, 1994), and more often in some situations (e.g., at work) than others (Basow, 1992; Benokraitis & Feagin, 1986; Burn, 1996). These negative beliefs about women help maintain the power and dominance of men over women, and this is a strong motivation for men to maintain gender stereotypes about women. Discrimination against women takes many forms. Next we examine the factors that lead to interpersonal and institutional discrimination against women.

Distancing Behavior

Much research indicates that gender stereotypes about women lead men to expect lower performance, lower motivation, and lower ability, relative to men (Basow, 1992; Deaux & Kite, 1993; Ruble & Ruble, 1982). As a result, men have tended to ignore, devalue, or behave in a patronizing manner toward women (Heilman, Martell, & Simon, 1988). In an interesting program of research, Lott and her colleagues (Lott, 1989; Saris, Johnston, & Lott, 1995) examined a measure of interpersonal sexist discrimination—distancing behavior— among men and women. Measures of distancing behavior in interpersonal interactions have a long history in psychology (e.g., Bogartus' [1925] social-distance scale). Much research indicates that when people feel positive toward, and wish to interact with, another person, they will reduce the interpersonal distance between themselves and the other individual (Lott, 1989). Therefore, greater distance should indicate a lower interest in or more neutral/negative feelings toward another person. Lott and her colleagues reasoned that, to the degree that males or females show a gender bias in their interpersonal distancing behaviors, they would have evidence for interpersonal discrimination based solely on the target's gender.

To test this idea, males and females were asked to read about a hypothetical situation and then indicate where they would like to sit in an array of chairs drawn on a sheet of paper. Some of the chairs were designated as occupied by a male or female. Participants' attitudes toward egalitarian and traditional sex roles were measured by having them complete the traditional/egalitarian sex-role questionnaire (TESR; Larsen & Long, 1988). Higher scores (possible range of 20–100) indicated more egalitarian attitudes. Results suggested that although both women ($M = 86.03$) and men ($M = 77.10$) indicated strong support for egalitarian beliefs about sex roles, the difference between these scores was statistically significant ($p < .001$). After the responses to the distancing measure were examined, though, a different picture emerged. Men tended to distance either toward or away from women. Women participants were not influenced by the gender of the seated persons. The data further indicated that the scenario dictated whether men would choose to sit near a woman. In scenarios in which there were sexual cues (e.g., a bar), male participants indicated a stronger desire to be seated next to women. In these scenarios, women participants did not show a bias based on target gender for where they wished to be seated. However, in other scenarios, men tended to distance themselves from women. These results are consistent with other research that suggests that even male characters on television programs show greater distancing behaviors (any head or body movement away from another person) toward women than toward men, whereas women showed no evidence of gender bias in the amount of their distancing behaviors (Lott, 1989). Lott (1995) suggests that the data obtained in her interpersonal-distancing behavior program of research support the oft-reported experience of women that men tend to ignore them, either overtly, or in terms of their ideas, contributions, skills, or opinions.

Job Opportunities

Because women are perceived as naturally likely to have more communal characteristics (e.g., compassion, caring, emotionality, nurturing), people tend to believe that women are therefore especially qualified for positions that rely on these characteristics (teacher, day care worker, nurse; Eagly & Mladinic, 1994). Unfortunately, these positions tend to offer lower prestige and lower salaries than dominantly male jobs (Cejka & Eagly, 1999; Eagly & Karau, 2002) (e.g., doctor, CEO of a company, or other top-level management positions; Glick, 1991; Glick, Wilk, & Perreault, 1995). Heilman et al., (1988) found that when women apply for these positions, they tend to be rated as less competent, and their career progress was perceived in less favorable terms. Only when raters were provided with information indicating that the female applicant had high performance ability did they rate the applicant equal to (and in some instances, better than) male applicants. These results are supported by research by Locksley, Borgida, Brekke, and Hepburn (1980) that indicated that when people have individuating information about a target individual, they tend to neglect gender stereotypes and are more influenced by the personal and behavioral information about the target. Locksley et al. suggest that even a minimal amount of individual information about a target can help eliminate the effects of gender stereotypes in the perceiver's judgments about the target.

A recent study by Cuddy, Fiske, and Glick (in press) reveals that working mothers have a difficult time in the workplace, in no small part because of the stereotypes that people have about working mothers. The researchers found that when working women become mothers, they lose perceived competence but are rated higher in warmth. Interestingly, when men become fathers, they do not lose perceived competence but they also gain perceived warmth. This drop in perceived competence has serious career implications for the working mothers, because evaluators in this study were significantly less likely to hire, promote, or educate working mothers. These findings were supported by another study by Fuegen, Biernat, Haines, and Deaux (in press). Just looking masculine (e.g., shorter hair, strong jaw) is enough to be rated as more competent (and more likely to be considered a leader), and this holds for both men and women (Sczesny & Kühnen, 2004).

Researchers have pointed to several factors that may contribute to the negative perception and devaluation of women's competence in traditionally male-dominated fields. A big part of the equation is that many of these positions are regarded as jobs in which it is crucial to be agentic. Gender stereotypes of women as especially communal (and much less likely to be agentic) then bias the perceptions of potential employers or supervisors of women in such jobs. In other words, it is very difficult for women to break into such jobs (though it is becoming easier), and when they do get these jobs, their performance (past accomplishments and future potential) is seen through gender stereotypes, and they are regarded as less competent, less hard-working, and less committed to the company (Eagly & Mladinic, 1994).

Women who apply for male sex-typed jobs (e.g., construction worker or executive management) are perceived as violating stereotypes, and as encroaching on the power and dominance of men, and men tend to perceive such women as a threat (Basow, 1992; Glick & Fiske, 2001). Men who endorse more traditional sex roles are more likely to negatively perceive women who pursue nontraditional careers (Brabeck & Weisgerber, 1989). Finally, physically attractive women applicants for high-level executive positions tend to be seen as being less serious than men about the position (Heilman & Stopeck, 1985). While researchers have long found that a perceiver's attributions for a target's success vary depending on the gender of the target (i.e., the job performance of a woman is more likely to be attributed to luck or other external factors, rather than their own ability; e.g., Greenhaus & Parasuraman, 1993), a recent thorough meta-analysis by Swim and Sanna (1996) found that the literature is quite mixed on this issue. In fact, their results suggest that there is virtually no difference in the attributions for the performance of a woman and a man on various tasks.

Though the vast majority of sexist prejudice and discrimination is directed toward women, it is important to remember that sexism can apply to prejudice, stereotypes, and discrimination toward men. As we have been discussing, our society stereotypes women as having an inborn ability to be being nurturing. Men are stereotyped as being much less nurturing, and traditional stereotypes tend to discourage men from developing personality traits (such as caring, compassion, nurturing) that have typically been associated with females (Aubé & Koestner, 1992). Consider the job of child care worker. Such a position has been typically strongly associated with women due to the traditional sex role for women of being the parent in charge of raising the child (while the man went to work) and the pervasive belief that women, by virtue of their genetic makeup as a women, have an inborn ability to successfully nurture and care for children. Though there has not been much empirical attention devoted to gender prejudice against men in women-dominated fields, a recent study by Murray (1999) sheds some light on the problem. Murray interviewed and observed male child care workers and noted parent, child, and employer behavior and attitudes toward the male workers. She found that these men are often regarded with suspicion and hostility by parents, more positively by administrators, and quite positively by children. Male child care workers are viewed as more effeminate, or perverted, or simply incompetent. This often results in overt prejudice and discrimination from parents. In one unfortunately typical case, a male child care worker told Murray that on more than one occasion, when parents find out that a male child care worker is working at the facility, they decide not to enroll their child.

Even when applying for jobs that are not considered sex typed (e.g., accountant), women experience discrimination based on their gender. Firth (1982) sent nearly identical résumés to accounting firms that were seeking applications for an accountant position in their firm. The only differences were in the applicant's name, gender, marital status, and race. Responses to the applications indicated a significant degree of gender bias from the prospective employer. Males were significantly more successful than females in getting advertised jobs, even though they had the same level of experience and qualifications. More dramatically, women's marital status had a strong impact on the employer's reaction to the females'—but not the males'—applications. Women who were married with children were the least successful (i.e., least likely to be hired), followed by married women with no children, and the most successful group were unmarried women. This latter finding is evidence for the implicit assumption that a woman who has a family will put the family first, and she will not be a hard worker (whereas the assumption implies that men are always hard workers, whether or not they have families).

Another factor that inhibits women's advancement in the workplace is their expectations about careers. Jackson, Gardner, and Sullivan (1992) found that women tend to hold lower expectations about advancement, opportunities, and performance evaluations than men. Additionally, women may be discouraged by the perpetual gap in pay between men and women for the same jobs (Kay & Hagan, 1995). Since women have entered the workforce, they have been paid far less than men have for the same work, due to many factors, including individual and institutional discrimination, prejudice, and stereotypes about women. A 1993 report by the U.S. Department of Labor found that women earned about 70% of what men get paid for the same job. Some data suggest that a major reason for this disparity is a general undervaluing of any work performed by women (Lips, 2003). As a result, women may expect lower starting and maximum salaries than men receive. However, even when women have expectations of equal pay and opportunities when they apply for a position, and even when they negotiate with their prospective employer for these things, they may still be offered lower pay than men (Gerhart & Rynes, 1991). Because we tend to compare ourselves with similar others, men are more likely to compare themselves to other men and women to other women (Crocker & Major, 1989). Some researchers suggest that this can lead to a perpetuation of the gender pay gap (Aman & England, 1999). Specifically, when women compare their salaries and advancement opportunities to those of other women, they may believe that they are doing pretty well, and they are less likely to perceive any gender discrimination or pay gap (Major & Forcey, 1985).

The Glass Ceiling

Although women are moving into high-status, higher-paying, and male-dominated jobs with increasing frequency (Jacobs, 1992), the proportion of women to men in high-level, executive positions is still remarkably low. In 1993, women made up only 25.4% of managers (U.S. Department of Labor, 1997). What accounts for the disproportionate number of males in the upper levels of power in the workforce? In addition to the factors we have just discussed, researchers have identified another phenomenon, the **glass ceiling**, which limits the advancement of women into management (Weiss, 1999). The glass ceiling is defined as "those artificial barriers based on attitudinal or organizational bias that prevent qualified individuals from advancing in their organization into upper management positions" (U.S. Department of Labor). While the occurrence of overt discrimination against women is fairly rare today, there still exist many subtle forms of individual and institutional prejudice against women that limit their advancement opportunities in the workforce (Business and Professional Women's Foundation, 1995).

This subtle discrimination comes in many forms. In their research, Ohlott, Ruderman, and McCauley (1994) found that women did not have as many developmental opportunities as men to gain crucial skills for upper-management promotions. They were

Much recent research shows that, unfortunately, the glass ceiling is alive and well in today's corporate world. Today's executive boardrooms tend to comprise predominantly (and often exclusively) males.

not given important assignments, were left out of critical communication networks, and reported that they often had to exert extra effort to get recognition for their work. Lyness and Thompson (1997) reported that women were given less responsibility, received less in stock options, and reported lower satisfaction about their prospects for advancement. Other research suggests that, ironically, as corporations "feminize" the role of managers, toward a more inclusive, participatory managerial style, women who are more agentic (and therefore possess stereotypically masculine traits, like assertiveness) will be seen as a poor fit for management and therefore will be passed over in favor of those who have both agentic and feminine (so-called communal) traits, even if these latter individuals are less competent (Rudman & Glick, 1999).

Thus, the available research indicates that the glass ceiling is indeed a real phenomenon. In a recent study, 79% of top corporate executives admitted that there are identifiable barriers to the advancement of women into the upper echelons of corporate America (Catalyst, 1990, as cited in Burn, 1996). To change this, society must change its stereotypes that women cannot lead, are more emotional, and are more indecisive (Basow, 1992). The research discussed in this chapter should convince those who hold such stereotypes about women to reconsider their positions. The results of a meta-analysis of the literature on leadership styles by Eagly and Johnson (1990) revealed that there were insignificant differences between the ability of men and women to be leaders in the workplace. The data also showed that women tend to adopt a more democratic and participatory style, incorporating both male and female traits. Moreover, Eagly and Johnson found that women are just as capable of decisive leadership as men are. It turns out that such a leadership style is often more effective than the traditional autocratic, male leadership style (Cann & Siegfried, 1990). Research by LaFrance and Banaji (1992) showed that women are no more likely than men to be emotional, though they are more likely to express emotion. Thus, although women are just as effective and decisive as leaders as men, stereotypes about women, and society's expectations about sex roles tend to influence the career choices and opportunities that women pursue, and they place barriers in front of women wanting to enter and advance in male-dominated occupations (Deaux & LaFrance, 1998).

SUMMARY

The goal for society to eliminate stereotypes and prejudice based on gender is a significant challenge. This task is made even more difficult when many people do not know sexism, even when confronted with sexist material (Brant, 1999; Rudman & Borgida, 1995). Most research suggests that such a goal is somewhat unrealistic, given the entrenched nature of sexism within American culture, institutions, and among individuals (e.g., Deaux & Kite, 1993; Ruble & Ruble, 1982). However, some research has attempted to reduce sexist beliefs and endorsement of gender stereotypes. For example, Jones and Jacklin (1988) found that men's and women's sexist beliefs declined significantly after having taken an introductory women's or men's studies course. O'Neil (1996) reports that men who attended a therapy group designed to help them identify and recognize their own sexist beliefs were successful in changing those stereotypes and becoming more egalitarian in their thinking about the sexes. Unfortunately, there is little data to suggest that these attitudinal changes are more than temporary and that they also influence gender discrimination. Moreover, because gender stereotypes are so resistant to change, stereotype-inconsistent individuals tend to be isolated as special cases and placed in a subcategory, thereby allowing the perceiver to maintain the gender stereotype and not be confronted with dissonance-provoking inconsistent information (Weber & Crocker, 1983).

What can be done to reduce sexism? The consensus among most contemporary researchers is that sexism will only be reduced if changes occur on multiple levels (Albee & Perry, 1998; Basow, 1992; Baxter & Kane, 1995; Bigler, 1999a; Deaux & Kite, 1993). Specifically, individuals need to be made aware of what constitutes sexism and that it is important to avoid sexist thoughts, attitudes, and behaviors. Society needs to change the way it views men and women, recognize that men and women are more similar than they are different, understand that perceived differences are primarily due to differences in the way men and women are socialized, and demand that they be treated equally. Finally, institutions within society need to be changed. In other words, economic, political, and legislative power structures need to be reorganized such that women and men share power at all levels of society, so that the patriarchical structure of society is relegated to history. These changes are massive, complex, and extremely challenging, but they are not insurmountable goals. Change is already happening (albeit slowly) at all of the levels, and if and when its citizens want these changes to occur at a faster rate, more awareness, resources, and activism need to be directed toward that end.

GLOSSARY

agentic traits   Traits that have traditionally been associated with males and that indicate task orientation, assertiveness, and a striving for achievement.

ambivalent sexism   Sexism in which the individual has both positive, yet traditional, attitudes toward women, and negative, hostile attitudes toward women.

availability heuristic   States that our judgments about the probability of the event will be affected by the availability (or how fast an instance of the event comes to mind) of that event information.

benevolent sexism   Sexism marked by positive attitudes toward, and positive stereotypical beliefs about, women.

bipolar assumption   States that an individual has characteristics associated with either males or females, but not both.

communal traits   Traits that have traditionally been associated with women, such as the desire to foster relationships, to be sensitive, and to get along with others.

descriptive stereotype   Tells how most people in a group behave, think, and feel. It describes the group's motives, expectations, and other aspects of behavior.

dualistic view   States that people can have some of

both agentic and communal traits.

face-ism   The greater facial prominence of depictions of men in the media, versus the greater emphasis on the whole body of women.

glass ceiling   Artificial barriers based on attitudinal or organizational bias that prevent qualified individuals from advancing in their organization into upper-management positions.

hostile sexism   Negative attitudes toward, and negative beliefs about, women.

informational influence   A type of social influence that is exerted on the individual when they wish to be correct in their judgments, opinions, or perceptions. The individual will be better persuaded by information that is perceived to be accurate.

modern sexism   Sexism indicated by the denial of discrimination against women, a hostility toward equality for women, and nonsupport of programs and legislation designed to help women.

neosexism   Sexism marked by a manifestation of a conflict between egalitarian values and residual negative feelings toward women.

normative influence   A type of social influence that is exerted on the individual when they wish to get along with others. The individual will be more likely to conform to others' opinions in order to establish and maintain a friendly relationship with other persons.

old fashioned sexism   Sexism characterized by endorsement of traditional gender roles, differential treatment of women and men, and stereotypes about lesser female competence.

prescriptive stereotype   Suggests how stereotyped groups *should* think, feel, and act.

sexism   Negative attitudes, prejudice, or discrimination directed toward someone on the basis of their gender.

social roles theory   States that the reason for gender differences in social behavior is not biological differences between men and women but the different socialization processes for men and women that lead them to perform different roles in society.

DISCUSSION QUESTIONS

1. To what extent do you believe the average American adheres to the bipolar assumption with regard to gender? Do you believe that most Americans do not endorse the dualistic view? Why?

2. How are gender stereotypes communicated via television, movies, and magazines? Can you cite some examples?

3. Do you think there are some aspects of behavior or personality that are linked to the sex chromosome of an individual? Or do you believe that all behavior is learned and there are no behaviors determined by the sex chromosome?

4. In what ways are stereotypes a form of control? How can gender stereotypes control women and the attitudes and behavior of society toward women?)

5. Can you think of examples of sexist language that you have heard, or that are still used today?

6. To what extent do gender stereotypes affect career aspirations of women, and employment opportunities available for women in America today? What do you think accounts for why women still receive only 74¢ for every $1 a man earns, for the same work?

SUGGESTED KEY READINGS

Bem, S. L. (1981). Gender-schema theory: A cognitive account of gender-typing. *Psychological Review, 88,* 354–364.

Deaux, K., & LaFrance, M. (1998). Gender. In D. T. Gilbert, S. T. Fiske, & G. Lindzey (Eds.), *Handbook of social psychology* (Vol. 1, 4th ed., pp. 788–827). New York: McGraw-Hill.

Eagly, A. H. (1987). *Sex differences in social behavior: A social-role interpretation.* Hillsdale, NJ: Erlbaum.

Fiske, S. T., & Stevens, L. E. (1993). What's so special about sex? Gender stereotyping and discrimination. In S. Oskamp (Ed.), *Gender issues in contemporary society* (pp. 173–196). Newbury Park, CA: Sage.

INTERNET RESOURCES: RESEARCHERS, REFERENCES, AND ORGANIZATIONS DEVOTED TO THE STUDY OF PREJUDICE

www.apa.org/divisions/div51 Division 51 of APA: Society for the Psychological Study of Men and Masculinity.

www.ibiblio.org/cheryb/women/wresources.html Women's resources on the Internet.

http://about-face.org Combats negative and distorted images of women.

www.now.org National Organization for Women.

www.feminist.org Feminist Majority Foundation.

http://psych.la.psu.edu/jswim Home page of Janet Swim, a leading sexism researcher.

CHAPTER NINE

REDUCING PREJUDICE

One of the nice things about teaching at a university is the academic freedom professors enjoy with respect to how their courses are structured. Suppose that you heard that my courses are interesting and fun and that I have a wacky sense of humor (all true! at least I think so!), and so you register for one of my classes. But this particular semester, in this class, I have an ax to grind. I am fed up with male students. I announce to the class that males (1) will not be allowed to speak for any reason, or they will be given an F for the semester; (2) cannot ask questions in class—instead they must submit all questions in writing; (3) are not eligible for extra credit; (4) must wait for all female students to be seated before they may sit down and must remain seated at the end of class until all females have left the room; and (5) will be given a different—and more difficult—standard against which their final grades will be determined. Females will enjoy all these privileges. Day after day, the females and I refer to males not by their name, but, in a derogating tone, as "Ys" (after the male sex chromosome), and I talk about how males are disruptive, undisciplined, and intellectually slower than females. I give all my attention to female students and ignore the male students. Now, if you are a female student, the special treatment will likely make you feel special, and you will want to preserve the status quo by, for example, not talking to, eating lunch with, or interacting in any way with males—I mean Ys—and reminding the Ys of their "place in society."

For a while (until the American Civil Liberties Union, university administration, and student lawsuits intervene), my classroom is a model of fascist authoritarian rule, complete with arbitrary prejudice against half of the students in class. The males (er, Ys) begin to feel unworthy, with decreased self-esteem and self-efficacy for their classwork (indeed, this is reflected in their plummeting test scores), and they feel depressed, helpless, frustrated, anxious, and angry. Then, after about a month of this, I suddenly decide I am fed up with females. The privileges and status are given to males, with females being the objects of discrimination, stereotypes, and prejudice. They begin to feel the same way the males used to feel in response to their plight.

What does this bizarre social experiment teach us (other than perhaps I have some unresolved narcissistic power issues going on)? Before I answer that, would it surprise you to learn that a very similar experiment actually was conducted, with elementary-school children? In the late 1960s, Jane Elliott (Elliot, 1970) was teaching a third-grade class in Iowa that comprised almost all white children. She wanted to teach them about prejudice and what it felt like to be the target of prejudice. She announced one day that students with blue eyes were "better than" students with brown eyes. Blue-eyed children were called on more often, were able to go back for second helpings at the cafeteria, and could stay out on recess longer (Jones, 1997). The brown-eyed students had to wear brown arm bands, they quickly became withdrawn and depressed, and their performance in class suffered. Some even got into fights with blue-eyed students. The next day, she had students switch roles. Now the blue-eyed children were discriminated against and were the objects of prejudice. The next day, Elliott returned the class to its preexperimental state, much to the delight of the children, who now had a better understanding of what it was like to be the target of prejudice and were much more willing to accept people of different cultures, races, genders, and so forth.

Elliott's demonstration highlights just one way that researchers have attempted to combat prejudice, reduce stereotyping, and improve intergroup relations. Her temporarily disadvantaged students learned empathy for those who are the victims of prejudice and how much it hurts to be the target of stereotyping. In this way, they learned that, because they did not like anyone stereotyping and discriminating against them, they should not do it to others. Ever since Lippmann (1922) coined the term *stereotype,* researchers have been actively engaged in attempting to find the best way to reduce prejudice. In this chapter, we will review the research in several domains and show what does and does not seem to be effective in reducing prejudice. We start with a focus of early empirical efforts: the contact hypothesis.

THE CONTACT HYPOTHESIS

It seems to be a truism that people fear the unknown. We have all heard this from time to time, and almost all of us might be able to recall an experience we have had with some unknown situation or thing which, at first, was a bit scary because we did not know what to expect. For example, taking the S.A.T. (or A.C.T.) college entrance exam is an unknown situation for millions of high school students each year, and they can probably tell you that they approached it with some degree of anxiety. As you recall from our discussion of the outgroup homogeneity bias in Chapter 2, people tend to make assumptions about groups with which they have little contact, or about which they have little knowledge (i.e., their outgroups). Because they have little contact with the outgroups, they feel little motivation to be accurate in their assumptions, expectations, and generalizations. The combination of little or no meaningful contact with the outgroups and low motivation to be accurate in one's assessment of outgroup members provides the perfect situation for the formation of stereotypes about, and fear of, the outgroup. Looking at the problem of stereotyping and prejudice, one might suggest a simple remedy: eliminate the fear of the unknown by having the groups get to know each other. That is, why not encourage more contact between (racial, religious, sexual orientation, etc.) groups? It seems very logical. In fact, one of the earliest solutions to the problem of intergroup stereotyping, prejudice, and discrimination was the contact hypothesis (Williams, 1947). The **contact hypothesis** proposes that increasing exposure to members of various groups can increase positive evaluations of the outgroup and decrease prejudice and stereotyping. This idea is elegant in its simplicity and is an intuitively appealing notion of how society might reduce prejudice. The contact hypothesis was especially appealing at the time it was introduced, because of the segregation of African Americans and Caucasians in the United States. (Pettigrew, 1986).

Allport's Contact Hypothesis

At its most basic form, the contact hypothesis suggests that merely putting two groups together (i.e., mere contact) is sufficient for the reduction of stereotypes and prejudice. The idea is that people will naturally "work it out" and get to know one another when placed in contact with members of the outgroup. Much research has shown, however, that mere contact is ineffective in changing racial attitudes (Amir, 1969). That is, it became apparent that in order to understand why the contact hypothesis only occasionally seemed to work well in reducing intergroup prejudice, it was necessary to ask not, does intergroup contact reduce prejudice? but rather, in what types of contact situations, with what kinds of representatives of the disliked group, will interaction and attitude change of specified types occur, and how will this vary for subjects of differing characteristics? (Cook, 1962, p. 76). The reason is that, upon viewing the member of the outgroup, stereotypes and negative affect are elicited even prior to the interaction. The stereotype filters the perception of the interaction in ways that confirm the stereotypes about the outgroup, and "by the time [the interactants] part, the offishness each has shown has confirmed the other's suspicion. The casual contact has left matters worse than before" (Allport, 1954, p. 264). Research indicated that in many situations of mere contact, roughly 50% of the interactants felt more positive about the outgroup, but about 50% of the time, people felt more *negative* toward the outgroup (Allport, 1954; Stephan, 1985; Wilner, Walkley, & Cook, 1955). Wilner et al. (1955) found that when Whites only had casual contact with Blacks, only about 33% of them developed positive attitudes toward Blacks. However, among those Whites who had many interactions, and had many conversations with Blacks, nearly 75% reported more positive attitudes toward Blacks. Perhaps one reason such externally imposed attempts to foster more tolerant outgroup attitudes often tend to meet with failure is that the majority group reacts to such real (or imagined) pressure by feeling angry, threatened, and, perhaps as a result of reactance, they then respond to the outgroup with even-more negative attitudes (Plant & Devine, 2001).

Clearly, then, there must be more to making intergroup contact successful than mere contact. The first person to specify the conditions under which contact should successfully reduce intergroup prejudice and stereotyping was Gordon Allport (1954). Allport recognized that a whole host of factors affect the intergroup-contact context and influence whether participants emerge from the situation with more positive or more negative attitudes toward the outgroup. He insightfully noticed that "the effect of contact will depend upon the kind of association that occurs, and upon the kinds of persons who are involved" (p. 262). In order to fully understand any contact situation, and to make predictions about the outcome of such situations, it is important to know about characteristics of the situation, such as, the status of the members (are they equal, or who is superior?), the role (cooperative versus competitive) of the contact, the social atmosphere (is prejudice prevalent, or is equality promoted?), the personality of the interactants (is the person high or low in prejudice toward the outgroup, and do they have an intolerant—i.e., authoritarian—personality?), and the situations in which the contact takes place. Knowing these things will help the researcher understand the dynamics of the intergroup contact and allow for better accuracy in predicting the outcomes of the intergroup contact (i.e., in terms of subsequent behavior and attitudes of members toward the outgroup). Allport (1954) specified that at least four fundamental criteria must be met in order for positive intergroup contact to occur: equal-status members, common goals, intergroup cooperation, and the support of legitimate authority (i.e., government, or other institutional or cultural support). Since Allport's initial list of conditions necessary for positive intergroup interactions, other researchers have added more conditions. In surveying the literature, Amir (1969) offered two more variables: there must be a favorable climate for intergroup contact, and the contact must be of an intimate rather than a casual nature. Pettigrew (1998) adds just one factor to Allport's four: that the contact situation have "friendship potential." Stephan (1985) lists 13 variables (!) that influence the outcome of contact situations. Next, we examine the research testing many of these propositions, in an effort to specify the situations in which the contact hypothesis is (and is not) supported by the research evidence.

Tests of the Contact Hypothesis

Some initial evidence seemed to provide support for basic contact theory and for Allport's specifications. When Whites and Blacks were brought into contact in the work arena (after desegregation efforts began), each group reported more positive feelings about the other (Brophy, 1946). Deutsch and Collins (1951) found that in desegregated public housing,

According to the contact hypothesis, putting groups together should result in prejudice reduction. If prejudice is based on ignorance about the outgroup, then if one were to come into contact with the outgroup and start talking to outgroup members, stereotypes would dissipate as the perceiver realized that the outgroup is just as varied as their own ingroup. However, research shows that many conditions need to be in place for contact to work. In this photograph, as in many schools, group proximity during lunch does not lead to intergroup contact (or prejudice reduction).

equal-status contact between White and African American neighbors resulted in much more favorable attitudes of the White individuals toward equal-housing policies. In one of the rare studies investigating the attitudes of a minority toward a majority, Works (1961) found that African Americans in a desegregated housing project had more positive attitudes toward their White neighbors than did their segregated African American counterparts. Researchers have also examined multiple contact situations over time. For example, an experiment by Cook (1969) suggests that contact over a period of time (2 hours a day for 20 days) can significantly change intergroup attitudes. In their research, White women who were selected because of their highly negative attitudes toward African Americans interacted with an African American woman on a cooperative task. The contact was close, the interactants had equal status, and they had a superordinate goal that they were working toward. A comparison of the pre- and postinteraction racial attitudes revealed that 40% of the women in the experimental group showed a significant positive change in racial attitudes toward African Americans.

One of the reasons the contact hypothesis has fallen into disfavor among prejudice researchers since Allport's time is that it has grown into what appears to be an atheoretical laundry list of factors that facilitate the positive effects of ingroup–outgroup contact. According to Pettigrew (1998), a key point of confusion is that some researchers have confused factors that are *essential* with those what are merely *facilitative* in intergroup contact. Pettigrew also highlights two other problems with the contact-hypothesis research. One is that research tends to focus on when and why contact will result in positive intergroup attitudes, but it does not speak to *how* this change in attitudes occurs in the contact situation. Another issue is that the contact hypothesis does not specify how positive feelings toward an outgroup member in the contact situation can generalize to one's feelings for the whole outgroup, and recent research has shown that the member-to-group generalization does not occur (Paolini, Hewstone, & Rubin, 2004).

Pettigrew's Reformulated Contact Theory

To counteract these problems with the contact theory, Pettigrew (1986, 1998) proposed a longitudinal model of how the optimal contact situation should proceed and of the changes that need to take place before individuals start to think of outgroup members as potential friends, and as members of a bigger ingroup (see Figure 9.1).

Pettigrew suggests that first, researchers need to be aware that individuals bring their own intergroup experiences and biases and their own personality characteristics to the contact situation. The next element is that the situation must have Allport's four necessary conditions and Pettigrew's additional necessary condition—the potential to become friends with the outgroup members—in order for any prejudice and stereotype reduction to take place. Next, when ingroup and outgroup members encounter each other in an initial contact situation, the group members will regard each other with initial anxiety but then begin decategorization, in which they begin to see each other in terms of their personalities and characteristics rather than their group membership. In decategorization, the groups get together through interacting with outgroup individuals. By individuating members of the outgroup, one realizes that they are unique persons who have varying opinions and as much variability as one's own ingroup. Thus, the outgroup category becomes virtually

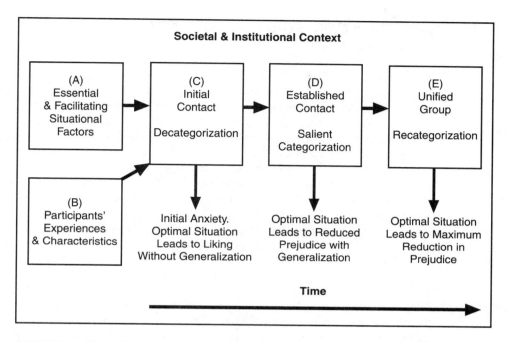

FIGURE 9.1   The reformulated contact theory.   (Reprinted with permission from *Annual Review of Psychology,* Volume 49, © 1998 by Annual Reviews. www.AnnualReviews.org.)

useless as a heuristic in understanding an individual member of that category. From here, established, prolonged contact (Tal-Or, Boninger, & Gleicher, 2002) facilitates salient categorization, whereby group members begin to think of the outgroup members as representative of the outgroup in general and begin to change their negative view of the entire outgroup (Hewstone & Brown, 1986). The last stage in the sequence entails recategorization. In recategorization, the intergroup context is configured to encourage a breakdown of "us" versus "them" distinct categories, and to form a broader "we" category, by making members of both groups aware that they have more in common on a number of other dimensions (i.e., arts, jobs, dreams, hobbies, values, and so forth), that far outweigh their differences in race, gender, or other broad category membership (Dovidio & Gaertner, 1999; Perdue, Dovidio, Gurtman, & Tyler, 1990). Unfortunately, most intergroup contact situations never reach this stage. Additionally, there is scant data (for an exception, see Nesdale & Todd, 1998) on how the recategorization generalizes to attitudes toward the whole outgroup (Pettigrew, 1998). Nevertheless, the empirical data gathered to date (Anastasio, Bachman, Gaertner, & Dovidio, 1997; Eller & Abrams, 2004; Gaertner, Dovidio, Banker, Houlette, Johnson, & McGlynn, 2000; Pettigrew, 1997; Pettigrew & Tropp, 2000) indicate that Pettigrew's reformulation of the contact situation is a promising model that not only integrates the somewhat disorganized research literature, it suggests fruitful directions for future empirical efforts (Hewstone, 2003).

SHERIF'S ROBBER'S CAVE STUDY: THE SUPERORDINATE GOAL

Recall from our discussion of the realistic conflict theory in Chapter 2 that one of the main tenets of the theory asserts that when two groups compete for scarce resources, prejudice and stereotypes between the two groups will result (Sherif et al., 1961). The theory also suggests that when groups are in conflict, they think of the outgroup in stereotyped ways, and they begin to feel hostility toward the outgroup. The groups also feel greater loyalty to their ingroup, as a result of this conflict. Remember that in his **Robber's Cave study,** Sherif had two groups of boys at a summer camp compete for a scarce resource. As predicted, prejudice erupted between the groups. Sherif then shifted the experiment to attempt to reduce prejudice. First, he discontinued the competitions. Sherif then reasoned that if intergroup competition increased prejudice, perhaps cooperation between groups would reduce or eliminate prejudice. He arranged for two problems (having a bus break down while it was full of boys, and an interrupted water supply to the camp) that the groups had to work on together to solve. These problems represented a **superordinate goal,** in that no group could remedy the situation alone. They needed to cooperate, to help each other, in order to solve the problem. They worked together, solved the crises, and both the counselors and Sherif noticed a change in the boys. When the counselors asked the boys who their friends were, they were much more likely to include members of the other group. The name calling was virtually eliminated, and the winning group chose to split their prize money from the competition with the other group members at an ice-cream shop on the way home from the camp (almost sounds like a 1950s sitcom script, huh?). Sherif's study nicely showed, in a very real setting, that prejudice and outgroup hostility can be caused by competition, but can be greatly reduced (or eliminated) via intergroup cooperation on a superordinate goal.

Common Ingroup Identity

What evidence since these early studies is there to bear on Sherif's very promising solution to the problem of reducing intergroup prejudice? As it turns out, there is good evidence to support the idea that prejudice can be greatly reduced through the encouragement of superordinate ingroup identities. Gaertner, Dovidio, Anastasio, Bachman, and Rust (1993) proposed that intergroup prejudice can be reduced by breaking down the salience of the groups' category membership and by getting the groups to reconceptualize themselves as all members of a larger, common ingroup identity (Gaertner & Dovidio, 2000; Dovidio, Vergert, Stewart, Gaertner, Johnson, Esses, Riek, & Pearson, 2004). The common ingroup identity model works through decategorization and recategorization (Anastasio, Bachman, Gaertner, & Dovidio, 1997).

In an experiment designed to test the common ingroup identity model, Dovidio, Gaertner, Isen, and Lowrance (1995) found that when participants in two separate groups felt more positive affect (via positive affect induction with candy, a common experimental technique; see Isen & Daubman, 1984), and when groups were made to feel less distinct, through similar clothes and similar goals, they were more likely to view their own group and the other group as members of one large group with shared goals. Prejudice, stereotyping, and outgroup bias or ingroup favoritism were greatly diminished. This experiment showed that, paradoxically, the processes that lead to ingroup favoritism can actually be used to promote a superordinate ingroup identity and to reduce ingroup/outgroup distinctions, thereby reducing prejudice. It should be noted that although the groups in this experiment were created via random assignment (i.e., they were what are called minimal groups), and critics (e.g., Billig, 1976) have suggested that the results may not generalize to real groups, other research (Gaertner, Rust, Dovidio, Bachman, & Anastasio, 1994) has found support for the common ingroup identity model in the real-world settings of a multiethnic high school (thereby involving long-standing racial attitudes, prejudices, and stereotypes) and the corporate world (Bachman, Gaertner, Anastasio, & Rust, 1993).

There is some evidence that holding two separate group identities (one's ingroup, and the common ingroup identity) can actually lead to *increased* likelihood of prejudice and discrimination toward outgroups. Wenzel and his colleagues (2003) found that group members tend to perceive their ingroup as prototypical of the common ingroup identity, and this projection of their ingroup to the overall identity of the common ingroup led them to regard all other common ingroup members as even more different from them. This perception led group members to be more likely to hold negative attitudes toward the other common ingroup members. The common ingroup identity model has a number of studies to support its basic tenets, but more research is clearly needed to further clarify the conditions under which forming a common ingroup identity leads to a reduction in prejudice toward outgroup members.

THE "CONFRONTATION TECHNIQUE" OF ROKEACH

Myrdal (1944) discussed what he termed the "American dilemma." Many White Americans have egalitarian beliefs but still harbor prejudiced tendencies, and therefore, they feel a moral conflict. According to Rokeach (1973), people should be dissatisfied with themselves (have feelings of guilt, etc.) when they are made aware of this discrepancy within themselves. Once this occurs, people should be willing to revise their prejudiced attitudes in order to alleviate their moral conflict and its attendant negative affect. This follows classic **cognitive-dissonance theory** (Festinger, 1957), which states that when people experience inconsistencies between their thoughts and behaviors, they will feel negative arousal. This arousal will motivate them to choose the easiest factor to change (almost always, it is one's attitude) to bring it in line with the other factor (usually, behavior; see Festinger & Carlsmith, 1959), and reduce the negative arousal. Rokeach (1973) empirically demonstrated support for the notion that when White subjects were made aware of the discrepancy between their self-views and their values, they changed their values (not an easy task!), and this value change led to changes in their attitude and behavior toward Blacks. However, other researchers reported no significant changes in intergroup attitudes and behavior as a result of Rokeach's value-confrontation technique (Cook & Flay, 1978; Penner, 1971). Thus, the data are a bit mixed on the effectiveness of the technique to reliably reduce prejudice and stereotyping. More research is needed to specify the conditions under which prejudice reduction is likely to occur following the value-confrontation technique.

Altemeyer (1994) used the confrontation procedure with individuals high in right-wing authoritarianism (RWA). Recall that RWA individuals are characterized by three main features: a high degree of submission, aggression, and conventionalism (traditionalism). As Adorno and his colleagues (Adorno et al., 1950) found in their pioneering research on authoritarianism, RWAs tend to be highly prejudiced against, well, basically everyone who is different from them. Correlations between high RWA scores and anti-homosexual attitudes range from .50 to .65 (Altemeyer, 1988), and from .53 to .69 for anti-Black attitudes (Duckitt, 1990). Altemeyer asked students to complete a scale measuring RWA and to rank 10 values (e.g., friendship, wisdom, equality, freedom, etc.) in terms of their personal importance. Most low and high RWAs ranked freedom ahead of equality. He then came back to the classroom several weeks later to provide the results of the rankings and to show them, according to Rokeach's technique, the discrepancy between their value of freedom and equality and how they feel about others' (minorities') struggle for equality. High-RWA participants' attitudes toward minorities and minority-related social issues such as affirmative action did not change as a result of the personal value confrontation technique, compared with high RWAs who were not confronted with the value discrepancy. Thus, although the technique tends to yield mixed results, Altemeyer (1994) is still optimistic that it can be useful in reducing prejudice. When the researcher is able to address the defensiveness sparked by the procedure, the technique can work with many high RWAs. Like most people, when high-RWA individuals realize a core discrepancy between their stated values and who they are (in terms of their RWA characteristics and tendencies), they usually show some willingness to change, if not motivated by benevolent insight, then at least by selfish desire to reduce their cognitive dissonance.

THE JIGSAW CLASSROOM

In 1954 the *Brown vs. Board of Education* decision by the U.S. Supreme Court ended segregation between Blacks and Whites. This presented an interesting real-life situation for social psychologists studying intergroup relations. Specifically, how would Blacks and Whites get along now that they would be intermingling in society? Would there be chaos? Or, would prejudice just disappear once people got to know members of the other group (as simple contact theory would suggest)? To examine how to reduce prejudice and stereotyping in the newly integrated schoolroom society, Aronson, Blaney, Stephan, Sikes, and Snapp (1978) conducted research in an Austin, Texas, elementary school, to examine the effects of a new, cooperative learning environment, compared with the traditional competitive environment, on the performance of Whites and Blacks and on their feelings about members of the outgroup.

Building on earlier work on cooperative groups by Deutsch (1949) and others (Phillips & D'Amico, 1956; Stendler, Damrin, & Haines, 1951), Aronson found that the typical elementary classroom environment in the United States is based on competition between individual students for the attention and praise of the teacher. Students who are called on frequently and who are correct in their answers feel better about themselves, and perform better than their classmates, yet are often resented by their peers (Aronson et al., 1978). When minorities were being bused to predominantly White schools, they were competing in an inherently unequal environment, because Whites had a more advantaged educational experience and were therefore much more likely to "win" in the competition for the teacher's attention and praise (Cohen, 1980). When the racial tensions that existed between the

Aronson's research on the jigsaw classroom shows that stereotypes and prejudice can be greatly reduced among children when they all must work together to teach each other information.

two groups were added to this competitive atmosphere, the negative feelings each group had for the other were often exacerbated.

Aronson and his colleagues wanted to attempt to eliminate competition and to structure interdependent cooperation between Blacks and Whites in the classroom in order to examine the impact of such a structure on prejudice and stereotyping. They placed students into small groups of 6 students each. The new structure of the classroom was such that the teacher was no longer the omniscient repository of all the answers. Rather, students were to use each other as resources. The researchers made individual competitiveness incompatible with success and set up the classroom such that success only resulted from cooperation. Each student in the small group was given a unique skill or piece of information. In order to complete the task, each group member must contribute and rely on the contributions of other group members. Then, each child was tested over all the material given to that group. Because of their mutual interdependence for task success, Aronson et al. referred to this model as the **jigsaw system** for intergroup cooperation. In this system, the interdependence reduced the need for competition, and it also discouraged ridicule of others in their group (on the basis of stereotypes, shyness, or being less bright that the others). Teachers informed students that such behavior would not help their group and could only hurt their chances of success. Thus, students were motivated (and reinforced) to help each other. In so doing, their preconceptions, fears, and stereotypes about the outgroup members slowly eroded in light of these positive experiences.

Results from the study indicated that children in the jigsaw classrooms liked their group members more than others in the classroom. Black and White children began to like each other more, their self esteem increased, and their performance was as good or better than competitive classrooms. Aronson's later research supported these findings (Aronson & Gonzalez, 1988). Indeed, much subsequent research has indicated that cooperative jigsaw settings are very effective in increasing positive intergroup attitudes and behavior and in decreasing stereotyping and prejudice (Cook, 1985; Desforges, Lord, Ramsey, Mason, Van Leeuwen, West, & Lepper, 1991; Johnson & Johnson, 1987). Other researchers report data that suggest that the impact of jigsaw cooperative groups will be even stronger in situations where the participants focus on getting to know the individual personalities (i.e., to individuate the person) of their group members. In this way, they are more likely to think of their group members in terms of their individual attributes and characteristics rather than in terms of their category (racial, gender, etc.) membership (Bettencourt, Brewer, Croak, & Miller, 1991; Perdue, et al., 1990). There seems to be good empirical support for this point from the lab experiments discussed above, and from real-world cooperative groups (Warring, Johnson, Maruyama, & Johnson, 1985).

Research has also demonstrated that the positive benefits of the cooperative group situation could be enhanced if additional factors characterized the situation. Specifically, cooperative groups foster more positive outgroup attitudes when (1) the group is successful (Sherif & Sherif, 1969; Wilson & Miller, 1961; Worchel & Norvell, 1980), (2) the outgroup members are seen as competent (Rosenfield, Stephan, & Lucker, 1981), (3) the group members self-disclose to each other (Ensari & Miller, 2002), and (4) the group members are seen as similar (Allen & Wilder, 1975; Blanchard & Cook, 1976).

In sum, the available empirical data indicate strong support for the efficacy of cooperative learning groups in reducing intergroup stereotyping and prejudice (Slavin & Cooper, 1999). Especially promising is the finding by Bettencourt et al. (1991) and others (Grack & Richman, 1996) that the positive attitudes and reduced prejudice generalizes to members of the outgroup other than those who were involved in the cooperative group experience. Indeed, research supports the idea that outcome dependence, or interdependence between groups (and not only those who are engaged in cooperative learning, as in the jigsaw classroom), facilitates individuation of outgroup members and reduces prejudice (Fiske, 2000). This may be the key to harnessing the full positive potential of cooperative groups, such as those modeled after the jigsaw system. Some research has uncovered a few important factors that can facilitate generalization from one's positive feelings about outgroup members in the small cooperative group to the entire outgroup. If the counterstereotypic information is spread across several outgroup members, they are less likely to be subtyped, and the perceiver is more likely to realize the variability of the outgroup and therefore less likely to think of the outgroup members in stereotyped terms (Weber & Crocker, 1983). If the counterstereotypic person in the small cooperative group is seen as typical of the outgroup, generalization to the outgroup is more likely to occur (Rothbart & Lewis, 1988). Finally, if people have time to consider the discrepancy between their feelings for the outgroup member in the cooperative group and their attitude toward the outgroup, they may be more likely to generalize their positive feelings toward the outgroup (Fiske & Taylor, 1991). More research is needed to address how participants in such groups can move toward viewing former outgroup members as ingroup members (Gaertner, Mann, Dovidio, Murrell, & Pomare, 1990).

EDUCATION, EMPATHY, AND ROLE PLAYING

If one assumes that prejudice is largely enhanced by the lack of information about the outgroup, fear of the outgroup, and an overall lack of understanding of the perspective of the outgroup, then it would stand to reason that prejudice could be greatly reduced by educating people about outgroups (i.e., showing them that the outgroup members are more similar to them than they are different), helping them understand what it is like to be the target of prejudice (so that they would not be prejudiced toward others), and helping them begin to understand that the outgroup individual is entitled to the same rights and respect as the perceiver. At the beginning of this chapter, we discussed one famous example—Elliott's (1970) brown-eye/blue-eye demonstration—of role playing and perspective taking, which, after the experiment, led to increased empathy and decreased prejudice. Next, we briefly discuss the research on the influence of education, empathy and role playing, on prejudice reduction.

It seems intuitive that if ignorance is a breeding ground for prejudice and stereotypes, then education about outgroups ought to be a perfect antidote for such attitudes. However, the evidence appears to be mixed as to the effectiveness of various cultural-training techniques, school courses, and the liberal, tolerance-enhancing effects the college experience should have on people (Devine, 1995). It is unclear why the data are so inconsistent. One problem is that many of the studies were not designed well and had no follow-up data, so we are unable to examine the true impact or any lasting impact of such educational experiences. Another problem may be that past programs designed to reduce children's racial and ethnic stereotyping may have failed because often they were based on simplistic models of attitude change (Bigler, 1999b). Aboud and Fenwick (1999) contend that those promoting prejudice-reduction efforts in schools cannot expect children's stereotypes to disappear as a result of the school merely promoting positive attitudes about stereotyped groups. Rather, evidence from their research (Study 2) suggests that when peers talk to each other in an open way to justify their racial evaluations, the prejudices of their fellow students tend to be reduced. Specifically, their data showed that when low-prejudice students honestly discussed their positive and negative evaluations of their own group and the stereotyped group, and when they cited stereotype-disconfirming examples (individuals) from the stereotyped group, and finally, when they asserted that all people can have positive and negative qualities, those students who were high in prejudice tended to attenuate their prejudice toward the outgroup. Thus, this research suggests that, under certain conditions, low-prejudice students can act as peer socializers and models of tolerance, and this can be an effective means of reducing prejudice in their fellow students.

Techniques designed to enhance empathy (largely through role playing) for the victim of prejudice have met with more success (Stephan & Finlay, 1999). The Elliott brown-eye/blue-eye study is a prime example of such a technique. White students learned how it feels to be treated in a prejudiced manner, were much less likely afterward to treat others (specifically those in minority outgroups) with prejudice, and they showed more positive attitudes toward the outgroup following the study. Recent experiments (Galinsky & Ku, 2004; Galinsky & Moskowitz, 2000; Vescio, Sechrist, & Paolucci, 2003) are also supportive of the benefits of empathy training in reducing intergroup bias. These researchers found that when people are asked to imagine life from a target individual's perspective, they are much less likely to stereotype that individual, and they show a decreased ingroup bias and more positive evaluations of the target person's group. Unfortunately, some data indicate that in the absence of continued salient antiprejudice norms, endorsement by authority of continued nonprejudiced attitudes and behavior, and once people leave the role playing setting, people often revert to their preempathy (i.e., more prejudiced) attitudes and behavior toward the outgroup (Fiske, 1998; Jones, 1997; Stephan, 1985).

THE COLOR-BLIND APPROACH

Perhaps prejudice and stereotyping could be reduced greatly if people were asked to not consider race (or age, gender, or other category information) when thinking about a person. The idea here is that people ought to be assessed according to their unique personality, talents, and contributions, and their group membership should not factor into one's thoughts about others. This is the rationale behind what has been called the color-blind approach. It suggests that, for example, employers, or college-admissions boards should not ask for gender, race, or other group-membership demographic information in their evaluation of whether an applicant should be hired/admitted. Thus, people would be assessed only on their merits and qualifications. In this way, according to this perspective, prejudice and stereotyping should decline greatly because it no longer would be considered by institutions and individuals in their evaluations of members from stereotyped groups.

Although well intentioned, the color-blind approach suffers from a number of problems and has been heavily criticized (Jones, 1997; Wittig, 1996). Jones (1997) argues that a major problem with the color-blind approach is that it fails to recognize the continuing significance of prejudice and discrimination in society. Moreover, critics argue, by saying that one's race, age, or gender, for example, does not matter, when in fact it does, it relegates the minority individual to a permanent position of diminished status. As we learned in Chapter 3 in our discussion of stereotype-suppression research, one cannot simply not think about stereotypes and group labels and expect that will be sufficient to eliminate prejudice. Research has demonstrated that attempts to suppress stereotypes and category information tend to fail quite dramatically. Even if such an approach were to be embraced, it is doubtful whether it could really be put into practice. Recent survey research from a number of studies indicates that although attitudes of contemporary Caucasians in the United States toward the principle of racial equality have become more positive, Caucasians are much less supportive of the actual implementation of policies concerning equal treatment (Shuman, Steeh, Bobo, & Krysan, 1997).

There is virtually no research on whether a color-blind approach does indeed work as a way to reduce stereotyping and prejudice. However, a recent series of experiments set out to address this question. In their research, Wolsko, Park, Judd, and Wittenbrink (2000) examined whether White participants would stereotype African Americans if the participants adopted either a perspective that emphasized the importance of embracing social diversity (the multicultural perspective) or a perspective that deemphasizes differences and emphasizes the need to regard each person as a unique individual (the color-blind perspective). In their research, Wolsko et al. asked participants to read essays that were said to be the collective opinion of sociologists, psychologists, economists, and political scientists about ethnic relations in America. The half-page essay described how ethnic tensions, prejudice, and stereotyping still exist and need to be addressed. Participants were assigned to either a multicultural perspective (MC) or a color-blind perspective (CB) condition. The essay for those in the MC condition stated that "intergroup harmony can be achieved if we better appreciate our diversity and recognize and accept each group's positive and negative qualities" (p. 638). The CB people read an essay that suggested that "intergroup harmony can be achieved if we recognize that at our core we are all the same, that all men and women are created equal, and that we are first and foremost a nation of individuals" (p. 638). Participants were then asked a series of questions about the content, and accuracy of stereotypes of Caucasians and African Americans.

The results were quite interesting. The data from Experiment 1 showed that the CB and MC perspectives yielded judgments that reflected less ingroup positivity (less ingroup bias). The MC participants' responses showed a stronger expression of stereotypes of African Americans, relative to Caucasians. The striking aspect to these findings is that although the MC individuals held more positive outgroup attitudes, they showed a heightened awareness of stereotypes about that outgroup. Experiment 2 revealed that MC participants were more accurate in estimating the real differences in prevalence of stereotypic and counterstereotypic attributes for African Americans and Caucasians. In this accuracy task, the MC participants showed less ingroup favoritism than the CB participants. However, the MC participants believed there was a greater difference between the values of Caucasians and those of African Americans. Experiment 3 assessed the types of information participants used to evaluate target individuals. MC participants used both ethnicity and individual information, whereas CB participants used only individual information, and ignored category information, in their evaluations.

These results suggest some intriguing conclusions about the best approach to reducing stereotyping and promoting intergroup harmony. The MC perspective suggests that we need to appreciate and embrace the positive and negative aspects of our group and other groups. Wolsko et al.'s data showed that this has the effect of increasing the salience of negative stereotypes for the perceiver. However, the data also showed that the MC perspective results in increased positive affect for the outgroup and decreased ingroup bias. Zaraté and Garza (2002) reported results of two studies that showed support for Wolsko et al.'s conclusions about the MC perspective. Their data showed that when people were directed to think about themselves (via a self-affirmation procedure), this created a heightened awareness of their ethnic identity, and when this occurs, participants' perceptions of hostility or competition between their group and outgroups is greatly reduced. In other words, when people are focused on their own self and made to think about how their groups differ from outgroups, their outgroup prejudice tends to be significantly reduced. These fascinating results support the idea that embracing our differences results in real changes in our intergroup perceptions. This contention is borne out in recent research that showed significantly greater racial bias in people who take a color-blind perspective than those who adopted a multicultural perspective (Richeson & Nussbaum, 2004).

So, increased awareness of stereotypes does not necessarily lead to a negative evaluation of the outgroup member. The important ingredient here is that the MC perspective emphasizes that it is critical to appreciate and value negative and positive group differences, and by doing so, one will form more positive attitudes toward outgroup members. This research showed that the CB and MC perspectives were equally potent in eliciting greater positive affect for the outgroup, and decreased ingroup bias. Wolsko et al. suggest that the greatest ingroup harmony will likely be attained through both an appreciation of positive and negative group differences and a concerted effort to disregard category information and evaluate each person as a unique individual. Steele (1991) summarized this approach nicely, "Difference can enrich only the common ground" (p. 148).

CURRENT APPROACHES TO PREJUDICE REDUCTION

Contemporary research on prejudice reduction differs from past research and theory in a number of respects. First, Allport and his colleagues were dealing with a different time (the late 1940s through the mid-1960s) and a different society. Racial prejudice was very overt, and even sanctioned by government laws and regulations that institutionalized segregation between Blacks and Whites. Thus, the contact hypothesis was an early attempt to identify the situations in which prejudice might be reduced. In other words, the reasoning was that if the two groups were merely brought together and got to know each other as human beings, they would not fear each other, and they would realize that their stereotypes and prejudices about the other group were unfounded. Other approaches focused on persuasion (attitude change), understanding the personality types that are associated with intergroup preju-

Research by Jones and Sigall, as well as later research on modern racism, has demonstrated that about one fourth of those who say they are not prejudiced still harbor deep, negative feelings about the outgroup. This research, and later research on implicit stereotyping, indicates that these feelings of prejudice, learned from childhood, still affect the individual's behavior toward the outgroup. These feelings also influence their thoughts and feelings when interacting with outgroup members, even though the perceiver may be unwilling (or unable) to realize that those negative attitudes and feelings are there.

dice (i.e., work on the authoritarian personality by Adorno et al. [1950]), and Rokeach's (1973) confrontation technique (Monteith et al., 1994). As the social (and legal) climate changed in the United States, so too did expressions of racial prejudice. Overt expressions of prejudice were discouraged, Whites and Blacks interacted more frequently (as a result of desegregation), and, over the decades, the attitudes of Whites toward Blacks have indeed become more positive (Schuman, Steeh, & Bobo, 1985). This brought about another significant change in the focus of research in stereotyping and prejudice. Researchers, using subtle and indirect techniques to assess attitudes, such as the bogus-pipeline technique (Jones & Sigall, 1971), found that there often was a dissociation between Whites' self-reported attitudes toward Blacks, and their indirectly assessed attitudes. In other words, a majority of Whites appeared low in prejudiced attitudes on direct measures of intergroup attitudes, yet on other, indirect measures of prejudice, they showed strong indications of lingering negative affect associated with the outgroup. Perhaps this phenomenon can best be described in an observation by Thomas Pettigrew, a leading prejudice researcher:

> Many Southerners have confessed to me, for instance, that even though in their minds they no longer feel prejudice toward Blacks, they still feel squeamish when they shake hands with a Black. These feelings are left over from what they learned in their families as children. (Pettigrew, 1987, p. 20, quoted from Devine, 1989)

A second way in which research on prejudice reduction is different from early empirical efforts is the shift toward identifying the measures that would help psychologists accurately assess the degree to which the individual's underlying attitudes (including those attitudes that may be socially unacceptable) do not match their overt attitudes on self-report questionnaires (see Chapter 5). As research on intergroup relations progressed, it became more sophisticated and specific. With the advent of the social-cognition approach in social psychology, researchers began to focus on the cognitive processes that underlie intergroup prejudice, stereotyping, and discrimination (Fiske & Taylor, 1991; Hamilton, 1981b). The cognitive approach to stereotyping yields much more precision in that it allows the researcher to understand the cognitive mechanisms, biases, errors, and structures that facilitate tendencies toward stereotypical thinking, and the conditions under which it is likely to occur (or flourish).

A third way in which the present approach to reducing prejudice and stereotyping differs from earlier approaches is in the assumptions researchers have about what lies at the foundation of the stereotype held by the individual. Upon what is the stereotype based? As already mentioned, earlier research suggested that stereotypes were the natural products of how people of certain personality types (i.e., Adorno et al., 1950) think. Others suggested that stereotypes originated in fear and ignorance (stemming from lack of experience with the outgroup member). In an interesting resurgence of empirical activity, researchers today are examining the functional utility of stereotypes (Snyder & Meine, 1994).

Functional Approach

Recall that the **functional approach** suggests that stereotypes exist and are utilized because they have a motivational foundation—they serve one or more important psychological functions for the individual—and, therefore, they are resistant to change or elimination.

Prejudice-reduction efforts are then directed at accurately assessing these functions and providing the individual with different motivational bases that satisfy the old motivations yet do not encourage the accompanying stereotyping of outgroups. Research is directed at understanding what needs, goals, and purposes are being met by the endorsement of the stereotype. Interestingly, this approach suggests that the same stereotypes may serve different psychological functions for different people (Snyder & Meine, 1994a). For example, some research (Katz & Hass, 1988) suggests that stereotypes may serve an expressive function. Specifically, many forms of prejudice center around the belief that the outgroup violates or does not subscribe to the same values as the ingroup (for Whites, these have traditionally been labeled the Protestant work ethic, which is characterized by self-reliance, hard work, obedience, and discipline). Derogating those who are perceived to violate these values allows the individual to reaffirm their sense of self and help solidify their values. Katz and Hass (1988) found increased expressions of prejudice and stereotyping among those for whom these values are made salient, compared with those who were not actively thinking about those values.

Another function that may allow individuals to maintain their stereotypes and prejudices is what Snyder and Meine (1994a) term the "detachment function." Prejudice that serves this function allows the individual to disregard, ignore, or detach the self from the target of the prejudice. Such a function enables prejudiced individuals to disown any personal responsibility for the plight and negative treatment of the victim of the prejudice. The detachment function is particularly likely to underlie prejudice between two groups when one group is advantaged and the other is disadvantaged. In this way, the advantaged group justifies their status and does nothing to change the inequality, because they feel little or no responsibility for the victim's situation. The functional approach to understanding the root of prejudice is a promising one. Though the functional perspective to prejudice has some empirical evidence to support it, more research is needed. At present, however, the approach is among the favored perspectives on understanding prejudice, because it allows researchers to understand the processes that underlie the prejudice, and the theoretical perspective of the approach is a great advance over earlier prejudice-reduction strategies, in that it represents a more broad-scope, multilevel focus on the problem of stereotyping and prejudice.

Normative Influence

Believe it or not, there was a time when it appeared that virtually everyone smoked. Movie stars, politicians, and all your friends and coworkers enjoyed puffing on cigarettes, cigars, and even pipes (a particular rarity these days!). However, that pesky surgeon general started looking into whether this was a healthy practice (he suspected it was not), and back in the 1960s the government realized that there was a sufficient amount of evidence being accumulated that linked smoking with all manner of nasty health consequences (high blood pressure, coronary heart disease, lung cancer, death). The government enacted laws restricting tobacco advertising and started restricting where people could smoke (i.e., no smoking on elevators, in hospitals, etc.). Then the big regulation: all tobacco companies were required by law to carry the surgeon general's warning about the health risks of tobacco on all the tobacco packaging. In the decades since this legislation was introduced, attitudes toward tobacco smoking have changed substantially. The United States is no longer a nation of mostly smokers, but of nonsmokers (National Center for Health Statistics, 1999).

This leads to an interesting question: can egalitarian attitudes be legislated (Allport, 1954)? Put another way, can stereotyping and prejudice be made against the law? This is already the case with respect to antidiscrimination legislation, but can more be done? If so, would it have a significant impact on the country's intergroup attitudes? There is compelling research to suggest that it might. This research focuses on changing the prevailing norms in the social context. The reasoning is that if social pressures existed that were strongly antistereotyping and antiprejudice, social sanctions may be enough to slowly but significantly change the intergroup climate in the United States (Dovidio & Gaertner, 1991; Pettigrew, 1985). Several experiments have shown that if social norms are salient for a particular (nonprejudiced) behavior in a given situation, then expressions of prejudice and discrimination are much less likely to occur in those situations (Dovidio & Gaertner, 1983; Gaertner & Dovidio, 1986; Blanchard, Lilly, & Vaughn, 1991). One way the social norms are made salient in a given situation is by members casually vocalizing their opinions about the outgroup. In the lab, a common technique has been to have confederates, posing as subjects, voice comments about the outgroup to each other, with the subjects overhearing their opinions. The question is, how does this social norm (made salient by the confederates' actions) affect the attitudes and prejudice of the subject toward the outgroup?

Research by Greenberg and Pyszczynski (1985) and colleagues (Kirkland, Greenberg, & Pyszczynski, 1987) has established that when Whites overheard ethnic slurs from White confederates (posing as subjects) about an African American target (also a confederate), their evaluations of the African American were more negative. However, it should be noted that the the social norm (the ethnic slur) only had an effect on the subject's evaluations when the target's performance was poor (i.e., when the Black confederate lost a mock debate). When the target performed well, the slur had no effect on participants' evaluations of the target. Greenberg and Pyszczynski suggest that this evidence supports the notion that social influence processes, and the social norms in a given context, play a strong role in perpetuating prejudice and stereotyping.

Given these data, a next logical question might be, can we use the social influence process to decrease expressions of prejudice? In two experiments, Blanchard et al. (1991) had research assistants interview White female students who were walking on campus between classes. Participants were interviewed with either one or two other White female confederates, who happened to walk up to the researcher at the same time. Participants expressed their opinions both orally (Experiment 1) and privately (Experiment 2) to 5 questions about anonymous racist e-mail messages that had been sent recently on campus. Confederates provided their responses before the participant did, and these responses were prefaced with either antiracist, neutral, or racist views. In both experiments, participants who overheard antiracist views tended to express more strongly antiracist opinions compared with those who overheard neutral or racist views. Research by Monteith, Deenen, and Tooman (1996), using Blanchard et al.'s methods with attitudes toward homosexuals and African Americans showed similar results. These results do not seem to be due to mere conformity effects, because participants' private opinions (which should be harder to influence than publicly stated opinions) were also strongly affected by the normative influence of the confederates. Monteith et al. (1996) suggest that these results and those reported by

Blanchard et al.'s (1991) study support the notion that hearing nonprejudiced opinions activates a strong social norm against showing prejudiced attitudes. However, it is important to note that some research suggests that such norms against prejudice are not always naturally salient in people's minds (even for low-prejudice persons), and that, in order for these norms to affect the expression of stereotypes and prejudice, they need to be made explicitly clear and unambiguously salient (Zuwerink, Devine, Monteith, & Cook, 1996, Experiment 1). Interestingly, both articles report a much weaker effect of hearing prejudiced responses, which may be attributable to the fact that today, the social norm promoting prejudice is weaker than that promoting antiprejudiced responses (Dovidio et al., 1996).

Self-Regulation

Monteith (1993) and her colleagues (Monteith, Zuwerink, & Devine, 1994) suggested a model of how prejudice reduction might occur, based on self-regulation principles. According to various theories of self-regulation (i.e., Carver & Scheier, 1981; Duval & Wicklund, 1972; Higgins, 1987), when behavior falls short of one's standards for that behavior, self-regulation tendencies may be engaged in order to attempt to match one's future behavior with one's standard. This notion of a real–ideal discrepancy can also be applied to intergroup attitudes and behavior. Monteith suggests that self-regulation tendencies may be activated in low-prejudice persons who experience a discrepancy between their thoughts and behavior and their egalitarian values and beliefs. This prejudice-reduction model is shown in Figure 9.2.

According to Monteith, when low-prejudice persons perceive cues about group membership of another individual, the associated stereotypes for that group are also made salient. The activation of the stereotype should often lead to stereotype-consistent behaviors or thoughts. When the individual is made aware of the discrepancy between an important aspect of their self (namely, their egalitarian values) and their thoughts or behavior in relation to the stereotyped outgroup, they should experience negative self-directed affect.

In this **dissociation model** (Devine, 1989), as in many theories of self-regulation, negative self-directed affect is key to the self-regulation process, in that it leads to heightened motivation to reduce prejudiced responses in the future. The salience of the discrepancy, along with negative self-directed affect, make one self-focused, and this, in turn, will cause the individual to pay attention to the discrepancy-producing stimuli in the environment and within the self), in order to prepare more appropriate responses to these stimuli in the future. The individual will then seek out further information about the prejudiced behavior or attitude in order to identify its impact. The end result of these steps is that the individual begins to build associations between cues present when the discrepant response occurred, the prejudice-related behavior or thought, and the guilty feelings that the low-prejudice person felt as a result of the discrepancy. The model suggests that in the future, when the cues for the outgroup and the attendant stereotypes are made salient, punishment cues (i.e., negative affect, such as guilt) will be quickly activated, and these will cause the system to more carefully cognitively process the information, such that stereotypes can be inhibited and replaced with more low-prejudice, egalitarian responses (Devine & Monteith, 1993).

Is this a valid model? Results of several experiments show that when low-prejudice persons were made aware that they had violated their egalitarian beliefs (by stereotyping

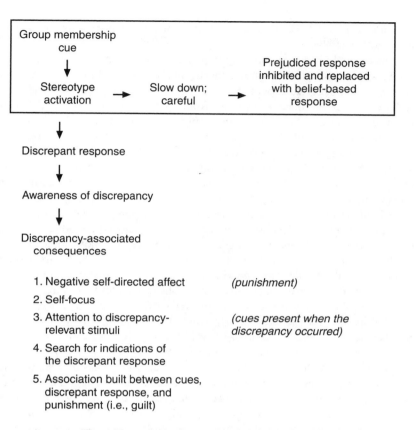

FIGURE 9.2   **The self-regulation of prejudiced responses.** (From "Prejudice and prejudice reduction: Classic challenges, contemporary approaches," by Monteith, Zuwerink, and Devine, copyright © 1994 by Academic Press, reproduced by permission of the publisher. All rights of reproduction in any form reserved.)

another person), they felt negative self-directed affect (e.g., guilt), increased self-focus, and greater attention to the prejudice-related response (Fazio & Hilden, 2001; Monteith, 1993; Monteith, Ashburn-Nardo, Voils, & Czopp, 2002). Participants' responses (to group-relevant cues) were slowed (i.e., slower—and presumably more careful, less stereo-typed—thinking about judgments of outgroup members) after the discrepancy between their egalitarian beliefs and their actions was made salient, which supports the notion that their prejudiced responses were beginning to be inhibited. It is important to note that later research has revealed that when low-prejudice persons are not thinking about their personal (egalitarian) standards, their discrepancy-associated negative affect is significantly diminished (Monteith, 1996a). This speaks to the importance of the negative self-directed affect (i.e., guilt) in initiating the self-regulatory processes that would inhibit future preju-dicial responses (Hing, Li, & Zanna, 2002). In fact, it may be the case that, in the absence of thinking about one's personal (egalitarian) standards, and the discrepancy-associated negative self-directed affect that follows, prejudiced responses may continue unabated in low-prejudice persons.

Interestingly, it appears that only prejudice-related (as compared to prejudice-unrelated) discrepancies improved low-prejudice participants' ability to inhibit the stereotype-consistent responses. This suggests support for the Cognitive-Dissonance theory (Festinger, 1957) which states that dissonance resulting from inconsistent thoughts and behavior in one domain can only be alleviated by changing one's attitude or behavior in that domain. Changing unrelated attitudes, or affirming another part of the self, as posited by the self-affirmation theory (Steele, 1988; e.g., "I get nervous around Hispanics, and I feel bad about that, because I like to think I am not prejudiced. I am really a good person, because I help so many people at the homeless shelter") did *not* decrease subsequent tendencies to respond with prejudice toward the outgroup.

Monteith notes that becoming aware of such discrepancies just one time, and even many times, may not be enough to unlearn well-entrenched prejudiced attitudes and behavior. However, with enough practice, and with enough motivation, people *can* drop prejudicial attitudes and beliefs associated with the outgroup and learn more egalitarian associations with the outgroup, making the latter the automatic, default association with the outgroup (Plant, Peruche, & Butz, 2005). She speculates that even high-prejudice persons value egalitarian ideals, and if the discrepancy between their values and their behavior and attitudes were made especially salient to them, they may be motivated to change their attitudes and behavior in order to avoid the negative affect and cognitive dissonance that accompanies such blatant discrepancies between attitudes and behavior.

Recent research supports the theory and data provided by Devine and Monteith (1999), in that it suggests that with enough motivation and practice, an individual can unlearn stereotyped associations between characteristics and a stereotyped group (Jacks & Devine, 2002). In a series of studies, Kawakami, Dovidio, Moll, Hermsen, and Russin (2000) asked people to negate their stereotypes of older persons, races, and skinheads. Participants were asked to hit a "no" button box as fast as possible when they saw a target category (e.g., skinheads) and a negative word typically associated with the group. If they saw the target category word and a trait not typically associated with skinheads, they were to hit the "yes" button as fast as possible. After extensive training and many trials of this activity, participants started showing faster reaction times to stereotype-unrelated traits when they were presented with the category prime, and slower reactions to stereotype-related traits. In this way, they broke the association between the category and the stereotyped characteristics and learned new associations between the category and stereotype-unrelated traits. Thus, recent theory and empirical evidence suggest that prejudice and stereotyping are not inevitable. They can be changed, with a lot of practice and strong internal motivation to respond without prejudice (Blair, 2002; Devine, Plant, Amodio, Harmon-Jones, & Vance, 2002). In a comparison between the efficacy of stereotype-suppression and perspective-taking methods in reducing stereotyping, Galinsky, Martorana, and Ku (2003) found that perspective-taking appears to be a more effective strategy. Perspective-taking (imagining how you would feel in the target's situation, or how the target feels or is influenced by his situation) engages an implicit process of self–other overlap, in that the perspective of the target and that of the perceiver tend to merge. Interestingly, this process appears to be impervious to increased cognitive load. This compelling conclusion is very encouraging, and certainly more empirical attention is needed to better understand how we might exploit perspective taking in the reduction of prejudice.

SUMMARY

We have covered discussed a number of early prejudice-reduction approaches. Which seems to work best, and offer the most promise for moving attitudes away from stereotypes? Before we answer that, let us consider how to characterize these approaches. According to Jones (1997), these prejudice-reduction approaches can be categorized in one of four ways. First, researchers looked at how prejudice could be reduced by *changing the prejudiced individual*. It seemed fairly obvious that because prejudice originated from the one who was doing the stereotyping, that if society wants to reduce or eliminate such behavior, it ought to direct its attention to changing that individual. Thus, we can characterize reduction efforts using education and role-playing, propoganda (see Stephan, 1985), and Rokeach's (1973) confrontation technique as examples (with varying degrees of mild to moderate success) of the attempt to reduce prejudice.

Second, a few studies have looked at *changing the victim*. The idea here is that if people are perceived in negative ways, or as otherwise deficient, society can reduce these stereotypes by helping to improve the situation of the prejudice victim. In other words, government help with jobs (e.g., social policies and laws such as affirmative action), housing, education, and child care would all work to help raise the status of the stereotyped group. As a result, the prejudiced individuals would have no reasons upon which to base any feelings of superiority over the outgroup, and (in theory) their prejudice would disappear once they come to the realization that the outgroup members were just like the individual's ingroup members. Unfortunately, there is little, if any, evidence to support such a notion.

Third, Jones (1997) suggests that some have argued that in order to reduce the tendency to think about others as outgroup members, which brings the danger of prejudice, society should attempt *to be colorblind* (note: this term is used to refer not only to race but to all major ways people characterize ingroups and outgroups). The idea here is quite simple: think of others as humans, and as individuals, not in terms of their race, sexual orientation, gender, age, or other category membership. In this way, there is no chance for prejudice to occur, because in the end we are all members of the same group, humanity. While this approach does seem to incorporate elements of Pettigrew's recategorization notion, it falls short as an effective prejudice-reduction strategy. First, it ignores reality, in that it is very difficult to avoid categorizing others, even in the most benign, general manner. Second, very little empirical evidence has been reported that tests this idea. Based on the data from Wolsko et al.'s (2000) experiments, it seems that a better approach to reducing intergroup prejudice may be to incorporate a colorblind approach with a multicultural perspective.

Fourth, is an approach that Jones (1997) calls the *transactional approach*. Very simply, to transact is to conduct a negotiation, or business between individuals toward some goal. Sound familiar? Exactly. Both the Robber's Cave study and the jigsaw-classroom study are prime examples of this type of approach. Of all the four approaches, the transactional approach, according to Jones, holds the most promise in future prejudice-reduction efforts. Jones argues that the first two approaches are ineffective because they only treat one individual in the prejudice interaction. The third colorblind approach is unrealistic, and has virtually no empirical support. The promise of superordinate goal techniques and the cooperative group-interaction techniques is that they may incorporate a number of nonreactive prejudice-reduction processes at many levels of the interaction, which explains why they are so successful. As Devine (1995) suggests, "The problem of intergroup prejudice is multifaceted, and as such, its solutions will have to be multifaceted as well" (p. 510).

While the transactional approach is a promising perspective, it is largely atheoretical. Why is this a drawback? As Devine (1995) notes, though there have been several theories of how prejudice and stereotypes form, there has been little theoretical focus on how to reduce prejudice. As a result, the earlier approaches to prejudice reduction have had a hit-or-miss quality, seeking to define isolated aspects of the prejudice situation (i.e., the characteristics of the individual, the target, or the interaction between the two) that may influence prejudice in one context but have little generalization to other situations or outgroups. Those approaches that are theory based and seek to understand the processes that underlie the formation and maintenance of prejudice are more likely to yield more promising answers to the question of how to reduce prejudice.

GLOSSARY

cognitive-dissonance theory   States that inconsistent thoughts and/or behaviors bring about negative arousal. The arousal will motivate the individual to change one, or both of the inconsistencies in order to make them consistent and to reduce the negative arousal.

confrontation technique   A process whereby the individual is reminded of their endorsement of egalitarian values then confronted with the fact that they also hold attitudes that are inconsistent with egalitarian values (i.e., stereotypes). When individuals are faced with this discrepancy, they will be motivated to change their attitudes (which are more malleable than values) to make them consistent with their values.

contact hypothesis   The notion that bringing two outgroups together in a situation will result in decreased prejudice and stereotyping.

dissociation model   States that low- and high-prejudice individuals automatically activate stereotypes of outgroups, but that low-prejudice persons also inhibit these thoughts with their egalitarian personal beliefs.

functional approach   Says that stereotyping and prejudice serve various motivational functions for different individuals. To reduce prejudice, it is important to understand what functions the stereotype serve and provide substitute psychological processes that do not entail stereotyping others but still allow the functions to be served.

jigsaw system   Technique for prejudice reduction in which outgroups are formed into small, cooperative, and interdependent groups that are working toward a common goal. Each group comprises an equal number of ingroup and outgroup members who contribute equally to the task success.

normative influence   Suggests that to reduce prejudice, it is important to make antiprejudice norms salient. Once people are made aware of the social sanctions against prejudice, they will be less likely to express and endorse prejudice.

realistic conflict theory   A theory on the origin of prejudice which suggests that when two groups compete for scarce resources, prejudice will arise between them.

Robber's Cave study Sherif's classic study that found support for the realistic-conflict theory and that also demonstrated how giving prejudiced groups a superordinate goal can greatly reduce prejudice by blurring the lines between ingroup and outgroup membership.

superordinate goal A task that requires the cooperation and efforts of two or more individuals to be completed successfully.

transactional approach Suggests that prejudice reduction is most likely to occur when people interact cooperatively toward a common goal, and when they have motivation and opportunity to form friendships with outgroup members in that context.

DISCUSSION QUESTIONS

1. Is it possible to not categorize, and thus stereotype, others? Why or why not?

2. Why do you think that merely bringing two groups together does not reduce prejudice between them?

3. Do you think that today's educational environment is structured to foster competition, or cooperation, between the students? Have you had any experiences in your education with classes that are structured to foster cooperation, like Aronson et al.'s (1978) jigsaw classroom? What did you think of the jigsaw-classroom method as a way of reducing racial prejudice? Do you think it can work in today's classrooms? Why or why not?

4. Do you think that prejudice and stereotyping would be more effectively reduced if people took a color-blind or a multicultural approach in their social judgments?

5. Can prejudice and stereotyping be legislated out of existence? Do you think that legislation on hate crimes, discrimination, and the like is effective in changing attitudes of society in the direction of more tolerance and egalitarian attitudes toward stereotyped groups?

6. What is the best way to reduce prejudice and stereotyping, in your opinion? Are there other methods, not discussed in this chapter, that you think work well in creating egalitarian attitudes in people?

SUGGESTED KEY READINGS

Altemeyer, R. (1994). Reducing prejudice in right-wing authoritarians. In M. Zanna & J. Olson (Eds.), *The psychology of prejudice: The Ontario symposium* (Vol. 7, pp. 131–148). Hillsdale, NJ: Erlbaum.

Aronson, E., Blaney, N., Stephan, C., Sikes, J., & Snapp, M. (1978). *The jigsaw classroom.* Beverly Hills, CA: Sage.

Gaertner, S. L., Dovidio, J. F., Banker, B. S., Houlette, M., Johnson, K. M., & McGlynn, E. A. (2000). Reducing intergroup conflict: From superordinate goals to decategorization, recategorization, and mutual differentiation. *Group Dynamics: Theory, Research, and Practice, 4,* 98–114.

Monteith, M. J., Zuwerink, J. R., & Devine, P. G. (1994). Prejudice and prejudice reduction: Classic challenges, contemporary approaches. In P. G. Devine, D. L. Hamilton, & T. M. Ostrom (Eds.), *Social cognition: Impact on social psychology* (pp. 323–346). New York: Academic Press.

INTERNET RESOURCES: RESEARCHERS, REFERENCES, AND ORGANIZATIONS DEVOTED TO THE STUDY OF PREJUDICE

www.jigsaw.org   Website about the Jigsaw Classroom research, designed with the help of the Jigsaw Classroom pioneer, Dr. Elliott Aronson.

http://psych.wisc.edu/faculty/bio/devine.html Home page of Dr. Patricia Devine, a prominent prejudice researcher.

www.uky.edu/ArtsSciences/Psychology/faculty/ monteith.html   Home page of Dr. Margo Monteith, social psychologist whose research focuses on prejudice reduction, as well as how to control prejudiced and stereotypic responses.

CHAPTER TEN

TRENDS AND UNANSWERED QUESTIONS IN PREJUDICE RESEARCH

Understanding prejudice is no easy task. Like most psychological phenomena, prejudice is complex and multiply determined. Prejudice emerges as a result of many motivational, affective, and cognitive processes and interactions thereof. Over the past 80 years, research has revealed volumes about the causes and consequences of prejudice, as well as ways to reduce prejudice and stereotyping. However, there remain many unanswered questions. In this, our final chapter, we address some of the biggest topics and areas yet to be explored by researchers. We begin with a brief survey of research on prejudice toward groups that have not received much empirical attention. We then examine the trends in the theory and research on prejudice and conclude by considering the future of prejudice research.

PREJUDICE AGAINST OTHER GROUPS

Throughout this text, we have covered three major types of prejudice: prejudice based on race, gender, and age. There are two major reasons why our discussion has been limited to these three types of prejudice. First, as we have discussed, the three main ways we categorize another person upon perceiving them is on the basis of their race, gender, and age. These groups for categorization are so pervasive in our social perceptions that they are virtually automatic. Of course, then, it is important for us to attempt to understand these fundamental bases for categorizing another person, because these provide the foundation (or bias) for the way we subsequently perceive other information about the individual. The second reason is that there is much more research on racism and sexism, and, to a lesser degree, on ageism, than any other types of prejudice. This allows us to get a much more detailed picture of the conditions under which race, age, or gender prejudice is fostered, maintained, and reduced. That said, it is equally important to recognize that there are other groups against which prejudice is directed. Although some research has examined prejudice and stereotyping against these groups, much more is needed. Indeed, more and more researchers are turning their attention toward these populations and examining the special challenges these group members face with respect to discrimination, stereotyping, and prejudice against their group. In addition, researchers are also attempting to understand the common factors that lead some people to form prejudice and stereotypes about these groups. Let us turn now to a discussion of what researchers are learning about prejudice against the overweight, homosexuals, and those who are physically challenged.

Attitudes toward Overweight Persons

It was not that long ago (a little over a century) that it was highly desirable to be overweight. The great painter Rubens achieved acclaim for his portraits of nude, overweight women. Back then, being overweight was a status symbol. In a time when most people were rather poor and barely able to keep food on the table, it was unheard of to have *too much food*. It was thus regarded as a symbol of wealth, privilege, and higher status to be overweight, because it said to the world, "I not only can afford to eat my share, I can eat more than my share, if I so desire, because I am wealthy enough to buy lots of food." With the increasing industrialization and growing economic wealth of various nations, being overweight was no longer the sole province of the wealthy. Indeed, working-class persons were increasingly able to purchase more food than they needed, and many also became overweight as a result. Thus, attitudes toward overweight persons have shifted quite dramatically since Rubens's era. Today, there is a significant prejudice against overweight persons (Blaine, DiBlasi, & Connor, 2002; Crandall, 1994). Nowhere is this more evident than in the most economically wealthy nation in the world, the United States (Crandall & Martinez, 1996). Americans seem to have a particularly strong aversion to persons who are overweight, and they are more likely to openly display their prejudice toward overweight individuals than toward other groups (Allon, 1982; Crandall, 1994). According to Allon (1982), one reason this is the case is that an individual who is overweight violates the American ideal of self-denial and self-restraint. The ideal for U.S. society has shifted to an image of an athletic, or at least thin, person who shows restraint and self-discipline in the face of the abundant food supply (Owen & Laurel-Seller, 2000).

Much research indicates that prejudice against overweight persons is quite pervasive and can have implications for the overweight individual's life in a number of domains. For example, in study after study, researchers have found that overweight people are perceived as gluttonous, lazy, weak-willed, unintelligent, morally inferior, unattractive, unlikable, and having low self-esteem (see Crandall, 1994, for a detailed discussion). Research has even concluded that overweight college students, particularly females (because the norms for being thin are stronger for females), have more difficulty paying for college, because they are less likely to get financial help for college from their parents (Crandall, 1991). In effect, parents are discriminating against their own children, believing, in part, that their daughter's weight is the result of poor self-control (Crandall, 1995). This effect is the strongest for those overweight students of politically conservative parents, who are more likely to endorse anti-overweight attitudes compared to more politically liberal parents. In a related vein, one study found that intense anti-fat attitudes were correlated with authoritarianism (Crandall & Biernat, 1990).

As this research indicates, most of this prejudice results from the attributions people make about the reasons for being overweight. As we learned earlier, the perceiver's attributions of the controllability of the target's stigmatized condition will have a strong impact on the evaluations, attitudes, and feelings the perceiver has about the target. Stigmatized conditions that are seen as uncontrollable tend to evoke sympathy and compassion. However, most people regard being overweight as entirely controllable and as an outward indicator of

Changing conceptions of a desirable physical image. In Europe, and particularly in the United States, culture tended to dictate a preference for a physical body type in men and women. In the past, as indicated in this painting by Rubens, it was considered quite fashionable to be overweight, since it conveyed the message that the individual was of higher socioeconomic status (because he or she could afford too much food). However, the decrease in the gap between the haves and the havenots has resulted in the preference for a slender body (as exemplified by today's models and movie and television celebrities, such as Lara Flynn Boyle of The Practice). Such an emphasis in society leads to stereotypes and prejudice against those who are overweight.

personal, intellectual, moral, emotional, and motivational deficiency (Blaine et al., 2002; Crandall, 1994; Crandall, D'Anello, Sakalli, Lazarus, Wieczorkowska, & Feather, 2001). As a result, they are more likely to feel prejudice against such individuals. Seeing examples of overweight people who have recently lost a lot of weight has the effect of further reinforcing the idea that being overweight is a controllable condition, and, unfortunately, it further polarizes the perceiver's negative attitudes against overweight persons (Blaine et al., 2002). The researchers in this study speculate that one reason the perceiver's attitudes would be more negative is that seeing examples of overweight people doing things to successfully lose weight is threatening to their stereotypes about overweight individuals (low motivation/lazy, hedonistic, gluttonous, etc.), and the threat translates to a further entrenchment of the stereotype and perhaps a dismissal (or a subcategorization) of the target as an aberrant outlier.

The strength and depth of the intense stereotypes and prejudices against overweight persons in America is difficult to overstate. One study found that when perceivers were asked to evaluate a male target who was seated by an overweight person, he was consistently rated significantly more negatively compared with those seated near a normal-weight person (Hebl & Mannix, 2003). This result held true regardless of the level of the perceived relationship between the seated individuals (from strangers to a closer relationship), and it was found even in those low in antifat prejudice. Another study found that 5 out of 11 landlords would not rent to an obese person, whereas all 11 readily would rent to normal-weight potential tenants (Karris, 1977). The strong antifat bias that people have in the United States (and other Westernized countries) is hard to counteract, even when the basis for the bias is directly being attacked. In one study, Teachman and her colleagues measured implicit and explicit antifat attitudes and found in their participants no explicit antifat attitudes but very strong implicit antifat attitudes (Teachman, Gapinski, Brownell, Rawlins, & Jeyaram, 2003). When the researchers told the participants that the overweight target's condition was a result of overeating (personal attribution), their implicit bias increased. When participants were told the target's condition was a result of genetic factors (external factors), implicit antifat attitudes were *not* reduced. Moreover, when participants read stories designed to induce empathy for overweight targets (stories about prejudice and discrimination against overweight persons) their implicit antifat attitudes did not diminish.

Interestingly, research suggests that obesity is only slightly related to diet (i.e., eating bad foods, or eating too much) and is more significantly the result of a combination of metabolic and genetic factors (Stunkard, Srensen, Hanis, Teasdale, Chakraborty, Schull, & Schulsinger, 1986). Indeed, research indicates that the genetic contribution to obesity is between 40% (Bouchard, 1997) and 80% (Echwald, 1999).

Attitudes toward Lesbians and Gay Men

Lesbians and gay men have a long history of persecution and have been consistent targets of prejudice, stereotypes, and discrimination (D'Emilio, 1983). This heterosexism (a stigmatizing of any sexual orientation other than heterosexual) often has a significant impact on the gay or lesbian target. One recent study found that workplace heterosexism and a lack of supportive interactions with others about that environment led to a greater incidence of depression and distress for the gay or lesbian target (Smith & Ingram, 2004). The authors make the good point that the impact of such treatment on the stigmatized individual depends not only on the number of supportive relationships they have, but also the number of nonsupportive interactions in that context, such as workplace, home, or school (see also, Brooks, 1981). Even comments from people who believe they are being supportive can be interpreted by the gay or lesbian person as unsupportive. Much more research is needed to understand the impact of the context and the dynamics of the interactants on how heterosexism affects gay and lesbian individuals.

Research indicates that the attitudes of heterosexuals toward lesbians and gay men depends on the gender of the respondent and the target of their evaluation (Kite & Whitley, 1996). Specifically, there has emerged a robust finding that heterosexual men (HM) and women (HW) indicate different attitudes toward gay men and lesbians. Although both HM and HW hold negative attitudes toward gays and lesbians, the attitudes of HM toward gay males are significantly more negative and prejudicial than they are toward lesbians, and HW hold more prejudicial attitudes against lesbians (Kite, 1984; Whitley, 1988). Some findings have also indicated that HW tend to have more positive attitudes than HM toward gay men (Kite & Whitley, 2003; Levina, Waldo, & Fitzgerald, 2000). Even within-group prejudice exists for some gay men. Taywaditep (2001) found that gay men who are effeminate tend to be regarded with contempt and hostility by more masculine gay men. Recall from Chapter 2 that the social-identity theory predicts such hostility toward a stereotype-confirming individual in one's group. That is, people in one's group who are a perceived detriment to the group (in the way they conform to negative stereotypes about the group) are shunned by their in-group, so that the overall status of the group is not harmed. Interestingly, some research also shows that the greater the interpersonal contact with gay men and lesbians in various contexts, the less likely the heterosexual individual will be prejudiced against lesbians and gay men (Harmon, 1997; Herek & Capitanio, 1996). However, the impact of education on attitudes about homosexuality seems to primarily have an impact on HWs, and little noticeable change tends to occur in the antigay attitudes of HM (Finken, 2002). Where do these negative attitudes come from? The research literature is less clear on this question.

As with the research on the stigma associated with being overweight, the perception of the controllability of one's sexual orientation has a large role in heterosexuals' attitudes toward lesbians and gay men (Sakalli, 2002). Research indicates that about half of all Americans believe that homosexuality is a "lifestyle," and that people choose to be homosexual (Whitley, 1990). The question of whether there is a genetic basis for homosexuality is the subject of controversy and heated debate in the scientific community, and it has generated mixed findings. Some studies claim no evidence for a genetic contribution (Byne & Parsons, 1993; King & McDonald, 1992; McGuire, 1995), some studies report less-than-definite results, with encouragement to pursue the question (Buhrich, Bailey, & Martin, 1991), and others find evidence that supports the idea that homosexuality has a genetic component (Haynes, 1995; Whitam, Diamond, & Martin, 1993). Thus, at this time, the jury is still out on the question of the genetic basis of sexual orientation.

Other studies on the origin of prejudice toward lesbians and gay men indicate support for an authoritarian-like origin, in that people who are less accepting of gender equality tend to also be less tolerant of (and more prejudiced against) gay men and lesbians (Haddock, Zanna, & Esses, 1993, Study 1; MacDonald & Games, 1974). Other studies suggest that antigay attitudes and prejudice are more likely to be found in heterosexuals who perceive homosexuality as a violation of the conventional social order and traditional values (Haddock et al., 1993, Study 2; Kurdek, 1988). Cullen, Wright, and Alessandri (2002) found that the degree of contact a person has with lesbians and gay men was the most significant predictor of subsequent homophobia: the greater the interpersonal contact, the less likely the person is to hold prejudiced attitudes toward lesbians and gay men. A limitation to a majority of the studies and surveys on prejudice against lesbians and gay men is that they provide some descriptive and correlational information, but they do not allow us to understand the true complexity of attitudes toward lesbians and gay men (Herek, 2000). Kite and her colleagues (Kite & Whitley, 1996; LaMar & Kite, 1998) have argued persuasively that researchers need to do more sophisticated modeling of prejudiced attitudes in order to understand the multiple bases upon which attitudes toward lesbians and gay men are founded, and why, for example, some people can hold two different attitudes toward homosexuals, depending on the salient situational context and norms available (Kite & Whitley, 1996).

Attitudes toward the Physically Challenged

Of all the major forms of prejudice that have been studied, the type that has been studied the least is prejudice against people who are physically challenged. This type of prejudice has alternatively been called **ableism**, or **handicapism** (Bogdan & Biklen, 1993). People with physical conditions (e.g., physical deformities, handicaps) are often the subject of derision, fear, disgust, prejudice, stereotypes, and discrimination, (Anderson, 1988–1989), and the media often perpetuates these stereotypes by portraying the physically challenged as objects of pity or ridicule, or even as dangerous (Bogdan, Biklen, Shapiro, & Spelkoman, 1990). In the news and communications business, some of this bias may reflect the type of training young journalists receive in college. One study of 216 journalism/mass communication programs found that little if any emphasis or training is devoted to the reporting of ableism (Dickson, 1994). Like other types of prejudice, ableism has negative effects on those against whom the negative attitudes are directed. Physically challenged persons report that such prejudice makes them feel as if there is something wrong with them, and that they are unacceptable (Hebl & Kleck, 2000; Weeber, 1999). Prejudice against people with physical challenges appears to be learned early in childhood (Anderson, 1988–1989). In one study (Richardson & Green, 1971), Black and White children were asked to rank order pictures showing Black or White people, who either did or did not have a physical disability. Children showed a strong preference for the pictures depicting the physically able, and the White children ranked the picture of the physically disabled person lower than the picture of the Black person. In a helping study, Juni and Roth (1981) found that handicapped confederates were helped more than nonhandicapped confederates. The researchers suggest that this may indicate a belief that handicapped persons need more assistance, and this assumption may be a symptom of underlying prejudice against handicapped persons. Even more than 10 years after the passage of the Americans with Disabilities Act in 1990, research indicates that people with disabilities are still the object of much discrimination in hiring. A study by Gouvier, Sytsma-Jordan, and Mayville (2003) found that people's ratings of the suitability of a person for a job depended on whether the applicant had a disability. Those who had a disability were given significantly lower ratings. However, the ratings of the applicants with disabilities varied according to the type of disability. Those with physical disabilities were rated much higher than those with mental disabilities.

Although research is continuing to examine the factors that contribute to prejudice against overweight persons, homosexuals, and the physically challenged, much more research is needed. Specifically, we need more information on the factors that enhance and inhibit the development of prejudice and stereotypes directed at these groups. Additionally, it is important to know the personality types and other individual-difference variables that are correlated with an enhanced likelihood of endorsing stereotypes about these groups. More research also needs to focus on understanding the institutional versus individual levels of prejudice toward these groups. There is much that researchers do not know about prejudice toward overweight persons, lesbians and gay men, and, especially the physically challenged. Hopefully, the future will bring more empirical and theoretical work on these understudied types of prejudice. Speaking of the future, let us now turn to a discussion of trends in the study of prejudice.

UNDERSTANDING THE DYNAMIC NATURE
OF INTERGROUP INTERACTIONS

In psychology (indeed, in any science), good theories suggest specific causal links between variables. One variable (or a number of variables) is predicted to cause a change in the level of the dependent variable(s). This prediction is based on the fact that, to prove causality, one event (*A*) must necessarily occur before the other event (*B*) in time, if we are to suggest that *A* caused a change in *B*. This seems clear enough, and theory and research in psychology has tended to follow this truism. In the lab, we try to isolate the influence of one (or more) variables on one (or more) dependent variables. However, there is a limitation to this approach to understanding human behavior. It represents a simplistic, unidirectional type of linear causation (i.e., a one-way street from a causal variable to an affected variable). As theory and research have progressed, our models of human interactions have become more and more sophisticated. We know that our interactions and perceptions of the world are not merely episodes of unidirectional causation. Rather, human interactions and perceptions are far more complex.

In 1960 Miller, Galanter, and Pribram published an early version of what has been called **control theory**, or **feedback theory** (see Powers, 1973). Essentially, this was a perspective on human behavior that said that we are continually seeking to match our behavior to internal standards for that behavior, and we are motivated to reduce discrepancies between our standards and our behavior. It seems a fairly straightforward proposition, and one that really ought not to arouse the hackles of any psychological researcher. But critics charged that this view of human behavior muddied the empirical water by stating that people are constantly behaving to internal standards, complicating which is the cause and which is the effect. No longer were people subject to the influence of a clear, identifiable causal variable, but they were affected by, *and affecting,* their environment. We are constantly responding to feedback from the environment (including other people) and adjusting our behavior accordingly, such that our goal of matching our perceptions to our standards is closer to being achieved.

A small but devoted group of psychologists, mathematicians, and engineers developed control theory further and attempted to apply it to the study of behavior (Powers, 1978, 1989). However, for a number of reasons, mainstream psychology would have none of it, and control theory never got a foothold in the psychological scientific literature. The main problem (aside from the blasphemy in saying—as control theorists did—that behavior was merely a by-product of our attempt to control our perceptions, such that they match our standards; see Powers [1973] for more information) was a methodological one. How do you measure causation in a model of continuous feedback on behavior? Such a model would have to be enormously complex, too complex, for a concise explanation of behavior. Thus, you could say that control theory was put on the shelf, to wait for theory and research to become sophisticated enough to begin to address the complex task of modeling feedback loops of behavior.

According to some, that time has come (Nowak & Vallacher, 1998; Vallacher & Nowak, 1997). So-called dynamic models of behavior stipulate that a particular behavior can at the same time be both an effect of the preceding moment's cause and a causal agent upon a variable in the following moment. As a result, these researchers argue, we should conceptualize the relationships between variables in terms of multiple feedback loops, with variables simultaneously being affected by, and affecting, other variables. Such a model would come closer to approximating the actual complexity of human behavior. Now, let us bring all of this back to the discussion of prejudice and stereotyping.

In 1996, Devine et al. wrote a chapter on prejudice and stereotyping. This chapter was unusual compared to the hundreds of scholarly chapters written in psychology each year. Devine and her colleagues were calling for prejudice researchers to begin to examine how prejudice and stereotyping emerge as a result of the interaction between the majority and minority groups. Devine et al. explained that, unless we begin to examine how each individual is affected by, and affects, the other individual in an interaction, we will have an incomplete, simplistic understanding of intergroup behavior. The thesis of the chapter is that stereotypes, anxiety, and prejudice toward outgroups tend to promote misunderstandings and negative expectations about interactions with outgroup members. Although that thesis is not new (many others have discussed the influence of expectancies on intergroup attitudes; e.g., Darley & Fazio, 1980; Neuberg, 1994; Olson, Roese, & Zanna, 1996), Devine and her colleagues used this discussion of expectancies as a backdrop for discussing two important aspects of intergroup encounters.

The first is an important distinction between two types of low-prejudice members of the majority (the majority refers to the numerical majority in any category, race, gender, religion, sexual orientation, etc.): those who have had extensive contact (EC) and interactions with members of the stereotyped minority group, and those who have had little contact (LC) and few interactions with the stereotyped outgroup. On paper-and-pencil measures of prejudiced attitudes, both are identical in that they each endorse egalitarian beliefs. However, in an interaction with a member of the stereotyped outgroup, an important difference emerges. Suppose we are talking about an interaction between an African American male and a White male. If the White is an EC individual, he will likely feel at ease with the African American interaction partner, and it is highly likely that their conversation will proceed with no negative reactions from either source. However, if the White is an LC individual (see Figure 10.1), he could say the exact same things as the EC individual, but the content of what he is saying tends to be obscured by the clear nonverbal indicators of anxiety the LC White is showing, and that discomfort will often lead the LC White to avoid interacting with African Americans (Towles-Schwen & Fazio, 2003). As Devine et al. (1996) point out, such interactions may appear to proceed uneventfully, but each interactant's view of the other will likely be negative. Why would that be the case?

To answer that question, we need to turn to the second aspect of intergroup interactions discussed by Devine et al. (1996). They suggest that our understanding of the factors that give rise to and maintain prejudice and stereotyping, and those factors that inhibit

FIGURE 10.1 The anxiety of the low-prejudice, intergroup-inexperienced majority member. (Cartoon by C. Headrick. Copyright © 1996 by Guilford Publishing. Reprinted with permission.)

positive intergroup encounters, will be incomplete unless we attempt to understand how the expectations of both the perceiver and the target influence their verbal and nonverbal behavior, and how subsequent impressions and behaviors within the interaction influence the other individual, which in turn influences their reaction to us, which influences our reaction to them, and so on (Shelton [2000] makes a similar argument in favor of examining the active role that the minority target plays in shaping the dynamic intergroup interaction). Sound familiar? Devine et al. (1996) are saying that we need to understand the dynamic process of intergroup interactions, by trying to model the feedback nature of the interaction, so that we can conceptualize the moment-by-moment impact of certain verbal and nonverbal events, along with cognitions, affect, and expectations (which would be biased by stereotypes about the outgroup). If this sounds incredibly complex, you are correct: it is. Which is perhaps the main reason why Devine and her colleagues found few studies that have attempted to even come close to tackling this problem. One recent paper, however, has reported evidence that supports core aspects of Devine's model. Blair, Park, and Bachelor (2003) found that prejudiced persons and those with little outgroup contact reported greater anxiety about imagined and real interactions with a stigmatized outgroup member. Thus, it may be that those who are just anxious about any intergroup interaction may be more likely to then form stereotypes and prejudice, or it may be the other way around: that those who are more prejudiced (or who have little outgroup contact) are more likely to interpret an interaction as threatening. Blair et al.'s data do not suggest which causal direction is more probable; therefore, this is an unanswered question that requires more empirical attention.

Let us return to the interaction between the LC individual and the African American partner. Recall that I said that it is likely that the interaction would result in each individual having a more negative view of the other person. Here is why. Devine et al. (1996) point out that LC individuals want to convey to their interaction partner that they are low preju-dice, and so they are especially nervous and concerned about doing or saying anything that would communicate otherwise. Some data suggest that when nonstigmatized persons interact with a person from a stigmatized group, they perceive the interaction as a chal-lenge and/or threat (Blascovich, Mendes, Hunter, Lickel, & Kowai-Bell, 2001). That is, the perceiver may feel heightened uncertainty, danger, an increased feeling of nervousness and doubt about one's ability to effectively interact with the stigmatized person (Hebl, Tickle, & Heatherton, 2000). In this research, these thoughts and feelings corresponded to heightened cardiovascular reactivity in the perceivers and poorer interpersonal perfor-mance. Indeed, research by Vorauer and Turpie (in press) showed that when low prejudice persons try to monitor their behavior toward outgroup members, their nervousness leads them to "choke" interpersonally, and they treat the outgroup member less positively than their counterparts who were not told to monitor their own behavior toward the outgroup member.

This heightened nervousness also leads to avoidant behaviors, such as more pauses in one's speech (and more "ums" and "uhs" peppering one's dialogue), decreased eye contact, increased interpersonal distance, and increased nervous fidgeting. This behav-ior becomes especially unfortunate if the minority-group member (the African American male, in our example) is suspicious of majority-group members. Devine and her colleagues (1996) point out that research on prejudice and stereotyping is only getting half of the pic-ture in examining the attitudes, affect, and behavior of the majority-group member toward the minority-group member. We also need to understand the expectations, prejudices, and stereotypes that the minority group member has about the majority-group member (as discussed in Chapter 6). Each person comes to the interaction with these expectations (unfortunately, these are often negative, having been tainted by stereotypes and prejudice), and as we have learned throughout this text, these expectations influence the verbal and nonverbal behavior of the individual and bias the way we perceive the behavior of the other individual in ways that confirm our expectations. Thus, the interaction involving the LC White and the African American might likely proceed as follows. They each enter the interaction with their expectations and stereotypes of the other. The African American, upon noticing the nervous behavior of the Caucasian, may think, why is he so nervous? This is just a simple interaction. He must be nervous because I am Black. Such an attribu-tion may be entirely reasonable, given the lack of a good reason why the White would be showing the avoidant behaviors. At that, the African American may become irritated at the (perceived) prejudiced behavior and behave in an aloof or cold manner toward the LC individual. The LC individual perceives only that suddenly his interaction partner is being rude to him (by being so aloof), and at that perception the LC person becomes irritated and decides to reciprocate with similar behavior. They both leave the interaction with reinforced stereotypes and one more negative intergroup interaction as "evidence" to support their stereotypes and prejudices. A recent paper by Plant (2004) reports two experiments that showed that this is exactly what happens. When participants had more interracial anxiety, they were more motivated to avoid interactions with outgroup members, and their interracial interactions were less positive.

As research and theory become more sophisticated, researchers will be better able to address the methodological challenges that confront them as they try to measure online social perception in the intergroup interaction. Understanding the complexity of the feedback dynamics in the intergroup situation represents one of the biggest challenges and most exciting areas of prejudice research for the future.

MOTIVATION AND PREJUDICE

As with other fields of scientific inquiry, psychology is characterized by trends in the research areas that receive empirical attention. Certain questions or approaches to studying human behavior become popular for a while, perhaps years, and then the field moves on to another, new area of inquiry. Such has been the case with the motivational approach to behavior, and for explaining intergroup behavior in particular. The motivational approach suggests that our affect, cognition, and behavior are guided by our needs and goals. So, the reason we do something is that we believe that the action will bring us closer to a desired goal. In this text we have discussed a number of motivational theories—most notably, the authoritarian-personality approach, relative deprivation, and the realistic conflict theory, to name a few. Generally speaking, each of these theories suggests that prejudice, stereotyping, and discrimination are the result of individuals trying to maintain their group's advantaged status in society, and/or maintain or raise their self-esteem. Although these theories were intuitive and had good empirical support, the emphasis on the motivational approach to understanding prejudice waned in the late 1960s with the growing influence of cognition in social psychology. Researchers became disenchanted with the motivational approach because it presented a few problems that could not be adequately addressed in experiments. Primary among them was the issue of defining motivation. Researchers differed on how we ought to define motivation, and definitions of motivation were notoriously vague. Generally, the definition of *motivation* was on the order of the following: "a psychological force that impels us toward a goal." Such definitions did not explain, but further muddied the water. For instance, what does *psychological force* mean and how do you know that such a force is present? The lack of a precise definition of *motivation* made it nearly impossible to construct a measure of it.

As we discussed in Chapter 3, the mid-1980s brought about advances in the study of emotions, and researchers began to once again take a look at motivational explanations for prejudice and stereotyping (e.g., Tajfel & Turner, 1986). Theorists were not as concerned about specific definitions of *motivation,* per se, but instead, they focused on the broad understanding of motivation as a movement toward some goal (usually a self-serving goal, as mentioned earlier). Such an approach was methodologically tighter, in that it is simpler to measure one's goals, rather than to define and measure a "psychological force."

Today, motivational approaches to understanding behavior are very popular, reflecting theoretical and empirical advances in understanding the influences of goal-directed action (e.g., see Gollwitzer & Moskowitz, 1996; Kruglanski, 1996). This renewed interest has taken researchers in a number of directions. One approach has focused on understanding what motives seem to dominate human behavior. For example, Smith and Mackie (1997) posit that there are three main motives that underlie our actions: the desire for mastery, the desire to feel connected to other people and groups, and the desire to have a positive view of oneself and one's ingroups. Using this as a theoretical foundation, researchers might begin to examine whether there are more than three major motives, and how these motives interact and influence cognition, affect, and behavior in various intergroup contexts. A second approach has focused on what is termed **motivated reasoning** (Kunda & Sinclair, 1999; Stangor & Ford, 1992). Motivated reasoning is simply the idea that our judgments are biased by the motivations that are salient at a particular moment. Research from this perspective tries to understand how our attitudes toward and impressions of others are influenced by motivation, and what conditions and situations seem to evoke certain types of motivated reasoning.

Research from the motivated-reasoning approach has confirmed that our judgments and attitudes tend to be biased by our motivational goals (see Kunda [1999] for a detailed discussion of the influence of motivated expectancies on social perception and memory). In other words, we are motivated to pay attention to (and remember) information about our self and our ingroups that confirms our positive view of our self and our groups, and we are motivated to disregard information that violates these views. Most behaviors, affect, and cognitions (including discrimination, prejudice, and stereotypes) are therefore in the service of such motives, and thus, in certain instances, an individual perceiver will be more likely to think of a target person in terms of a stereotype when it would be effective in moving the perceiver toward their goal of positive self esteem, and higher ingroup status, relative to the target individual's group (Kunda & Sinclair, 1999; Kunda & Thagard, 1996). The task for future researchers is to address the following questions: Which motives dominate mental life? What determines whether one will be motivated to activate, apply, or inhibit a stereotype when thinking about another individual? (Kunda & Sinclair, 1999), and how can we measure such motivations (Dunton & Fazio, 1997; Plant & Devine, 1998)? Under what circumstances does each motive operate? Finally, how do specific motives influence cognition, affect, and behavior?

THE NEUROBIOLOGY OF PREJUDICE

In science, new theories are proposed, and advances in knowledge are attained, by advances in methods used to investigate a concept or phenomenon. Over the past 5 years, our understanding about the way we think and behave with respect to stereotyped outgroups has advanced in dramatic fashion via experiments utilizing neuroimaging (Phelps, 2003). These experiments take place in the dawn of a new approach to understanding social behavior, which has been alternatively termed "social cognitive neuroscience" (Ochsner & Lieberman, 2001) or simply "social neuroscience" (Cacioppo, Berntson, Adolphs, Carter, Davidson, McClintock et al., 2002). In this approach, researchers seek to understand the linkages between the functioning of the brain, the thoughts that come from those functions, and the affect and behavior that emerge from those cognitions. Social-cognitive neuroscience (SCN) represents a fascinating and complex attempt to integrate otherwise distinct subfields of psychology, and though still in its relative infancy, SCN is already shedding light on classic unanswered questions about the nature of prejudice. For example, the amygdala is an area of the brain that is strongly associated with the experience of fear (LeDoux, 1996). One reason people may want to avoid outgroups is that they may be afraid (perhaps based on stereotypes about them) of outgroup members. In this case, one would expect an elevated amount of amygdala activity in such individuals when they think about or view an outgroup member, relative to an ingroup member. Using functional magnetic resonance imaging (fMRI), a method of pinpointing the activity levels of the brain from moment to moment, Phelps, O'Connor, Cunningham, Funayama, Gatenby, and Gore (2000) found that Whites who showed outgroup bias on an implicit measure of racial attitudes (IAT) were also more likely to show a stronger amygdala response when viewing photos of Blacks than when they viewed other photos of Whites. Later research by Cunningham and his colleagues (2004) showed similar results. Additionally, Cunningham et al. found that the significant difference in amygdala activity between White perceivers regarding a Black face for 30 milliseconds and Whites viewing a White face decreased to nonsignificant differences when viewing time was increased to 525 milliseconds. This suggests that automatic stereotyping and prejudice reactions appear to be brought under control once the individual is conscious of the initial automatic (prejudiced) reaction, or if the individual is motivated to individuate the target (Wheeler & Fiske, 2005).

While it is interesting to use fMRI and other brain-imaging methods to understand brain activity during social perception or social evaluation, it is important to keep in mind that this research is still quite new, and it would be imprudent to suggest that the results from these studies are more informative than traditional psychological studies of social evaluation (Phelps & Thomas, 2003). There is much we do not know yet about the linkages between brain activity, cognition, attitudes, and behavior, and much more research is needed before we can understand how brain, thoughts, and actions are connected in the formation and perpetuation of prejudice. Social-cognitive neuroscience is one example of new approaches and perspectives that researchers are bringing to bear on the problem of prejudice, and the use of brain-imaging technology is rapidly increasing in popularity among prejudice researchers.

IMPLICIT AND AUTOMATIC STEREOTYPING

When are we aware that a stereotype has influence on our perceptions of others? Can our evaluations of other individuals be biased according to stereotype-consistent expectancies without our awareness? Is stereotyping uncontrollable? In various forms, these questions have occupied prejudice researchers over the decades. Today, they take the form of research on implicit stereotyping (see Chapter 3) and the automaticity of stereotyping (Chapters 1 and 3). In their research on implicit stereotyping, Banaji, Greenwald, and others (Banaji et al., 1993; Bargh, Chen, and Burrows, 1996; Kawakami & Dovidio, 2001; Greenwald & Banaji, 1995) have shown that our evaluations of other people can be biased by prior exposure to information, and this biasing influence occurs even when we are not consciously aware of it. The fascinating findings related to implicit stereotyping have led some to believe that stereotyping is inevitable and cannot be controlled (Banaji & Greenwald, 1994). The argument is that if we are not aware of the biasing effects of prior information on our current judgments, we cannot control the outcome of our judgments, and thus whether we use a stereotype to evaluate someone else is merely up to chance (i.e., the likelihood that we were exposed to stereotype-priming or stereotype-consistent information some time earlier). The argument has some merit, in that there is a degree of automatic stereotyping that occurs in daily cognition. However, such an argument tends to obscure an important distinction between the activation and application of stereotypes (Kunda, 1999). Activation of the stereotype refers to whether, upon viewing or thinking of the target individual, a stereotype will be cognitively activated, even if one is not aware of its activation. Application refers to whether the perceiver will then use the activated stereotype in their assessment of the target.

TO INDIVIDUATE OR STEREOTYPE? THAT *IS* THE QUESTION

Most researchers agree that stereotype activation becomes an automatic process early in childhood (Katz, 1976) and that it is difficult to control its onset. Researchers also have tended to agree with Devine (1989), that high- and low-prejudice persons differ in their tendency to endorse and apply the activated stereotype to a target individual. However, the disagreement comes about on the issue of the controllability of the stereotype activation. Devine and her colleagues (Devine & Monteith, 1993) have reported compelling evidence to suggest that automatically activated stereotypes *can* be deleted and substituted with an evaluatively neutral attitude. Such an attitude would encourage the perceiver to not rush to any hasty judgments about an individual but instead try to evaluate the person based on information about the target individual as a person (i.e., to individuate, and assess each person based on their own personality, talents, etc.). Devine and her colleagues suggest that this is precisely what low-prejudice persons do, and in so doing, they are breaking the prejudice habit (Devine & Monteith, 1993; Monteith, 1993). Devine's research suggests that if a low-prejudice person is motivated enough and devotes enough conscious cognitive effort to the task, they can override the automatic activation of a stereotype and substitute a more egalitarian response to the target person. Indeed, this type of individual should be more likely to abandon most if not all of their stereotypes, toward the goal of evaluating each person on that person's own merits, and not according to stereotypes. Can this really be done? Unfortunately, most people are not that motivated, and the cognitive benefits of having stereotypes tend to outweigh the costs associated with the intense cognitive work and perceived small benefits that they would get from abandoning their stereotypes. Even an ardent critic of the controllability of automatic stereotyping like Bargh (1999) concedes that automatic stereotyping *can* be overcome but that such an effort requires a near-herculean motivation and cognitive attention, thus making automatic egalitarianism a far rarer occurrence than Devine proposes. Devine and her colleagues acknowledge this, but they suggest that some people are so motivated that they can supplant their automatic stereotypes with an automatic egalitarian attitude toward others (Devine & Monteith, 1999). Recent research suggests support for this contention. Moskowitz, Salomon, and Taylor (2000) exposed White participants to computer-presented primes (presented at a subliminal rate of 200 milliseconds) of faces of either a White or African American person. They were then asked to pronounce subsequent stereotype-relevant or stereotype-irrelevant words on a computer screen as quickly as possible. Two weeks earlier, participants had been asked about their goals in life. Those who listed egalitarian goals, specifically with reference to equal treatment for African Americans, were classified as chronic egalitarians. Those who did not list such goals were classified as nonchronics. Moskowitz et al. (2000) found that when chronic egalitarians were exposed to an African American prime, they did not activate cultural stereotypes of African Americans, and indeed, they were equally fast at recognizing stereotype-relevant and -irrelevant words. However, nonchronics in the African American prime condition responded faster to stereotype-relevant words than to stereotype-irrelevant words. This indicates that the prime activated the stereotype of African Americans, and this facilitated recognition of stereotype-relevant words. A second experiment revealed that chronic egalitarians respond faster to egalitarian-relevant words (and not egalitarian-irrelevant words) when they followed stereotypic primes. These are perhaps the strongest data gathered thus far that suggest that, for some people (chronic egalitarians), automatic stereotype activation does not occur when encountering a member of a stereotyped group. Rather, in these people, what tends to be automatically activated are egalitarian ideals and beliefs.

SUMMARY

The father of modern social psychology, Kurt Lewin, believed a good theory ought to have practical applications. Certainly this can be said of many theories about prejudice that we have discussed in this text. Because prejudice has been (and of course, still is) regarded as undesirable, psychologists have long been interested in understanding the nature of prejudice, in order to ascertain ways to eliminate, or at least reduce, its influence on our social perceptions. In this book, we have covered a broad landscape of topics, questions, and theories of prejudice, and we have explored in some depth the many important experiments that researchers have used to provide some answers to various questions about prejudice. At its heart, research on prejudice is very practical, and we are continually seeking to understand more about prejudice and stereotyping, because most researchers believe, as Myrdal (1944) did, that "scientific theories of causal relations will be seen as instrumental in planning controlled social change" (p. 1023).

Hopefully, like a good scientist, you had some questions answered in reading this text but you also had more questions that arose as a result of reading about the theories and experiments within this volume. Prejudice is multifaceted and multidetermined, and, as we have learned, it is much more complex than many think. Though stereotypes and prejudice are difficult to break, the hopeful news is that they *can* be replaced with more egalitarian attitudes (Hamilton & Sherman, 1994). With that in mind, we are much closer to answering yes to Allport's (1954) last question:

> The question before us is whether progress toward tolerance will continue, or whether as in many regions of the world, a fatal retrogression will set in. The whole world watches to see whether the democratic ideal in human relationships is viable. Can citizens learn to seek their own welfare and growth not at the expense of their fellow men, but in concert with them? The human family does not yet know the answer, but hopes it will be affirmative. (p. 518)

GLOSSARY

ableism (handicapism)   Prejudice against individuals who are physically challenged.

control theory (feedback theory)   States that we constantly are comparing our behavior to a standard, and our behavior is regulated by a negative feedback loop, in order to keep our

perceptions of the world consistent with our standards.

motivated reasoning   The idea that our judgments are biased by the motivations that are salient at that particular moment.

DISCUSSION QUESTIONS

1. Is prejudice against people who are overweight increasing or decreasing in America? Why (as Crandall [1991] found) do some parents even feel prejudice or endorse stereotypes about their overweight children?

2. If medical research were to prove that sexual orientation is almost entirely determined by genetic factors (i.e., homosexuality and heterosexuality are not chosen or a lifestyle, but it inherent in our genes), prejudice against homosexuals would diminish (as research on the controllability of stigmas would suggest)?

3. How pervasive is prejudice against those who have a physical disability? Is America doing enough to reduce stereotypes and prejudice against the physically challenged? Why do some people develop a prejudice against the physically challenged?

4. Are there other prejudices that ought to be examined by researchers, that have not been discussed in this text? What are some stereotyped groups that have garnered no, or very little, empirical attention?

SUGGESTED KEY READINGS

Crandall, C. S., & Martinez, R. (1996). Culture, ideology, and antifat attitudes. *Personality and Social Psychology Bulletin, 22*(11), 1165–1176.

Haddock, G., Zanna, M. P., & Esses, V. M. (1993). Assessing the structure of prejudicial attitudes: The case of attitudes toward homosexuals. *Journal of*

Personality and Social Psychology, 65(6), 1105–1118.

Herek, G. M. (2000). The psychology of sexual prejudice. *Current Directions in Psychological Science, 9,* 19–22.

INTERNET RESOURCES: RESEARCHERS, REFERENCES, AND ORGANIZATIONS DEVOTED TO THE STUDY OF PREJUDICE

www.apa.org/pubinfo/answers.html   APA's report on sexual orientation.

psychology.ucdavis.edu/herek   Website for Dr. Greg Herek, a prominent researcher of prejudice against homosexuals.

www.glaad.org/org/index.html   Gay and Lesbian Alliance Against Defamation.

www.eskimo.com/~largesse   Network for size esteem.

www.naafa.org   National Association to Advance Fat Acceptance.

www.jan.wvu.edu/links/adalinks.htm Document center for information related to the Americans with Disabilities Act.

www.ncd.gov National Council on Disability.

www.psych.nyu.edu/phelpslab/ Lab page for Elizabeth Phelps, a leading neuroscientist doing fMRI studies of how the brain processes facial information of outgroups.

REFERENCES

■   ■   ■   ■

Abeles, R. P. (1976). Relative deprivation, rising expectations and black militancy. *Journal of Social Issues, 32*(2), 119–137.

Abeles, R. (1987). *Life-span perspectives and social psychology.* Hillsdale, NJ: Erlbaum.

Aberson, C. L., & Ettlin, T. E. (2004). The aversive racism paradigm and responses favoring African Americans: Meta-analytic evidence of two types of favoritism. *Social Justice Research, 17*(1), 25–46.

Aboud, F. (1988). *Children and prejudice.* Cambridge, MA: Blackwell.

Aboud, F. E. (2003). The formation of in-group favoritism and out-group prejudice in young children: Are they distinct attitudes? *Developmental Psychology, 39,* 48–60.

Aboud, F. E., & Fenwick, V. (1999). Exploring and evaluating school-based interventions to reduce prejudice. *Journal of Social Issues, 55*(4), 767–786.

Abrams, C., Viki, G. T., Masser, B., & Bohner, G. (2003). Perceptions of stranger and acquaintance rape: The role of benevolent and hostile sexism in victim blame and rape proclivity. *Journal of Personality and Social Psychology, 84,* 111–125.

Abrams, D., & Hogg, M. (1988). Comments on the motivational status of self-esteem in social identity and intergroup discrimination. *European Journal of Social Psychology, 18,* 317–334.

Adorno, T. W., Frenkel-Brunswik, E. Levinson, D. J., & Sanford, R. N. (1950). *The authoritarian personality.* New York: Harper & Row.

Albee, G. W., & Perry, M. (1998). Economic and social causes of sexism and of the exploitation of women. *Journal of Community and Applied Social Psychology, 8,* 145–160.

Allen, B. P. (1971). Impressions of persuasive communicators: A test of a belief congruence hypothesis. *Journal of Social Psychology, 85,* 145–146.

Allen, B. P. (1995). Gender stereotypes are not accurate: A replication of Martin (1987) using diagnostic vs. self-report and behavioral criteria. *Sex Roles, 32*(9/10), 583–600.

Allen, B. P. (1996). African Americans' and European Americans' mutual attributions: Adjective generation technique (AGT) stereotyping. *Journal of Applied Social Psychology, 26*(10), 894–910.

Allen, R. O., & Spilka, B. (1967). Committed and consensual religion: A specification of religion-prejudice relationships. *Journal for the Scientific Study of Religion, 6*(2), 191–206.

Allen, V. L., & Wilder, D. A. (1975). Categorization, belief, similarity, and intergroup discrimination. *Journal of Personality and Social Psychology, 32,* 971–977.

Allon, N. (1982). The stigma of overweight in everyday life. In B. Wolman (Ed.), *Psychological aspects of obesity: A handbook* (pp. 130–174). New York: Van Nostrand Reinhold.

Allport, G. W. (1935). Attitudes. In C. Murchison (Ed.), *A handbook of social psychology* (pp. 798–844). Worcester, MA: Clark University Press.

Allport, G. W. (1954). *The nature of prejudice.* Reading, MA: Addison-Wesley.

Allport, G. W., & Kramer, B. M. (1946). Some roots of prejudice. *Journal of Psychology, 22,* 9–39.

Allport, G. W., & Ross, J. M. (1967). Personal religious orientation and prejudice. *Journal of Personality and Social Psychology, 5,* 432–443.

Altemeyer, B. (1981). *Right-wing authoritarianism.* Winnipeg, Canada: University of Manitoba Press.

Altemeyer, B. (1988). *Enemies of freedom: Understanding right-wing authoritarianism.* San Francisco: Jossey-Bass.

Altemeyer, B. (1994). Reducing prejudice in right-wing authoritarians. In M. P. Zanna & J. M. Olson (Eds.), *The psychology of prejudice* (Vol. 7, pp. 131–148). Hillsdale, NJ: Erlbaum.

Altemeyer, B. (1996). *The authoritarian specter.* Cambridge, MA: Harvard University Press.

Altemeyer, B., & Hunsberger, B. (1992). Authoritarianism, religious fundamentalism, quest, and prejudice. *The International Journal for the Psychology of Religion, 2*(2), 113–133.

Aman, C. J., & England, P. (1999). Comparable worth: When do two jobs deserve the same pay? In N. Benokraitis (Ed.), *Subtle sexism: Current practice and prospects for change* (pp. 297–314). Thousand Oaks, CA: Sage.

Ambady, N., Paik, S. K., Steele, J., Owen-Smith, A., & Mitchell, J. P. (2004). Deflecting negative self-relevant stereotype activation: The effects of individuation. *Journal of Experimental Social Psychology, 40,* 401–408.

Ambady, N., Shih, M., Kim, A., & Pittinsky, T. L. (2001). Stereotype susceptibility in children: Effects of identity activation on quantitative performance. *Psychological Science, 12*(5), 385–390.

American Psychiatric Association (2000). *Diagnostic and statistical manual for mental disorders* (4th ed. Revised). Washington, D.C.: American Psychiatric Association.

Amir, Y. (1969). Contact hypothesis in ethnic relations. *Psychological Bulletin, 71*(5), 319–342.

Anastasio, P., Bachman, B., Gaertner, S., & Dovidio, J. (1997). Categorization, recategorization, and common ingroup identity. In R. Spears, P. J. Oakes, N. Ellemers, & S. A. Haslam (Eds.), *The social psychology of stereotyping and group life* (pp. 236–256). Cambridge, MA: Blackwell.

Anderson, P. M. (1988–1989). American humor, handicapism, and censorship. *Journal of Reading, Writing, and Learning Disabilities International, 4*(2), 79–87.

Ansello, E. F. (1978). Age-ism: The subtle stereotype. *Childhood Education, 54*(3), 118–122.

Archer, D., Iritani, B., Kimes, D. D., & Barrios, M. (1983). Face-ism: Five studies of sex differences in facial prominence. *Journal of Personality and Social Psychology, 45*(4), 725–735.

Archer, J. (1996). Sex differences in social behavior: Are the social role and evolutionary explanations compatible? *American Psychologist, 51*(9), 909–917.

Arkin, R. M., & Baumgardner, A. H. (1985). Self-handicapping. In J. Harvey & G. Weary (Eds.), *Attribution: Basic issues and applications* (pp. 169–202). New York: Academic Press.

Arluke, A., & Levin, J. (1984, August/September). Another stereotype: Old age as a second childhood. *Aging, 7*–11.

Arndt, J., Greenberg, J., Schimel, J., Pyszczynski, T., & Solomon, S. (2002). To belong or not to belong, that is the question: Terror management and identification with gender and ethnicity. *Journal of Personality and Social Psychology, 83,* 26–43.

Aronson, E., Blaney, N., Stephan, C., Sikes, J., & Snapp, M. (1978). *The jigsaw classroom.* Beverly Hills, CA: Sage.

Aronson, E., & Bridgeman, D. (1979). Jigsaw groups and the desegregated classroom: In pursuit of common goals. *Personality and Social Psychology Bulletin, 5,* 438–445.

Aronson, E., & Gonzalez, A. (1988). Desegregation, jigsaw, and the Mexican-American experience. In P. Katz & D. Taylor (Eds.), *Eliminating racism: Profiles in controversy* (pp. 310–314). New York: Plenum.

Aronson, J., Fried, C. B., & Good, C. (2001). Reducing the effects of stereotype threat on African American college students by shaping theories of intelligence. *Journal of Experimental Social Psychology, 38,* 113–125.

Aronson, J., & Inzlicht, M. (2004). The ups and downs of attributional ambiguity: Stereotype vulnerability and the academic self-knowledge of African American college students. *Psychological Science.*

Aronson, J., Quinn, D. M., & Spencer, S. J. (1998). Stereotype threat and the academic underperformance of minorities and women. In J. K. Swim & C. Stangor (Eds.), *Prejudice: The target's perspective* (pp. 83–103). New York: Academic Press.

Arroyo, C. G., & Zigler, E. (1995). Racial identity, academic achievement, and the psychological well-being of economically disadvantaged adolescents. *Journal of Personality and Social Psychology, 69*(5), 903–914.

Ashburn-Nardo, L., Knowles, M. L., & Monteith, M. J. (2003). Black Americans' implicit racial associations and their implications for intergroup judgment. *Social Cognition, 21,* 61–87.

Ashmore, R. D., & Del Boca, F. K. (1979). Sex stereotypes and implicit personality theory: Toward a cognitive-social psychological conceptualization. *Sex Roles, 5,* 219–248.

Ashmore, R. D., & Del Boca, F. K. (1981). Conceptual approaches to stereotypes and stereotyping. In D. L. Hamilton (Ed.), *Cognitive processes in stereotyping and intergroup behavior* (pp. 1–35). Hillsdale, NJ: Erlbaum.

Atchley, R. (1977). *The social forces in later life* (2nd ed.). Belmont, CA: Wadsworth.

Atchley, R. (1982). The aging self. *Psychotherapy: Theory, Research, and Practice, 19*(4), 388–396.

Aubé, J., & Koestner, R. (1992). Gender characteristics and adjustment: A longitudinal study. *Journal of Personality and Social Psychology, 63*(3), 485–493.

Avorn, J., & Langer, E. (1982). Induced disability in nursing home patients: A controlled trial. *Journal of the American Geriatrics Society, 20,* 297–300.

Bachman, B. A., Gaertner, S. L., Anastasio, P., & Rust, M. (1993). *When corporations merge: Organizational identification among employees of acquiring and acquired organizations.* Paper presented at the 64th annual meeting of the Eastern Psychological Association, Crystal City, VA.

Banaji, M., & Greenwald, A. G. (1994) Implicit stereotypes and prejudice. In M. P. Zanna & J. M. Olson (Eds.), *The psychology of prejudice: The Ontario symposium* (Vol. 7, pp. 55–76). Hillsdale, NJ: Erlbaum.

Banaji, M., & Greenwald, A. G. (1995). Implicit gender stereotyping in judgments of fame. *Journal of Personality and Social Psychology, 68,* 181–198.

Banaji, M., Hardin, C., & Rothman, A. J. (1993). Implicit stereotyping in person judgment. *Journal of Personality and Social Psychology, 65,* 272–281.

Banaji, M. R., & Hardin, C. D. (1996). Automatic Stereotyping. *Psychological Science, 7*(3), 136–141.

Bandura, A., Ross, D., & Ross, S. A. (1961). Transmission of aggression through imitation of aggressive models. *Journal of Abnormal and Social Psychology, 63,* 575–582.

Bandura, A., & Walters, R. H. (1963). *Social learning and personality development.* New York: Holt, Rinehart & Winston.

Banziger, G., & Drevenstedt, J. (1982). Achievement attributions by young and old judges as a function of perceived age of stimulus persons. *Journal of Gerontology, 37*(4), 468–474.

Barak, B. (1987). Cognitive age: A new multidimensional approach to measuring age identity. *International Journal of Aging and Human Development, 25*(2), 109–128.

Bargh, J. A. (1989). Conditional automaticity: Varieties of automatic influence in social perception and cognition. In J. S. Uleman & J. A. Bargh (Eds.), *Unintended thought* (pp. 3–51). New York: Guilford.

Bargh, J. A. (1994). The four horsemen of automaticity: Awareness, intention, efficiency, and control in social cognition. In R. S. Wyer Jr. & T. K. Srull (Eds.), *Handbook of Social Cognition* (Vol. 1, 2nd ed., pp. 3–51). Hillsdale, NJ: Erlbaum.

Bargh, J. A. (1999). The cognitive monster: The case against the controllability of automatic stereotype effects. In S. Chaiken & Y. Trope (Eds.), *Dual-process theories in social psychology* (pp. 361–382). New York: Guilford.

Bargh, J. A., Chen, M., & Burrows, L. (1996). Automaticity of social behavior: Direct effects of trait construct and stereotype activation on action. *Journal of Personality and Social Psychology, 71*(2), 230–244.

Baron, R. S., Inman, M. B., Kao, C. F., & Logan, H. (1992). Emotion and superficial social processing. *Motivation and Emotion, 16,* 323–345.

Baron, R. S., Logan, H. & Lilly, J. (1994). Negative emotion and message processing. *Journal of Experimental Social Psychology, 30*(2), 181–201.

Barreto, M., & Ellemers, N. (in press). The perils of political correctness: Responses of men and women to old-fashioned and modern sexist views. *Social Psychology Quarterly.*

Barrett, K. C. (1995). A functionalist approach to shame and guilt. In J. P. Tangney & K. W. Fischer (Eds.), *Self-conscious emotions: The psychology of shame, guilt, embarrassment and pride* (pp. 25–63). New York: Guilford.

Barrett, K. C., Zahn-Waxler, C., & Cole, P. M. (1993). Avoiders versus amenders: Implications for the investigation of guilt and shame during toddlerhood? *Cognition and Emotion, 7*(6), 481–505.

Barrow, G. M., & Smith, P. A. (1979). *Aging, ageism, and society.* New York: West Publishing.

Basow, S. A. (1992). *Gender: Stereotypes and roles* (3rd ed.). Pacific Grove, CA: Brooks/Cole.

Basso, M. R., Schefft, B. K., & Hoffman, R. G. (1994). Mood-moderating effects of affect intensity on cognition: Sometimes euphoria is not beneficial and dysphoria is not detrimental. *Journal of Personality and Social Psychology, 66*(2), 363–368.

Bassili, J. N., & Reil, J. E. (1981). On the dominance of the old-age stereotype. *Journal of Gerontology, 36*(6), 682–688.

Batson, C. D. (1976). Religion as prosocial: Agent or double agent. *Journal for the Scientific Study of Religion, 15,* 29–45.

Batson, C. D., & Burris, C. T. (1994). Personal religion: Depressant or stimulant of prejudice and discrimination? In M. P. Zanna & J. M. Olson (Eds.), *The psychology of prejudice* (Vol. 7, pp. 149–169). Hillsdale, NJ: Erlbaum.

Batson, C. D., Flink, C. H., Schoenrade, P. A., Fultz, J., & Pych, V. (1986). Religious orientation and overt versus covert racial prejudice. *Journal of Personality and Social Psychology, 50,* 175–181.

Batson, C. D., Naifeh, S. J., & Pate, S. (1978). Social desirability, religious orientation, and racial prejudice. *Journal for the Scientific Study of Religion, 17,* 31–41.

Batson, C. D., & Ventis, W. L. (1982). *The religious experience: A social-psychological perspective.* New York: Oxford University Press.

Baumeister, R. F. (1984). Choking under pressure: Self-consciousness and paradoxical effects of incentives on skillful performance. *Journal of Personality and Social Psychology, 46,* 610–620.

Baumeister, R. F., Reis, H. T., & Delespaul, P. (1995). Subjective and experiential correlates of guilt in daily life. *Personality and Social Psychology Bulletin, 21*(12), 1256–1268.

Baumeister, R. F., Stillwell, A. M., & Heatherton, T. F. (1994). Guilt: An interpersonal approach. *Psychological Bulletin, 115*(2), 243–267.

Baxter, J., & Kane, E. W. (1995). Dependence and independence: A cross-national analysis of gender inequality and gender attitudes. *Gender and Society, 9*(2), 193–215.

Beaton, A. M., Tougas, F., & Joly, S. (1996). Neosexism among male managers: Is it a matter of numbers? *Journal of Applied Social Psychology, 26*(24), 2189–2203.

Bell, J. (1992). In search of a discourse on aging: The elderly on television. *The Gerontologist, 32,* 305–311.

Bem, S. L. (1974). The measurement of psychological androgyny. *Journal of Consulting and Clinical Psychology, 42,* 155–162.

Bem, S. L. (1981). Gender-schema theory: A cognitive account of gender-typing. *Psychological Review, 88,* 354–364.

Bem, S. L. (1993). *The lenses of gender.* New Haven, CT: Yale University Press.

Bem, S. L., & Bem, D. J. (1970). Training the woman to know her place. In D J. Bem (Ed.), *Beliefs, attitudes, and human affairs.* Belmont, CA: Brooks/Cole.

Bennett, R. (1976). Can the young believe they'll get old? *Personnel and Guidance Journal, 55*(3), 136–139.

Benokraitis, N. V. (1997). *Subtle sexism: Current practice and prospects for change.* Thousand Oaks, CA: Sage.

Benokraitis, N. V., & Feagin, J. R. (1986). *Modern sexism: Blatant, subtle, and covert discrimination.* Englewood Cliffs, NJ: Prentice-Hall.

Benson, P. L., & Vincent, S. (1980). Development and validation of the Sexist Attitudes toward Women Scale (SATWS). *Psychology of Women Quarterly, 5*(2), 276–291.

Bergen, D. J., & Williams, J. E. (1991). Sex stereotypes in the United States revisited: 1972–1988. *Sex Roles, 24*(70–8), 413–423.

Berglas, S., & Jones, E. E. (1978). Drug choice as a self-handicapping strategy in response to noncontingent success. *Journal of Personality and Social Psychology, 36,* 405–417.

Berkowitz, L. (1989). Frustration-aggression hypothesis: Examination and reformulation. *Psychological Bulletin, 106,* 59–73.

Berkowitz, L., & Green, J. A. (1962). The stimulus qualities of the scapegoat. *Journal of Abnormal and Social Psychology, 64*(4), 293–301.

Bernstein, M., & Crosby, F. (1980). An empirical examination of relative deprivation theory. *Journal of Experimental Social Psychology, 16*(5), 442–456.

Bettencourt, B. A., Brewer, M. B., Croak, M. R., & Miller, N. (1991). Cooperation and the reduction of intergroup bias: The role of reward structure and social orientation. *Journal of Experimental Social Psychology, 28*(4), 301–319.

Biernat, M., & Crandall, C. S. (1999). Racial attitudes. In J. Robinson, P. Shaver, & L. Wrightsman (Eds.), *Measures of political attitudes* (pp. 297–411). New York: Academic Press.

Bigler, R. S. (1999a). Psychological interventions designed to counter sexism in children: Empirical limitations and theoretical foundations. In W. B. Swann, J. H. Langlois, & L. A. Gilbert (Eds.), *Sexism and stereotypes in modern society: The gender science of Janet Taylor Spence* (pp. 129–151). Washington, DC: American Psychological Association.

Bigler, R. S. (1999b). The use of multicultural curricula and materials to counter racism in children. *Journal of Social Issues, 55*(4), 687–705.

Bill, B., & Naus, P. (1992). The role of humor in the interpretation of sexist incidents. *Sex Roles, 27*(11/12), 645–664.

Billig, M. (1976). *Social psychology and intergroup relations.* London: Academic Press.

Billig, M., & Tajfel, H. (1973). Social categorization and similarity in intergroup behavior. *European Journal of Social Psychology, 3,* 27–52.

Bird, C. E. (1999). Gender, household labor, and psychological distress: The impact of the amount and division of housework. *Journal of Health and Social Behavior, 40,* 32–45.

Blaine, B., Crocker, J., & Major, B. (1995). The unintended negative consequences of sympathy for the stigmatized. *Journal of Applied Social Psychology, 25*(10), 889–905.

Blaine, B. E., DiBlasi, D. M., & Connor, J. M. (2002). The effect of weight loss on perceptions of weight controllability: Implications for prejudice against overweight people. *Journal of Applied Biobehavioral Research, 7,* 44–56.

Blair, I. V. (2002). The malleability of automatic stereotypes and prejudice. *Personality and Social Psychology Review, 6*(3), 242–261.

Blair, I., & Banaji, M. (1996). Automatic and controlled processes in stereotype priming. *Journal of Personality and Social Psychology, 70,* 1142–1163.

Blair, I. V., Judd, C. M., & Chapleau, K. M. (2004). The influence of afrocentric facial features in criminal sentencing. *Psychological Science, 15*(10), 674–679.

Blair, I. V., Park, B., & Bachelor, J. (2003). Understanding intergroup anxiety: Are some people more anxious than others? *Group Processes & Intergroup Relations, 6*(2), 151–169.

Blanchard, F., & Cook, S. (1976). Effect of helping a less competent member of a cooperating interracial group on the development of interpersonal attraction. *Journal of Personality and Social Psychology, 34,* 1245–1255.

Blanchard, F. A., & Crosby, F. J. (Eds.). (1989). *Affirmative action in perspective.* New York: Springer-Verlag.

Blanchard, F. A., Lilly, T., & Vaughn, L. A. (1991). Reducing the expression of racial prejudice. *Psychological Science, 2*(2), 101–105.

Blascovich, J., Mendes, W. B., Hunter, S. B., Lickel, B., & Kowai-Bell, N. (2001). Perceiver threat in social interactions with stigmatized others. *Journal of Personality and Social Psychology, 80*(2), 253–267.

Blascovich, J., Spencer, S. J., Quinn, D., & Steele, C. (2001). African Americans and high blood pressure: The role of stereotype threat. *Psychological Science, 12*(3), 225–229.

Bless, H., Bohner, G., Schwarz, N., & Strack, F. (1990). Mood and persuasion: A cognitive response analysis. *Personality and Social Psychology Bulletin, 16,* 331–345.

Bless, H., Hamilton, D. L., & Mackie, D. M. (1992). Mood effects on the organization of person information. *European Journal of Social Psychology, 22*(5), 497–509.

Bobo, L. (1983). Whites' opposition to busing: Symbolic racism or realistic group conflict? *Journal of Personality and Social Psychology, 45,* 1196–1210.

Bobo, L. (1988). Group conflict, prejudice, and the paradox of contemporary racial attitudes. In P. A. Katz & D. A. Taylor (Eds.), *Eliminating racism: Profiles in controversy* (pp. 85–114). New York: Plenum.

Bodenhausen, G. V. (1988). Stereotypic biases in social decision making and memory: Testing process models of stereotype use. *Journal of Personality and Social Psychology, 55,* 726–737.

Bodenhausen, G. V. (1990). Stereotypes as judgmental heuristics: Evidence of circadian variations in discrimination. *Psychological Science, 1*(5), 319–322.

Bodenhausen, G. V. (1993). Emotions, arousal and stereotypic judgments: A heuristic model of affect and stereotyping. In D. M. Mackie & D. L. Hamilton (Eds.), *Affect, cognition and stereotyping: Interactive processes in group perception* (pp. 13–37). New York: Academic Press.

Bodenhausen, G. V., Kramer, G. P., & Süsser, K. (1994). Happiness and stereotypic thinking in social judgment. *Journal of Personality and Social Psychology, 66*(4), 621–632.

Bodenhausen, G. V., & Lichtenstein, M. (1987). Social stereotypes and information processing strategies: The impact of task complexity. *Journal of Personality and Social Psychology, 52,* 871–880.

Bodenhausen, G. V., & Macrae, C. N. (1996). The self-regulation of intergroup perception: Mechanisms and consequences of stereotype suppression. In C. N. Macrae, M. Hewstone, & C. Stangor (Eds.), *Foundations of stereotypes and stereotyping.* New York: Guilford.

Bodenhausen, G. V., & Macrae, C. N. (1998). Stereotype activation and inhibition. In R. S. Wyer (Ed.), *Advances in social cognition* (Vol. 11, pp. 1–52). Mahwah, NJ: Erlbaum.

Bodenhausen, G. V., Schwarz, N., Bless, H., & Wanake, M. (1995). Effects of atypical exemplars on racial beliefs: Enlightened racism or generalized appraisals? *Journal of Experimental Social Psychology, 31,* 48–63.

Bodenhausen, G. V., Sheppard, L. A., & Kramer, G. P. (1994). Negative affect and social judgment: The differential impact of anger and sadness. *European Journal of Social Psychology, 24,* 45–62.

Bogartus, E. (1925). Measuring social distance. *Journal of Applied Sociology, 9,* 299–308.

Bogdan, R., & Biklen, D. (1993). Handicapism. In M. Nagler (Ed.), *Perspectives on disability* (2nd ed., pp. 69–76). Palo Alto, CA: Health Markets Research.

Bogdan, R., Biklen, D., Shapiro, A., & Spelkoman, D. (1990). The disabled: Media's monster. In M. Nagler (Ed.), *Perspectives on disability* (pp. 138–142). Palo Alto, CA: Health Markets Research.

Boldry, J. G., & Kashy, D. A. (1999). Intergroup perception in naturally occurring groups of differential status: A social relations perspective. *Journal of Personality and Social Psychology, 77*(6), 1200–1212.

Boone, D., Bayles, K., & Koopmann, C. (1982). Communicative aspects of aging. *Otolaryngologic Clinics of North America, 15*(2), 313–327.

Bornstein, R., & Pittman, T. (Eds.). (1992). *Perception without awareness.* New York: Guilford.

Bouchard, C. (1997). Genetics of human obesity: Recent results from linkage studies. *Journal of Nutrition, 127*(9), 1887–1890.

Bouman, W. P., & Arcelus, J. (2001). Are psychiatrists guilty of 'ageism' when it comes to taking a sexual history? *International Journal of Geriatric Psychiatry, 16,* 27–31.

Bower, G. H. (1981). Mood and memory. *American Psychologist, 36,* 129–148.

Bower, G. H., & Cohen, P. R. (1982). Emotional influences in memory and thinking: Data and theory. In M. S. Clark & S. T. Fiske (Eds.), *Affect and cognition.* Hillsdale, NJ: Erlbaum.

Bowman, M. (1984). *Why we burn: Sexism exorcised.* San Jose, CA: Hot Flash Press.

Brabeck, M. M., & Weisgerber, K. (1989). College students' perceptions of men and women choosing teaching and management: The effects of gender and sex role egalitarianism. *Sex Roles, 21,* 841–857.

Braithwaite, V., Gibson, D., & Holman, J. (1986). Age stereotyping: Are we oversimplifying the phenomenon? *International Journal of Aging and Human Development, 22*(4), 315–325.

Braithwaite, V., Lynd-Stevenson, R., & Pigram, D. (1993). An empirical study of ageism: From polemics to scientific utility. *Australian Psychologist, 28,* 9–15.

Branco, K. J., & Williamson, J. B. (1982). Stereotyping and the life cycle: Views of aging and the aged. In A. G. Miller (Ed.), *In the eye of the beholder: Contemporary issues in stereotyping* (pp. 364–410). New York: Praeger.

Branscombe, N. R., & Wann, D. L. (1994). Collective self-esteem consequences of outgroup derogation when a valued social identity is on trial. *European Journal of Social Psychology, 24,* 641–657.

Brant, C. R. (1999, June). *Judgments about sexism: A tendency to choose information that confirms a hypothesis.* Paper presented at the annual meeting of the American Psychological Society, Washington, DC.

Breckler, S. J. (1984). Empirical validation of affect, behavior and cognition as distinct components of attitude. *Journal of Personality and Social Psychology, 47,* 1191–1205.

Breckler, S. J., & Wiggins, E. C. (1989). On defining attitude and attitude theory: Once more with feeling. In A. R. Pratkanis, S. J. Breckler, & A. G. Greenwald (Eds.), *Attitude structure and function* (pp. 407–427). Hillsdale, NJ: Erlbaum.

Brewer, M. B. (1979). In-group bias in the minimal intergroup situation: A cognitive-motivational analysis. *Psychological Bulletin, 86,* 307–324.

Brewer, M. B. (1988). A dual-process model of impression formation. In T. K. Srull & R. S. Wyer (Eds.), *Advances in social cognition* (Vol. 1, pp. 1–36). Hillsdale, NJ: Erlbaum.

Brewer, M. B. (1991). The social self: On being the same and different at the same time. *Personality and Social Psychology Bulletin, 17,* 475–482.

Brewer, M. B. (1998). Intergroup relations. In D. T. Gilbert, S. T. Fiske, & G. Lindzey (Eds.), *Handbook of social psychology* (Vol. 2, 4th ed., pp. 554–594). New York: McGraw-Hill.

Brewer, M. B. (1999). The psychology of prejudice: Ingroup love, or outgroup hate? *Journal of Social Issues, 55*(3), 429–444.

Brewer, M. B., & Brown, R. J. (1998). Intergroup relations. In D. T. Gilbert, S. T. Fiske, & G. Lindzey (Eds.), *Handbook of social psychology* (Vol. 2, 4th ed., pp. 554–594). New York: McGraw-Hill.

Brewer, M. B., Dull, V., & Lui, L. (1981). Perceptions of the elderly: Stereotypes as prototypes. *Journal of Personality and Social Psychology, 41*(4), 656–670.

Brewer, M. B., & Kramer, R. M. (1985). The psychology of intergroup attitudes and behavior. *Annual Review of Psychology, 36,* 219–243.

Brewer, M. B., & Lui, L. (1984). Categorization of the elderly by the elderly: Effects of perceiver's category membership. *Personality and Social Psychology Bulletin, 10*(4), 585–595.

Brewer, M. B., Manzi, J. M., & Shaw, J. S. (1993). In-group identification as a function of depersonalization, distinctiveness, and status. *Psychological Science, 4*(2), 88–92.

Brewer, M. B., & Miller, N. (1996). *Intergroup relations.* Pacific Grove, CA: Brooks/Cole.

Briere, J., & Lanktree, C. (1983). Sex-role related effects of bias in language. *Sex Roles, 9,* 625–632.

Brigham, J. C. (1971). Ethnic stereotypes. *Psychological Bulletin, 76,* 15–38.

Britt, T. W., & Crandall, C. S. (2000). Acceptance of feedback by the stigmatized and non-stigmatized: The mediating role of the motive of the evaluator. *Group Processes and Intergroup Relations, 3,* 79–95.

Brooks, V. R. (1981). *Minority stress and lesbian women.* Lexington, MA: D.C. Heath.

Brophy, I. N. (1946). The luxury of anti-Negro prejudice. *Public Opinion Quarterly, 9,* 456–466.

Broverman, I. K., Bloom, L. M., Gunn, S. P., & Torok, T. (1974). Attitude measurement via the bogus pipeline: A dry well? *Representative Research in Social Psychology, 5,* 97–114.

Broverman, I., Vogel, S. R., Broverman, D. M., Clarkson, F. E., & Rosenkrantz, P. S. (1972). Sex role stereotypes: A current appraisal. *Journal of Social Issues, 28*(2), 59–78.

Brown, R. (1965). *Social psychology.* New York: Free Press.

Brown, R. (1995). *Prejudice: Its social psychology.* Cambridge, MA: Blackwell.

Brown, R. P., Charnsangavej, T., Keough, K. A., Newman, M. L., & Rentfrow, P. J. (2000). Putting the "affirm" into affirmative action: Preferential selection and academic performance. *Journal of Personality and Social Psychology, 79*(5), 736–747.

Brown, R. P., & Pinel, E. C. (2003). Stigma on my mind: Individual differences in the experience of stereotype threat. *Journal of Experimental Social Psychology, 39,* 626–633.

Bruner, J. S. (1958). Social psychology and perception. In E. E. Maccoby, T. M. Newcomb, & E. L. Hartley (Eds.), *Readings in social psychology* (3rd ed., pp. 85–94). New York: Holt, Rinehart & Winston.

Bryant, J., Brown, D., Parks, S. L., & Zillman, D. (1983). Children's imitation of a ridiculed model. *Human Communication Research, 10*(2), 243–255.

Buhrich, N., Bailey, J. M., & Martin, N. G. (1991). Sexual orientation, sexual identity, and sex-dimorphic behaviors in male twins. *Behavior Genetics, 21,* 75–96.

Bunzel, J. (1972). Note on the history of a concept—Gerontophobia. *The Gerontologist, 12,* 116–203.

Burn, S. M. (1996). *The social psychology of gender.* New York: McGraw-Hill.

Burt, M. R. (1980). Cultural myths and support for rape. *Journal of Personality and Social Psychology, 38*(2), 217–230.

Business and Professional Women's Foundation (1995). A glass ceiling limits women's roles at work. In J. S. Petrikin (Ed.), *Male/female roles: Opposing viewpoints* (pp. 85–91). San Diego, CA: Greenhaven Press.

Buss, D. M. (1995). Evolutionary psychology: A new paradigm for psychological science. *Psychological Inquiry, 6,* 1–30.

Buss, D. M. (1996). The evolutionary psychology of human social strategies. In E. T. Higgins & A. Kruglanski (Eds.), *Social psychology: A handbook of principles* (pp. 3–38). New York: Guilford.

Butler, R. (1969). Age-ism: Another form of bigotry. *The Gerontologist, 9,* 243–246.

Butler, R. (1980). Ageism: A foreword. *Journal of Social Issues, 36(2),* 8–11.

Butler, R., Lewis, M., & Sunderland, T. (1991). *Aging and mental health: Positive psychosocial and biomedical approaches.* New York: Macmillan.

Byne, W., & Parsons, B. (1993). Human sexual orientation. The biologic theories reappraised. *Archives of General Psychiatry, 50*(3), 228–239.

Bytheway, B. (1995). *Ageism.* Philadelphia: Open University Press.

Cacioppo, J. T., Berntson, G. G., Adolphs, R., Carter, C. S., Davidson, R. J., McClintock, M. K. et al. (Eds.). (2002). *Foundations in social neuroscience.* Cambridge, MA: MIT Press.

Cacioppo, J. T., & Petty, R. E. (1982). The need for cognition. *Journal of Personality and Social Psychology, 42,* 116–131.

Cacioppo, J. T., Petty, R. E., Feinstein, J. A., & Jarvis, W. B. G. (1996). Dispositional differences in cognitive motivation:

The life and times of individuals varying in the need for cognition. *Psychological Bulletin, 119*(2), 197–253.

Cacioppo, J. T., & Tassinary, L. G. (Eds.). (1990). *Principles of psychophysiology: Physical, social, and inferential elements.* Cambridge: Cambridge University Press.

Campbell, D. T. (1965). Ethnocentric and other altruistic motives. In D. Levine (Ed.), *Nebraska symposium on motivation.* Lincoln: University of Nebraska Press.

Cann, A., & Haight, J. M. (1983). Children's perceptions of relative competence in sex-typed occupations. *Sex Roles, 9*(7), 767–773.

Cann, A., & Siegfried, W. D. (1990). Gender stereotypes and dimensions of effective leader behavior. *Sex Roles, 23,* 413–419.

Caporael, L. (1981). The paralanguage of caregiving: Baby talk to the institutionalized aged. *Journal of Personality and Social Psychology, 40,* 876–884.

Caporael, L. R., & Brewer, M. B. (1995). Hierarchical evolutionary theory: There *Is* an alternative, and it's not creationism. *Psychological Inquiry, 6,* 31–34.

Caporael, L., & Culbertson, G. (1986). Verbal response modes of baby talk and other speech at institutions for the aged. *Language and Communication, 6,* 99–112.

Caporael, L., Lukaszewski, M., & Culbertson, G. (1983). Secondary baby talk: Judgments by institutionalized elderly and their caregivers. *Journal of Personality and Social Psychology, 44,* 746–754.

Carroll, J. B. (Ed.). (1956). *Language, thought, and reality: Selected writings of Benjamin Lee Whorf.* Cambridge, MA: MIT Press.

Carter, J. D., Hall, J. A., Carney, D. R., & Rosip, J. C. (2004). *Individual differences in the acceptance of stereotyping.* Unpublished manuscript.

Carver, C. S., & de la Garza, N. H. (1984). Schema-guided information search in stereotyping of the elderly. *Journal of Applied Social Psychology, 14,* 69–81.

Carver, C. S., Glass, D. C., & Katz, I. (1978). Favorable evaluations of Blacks and the handicapped: Positive prejudice, unconscious denial, or social responsibility? *Journal of Applied Social Psychology, 8*(2), 97–106.

Carver, C. S., Glass, D. C., Snyder, M. L., & Katz, I. (1977). Favorable evaluations of stigmatized others. *Personality and Social Psychology Bulletin, 3,* 232–235.

Carver, C. S., & Scheier, M. F. (1981). *Attention and self-regulation: A control-theory approach to human behavior.* New York: Springer-Verlag.

Catalyst. (1990). *Catalyst's study of women in corporate management.* New York: Catalyst.

Center for Media Education. (1997). Children and television: Frequently asked questions. (Brochure retrieved 2/9/05, from www.cme.org/children/kids_tv/c_and_t.html.

Cejka, M. A., & Eagly, A. H. (1999). Gender-stereotypic images of occupations correspond to the sex segregation of employment. *Personality and Social Psychology Bulletin, 25*(4), 413–423.

Chaiken, S., Giner-Sorolla, R., & Chen, S. (1996). Beyond accuracy: Defense and impression motives in heuristic and systematic information processing. In P. M. Gollwitzer & J. A. Bargh (Eds.), *The psychology of action: Linking cognition and motivation to behavior* (pp. 553–578). New York: Guilford.

Chasteen, A. L., Schwarz, N., & Park, D. C. (2002). The activation of aging stereotypes in younger and older adults. *Journal of Gerontology: Psychological Sciences, 57B*(6), 540–547.

Chen, M., & Bargh, J. A. (1997). Nonconscious behavioral confirmation processes: The self-fulfilling consequences of automatic stereotype activation. *Journal of Experimental Social Psychology, 33,* 541–560.

Cherry, F., Byrne, D. E., & Mitchell, H. E. (1976). Clogs in the bogus pipeline: Demand characteristics and social desirability. *Journal of Research in Personality, 10,* 69–75.

Cheryan, S., & Bodenhausen, G. V. (2000). When positive stereotypes threaten intellectual performance: The psychological hazards of "model minority" status. *Psychological Science, 11*(5), 399–402.

Chideya, F. (1995). *Don't believe the hype: Fighting cultural misinformation about African-Americans.* New York: Penguin.

Chin, M. G. (1995). An evaluation of social identity theory: Relating ingroup bias, transitory self-esteem, and mood state. *Dissertation Abstracts International, 55,* 10B. (University Microfilms No. AAM9507767)

Chiu, C., Hong, Y., Lam, I. C., Fu, J. H., Tong, J. Y., & Lee, V. S. (1998). Stereotyping and self-presentation: Effects of gender stereotype activation. *Group Processes and Intergroup Relations, 1,* 81–96.

Cjeka, M. A., & Eagly, A. H. (1999). Gender-stereotypic images of occupations correspond to the sex segregation of employment. *Personality and Social Psychology Bulletin, 25*(4), 413–423.

Clark, K. B. (1963). *Prejudice and your child.* Boston, MA: Beacon Press.

Clark, M. S., Milberg, S., & Erber, R. (1988). Arousal-state-dependent memory: Evidence and implications for understanding social judgments and social behavior. In K. Fiedler & J. P. Forgas (Eds.), *Affect, cognition and social behavior* (pp. 63–83). Toronto, Ontario, Canada: Hogrefe.

Clore, G. L., Schwarz, N., & Conway, M. (1994). Affective causes and consequences of social information processing. In R. S. Wyer Jr. & T. K. Srull (Eds.), *Handbook of social cognition: Basic processes* (Vol. 1, pp. 323–417). Hillsdale, NJ: Erlbaum.

Coates, J. (1986). *Women, men, and language.* New York: Longman.

Cohen, E. (1980). Design and redesign of the desegregated school: Problems of status, power, and conflict. In W. G. Stephan & J. Feagin (Eds.), *School desegregation* (pp. 251–280). New York: Plenum.

Collins, A. M., & Loftus, E. F. (1975). A spreading-activation theory of semantic processing. *Psychological Review, 82,* 407–428.

Collins, A., & Quillian, M. (1969). Retrieval time from semantic memory. *Journal of Verbal Learning and Verbal Behavior, 8,* 240–247.

Conrey, F. R., Sherman, J. W., Gawronski, B., Hugenberg, K., & Groom, C. J. (2004). *Separating multiple processes in implicit social cognition: The Quad model of implicit task performance.* Unpublished manuscript.

Cook, F. (1992). Ageism: Rhetoric and reality. *The Gerontologist, 32*(3), 292–293.

Cook, S. W. (1962). The systematic analysis of socially significant events: A strategy for social research. *Journal of Social Issues, 18*(2), 257–263.

Cook, S. W. (1969). Motives in a conceptual analysis of attitude-related behavior. *Nebraska symposium on motivation* (Vol. 17, pp. 179–231). Lincoln: University of Nebraska Press.

Cook, S. W. (1985). Experimenting on social issues: The case of school desegregation. *American Psychologist, 40*(4), 452–460.

Cook, T. D., & Flay, B. R. (1978). The persistence of experimentally induced attitude change. In L. Berkowitz (Ed.), *Advances in experimental social psychology* (Vol. 11, pp. 2–57). New York: Academic Press.

Cooley, C. (1902). *Human nature and the social order.* New York: Scribners.

Corenblum, B. (2003). What children remember about ingroup and outgroup peers: Effects of stereotypes on children's processing of information about group members. *Journal of Experimental Child Psychology, 86,* 32–66.

Corenblum, B., Annis, R. C., & Young, S. (1996). Effects of own group success or failure on judgments of task performance by children of different ethnicities. *European Journal of Social Psychology, 26*(5), 777–798.

Cose, E. (1993). *The rage of a privileged class.* New York: HarperCollins.

Cota, A. A., & Dion, K. L. (1986). Salience of gender and sex comparison of ad hoc groups: An experimental test of distinctiveness theory. *Journal of Personality and Social Psychology, 37,* 131–146.

Cottrell, W., & Atchley, R. (1969). Women in retirement: A preliminary report. Oxford, OH: Scripps Foundation.

Coupland, N., & Coupland, J. (1993). Discourses of ageism and anti-ageism. *Journal of Aging Studies, 7*(3), 279–301.

Coupland, N., Coupland, J., Giles, H., Henwood, K., & Weimann, J. (1988). Elderly self-disclosure: Interactional and intergroup issues. *Language and Communication, 8*(2), 109–133.

Courtney, A. E., & Whipple, T. W. (1983). *Sex stereotyping in advertising.* Lexington, Mass: D.C. Heath.

Crandall, C. S. (1991). Do heavy-weight students have more difficulty paying for college? *Personality and Social Psychology Bulletin, 17*(6), 606–611.

Crandall, C. S. (1994). Prejudice against fat people: Ideology and self-interest. *Journal of Personality and Social Psychology, 66*(5), 882–894.

Crandall, C. S. (1995). Do parents discriminate against their heavyweight daughters? *Personality and Social Psychology Bulletin, 21*(7), 724–735.

Crandall, C. S. (2000). Ideology and lay theories of stigma: The justification of stigmatization. In T. F. Heatherton, R. E. Kleck, M. R. Hebl, & J. G. Hull (Eds.), *The social psychology of stigma* (pp. 126–150). New York: Guilford.

Crandall, C. S., & Biernat, M. (1990). The ideology of anti-fat attitudes. *Journal of Applied Social Psychology, 20*(3), 227–243.

Crandall, C. S., D'Anello, S., Sakalli, N., Lazarus, E., Wieczorkowska, G., & Feather, N. T. (2001). An attribution-value model of prejudice: Anti-fat attitudes in six nations. *Personality and Social Psychology Bulletin, 27,* 30–37.

Crandall, C. S., & Eshleman, A. (2003). A justification–suppression model of the expression and experience of prejudice. *Psychological Bulletin, 129*(3), 414–446.

Crandall, C. S., & Martinez, R. (1996). Culture, ideology, and antifat attitudes. *Personality and Social Psychology Bulletin, 22*(11), 1165–1176.

Crawford, M. T., & Skowronski, J. J. (1998). When motivated thoughts lead to heightened bias: High need for cognition can enhance the impact of stereotypes on memory. *Personality and Social Psychology Bulletin, 24*(10), 1075–1088.

Crocker, J., Cornwell, B., & Major, B. (1993). The stigma of overweight: Affective consequences of attributional ambiguity. *Journal of Personality and Social Psychology, 64,* 60–70.

Crocker, J., & Major, B. (1989). Social stigma and self-esteem: The self-protective properties of stigma. *Psychological Review, 96,* 608–630.

Crocker, J., & Major, B. (1994). Reactions to stigma: The moderating role of justifications. In M. P. Zanna & J. M. Olson (Eds.), *The psychology of prejudice: The Ontario symposium* (Vol. 7, pp. 289–314). Hillsdale, NJ: Erlbaum.

Crocker, J., Major, B., & Steele, C. (1998). Social stigma. In D. T. Gilbert, S. T. Fiske, & G. Lindzey (Eds.), *Handbook of social psychology* (Vol. 2, 4th ed., pp. 504–553). New York: McGraw-Hill.

Crocker, J., & Quinn, D. M. (2000). Social stigma and the self: Meanings, situations, and self-esteem. In T. F. Heatherton, R. E. Kleck, M. R. Hebl, & J. G. Hull (Eds.), *The social psychology of stigma* (pp. 153–183). New York: Guilford.

Crocker, J., Voelkl, K., Testa, M., & Major, B. (1991). Social stigma: The affective consequences of attributional ambiguity. *Journal of Personality and Social Psychology, 60*(2), 218–228.

Crockett, W. H., & Hummert, M. L. (1987). Perceptions of aging and the elderly. In K. Schaie & C. Eisdorfer (Eds.), *Annual review of gerontology and geriatrics* (Vol. 7, pp. 217–241). New York: Springer-Verlag.

Croizet, J., & Claire, T. (1998). Extending the concept of stereotype threat to social class: The intellectual underperformance of students from low socioeconomic backgrounds. *Personality and Social Psychology Bulletin, 24*(6), 588–594.

Crosby, F. (1976). A model of egoistical relative deprivation. *Psychological Review, 83*(2), 85–113.

Crosby, F. (1984). The denial of personal discrimination. *American Behavioral Scientist, 27*(3), 371–386.

Crosby, F. J. (1991). *Juggling: The unexpected advantages of balancing a career and home for women and their families.* New York: Free Press.

Crosby, F., Bromley, S., & Saxe, L. (1980). Recent unobtrusive studies of black and white discrimination and prejudice: A literature review. *Psychological Bulletin, 87,* 546–563.

Crosby, F. J., Iyer, A., Clayton, S., & Downing, R. A. (2003). Affirmative action: Psychological data and the policy debates. *American Psychologist, 58*(2), 93–115.

Crosby, F. J., & Jaskar, K. L. (1993). Women and men at home and at work: Realities and illusions. In S. Oskamp & M. Costanzo (Eds.), *Gender issues in contemporary society* (pp. 143–171). Newbury Park, CA: Sage.

Cross, W. E., & Strauss, L. (1998). The everyday functions of African American identity. In J. K. Swim & C. Stangor

(Eds.), *Prejudice: The target's perspective* (pp. 267–279). New York: Academic Press.

Cuddy, A. J. C., & Fiske, S. T. (2002). Doddering but dear: Process, content, and function in stereotyping older adults. In T. D. Nelson (Ed.), *Ageism: Stereotyping and prejudice against older persons* (pp. 3–26). Cambridge, MA: MIT Press.

Cuddy, A. J. C., Fiske, S. T., & Glick, P. (in press). When professionals become mothers, warmth doesn't cut the ice. *Journal of Social Issues.*

Cullen, J. M., Wright, L. W., & Alessandri, M. (2002). The personality variable: Openness to experience as it relates to homophobia. *Journal of Homosexuality, 42*(4), 119–134.

Cunningham, W. A., Johnson, M. K., & Raye, C. L. (2004). Separable neural components in the processing of black and white faces. *Psychological Science, 15*(12), 806–813.

Cunningham, W. A., Nezlek, J. B., & Banaji, M. R. (2004). Implicit and explicit ethnocentrism: Revisiting the ideologies of prejudice. *Personality and Social Psychology Bulletin, 30*(10), 1332–1346.

Cunningham, W. A., Preacher, K. J., & Banaji, M. R. (2001). Implicit attitude measures: Consistency, stability, and convergent validity. *Psychological Science, 12*(2), 163–170.

Czaja, S. J., & Sharit, J. (1998). Ability-performance relationships as a function of age and task experience for a data entry task. *Journal of Experimental Psychology: Applied, 4*(4), 332–351.

Czopp, A. M., & Monteith, M. J. (2003). Confronting prejudice (literally): Reactions to confrontations of racial and gender bias. *Personality and Social Psychology Bulletin, 29*(4), 532–544.

Darley, J. M., & Fazio, R. H. (1980). Expectancy confirmation processes arising in the social interaction sequence. *American Psychologist, 35,* 867–881.

Darwin, C. (1859). *On the origin of the species by means of natural selection, or preservation of favoured races in the struggle for life.* London: Murray.

Dasgupta, N. (2004). Implicit ingroup favoritism, outgroup favoritism, and their behavioral manifestations. *Social Justice Research, 17*(2), 143–169.

Dasgupta, N., & Asgari, S. (in press). Seeing is believing: Exposure to counterstereotypic women leaders and its effect on the malleability of automatic gender stereotyping. *Journal of Experimental Social Psychology.*

Davis, J. A. (1959). A formal interpretation of the theory of relative deprivation. *Sociometry, 22,* 280–296.

Davis, J., & Smith, T. (1990). *General social surveys, 1972–1990.* Chicago, IL: National Opinion Research Center.

Deaux, K. (1996). Social identification. In E. T. Higgins & A. Kruglanski (Eds.), *Social psychology: Handbook of principles* (pp. 777–798). New York: Guilford.

Deaux, K., & Kite, M. (1993). Gender stereotypes. In F. Denmark & M. Paludi (Eds.), *Psychology of women: A handbook of issues and theories* (pp. 107–139). Westport, CT: Greenwood Press.

Deaux, K., & LaFrance, M. (1998). Gender. In D. T. Gilbert, S. T. Fiske, & G. Lindzey (Eds.), *Handbook of social psychology* (Vol. 1, 4th ed., pp. 788–827). New York: McGraw-Hill.

Deaux, K., & Lewis, L. L. (1984). Structure of gender stereotypes: Interrelationships among components and gender

label. *Journal of Personality and Social Psychology, 46*(5), 991–1004.

de Dreu, C. K. W., Koole, S. L., & Oldersma, F. L. (1999). On the seizing and freezing of negotiator inferences: Need for cognitive closure moderates the use of heuristics in negotiation. *Personality and Social Psychology Bulletin, 25*(3), 348–362.

Deiner, E., & Srull, T. K. (1979). Self-awareness, psychological perspective, and self-reinforcement in relation to personal and social standards. *Journal of Personality and Social Psychology, 37,* 413–423.

Deiner, E., & Wallbom, M. (1976). Effects of self-awareness on antinormative behavior. *Journal of Research in Personality, 10,* 107–111.

D'Emilio, J. (1983). *Sexual politics, sexual communities: The making of a homosexual minority in the United States, 1940–1970.* Chicago: University of Chicago Press.

Descartes, R. (1637; reprinted 1972). *Treatise of man.* (T. S. Hall, trans.) Cambridge, MA: Harvard University Press.

Desforges, D. M., Lord, C. G., Ramsey, S. L., Mason, J. A., Van Leeuwen, M. D., West, S. C., & Lepper, M. R. (1991). Effects of structured cooperative contact on changing negative attitudes towards stigmatized groups. *Journal of Personality and Social Psychology, 60,* 531–544.

Deutsch, M. (1949). An experimental study of the effects of cooperation and competition upon group process. *Human Relations, 2,* 199–232.

Deutsch, M., & Collins, M. E. (1951). *Interracial housing: A psychological evaluation of a social experiment.* Minneapolis: University of Minnesota Press.

Deutsch, M., & Gerard, H. B. (1955). A study of normative and informational social influences upon individual judgment. *Journal of Abnormal and Social Psychology, 51,* 629–636.

Devine, P. G. (1989). Stereotypes and prejudice: Their automatic and controlled components. *Journal of Personality and Social Psychology, 56,* 5–18.

Devine, P. G. (1995). Prejudice and out-group perception. In A. Tesser (Ed.), *Advanced social psychology* (pp. 467–524). New York: McGraw-Hill.

Devine, P. G., & Elliot, A. J. (1995). Are racial stereotypes really fading? The Princeton trilogy revisited. *Personality and Social Psychology Bulletin, 21*(11), 1139–1150.

Devine, P. G., Evett, S. R., & Vasquez-Suson, K. A. (1996). Exploring the interpersonal dynamics of intergroup contact. In R. M. Sorrentino & E. T. Higgins (Eds.), *Handbook of motivation and cognition: The interpersonal context* (Vol. 3, pp. 423–464). New York: Guilford.

Devine, P. G., & Monteith, M. J. (1993). The role of discrepancy-associated affect in prejudice reduction. In D. M. Mackie, & D. L. Hamilton (Eds.), *Affect, cognition, and stereotyping: Interactive processes in group perception* (pp. 317–344). New York: Academic Press.

Devine, P. G., & Monteith, M. J. (1999). Automaticity and control in stereotyping. In S. Chaiken & Y. Trope (Eds.), *Dual-process theories in social psychology* (pp. 339–360). New York: Guilford.

Devine, P. G., Monteith, M. J., Zuwerink, J. R., & Elliot, A. (1991). Prejudice with and without compunction. *Journal of Personality and Social Psychology, 60*(6), 817–830.

Devine, P. G., Plant, E. A., Amodio, D. M., Harmon-Jones, E., & Vance, S. L. (2002). The regulation of explicit and implicit race bias: The role of motivations to respond without prejudice. *Journal of Personality and Social Psychology, 82*(5), 835–848.

Dickson, T. (1994, August). *How JMC education rates in its efforts to sensitize students to ableism issues.* Paper presented at the annual meeting of the Association for Education in Journalism and Mass Communication, Atlanta, GA.

Dijker, A. J. M. (1987). Emotional reactions to ethnic minorities. *European Journal of Social Psychology, 17,* 305–325.

Dijker, A. J. M., & Frijda, N. H. (1988). *Towards a model of stereotype-based emotions.* Paper presented at the annual meeting of the American Psychological Association, Atlanta, GA.

Dijksterhuis, A., & Knippenberg, A. (1996). The knife that cuts both ways: Facilitated and inhibited access to traits as a result of stereotype activation. *Journal of Experimental Social Psychology, 32,* 271–288.

Dijksterhuis, A., Knippenberg, A., Kruglanski. A. W., & Schaper, C. (1996). Motivated social cognition: Need for closure effects on memory and judgment. *Journal of Experimental Social Psychology, 32,* 254–270.

Dion, K. L., & Earn, B. M. (1975). The phenomenology of being a target of prejudice. *Journal of Personality and Social Psychology, 32*(5), 944–950.

Dixon, T. L., & Maddox, K. B. (in press). Skin tone, crime news, and social reality judgments: Priming the schema of the dark and dangerous Black criminal. *Journal of Applied Social Psychology.*

Dollard, J., Miller, N. E., Doob, L. W., Mowrer, O. H., & Sears, R. R. (1939). *Frustration and aggression.* New Haven, CT: Yale University Press.

Doosje, B., & Ellemers, N. (1997). Stereotyping under threat: The role of group identification. In R. Spears, P. J. Oakes, N. Ellemers, & S. A. Haslam (Eds.), *The social psychology of stereotyping and group life* (pp. 257–272). Cambridge, MA: Blackwell.

Dovidio, J. F., Brigham, J. C., Johnson, B. T., & Gaertner, S. L. (1996). Stereotyping, prejudice, and discrimination: Another look. In C. N. Macrae, C. Stangor, & M. Hewstone (Eds.), *Stereotypes and stereotyping* (pp. 276–319). New York: Guilford.

Dovidio, J. F., Evans, N., & Tyler, R. B. (1986). Racial stereotypes: The contents of their cognitive representations. *Journal of Experimental Social Psychology, 22,* 22–37.

Dovidio, J. F., & Fazio, R. H. (1992). New technologies for the direct and indirect assessment of attitudes. In J. Tanur (Ed.), *Questions about questions: Inquiries into the cognitive bases of surveys* (pp. 204–237). New York: Sage.

Dovidio, J. F., & Gaertner, S. L. (1983). Race, normative structure, and help seeking. In B. M. Depaulo, A. Nadler, & J. Fisher (Eds.), *New directions in helping* (Vol. 2, pp. 285–303). New York: Academic Press.

Dovidio, J. F., & Gaertner, S. L. (1986). Prejudice, discrimination, and racism: Historical trends and contemporary approaches. In J. Dovidio & S. Gaertner (Eds.), *Prejudice, discrimination, and racism* (pp. 1–34). New York: Academic Press.

Dovidio, J. F., & Gaertner, S. L. (1991). Changes in the expression of racial prejudice. In H. Knopke, J. Norrell, & R. Rogers (Eds.), *Opening doors: An appraisal of race relations in contemporary America* (pp. 201–241). Tuscaloosa: University of Alabama Press.

Dovidio, J. F., & Gaertner, S. L. (1993). Stereotypes and evaluative intergroup bias. In D. M. Mackie & D. L. Hamilton (Eds.), *Affect, cognition, and stereotyping: Interactive processes in group perception* (pp. 167–194). New York: Academic Press.

Dovidio, J. F., & Gaertner, S. L. (1996). Affirmative action, unintentional racial biases, and intergroup relations. *Journal of Social Issues, 52*(4), 51–75.

Dovidio, J. F., & Gaertner, S. L. (1999). Reducing prejudice: Combating intergroup biases. *Current Directions in Psychological Science, 8*(4), 101–105.

Dovidio, J. F., & Gaertner, S. L. (2000). Aversive racism and selection decisions: 1989 and 1999. *Psychological Science, 11*(4), 315–319.

Dovidio, J. F., Gaertner, S. L., Isen, A. M., & Lowrance, R. (1995). Group representations and intergroup bias: Positive affect, similarity, and group size. *Personality and Social Psychology Bulletin, 21*(8), 856–865.

Dovidio, J. F., Kawakami, K., Johnson, C., Johnson, B., & Howard, A. (1997). On the nature of prejudice: Automatic and controlled processes. *Journal of Experimental Social Psychology, 33,* 510–540.

Dovidio, J. F., Vergert, M. T., Stewart, T. L., Gaertner, S. L., Johnson, J. D., Esses, V. M., Riek, B. M., & Pearson, A. R. (2004). Perspective and prejudice: Antecedents and mediating mechanisms. *Personality and Social Psychology Bulletin, 30*(12), 1537–1549.

Downs, A. C., & Harrison, S. K. (1985). Embarrassing age spots or just plain ugly? Physical attractiveness stereotyping as an instrument of sexism on American television commercials. *Sex Roles, 13*(1/2), 9–19.

Duckitt, J. H. (1990). *A social psychological investigation of racial prejudice among white South Africans.* Unpublished doctoral dissertation, University of Witwatersrand, Johannesburg, South Africa.

Duckitt, J. (1992). Psychology and prejudice: A historical analysis and integrative framework. *American Psychologist, 47*(10), 1182–1193.

Duckitt, J., Wagner, C., du Plessis, I, & Birum, I. (2002). The psychological bases of ideology and prejudice: Testing a dual process model. *Journal of Personality and Social Psychology, 83,* 75–93.

Dunn, E. W., & Spellman, B. A. (2003). Forgetting by remembering: Stereotype inhibition through rehearsal of alternative aspects of identity. *Journal of Experimental Social Psychology, 39*(5), 420–433.

Dunton, B. C., & Fazio, R. H. (1997). An individual difference measure of motivation to control prejudiced reactions. *Personality and Social Psychology Bulletin, 23*(3), 316–326.

Dutton, D. G., & Lake, R. A. (1973). Threat of own prejudice and reverse discrimination in interracial situations. *Journal of Personality and Social Psychology, 28,* 94–100.

Dutton, D. G., & Lennox, V. L. (1974). Effect of prior "token" compliance on subsequent interracial behavior. *Journal of Personality and Social Psychology, 29,* 65–71.

Duval, S., & Wicklund, R. A. (1972). *A theory of objective self-awareness.* San Diego, CA: Academic Press.

Dye, C. (1978). Psychologists' role in the provision of mental health care for the elderly. *Professional Psychology, 9,* 38–49.

Eagly, A. H. (1987). *Sex differences in social behavior: A social-role interpretation.* Hillsdale, NJ: Erlbaum.

Eagly, A. H., & Chaiken, S. (1993). *The psychology of attitudes.* New York: Harcourt Brace Jovanovich.

Eagly, A. H., & Chaiken, S. (1998). Attitude structure and function. In. D. T. Gilbert, S. T. Fiske, & G. Lindzey (Eds.), *The handbook of social psychology* (Vol. 1, 4th ed., pp. 269–322). New York: McGraw-Hill.

Eagly, A. H., & Diekman, A. B. (2005). What is the problem? Prejudice as an attitude-in-context. In J. F. Dovidio, P. Glick, & L. Rudman (Eds.), *Reflecting on the nature of prejudice: Fifty years after Allport.* Malden, MA: Blackwell.

Eagly, A. H., & Johnson, B. T. (1990). Gender and leadership style: A meta-analysis. *Psychological Bulletin, 108,* 233–256.

Eagly, A. H., & Karau, S. J. (2002). Role congruity theory of prejudice toward female leaders. *Psychological Review, 109*(3), 573–598.

Eagly, A. H., & Mladinic, A. (1989). Gender stereotypes and attitudes toward women and men. *Personality and Social Psychology Bulletin, 15*(4), 543–558.

Eagly, A. H., & Mladinic, A. (1994). Are people prejudiced against women? Some answers from research on attitudes, gender stereotypes, and judgments of competence. In W. Strobe & M. Hewstone (Eds.), *European review of social psychology* (Vol. 5, pp. 1–35). New York: Wiley.

Eagly, A. H., & Steffen, V. J. (1986). Gender and aggressive behavior: A meta-analytic review of the social psychological literature. *Psychological Bulletin, 100*(3), 309–330.

Eagly, A. H., & Wood, W. (1991). Explaining sex differences in social behavior: A meta-analytic perspective. *Personality and Social Psychological Bulletin, 17*(3), 306–315.

Eagly, A. H., & Wood, W. (1999). The origins of sex differences in human behavior. *American Psychologist, 54*(6), 408–423.

Eberhardt, J. L., & Fiske, S. T. (1996). Motivating individuals to change: What is a target to do? In C. N. Macrae, C. Stangor, & M. Hewstone (Eds.), *Stereotypes and stereotyping* (pp. 369–415). New York: Guilford.

Eccles, J. S., Jacobs, J. E., Harold, R. D., Yoon, K. S., Arbreton, A., & Freedman-Doan, C. (1993). Parents and gender-role socialization during the middle childhood and adolescent years. In S. Oskamp & M. Costanzo (Eds.), *Gender issues in contemporary society* (pp. 59–83). Newbury Park, CA: Sage.

Echwald, S. M. (1999). Genetics of human obesity: Lessons from mouse models and candidate genes. *Journal of Internal Medicine, 245*(6), 653–666.

Eckman, P., & Friesen, W. V. (1982). Felt, false, and miserable smiles. *Journal of Nonverbal Behavior, 6*(4), 238–258.

Edelbrock, C., & Sugawara, A. I. (1978). Acquisition of sex-typed preferences in preschool aged children. *Developmental Psychology, 14,* 614–623.

Edwards, K., & Wetzler, J. (1998). *Too young to be old: The roles of self threat and psychological distancing in social categorization of the elderly.* Unpublished manuscript.

Ehrlich, H. D., & Rinehart, J. W. (1965). A brief report on the methodology of stereotype research. *Social Forces, 43*(4), 564–575.

Eidelson, R. J., & Eidelson, J. I. (2003). Dangerous ideas: Five beliefs that propel groups toward conflict. *American Psychologist, 58*(3), 182–192.

Eller, A., & Abrams, D. (2004). Come together: Longitudinal comparisons of Pettigrew's reformulated intergroup contact model and the common ingroup identity model in Anglo-french and Mexican-American contexts. *European Journal of Social Psychology, 34,* 229–256.

Elliott, J. (1970). *The eye of the storm.* [Videotape.] Mount Kisco, NY: Center for the Humanities.

Ellis, H. C., & Ashbrook, P. W. (1988). Resource allocation model of the effects of depressed mood states on memory. In K. Kiedler & J. Forgas (Eds.), *Affect cognition, and social behavior* (pp. 25–43). Toronto, Ontario, Canada: Hogrefe.

Elms, A. C. (1975). The crisis of confidence in social psychology. *American Psychologist, 30*(10), 967–976.

Ensari, N., & Miller, N. (2002). The out-group must not be so bad after all: The effects of disclosure, typicality, and salience on intergroup bias. *Journal of Personality and Social Psychology, 83*(2), 313–329.

Epstein, S. (1972). The nature of anxiety with emphasis upon its relationship to expectancy. In C. D. Spielberger (Ed.), *Anxiety: Current trends in theory and research* (Vol. 2). New York: Academic Press.

Esses, V. M., Haddock, G., & Zanna, M. P. (1993). Values, stereotypes, and emotions as determinants of intergroup attitudes. In D. M. Mackie & D. L. Hamilton (Eds.), *Affect, cognition, and stereotyping: Interactive processes in group perception* (pp. 137–166). New York: Academic Press.

Esses, V. M., Haddock, G., & Zanna, M. P. (1994). The role of mood in the expression of intergroup stereotypes. In M. P. Zanna & J. M. Olson (Eds.), *The psychology of prejudice: The Ontario symposium* (Vol. 7, pp. 77–101). Hillsdale, NJ: Erlbaum.

Esses, V. M., & Zanna, M. P. (1995). Mood and the expression of ethnic stereotypes. *Journal of Personality and Social Psychology, 69*(6), 1052–1068.

Evans, R. I. (1952). Personal values as factors in anti-Semitism. *Journal of Abnormal and Social Psychology, 47,* 749–756.

Evans, R. I., Hansen, W. B., & Mittelmark, M. B. (1977). Increasing the validity of self-reports of smoking behavior in children. *Journal of Applied Psychology, 62,* 521–523.

Falk, U., & Falk, G. (1997). *Ageism, the aged and aging in America.* Springfield, IL: Charles Thomas.

Fazio, R. H. (1990). A practical guide to the use of response latency in social psychological research. In C. Hendrick, & M. Clark (Eds.), *Review of Personality and Social Psychology* (Vol. 11, pp. 74–97). Newbury Park, CA: Sage.

Fazio, R. H., & Dunton, B. C. (1997). Categorization by race: The impact of automatic and controlled components of racial prejudice. *Journal of Experimental Social Psychology, 33,* 451–470.

Fazio, R. H., & Hilden, L. E. (2001). Emotional reactions to a seemingly prejudiced response: The role of automatically activated racial attitudes and motivation to control prejudiced reactions. *Personality and Social Psychology Bulletin, 27*(5), 538–549.

Fazio, R. H., Jackson, J. R., Dunton, B. C., & Williams, C. J. (1995). Variability in automatic activation as an unobtrusive measure of racial attitudes: A bona fide pipeline? *Journal of Personality and Social Psychology, 69*(6), 1013–1027.

Fazio, R. H., & Olson, M. A. (2003). Attitudes: Foundations, functions, and consequences. In M. A. Hogg & J. Cooper (Eds.), *The Sage handbook of social psychology* (pp. 139–160). Thousand Oaks, CA: Sage.

Fazio, R. H., Powell, M. C., & Herr, P. M. (1983). Toward a process model of the attitude-behavior relation: Accessing one's attitude on mere observation of the attitude object. *Journal of Personality and Social Psychology, 44,* 723–735.

Fazio, R. H., Sanbonmatsu, D. M., Powell, M. C., & Kardes, F. R. (1986). On the automatic activation of attitudes. *Journal of Personality and Social Psychology, 50,* 229–238.

Federico, C. M., & Sidanius, J. (2002). Racism, ideology, and affirmative action revisited: The antecedents and consequences of "principled objections" to affirmative action. *Journal of Personality and Social Psychology, 82*(4), 488–502.

Fein, S., & Spencer, S. J. (1997). Prejudice as self-image maintenance: Affirming the self through derogating others. *Journal of Personality and Social Psychology, 73,* 31–44.

Festinger, L. (1954). A theory of social comparison processes. *Human Relations, 7,* 117–140.

Festinger, L. (1957). *A theory of cognitive dissonance.* Palo Alto, CA: Stanford University Press.

Festinger, L., & Carlsmith, J. M. (1959). Cognitive consequences of forced compliance. *Journal of Abnormal and Social Psychology, 58,* 203–210.

Finkelstein, L. M. (April, 1997). *Age identity and economic stereotyping: Some surprising findings.* Paper presented at the 12th annual meeting of the Society for Industrial and Organizational Psychology, St. Louis.

Finkelstein, L., Burke, M., & Raju, N. (1995). Age discrimination in simulated employment contexts: An integrative analysis. *Journal of Applied Psychology, 80*(6), 652–663.

Finken, L. L. (2002). The impact of a human sexuality course on anti-gay prejudice: The challenge of reaching male students. *Journal of Psychology and Human Sexuality, 14,* 37–46.

Firth, M. (1982). Sex discrimination in job opportunities for women. *Sex Roles, 8*(8), 891–901.

Fishbein, M., & Ajzen, I. (1975). *Belief, attitude, intention, and behavior: An introduction to theory and research.* Reading, MA: Addison-Wesley.

Fisher, J. D., Nadler, A., & Whitcher-Alagna, S. (1982). Recipient reactions to aid. *Psychological Bulletin, 91,* 27–54.

Fishman, J. A. (1956). An examination of the process and function of social stereotyping. *Journal of Social Psychology, 43,* 26–64.

Fiske, S. T. (1982). Schema-triggered affect: Applications to social perception. In M. S. Clark & S. T. Fiske (Eds.), *Affect and cognition* (pp. 55–78). Hillsdale, NJ: Erlbaum.

Fiske, S. T. (1989). Examining the role of intent: Toward understanding its role in stereotyping and prejudice. In J. S. Uleman & J. A. Bargh (Eds.), *Unintended thought* (pp. 253–283). New York: Guilford.

Fiske, S. T. (1993). Controlling other people: The impact of power on stereotyping. *American Psychologist, 48*(6), 621–628.

Fiske, S. T. (1998). Stereotyping, prejudice, and discrimination. In D. T. Gilbert, S. T. Fiske, & G. Lindzey (Eds.), *The Handbook of social psychology* (Vol. 2, 4th ed., pp. 357–411). New York: McGraw-Hill.

Fiske, S. T. (2000). Interdependence and the reduction of prejudice. In S. Oskamp (Ed.), *Reducing prejudice and discrimination* (pp. 115–135). Mahwah, NJ: Erlbaum.

Fiske, S. T. (2002). What we know now about bias and intergroup conflict, the problem of the century. *Current Directions in Psychological Science, 11*(4), 123–128.

Fiske, S. T. (2004). Intent and ordinary bias: Unintended thought and social motivation create casual prejudice. *Social Justice Research, 17*(2), 117–127.

Fiske, S. T., Cuddy, A. J. C., Glick, P., & Xu, J. (2002). A model of (often mixed) stereotype content: Competence and warmth respectively follow from perceived status and competition. *Journal of Personality and Social Psychology, 82*(6), 878–902.

Fiske, S. T., Lin, M., & Neuberg, S. L. (1999). The continuum model: Ten years later. In S. Chaiken & Y. Trope (Eds.), *Dual-process theories in social psychology* (pp. 231–254). New York: Guilford.

Fiske, S. T., Morling, B., & Stevens, L. E. (1996). Controlling self and others: A theory of anxiety, mental control, and social control. *Personality and Social Psychology Bulletin, 22*(2), 115–123.

Fiske, S. T., & Neuberg, S. L. (1990). A continuum of impression formation, from category-based to individuating processes: Influences of information and motivation on attention and interpretation. In M. P. Zanna (Ed.), *Advances in experimental social psychology* (Vol. 23, pp. 1–74). New York: Academic Press.

Fiske, S. T., & Pavelchak, M. A. (1986). Category-based versus piecemeal-based affective responses: Developments in schema-triggered affect. In R. M. Sorrentino & E. T. Higging (Eds.), *Handbook of motivation and cognition: Foundations of social behavior* (pp. 167–203). New York: Guilford.

Fiske, S. T., & Rusher, J. B. (1993). Negative interdependence and prejudice: Whence the affect? In D. M. Mackie & D. L. Hamilton (Eds.), *Affect, cognition, and stereotyping: Interactive processes in group perception* (pp. 239–268). New York: Academic Press.

Fiske, S. T., & Stevens, L. E. (1993). What's so special about sex? Gender stereotyping and discrimination. In S. Oskamp (Ed.), *Gender issues in contemporary society* (pp. 173–196). Newbury Park, CA: Sage.

Fiske, S. T., & Taylor, S. E. (1991). *Social cognition* (2nd ed.). New York: McGraw-Hill.

Fiske, S. T., Xu, J., Cuddy, A. C., & Glick, P. (1999). (Dis)respecting versus (dis)liking: Status and interdependence predict ambivalent stereotypes of competence and warmth. *Journal of Social Issues, 55*(3), 473–489.

Ford, C., & Sbordonne, R. (1980). Attitudes of psychiatrists toward elderly patients. *American Journal of Psychiatry, 137,* 571–575.

Fordham, S. (1988). Racelessness as a factor in Black students' school success: Pragmatic strategy or pyrrhic victory? *Harvard Educational Review, 58,* 54–84.

Fordham, S., & Ogbu, J. U. (1986). Black students' school success: "Coping with the burden of 'acting white.'" *The Urban Review, 18,* 176–206.

Forgas, J. P. (1989). Mood effects on decision making strategies. *Australian Journal of Psychology, 41,* 197–214.

Forgas, J. P. (1990). Affect and social judgments: An introductory review. In J. P. Forgas (Ed.), *Emotion and social judgments* (pp. 3–29). Oxford: Pergamon.

Forgas, J. P. (1992). Affect in social judgments and decisions: A multiprocess model. In M. P. Zanna (Ed.), *Advances in experimental social psychology* (Vol. 25, pp. 227–275). New York: Academic Press.

Forgas, J. P., & Bower, G. H. (1988). Mood effects on social and personal judgments. In K. Fiedler & J. Forgas (Eds.), *Affect, cognition, and social behavior* (pp. 183–208). Toronto, Ontario, Canada: Hoegrefe.

Forsyth, D. R. (1999). *Group dynamics* (3rd ed.). Belmont, CA: Wadsworth.

Foster, L. D., Hooker, K., Johnson, P. M., & Kaus, C. R. (2000). Continuity and change in possible selves in later life: A 5 year longitudinal study. *Basic and Applied Social Psychology, 22*(3), 237–243.

Frable, D. E. S. (1989). Sex typing and gender ideology: Two facets of the individual's gender psychology that go together. *Journal of Personality and Social Psychology, 56,* 95–108.

Frable, D. E. S., Blackstone, T., & Scherbaum, C. (1990). Marginal and mindful: Deviants in social interaction. *Journal of Personality and Social Psychology, 59,* 140–149.

Frantz, C. M., Cuddy, A. J. C., Burnett, M., Ray, H., & Hart, A. (2004). A threat in the computer: The race Implicit Association Test as a stereotype threat experience. *Personality and Social Psychology Bulletin, 30*(12), 1611–1624.

Frazier, L. D., Hooker, K., Johnson, P. M., & Kaus, C. R. (2000). Continuity and change in possible selves in later life: A 5-year longitudinal study. *Basic and Applied Social Psychology, 22*(3), 237–243.

Freud, S. (1953). The interpretation of dreams. In J. Strachey (Ed. & Trans.), *The standard edition of the complete psychological works of Sigmund Freud* (Vols. 4 & 5). London: Hogarth Press (Original work published 1900).

Frijda, N. H. (1988). The laws of emotion. *American Psychologist, 43,* 349–358.

Froming, W. J., Walker, G. R., & Lopyan, K. J. (1982). Public and private self-awareness: When personal attitudes conflict with societal expectations. *Journal of Experimental Social Psychology, 18,* 476–487.

Fuegen, K., Biernat, M., Haines, E., & Deaux, K. (in press). Mothers and fathers in the workplace: How gender and parental status influence judgments of job-related competence. *Journal of Social Issues.*

Gaertner, S. L. (1976). Nonreactive measures in racial attitude research: A focus on "liberals." In P. Katz (Ed.), *Toward the elimination of racism* (pp. 183–211). New York: Pergamon.

Gaertner, S. L., & Dovidio, J. F. (1977). The subtlety of white racism, arousal, and helping behavior. *Journal of Personality and Social Psychology, 35*(10), 691–707.

Gaertner, S. L., & Dovidio, J. F. (1981). Racism among the well-intentioned. In E. G. Clausen & J. Bermingham (Eds.), *Pluralism, racism, and public policy: The search for equality* (pp. 208–222). Boston: G. K. Hall.

Gaertner, S. L., & Dovidio, J. F. (1986). The aversive form of racism. In J. F. Dovidio & S. L. Gaertner (Eds.), *Prejudice, discrimination, and racism* (pp. 61–89). New York: Academic Press.

Gaertner, S. L., & Dovidio, J. F. (2000). *Reducing intergroup bias: The common ingroup identity model.* New York, NY: Psychology Press.

Gaertner, S. L., Dovidio, J. F., Anastasio, P. A., Bachman, B. A., & Rust, M. C. (1993). The common ingroup identity model: Recategorization and the reduction of intergroup bias. In W. Stroebe & M. Hewstone (Eds.), *European review of social psychology* (Vol. 4, pp. 1–26). New York: Wiley.

Gaertner, S. L., Dovidio, J. F., Banker, B. S., Houlette, M., Johnson, K. M., & McGlynn, E. A. (2000). Reducing intergroup conflict: From superordinate goals to decategorization, recategorization, and mutual differentiation. *Group Dynamics: Theory, Research, and Practice, 4,* 98–114.

Gaertner, S. L., Mann, J., Dovidio, J. F., Murrell, A., & Pomare, M. (1990). How does cooperation reduce intergroup bias? *Journal of Personality and Social Psychology, 59,* 692–704.

Gaertner, S. L., & McLaughlin, J. P. (1983). Racial stereotypes: Associations and ascriptions of positive and negative characteristics. *Social Psychology Quarterly, 46,* 23–30.

Gaertner, S. L., Rust, M. C., Dovidio, J. F., Bachman, B. A., & Anastasio, P. A. (1994). The contact hypothesis: The role of a common in-group identity in reducing intergroup bias. *Small Groups, 25,* 224–249.

Galinsky, A. D., & Ku, G. (2004). The effects of perspective-taking on prejudice: The moderating role of self-evaluation. *Personality and Social Psychology Bulletin, 30*(5), 594–604.

Galinsky, A. D., Martorana, P. V., & Ku, G. (2003). To control or not to control stereotypes: Separating the implicit and explicit processes of perspective-taking and suppression. In J. P. Forgas & K. D. Williams (Eds.), *Social judgments: Implicit and explicit processes* (pp. 343–363). New York, NY: Cambridge University Press.

Galinsky, A. D., & Moskowitz, G. B. (2000). Perspective-taking: Decreasing stereotype expression, stereotype accessibility and in-group favoritism. *Journal of Personality and Social Psychology, 78*(4), 708–724.

Garcia-Marques, L., & Mackie, D. M. (1999). The impact of stereotype-incongruent information on perceived group variability and stereotype change. *Journal of Personality and Social Psychology, 77*(5), 979–990.

Gardner, H. (1985). *The mind's new science: A history of the cognitive revolution.* New York: Basic Books.

Gardner, R. C. (1994). Stereotypes as consensual beliefs. In M. P. Zanna & J. M. Olson (Eds.), *The psychology of prejudice: The Ontario symposium* (Vol. 7, pp. 1–31). Hillsdale, NJ: Erlbaum.

Garfinkel, R. (1975). The reluctant therapist: 1975. *The Gerontologist, 15,* 136–137.

Gastil, J. (1990). Generic pronouns and sexist language: The oxymoronic character of masculine generics. *Sex Roles, 23*(11/12), 629–643.

Gates, H. L. (1995). Thirteen ways of looking at a Black man. *The New Yorker, LXXI,* October 23, 56–65.

Gatz, M., & Pearson, C. (1988). Ageism revised and the provision of psychological services. *American Psychologist, 43*(3), 184–188.

Gatz, M., Popkin, S., Pino, C., & VandenBos, G. (1984). Psychological interventions with older adults. In J. E. Birren & K. W. Shaie (Eds.), *Handbook of the psychology of aging* (2nd ed., pp. 755–787). New York: Reinhold.

Gawronski, B. (2002). What does the Implicit Association Test measure? A test of the convergent and discriminant validity of prejudice-related IAT's. *Experimental Psychology, 49*(3), 171–180.

Geen, R. (1995). *Human motivation: A social-psychological approach.* Pacific Grove, CA: Brooks/Cole.

Geis, F. L., Brown, V., Jennings, J., & Porter, N. (1984). TV commercials as achievement scripts for women. *Sex Roles, 10*(7/8), 513–525.

Gekoski, W., & Knox, V. (1990). Ageism or healthism? Perceptions based on age and health status. *Journal of Aging and Health, 2,* 15–27.

Gerhart, B., & Rynes, S. (1991). Determinants and consequences of salary negotiations by male and female MBA graduates. *Journal of Applied Psychology, 76,* 256–262.

Gilbert, D. T. (1989). Thinking lightly about others: Automatic components of the social inference process. In J. S. Uleman & J. A. Bargh (Eds.), *Unintended thought* (pp. 189–211). New York: Guilford.

Gilbert, D. T. (1991). The trouble of thinking: Activation and application of stereotypic beliefs. *Journal of Personality and Social Psychology, 60,* 509–517.

Gilbert, D. T., & Hixon, J. G. (1991). The trouble of thinking: Activation and application of stereotypic beliefs. *Journal of Personality and Social Psychology, 60,* 509–517.

Gilbert, G. M. (1951). Stereotype persistence and change among college students. *Journal of Abnormal and Social Psychology, 46,* 245–254.

Giles, H., & Coupland, N. (1991). *Language, ageing, and health.* Pacific Grove, CA: Brooks/Cole.

Giles, H., Fox, S., Harwood, J., & Williams, A. (1994). Taking age and aging talk: Communicating through the life span. In M. Hummert, J. Wiemann, & J. Nussbaum (Eds.), *Interpersonal communication in older adulthood: Interdisciplinary theory and research* (pp. 130–161). Thousand Oaks, CA: Sage.

Giles, H., Fox, S., & Smith, E. (1993). Patronizing the elderly: Intergenerational evaluations. *Research on Language and Social Interaction, 26*(2), 129–149.

Giles, H., Henwood, K., & Coupland, N. (1992). Language attitudes and cognitive mediation. *Human Communication Research, 18,* 500–527.

Giles, H., & Williams, A. (1994). Patronizing the young: Forms and evaluations. *International Journal of Aging and Human Development, 39,* 33–53.

Gill, M. J. (2004). When information does not deter stereotyping: Prescriptive stereotyping can foster bias under conditions that deter descriptive stereotyping. *Journal of Experimental Social Psychology, 40*(5), 619–632.

Glass, C., & Trent, C. (1980). Changing ninth graders' attitudes toward older persons: Possibility and persistence through education. *Research on Aging, 2*(4), 499–512.

Glick, P. (1991). Trait-based and sex-based discrimination in occupational prestige, occupational salary, and hiring. *Sex Roles, 25,* 351–378.

Glick, P., Diebold, J., Bailey-Werner, B., & Zhu, L. (1997). The two faces of Adam: Ambivalent sexism and polarized attitudes toward women. *Personality and Social Psychology Bulletin, 23*(12), 1323–1334.

Glick, P., & Fiske, S. T. (1996). The Ambivalent Sexism Inventory: Differentiating hostile and benevolent sexism. *Journal of Personality and Social Psychology, 70*(3), 491–512.

Glick, P., & Fiske, S. T. (1999). Sexism and other "isms": Interdependence, status, and the ambivalent content of stereotypes. In W. B. Swann Jr., J. H. Langlois, & L. A. Gilbert (Eds.), *Sexism and stereotypes in modern society: The gender science of Janet Taylor Spence* (pp. 193–221). Washington, DC: American Psychological Association.

Glick, P., & Fiske, S. T. (2001). Ambivalent stereotypes as legitimizing ideologies: Differentiating paternalistic and envious prejudice. In J. T. Jost & B. Major (Eds.), *The psychology of legitimacy: Ideology, justice, and intergroup relations* (pp. 278–306). New York: Cambridge University Press.

Glick, P., Lameiras, M., & Castro, Y. R. (2002). Education and Catholic religiosity as predictors of hostile and benevolent sexism toward women and men. *Sex Roles, 47*(9/10), 433–441.

Glick, P., Sakalli-Ugurlu, N., Ferreira, M. C., & de Souza, M. A. (2002). Ambivalent sexism and attitudes toward wife abuse in Turkey and Brazil. *Psychology of Women Quarterly, 26,* 292–297.

Glick, P., Wilk, K., & Perreault, M. (1995). Images of occupations: Components of gender and status in occupational stereotypes. *Sex Roles, 32*(9/10), 565–582.

Goffman, E. (1963). *Stigma: Notes on the management of spoiled identity.* Englewood Cliffs, NJ: Prentice-Hall.

Goffman, E. (1979). *Gender advertisements.* Cambridge, MA: Harvard University Press.

Gold, D., Andres, D., Arbuckle, T., & Schwartzman, A. (1988). Measurements and correlates of verbosity in elderly people. *Journal of Gerontology: Psychological Sciences, 43,* 27–33.

Goldhagen, D. J. (1996). *Hitler's willing executioners: Ordinary Germans and the Holocaust.* New York: Knopf.

Goldsmith, R., & Heiens, R. (1992). Subjective age: A test of five hypotheses. *The Gerontologist, 32*(3), 312–317.

Gollwitzer, P. M., & Moskowitz, G. B. (1996). Goal effects on action and cognition. In E. T. Higgins & A. W. Kruglanski (Eds.), *Social psychology: Handbook of principles* (pp. 361–399). New York: Guilford.

Golub, S. A., Filipowicz, A., & Langer, E. J. (2002). Acting your age. In T. D. Nelson (Ed.), *Ageism: Stereotyping and prejudice against older persons* (pp. 277–294). Cambridge, MA: MIT Press.

Goodman, M. (1952). *Race awareness in young children.* Cambridge, MA: Addison-Wesley.

Gordijn, E. H., Hindriks, I., & Koomen, W. (2004). Consequences of stereotype suppression and internal suppression motivation: A self-regulation approach. *Personality and Social Psychology Bulletin, 30*(2), 212–224.

Gough, H. G. (1951). Studies of social intolerance: IV. Related social attitudes. *Journal of Social Psychology, 33,* 263–269.

Gouvier, W. D., Sytsma-Jordan, S., & Mayville, S. (2003). Patterns of discrimination in hiring job applicants with disabilities: The role of disability type, job complexity, and public contact. *Rehabilitation Psychology, 48*(3), 175–181.

Govan, C. L., & Williams, K. D. (2004). Changing the affective valence of the stimulus items influences the IAT by redefining the category labels. *Journal of Experimental Social Psychology, 40*(3), 357–365.

Grack, C., & Richman, C. L. (1996). Reducing general and specific heterosexism through cooperative contact. *Journal of Psychology and Human Sexuality, 8*(4), 59–68.

Graf, P., & Schacter, D. (1985). Implicit and explicit memory for new associations in normal and amnesic subjects. *Journal of Experimental Psychology: Learning, Memory, and Cognition, 11*, 501–518.

Grainger, K., Atkinson, K., & Coupland, N. (1990). Responding to the elderly: Troubles-talk in the caring context. In H. Giles, N. Coupland, & J. Weimann (Eds.), *Communication health and the elderly* (pp. 192–212). Manchester, England: Manchester University Press.

Grant, L. (1996). Effects of ageism on individual and health care providers' responses to healthy aging. *Health and Social Work, 21*, 9–15.

Gray-Little, B., & Hafdahl, A. R. (2000). Factors influencing racial comparisons of self-esteem: A quantitative review. *Psychological Bulletin, 126*, 26–54.

Graziano, W. G., Bruce, J. W., Sheese, B. E., & Tobin, B. E. (2004). *Negative evaluations of other people: Prejudice or misanthropy?* Unpublished manuscript.

Green, D. P., Glaser, J., & Rich, A. (1998). From lynching to gay bashing: The elusive connection between economic conditions and hate crime. *Journal of Personality and Social Psychology, 75*, 82–92.

Green, R. J., & Ashmore, R. D. (1998). Taking and developing pictures in the head: Assessing the physical stereotypes of eight gender types. *Journal of Applied Social Psychology, 28*(17), 1609–1636.

Green, S. K. (1981). Attitudes and perceptions about the elderly: Current and future perspectives. *International Journal of Aging and Human Development, 13*, 99–119.

Greenberg, J., & Pyszczynski, T. (1985). The effect of an overheard ethnic slur on evaluations of the target: How to spread a social disease. *Journal of Experimental Social Psychology, 21*, 61–72.

Greenberg, J., Pyszczynski, T., & Solomon, S. (1986). The causes and consequences of a need for self-esteem: A terror management theory. In R. F. Baumeister (Ed.), *Public self and private self* (pp. 188–212). New York: Springer.

Greenberg, J., Schimel, J., & Mertens, A. (2002). Ageism: Denying the face of the future. In T. D. Nelson (Ed.), *Ageism: Stereotyping and prejudice against older persons* (pp. 27–48). Cambridge, MA: MIT Press.

Greenhaus, J. H., & Parasuraman, S. (1993). Job performance attributions and career advancement prospects: An examination of gender and race effects. *Organizational Behavior and Human Decision Processes, 55*, 273–297.

Greenwald, A. G., & Banaji, M. R. (1995). Implicit social cognition: Attitudes, self-esteem, and stereotypes. *Psychological Review, 102*, 4–27.

Greenwald, A. G., McGhee, D. E., & Schwartz, J. K. L. (1998). Measuring individual differences in implicit cognition: The implicit association test. *Journal of Personality and Social Psychology, 74*, 1464–1480.

Greenwald, A. G. & Nosek, B. A. (2001). Health of the Implicit Association Test at age 3. *Zeitschrift für Experimentelle Psychologie, 48*, 85–93.

Greenwald, A. G., Spangenberg, E. R., Pratkanis, A. R., & Eskenazi, J. (1991). Double-blind tests of subliminal self-help audiotapes. *Psychological Science, 2*(2), 119–122.

Gresham, M. (1973). The infantilization of the elderly. *Nursing Forum, 15*, 196–209.

Griffin, G. A. E., Gorsuch, R. L., & Davis, A. (1987). A crosscultural investigation of religious orientation, social norms, and prejudice. *Journal for the Scientific Study of Religion, 26*(3), 358–365.

Guimond, S., Dambrun, M., Michinov, N., & Duarte, S. (2003). Does social dominance generate prejudice? Integrating individual and contextual determinants of intergroup cognitions. *Journal of Personality and Social Psychology, 84*(4), 697–721.

Guimond, S., & Dube-Simard, L. (1983). Relative deprivation theory and the Quebec nationalist movement: The cognition-emotion distinction and the personal-group deprivation issue. *Journal of Personality and Social Psychology, 44*(3), 526–533.

Guindon, M. H., Green, A. G., & Hanna, F. J. (2003). Intolerance and psychopathology: Toward a general diagnosis for racism, sexism, and homophobia. *American Journal of Orthopsychiatry, 73*(2), 167–176.

Gunter, B. (1986). *Television and sex role stereotyping*. London: John Libbey.

Haddock, G., & Zanna, M. P. (1994). Preferring "housewives" to "feminists": Categorization and the favorability of attitudes toward women. *Psychology of Women Quarterly, 18*, 25–52.

Haddock, G., Zanna, M. P., & Esses, V. M. (1993). Assessing the structure of prejudicial attitudes: The case of attitudes toward homosexuals. *Journal of Personality and Social Psychology, 65*(6), 1105–1118.

Haines, E. L., & Jost, J. T. (2000). Placating the powerless: Effects of legitimate and illegitimate explanation on affect, memory, and stereotyping. *Social Justice Research, 13*(3), 219–236.

Hall, E. T. (1966). *The hidden dimension*. New York: Doubleday.

Hambrick, D. Z., Salthouse, T. A., & Meinz, E. J. (1999). Predictors of crossword puzzle proficiency and moderators of age-cognition relations. *Journal of Experimental Psychology: General, 128*(2), 131–164.

Hamilton, D. L. (1976). Cognitive biases in the perception of social groups. In J. S. Carroll & J. W. Payne (Eds.), *Cognition and social behavior* (pp. 81–93). Hillsdale, NJ: Erlbaum.

Hamilton, D. L. (1981a). Illusory correlation as a basis for stereotyping. In D. L. Hamilton (Ed.), *Cognitive processes in stereotyping and intergroup behavior* (pp. 115–144). Hillsdale, NJ: Erlbaum.

Hamilton, D. L. (1981b). Stereotyping and intergroup behavior: Some thoughts on the cognitive approach. In D. L. Hamilton (Ed.), *Cognitive processes in stereotyping and intergroup behavior* (pp. 333–353). Hillsdale, NJ: Erlbaum.

Hamilton, D. L., & Gifford, R. K. (1976). Illusory correlation in interpersonal perception: A cognitive basis of stereotypic judgments. *Journal of Experimental Social Psychology, 12,* 392–407.

Hamilton, D. L., & Mackie, D. M. (1993). Cognitive and affective processes in intergroup perception: The developing interface. In D. M. Mackie & D. L. Hamilton (Eds.), *Affect, cognition, and stereotyping: Interactive processes in intergroup perception* (pp. 1–11). New York: Academic Press.

Hamilton, D. L., & Rose, T. L. (1980). Illusory correlation and the maintenance of stereotypic beliefs. *Journal of Personality and Social Psychology, 39*(5), 832–845.

Hamilton, D. L., & Sherman, J. W. (1989). Illusory correlations: Implications for stereotype theory and research. In D. Bar-Tal, C. F. Graumann, A. W. Kruglanski, & W. Stroebe (Eds.), *Stereotyping and prejudice: Changing conceptions* (pp. 59–82). New York: Academic Press.

Hamilton, D. L., & Sherman, J. W. (1994). Stereotypes. In R. S. Wyer & T. K. Srull (Eds.), *Handbook of social cognition* (Vol. 2, 2nd ed., pp. 1–68). Hillsdale, NJ: Erlbaum.

Hamilton, D. L., Stroessner, S. J., & Driscoll, D. M. (1994). Social cognition and the study of stereotyping. In P. G. Devine, D. L. Hamilton, & T. M. Ostrom (Eds.), *Social cognition: Impact on social psychology* (pp. 291–321). New York: Academic Press.

Hamilton, D. L., Stroessner, S. J., & Mackie, D. M. (1993). The influence of affect on stereotyping: The case of illusory correlations. In D. Mackie & D. Hamilton (Eds.), *Affect, cognition, and stereotyping: Interactive processes in group perception* (pp. 39–61). New York: Academic Press.

Hamilton, D. L., & Trolier, T. K. (1986). Stereotypes and stereotyping: An overview of the cognitive approach. In J. F. Dovidio & S. L. Gaertner (Eds.), *Prejudice, discrimination, and racism* (pp. 127–163). New York: Academic Press.

Handbook of social cognition. (1994). (Vol. 2, pp. 1–68). Hillsdale, NJ: Erlbaum.

Harding, J., Proshansky, H., Kutner, B., & Chein, I. (1969). Prejudice and ethnic relations. In G. Lindzey & E. Aronson (Eds.), *The handbook of social psychology* (Vol. 5, 3rd ed., pp. 1–76). Reading, MA: Addison-Wesley.

Harmon, M. L. (1997). Heterosexuals' attitudes toward gay men and lesbians: The effects of interpersonal contact, sex role orientation, gender, and religiosity. *Dissertation Abstracts International, 58,* 5-B, 2749. (University Microfilms No. AAM9734473)

Harris, J. R. (1998). *The nurture assumption: Why children turn out the way they do.* New York: Free Press.

Harris, M., Moniz, A., Sowards, B., & Krane, K. (1994). Mediation of interpersonal expectancy effects: Expectancies about the elderly. *Social Psychology Quarterly, 57,* 36–48.

Harwood, J., Giles, H., Fox, S., Ryan, E., & Williams, A. (1993). Patronizing speech and reactive responses. *Journal of Applied Communication Research, 21,* 211–226.

Haslam, S. A., Oakes, P. J., Reynolds, K. J., & Turner, J. C. (1999). Social identity salience and the emergence of stereotype consensus. *Personality and Social Psychology Bulletin, 25*(7), 809–818.

Haynes, J. D. (1995). A critique of the possibility of genetic inheritance of homosexual orientation. *Journal of Homosexuality, 28*(1/2), 91–113.

Heatherton, T. F., Kleck, R. E., Hebl, M. R., & Hull, J. G. (Eds.). (2000). *The social psychology of stigma.* New York: Guilford.

Heaven, P. C. L., & St. Quintin, D. (2003). Personality factors predict racial prejudice. *Personality and Individual Differences, 34*(4), 625–634.

Hebl, M. R., & Kleck, R. E. (2000). The social consequences of physical disability. In T. F. Heatherton, R. E. Kleck, M. R. Hebl, & J. G. Hull (Eds.), *The social psychology of stigma* (pp. 419–439). New York: Guilford.

Hebl, M. R., & Kleck, R. E. (2002). Acknowledging one's stigma in the interview setting: Effective strategy or liability? *Journal of Applied Social Psychology, 32*(2), 223–249.

Hebl, M. R., & Mannix, L. M. (2003). The weight of obesity in evaluating others: A mere proximity effect. *Personality and Social Psychology Bulletin, 29,* 28–38.

Hebl, M. R., Tickle, J., & Heatherton, T. F. (2000). Awkward moments in interactions between nonstigmatized and stigmatized individuals. In T. F. Heatherton, & R. E. Kleck (Eds.), *The social psychology of stigma* (pp. 275–306). New York, NY: Guilford.

Heider, F. (1958). *The psychology of interpersonal relations.* Hillsdale, NJ: Erlbaum.

Heilman, M. E., Block, C. J., & Lucas, J. A. (1992). Presumed incompetent? Stigmatization and affirmative action efforts. *Journal of Applied Psychology, 77,* 536–544.

Heilman, M. E., Martell, R. F., & Simon, M. C. (1988). The vagaries of sex bias: Conditions regulating the undervaluation, equivaluation, and overvaluation of female job applicants. *Organizational Behavior and Human Decision Processes, 41,* 98–110.

Heilman, M. E., Rivero, J. C., & Brett, J. F. (1991). Skirting the competence issue: Effects of sex-based preferential selection on task choices of women and men. *Journal of Applied Psychology 76,* 99–105.

Heilman, M. E., & Stopeck, M. H. (1985). Attractiveness and corporate success: Different causal attributions for males and females. *Journal of Applied Psychology, 70,* 379–388.

Henderson-King, E. (1994). Minimizing intergroup contact: An urban field study. *Journal of Applied Social Psychology, 24*(16), 1428–1432.

Henderson-King, E. (1999). The impact of a passing reference to race on perceptions of out-group differentiation: "If you've seen one . . . " *Group Processes and Intergroup Relations.*

Henderson-King, E., & Nisbett, R. E. (1996). Anti-Black prejudice as a function of exposure to the negative behavior of a single Black person. *Journal of Personality and Social Psychology, 71*(4), 654–664.

Hense, R. L., Penner, L. A., & Nelson, D. L. (1995). Implicit memory for age stereotypes. *Social Cognition, 13*(4), 399–415.

Hepworth, J. T., & West, S. G. (1988). Lynching and the economy: A time-series reanalysis of Hovland and Sears (1940). *Journal of Personality and Social Psychology, 55,* 239–247.

Herek, G. M. (1987). Religious orientation and prejudice: A comparison of racial and sexual attitudes. *Personality and Social Psychology Bulletin, 13,* 34–44.

Herek, G. M. (2000). The psychology of sexual prejudice. *Current Directions in Psychological Science, 9,* 19–22.

Herek, G. M., & Capitanio, J. P. (1996). "Some of my best friends": Intergroup contact, concealable stigma, and heterosexuals' attitudes toward gay men and lesbians. *Personality and Social Psychology Bulletin, 22*(4), 412–424.

Hess, T. M., Auman, C., Colcombe, S. J., & Rahhal, T. A. (2003). The impact of stereotype threat on age differences in memory performance. *Journal of Gerontology: Psychological Sciences, 58B,* 3–11.

Hewstone, M. (2003). Intergroup contact: Panacea for prejudice? *The Psychologist, 16*(7), 352–355.

Hewstone, M., & Brown, R. (1986). Contact is not enough: An intergroup perspective on the "contact hypothesis." In M. Hewstone & R. Brown (Eds.), *Contact and conflict in intergroup encounters* (pp. 1–44). New York: Basil Blackwell.

Higgins, E. T. (1987). Self-discrepancy: A theory relating self and affect. *Psychological Review, 94,* 319–340.

Hill, P. C., Henderson, A. H., Bray, J. H., & Evans, R. I. (1981). Generalizing a self-report validator of cigarette smoking to older adolescents. *Replications in Social Psychology, 1,* 38–40.

Hillerbrand, E., & Shaw, D. (1990). Age bias in a general hospital: Is there ageism in psychiatric consultation? *Clinical Gerontologist, 2*(2), 3–13.

Hilton, J. L., & Darley, J. M. (1985). Constructing other persons: A limit on the effect. *Journal of Experimental Social Psychology, 21,* 1–18.

Hilton, J. L., & Darley, J. M. (1991). The effects of interaction goals on person perception. In M. P. Zanna (Ed.), *Advances in experimental social psychology* (Vol. 24, pp. 235–267). San Diego, CA: Academic Press.

Hing, L. S. S., Li, W., & Zanna, M. P. (2002). Inducing hypocrisy to reduce prejudicial responses among aversive racists. *Journal of Experimental Social Psychology, 38,* 71–78.

Hirt, E. R., Zillman, D., Erickson, G. A., & Kennedy, G. (1992). Costs and benefits of allegiance: Changes in fans' self-ascribed competencies after team victory versus defeat. *Journal of Personality and Social Psychology, 63*(5), 724–738.

Hodson, G., & Esses, V. M. (2002). Distancing oneself from negative attributes and the personal/group discrimination discrepancy. *Journal of Experimental Social Psychology, 38,* 500–507.

Hogg, M. A., & Abrams, D. (1990). Social motivation, self-esteem, and social identity. In D. Abrams and M. Hogg (Eds.), *Social identity theory: Constructive and critical advances* (pp. 28–47). London: Harvester Wheatsheaf.

Hogg, M. A., & Turner, J. C. (1987). Intergroup behavior, self-stereotyping, and the salience of social categories. *British Journal of Social Psychology, 26,* 325–340.

Hornsey, M. J., & Hogg, M. A. (1999). Subgroup differentiation as a response to an overly- inclusive group: A test of optimal distinctiveness theory. *European Journal of Social Psychology, 29*(4), 543–550.

Hornsey, M. J., & Hogg, M. A. (2000). Assimilation and diversity: An integrative model of subgroup relations. *Personality and Social Psychology Review, 4*(2), 143–156.

Horwitz, M., & Rabbie, J. M. (1989). Stereotypes of groups, group members, and individuals in categories: A differential analysis. In D. Bar-Tal, C. F. Graumann, A. W. Kruglanski, & W. Stroebe (Eds.), *Stereotyping and prejudice: Changing conceptions* (pp. 105–129). New York: Springer-Verlag.

Hovland, C. I., Janis, I. L., & Kelley, H. H. (1953). *Communication and persuasion: Psychological studies of opinion change.* New Haven, CT: Yale University Press.

Hovland, C. I., & Sears, R. R. (1940). Minor studies in aggression: VI: Correlation of lynchings with economic indices. *Journal of Psychology, 9,* 301–310.

Huff, D. (1954). *How to lie with statistics.* New York: Norton.

Hull, C. L. (1943). *Principles of behavior: An introduction to behavior theory.* New York: Appleton-Century-Crofts.

Hummert, M. L. (1990). Multiple stereotypes of elderly and young adults: A comparison of structure and evaluations. *Psychology and Aging, 5*(2), 182–193.

Hummert, M. L. (1994). Physiognomic cues to age and the activation of stereotypes of the elderly in interaction. *International Journal of Aging and Human Development, 39,* 5–19.

Hummert, M., Garstka, T., Shaner, J., & Strahm, S. (1995). Judgments about stereotypes of the elderly: Attitudes, age associations, and typicality ratings of young, middle-aged, and elderly adults. *Research on Aging, 17*(2), 168–189.

Hunsberger, B. (1995). Religion and prejudice: The role of religious fundamentalism, quest, and right-wing authoritarianism. *Journal of Social Issues, 51*(2), 113–129.

Hunt, R. A., & King, M. B. (1971). The intrinsic-extrinsic concept: A review and evaluation. *Journal for the Scientific Study of Religion, 10,* 339–356.

Hyde, J. S. (1984). Children's understanding of sexist language. *Developmental Psychology, 20,* 722–736.

Hyers, L. L., & Swim, J. K. (1998). A comparison of the experiences of dominant and minority group members during an intergroup encounter. *Group Processes and Intergroup Relations, 1*(2), 143–163.

Ickes, W. (1984). Compositions in black and white: Determinants of interaction in interracial dyads. *Journal of Personality and Social Psychology, 47*(2), 330–341.

Ikels, C., Keith, J., Dickerson-Putman, J., Draper, P., Fry, C., Glascock, A., & Harpending, H. (1992). Perceptions of the adult life course: A cross-cultural analysis. *Aging and Society, 12,* 49–84.

Innes, J. M., & Ahrens, C. R. (1991). Positive mood, processing goals and the effects of information on evaluative judgment. In J. Forgas (Ed.), *Emotion and social judgments* (pp. 221–239). Oxford, England: Pergamon.

Inzlicht, M., & Ben-Zeev, T. (2000). A threatening intellectual environment: Why females are susceptible to experiencing problem-solving deficits in the presence of males. *Psychological Science, 11*(5), 365–371.

Isaacs, L., & Bearison, D. (1986). The development of children's prejudice against the aged. *International Journal of Aging and Human Development, 23,* 175–194.

Isen, A. M. (1987). Positive affect, cognitive processes, and social behavior. In L. Berkowitz (Ed.), *Advances in experimental social psychology* (Vol. 20, pp. 203–253). New York: Academic Press.

Isen, A. M., & Daubman, K. A. (1984). The influence of affect on categorization. *Journal of Personality and Social Psychololgy, 47*(6), 1206–1217.

Isen, A. M., Means, B., Patrick, R., & Nowicki, G. (1982). Some factors influencing decision-making and risk taking. In M. S. Clark & S. T. Fiske (Eds.), *Affect and cognition* (pp. 243–261). Hillsdale, NJ: Erlbaum.

Isen, A. M., & Simmonds, S. (1978). The effect of feeling good on a task that is incompatible with good mood. *Social Psychology Quarterly, 41,* 346–349.

Islam, R. M., & Hewstone, M. (1993). Dimensions of contact as predictors of intergroup anxiety, perceived outgroup variability, and out-group attitude: An integrative model. *Personality and Social Psychology Bulletin, 19,* 700–710.

Ivester, C., & King, K. (1977). Attitudes of adolescents toward the aged. *The Gerontologist, 17,* 85–89.

Izard, C. E. (1972). *Patterns of emotions: A new analysis of anxiety and depression.* New York: Academic Press.

Jacklin, C. N., & Baker, L. A. (1993). Early gender development. In S. Oskamp & M. Costanzo (Eds.), *Gender issues in contemporary society* (pp. 41–57). Newbury Park, CA: Sage.

Jacks, J. Z., & Devine, P. G. (2002). Prejudice, internalization, and the accessibility of personal standards for responding to gay men. *Journal of Homosexuality, 43,* 39–58.

Jackson, J. R., & Fazio, R. H. (1995, May). *The effect of race of experimenter on responses to the Modern Racism Scale: A test of reactivity.* Paper presented at the meeting of the Midwestern Psychological Association, Chicago, IL.

Jackson, L. A., Gardner, P., & Sullivan, L. (1992). Explaining gender differences in self-pay expectations: Social comparison standards and perceptions of fair pay. *Journal of Applied Psychology, 77,* 651–663.

Jackson, L. A., Hodge, C. N., Gerard, D. A., Ingram, J. M., Ervin, K. S., & Sheppard, L. A. (1996). Cognition, affect, and behavior in the prediction of group attitudes. *Personality and Social Psychology Bulletin, 22*(3), 306–316.

Jacobs, J. A. (1992). Women's entry into management: Trends in earnings, authority, and values among salaried managers. *Administrative Science Quarterly, 37,* 282–301.

Jacoby, L. L., & Dallas, M. (1981). On the relationship between autobiographical memory and perceptual learning. *Journal of Experimental Psychology: General, 110,* 306–340.

Jacoby, L. L., & Witherspoon, D. (1982). Remembering without awareness. *Canadian Journal of Psychology, 36,* 300–324.

James, J., & Haley, W. (1995). Age and health bias in practicing clinical psychologists. *Psychology and Aging, 10*(4), 610–616.

James, W. (1890). *The principles of psychology.* New York: Holt.

Jamieson, D. W., & Zanna, M. P. (1989). Need for structure in attitude formation and expression. In A. R. Pratkanis, S. J. Breckler, & A. G. Greenwald (Eds.), *Attitude structure and function* (pp. 383–406). Hillsdale, NJ: Erlbaum.

Janis, I. L. (1968). Group identification under conditions of external danger. In D. Cartwright & A. Zander (Eds.), *Group dynamics: Research and theory* (3rd ed.). New York: Harper & Row.

Janssen-Jurreit, M. (1982). *Sexism: The male monopoly on history and thought.* New York: McGraw-Hill.

Jantz, R., Seefeldt, C., Caalper, A., & Serock, K. (1976). *Children's attitudes toward the elderly.* Washington, DC: National Retired Teachers Association.

Jensen, G. D., & Oakley, F. B. (1982–1983). Ageism across cultures and in perspective of sociobiologic and psychodynamic theories. *International Journal of Aging and Human Development, 15,* 17–26.

Jetten, J., Spears, R., & Manstead, A. S. R. (1996). Intergroup norms and intergroup discrimination: Distinctive self-categorization and social identity effects. *Journal of Personality and Social Psychology, 71,* 1222–1233.

Johnson, D. W., & Johnson, R. T. (1987). *Learning together and alone: Cooperative, competitive, and individualistic learning* (2nd ed.). Englewood Cliffs, NJ: Prentice Hall.

Jones, E. E. (1985). Major developments in social psychology during the past five decades. In G. Lindzey & E. Aronson (Eds.), *Handbook of social psychology* (Vol. 1, 3rd ed., pp. 47–107). New York: Random House.

Jones, E. E. (1990). *Interpersonal perception.* New York: W. H. Freeman.

Jones, E. E., Farina, A., Hastorf, A. H., Markus, H., Miller, D. T., Scott, R. A., et al. (1984). *Social stigma: The psychology of marked relationships.* New York: W. H. Freeman.

Jones, E. E., Kanouse, D., Kelley, H. H., Nisbett, R. E., Valins, S., & Weiner, B. (1972). *Attribution: Perceiving the causes of behavior.* Morristown, NJ: General Learning Press.

Jones, E. E., & Sigall, H. (1971). The bogus pipeline: A new paradigm for measuring affect and attitude. *Psychological Bulletin, 76*(5), 349–364.

Jones, G. P., & Jacklin, C. N. (1988). Changes in sexist attitudes toward women during introductory women's and men's studies courses. *Sex Roles, 18*(9/10), 611–622.

Jones, J. M. (1997a). *Prejudice and racism* (2nd ed.). New York: McGraw-Hill.

Jones, J. M. (1997b). Whites are from Mars, O. J. is from Planet Hollywood: Blacks don't support O. J. and Whites just don't get it. In M. Fine, L. Weis, L. Powell, & L. Wong (Eds.), *Off white: Readings on rage, power, and society* (pp. 251–258). New York: Routledge.

Jones, R. A. (1982). Perceiving other people: Stereotyping as a process of social categorization. In A. Miller (Ed.), *In the eye of the beholder: Contemporary issues in stereotyping* (pp. 41–91). New York: Praeger.

Jost, J. J., Glaser, J., Kruglanski, A. W., & Sulloway, F. J. (2003). Political conservatism as motivated social cognition. *Psychological Bulletin, 129*(3), 339–375.

Juni, S., & Roth, M. M. (1981). Sexism and handicapism in interpersonal helping. *Journal of Social Psychology, 115*(2), 175–181.

Jussim, L., & Fleming, C. (1996). Self-fulfilling prophecies and the maintenance of social stereotypes: The role of dyadic interactions and social forces. In C. N. Macrae, C. Stangor, & M. Hewstone (Eds.), *Stereotypes and stereotyping* (pp. 161–192). New York: Guilford.

Kahneman, D., Slovic, P., & Tversky, A. (Eds.). (1982). *Judgment under uncertainty: Heuristics and biases.* New York: Cambridge University Press.

Kaiser, C. R., Major, B., & McCoy, S. K. (2004). Expectations about the future and the emotional consequences of perceiving prejudice. *Personality and Social Psychology Bulletin, 30*(2), 173–184.

Kaiser, C. R., & Miller, C. T. (2001). Stop complaining! The social costs of making attributions to discrimination. *Personality and Social Psychology Bulletin, 27*(2), 254–263.

Kaiser, C. R., & Miller, C. T. (2003). Derogating the victim: The interpersonal consequences of blaming events on discrimination. *Group Processes & Intergroup Relations, 6*(3), 227–237.

Kane, M. N. (2002). Awareness of ageism, motivation, and countertransference in the care of elders with Alzheimer's disease. *American Journal of Alzheimer's Disease and Other Dementias, 17*(2), 101–109

Kaplan, M. F., Wanshula, L. T., & Zanna, M. P. (1993). Time pressure and information integration in social judgment: The effect of need for structure. In O. Svenson & A. J. Maule (Eds.), *Time pressure and stress in human judgment and decision making* (pp. 255–267). New York: Plenum.

Karlins, M., Coffman, T. L., & Walters, G. (1969). On the fading of social stereotypes: Studies in three generations of college students. *Journal of Personality and Social Psychology, 13,* 1–16.

Karris, L. (1977). Prejudice against obese renters. *Journal of Social Psychology, 101,* 159–160.

Kastenbaum, R. (1964). The reluctant therapist. In R. Kastenbaum (Ed.), *New thoughts on old age* (pp. 139–145). New York: Springer.

Kastenbaum, R., & Durkee, N. (1964). Young people view old age. In R. Kastenbaum (Ed.), *New thoughts on old age* (pp. 237–249). New York: Springer.

Katz, D. (1981). *Stigma: A social psychological analysis.* Hillsdale, NJ: Erlbaum.

Katz, D., & Braly, K. (1933). Racial stereotypes in one hundred college students. *Journal of Abnormal and Social Psychology, 28,* 280–290.

Katz, D., & Braly, K. W. (1935). Racial prejudice and racial stereotypes. *Journal of Abnormal and Social Psychology, 30,* 175–193.

Katz, I. (1981). *Stigma: A social psychological analysis.* Hillsdale, NJ: Erlbaum.

Katz, I., & Hass, R. G. (1988). Racial ambivalence and American value conflict: Correlational and priming studies of dual cognitive structures. *Journal of Personality and Social Psychology, 55*(6), 893–905.

Katz, P. A. (1976). The acquisition of racial attitudes in children. In P. A. Katz (Ed.), *Towards the elimination of racism* (pp. 125–154). New York: Pergamon.

Katz, P. A. (1983). Developmental foundations of gender and racial attitudes. In R. L. Leahy (Ed.), *The child's construction of social inequality* (pp. 41–78). New York: Academic Press.

Kawakami, K., & Dovidio, J. F. (2001). The reliability of implicit stereotyping. *Personality and Social Psychology Bulletin, 27*(2), 212–225.

Kawakami, K., Dovidio, J. F., Moll, J., Hermsen, S., & Russin, A. (2000). Just say no (to stereotyping): Effects of training in the negation of stereotypic associations on stereotype activation. *Journal of Personality and Social Psychology, 78*(5), 871–888.

Kay, F. M., & Hagan, J. (1995). The persistent glass ceiling: Gendered inequalities in the earnings of lawyers. *British Journal of Sociology, 46*(2), 279–310.

Kelley, H. H. (1967). Attribution theory in social psychology. In D. Levine (Ed.), *Nebraska symposium on motivation* (Vol. 15, pp. 192–238). Lincoln: University of Nebraska Press.

Keltner, D., Gruenfeld, D. H., & Anderson, C. (2003). Power, approach, and inhibition. *Psychological Review, 110*(2), 265–284.

Kemper, S. (1994). Elderspeak: Speech accommodations to older adults. *Aging and Cognition, 1,* 17–28.

Kihlstrom, J. (1990). The psychological unconscious. In L. A. Pervin (Ed.), *Handbook of personality: Theory and research* (pp. 445–464). New York: Guilford Press.

Kilianski, S. E., & Rudman, L. A. (1998). Wanting it both ways: Do women approve of benevolent sexism? *Sex Roles, 39*(5/6), 333–352.

Kim, H., & Baron, R. S. (1988). Exercise and illusory correlation: Does arousal heighten stereotypic processing? *Journal of Experimental Social Psychology, 24,* 366–380.

Kinder, D. R., & Sears, D. O. (1981). Prejudice and politics: Symbolic racism versus racial threats to the good life. *Journal of Personality and Social Psychology, 40,* 414–431.

King, K. R. (2003). Racism or sexism? Attributional ambiguity and simultaneous membership in multiple oppressed groups. *Journal of Applied Social Psychology, 33*(2), 223–247.

King, M., & McDonald, E. (1992). Homosexuals who are twins. A study of 46 probands. *British Journal of Psychiatry, 160,* 407–409.

Kirkland, S. L., Greenberg, J., & Pyszczynski, T. (1987). Further evidence of the deleterious effects of overheard derogatory ethnic labels: Derogation beyond the target. *Personality and Social Psychology Bulletin, 13,* 216–227.

Kite, M. E. (1984). Sex differences in attitudes toward homosexuals: A meta-analytic review. *Journal of Homosexuality, 10*(1/2), 69–81.

Kite, M. E., & Johnson, B. T. (1988). Attitudes toward older and younger adults: A meta-analysis. *Psychology and Aging, 3*(3), 233–244.

Kite, M. E., Stockdale, G. D., Whitley, B. E., & Johnson, B. T. (2005). Attitudes toward older and younger adults: An updated meta-analytic review. *Journal of Social Issues, 61*(2), 241–266.

Kite, M. E., & Wagner, L. S. (2002). Attitudes toward older adults. In T. D. Nelson (Ed.), *Ageism: Stereotyping and prejudice against older persons* (pp. 129–161). Cambridge, MA: MIT Pess.

Kite, M. E., & Whitley, B. E. (1996). Sex differences in attitudes toward homosexual persons, behaviors, and civil rights: A meta-analysis. *Personality and Social Psychology Bulletin, 22*(4), 336–353.

Kite, M. E., & Whitley, B. E. (2003). Do heterosexual women and men differ in their attitudes toward homosexuality? A conceptual and methodological analysis. In L. D. Garnets & D. C. Kimmel (Eds.), *Psychological perspectives on lesbian, gay, & bisexual* experiences (2nd ed., pp. 165–187). New York: Columbia University Press.

Kleck, R. E., & Strenta, A. (1980). Perceptions of the impact of negatively valued physical characteristics on social interaction. *Journal of Personality and Social Psychology, 39*(5), 861–873.

Klein, W. M., & Kunda, Z. (1992). Motivated person perception: Constructing justifications for desired beliefs. *Journal of Experimental Social Psychology, 28,* 145–168.

Kleinpenning, G., & Hagendoorn, L. (1993). Forms of racism and the cumulative dimension of ethnic attitudes. *Social Psychology Quarterly, 56,* 21–36.

Knowles, E. S. (1980). An affiliative-conflict theory of personal and group spatial behavior. In P. B. Paulus (Ed.), *Psychology of group influence* (pp. 133–188). Hillsdale, NJ: Erlbaum.

Knox, V. J., Gekoski, W. L., & Johnson, E. A. (1986). Contact with and perceptions of the elderly. *The Gerontologist, 26*(3), 309–313.

Koomen, W., & Dijker, A. J. (1997). Ingroup and outgroup stereotypes and selective processing. *European Journal of Social Psychology, 27*, 589–601.

Koyano, W. (1989). Japanese attitudes toward the elderly: A review of research findings. *Journal of Cross-Cultural Gerontology, 4*, 335–345.

Krauth-Gruber, S., & Ric, F. (2000). Affect and stereotypic thinking: A test of the mood-and-general-knowledge-model. *Personality and Social Psychology Bulletin, 26*(12), 1587–1597.

Kravitz, D. A., Klineberg, S. L., Avery, D. R., Nguyen, K., Lund, C., & Fu, E. J. (2000). Attitudes toward affirmative action: Correlations with demographic variables and with beliefs about targets, actions, and economic effects. *Journal of Applied Social Psychology, 30*(6), 1109–1136.

Kruglanski, A. W. (1980). Lay epistemo-logic-process and contents: Another look at attribution theory. *Psychological Review, 87*, 70–87.

Kruglanski, A. W. (1990). Motivations for judging and knowing: Implications for causal attribution. In E. T. Higgins and R. M. Sorrentino (Eds.), *Handbook of motivation and cognition: Foundations of social behavior* (Vol. 2, pp. 333–368). New York: Guilford.

Kruglanski, A. W. (1996). Motivated social cognition: Principles of the interface. In E. T. Higgins & A. W. Kruglanski (Eds.), *Social psychology: Handbook of basic principles* (pp. 493–520). New York: Guilford.

Kruglanski, A. W., & Freund, T. (1983). The freezing and unfreezing of lay-inferences: Effects on impressional primacy, ethnic stereotyping, and numerical anchoring. *Journal of Experimental Social Psychology, 19*, 448–468.

Kruglanski, A. W., & Webster, D. M. (1996). Motivated closing of the mind: "Seizing" and "freezing." *Psychological Review, 103*(2), 263–283.

Kuhn, T. S. (1970). *The structure of scientific revolutions* (2nd ed.). Chicago: University of Chicago Press.

Kunda, Z. (1990). The case for motivated reasoning. *Psychological Bulletin, 108*, 480–498.

Kunda, Z. (1999). *Social cognition: Making sense of people.* Cambridge, MA: MIT Press.

Kunda, Z., & Oleson, K. C. (1995). Maintaining stereotypes in the face of disconfirmation: Constructing grounds for subtyping deviants. *Journal of Personality and Social Psychology, 68*(4), 565–579.

Kunda, Z., & Sinclair, L. (1999). Motivated reasoning with stereotypes: Activation, application, and inhibition. *Psychological Inquiry, 10*, 12–22.

Kunda, Z., & Thagard, P. (1996). Forming impressions from stereotypes, traits, and behaviors: A parallel-constraint satisfaction theory. *Psychological Review, 103*, 284–308.

Kurdek, L. A. (1988). Correlates of negative attitudes toward homosexuals in heterosexual college students. *Sex Roles, 18*(11/12), 727–738.

LaFrance, M., & Banaji, M. (1992). Toward a reconsideration of the gender-emotion relationship. In M. Clark (Ed.), *Emotion and social behavior* (pp. 178–201). Newbury Park, CA: Sage.

LaFrance, M., & Woodzicka, J. A. (1998). No laughing matter: Women's verbal and nonverbal reactions to sexist humor. In J. K. Swim & C. Stangor (Eds.), *Prejudice: The target's perspective* (pp. 62–80). New York: Academic Press.

LaMar, L., & Kite, M. E. (1998). Sex differences in attitudes toward gay men and lesbians: A multidimensional perspective. *Journal of Sex Research, 35*(2), 189–196.

Lambert, A. J., Payne, B. K., & Ramsey, S. (2005). On the predictive validity of implicit attitude measures: The moderating effect of perceived group variability. *Journal of Experimental Social Psychology, 41*(2), 114–128.

Langer, E. (1989). *Mindfulness.* Reading, MA: Addison-Wesley.

Langer, E. J., Fiske, S., Taylor, S. E., & Chanowitz, B. (1976). Stigma, staring, and discomfort: A novel-stimulus hypothesis. *Journal of Experimental Social Psychology, 12*, 451–463.

LaPiere, R. T. (1934). Attitudes versus actions. *Social forces, 13*, 230–237.

Larsen, K. S., & Long, E. (1988). Attitudes toward sex-roles: Traditional or egalitarian? *Sex Roles, 19*, 1–12.

Lea, S. J., Bokhorst, F. D., & Colenso, J. (1995). The empirical relationship between the constructs of traditional and symbolic racism. *South African Journal of Psychology, 25*(4), 224–228.

LeDoux, J. E. (1996). *The emotional brain.* New York: Simon & Schuster.

Lee, Y., Jussim, L. J., & McCauley, C. R. (1995). *Stereotype accuracy: Toward appreciating group differences.* Washington, DC: American Psychological Association.

Lee, Y., & Ottati, V. (1995). Perceived in-group homogeneity as a function of group membership salience and stereotype threat. *Personality and Social Psychology Bulletin, 21*(6), 610–619.

Lehr, U. (1983). In J. Birren, J. Munnichs, H. Thomae, & M. Marois (Eds.), *Aging: A challenge to science and society* (Vol. 3, pp. 101–112). New York: Oxford University Press.

Leonardelli, G. J., & Brewer, M. B. (2001). Minority and majority discrimination: When and why. *Journal of Experimental Social Psychology, 37*(6), 468–485.

Lepore, L., & Brown, R. (1997). Category and stereotype activation: Is prejudice inevitable? *Journal of Personality and Social Psychology, 72*(2), 275–287.

Lerner, M. J. (1980). *The belief in a just world: A fundamental delusion.* New York: Plenum.

Levenson, A. J. (1981). Ageism: A major deterrent to the introduction of curricula in aging. *Gerontology and Geriatrics Education, 1*, 161–162.

Levin, J., & Levin, W. (1980). *Ageism: Prejudice and discrimination against the elderly.* Belmont, CA: Wadsworth.

Levina, M., Waldo, C. R., & Fitzgerald, L. F. (2000). We're here, we're queer, we're on TV: The effects of visual media on heterosexuals' attitudes toward gay men and lesbians. *Journal of Applied Social Psychology, 30*(4), 738–758.

Levy, B. R. (2003). Mind matters: Cognitive and physical effects of aging self-stereotypes. *Journal of Gerontology: Psychological Sciences, 58B*(4), 203–211.

Levy, B., & Langer, E. (1994). Aging free from negative stereotypes: Successful memory in China and among the American deaf. *Journal of Personality and Social Psychology, 66*(6), 989–997.

Levy, B. R., Slade, M. D., Kunkel, S. R., & Kasl, S. V. (2003). Longevity increased by positive self-perceptions of aging. *Journal of Personality and Social Psychology, 83*(2), 261–270.

Levy, S. R., Plaks, J. E., & Dweck, C. S. (1999). Modes of social thought: Implicit theories and social understanding. In S. Chaiken & Y. Trope (Eds.), *Dual-process theories in social psychology* (pp. 179–202). New York: Guilford.

Levy, S. R., Stroessner, S. J., & Dweck, C. S. (1998). Stereotype formation and endorsement: The role of implicit theories. *Journal of Personality and Social Psychology, 74*(6), 1421–1436.

Lewicki, P., Hill, T., & Czyzewska, M. (1992). Nonconscious acquisition of information. *American Psychologist, 47*(6), 796–801.

Lewin, K. (1948). *Resolving social conflicts.* New York: Harper & Row.

Lewin, K. (1951a). *Field theory in social science: Selected theoretical papers.* New York: Harper.

Lewin, K. (1951b). Problems of research in social psychology. In D. Cartwright (Ed.), *Field theory in social science.* New York: Harper & Row.

Lieberman, J. D. (1999). Terror management, illusory correlation, and perceptions of minority groups. *Basic and Applied Social Psychology, 21,* 13–23.

Lieberman, M., & Peskin, H. (1992). Adult life crises. In J. Birren, R. Sloane, & G. Cohen (Eds.), *Handbook of mental health and aging* (2nd ed., pp. 119–143). San Diego, CA: Academic Press.

Lin, M. H., Kwan, V. S. Y., & Cheung, A. (2005). Stereotype content model explains prejudice for an envied outgroup: Scale of anti-asian American stereotypes. *Personality and Social Psychology Bulletin, 31,* 34–47.

Linville, P. W. (1987). Self-complexity as a cognitive buffer against stress-related illness and depression. *Journal of Personality and Social Psychology, 52,* 663–676.

Lippmann, W. (1922). *Public opinion.* New York: Harcourt, Brace, Jovanovich.

Lips, H. M. (2003). The gender pay gap: Concrete indicator of women's progress toward equality. *Analysis of Social Issues and Public Policy, 3*(1), 87–109.

Locksley, A., Borgida, E., Brekke, N., & Hepburn, C. (1980). Sex stereotypes and social judgment. *Journal of Personality and Social Psychology, 39*(5), 821–831.

Loehlin, J. C., Lindzeg, G., & Spuhler, J. N. (1975). *Race differences in intelligence.* San Francisco: Freeman.

Long, K., & Spears, R. (1997). The self-esteem hypothesis revisited: Differentiation and the disaffected. In R. Spears, P. J. Oakes, N. Ellemers, & S. A. Haslam (Eds.), *The social psychology of stereotyping and group life* (pp. 296–317). Cambridge, MA: Blackwell.

Lorenzi-Cioldi, F. (1991). Self-stereotyping and self-enhancement in gender groups. *European Journal of Social Psychology, 21,* 403–417.

Lott, B. (1989). Sexist discrimination as distancing behavior: II. Primetime television. *Psychology of Women Quarterly, 13,* 341–355.

Lott, B. (1995). Distancing from women: Interpersonal sexist discrimination. In B. Lott & D. Maluso (Eds.), *The social psychology of interpersonal discrimination* (pp. 12–49). New York: Guilford.

Love, A. M., & Deckers, L. H. (1989). Humor appreciation as a function of sexual, aggressive, and sexist content. *Sex Roles, 20*(11/12), 649–654.

Lundin, R. W. (1979). *Theories and systems of psychology* (2nd ed.). Lexington, MA: D.C. Heath.

Lutsky, N. S. (1980). Attitudes toward old age and elderly persons. In C. Eisdorfer (Ed.), *Annual review of gerontology and geriatrics* (Vol. 1, pp. 287–336). New York: Springer.

Lyness, K. S., & Thompson, D. E. (1997). Above the glass ceiling? A comparison of matched samples of female and male executives. *Journal of Applied Psychology, 82*(3), 359–375.

Lytton, H., & Romney, D. M. (1991). Parents' differential socialization of boys and girls: A meta-analysis. *Psychological Bulletin, 109*(2), 267–296.

MacDonald, A. P., & Games, R. G. (1974). Some characteristics of those who hold positive and negative attitudes toward homosexuals. *Journal of Homosexuality, 1*(1), 9–27.

MacKay, D. G. (1980). Psychology, presciptive grammar, and the pronoun problem. *American Psychologist, 35*(5), 444–449.

Mackie, D. M., Asuncion, A. G., & Rosselli, F. (1992). The impact of positive affect on persuasion processes. In M. S. Clark (Ed.), *Review of Personality and Social Psychology* (Vol. 14, pp. 247–270). Newbury Park, CA: Sage.

Mackie, D. M., & Hamilton, D. L. (Eds.). (1993). *Affect, cognition, and stereotyping: Interactive processes in group perception.* New York: Academic Press.

Mackie, D. M., & Worth, L. T. (1989). Cognitive deficits and the mediation of positive affect in persuasion. *Journal of Personality and Social Psychology, 57,* 27–40.

Mackie, D. M., & Worth, L. T. (1991). Feeling good, but not thinking straight: The impact of positive mood on persuasion. In J. P. Forgas (Ed.), *Emotion and social judgments* (pp. 201–219). New York: Pergamon.

Macrae, C. N., Bodenhausen, G. V., & Milne, A. B. (1995). The dissection of selection in person perception: Inhibitory processes in social stereotyping. *Journal of Personality and Social Psychology, 69*(3), 397–407.

Macrae, C. N., Bodenhausen, G. V., & Milne, A. B. (1998). Saying no to unwanted thoughts: Self- focus and the regulation of mental life. *Journal of Personality and Social Psychology, 74*(3), 578–589.

Macrae, C. N., Bodenhausen, G. V., Milne, A. B., & Jetten, J. (1994). Out of mind but back in sight: Stereotypes on the rebound. *Journal of Personality and Social Psychology, 67*(5), 808–817.

Macrae, C. N., Bodenhausen, G. V., Milne, A. B., Thorn, T. M. J., & Castelli, L. (1997). On the activation of social stereotypes: The moderating role of processing objectives. *Journal of Experimental Social Psychology, 33,* 471–489.

Macrae, C. N., Bodenhausen, G. V., Milne, A. B., & Wheeler, V. (1996). On resisting the temptation for simplification: Counterintentional effects of stereotype suppression on social memory. *Social Cognition, 14,* 1–20.

Macrae, C. N., Milne, A. B., & Bodenhausen, G. V. (1994). Stereotypes as energy-saving devices: A peek inside the cognitive toolbox. *Journal of Personality and Social Psychology, 66,* 37–47.

Macrae, C. N., Stangor, C., & Milne, A. B. (1994). Activating social stereotypes: A functional analysis. *Journal of Experimental Social Psychology, 30,* 370–389.

Madan, A. K., Aliabadi-Wahle, S., & Beech, D. J. (2001). Ageism in medical students' treatment recommendations: The example of breast-conserving procedures. *Academic Medicine, 76*(3), 282–284.

Maddox, K. B. (2004). Perspectives on racial phenotypicality bias. *Personality and Social Psychology Review, 8*(4), 383–401.

Madey, S. F., & Gomez, R. (2003). Reduced optimism for perceived age-related medical conditions. *Basic and Applied Social Psychology, 25*(3), 213–219.

Major, B., & Crocker, J. (1993). Social stigma: The consequences of attributional ambiguity. In D. M. Mackie & D. L. Hamilton (Eds.), *Affect, cognition, and stereotyping: Interactive processes in group perception* (pp. 345–370). New York: Academic Press.

Major, B., Feinstein, J., & Crocker, J. (1994). Attributional ambiguity of affirmative action. *Basic and Applied Social Psychology, 15*(1/2), 113–141.

Major, B., & Forcey, B. (1985). Social comparisons and pay evaluations: Preferences for same-sex and same-job wage comparisons. *Journal of Experimental Social Psychology, 21*, 393–405.

Major, B., Gramzow, R. H., McCoy, S. K., Levin, S., Schmader, T., & Sidanius, J. (2002). Perceiving personal discrimination: The role of group status and legitimizing ideology. *Journal of Personality and Social Psychology, 82*(3), 269–282.

Major, B., Kaiser, C. R., & McCoy, S. K. (2003). It's not my fault: When and why attributions to prejudice protect self-esteem. *Personality and Social Psychology Bulletin, 29*(6), 772–781.

Major, B., Quinton, W. J., & McCoy, S. K. (2002). Antecedents and consequences of attributions to discrimination: Theoretical and empirical advances. In M. Zanna (Ed.), *Advances in experimental social psychology* (Vol. 34, pp. 251–330). New York: Academic Press.

Major, B., & Schmader, T. (1998). Coping with stigma through psychological disengagement. In J. K. Swim & C. Stangor (Eds.), *Prejudice: The target's perspective* (pp. 219–241). New York: Academic Press.

Major, B., Spencer, S., Schmader, T., Wolfe, C., & Crocker, J. (1998). Coping with negative stereotypes about intellectual performance: The role of psychological disengagement. *Personality and Social Psychology Bulletin, 24*, 34–50.

Malamuth, N. M. (1989). The attraction to sexual aggression scale: Part one. *Journal of Sex Research, 26*, 26–49.

Markus, H., & Herzog, A. R. (1991). The role of the self-concept in aging. In K. W. Schaie (Ed.), *Annual Review of Gerontology and Geriatrics* (Vol. 11, pp. 110–143). New York: Springer.

Markus, H., & Kunda, Z. (1986). Stability and malleability of the self-concept. *Journal of Personality and Social Psychology, 51*, 858–866.

Markus, H., & Nurius, P. (1986). Possible selves. *American Psychologist, 41*, 954–969.

Markus, H., & Zajonc, R. (1985). The cognitive perspective in social psychology. In G. Lindzey & E. Aronson (Eds.), *Handbook of social psychology* (Vol. 1, 3rd ed., pp. 137–230). New York: Random House.

Martens, A., Greenberg, J., Schimel, J., & Landau, M. J. (2004). Ageism and death: Effects of mortality salience and perceived similarity to elders on reactions to elderly people.

Personality and Social Psychology Bulletin, 30(12), 1524–1536.

Martin, C. L. (1987). A ratio measure of sex stereotyping. *Journal of Personality and Social Psychology, 52*(3), 489–499.

Martin, C., & Nichols, R. C. (1962). Personality and religious belief. *Journal of Social Psychology, 56*, 3–8.

Martin, J. G., & Westie, F. R. (1959). The tolerant personality. *American Sociological Review, 24*, 521–528.

Maslow, A. H. (1970). *Motivation and personality.* New York: Harper & Row.

McCann, R., & Giles, H. (2002). Ageism in the workplace: A communication perspective. In T. D. Nelson (Ed.), *Ageism: Stereotyping and prejudice against older persons* (pp. 163–199). Cambridge, MA: MIT Press.

McCauley, C., & Stitt, C. L. (1978). An individual and quantitative measure of stereotypes. *Journal of Personality and Social Psychology, 36*(9), 929–940.

McCauley, C., Stitt, S. L., & Segal, M. (1980). Stereotyping: From prejudice to prediction. *Psychological Bulletin, 87*, 195–208.

McConahay, J. B. (1983). Modern racism and modern discrimination: The effects of race, racial attitudes, and context on simulated hiring decisions. *Personality and Social Psychology Bulletin, 9*(4), 551–558.

McConahay, J. B. (1986). Modern racism, ambivalence, and the modern racism scale. In J. F. Dovidio & S. L. Gaertner (Eds.), *Prejudice, discrimination, and racism* (pp. 91–125). New York: Academic Press.

McConahay, J. B., Hardee, B. B., & Batts, V. (1981). Has racism declined in America? It depends on who is asking and what is asked. *Journal of Conflict Resolution, 25*, 563–579.

McConahay, J. B., & Hough, J. C. (1976). Symbolic racism. *Journal of Social Issues, 32*, 23–45.

McConnell, A. R., & Leibold, J. M. (2001). Relations among the Implicit Association Test, discriminatory behavior, and explicit measures of racial attitudes. *Journal of Experimental Social Psychology, 37*(5), 435–442.

McFarland, S. G. (1989). Religious orientations and the targets of discrimination. *Journal for the Scientific Study of Religion, 28*, 324–336.

McFarland, S. G., & Crouch, Z. (2002). A cognitive skill confound on the Implicit Association Test. *Social Cognition, 20*(6), 483–510.

McGuire, T. R. (1995). Is homosexuality genetic? A critical review and some suggestions. *Journal of Homosexuality, 28*(1/2), 115–145.

McGuire, W. J., & McGuire, C. V. (1981). The spontaneous self-concept as affected by personal distinctiveness. In M. D. Lynch, A. A. Norem-Hebeisen, & K. J. Gergen (Eds.), *Self-concept: Advances in theory and research.* Cambridge, MA: Ballinger.

McIntyre, R. B., Paulson, R. M., & Lord, C. G. (2003). Alleviating women's mathematics stereotype threat through salience of group achievements. *Journal of Experimental Social Psychology, 39*, 83–90.

McKown, C., & Weinstein, R. S. (2003). The development and consequences of stereotype consciousness in middle childhood. *Child Development, 74*(2), 498–515.

McVittie, C., McKinlay, A., & Widdicombe, S. (2003). *British Journal of Social Psychology, 42*, 595–612.

Mellor, D. (2003). Contemporary racism in Australia: The experiences of Aborigines. *Personality and Social Psychology Bulletin, 29*(4), 474–486.

Meltzer, H. (1962). Age differences in status and happiness of workers. *Geriatrics, 17*, 831–837.

Mendoza-Denton, R., Downey, G., Purdie, V. J., Davis, A., & Pietrzak, J. (2002). Sensitivity to status-based rejection: Implications for African American students' college experience. *Journal of Personality and Social Psychology, 83*(4), 896–918.

Miller, G. A. (1956). The magical number seven, plus or minus two: Some limits on our capacity for processing information. *Psychological Review, 63*, 81–97.

Miller, G. A., Galanter, E., & Pribram, K. (1960). *Plans and the structure of behavior.* New York: Holt.

Miller, N., & Brewer, M. B. (1986). Categorization effects on ingroup and outgroup perception. In J. Dovidio & S. L. Gaertner (Eds.), *Prejudice, discrimination, and racism* (pp. 209–230). New York: Academic Press.

Miller, N. E., & Dollard, J. (1941). *Social learning and imitation.* New Haven, CT: Yale University Press.

Mischel, W. (1966). A social learning view of sex differences in behavior, In E. E. Maccoby (Ed.), *The development of sex differences* (pp. 56–81). Stanford, CA: Stanford University Press.

Mischel, W. (1977). The interaction of person and situation. In D. Magnusson & N. S. Endler (Eds.), *Personality at the crossroads: Current issues in interactional psychology.* Hillsdale, NJ: Erlbaum.

Mitchell, C. J. (2004). Mere acceptance produces apparent attitude in the Implicit Association Test. *Journal of Experimental Social Psychology, 40*(3), 366–373.

Monteith, M. J. (1993). Self-regulation of prejudiced responses: Implications for progress in prejudice-reduction efforts. *Journal of Personality and Social Psychology, 65*, 469–485.

Monteith, M. J. (1996a). Affective reactions to prejudice-related discrepant responses: The impact of standard salience. *Personality and Social Psychology Bulletin, 22*, 48–59.

Monteith, M. J. (1996b). Contemporary forms of prejudice-related conflict: In search of a nutshell. *Personality and Social Psychology Bulletin, 22*(5), 461–473.

Monteith, M. J., Ashburn-Nardo, L., Voils, C. I., & Czopp, A. M. (2002). Putting the brakes on prejudice: On the development and operation of cues for control. *Journal of Personality and Social Psychology, 83*(5), 1029–1050.

Monteith, M. J., Deneen, N. E., & Tooman, G. D. (1996). The effect of social norm activation on the expression of opinions concerning gay men and blacks. *Basic and Applied Social Psychology, 18*(3), 267–288.

Monteith, M. J., Spicer, C. V., & Tooman, G. D. (1998). Consequences of stereotype suppression: Stereotypes on and not on the rebound. *Journal of Experimental Social Psychology, 34*, 355–377.

Monteith, M. J., Zuwerink, J. R., & Devine, P. G. (1994). Prejudice and prejudice reduction: Classic challenges, contemporary approaches. In P. G. Devine, D. L. Hamilton, & T. M. Ostrom (Eds.), *Social cognition: Impact on social psychology* (pp. 323–346). New York: Academic Press.

Montepare, J. M., & Lachman, M. E. (1989). "You're only as old as you feel": Self-perceptions of age, fears of aging, and life satisfaction from adolescence to old age. *Psychology and Aging, 4*, 73–78.

Montepare, J. M., & Zebrowitz, L. A. (1998). Person perception comes of age: The salience and significance of age in social judgments. In M. Zanna (Ed.), *Advances in experimental social psychology* (Vol. 30, pp. 93–161) New York: Academic Press.

Montepare, J. M., & Zebrowitz, L. A. (2002). A social-developmental view of ageism. In T. D. Nelson (Ed.), *Ageism: Stereotyping and prejudice against older persons* (pp. 77–125). Cambridge, MA: MIT Press.

Montessori, M. (1974). *Childhood education.* Chicago: Regnery.

Moore, T. E., Griffiths, K., & Payne, B. (1987). Gender, attitudes towards women, and the appreciation of sexist humor. *Sex Roles, 16*(9/10), 521–531.

Moreno, K. N., & Bodenhausen, G. V. (1999). Resisting stereotype change: The role of motivation and attentional capacity in defending social beliefs. *Group processes and intergroup relations, 2*, 5–16.

Morgan, M. Y. (1987). The impact of religion on gender-role attitudes. *Psychology of Women Quarterly, 11*, 301–310.

Morris, R. J., Hood, R. W., & Watson, P. J. (1989). A second look at religious orientation, social desirability, and prejudice. *Bulletin of the Psychonomic Society, 27*, 81–84.

Moskowitz, D. S., Suh, E. J., & Desaulniers, J. (1994). Situational influences on gender differences in agency and communion. *Journal of Personality and Social Psychology, 66*, 753–761.

Moskowitz, G. B. (1993). Individual differences in social categorization: The influence of personal need for structure on spontaneous trait inferences. *Journal of Personality and Social Psychology, 65*, 132–142.

Moskowitz, G. B., Salomon, A. R., & Taylor, C. M. (2000). Preconsciously controlling stereotyping: Implicitly activated egalitarian goals prevent the activation of stereotypes. *Social Cognition 18*(2), 151–177.

Murphey, M., Myers, J., & Drennan, P. (1982). Attitudes of children toward older persons: What they are, what they can be. *The School Counselor, 29*(4), 281–288.

Murray, S. B. (1999). It's safer this way: The subtle and not-so-subtle exclusion of men in child care. In N. V. Benokraitis (Ed.), *Subtle sexism: Current practice and prospects for change* (pp. 136–153). New York: Sage.

Murrell, A. J., & Jones, R. (1996). Assessing affirmative action: Past, present, and future. *Journal of Social Issues, 52*(4), 77–92.

Myrdal, G. (1944). *An American dilemma.* New York: Harper.

Nacoste, R. W. (1985). Selection procedure and responses to affirmative action: The case of favorable treatment. *Law and Human Behavior, 9*, 225–242.

Nadler, A., & Fisher, J. D. (1986). The role of threat to self-esteem and perceived control in recipient reaction to help: Theory development and empirical validation. In L. Berkowitz (Ed.), *Advances in experimental social psychology* (Vol. 19, pp. 81–122). New York: Academic Press.

National Center for Health Statistics (1999). *Healthy people 2000 review, 1998–1999.* Hyattsville, MD: Public Health Service.

Nelson, L. J., & Wischusen, J. (1999, June). *Mortality salience and intergroup bias: Nationalism versus racism. Which worldview is defended in a situation of multiple group identities?* Poster presented at the annual meeting of the American Psychological Society, Denver, CO.

Nelson, T. D. (1993). The hierarchical organization of behavior: A useful feedback model of self-regulation. *Current Directions in Psychological Science, 2*(4), 121–126.

Nelson, T. D. (1996). *The effects of interpersonal discomfort on intergroup attitudes and behavior* Unpublished doctoral dissertation, Michigan State University, East Lansing.

Nelson, T. D. (Ed.). (2002). *Ageism: Stereotyping and prejudice against older persons.* Cambridge, MA: MIT Press.

Nelson, T. E., Acker, M., & Manis, M. (1996). Irrepressible stereotypes. *Journal of Experimental Social Psychology, 32,* 13–38.

Nesdale, D., & Todd, P. (1998). Intergroup ratio and the contact hypothesis. *Journal of Applied Social Psychology, 28*(13), 1196–1217.

Neuberg, S. L. (1994). Expectancy-confirmation processes in stereotype-tinged social encounters: The moderating role of social goals. In M. P. Zanna & J. M. Olson (Eds.), *The psychology of prejudice: The Ontario symposium* (Vol. 7, pp. 103–130). Hillsdale, NJ: Erlbaum.

Neuberg, S. L., & Newsom, J. T. (1993). Personal need for structure: Individual differences in the desire for simple structure. *Journal of Personality and Social Psychology, 65,* 113–131.

Neuberg, S. L., Smith, D. M., & Asher, T. (2000). Why people stigmatize: Toward a biocultural framework. In T. F. Heatherton, R. E. Kleck, M. R. Hebl, & J. G. Hull (Eds.), *The social psychology of stigma* (pp. 31–61). New York: Guilford.

Neufeldt, V. (1989). *Webster's new world dictionary.* New York: Webster's New World Dictionaries.

Neugarten, B. (1974). Age groups in American society and the rise of the young-old. *The Annals of the American Academy of Political and Social Science* (September), 187–198.

Neugarten, B. (1982). *Age or need? Public policies for older people.* Beverly Hills, CA: Sage.

Newcomb, T. M. (1959). *Social psychology.* New York: Holt-Dryden.

Newman, L. S., Caldwell, T., Chamberlin, B. W., & Griffin, T. D. (in press). Thought suppression, projection, and the development of stereotypes. *Basic and Applied Social Psychology.*

Newsom, J. T. (1999). Another side to caregiving: Negative reactions to being helped. *Current Directions in Psychological Science, 8*(6), 183–187.

Ng, S. H. (2002). Will families support their elders? Answers from across cultures. In T. D. Nelson (Ed.), *Ageism: Stereotyping and prejudice against older persons* (pp. 295–309). Cambridge, MA: MIT Press.

Niemann, Y. F., Jennings, L., Rozelle, R. M., Baxter, J. C., & Sullivan, E. (1994). Use of free responses and cluster analysis to determine stereotypes of eight groups. *Personality and Social Psychology Bulletin, 20*(4), 379–390.

Nisbett, R. E., & Ross, L. (1980). *Human inference: Strategies and shortcomings of social judgment.* Englewood Cliffs, NJ: Prentice-Hall.

Nosek, B. A., Banaji, M. R., & Greenwald, A. G. (2002). Math = male, me = female, therefore math ≠ me. *Journal of Personality and Social Psychology, 83,* 44–59.

Nowak, A., & Vallacher, R. (1998). *Dynamical social psychology.* New York: Guilford.

Nuessel, F. (1982). The language of ageism. *The Gerontologist, 22*(3), 273–276.

O'Malley, P. M., & Bachman, J. G. (1983). Self esteem: Change and stability between age 13 and 23. *Developmental Psychology, 19,* 257–268.

O'Neil, J. M. (1996). The gender role journey workshop: Exploring sexism and gender role conflict in a coeducational setting. In M. P. Andronico (Ed.), *Men in groups: Insights, interventions, and psychoeducational work* (pp. 193–213). Washington, DC: American Psychological Association.

Oatley, K. (1993). Social construction in emotions. In M. Lewis & J. M. Haviland (Eds.), *Handbook of emotions* (pp. 341–352). New York: Guilford.

Ochsner, K. N., & Lieberman, M. D. (2001). The emergence of social cognitive neuroscience. *American Psychologist, 56*(9), 717–734.

Ohlott, P. J., Ruderman, M. N., & McCauley, C. D. (1994). Gender differences in managers' developmental job experiences. *Academy of Management Journal, 37,* 46–67.

Olson, J. M., Roese, N. J., & Zanna, M. P. (1996). Expectancies. In E. T. Higgins & A. W. Kruglanski (Eds.), *Social psychology: Handbook of principles* (pp. 211–238). New York: Guilford.

Olson, M. A., & Fazio, R. H. (2003). Relations between implicit measures of prejudice: What are we measuring? *Psychological Science, 14*(6), 636–639.

Olson, M. A., & Fazio, R. H. (2004a). Reducing the influence of extrapersonal associations on the Implicit Association Test: Personalizing the IAT. *Journal of Personality and Social Psychology, 86*(5), 653–667.

Olson, M. A. & Fazio, R. H. (2004b). Trait inferences as a function of automatically activated racial attitudes and motivation to control prejudiced reactions. *Basic and Applied Social Psychology, 26,* 1–11.

Ortony, A., Clore, G. L., & Collins, A. (1988). *The cognitive structure of emotions.* New York: Cambridge University Press.

Osborne, J. W. (1995). Academics, self-esteem, and race: A look at the underlying assumptions of the disidentification hypothesis. *Personality and Social Psychology Bulletin, 21*(5), 449–455.

Oskamp, S. (1991). *Attitudes and opinions.* Englewood Cliffs, NJ: Prentice-Hall.

Ostrom, T. M., & Sedikides, C. (1992). Out-group homogeneity effects in natural and minimal groups. *Psychological Bulletin, 112,* 536–552.

Ottati, V., & Lee, Y. (1995). Accuracy: A neglected component of stereotype research. In Y. Lee, L. J. Jussim, & C. R. McCauley (Eds.), *Stereotype accuracy: Toward appreciating group differences* (pp. 29–59). Washington, DC: American Psychological Association.

Ottaway, S. A., Hayden, D. C., & Oakes, M. A. (2001). Implicit attitudes and racism: Effects of word familiarity and frequency on the implicit association test. *Social Cognition, 19*(2), 97–144.

Owen, P. R., & Laurel-Seller, E. (2000). Weight and shape ideals: Thin is dangerously in. *Journal of Applied Social Psychology, 30*(5), 979–990.

Page, R. A., & Moss, M. K. (1975). Attitude similarity and attraction: The effects of the bogus pipeline. *Bulletin of the Psychonomic Society, 5,* 63–65.

Palmore, E. B. (1982). Attitudes toward the aged: What we know and need to know. *Research on Aging, 4,* 333–348.

Palmore, E. B. (1999). *Ageism: Negative and positive* (2nd ed.). New York: Springer.

Paolini, S., Hewstone, M., & Rubin, M. (2004). Increased group dispersion after exposure to one deviant group member: Testing Hamburger's model of member-to-group generalization. *Journal of Experimental Social Psychology, 40*(5), 569–585.

Park, J., & Banaji, M. R. (2000). Mood and heuristics: The influence of happy and sad states on sensitivity and bias in stereotyping. *Journal of Personality and Social Psychology, 78*(6), 1005–1023.

Park, J., & Rothbart, M. (1982). Perception of out-group homogeneity and levels of social categorization: Memory for the subordinate attributes of in-group and out-group members. *Journal of Personality and Social Psychology, 42*(6), 1051–1068.

Parry, H. J. (1949). Protestants, Catholics and prejudice. *International Journal of Opinion and Attitude Research, 3,* 205–213.

Pasupathi, M., Carstensen, L., & Tsai, J. (1995). Ageism in interpersonal settings. In B. Lott & D. Maluso (Eds.), *The social psychology of interpersonal discrimination* (pp. 160–182). New York: Guilford.

Peacock, E., & Talley, W. (1984). Intergenerational contact: A way to counteract ageism. *Educational Gerontology, 10,* 13–24.

Pendry, L. F., & Macrae, C. N. (1994). Stereotypes and mental life: The case of the motivated but thwarted tactician. *Journal of Experimental Social Psychology, 30*(4), 303–325.

Pendry, L. F., & Macrae, C. N. (1996). What the disinterested perceiver overlooks: Goal-directed social categorization. *Personality and Social Psychology Bulletin, 22*(3), 249–256.

Penner, L. A. (1971). Interpersonal attraction toward a Black person as a function of value importance. *Personality, 2,* 175–187.

Perdue, C. W., Dovidio, J. F., Gurtman, M. B., & Tyler, R. B. (1990). "Us" and "them": Social categorization and the process of intergroup bias. *Journal of Personality and Social Psychology, 59,* 475–486.

Perdue, C. W., & Gurtman, M. B. (1990). Evidence for the automaticity of ageism. *Journal of Experimental Social Psychology, 26,* 199–216.

Pettigrew, T. F. (1958). Personality and sociocultural factors in intergroup attitudes: A cross-national comparison. *Journal of Conflict Resolution, 2,* 29–42.

Pettigrew, T. F. (1959). Regional differences in an anti-Negro prejudice. *Journal of Abnormal and Social Psychology, 59,* 28–36.

Pettigrew, T. F. (1979). The ultimate attribution error: Extending Allport's cognitive analysis of prejudice. *Personality and Social Psychology Bulletin, 5*(4), 461–476.

Pettigrew, T. F. (1985). New black-white patterns: How best to conceptualize them? In R. H. Turner & J. F. Short (Eds.), *Annual review of sociology* (Vol. 11, pp. 75–91). Palo Alto, CA: Annual Reviews.

Pettigrew, T. F. (1986). The intergroup contact hypothesis reconsidered. In M. Hewstone & R. Brown (Eds.), *Contact and conflict in intergroup encounters* (pp. 169–195). New York: Basil Blackwell.

Pettigrew, T. F. (1987, May 12). "Useful" modes of thought contribute to prejudice. *New York Times,* 17–20.

Pettigrew, T. F. (1997). Generalized intergroup contact effects on prejudice. *Personality and Social Psychology Bulletin, 23*(2), 173–185.

Pettigrew, T. F. (1998). Intergroup contact theory. *Annual review of psychology* (Vol. 49, pp. 65–85). Palo Alto, CA: Annual Reviews.

Pettigrew, T. F., & Meertens, R. W. (1995). Subtle and blatant prejudice in Western Europe. *European Journal of Social Psychology, 25,* 57–75.

Pettigrew, T. F., & Tropp, L. R. (2000). Does intergroup contact reduce prejudice? Recent meta-analytic findings. In S. Oskamp (Ed.), *Reducing prejudice and discrimination* (pp. 93–114). Mahwah, NJ: Erlbaum.

Petty, R. E., & Cacioppo, J. T. (1981). *Attitudes and persuasion: Classic and contemporary approaches.* Dubuque, IA: William Brown.

Petty, R. E., & Wegener, D. T. (1998). Attitude change: Multiple roles for persuasion variables. In D. T. Gilbert, S. T. Fiske, & G. Lindzey (Eds.), *The handbook of social psychology* (Vol. 1, 4th ed., pp. 323–390). New York: McGraw-Hill.

Phelps, E. A., O'Connor, K. J., Cunningham, W. A., Funayama, E. S., Gatenby, J. C., Gore, J. C., et al. (2000). Performance on indirect measures of race evaluation predicts amygdala activation. *Journal of Cognitive Neuroscience, 12*(5), 729–738.

Phelps, E. A., & Thomas, L. A. (2003). Race, behavior, and the brain: The role of neuroimaging in understanding complex social behaviors. *Political Psychology, 24*(4), 747–758.

Phillips, B. N., & D'Amico, L. A. (1956). Effects of cooperation and competition on the cohesiveness of small face-to-face groups. *Journal of Educational Psychology, 47,* 65–70.

Pinel, E. C. (2002). Stigma consciousness in intergroup contexts: The power of conviction. *Journal of Experimental Social Psychology, 38,* 178–185.

Plant, E. A. (2004). Responses to interracial interactions over time. *Personality and Social Psychology Bulletin, 30*(11), 1458–1471.

Plant, E. A., & Devine, P. G. (1998). Internal and external motivation to respond without prejudice. *Journal of Personality and Social Psychology, 75*(3), 811–832.

Plant, E. A., & Devine, P. G. (2001). Responses to other-imposed pro-Black pressure: Acceptance or backlash? *Journal of Experimental Social Psychology, 37*(6), 486–501.

Plant, E. A., Peruche, B. M., & Butz, D. A. (2005). Eliminating automatic racial bias: Making race non-diagnostic for responses to criminal suspects. *Journal of Experimental Social Psychology, 41*(2), 141–156.

Plous, S. (1993). *The psychology of judgment and decision making.* New York: McGraw-Hill.

Porter, J. R., & Washington, R. E. (1979). Black identity and self-esteem: A review of the studies of Black self-concept, 1968–1978. *Annual Review of Sociology, 5,* 53–74.

Potkay, C. R., & Allen, B. P. (1988). The adjective generation technique (AGT): Assessment via word descriptions of self and others. In C. Spielberger & J. N. Butcher (Eds.),

Advances in personality assessment (Vol. 7, pp. 127–159). Hillsdale, NJ: Erlbaum.

Powers, W. T. (1973). *Behavior: The control of perception.* Chicago: Aldine.

Powers, W. T. (1978). Quantitative analysis of purposive systems: Some spadework at the foundations of psychology. *Psychological Review, 85*(5), 417–435.

Powers, W. T. (1989). *Living control systems.* Gravel Switch, KY: The Control Systems Group.

Pozo, C., Carver, C. S., Wellens, A. R., & Scheier, M. F. (1991). Social anxiety and social perception: Construing others' reactions to the self. *Personality and Social Psychology Bulletin, 17*(4), 355–362.

Pratkanis, A. R., & Turner, M. E. (1996). The proactive removal of discriminatory barriers: Affirmative action as effective help. *Journal of Social Issues, 52*(4), 111–132.

Pratto, F., & Shih, M. (2000). Social dominance orientation and group context in implicit group prejudice. *Psychological Science, 11*(6), 515–518.

Pratto, F., Sidanius, J., Stallworth, L. M., & Malle, B. F. (1994). Social dominance orientation: A personality variable predicting social and political attitudes. *Journal of Personality and Social Psychology, 67*(4), 741–763.

Pratto, F., Stallworth, L. M., & Sidanius, J. (1997). The gender gap: Differences in political attitudes and social dominance orientation. *British Journal of Social Psychology, 36,* 49–68.

Pratto, F., Stallworth, L. M., Sidanius, J., & Siers, B. (1997). The gender gap in occupational role attainment: A social dominance approach. *Journal of Personality and Social Psychology, 72,* 37–53.

Pressly, S. L., & Devine, P. G. (1992). Sex, sexism, and compunction: Group membership or internalization of standards? Paper presented at the 64th annual meeting of the Midwestern Psychological Association, Chicago, May.

Pronin, E., Steele, C. M., & Ross, L. (2004). Identity bifurcation in response to stereotype threat: Women and mathematics. *Journal of Experimental Social Psychology, 40,* 152–168.

Pyszczynski, T., Greenberg, J., Solomon, S., Arndt, J., & Shimel, J. (2004). Why do people need self-esteem? A theoretical and empirical review. *Psychological Bulletin, 130*(3), 435–468.

Quattrone, G. A., & Jones, E. E. (1980). The perception of variability within in-groups and out-groups: Implications for the law of small numbers. *Journal of Personality and Social Psychology, 38,* 141–152.

Quigley-Fernandez, B., & Tedeschi, J. T. (1978). The bogus pipeline as lie detector: Two validity studies. *Journal of Personality and Social Psychology, 36,* 247–256.

Quinn, D. M., & Spencer, S. J. (1996, August). *Stereotype threat and the effect of test diagnosticity on women's math performance.* Paper presented at the annual American Psychological Association conference, Toronto, Canada.

Quist, R. M., & Resendez, M. G. (2002). Social dominance threat: Examining social dominance theory's explanation of prejudice as legitimizing myths. *Basic and Applied Social Psychology, 24*(4), 287–293.

Rabbie, J. M., & Horwitz, M. (1969). Arousal of ingroup-outgroup bias by a chance win or loss. *Journal of Personality and Social Psychology, 13*(3), 269–277.

Raden, D. (1994). Are symbolic racism and traditional prejudice part of a contemporary authoritarian attitude syndrome? *Political Behavior, 16*(3), 365–384.

Radke, M., Trager, H., & Davis, H. (1949). Social perceptions and attitudes of children. *Genetic Psychology Monographs, 40,* 327–447.

Rakow, L. F., & Wackwitz, L. A. (1998). Communication of sexism. In M. L. Hecht (Ed.), *Communicating prejudice* (pp. 99–111). Thousand Oaks, CA: Sage.

Ramsey, J. L., Langlois, J. H., & Hoss, R. A. (2004). Origins of a stereotype: Categorization of facial attractiveness by 6-month old infants. *Developmental Science, 7*(2), 201–211.

Rankin, R. E., & Campbell, D. T. (1955). Galvanic skin response to Negro and White experimenters. *Journal of Abnormal and Social Psychology, 51,* 30–33.

Reeve, J. M. (1997). *Understanding motivation and emotion* (2nd ed.). Orlando, FL: Harcourt Brace.

Resendez, M. G. (2002). The stigmatizing effects of affirmative action: An examination of moderating variables. *Journal of Applied Social Psychology, 32,* 185–206.

Reyes-Ortiz, C. (1997). Physicians must confront ageism. *Academic Medicine, 72*(10), 831.

Reynolds, K. J., Turner, J. C., Haslam, S. A., & Ryan, M. K. (2001). The role of personality and group factors in explaining prejudice. *Journal of Experimental Social Psychology, 37,* 427–434.

Ric, F. (2004). Effects of the activation of affective information on stereotyping: When sadness increases stereotype use. *Personality and Social Psychology Bulletin, 30*(10), 1310–1321.

Richardson, S. A., & Green, A. (1971). When is black beautiful? Coloured and white children's reactions to skin color. *British Journal of Educational Psychology, 41,* 62–69.

Richeson, J. A., & Nussbaum, R. J. (2004). The impact of multiculturalism versus color-blindness on racial bias. *Journal of Experimental Social Psychology, 40*(3), 417–423.

Riess, M., Kalle, R. J., & Tedeschi, J. T. (1981). Bogus pipeline attitude assessment, impression management, and misattribution in induced compliance settings. *Journal of Social Psychology, 115,* 247–258.

Roberts, T., & Pennebaker, J. W. (1995). Gender differences in perceiving internal state: Toward a his-and-hers model of perceptual cue use. In M. Zanna (Ed.), *Advances in experimental social psychology* (Vol. 27, pp. 143–175). New York: Academic Press.

Rodin, J., & Langer, E. (1980). The decline of control and the fall of self-esteem. *Journal of Social Issues, 36,* 12–29.

Rodin, M., Price, J., Sanchez, F., & McElligot, S. (1989). Derogation, exclusion, and unfair treatment of persons with social flaws: Controllability of stigma and the attribution of prejudice. *Personality and Social Psychology Bulletin, 15*(3), 439–451.

Roediger, H. L. (1990). Implicit memory: Retention without awareness. *American Psychologist, 45,* 1043–1056.

Roese, N. J., & Jamieson, D. W. (1993). Twenty years of bogus pipeline research: A critical review and meta-analysis. *Psychological Bulletin, 114*(2), 363–375.

Rohan, M. J., & Zanna, M. P. (1996). Value transmission in families. In C. Seligman, J. M. Olson, & M. P. Zanna (Eds.), *The psychology of values: The Ontario symposium* (Vol. 8, pp. 253–276). Mahwah, NJ: Erlbaum.

Rokeach, M. (1973). *The nature of human values.* New York, NY: Free Press.

Rollins, J. H. (1973). Reference identification of youth of differing ethnicity. *Journal of Personality and Social Psychology, 26,* 222–231.

Romer, D., Jamieson, K. H., & deCoteau, N.J. (1998). The treatment of persons of color in local television news: Ethnic blame discourse or realistic group conflict? *Communication Research, 25*(3), 286–305.

Rosch, E., & Lloyd, B. (1978). *Cognition and categorization.* Hillsdale, NJ: Erlbaum.

Rosen, B., & Jerdee, T. (1976). The nature of job related stereotypes. *Journal of Applied Psychology, 61,* 180–183.

Rosenberg, M. (1979). *Conceiving the self.* New York: Basic Books.

Rosenfield, D., Greenberg, J., Folger, R., & Borys, R. (1982). Effect of an encounter with a black panhandler on subsequent helping for Blacks: Tokenism or confirming a negative stereotype? *Personality and Social Psychology Bulletin, 8,* 664–671.

Rosenfield, D., & Stephan, W. G. (1981). Intergroup relations among children. In S. Brehm, S. Kassin, & F. Gibbons (Eds.), *Developmental social psychology* (pp. 271–297). New York: Oxford University Press.

Rosenfield, D., Stephan, W. G., & Lucker, G. W. (1981). Attraction to competent and incompetent members of cooperative and competitive groups. *Journal of Applied Social Psychology, 11*(5), 416–433.

Rosenhan, D. L. (1973). On being sane in insane places. *Science, 179,* 250–258.

Rosenthal, R., & Jacobson, L. (1968). *Pygmalion in the classroom.* New York: Holt, Rinehart & Winston.

Rosenthal, R., & Rubin, D. B. (1978). Interpersonal expectancy effects: The first 345 studies. *Behavioral and Brain Sciences, 3,* 377–386.

Ross, L., & Nisbett, R. E. (1991). *The person and the situation: Perspectives of social psychology.* New York: McGraw-Hill.

Rothbart, M., Evans, M., & Fulero, S. (1979). Recall for confirming events: Memory processes and the maintenance of social stereotyping. *Journal of Experimental Social Psychology, 15,* 343–355.

Rothbart, M., & Lewis, S. (1988). Inferring category attributes from exemplar attributes: Geometric shapes and social categories. *Journal of Personality and Social Psychology, 55,* 861–872.

Rothbart, M., & Lewis, S. (1994). Cognitive processes and intergroup relations: A historical perspective. In P. G. Devine, D. L. Hamilton, & T. M. Ostrom (Eds.), *Social cognition: Impact on social psychology* (pp. 347–382). New York: Academic Press.

Rothbaum, F. (1983). Aging and age stereotypes. *Social Cognition, 2*(2), 171–184.

Rowatt, W. C., & Franklin, L. M. (2004). Christian orthodoxy, religious fundamentalism, and right-wing authoritarianism as predictors of implicit racial prejudice. *International Journal for the Psychology of Religion, 14*(2), 125–138.

Rowatt, W. C., Tsang, J., Kelly, J., LaMartina, B., McCullers, M., & McKinley, A. (2004). *Associations between religious personality dimensions and implicit homosexual prejudice.* Manuscript submitted for publication.

Ruble, D. N., & Ruble, T. L. (1982). Sex stereotypes. In A. G. Miller (Ed.), *In the eye of the beholder: Contemporary issues in stereotyping* (pp. 188–252). New York: Praeger.

Rudman, L. A., Ashmore, R. D., & Gary, M. L. (2001). Unlearning automatic biases: The malleability of implicit prejudice and stereotypes. *Journal of Personality and Social Psychology, 81*(5), 856–868.

Rudman, L. A., & Borgida, E. (1995). The afterglow of construct accessibility: The behavioral consequences of priming men to view women as sexual objects. *Journal of Experimental Social Psychology, 31,* 493–517.

Rudman, L. A., Feinberg, J., & Fairchild, K. (2002). Minority members' implicit attitudes: Automatic ingroup bias as a function of group status. *Social Cognition, 20*(4), 294–320.

Rudman, L. A., & Glick, P. (1999). Feminized management and backlash toward agentic women: The hidden costs to women of a kinder, gentler image of middle managers. *Journal of Personality and Social Psychology, 77*(5), 1004–1010.

Runciman, W. G. (1968). Problems of research on relative deprivation. In H. H. Hyman & E. Singer (Eds.), *Readings in reference group theory and research.* New York: Free Press.

Ryan, K. M., & Kanjorski, J. (1998). The enjoyment of sexist humor, rape attitudes, and relationship aggression in college students. *Sex Roles, 38*(9/10), 743–756.

Sackett, P. R., Hardison, C. M., & Cullen, M. J. (2004). On interpreting stereotype threat as accounting for African American–White differences on cognitive tests. *American Psychologist, 59,* 7–13.

Sakalli, N. (2002). Application of the attribution-value model of prejudice to homosexuality. *Journal of Social Psychology, 142*(2), 264–271.

Sales, S. M. (1973). Threat as a factor in authoritarianism: An analysis of archival data. *Journal of Personality and Social Psychology, 28,* 44–57.

Santuzzi, A. M., & Ruscher, J. B. (2002). Stigma salience and paranoid social cognition: Understanding variability in metaperceptions among individuals with recently-acquired stigma. *Social Cognition, 20*(3), 171–197.

Saris, R. N., Johnston, I., & Lott, B. (1995). Women as cues for men's approach or distancing behavior: A study of interpersonal sexist discrimination. *Sex Roles, 33*(3/4), 289–298.

Saucier, D. A., & Miller, C. T. (2003). The persuasiveness of racial arguments as a subtle measure of racism. *Personality and Social Psychology Bulletin, 29*(10), 1303–1315.

Saucier, D. A., Miller, C. T., Doucet, N. (in press). Differences in helping Whites and Blacks: A meta-analysis. *Personality and Social Psychology Review.*

Schacter, D. (1987). Implicit memory: History and current status. *Journal of Experimental Psychology: Learning, Memory, and Cognition, 12,* 432–444.

Schacter, D. L. (1992). Understanding implicit memory: A cognitive neuroscience approach. *American Psychologist, 47*(4), 559–569.

Schacter, S., & Singer, J. E. (1962). Cognitive, social and physiological determinants of emotional states. *Psychological Review, 69,* 379–399.

Schaller, M., Boyd, C., Yohannes, J., & O'Brien, M. (1995). The prejudiced personality revisited: Personal need for structure and formation of erroneous group stereotypes. *Journal of Personality and Social Psychology, 68*(3), 544–555.

Scheier, M. F., Carver, C. S., & Matthews, K. A. (1983). Attentional factors in the perception of bodily states. In J. T. Cacioppo & R. E. Petty (Eds.), *Social psychophysiology: A sourcebook* (pp. 510–542). New York: Guilford.

Schiele, J. H. (1991). An epistemological perspective on intelligence assessment among African American children. *Journal of Black Psychology, 17,* 23–36.

Schlenker, B. R., Bonoma, T. V., Hutchinson, D., & Burns, L. (1976). The bogus pipeline and stereotypes toward blacks. *Journal of Psychology, 93,* 319–329.

Schmader, T. (2001). Gender identification moderates stereotype threat effects on woman's math performance. *Journal of Experimental Social Psychology, 38,* 194–201.

Schmader, T., & Johns, M. (2003). Converging evidence that stereotype threat reduces working memory capacity. *Journal of Personality and Social Psychology, 85*(3), 440–452.

Schmidt, D., & Boland, S. (1986). Structure of perceptions of older adults: Evidence for multiple stereotypes. *Psychology and Aging, 1*(3), 255–260.

Schneider, D. J. (1973). Implicit personality theory: A review. *Psychological Bulletin, 79,* 294–309.

Schneider, D. J. (2004). *The psychology of stereotyping.* New York: Guilford.

Schneider, M. E., Major, B., Luhtanen, R., & Crocker, J. (1996). Social stigma and the potential costs of assumptive help. *Personality and Social Psychology Bulletin, 22*(2), 201–209.

Schroeder, D. A., Penner, L. A., Dovidio, J. F., & Piliavin, J. A. (1995). *The psychology of helping and altruism: Problems and puzzles.* New York: McGraw-Hill.

Schuman, H., & Kalton, G. (1985). Survey methods. In G. Lindzey & E. Aronson (Eds.), *Handbook of social psychology* (3rd ed., pp. 635–697). New York: Guilford.

Schuman, H., Steeh, C., & Bobo, L. (1985). *Racial attitudes in America: Trends and interpretations.* Cambridge, MA: Harvard University Press.

Schuman, H., Steeh, C., Bobo, L., & Krysan, M. (1997). *Racial attitudes in America* (2nd ed.). Cambridge, MA: Harvard University Press.

Schwarz, N. (1990). Feelings as information: Informational and motivational functions of affective states. In R. Sorrentino & E. T. Higgins (Eds.), *Handbook of motivation and cognition* (Vol. 2, pp. 527–561). New York: Guilford.

Schwarz, N., & Bless, H. (1991). Happy and mindless, but sad and smart? The impact of affective states on analytic reasoning. In J. Forgas (Ed.), *Emotion and social judgments* (pp. 55–71). London: Pergamon.

Schwarz, N., Bless, H., & Bohner, G. (1991). Mood and persuasion: Affective states influence the processing of persuasive communications. In M. P. Zanna (Ed.), *Advances in experimental social psychology* (Vol. 24, pp. 161–201). New York: Academic Press.

Schwarz, N., & Clore, G. (1988). How do I feel about it? Informative functions of affective states. In K. Fiedler & J. Forgas (Eds.), *Affect, cognition, and social behavior.* Toronto, Ontario, Canada: Hogrefe.

Schwarz, N., Wagner, D., Bannert, M., & Mathes, L. (1987). Cognitive accessibility of sex role concepts and attitudes toward political participation: The impact of sexist advertisements. *Sex Roles, 17*(9/10), 593–601.

Sczesny, S., & Kühnen, U. (2004). Meta-cognition about biological sex and gender-stereotypic physical appearance: Consequences for the assessment of leadership competence. *Personality and Social Psychology Bulletin, 30,* 13–21.

Sears, D. O. (1988). Symbolic racism. In P. A. Katz & D. A. Taylor (Eds.), *Eliminating racism: Profiles in controversy* (pp. 53–84). New York: Plenum.

Sears, D. O., & Allen, H. M., Jr. (1984). The trajectory of local desegregation controversies and whites' opposition to busing. In N. Miller & M. B. Brewer (Eds.), *Groups in contact: The psychology of desegregation* (pp. 123–151). New York: Academic Press.

Sears, D. O., & Henry, P. J. (2003). The origins of symbolic racism. *Journal of Personality and Social Psychology, 85*(2), 259–275.

Secouler, L. M. (1992). Our elders: At high risk for humiliation. *Journal of Primary Prevention, 12*(3), 195–208.

Sekaquaptewa, D., & Thompson, M. (2003). Solo status, stereotype threat, and performance expectancies: Their effects on women's performance. *Journal of Experimental Social Psychology, 39,* 68–74.

Serbin, L. A., Powlishta, K. K., & Gulko, J. (1993). The development of sex typing in middle childhood. *Monographs of the Society for Research in Child Development, 58,* 1–74.

Shah, J. Y., Kruglanski, A. W., & Thompson, E. P. (1998). Membership has its (epistemic) rewards: Need for closure effects on in-group bias. *Journal of Personality and Social Psychology, 75*(2), 383–393.

Shaller, M., Boyd, C., & Yohannes, J. (1995). The prejudiced personality revisited: Personal need for structure and formation of erroneous group stereotypes. *Journal of Personality and Social Psychology, 68*(3), 544–555.

Shelton, J. N. (2000). A reconceptualization of how we study issues of racial prejudice. *Personality and Social Psychology Review, 4*(4), 374–390.

Shepelak, N. J., Ogden, D., & Tobin-Bennett, D. (1984). The influence of gender labels on the sex typing of imaginary occupations. *Sex Roles, 11,* 983–996.

Sherif, M. (1956). Experiments in group conflict. *Scientific American, 195,* 54–58.

Sherif, M., Harvey, O. J., White, B. J., Hood, W. R., & Sherif, C. W. (1961). *Intergroup conflict and cooperation: The Robber's Cave experiment.* Norman: Oklahoma Book Exchange.

Sherif, M., & Sherif, C. W. (1969). *Social psychology.* New York: Harper & Row.

Sherman, J. W. (1996). Development and mental representation of stereotypes. *Journal of Personality and Social Psychology, 70*(6), 1126–1141.

Sherman, J. W., & Bessenoff, G. R. (1999). Stereotypes as source-monitoring cues: On the interaction between episodic and semantic memory. *Psychological Science, 10*(2), 106–110.

Sherman, J. W., & Frost, L. A. (2000). On the encoding of stereotype-relevant information under cognitive load. *Personality and Social Psychology Bulletin, 26,* 26–34.

Sherman, J. W., Klein, S. B., Laskey, A., & Wyer, N. A. (1998). Intergroup bias in group judgment processes: The role of behavioral memories. *Journal of Experimental Social Psychology, 34,* 51–65.

Sherman, J. W., Lee, A. Y., Bessenoff, G. R., & Frost, L. A. (1998). Stereotype efficiency reconsidered: Encoding flexibility under cognitive load. *Journal of Personality and Social Psychology, 75*(3), 589–606.

Sherman, J. W., Stroessner, S. J., Conrey, F. R., & Azam, O. (in press). Prejudice and stereotype maintenance processes: Attention, attribution, and individuation. *Journal of Personality and Social Psychology.*

Sherman, J. W., Stroessner, S. J., Loftus, S. J., & Deguzman, G. (1997). Stereotype suppression and recognition memory for stereotypical and nonstereotypical information. *Social Cognition, 15*(3), 205–215.

Sherman, S. J. (1970). Effects of choice and incentive on attitude change in a discrepant behavior situation. *Journal of Personality and Social Psychology, 15,* 245–252.

Sherman, S. J., & Gorkin, L. (1980). Attitude bolstering when behavior is inconsistent with central attitudes. *Journal of Experimental Social Psychology, 16,* 388–403.

Shih, M., Pittinsky, T. L., & Ambady, N. (1999). Stereotype susceptibility: Identity salience and shifts in quantitative performance. *Psychological Science, 10,* 80–83.

Showers, C., & Cantor, N. (1985). Social cognition: A look at motivated strategies. *Annual review of psychology* (Vol. 36, pp. 275–305).

Shuman, H., Steeh, C., Bobo, L., & Krysan, M. (1997). *Racial attitudes in America* (2nd ed.). Cambridge, MA: Harvard University Press.

Sidanius, J. (1993). The psychology of group conflict and the dynamics of oppression: A social dominance perspective. In W. McGuire & S. Iyengar (Eds.), *Current approaches to political psychology* (pp. 183–219). Durham, NC: Duke University Press.

Sidanius, J., Devereux, E., & Pratto, F. (1992). A comparison of symbolic racism theory and social dominance theory as explanations for racial policy attitudes. *Journal of Social Psychology, 132*(3), 377–395.

Sidanius, J., Liu, J. H., Shaw, J. S., & Pratto, F. (1994). Social dominance orientation, hierarchy attenuators and hierarchy enhancers: Social dominance theory and the criminal justice system. *Journal of Applied Social Psychology, 24*(4), 338–366.

Sidanius, J., Pratto, F., & Bobo, L. (1994). Social dominance orientation and the political psychology of gender: A case of invariance? *Journal of Personality and Social Psychology, 67*(6), 998–1011.

Sidanius, J., Pratto, F., & Bobo, L. (1996). Racism, conservatism, affirmative action, and intellectual sophistication: A matter of principled conservatism or group dominance? *Journal of Personality and Social Psychology, 70*(3), 476–490.

Sidanius, J., Pratto, F., Martin, M., & Stallworth, L. (1991). Consensual racism and career track: Some implications of social dominance theory. *Political Psychology, 12,* 691–721.

Sigall, H., & Page, R. (1971). Current stereotypes: A little fading, a little faking. *Journal of Personality and Social Psychology, 18*(2), 247–255.

Sigelman, L., & Sigelman, C. (1982). Sexism, racism, and ageism in voting behavior: An experimental analysis. *Social Psychology Quarterly, 45*(4), 263–269.

Sigelman, L., & Tuch, S. A. (1997). Metastereotypes: Blacks' perceptions of Whites' stereotypes of Blacks. *Public Opinion Quarterly, 61,* 87–101.

Silberman, E. K., Weingartner, H., & Post, R. M. (1983). Thinking disorder in depression: Logic and strategy in an abstract reasoning task. *Archives of General Psychiatry, 40,* 775–780.

Simmons, L. W. (1945). *The role of the aged in primitive society.* New Haven, CT: Yale University Press.

Simmons, R. G., Brown, L., Bush, D. M., & Blyth, D. A. (1978). Self-esteem and achievement of Black and White adolescents. *Social Problems, 26,* 86–96.

Simonton, D. K. (1990). Personality and politics. In L. A. Pervin (Ed.), *Handbook of personality: Theory and research* (pp. 670–692). New York: Guilford.

Simpson, J. A., & Kenrick, D. T. (1997). *Evolutionary social psychology.* Mahwah, NJ: Erlbaum.

Sinclair, R. C. (1988). Mood, categorization breadth, and performance appraisal: The effects of order of information acquisition and affective state on halo, accuracy, information retrieval, and evaluations. *Organizational Behavior and Human Decision Processes, 42,* 22–46.

Skinner, B. F. (1953). *Science and human behavior.* New York: Macmillan.

Skitka, L. J., Bauman, C. W., & Mullen, E. (2004). Political tolerance and coming to psychological closure following the September 11, 2001 terrorist attacks: An integrative approach. *Personality and Social Psychology Bulletin, 30*(6), 743–756.

Slater, P. E. (1964). Cross cultural views of the aged. In R. Kastenbaum (Ed.), *New thoughts on old age* (pp. 229–236). New York: Springer.

Slavin, R. E., & Cooper, R. (1999). Improving intergroup relations: Lessons learned from cooperative learning programs. *Journal of Social Issues, 55*(4), 647–663.

Smith, C. A., & Ellsworth, P. C. (1987). Patterns of appraisal and emotion related to taking an exam. *Journal of Personality and Social Psychology, 52*(3), 475–488.

Smith, E. (1990). Content and process specificity in the effects of prior experiences. In T. K. Srull & R. S. Wyer (Eds.), *Advances in social cognition* (pp. 1–59). Hillsdale, NJ: Erlbaum.

Smith, E. (1993). Social identity and social emotions: Toward new conceptualizations of prejudice. In D. M. Mackie & D. L. Hamilton (Eds.), *Affect, cognition, and stereotyping: Interactive processes in group perception* (pp. 297–315). New York: Academic Press.

Smith, E. R., & Branscombe, N. R. (1988). Category accessibility as implicit memory. *Journal of Experimental Social Psychology, 24,* 490–504.

Smith, E. R., & Mackie, D. M. (1997). Integrating the psychological and the social to understand human behavior. In C. McGarty & S. A. Haslam (Eds.), *The message of social psychology* (pp. 305–314). Cambridge, MA: Blackwell.

Smith, H. P., & Rosen, E. W. (1958). Some psychological correlates of worldmindedness and authoritarianism. *Journal of Personality, 26,* 170–183.

Smith, J. L., & White, P. H. (2002). An examination of implicitly activated, explicitly activated, and nullified stereotypes on mathematical performance: It's not just a woman's issue. *Sex Roles, 47*(3/4), 179–191.

Smith, N. G., & Ingram, K. M. (2004). Workplace heterosexism and adjustment among lesbian, gay, and bisexual individuals: The role of unsupportive social interactions. *Journal of Counseling Psychology, 51,* 57–67.

Sniderman, P. M., & Tetlock, P. E. (1986). Symbolic racism: Problems of motive attribution in political analysis. *Journal of Social Issues, 42*(2), 129–150.

Snyder, M. (1987). *Public appearances, private realities: The psychology of self-monitoring.* New York: Freeman.

Snyder, M. (1993). Basic research and practical problems: The promise of a "functional" personality and social psychology. *Personality and Social Psychology Bulletin, 19*(3), 251–264.

Snyder, M. L., Kleck, R. E., Strenta, A., & Mentzer, S. J. (1979). Avoidance of the handicapped: An attributional ambiguity analysis. *Journal of Personality and Social Psychology, 37*(12), 2297–2306.

Snyder, M., & Miene, P. (1994a). On the functions of stereotypes and prejudice. In M. P. Zanna & J. M. Olson (Eds.), *The psychology of prejudice: The Ontario symposium* (Vol. 7, pp. 33–54). Hillsdale, NJ: Erlbaum.

Snyder, M., & Miene, P. (1994b). Stereotyping of the elderly: A functional approach. *British Journal of Social Psychology, 33,* 63–82.

Snyder, M., & Swann, W. B. (1978). Behavioral confirmation in social interaction. *Journal of Experimental Social Psychology, 14,* 148–162.

Solomon, S., Greenberg, J., & Pyszczynski, T. (1991a). Terror management theory of self-esteem. In C. R. Snyder & D. R. Forsyth (Eds.), *Handbook of social and clinical psychology* (pp. 21–40). New York: Pergamon.

Solomon, S., Greenberg, J., & Pyszczynski, T. (1991b). A terror management theory of social behavior: The psychological functions of self-esteem and worldviews. In M. P. Zanna (Ed.), *Advances in experimental social psychology* (Vol. 24, pp. 91–159). New York: Academic Press.

Solomon, S., Greenberg, J., & Pyszczynski, T. (1997). A terror management theory of social behavior: The psychological functions of self-esteem and cultural worldviews. In M. Zanna (Ed.), *Advances in experimental social psychology* (Vol. 24, pp. 93–159). New York: Academic Press.

Solomon, S., Greenberg, J., & Pyszczynski, T. (2000). Pride and prejudice: Fear of death and social behavior. *Current Directions in Psychological Science, 9*(6), 200–204.

Sorgman, M., & Sorensen, M. (1984). Ageism: A course of study. *Theory Into Practice, 23*(2), 117–123.

Spears, R., Doosje, B., & Ellemers, N. (1997). Self-stereotyping in the face of threats to group status and distinctiveness: The role of group identification. *Personality and Social Psychology Bulletin, 23,* 538–553.

Spears, R., Oakes, P. J., Ellemers, N., & Haslam, S. A. (1997). Introduction: The social psychology of stereotyping and group life. In R. Spears, P. J. Oakes, N. Ellemers, & S. A. Haslam (Eds.), *The social psychology of stereotyping and group life* (pp. 1–19). Cambridge, MA: Blackwell.

Spence, J. T. (1993). Women, men, and society: Plus ca change, plus c'est la meme chose. In S. Oskamp & M. Costanso (Eds.), *Gender issues in contemporary society* (pp. 3–17). Newbury Park, CA: Sage.

Spence, J. T., & Helmreich, R. L. (1978). *Masculinity and femininity.* Austin: University of Texas Press.

Spencer, S. J., Steele, C. M., & Quinn, D. M. (1999). Stereotype threat and women's math performance. *Journal of Experimental Social Psychology, 35,* 4–28.

Srinivas, K. & Roediger, H. L. (1990). Classifying implicit memory tests: Category association and anagram solution. *Journal of Memory and Language, 29*(4), 389–412.

Stangor, C. (1988). Stereotype accessibility and information processing. *Personality and Social Psychology Bulletin, 14*(4), 694–708.

Stangor, C. (1990). Arousal, accessibility of trait constructs, and person perception. *Journal of Experimental Social Psychology, 26,* 305–321.

Stangor, C., & Ford, T. E. (1992). Accuracy and expectancy-confirming processing orientations and the development of stereotypes and prejudice. *European Review of Social Psychology, 3,* 57–89.

Stangor, C., & Lange, J. E. (1994). Mental representations of social groups: Advances in understanding stereotypes and stereotyping. In M. P. Zanna (Ed.), *Advances in experimental social psychology* (Vol. 26, pp. 357–416). New York: Academic Press.

Stangor, C., & McMillan, D. (1992). Memory for expectancy-congruent and expectancy-incongruent information: A review of the social and social developmental literatures. *Psychological Bulletin, 111,* 42–61.

Stangor, C., & Schaller, M. (1996). Stereotypes as individual and collective representations. In C. N. Macrae, C. Stangor, & M. Hewstone (Eds.), *Stereotypes and stereotyping* (pp. 3–37). New York: Guilford.

Stangor, C., Sullivan, L. A., & Ford, T. E. (1991). Affective and cognitive determinants of prejudice. *Social Cognition, 9*(4), 359–380.

Stapel, D. A., & Koomen, W. (1998). When stereotype activation results in (counter)stereotypical judgments: Priming stereotype-relevant traits and exemplars. *Journal of Experimental Social Psychology, 34,* 136–163.

Steele, C. M. (1988). The psychology of self-affirmation: Sustaining the integrity of the self. In L. Berkowitz (Ed.), *Advances in experimental social psychology* (Vol. 21, pp. 261–346). New York: Academic Press.

Steele, C. M. (1992, April). Race and the schooling of Black Americans. *The Atlantic Monthly,* 68–78.

Steele, C. M. (1995). Stereotype threat and the intellectual performance of African Americans. *Journal of Personality and Social Psychology, 69*(5), 797–811.

Steele, C. M. (1997). A threat in the air: How stereotypes shape intellectual identity and performance. *American Psychologist, 52*(6), 613–629.

Steele, C. M., & Aronson, J. (1995). Stereotype threat and the intellectual test performance of African Americans. *Journal of Personality and Social Psychology, 69*(5), 797–811.

Steele, C. M., Spencer, S. J., & Aronson, J. (2002). Contending with group image: The psychology of stereotype and social identity threat. In M. Zanna (Ed.), *Advances in Experimental Social Psychology* (Vol. 34, pp. 379–440). New York: Academic Press.

Steele, C. M., Spencer, S. J., Hummel, M., Carter, K., Harber, K., Schoem, D., & Nisbett, R. (1998). African-American college achievement: A "wise" intervention. In C. Jencks & M. Phillips (Eds.), *Test score differences between Blacks and Whites.* Cambridge, MA: Harvard University Press.

Steele, S. (1990). *The content of our character.* New York: St. Martin's Press.

Steele, S. (1991). *The content of our character: A new vision of race in America.* New York: Harper Collins.

Steffens, M. C. & Buchner, A. (2003). Implicit Association Test: Separating transsituationally stable and variable components of attitudes toward gay men. *Experimental Psychology, 50,* 33–48.

Stendler, C. D., Damrin, D., & Haines, A. C. (1951). Studies in cooperation and competition 1: The effects of working for group and individual rewards on the social climate of groups. *Journal of Genetic Psychology, 79,* 173–197.

Stephan, W. G. (1985). Intergroup relations. In G. Lindzey & E. Aronson (Eds.), *Handbook of social psychology* (Vol. 2, 3rd ed., pp. 599–658). New York: Random House.

Stephan, W. G. (1989). A cognitive approach to stereotyping. In D. Bar-Tal, C. F. Graumann, A. W. Kruglanski, & W. Stroebe (Eds.), *Stereotyping and prejudice: Changing conceptions* (pp. 37–57). New York: Springer-Verlag.

Stephan, W. G., & Finlay, K. (1999). The role of empathy in improving intergroup relations. *Journal of Social Issues, 55*(4), 729–743.

Stephan, W. G., & Rosenfield, D. (1982). Racial and ethnic stereotypes. In A. Miller (Ed.), *In the eye of the beholder: Contemporary issues in stereotyping* (pp. 92–136). New York: Praeger.

Stephan, W. G., & Stephan, C. W. (1985). Intergroup anxiety. *Journal of Social Issues, 41*(3), 157–175.

Stephan, W. G., & Stephan, C. W. (1993). Cognition and affect in stereotyping: Parallel interactive networks. In D. M. Mackie & D. L. Hamilton (Eds.), *Affect, cognition, and stereotyping: Interactive processes in group perception* (p. 111–136). New York, NY: Academic Press.

Stewart, M. W., Verstraate, C. D., & Fanslow, J. L. (1990). Sexist language and university academic staff: Attitudes, awareness, and recognition of sexist language. *New Zealand Journal of Educational Studies, 25*(2), 115–125.

Stewart, T. L., Weeks, M., & Lupfer, M. B. (2003). Spontaneous stereotyping: A matter of prejudice? *Social Cognition, 21*(4), 263–298.

Stone, J. (2002). Battling doubt by avoiding practice: The effects of stereotype threat on self-handicapping in white athletes. *Personality and Social Psychology Bulletin, 28*(12), 1667–1678.

Stone, J., Lynch, C. I., Sjomeling, M., & Darley, J. M. (1999). Stereotype threat effects on Black and white athletic performance. *Journal of Personality and Social Psychology, 77*(6), 1213–1227.

Strickland, B. R., & Weddell, S. C. (1972). Religious orientation, racial prejudice, and dogmatism: A study of Baptists and Unitarians. *Journal for the Scientific Study of Religion, 11*(4), 395–399.

Stroebe, W., & Insko, C. A. (1989). Stereotype, prejudice, and discrimination: Changing conceptions in theory and research. In D. Bar-Tal, C. F. Graumann, A. W. Kruglanski, & W. Stroebe (Eds.), *Stereotyping and prejudice: Changing conceptions* (pp. 3–34). New York: Springer-Verlag.

Stroessner, S. J., & Mackie, D. M. (1993). Affect and perceived group variability: Implications for stereotyping and prejudice. In D. M. Mackie & D. L. Hamilton (Eds.), *Affect, cognition, and stereotyping: Interactive processes in group perception* (pp. 63–86). New York: Academic Press.

Strunk, W., & White, E. B. (1979). *The elements of style* (3rd ed.). New York: Macmillan.

Stunkard, A., Srensen, T., Hanis, C., Teasdale, T. Chakraborty, R., Schull, W., & Schulsinger, F. (1986). An adoption study of human obesity. *New England Journal of Medicine, 314*(4), 193–198.

Sullivan, M. J., & Conway, M. (1989). Negative affect leads to low-effort cognition: Attributional processing for observed social behavior. *Social Cognition, 7,* 315–337.

Swann, W. B., Langlois, J. H., & Gilbert, L. A. (Eds.). (1999). *Sexism and stereotypes in modern society.* Washington, DC: American Psychological Association.

Swim, J. (1993). In search of gender bias in evaluations and trait inferences: The role of diagnosticity and gender stereotypicality of behavioral information. *Sex Roles, 29*(3/4), 213–237.

Swim, J. K. (1994). Perceived versus meta-analytic effect sizes: An assessment of the accuracy of gender stereotypes. *Journal of Personality and Social Psychology, 66,* 21–36.

Swim, J. K., Aikin, K. J., Hall, W. S., & Hunter, B. A. (1995). Sexism and racism: Old-fashioned and modern prejudices. *Journal of Personality and Social Psychology, 68*(2), 199–214.

Swim, J., Borgida, E., Maruyama, G., & Myers, D. G. (1989). Joan McKay versus John McKay: Do gender stereotypes bias evaluations? *Psychological Bulletin, 105*(3), 409–429.

Swim, J. K., Cohen, L. L., & Hyers, L. L. (1998). Experiencing everyday prejudice and discrimination. In J. K. Swim & C. Stangor (Eds.), *Prejudice: The target's perspective* (pp. 37–60). New York: Academic Press.

Swim, J., & Hyers, L. L. (1999). Excuse me—What did you just say?! Women's public and private responses to sexist remarks. *Journal of Experimental Social Psychology, 35,* 68–88.

Swim, J. K., & Sanna, L. J. (1996). He's skilled, she's lucky: A meta-analysis of observers' attributions for women's and men's successes and failures. *Personality and Social Psychology Bulletin, 22*(5), 507–519.

Swim, J. K., & Stangor, C. S. (Eds.). (1998). *Prejudice: The target's perspective.* New York: Academic Press.

Tajfel, H. (1969). Cognitive aspects of prejudice. *Journal of Social Issues, 25*(4), 79–97.

Tajfel, H. (1970). Experiments in intergroup discrimination. *Scientific American, 223*(5), 96–102.

Tajfel, H., Flament, C., Billig, K., & Bundy, R. (1971). Social categorization and intergroup behavior. *European Journal of Social Psychology, 1,* 149–175.

Tajfel, H., & Turner, J. (1979). An integrative theory of intergroup conflict. In W. G. Austin & S. Worchel (Eds.), *The social psychology of intergroup relations* (pp. 33–47). Monterey, CA: Brooks/Cole.

Tajfel, H., & Turner, J. C. (1986). The social identity theory of intergroup behavior. In S. Worchel & W. G. Austin (Eds.), *The psychology of intergroup relations* (pp. 7–24). Chicago: Nelson-Hall.

Tal-Or, N., Boninger, D., & Gleicher, F. (2002). Understanding the conditions and processes necessary for intergroup contact to reduce prejudice. In G. Salomon & B. Nevo (Eds.), *Peace education: The concept, principles, and practices around the world* (pp. 89–107). Mahwah, NJ: Erlbaum.

Taylor, D. M., & Dube, L. (1986). Two faces of identity: The "I" and the "we." *Journal of Social Issues, 42,* 81–98.

Taylor, S. E. (1981). A categorization approach to stereotyping. In D. L. Hamilton (Ed.), *Cognitive processes in stereotyping*

312 REFERENCES

and intergroup behavior (pp. 88–114). Hillsdale, NJ: Erlbaum.

Taylor, S. E., & Crocker, J. (1981). Schematic bases of social information processing. In E. T. Higgins, C. P. Herman, & M. P. Zanna (Eds.), *Social cognition: The Ontario symposium* (Vol. 1, pp. 89–134). Hillsdale, NJ: Erlbaum.

Taylor, S. E., & Fiske, S. T. (1991). *Social cognition* (2nd ed.). New York: McGraw-Hill.

Taylor, S. E., Fiske, S. T., Etcoff, N. L., & Ruderman, A. J. (1978). Categorical bases of person memory and stereotyping. *Journal of Personality and Social Psychology, 36,* 778–793.

Taylor, S. E., Helgeson, V. S., Reed, G. M., & Skokan, L. A. (1991). Self-generated feelings of control and adjustment to physical illness. *Journal of Social Issues, 47*(4), 91–109.

Taywaditep, K. J. (2001). Marginalization among the marginalized: Gay men's anti-effeminacy attitudes. *Journal of Homosexuality, 42,* 1–28.

Teachman, B. A., Gapinski, K. D., Brownell, K. D., Rawlins, M., & Jeyaram, S. (2003). Demonstrations of implicit anti-fat bias: The impact of providing causal information and evoking empathy. *Health Psychology, 22,* 68–78.

Thoits, P. A. (1987). *Negotiating roles.* In F. J. Crosby (Ed.), *Spouse, parent, worker: On gender and multiple roles* (pp. 11–22). New Haven, CT: Yale University Press.

Thompson, M. M., Zanna, M. P., & Griffin, D. W. (1995). Let's not be indifferent about (attitudinal) ambivalence. In R. E. Petty & J. A. Krosnick (Eds.), *Attitude strength: Antecedents and consequences* (pp. 361–386). Mahwah, NJ: Erlbaum.

Thompson, T. L., & Zerbinos, E. (1995). Gender roles in animated cartoons: Has the picture changed in 20 years? *Sex Roles, 32*(9/10), 651–673.

Thorndike, E. L. (1911). *Animal intelligence: Experimental studies.* New York: Macmillan.

Tien-Hyatt, J. L. (1986–1987). Self-perceptions of aging across cultures: Myth or reality? *International Journal of Aging and Human Development, 24*(2), 129–148.

Todd-Mancillas, W. (1981). Masculine generics = sexist language. *Communication Quarterly, 29*(2), 107–115.

Tougas, F., Brown, R., Beaton, A. M., & Joly, S. (1995). Neosexism: Plus ca change, plus c'est pareil. *Personality and Social Psychology Bulletin, 21*(8), 842–849.

Towles-Schwen, T., & Fazio, R. H. (2003). Choosing social situations: The relation between automatically activated racial attitudes and anticipated comfort interacting with African Americans. *Personality and Social Psychology Bulletin, 29*(2), 170–182.

Triandis, H. C. (1994). *Culture and social behavior.* New York: McGraw-Hill.

Troll, L., & Schlossberg, N. (1971). How age-biased are college counselors? *Industrial Gerontology, 10,* 14–20.

Tuckman, J., & Lorge, I. (1953). Attitudes toward old people. *Journal of Social Psychology, 37,* 249–260.

Turner, J. C. (1987). *Rediscovering the social group: A self-categorization theory.* Oxford: Blackwell.

Tversky, A., & Kahneman, D. (1973). Availability: A heuristic for judging frequency and probability. *Cognitive Psychology, 5,* 207–232.

Twenge, J. M., & Crocker, J. (2002). Race and self-esteem: Meta-analyses comparing Whites, Blacks, Hispanics, Asians, and American Indians and comment on Gray-Little and Hafdahl (2000). *Psychological Bulletin, 128*(3), 371–408.

Uleman, J., & Bargh, J. (Eds.). (1989). *Unintended thought.* New York: Guilford Press.

Unger, R. K. & Saundra (1993). Sexism: An integrated perspective. In F. L. Denmark & M. Paludi (Eds.). *Psychology of women: A handbook of issues and theories* (pp. 141–188). Westport, CT: Greenwood Press.

U.S. Census Bureau (2000). Projections of the total resident population by 5-year age groups, and sex with special age categories: Middle series, 2025 to 2045. Washington, D.C. Population projections program, U.S. Census Bureau.

U.S. Department of Labor. (1997). *The glass ceiling initiative: Are there cracks in the ceiling?* Washington, DC: U.S. Department of Labor.

U.S. Department of Transportation. (1999). *Traffic safety facts: 1998.* Washington, DC: U.S. Department of Transportation.

Vallacher, R., & Nowak, A. (1997). The emergence of dynamical social psychology. *Psychological Inquiry, 8*(2), 73–99.

van Dijk, T. A. (1991). *Racism and the press.* New York: Routledge.

Vanman, E. J., Saltz, J. L., & Nathan, L. R. (2004). Racial discrimination by low-prejudiced whites. *Psychological Science, 15*(11), 711–714.

Vanneman, R. D., & Pettigrew, T. F. (1972). Race and relative deprivation in the urban United States. *Race, 13,* 461–486.

Vescio, T. K., Sechrist, G. B., & Paolucci, M. P. (2003). Perspective taking and prejudice reduction: The mediational role of empathy arousal and situational attributions. *European Journal of Social Psychology, 33*(4), 455–472.

Viki, G. T., & Abrams, D. (2002). But she was unfaithful: Benevolent sexism and reactions to rape victims who violate traditional gender role expectations. *Sex Roles, 47*(5/6), 289–293.

Vinacke, W. E. (1957). Stereotypes as social concepts. *The Journal of Social Psychology, 46,* 229–243.

Von Hippel, W., Sekaquaptewa, D., & Vargas, P. (1995). On the role of encoding processes in stereotype maintenance. In M. Zanna (Ed.), *Advances in experimental social psychology,* (Vol. 27, pp. 177–254). New York: Academic Press.

Von Neumann, J. (1958). *The computer and the brain.* New Haven, CT: Yale University Press.

Vorauer, J. D., Main, K. J., & O'Connell, G. B. (1998). How do individuals expect to be viewed by members of lower status groups? Content and implications of meta-stereotypes. *Journal of Personality and Social Psychology, 75*(4), 917–937.

Wagner, L. S., & Wagner, T. H. (2003). The effect of age on the use of health and self-care information: Confronting the stereotype. *Gerontologist, 43*(3), 318–324.

Walker, I., & Smith, H. J. (2002). *Relative deprivation: Specification, development and integration.* New York, NY: Cambridge University Press.

Walton, G. M. & Cohen, G. L. (2003). Stereotype lift. *Journal of Experimental Social Psychology, 39*(5), 456–467.

Ward, D. (1985). Generations and the expression of symbolic racism. *Political Psychology, 6,* 1–18.

Warring, D., Johnson, D. W., Maruyama, G., & Johnson, R. (1985). Impact of different types of cooperative learning on cross-ethnic and cross-sex relationships. *Journal of Educational Psychology, 77,* 53–59.

Warrington, E. K., & Weiskrantz, L. (1970). The amnesic syndrome: Consolidation or retrieval? *Nature, 228,* 628–630.

Weber, R., & Crocker, J. (1983). Cognitive processes in the revision of stereotypic beliefs. *Journal of Personality and Social Psychology, 45*(5), 961–977.

Webster, D. M. (1993). Motivated augmentation and reduction of the overattribution bias. *Journal of Personality and Social Psychology, 65*(2), 261–271.

Webster, D. M., & Kruglanski, A. W. (1994). Individual differences in need for cognitive closure. *Journal of Personality and Social Psychology, 67*(6), 1049–1062.

Webster, D. M., Kruglanski, A. W., & Pattison, D. A. (1997). Motivated language use in intergroup contexts: Need-for-closure effects on the linguistic intergroup bias. *Journal of Personality and Social Psychology, 72*(5), 1122–1131.

Weeber, J. E. (1999). What could I know of racism? *Journal of Counseling and Development, 77,* 21–23.

Wegener, D. T., & Petty, R. E. (1994). Mood-management across affective states: The hedonic contingency hypothesis. *Journal of Personality and Social Psychology, 66,* 1034–1048.

Wegner, D. M. (1989). *White bears and other unwanted thoughts: Suppression, obsession, and the psychology of mental control.* New York: Penguin Books.

Wegner, D. M. (1994). Ironic processes of mental control. *Psychological Review, 101,* 34–52.

Wegner, D. M., & Erber, R. (1992). The hyperaccessibility of suppressed thoughts. *Journal of Personality and Social Psychology, 63*(6), 903–912.

Wegner, D. M., Erber, R., & Zanakos, S. (1993). Ironic processes in the mental control of mood and mood-related thought. *Journal of Personality and Social Psychology, 65,* 1093–1104.

Wegner, D. M., & Giuliano, T. (1980). Arousal-induced attention to the self. *Journal of Personality and Social Psychology, 38,* 719–726.

Wegner, D. M., & Pennebaker, J. W. (Eds.). (1993). *Handbook of mental control.* Englewood Cliffs, NJ: Prentice-Hall.

Weigel, R. H., & Howes, P. W. (1985). Conceptions of racial prejudice: Symbolic racism reconsidered. *Journal of Social Issues, 41*(3), 117–138.

Weiner, B., Perry, R. P., & Magnusson, J. (1988). An attributional analysis of reactions to stigmas. *Journal of Personality and Social Psychology, 55*(5), 738–748.

Weiss, A. E. (1999). *The glass ceiling: A look at women in the workforce.* Brookfield, CT: Twenty-First Century Books.

Weitz, S. (1972). Attitude, voice, and behavior: A repressed affect model of interracial interaction. *Journal of Personality and Social Psychology, 24,* 14–21.

Wentura, D., & Brandtstadter, J. (2003). Age stereotypes in younger and older women: Analyses of accommodative shifts with a sentence-priming task. *Experimental Psychology, 50,* 16–26.

Wenzel, M., Mummendey, A., Weber, U., & Waldzus, S. (2003). The ingroup as pars pro toto: Projection from the ingroup onto the inclusive category as a precursor to social discrimination. *Personality and Social Psychology Bulletin, 29*(4), 461–473.

Westman, J. (1991). Juvenile ageism: Unrecognized prejudice and discrimination against the young. *Child Psychiatry and Human Development, 21*(4), 237–256.

Wheeler, M. E., & Fiske, S. T. (2005). Social-cognitive goals affect amygdala and stereotype activation. *Psychological Science, 16,* 56–63.

Whitam, F. L., Diamond, M., & Martin, J. (1993). Homosexual orientation in twins: A report on 61 pairs and three triplet sets. *Archives of Sexual Behavior, 22*(3), 187–206.

Whitbourne, S. (1976). Test anxiety in elderly and young adults. *International Journal of Aging and Human Development, 7*(3), 201–210.

Whitbourne, S. K., & Hulicka, I. M. (1990). Ageism in undergraduate psychology texts. *American Psychologist, 45*(10), 1127–1136.

Whitley, B. E. (1988). Sex differences in heterosexuals' attitudes toward homosexuals: It depends upon what you ask. *Journal of Sex Research, 24,* 287–291.

Whitley, B. E. (1990). The relationship of heterosexuals' attributions for the causes of homosexuality to attitudes towards lesbians and gay men. *Personality and Social Psychology Bulletin, 16,* 369–377.

Wicker, A. W. (1969). Attitude versus actions: The relationship of verbal and overt behavioral responses to attitude objects. *Journal of Social Issues, 25*(4), 41–78.

Wigboldus, D. H. J., Dijksterhuis, A., & Van Knippenberg, A. (2003). When stereotypes get in the way: Stereotypes obstruct stereotype-inconsistent trait inferences. *Journal of Personality and Social Psychology, 84*(3), 470–484.

Wigdor, B. (1983). Mental health and social conditions. In J. Birren, J. Munnichs., H. Thomae, & M. Marois (Eds.), *Aging: A challenge to science and society* (Vol. 3, pp. 49–57). New York: Oxford University Press.

Wilder, D. A. (1981). Perceiving persons as a group: Categorization and intergroup relations. In D. L. Hamilton (Ed.), *Cognitive processes in stereotyping and intergroup behavior* (pp. 213–258). Hillsdale, NJ: Erlbaum.

Wilder, D. A. (1993). The role of anxiety in facilitating stereotypic judgments of outgroup behavior. In D. M. Mackie & D. L. Hamilton (Eds.), *Affect, cognition, and stereotyping: Interactive processes in group perception* (pp. 87–109). New York: Academic Press.

Wilder, D. A., & Shapiro, P. (1989). Role of competition-induced anxiety in limiting the beneficial impact of positive behavior by an out-group member. *Journal of Personality and Social Psychology, 56,* 60–69.

Williams, A., Ota, H., Giles, H., Pierson, H., Gallois, C., Ng, S., Lim, T., et al. (1997). Young people's beliefs about intergenerational communication: An initial cross-cultural comparison. *Communication Research, 24*(4), 370–393.

Williams, J. E., & Best, D. L. (1982). *Measuring sex stereotypes: A thirty-nation study.* Beverly Hills, CA: Sage.

Williams, R. M. (1947). *Reduction of intergroup tension.* New York: Social Science Research Council.

Wilner, D. M., Walkley, R., & Cook, S. W. (1955). *Human relations in interracial housing: A test of the contact hypothesis.* Minneapolis: University of Minnesota Press.

Wilson, W., & Miller, N. (1961). Shifts in evaluation of participants following intergroup competition. *Journal of Abnormal and Social Psychology, 63,* 428–431.

Wise, E., & Rafferty, J. (1982). Sex bias and language. *Sex Roles, 8,* 1189–1196.

Wittenbrink, B., Judd, C. M., & Park, B. (1997). Evidence for racial prejudice at the implicit level and its relationship with questionnaire measures. *Journal of Personality and Social Psychology, 72*(2), 262–274.

Wittig, M. A. (1996). Taking affirmative action in education and employment. *Journal of Social Issues, 52*(4), 145–160.

Wolfe, C. T., & Spencer, S. J. (1996). Stereotypes and prejudice: Their overt and subtle influence in the classroom. *American Behavioral Scientist, 40*(2), 176–185.

Wolsko, C., Park, B., Judd, C. M., & Wittenbrink, B. (2000). Framing interethnic ideology: Effects of multicultural and color-blind perspectives on judgments of groups and individuals. *Journal of Personality and Social Psychology, 78*(4), 635–654.

Wood, J. (1994). Is "symbolic racism" racism? A review informed by intergroup behavior. *Political Psychology, 15*(4), 673–686.

Wood, P. B., & Sonleitner, N. (1996). The effect of childhood interracial contact on adult antiblack prejudice. *International Journal of Intercultural Relations, 20,* 1–17.

Word, C. O., Zanna, M. P., & Cooper, J. (1974). The nonverbal mediation of self-fulfilling prophecies in interracial interaction. *Journal of Experimental Social Psychology, 10,* 109–120.

Works, E. (1961). The prejudice-interaction hypothesis from the point of view of the Negro minority group. *American Journal of Sociology, 67,* 47–52.

Worschel, S., & Norvell, N. (1980). Effect of perceived environmental conditions during cooperation on intergroup attraction. *Journal of Personality and Social Psychology, 38,* 764–772.

Worschel, S., & Rothgerber, H. (1997). Changing the stereotype of the stereotype. In R. Spears, P. J. Oakes, N. Ellemers, & S. A. Haslam (Eds.), *The social psychology of stereotyping and group life* (pp. 72–93). Cambridge, MA: Blackwell.

Worth, L. T., & Mackie, D. M. (1987). Cognitive mediation of positive affect in persuasion. *Social Cognition, 5,* 76–94.

Wright, S. C., & Taylor, D. M. (2003). The social psychology of cultural diversity: Social stereotyping, prejudice, and discrimination. In M. A. Hogg & J. Cooper (Eds.), *The Sage handbook of social psychology* (pp. 432–457). Thousand Oaks, CA: Sage.

Wyatt, D. F., & Campbell, D. T. (1951). On the liability of stereotype or hypothesis. *Journal of Abnormal and Social Psychology, 46,* 496–500.

Wyer, N. A. (2004). Not all stereotypic biases are created equal: Evidence for a stereotype-disconfirming bias. *Personality and Social Psychology Bulletin, 30*(6), 706–720.

Wyer, R. S., Jr., & Srull, T. K. (1989). *Memory and cognition in its social context.* Hillsdale, NJ: Erlbaum.

Zajonc, R. B. (1980). Cognition and social cognition: A historical perspective. In L. Festinger (Ed.), *Retrospections on social psychology* (pp. 180–204). New York: Oxford University Press.

Zajonc, R. B. (1998). Emotions. In D. T. Gilbert, S. T. Fiske, & G. Lindzey (Eds.), *The handbook of social psychology* (Vol. 1, 4th ed., pp. 591–632). New York: McGraw-Hill.

Zanna, M. P., & Rempel, J. K. (1988). Attitudes: A new look at an old concept. In D. Bar-Tal & A. Kruglanski (Eds.), *The social psychology of knowledge* (pp. 315–334). New York: Cambridge.

Zárate, M. A., Garcia, B., & Garza, A. A., & Hitlan, R. (2004). Cultural threat and perceived realistic group conflict as predictors of attitudes towards Mexican immigrants. *Journal of Experimental Social Psychology, 40,* 99–105.

Zárate, M. A., & Garza, A. A. (2002). In-group distinctiveness and self-affirmation as dual components of prejudice reduction. *Self and Identity, 1,* 235–249.

Zebrowitz, L. A., & Montepare, J. M. (2000). "Too young, too old": Stigmatizing adolescents and elders. In T. F. Heatherton, R. E. Kleck, M. R. Hebl, & J. G. Hull (Eds.), *The Social Psychology of Stigma.* (pp. 334–373). New York: Guilford.

Zillman, D. (1983). Disparagement humor. In P. E. McGhee & J. H. Goldstein (Eds.), *Handbook of humour research* (Vol. 1). New York: Springer-Verlag.

Zuwerink, J. R., Devine, P. G., Monteith, M. J., & Cook, D. A. (1996). Prejudice toward blacks: With and without compunction? *Basic and Applied Social Psychology, 18*(2), 131–150.

NAME INDEX

SUBJECT INDEX